Cisco IP Routing

Cisco IP Routing

Packet Forwarding and Intra-domain Routing Protocols

A l e x   Z i n i n

✦ Addison-Wesley

Boston • San Francisco • New York • Toronto • Montreal
London • Munich • Paris • Madrid
Capetown • Sydney • Tokyo • Singapore • Mexico City

Many of the designations used by manufacturers and sellers to distinguish their products are claimed as trademarks. Where those designations appear in this book, and Addison-Wesley was aware of a trademark claim, the designations have been printed with initial capital letters or in all capitals.

The author and publisher have taken care in the preparation of this book, but make no expressed or implied warranty of any kind and assume no responsibility for errors or omissions. No liability is assumed for incidental or consequential damages in connection with or arising out of the use of the information or programs contained herein.

The publisher offers discounts on this book when ordered in quantity for special sales. For more information, please contact:

Pearson Education Corporate Sales Division
201 W. 103rd Street
Indianapolis, IN 46290
(800) 428-5331
corpsales@pearsoned.com

Visit AW on the Web: www.aw.com/cseng/

Library of Congress Cataloging-in-Publication Data
Zinin, Alex.
   Cisco IP routing : packet forwarding and intra-domain routing protocols / Alex Zinin.
      p. cm.
   Includes bibliographical references and index.
   ISBN 0-201-60473-6 (alk. paper)
1   . Routers (Computer networks) 2. Packet switching (Data transmission) I. Title.
TK5105.543 .Z56 2002
004.6'2--dc21   2001046234

ISBN : 0-201-60473-6
Text printed on recycled paper
1 2 3 4 5 6 7 8 9 10—MA—0504030201
First printing, October 2001

To my wife Liza for her love and support.

*To my children Alexey and Artem for accepting
me the way I am and making sure I don't
forget the world is beautiful.*

To my parents for giving me this world.

Contents

Preface xv

Chapter One: Overview of Cisco Routers 1

1.1 Description of a Cisco Router 1

1.2 Interfacing with Routers 3

1.3 Router Configuration 5

1.4 Monitoring and Troubleshooting Tools 11

1.5 The Test Lab 14

1.6 References 14

Chapter Two: Review of IP Addressing 15

2.1 IP Addressing 15

2.2 Subnetting 18

2.3 Special Addressing Rules 20

2.4 Classful and Classless Addressing 22

2.5 Variable-Length Subnet Masks 22

2.6 IP Addressing Details in Cisco Routers 25

2.7 Frequently Asked Questions 30

2.8 References 31

Chapter Three: Routing and Forwarding Processes 33

3.1 Packet-Switched Technologies 33

3.2 Router Operation Overview 35

3.3 Routing Information Sources 41

3.4 Static Routing 42

3.5 Dynamic Routing 44

3.6 Default Routing 46

3.7 Basic Forwarding Algorithm 47

3.8 Classful Routing Operations 52

3.9 Classless Routing Operations 59

Chapter Four: Routing Table Maintenance 65

4.1 Routing Information Sources 65
4.1.1 Directly Attached Networks and Interface Routes 67
4.1.2 Static Routes 72
4.1.3 Dynamic Routes 76
4.1.4 Comparison of the Route Sources 78

4.2 Routing Table Maintenance **80**
4.2.1 Representation of Routing Information and Interfaces 80
4.2.2 Routing Table Structure 81
4.2.3 Route Source Selection 99
4.2.4 Routing Table Initialization 110
4.2.5 Asynchronous Table Maintenance 111
4.2.6 Route Resolvability 115
4.2.7 Change of an Interface State 118
4.2.8 Change of Interface Address 121
4.2.9 Dynamic Route Processing 124
4.2.10 Static Route Processing 126
4.2.11 Manual Routing Table Clearance 144
4.2.12 Defining Default Routes 147
4.2.13 Default Route Selection 151

4.3 Summary **155**

4.4 Frequently Asked Questions **155**

Chapter Five: Packet Forwarding **161**

5.1 Overview of IP Forwarding **161**

5.2 Packet Input **165**

5.3 Forwarding Engine **170**
5.3.1 Route Lookup 173
5.3.2 Policy Routing 177

5.4 Packet Delivery **182**
5.4.1 Network Interface Types 182
5.4.2 General Packet-Delivery Functionality 187
5.4.2.7 Packet Delivery on Null Interface 204

5.5 Forwarding Methods in Cisco IOS **205**

5.5.1 Fast Switching 207

5.5.2 Autonomous and SSE Switching 214

5.5.3 Optimum Switching 215

5.5.4 Distributed Switching 216

5.5.5 Cisco Express Forwarding 220

5.5.6 NetFlow Switching 225

5.6 Load Sharing in Cisco IOS 229

5.6.1 Per Packet Load Sharing in Process-Switching Path 230

5.6.2 Per Destination Load Sharing in Fast Switching Path 232

5.6.3 Load Sharing in Cisco Express Forwarding 234

5.7 Summary 237

5.8 Frequently Asked Questions 238

5.9 References 239

Chapter Six: Static Routes 241

6.1 Static Routes in Cisco Routers 241

6.2 Backup Static Routes 244

6.3 Using Static Routes in NBMA and Dial-Up Environments 247

6.4 Default Routes 248

6.5 Routing Loops and Discard Routes 250

6.6 Implementation Scenarios 255

6.6.1 ISP and a Customer 255

6.6.2 Central Office and Branch Offices (Partial Mesh) 259

6.7 Frequently Asked Questions 266

Chapter Seven: Dynamic Routing Protocols in Cisco IOS 269

7.1 Common Functionality of Dynamic Routing Protocols 269

7.2 Routing Protocol Configuration 271

7.3 Routing Protocol Data Structures 276

7.4 Route Redistribution 281

7.5 Events Processed by Routing Protocols 290

7.6 Summary 291

7.7 Frequently Asked Questions 292

References 293

Chapter Eight: Distance-Vector Routing Protocols 295

8.1 Distance-Vector Principles 295
8.1.1 Topology Discovery 296
8.1.2 Counting-to-Infinity Problem 301
8.1.3 Split Horizon 303
8.1.4 Holddown Timers 305
8.1.5 Triggered Updates 306
8.1.6 Counting to Infinity Again 307
8.1.7 The Bellman-Ford Algorithm 307

8.2 Routing Information Protocol 310
8.2.1 Basic Description and History 310
8.2.2 Configuration Parameters 311
8.2.3 Message Format 315
8.2.4 Input Processing 318
8.2.5 Event Processing 329
8.2.6 Sending RIP Updates 338

8.2.7 RIP version 2 347
8.2.8 RIP Demand Circuits Extensions 350
8.2.9 RIP Configuration 352
8.2.10 Summary 371
8.2.11 Frequently Asked Questions 372

8.3 Interior Gateway Routing Protocol **374**
8.3.1 Basic Description and History 375
8.3.2 Protocol Parameters 380
8.3.3 Message Format 383
8.3.4 Input Processing 386
8.3.5 Event Processing 388
8.3.6 IGRP Configuration 388
8.3.7 Summary 401
8.3.8 Frequently Asked Questions 402

8.4 References **403**

Chapter Nine: Link-State Routing Protocols **405**

9.1 Introduction to Link-State Routing **405**
9.1.1 Theoretical Basis 405
9.1.2 Dijkstra Algorithm 408
9.1.3 Database Synchronization and Flooding Algorithm 413
9.1.4 Calculating Routing Information 418
9.1.5 Overview of Link-State Routing Protocols 419

9.2 Open Shortest Path First (OSPF) **419**
9.2.1 Basic Characteristics 420
9.2.2 General Data Structures 428
9.2.3 Intra-Area Routing 436
9.2.4 Inter-Area Routing 483
9.2.5 Routing to External Networks in OSPF 493

9.2.6 Summary of Routing Table Calculation and Route
      Preference Rules 505
9.2.7 Demand Circuit OSPF Extensions 506
9.2.8 Details of Cisco OSPF Implementation 508
9.2.9 OSPF Configuration 509
9.2.10 Configuration Examples 524
9.2.11 Summary 547

9.3 References **548**

Chapter Ten: Enhanced IGRP **551**

10.1 Basic Description and History **551**

10.2 Theoretical Basis **552**

10.3 Subsystems and Data Structures **560**

10.4 Message Format **565**

10.5 Input Processing **571**
10.5.1 Generic Packet Processing 571
10.5.2 Processing EIGRP Updates 573
10.5.3 Processing EIGRP Queries 574
10.5.4 Processing EIGRP Replies 574

10.6 Internal Event Processing **574**

10.7 Sending EIGRP Packets **575**
10.7.1 Sending EIGRP Hellos 576
10.7.2 Sending Updates and Queries 576
10.7.3 Sending Replies 577

10.8 Shortest-Path Calculation **577**

10.9 Default Route Support **578**

10.10 Route Aggregation **579**

10.11 EIGRP Stub Router Extension **579**

10.12 EIGRP Configuration **581**

10.13 Configuration Examples **586**
10.13.1 Basic EIGRP Configuration 587
10.13.2 Local and Distributed Route Calculation 592
10.13.3 Configuring Variance Parameter 596
10.13.4 Injecting the Default Route 597
10.13.5 Manual Route Summarization 605
10.13.6 Route Redistribution, Filtering, and Route Maps 607

10.4 Frequently Asked Questions **612**

Bibliography **615**

Index **621**

Preface

Introduction

The role of the Internet today cannot be overestimated. It has become a part of our culture. Children learn how to use the Internet at school. Millions of people start their day by checking the e-mail messages. Internet connectivity is not considered as something extraordinary anymore. People use the Internet every day, as they have been using cars or TV sets for decades. More and more devices become connected to the Internet. These are not limited to servers and personal computers anymore. Electronic organizers, cellular phones, TV sets, and many other types of equipment come with the Internet applications. Digital video cameras and phones are connected to the Internet to instantly cast data to remote users around the globe.

The value of the Internet is definitely not in its just being a global network, but in the resources available through this network. Resources are provided and used by the end devices (for example, servers and personal computers)—the largest part of the Internet. The other part of it is the intermediate network devices or routers. The role of the routers is to provide connectivity between the end devices by properly forwarding the packets of the Internet Protocol (IP) that end devices send to each other in order to exchange data such as e-mail messages or the contents of the web pages. In order to deliver IP packets to their destinations successfully, routers communicate the network reachability information to each other using routing protocols. The information provided by the routing protocols allows the routers to calculate the paths to remote networks. All routing protocols are divided into two groups—intra-domain and inter-domain. Intra-domain routing protocols (for example, RIP or OSPF) are used for routing within an elementary block of the Internet architecture (an autonomous system or domain), while inter-domain protocols (the Internet is using BGPv4 today) are used to exchange routing information among these blocks.

Cisco routers are the most widely spread network devices in the Internet today. They are used to provide connectivity to the end users, aggregate traffic from multiple access devices, and perform routing in the Internet backbone. This book describes very deep details of Cisco routers functionality with the emphasis on packet forwarding and intra-domain dynamic routing protocols.

Objectives

Quite a few very high quality books on IP, IP routing, IP network design, and configuration of Cisco routers have recently become available. However, it is still hard to find detailed explanation of the processes happening inside the routers. Nevertheless, this knowledge is vital for network professionals to be able to properly configure and efficiently troubleshoot Cisco routers.

This book does not teach how to build networks. It also does not teach the basics of the IP protocol or Cisco routers. Instead, it is written to thoroughly explain a very limited set of questions—IP routing and IP forwarding inside Cisco routers. The goal of this book is to give the reader a very deep understanding of the routing and forwarding technologies in general and in connection with their implementation in Cisco routers. The contents are intended to make sure the reader feels the details instead of just memorizing them. The book also clarifies a great number of very common misunderstandings about IP routing technologies and Cisco routers in particular.

Audience

An important condition that applies to the readers of this book is the presence of at least basic knowledge of IP and Cisco routers. Even though the book provides some introduction to these topics, the reader is assumed to have spent some time in the lab with Cisco routers and be familiar with such notions as TCP/IP, ARP, or Ethernet.

Except for this reservation, the book is addressed to a wide range of readers. This includes IP network architects, engineers and operators that would like to know more details on IP routing technologies and processes inside Cisco routers, network engineers preparing for the Cisco certified internetworking engineer (CCIE) examination, network support and consulting engineers, and so on.

Organization

The book consists of ten chapters. The first three chapters refresh the knowledge of Cisco routers, IP addressing and routing technologies that is required for the rest of the book. Remain chapters guide the reader through a thorough explanation of the generic routing and forwarding mechanisms inside Cisco routers and intra-domain IP routing protocols. Brief description of each chapter of the book follows.

Chapter 1—Introduction. Chapter 1 provides brief overview of Cisco routers including basic information on routers' hardware and software, configuration and monitoring. This chapter clarifies some points important for other chapters and describes the lab network used in the illustrations.

Chapter 2—IP addressing review. This part of the book explains topics that are important for the routing discussion—classful IP addressing and subnetting, classless IP addressing, and variable length subnet masks.

Chapter 3—Routing and forwarding processes. This chapter sets required background for a detailed discussion on specific routing technologies. The reader is familiarized with the fundamental networking concepts and router operation algorithms. The difference between routing and forwarding processes is explained. It is followed by a description of the sources of routing information and more detailed discussions on each source and the principles of default routing. The chapter also explains the basic forwarding algorithm and the differences between classful and classless routing operations.

Chapter 4—Routing table maintenance. Chapter 4 provides a very detailed discussion on how routing information is organized and maintained in Cisco routers. The chapter starts with a thorough explanation of each source of routing information. The second part of the chapter is dedicated to the routing table maintenance process. This includes processing of connected, static and dynamic routes, as well as the default route selection algorithm.

Chapter 5—Packet forwarding. Chapter 5 describes in detail the IP packet forwarding process—the module that actually uses information in the routing table to move packets from one interface to another. The chapter starts with the forwarding process overview, followed by a systematic explanation of each stage. Packet switching mechanisms available in Cisco IOS, including fast, optimum, distributed, NetFlow switching and Cisco Express Forwarding are described in the following section. The chapter ends with a discussion on the load sharing techniques available in Cisco routers.

Chapter 6—Static routes. This chapter provides a complete description of static routes in Cisco IOS. This includes the details on recursive static routes, static routes via interfaces, backup (floating), default and discard static routes. The chapter also includes implementation scenarios that help the reader understand the issues and tradeoffs involved into managing of a network using static routes.

Chapter 7—Dynamic routing protocols in Cisco IOS. Chapter 7 provides information about generic mechanisms used by the dynamic routing protocols. This includes basic routing protocol configuration, data structures, routes redistribution and event processing.

Chapter 8—Distance vector routing protocols. This chapter begins with a discussion on principles of distance-vector routing and, specifically, the Bellman-Ford algorithm. Very detailed descriptions of two distance-vector IP routing protocols—Routing Information Protocol (RIP) and Interior Gateway Routing Protocol (IGRP)—are provided. Each protocol description includes information on protocol packet formats, input message and event processing, outbound message generation, as well as the configuration commands and examples.

Chapter 9—Link-state routing protocols. Chapter 9 describes the mechanisms of link-state routing in general and a link-state routing protocol—Open Shortest Path First (OSPF). The first part of the chapter gives a very detailed explanation of the link-state routing concepts, including the Dijkstra algorithm, link-state database synchronization and flooding. An overview of the two link-state routing protocols (integrated IS-IS, and OSPF) currently used in IP world is given as well. The second part of the chapter provides a complete guide to the OSPF protocol and details of Cisco's OSPF implementation. Practically every aspect of the protocol is explained very thoroughly in this section. The chapter is completed with information on OSPF configuration commands and configuration examples.

Chapter 10—Enhanced IGRP. This chapter gives a detailed explanation of enhanced IGRP (EIGRP)—a Cisco's proprietary routing protocol, based on the diffusing update calculation algorithm. The chapter introduces the concepts of EIGRP by showing how the protocol solves real-life problems in the distance-vector protocols. As in the previous chapters, full description of EIGRP packets, message and event processing, as well as update generation is included. The chapter also discusses the topics of the default route support and route aggregation in EIGRP, followed by a description of the EIGRP stub router extension. Sections on EIGRP configuration and configuration examples conclude the chapter.

Approach

When this book was being written, the emphasis was made on explaining why certain things work in a specific way, not just how they work. This is why practically every chapter in the book contains a theoretical introduction to the topic. The core of every chapter is the actual explanation of specific mechanisms inside the router. In most of the cases, discussions on specific topics are given in the context of Cisco's implementation of the algorithms and mechanisms, illustrated with logs from real Cisco routers.

The book contains description of many algorithms. All of them are described in human language, and for some of them a pseudocode definition is given for better under-standing.

Chapters 4 through 10 also contain sections that answer the most frequently asked questions about a specific technology.

Disclaimer

The author would like to note that pseudocode used in this book is not a recompilation of the Cisco IOS source code and any similarity between the two is accidental.

Chapter One

Overview of Cisco Routers

This chapter provides an overview of the architecture, configuration, and monitoring of Cisco routers—information essential for understanding the other topics in the book. This chapter does not teach in depth, though, as readers are expected to have at least some prior experience with Cisco devices.

After presenting basic information about the hardware and software architecture of the routers, we discuss Cisco's command line interface (CLI), which includes a set of embedded configuration, monitoring, and debugging commands. Next, we address the configuration of Cisco routers, including the commands to modify, store, and download router settings, followed by a description of the monitoring and troubleshooting tools necessary to follow the examples given in this book. The chapter ends with a description of the test lab used to illustrate most of the theoretical and practical topics presented in the rest of the book.

1.1 Description of a Cisco Router

Cisco routers are specialized computers used in data networks to provide connectivity between remote computers (also called hosts) and network segments. Cisco routers operate on the third—network—layer of the OSI (Open Systems Interconnection) reference model and perform such functions as packet forwarding and best-path determination.

The architecture of Cisco routers is very similar to that of other computers. Routers have memory and a processor, which are used to execute the operating system and numerous processes or programs. Generally speaking, the Cisco IOS (Internetwork Operating System) is a set of processes running inside a router. Examples of such processes are the forwarding engines for network-layer protocols—for example, IP, IPX, AppleTalk—routing protocols—RIP, OSPF, BGP—data link layer protocols—PPP, HDLC, Frame Relay—as well as numerous other tasks.

The type of central processor used in Cisco routers varies, depending on the router model. For example, Cisco 2500-series routers use the 20MHz Motorola 68EC030, whereas the more powerful routers, such as the Gigabit Switch Router (GSR), use the 200MHz IDT R5000 RISC (reduced instruction set computer). The internal architecture of routers also depends on the router model. The architecture can be as simple as "one bus, one CPU" in the case of the 2500 series and as complex as the switch fabric with up to 320Gbps (gigabits per second) capacity and distributed traffic processing used by the GSR 12416.

Every Cisco router uses at least four types of memory:

- Read-only memory (ROM)
- Random-access memory (RAM)
- Nonvolatile random-access memory (NVRAM)
- Flash memory

Read-only memory is used to store the start-up code that bootstraps the router. This code checks the hardware and loads the main IOS image, which is usually stored in flash memory, into RAM. (Some models of Cisco routers, such as the 2500 series, can run IOS directly from flash memory, which is addressable by the CPU [central processing unit]. This method is called "run from flash.") When the main IOS image has been loaded and given control, it copies the router configuration from NVRAM to a buffer in RAM and passes it to the parser for processing. The parser then dynamically processes corresponding configuration commands.

In addition to the CPU and memory, Cisco routers also have *input/output* (I/O) devices, such as *network interface controllers* (NICs) or asynchronous serial management ports. Network interface controllers, hardware devices inside the router, provide low-level functionality for network attachments, such as LAN (local area network) or WAN (wide area network) interfaces. Controllers send and receive frames on given physical media, using appropriate data formatting and transmission techniques. Controllers also calculate and check the *frame check sequence* (FCS) fields that ensure data integrity. The process of communication between I/O controllers and the CPU depends largely on the architecture of the router. Controllers can either involve the CPU in packet processing by sending an interrupt request—as it's implemented in lower-end routers—or process packets communicating with other controllers directly, as in high-end routers, such as the Cisco 7500 or GSR.

Every Cisco router is equipped with a console port (CON), which is a simple asynchronous serial controller used to provide access to the router via a terminal. Most models also include an auxiliary asynchronous serial port (AUX) that can be used for both direct terminal connection and remote out-of-band management via a modem.

IOS, the operating system used in Cisco routers, is a special type of multitasking software, providing users and administrators with a command line interface and a set of processes and utilities. IOS multitasking is nonpreemptive and cooperative, which means that processes are responsible for returning control to the task scheduler to let other running processes work, much like user-level threads in UNIX operating systems. The administrator does not have direct control over all processes running in the router. It's not possible to explicitly start or stop a process as is done in operating systems like UNIX. Implicit control is achieved via groups of configuration and management commands that the administrator can issue after gaining access to the router and switching to the privileged mode.

1.2 Interfacing with Routers

Among the programs executed in a router is a group of processes that allow the administrator to remotely access the router and use its *command line interface*. CLI functionality in Cisco IOS is provided by the process called EXEC, which is analogous to UNIX's shell and allows users and administrators to configure and to monitor the router. EXEC can be accessed by using a direct connection from a terminal to the console port of the router or remotely via TELNET, secure shell (SSH), X.25 PAD (packet assembler/disassembler), or LAT (local-area transport) services (Figure 1-1).

Figure 1-2 shows how the EXEC process cooperates with other modules of the operating system. As you can see, TELNET daemon, PAD, and LAT processes are used to provide virtual terminal functionality. The terminal lines—CON, AUX, TTYs (terminal teletype), and VTYs (virtual teletype)—terminate the virtual connections, established

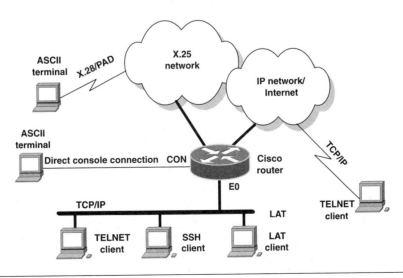

Figure 1-1. *Accessing a router's command line interface*

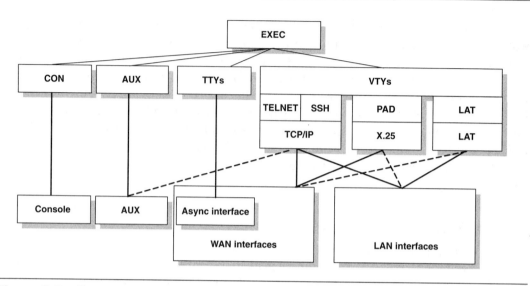

Figure 1-2. *Command line interface protocol stack*

from remote hosts, with EXEC run on top of them. It doesn't really matter how you access the router; once you're logged into it, the interface is uniform.

When a new terminal connection is established, the router requests a user name and the password, as shown in Listing 1-1. (This requires user database configuration on the router or on an external server; see [SecConf]. If no user database is provided, the administrator may configure only the password.) If the user name and the password are entered correctly, a new instance of EXEC is created, and the user receives the prompt.

```
con>telnet 20.1.1.1
Trying 20.1.1.1 ... Open

User Access Verification

Username: adm
Password:
R1>
```

Listing 1-1. *Using TELNET to access a router*

It's important to note the difference between the CON port and other terminal lines, including the AUX port, TTYs associated with asynchronous interfaces, and VTYs used for remote connections. By default, Cisco routers do not send log, system, or debug messages to any line other than CON. So, when default settings are used, no debug messages from the router will be seen in a TELNET session, for example. The reason is that a router can have multiple terminal sessions from different points within the network. Sessions can be initiated by people with different privileges. It wouldn't be smart to send debugging or system event information useful only for the system administrator to all sessions.

Listing 1-2 shows how this default behavior is affected by the **terminal monitor** command, which is issued at the current (privileged mode) prompt.

```
R1#show logging
Syslog logging: enabled (0 messages dropped, 0 flushes, 0 overruns)
    Console logging: level debugging, 10070 messages logged
    Monitor logging: level debugging, 0 messages logged
    Trap logging: level informational, 84 message lines logged
    Buffer logging: disabled
R1#
R1#terminal monitor
R1#show logging
Syslog logging: enabled (0 messages dropped, 0 flushes, 0 overruns)
    Console logging: level debugging, 10071 messages logged
    Monitor logging: level debugging, 0 messages logged
        Logging to: vty11(0)
    Trap logging: level informational, 85 message lines logged
    Buffer logging: disabled
R1#
```

Listing 1-2. *Using* **terminal monitor** *to change default logging behavior*

When the **terminal monitor** command is entered, the router adds another logging destination—VTY11(0), the VTY line corresponding to the current TELNET session. This means that whenever it needs to log a message, the router will also send it to the TELNET session where the command was issued.

The **terminal monitor** command is the only way to get system or debug messages to show up on a remote terminal session. You will typically use this command when monitoring or troubleshooting a router. This command is not in the examples used in this book, however, because access to all routers in the test lab is via the console ports. Don't forget about the command while reproducing the examples.

1.3 Router Configuration

Because it is a rather complex combination of sophisticated hardware and software, a Cisco router provides the administrator with a large set of configurable parameters and options. Unlike other configurable devices, Cisco routers store their configurations as easily readable text. This approach is useful, as it simplifies the process of troubleshooting and preparing configurations; no additional software is needed to read, analyze, and edit configuration files. A portion of a simple configuration file follows.

```
!
version 11.3
service timestamps debug datetime msec
!
hostname R1
!
enable secret 5 ...
!
ip subnet-zero
no ip domain-lookup
!
interface Ethernet0
 ip address 10.1.1.1 255.255.255.224

...
```

As you can see, the configuration syntax is intuitive and very close to plain language, so there's no need to remember arcane abbreviations. The sequence of commands is also easy to understand once you are used to the principle of nested configuration and the configuration context.

In order to change the parameters of a running process, the administrator must have terminal access to the router—direct terminal or a remote TELNET connection—and know the password used to switch to the privileged mode via the **enable** command (Listing 1-3).

```
R1>enable
Password:
R1#
```

Listing 1-3. *Switching to privileged mode*

When the password is entered, the administrator can change any part of the router's configuration. The parser—a part of the EXEC process responsible for command processing—is switched into the configuration context, using the **configure** command, which is usually given an optional parameter specifying the source of configuration (see Listing 1-4).

```
R1#configure ?
  memory             Configure from NV memory
  network            Configure from a TFTP network host
  overwrite-network  Overwrite NV memory from TFTP network host
```

```
terminal            Configure from the terminal
<cr>

R1#configure
```

Listing 1-4. *List of parameters for the* **configure** *command*

The terminal keyword specifies that the parser should use the current terminal session as input and output streams for command processing.

Commands entered by the administrator are instantly processed and applied to the running software modules, as shown in Listing 1-5, where an interface is dynamically shut down and brought up.

```
R1#configure terminal
Enter configuration commands, one per line.  End with CNTL/Z.
R1(config)#int s0
R1(config-if)#shutdown
R1(config-if)#
%LINEPROTO-5-UPDOWN: Line protocol on Interface Serial0, changed state to
down
R1(config-if)#
%LINK-5-CHANGED: Interface Serial0, changed state to administratively down
R1(config-if)#no shutdown
R1(config-if)#
%LINK-3-UPDOWN: Interface Serial0, changed state to up
%LINEPROTO-5-UPDOWN: Line protocol on Interface Serial0, changed state to up
R1(config-if)#^Z
R1#
```

Listing 1-5. *Making dynamic changes to a router's configuration*

The **configure terminal** command is the method of using manually entered commands to change a router's configuration online via a terminal session. If the memory keyword is specified for the **configure** command, the router reads the backed-up copy of the configuration from NVRAM and passes it to the parser. This is exactly what routers do on start-up. NVRAM is used to store the configuration, which is used the next time the router is reloaded. Usually, the **configure memory** command is used to restore the router's configuration after some or all its current settings have been reset.

If the **configure network** command is entered, the router tries to download a configuration file from a TFTP (trivial file transfer protocol) server to a portion of RAM and then passes it to the parser for processing. Before the download procedure starts, several questions about the IP address of the TFTP server and the name of the file are asked (Listing 1-6).

```
R1#configure network
Host or network configuration file [host]?
Address of remote host [255.255.255.255]? 10.1.1.1
Name of configuration file [r1-confg]?
Configure using r1-confg from 10.1.1.1? [confirm]
...
```

Listing 1-6. *The* configure network *command, used to apply a configuration file from a TFTP server*

The difference between the host and the network configuration files is in the name of the file the router suggests downloading. For the host configuration file, the name is in the form *<Router-name>*-confg, where *<Router-name>* is the name of the router. This file name shows up in the user prompt and can be changed by using the **hostname** global configuration command. The suggested name of the network configuration file is always *network*-confg. It is possible to change the suggested file name to the one that needs to be loaded.

The concept behind the **configure** command is changing, or configuring, active parameters by processing configuration commands from a source. The **configure overwrite-network** version of the command is an exception, though. When this command is entered, it copies a configuration file from a TFTP server to the NVRAM, without any processing.

When the active configuration of the router provides the desired results, the router's settings can be saved to the NVRAM to make sure that the router works properly after reload. The command responsible for copying the running configuration to other destinations is **copy** (see Listing 1-7).

```
R1#copy ?
  /erase          Erase destination file system.
  flash:          Copy from flash: file system
  ftp:            Copy from ftp: file system
  null:           Copy from null: file system
  nvram:          Copy from nvram: file system
  rcp:            Copy from rcp: file system
  running-config  Copy from current system configuration
  startup-config  Copy from startup configuration
  system:         Copy from system: file system
  tftp:           Copy from tftp: file system
  xmodem:         Copy from xmodem: file system
  ymodem:         Copy from ymodem: file system

R1#copy running-config ?
  flash:          Copy to flash: file system
  ftp:            Copy to ftp: file system
  null:           Copy to null: file system
  nvram:          Copy to nvram: file system
```

```
rcp:             Copy to rcp: file system
running-config   Update (merge with) current system configuration
startup-config   Copy to startup configuration
system:          Copy to system: file system
tftp:            Copy to tftp: file system

R1#copy running-config
```

Listing 1-7. *List of parameters for the* **copy** *command*

The **copy running-config startup-config** command creates the backup copy of the running configuration in the NVRAM. The **show configuration** command can be used to check the contents of the NVRAM. The **show running-config** command displays active settings in the current terminal session (see Listing 1-8).

```
R1#show running
Building configuration...


Current configuration:
!
version 11.3
service timestamps debug datetime msec
no service password-encryption
!
hostname R1
!
...
```

Listing 1-8. *Example of using the* **show running-config** *command*

The **copy running tftp** command can be used to store the router's active configuration to a TFTP server. When this command is entered, several additional parameters, such as the IP address and the file name, need to be specified. An exception to the idea of the **copy** command is its **copy /erase** version. It does not process the running configuration but instead clears the contents of the specified destination.

The configuration management commands given here were introduced in IOS v10.3. The operating system still supports old-style commands. Table 1-1 shows the corresponding old and new versions of the commands. Most people find the new set of commands more logical and prefer using the new ones. However, old habits are difficult to break, and because the old syntax is supported, people still type **write mem** instead of **copy running startup**.

An important detail about making changes to the router's active configuration is that the new configuration file does not substitute the current settings as occurs during a file copy operation. Rather, new commands are merged with the existing settings. It is usually

Table 1-1. *Command Equivalences*

Old-Style (Pre 10.3) Commands	New-Style (10.3 and Later) Commands
Configure terminal	configure terminal
Configure memory	copy startup-config running-config
Configure network	copy tftp running-config
Configure overwrite-network	copy tftp startup-config
write terminal	show running-config
write memory	copy running-config startup-config
write network	copy running-config tftp
write erase	erase startup-config
show configuration	show startup-config

no problem to understand the manual changes made using the **configure terminal** command. However, people tend to incorrectly imagine the way the **copy startup-config running-config** and the **copy tftp running-config** commands work as substitution. Consider an example. The following is the initial configuration of a router's interface Serial0:

```
interface serial 0
 no ip address
 shutdown
```

It is updated with following configuration file on a TFTP server:

```
interface serial 0
 ip address 10.1.1.1 255.255.255.0
```

Will the router be able to forward IP packets over the Serial0 interface after applying the configuration file from the TFTP server by using the **copy tftp running** or the **configure network** command? People usually answer yes because the new configuration enables IP processing on the interface by assigning an IP address. The correct answer, however, is no because the configuration fragment downloaded from the server does not explicitly disable the **shutdown** interface command. The final configuration, therefore, is as follows, and the interface is administratively down until the administrator enters the **no shutdown** command:

```
interface serial 0
ip address 10.1.1.1 255.255.255.0
shutdown
```

Note the difference between the applied and the final configurations. To understand why they are different, just imagine how the process of configuration parsing occurs. The parser doesn't care about the source of commands; it just processes them and applies changes to the software modules. Processing commands from a file on a TFTP server or from the NVRAM has the same result as entering the commands from a terminal session by using the **configure terminal** command.

1.4 Monitoring and Troubleshooting Tools

Today, network administrators have a wide choice of troubleshooting equipment, including the packet decoders for LAN and WAN links from several vendors. The tool may be a software package that makes a protocol analyzer from a PC, or it may be a dedicated piece of equipment. These tools become helpful when you have to find what is on the wire and have physical access to it. However, it's not very likely that to troubleshoot a routing problem you will need to chase frames all over the network, eavesdropping on the links with your beloved analyzer. In fact, the majority of problems in Cisco-based networks can be solved or at least identified with the tools built into the routers.

As you may have guessed, only built-in tools are used in this book to see what's happening inside the network. These tools include a number of **show** commands, allowing the administrator to display the contents of certain data structures, such as the routing tables or internal protocol databases. All dynamic data is collected with a set of **debug** commands, the output of which can be obtained from the routers' console ports or a TELNET session by using the **terminal monitor** command discussed earlier.

Because the book is dedicated to IP routing, we will be interested mostly in the routing tables of the routers in the lab. We use the **show ip route** set of commands to display the contents of the routing table and details of specific routes. Interesting parts of the output are marked as shown in Listing 1-9, which illustrates how the **show ip route** command can be used to show the routing table and the details of a specific route.

```
R1#show ip rou
...
Gateway of last resort is 200.1.0.2 to network 0.0.0.0

S    50.0.0.0/8 is directly connected, Null0
C    200.0.0.0/24 is directly connected, Loopback0
...
R    40.0.0.0/8 [120/1] via 20.1.0.2, 00:00:15, Serial0
```

```
        10.0.0.0/24 is subnetted, 1 subnets
C          10.0.1.0 is directly connected, Ethernet0
        30.0.0.0/8 is variably subnetted, 2 subnets, 2 masks
R          30.1.16.0/22 [120/1] via 20.1.0.2, 00:00:17, Serial0
R          30.1.16.0/24 [120/1] via 20.1.0.2, 00:00:17, Serial0
R*      0.0.0.0/0 [120/1] via 20.1.0.2, 00:00:17, Serial0
R1#
R1#show ip route 30.1.16.0
Routing entry for 30.1.16.0/24
  Known via "rip", distance 120, metric 1
  Redistributing via rip
  Advertised by rip (self originated)
  Last update from 20.1.0.2 on Serial0, 00:00:22 ago
  Routing Descriptor Blocks:
  * 20.1.0.2, from 20.1.0.2, 00:00:22 ago, via Serial0
      Route metric is 1, traffic share count is 1
R1#
```

Listing 1-9. *Output of the* show ip route *command*

Ellipsis (...) points are used whenever some information is deleted from the output. As in the outputs shown throughout the book, the first part of the output, showing the origin and other codes, is stripped out to save space for more valuable information.

By default, Cisco routers do not include date and time when displaying debugging and logging messages. Instead, the **service timestamps** command is used to make the router add the current date and time to the messages it sends (see Listing 1-10).

```
R1#debug serial interface
R1#
Serial2(in): StEnq, myseq 72
Serial2(out): Status, myseq 73, yourseen 76, DCE up
R1#conf t
Enter configuration commands, one per line.  End with CNTL/Z.
R1(config)# service timestamps debug datetime msec
R1(config)#^Z
R1#
%SYS-5-CONFIG_I: Configured from console by console
R1#
*Mar  4 04:55:02.148: Serial2(in): StEnq, myseq 73
*Mar  4 04:55:02.156: Serial2(out): Status, myseq 74, yourseen 77, DCE up
R1#
```

Listing 1-10. *Using the* service timestamps *command*

Listing 1-11, a part of the **debug ip** commands available on Cisco routers, shows the potential of the debugging commands in Cisco IOS.

```
R1#debug ip ?
  bgp        BGP information
  cache      IP cache operations
  egp        EGP information
  eigrp      IP-EIGRP information
  error      IP error debugging
  icmp       ICMP transactions
  igrp       IGRP information
  mobile     Mobility protocols
  ospf       OSPF information
  policy     Policy routing
  rip        RIP protocol transactions
  routing    Routing table events
  ...
R1#debug ip ospf ?
  adj              OSPF adjacency events
  events           OSPF events
  flood            OSPF flooding
  lsa-generation   OSPF lsa generation
  packet           OSPF packets
  retransmission   OSPF retransmission events
  spf              OSPF spf
  tree             OSPF database tree
```

Listing 1-11. *List of parameters for the* **debug ip** *command*

Other helpful tools are Ping and Traceroute. Ping is used to test end-to-end connectivity between routers; Traceroute, to find out what network path packets take when going from one point of a network to another.

Listing 1-12 shows how Ping works.

```
R1#ping 20.1.1.2

Type escape sequence to abort.
Sending 5, 100-byte ICMP Echos to 20.1.1.2, timeout is 2 seconds:
!!!!!
Success rate is 100 percent (5/5), round-trip min/avg/max = 28/30/32 ms
R1#
R1#ping 33.33.33.33

Type escape sequence to abort.
Sending 5, 100-byte ICMP Echos to 33.33.33.33, timeout is 2 seconds:
.....
Success rate is 0 percent (0/5)
R1#
```

Listing 1-12. *Example of using the* **ping** *command to test connectivity*

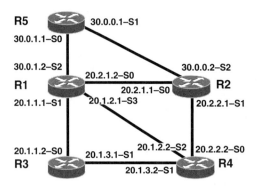

Figure 1-3. *Topology of the test lab network*

As you can see, two addresses were pinged with different results. The first ping was addressed to a host with IP address 20.1.1.2, the address of one of the routers in the lab. The exclamation points mean that ping requests were successfully answered and the router received the replies. The last line shows the percentage of successful attempts. The second ping was destined to 33.33.33.33. Because this address doesn't exist in the lab, the packets were dropped, and no reply was received, as indicated by the periods.

1.5 The Test Lab

Throughout this book, five Cisco routers are used to illustrate topics discussed. The exact models used in the lab vary from chapter to chapter, but the lab has been made as uniform as possible. Unless explicitly noted, all routers run IOS v12.1, Enterprise Feature Set. The topology of the lab network is shown in Figure 1-3. Whenever the network topology or the interface names are changed, the network diagram is provided. All links in the lab are assigned individual subnets with subnet mask 255.255.255.0. This addressing scheme is used in all cases unless it is changed to foster a better understanding of the subject. For the same reason, extra routers may be added to the network, and devices may be reconnected when necessary.

All serial connections are made back-to-back, using native Cisco V.35 DTE (data terminal equipment) and DCE (data communications equipment) cables, but this is not mandatory. While reconstructing the examples in your lab, remember that use of DCE cables on Cisco routers requires the **clock rate** interface command, which enables generation of the synchronization signal to time the DTE-side router.

1.6 References

[SecConf] Cisco Systems. Security Configuration. http://www.cisco.com/univercd/cc/td /doc/product/software/ios113ed/dsqcg/qcsecur.htm.

Chapter Two

Review of IP Addressing

This chapter provides a short summary of IP addressing in order to refresh readers' existing knowledge and to clarify several commonly misunderstood aspects. Information is provided on classful and classless IP addressing, subnets and variable-length subnet masks, and other topics.

2.1 IP Addressing

Working on the network layer of the OSI reference model, the Internet Protocol (IP) provides higher layers with logical addressing, routing, and best-path determination. Logical addressing is an important characteristic that allows network devices to disengage themselves from the details of physical topology and media access protocols. When two IP hosts communicate with each other, neither one knows or cares about the type of media used to connect the other host to the IP network. All they need to know is the IP address of the other host. The media could be Ethernet or Token Ring or an asynchronous connection using Point-to-Point Protocol (PPP) as its data link layer protocol. Logical addressing hides these details.

Every block of information sent over IP is encapsulated in an IP datagram. For example, when you type a **show version** command in your TELNET session to a Cisco router, the symbols you type are passed to a Transmission Control Protocol (TCP) connection over which this TELNET session is working. When it dispatches one or more symbols to IP, TCP adds its own TCP header in front. The IP layer in turn prefixes the TCP segment with its own IP header and passes the whole block as a single piece of data to the data link layer of the appropriate interface.

[RFC791] describes the format of the IP header, which is attached to the beginning of every data block sent via IP (Figure 2-1). As you can see, the header contains two 32-bit address fields—the *source address* and the *destination address*—that uniquely identify the sender and the receiver of a given IP datagram. The destination address is

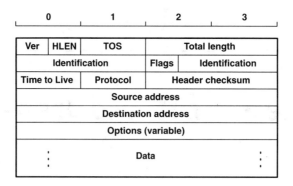

Figure 2-1. *Format of IP header*

the information routers use to forward IP datagrams from one interface to another. Having received an IP datagram, the receiver knows to reply to the source address.

IP addressing has always been hierarchical; it doesn't imply a flat addressing scheme whereby devices in the network maintain a path to each reachable host independently. Instead, the scheme presumes that although each host has a unique address within the network, all hosts are grouped into separately addressed networks, represented by LAN segments or WAN clouds. Each host inside a network is assigned a unique address. Therefore, every IP address can be divided into two parts: the part representing the network to which the host is attached and the part indicating which host on the network is the source or the destination of the communication stream. The network part of an IP address is used to identify a community of hosts, each of which is addressed with the host part.

The *address mask*, which too is a 32-bit number, is used in IP to split the IP address into the network and the host portions. Bits set to 1 in the address mask correspond to the network part of an address. Other bits correspond to the host part of it. Both IP addresses and masks are written as four decimal numbers—one for each byte—divided by dots: *dotted-decimal notation*. An example of an IP address is 20.1.2.2; an example of an address mask is 255.255.255.0.

The way address masks are used to segregate the network and the host parts of an IP address is simple. An IP host performs a binary AND operation between the IP address and the corresponding mask (Listing 2-1). The result of a binary (Address AND Mask) is the address of the network, or the network part; the result of a binary (Address AND (NOT Mask)) is the host address within the network.

```
Address:      200.1.2.2
Mask:         255.255.255.0
```

```
Address:        11001000.00000001.00000010.00000010
Mask:           11111111.11111111.11111111.00000000
                _____

Network:        11001000.00000001.00000010.00000000   <- Binary Address AND Mask
Host:           00000000.00000000.00000000.00000010   <- Binary Address AND (NOT Mask)

Network:        200.1.2.0
Host:           0.0.0.2
```

Listing 2-1. *Determining the network and the host parts of an IP address*

An obvious question is how the address masks are assigned to addresses. [RFC791], which described the first version of the IP addressing scheme, defined static mask assignment by dividing the whole IP address space into classes. Each of five address classes (A to E) is identified by the highest bits of the address value. Classes A through C are assigned specific address masks. Classes D and E do not have associated address masks. Figure 2-2 shows identification of address classes and the boundary between the network and the host parts. As you can see, the highest-order bits of the address function as class discriminators and are used by IP hosts and routers to determine the class of IP address referenced.

Each class is assigned its own address mask. The class of an address is identified by the high order bits of the address. Table 2-1 shows the address ranges and address masks for each class. Classes D and E are not assigned default address masks, because they are not used for normal IP addressing but rather for IP multicasting (class D) and for research needs (class E). Classes A through C have default address masks, which makes it possible to break a given IP address into network and host parts. The address range 248–254 is reserved, and network 255 is used for local subnet broadcast (discussed later).

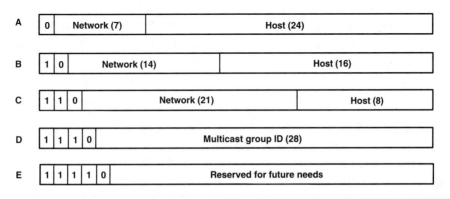

Figure 2-2. *IP address classes (binary notation)*

Table 2-1. *Class Address Ranges and Default Masks (decimal notation)*

Class	First Byte Range	Default Mask
A	1–126	255.0.0.0
B	128–191	255.255.0.0
C	192–223	255.255.255.0
D	224–239	Multicast
E	240–247	Experimental

If you look at class A's first byte range, you see that border values are not used, that is, values 0 and 127 are not in the range. This is not a mistake in mathematics but rather a basic IP addressing agreement to use network address 0 to identify the network a host is on at the moment. Network address 0 can be used by the Bootstrap protocol (BOOTP) while a station is trying to find out its IP address. Network address 127 is used for "loopback" IP addresses, which can be used by an IP host to direct packets to itself without sending them to a physical media. It implies that an IP packet sent to network 127 will never go out of the box but will be returned to the IP layer as if it were received from an external source.

Although the foregoing is a simple way to split the IP address into two parts, using default address masks is not efficient and wastes address space. Imagine that an organization receives a range of IP addresses as a class A network 123.0.0.0. If default address masks are used, the organization is supposed to use all three remaining bytes to identify specific hosts on a *single* LAN segment. Even today, when we have powerful LAN switches, it is not realistic to have a flat network consisting of 16,777,212 ($2^{24} - 2$) hosts. Furthermore, if the organization had multiple LAN segments, it would need to acquire additional networks to be able to address hosts on other segments. To solve this problem, the mechanism of subnetting was introduced in [RFC950].

2.2 Subnetting

The subnetting procedure allows an administrator to use some bits from the host part of an IP address to number individual IP segments within a network. To accomplish this, the administrator must extend the length of the address mask to the desired number of bits. Bits added to the standard address mask represent the part of the IP address used to number subnets. Listing 2-2 shows how a class B network, 131.10.0.0, is subnetted, using the third byte for numbering extension.

```
Address: 131.10.0.0
Standard mask 255.255.0.0   : 11111111. 11111111. 00000000. 00000000
Extended mask 255.255.255.0 : 11111111. 11111111. 11111111. 00000000
```

Listing 2-2. *Extending the address mask for subnetting*

Now all IP hosts in the network are assigned IP addresses with address mask 255.255.255.0, indicating that the third byte is used for subnetting. This is to let the hosts and the routers know which destination addresses belong to which subnets. To send packets destined to addresses belonging to remote—not directly attached—subnets, the host uses the default router as a relay. Packets addressed to hosts on attached subnets are sent to them directly.

Each address in form 131.10.X.0 is now called a subnet, whereas the class-derived network address 131.10.0.0 is called a major network. (Note that only one subnet mask per major network is allowed in classful addressing.) Table 2-2 shows the list of subnets and the host address ranges for the example.

While subnetting a given address space, it is not necessary to stick to the byte boundaries, because both the IP address and the address mask are considered 32-bit values, not four separate bytes. Thus, it is not necessary to use all eight bits of any byte in the address to number the subnets. Instead, most organizations are now given class C address networks for their use, which means that addresses must be split into subnet and host parts somewhere within the last byte. Listing 2-3 shows how this is done.

```
Address: 195.100.10.0
Standard mask 255.255.255.0  : 11111111. 11111111. 11111111. 00000000
Extended mask 255.255.255.224: 11111111. 11111111. 11111111. 11100000
```

Listing 2-3. *Using bits for subnetting*

Table 2-2. *Address Ranges for Subnets*

Subnet	Address Range*
131.10.1.0	131.10.1.1–131.10.1.254
131.10.2.0	131.10.1.2–131.10.2.254
131.10.3.0	131.10.1.3–131.10.3.254
….	
131.10.254.0	131.10.254.1–131.10.254.254

*All addresses are used with the address mask 255.255.255.0.

Three bits are used to number subnets; five bits, to number hosts. Skipping border values of all 0s and all 1s for both subnet and host numbers, explained later in this chapter, there can be 6 ($2^3 - 2$) subnets, each consisting of 30 ($2^5 - 2$) hosts. This is suitable for most midsize companies. This scheme implies using the address mask of 255.255.255.224 for every IP address assigned to a host within the entire network. Table 2-3 shows the ranges of IP addresses for each subnet.

2.3 Special Addressing Rules

You should have noticed by now that the complete mathematical range of addresses for network and host parts was not used. For example, when the address classes were discussed, the networks 0 and 127 were not used for class A. It was mentioned when considering subnetting examples, that border values of all 0s and all 1s are not used for subnet and host numbers. The reason for that is addressing conventions:

- *All 0s in all bits.* The address 0.0.0.0 is an obsolete form of local broadcast.
- *All 0s in the network part.* This case is described in [RFC791]. An address with all 0s in the network part may be used to specify *this network*, the network a host is currently on. This type of addressing is usually used in some Internet Control Message Protocol (ICMP) and BOOTP messages. An example is address 0.0.0.12, which designates an IP host with number 0.0.0.12 in the current network (the network address is unknown).
- *All 1s in the network and host parts.* This case is described in [RFC1812]. The IP address of all 1s (255.255.255.255) is considered to be a *local broadcast*. The local broadcasts are used to address all IP hosts on "this" segment.
- *All 0s in the host part.* This case is described in [RFC1812]. This kind of IP address—for example, 131.10.1.0—is an obsolete form of directed broadcast when

Table 2-3. *Address Ranges for Subnets*

Subnet	Address Range*
195.100.10.32	195.100.10.33–195.100.10.62
195.100.10.64	195.100.10.65–195.100.10.94
195.100.10.96	195.100.10.97–95.100.10.126
195.100.10.128	195.100.10.129–195.100.10.158
195.100.10.160	195.100.10.161–195.100.10.190
195.100.10.192	195.100.10.193–195.100.10.222

*All addresses are used with the address mask 255.255.255.224.

used as the destination address. This type of address is also used to keep information in the routing tables.

- *All 1s in the host part.* This case is described in [RFC1812]. An address with all 1s in the host part with the network part set to a network address is used as a *directed broadcast*, addressing all hosts on a given network/subnet. For example, 131.10.1.255 addresses all hosts in the subnet 131.10.1.0 of the major network 131.101.0.0. As another example, 195.100.10.63 addresses all hosts in the subnet 195.100.10.32 of the major network 195.100.10.0. [RFC2644] specifies that routers should provide the administrator with an option to control processing of directed broadcast packets (see Section 2.6.)

- *All 1s in the subnet and host parts.* So-called *all subnets broadcast* is a form of directed broadcast, when all hosts on all subnets are addressed. The example address 131.10.255.255 can be used to address all hosts in all subnets of the major network 131.10.0.0. Note that if no subnetting is used, this address can also be used to find all IP hosts in the major network.

These six rules are basic and critical for understanding. For additional information on special IP addressing cases, please read RFCs 791 and 1812.

Now you should understand why all 0s cannot be used in a network number. All 0s and all 1s in the subnet portion used to be a not-recommended configuration as well, mostly because of the confusion it could potentially cause in some routing protocols. (RIPv1 and IGRP do not explicitly differentiate between a route to the major network and a route to the zero subnet, as they do not announce route masks.) However, using border subnet values is a common practice today, as it saves IP address space. The problem with the routing protocols is solved by assuming that zero subnets are announced only within the network they belong to and that a route to the major network is never announced inside the network itself.

If you decide to use all 0s and all 1s combinations for subnet numbers, you can use only a single bit for two subnets instead of two bits when you don't use border values.

Even though you can use all 0s and all 1s in the subnet part of the address, you cannot do so in the host part of an address used for a real host. The host part *cannot* be all 0s or all 1s, as these combinations are used for specifying a given subnet and broadcasting.

An exception to this rule is documented in [RFC3021]. The document describes how a single bit can be used to assign IP addresses to the interfaces connected to point-to-point links.

2.4 Classful and Classless Addressing

All addressing principles explained in the previous sections are said to be *classful*, because they use address classes as the main concept. Classful addressing also calls for some rules of router operations, considered in Chapter 3.

Classful addressing is now used only in legacy networks. Moreover, even legacy networks are now going to classless addressing schemes. It sometimes is not understood why the IP community decided to move to it. To give you a better understanding, we consider the two basic parts of classless IP—classless addressing and classless routing—separately.

The main, and most obvious, problem with classful addressing is that the standard subnetting procedure is not really flexible, as it requires a single subnet mask to be used throughout the entire major network, regardless of how many hosts are actually on each segment. Imagine using four bits for subnetting and four bits for host numbering. Four bits can be used to address 14 hosts on one segment, which is okay for LANs but not for point-to-point links, where there are only two hosts. This is an obvious waste of address space.

Another problem with classful addressing is that route aggregation can be done only on the major network boundaries. That is, a route's mask can be either a subnet or a network one, thus making it impossible to represent a set of subnets or a set of major networks with a single route. (Aggregation is covered in Chapter 3.) This results in growth of the routing table in the routers.

Taking into consideration these and other problems, the Internet community proposed a special technique, called *variable-length subnet masks* (VLSM), that allowed administrators to split given address space into more adequate ranges, each reflecting the needs of a given part of the network. The VLSM technique is a part of the *classless interdomain routing* (CIDR) concept described in [RFC1519], which also implies some modifications to routers operation, considered in Chapter 3.

2.5 Variable-Length Subnet Masks

The most common misunderstanding about VLSM is that it was the first subnetting technique. This is not true, of course. As seen in the previous sections, classful addressing includes basic subnetting, and it was used in the real world long before VLSM appeared.

While considering classful addressing, it was mentioned that the entire major network is necessarily configured with IP addresses using one address mask, also called subnet mask. It is not correct to use, for example, mask 255.255.255.0 on some segments and mask 255.255.192.0 on other ones, although it would be more convenient.

Use of VLSM allows some subnets to be subdivided, thus making it possible to use different subnet masks on different network segments. For example, a company acquires an address range as a network 195.100.10.0. Now imagine that this small company has five LAN segments—one in the main office and four in remote sites, each consisting of not less than 20 and not more than 25 hosts. The company also has five point-to-point links: four links from the central site to the remote sites and one uplink to the Internet provider. The task is to assign IP subnets to each LAN segment and WAN link.

With classical subnetting, the problem can't be solved without asking for additional addresses. This comes from simple mathematical calculations: For ten subnets—five LANs and five point-to-point links—four bits would be needed for subnetting. The remaining four bits would permit only 14 hosts per subnet, which doesn't meet the requirements.

The VLSM technique addresses this problem. First, let's consider the LAN segments. Each of them contains from 20 to 25 hosts. This leads to the decision of using five bits for host numbering on these segments ($2^5 - 2 = 30$). Now we have three bits left for subnetting. This is not enough for classical subnetting, but VLSM is a different case. In Figure 2-3, which shows the subnetting boundaries, border values are not used for subnet numbering, which yields a total of six subnets with the given subnet mask. These subnets can be used successfully for LAN addressing, but what about WAN links? Take the last subnet in Figure 2-3 and subdivide it further using only two bits for host numbering. (Only two hosts per subnet are required for point-to-point links.) The result of this operation is illustrated in Figure 2-4. As you see, in addition to three original bits used for subnetting, we have three more bits, which permit six "subsubnets" within the last subnet. As a result, there are now enough addresses to use in the sample network.

After setting the borders, all the subnets and masks in the network can be listed (Table 2-4). If the network grew further, border values—all 0s and all 1s combinations—could be used to number subnets, which would make it possible to have two additional subnets for LANs and two for point-to-point links.

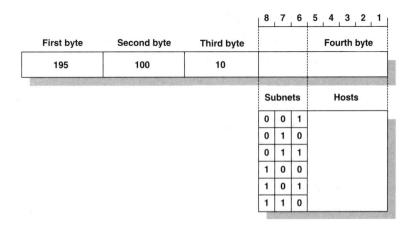

Figure 2-3. *Subnetting example*

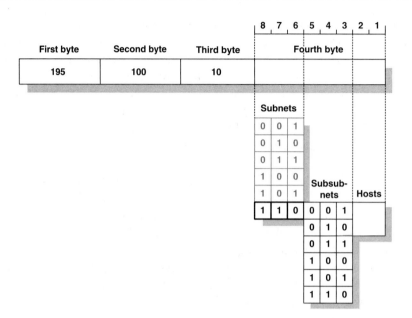

Figure 2-4. *VLSM subnetting*

Table 2-4. *Example Subnet Address and Host Address Ranges*

	Subnet Addresses	Host Address Ranges
LANs	195.100.10.32 255.255.255.224	195.100.10.33–195.100.10.62
	195.100.10.64 255.255.255.224	195.100.10.65–195.100.10.94
	195.100.10.96 255.255.255.224	195.100.10.97–195.100.10.126
	195.100.10.128 255.255.255.224	195.100.10.129–195.100.10.158
	195.100.10.160 255.255.255.224	195.100.10.161–195.100.10.170
Point-to-point	195.100.10.196 255.255.255.252	195.100.10.197–195.100.10.198
	195.100.10.200 255.255.255.252	195.100.10.201–195.100.10.202
	195.100.10.204 255.255.255.252	195.100.10.205–195.100.10.206
	195.100.10.208 255.255.255.252	195.100.10.209–195.100.10.210
	195.100.10.212 255.255.255.252	195.100.10.213–195.100.10.214
	195.100.10.216 255.255.255.252	195.100.10.217–195.100.10.218

When thinking about VLSM, you should understand that there are no address classes any more; nor is there any fixed border between the network and the host parts in the address. There are no subnets in the classful meaning. A given address space can now be split by using different address masks, provided that each prefix is distinguishable from the others. In normal language, you cannot use one prefix on a segment and subdivide it further to number other segments, because it leads to ambiguity in routing.

> Not all routing protocols support VLSM. RIPv1 and IGRP are classful protocols and cannot be used in CIDR environments. RIPv2, Enhanced IGRP (EIGRP), Open Shortest Path First (OSPF), Integrated Intermediate System to Intermediate System (IS-IS), and Border Gateway Protocol version 4 (BGPv4) are classless protocols.

2.6 IP Addressing Details in Cisco Routers

Cisco routers support both classful and classless addressing, and you don't have to enter any command to turn on the classless addressing.

> Note that the **ip classless** command enables classless routing table lookup, but it does not affect IP addressing. You don't have to enter any command to be able to use VLSM.

To assign an IP address to an interface, use the following command in the interface configuration mode.

ip address *ip-address mask*

Listing 2-4 shows an example of assigning an IP address to a router's interface.

```
R1#show int s0
Serial0 is up, line protocol is up
  Hardware is HD64570
  MTU 1500 bytes, BW 64 Kbit, DLY 20000 usec, rely 255/255, load 1/255
  Encapsulation PPP, loopback not set, keepalive set (10 sec)
...
R1#show ip int s0
Serial0 is up, line protocol is up
  Internet protocol processing disabled
R1#
R1#conf t
Enter configuration commands, one per line.  End with CNTL/Z.
```

```
R1(config)#int ser 0
R1(config-if)#ip address 20.1.1.2 255.255.255.0
R1(config-if)#^Z
R1#
R1#show int s0
Serial0 is up, line protocol is up
  Hardware is HD64570
  Internet address is 20.1.1.2/24
  MTU 1500 bytes, BW 64 Kbit, DLY 20000 usec, rely 255/255, load 1/255
  Encapsulation PPP, loopback not set, keepalive set (10 sec)
...
R1#show ip int s0
Serial0 is up, line protocol is up
  Internet address is 20.1.1.2/24
  Broadcast address is 255.255.255.255
  Address determined by setup command
  Peer address is 20.1.1.1
MTU is 1500 bytes
...
```

Listing 2-4. *Assigning IP address to an interface*

Note that the output of the first **show interface serial 0** command doesn't show an IP address, which means that IP processing is not enabled on the interface and no IP packets are sent over it. This is confirmed by the output of the **show ip interface serial 0** command. Only after using the **ip address** command in the interface configuration mode is IP processing enabled on it.

It is possible to have multiple IP networks on the same physical segment. In this case, hosts on different IP networks are not supposed to communicate with each other directly but rather to use a router that has attachments to all required networks. A Cisco router, if it is configured with multiple IP addresses on the same interface, can be used to route between different IP subnets on the same physical segment. The following interface configuration command can be used to configure additional IP addresses on an interface.

ip address *ip-address mask* **secondary**

An example of using this command is given in the Listing 2-5. Interface Serial0 is assigned a primary and a secondary IP address. Note that the secondary address is not displayed in the **show interface** commands. You can identify them by looking through the router's active configuration given by the **show running** command.

```
R1#conf t
Enter configuration commands, one per line.  End with CNTL/Z.
```

```
R1(config)#int s0
R1(config-if)#ip address 20.1.1.2 255.255.255.0
R1(config-if)#ip address 50.1.1.1 255.255.255.0 sec
R1(config-if)#^Z
R1#show ip int s0
Serial0 is up, line protocol is up
  Internet address is 20.1.1.2/24
  Broadcast address is 255.255.255.255
  Address determined by setup command
  Peer address is 20.1.1.1
  MTU is 1500 bytes
  Helper address is not set
...
R1#show run
Building configuration...

Current configuration:
!
...
interface Serial0
  ip address 50.1.1.1 255.255.255.0 secondary
  ip address 20.1.1.2 255.255.255.0
  encapsulation ppp
...
R1#
```

Listing 2-5. *Assigning secondary IP address*

Cisco IOS supports unnumbered point-to-point interfaces as described in [RFC1812]. Interfaces configured as unnumbered can be used to send and to receive IP packets without assigning separate IP addresses to them. As discussed in Chapter 4, an IP address does not have to be assigned to a point-to-point interface to make the router use it while forwarding packets. The reason is that the router does not need to know the IP address of the remote end of a link—the next-hop address—to construct the frame. The router can just push a packet over the link. To enable IP processing on a point-to-point link without assigning a specific IP address, use the following interface configuration command:

ip unnumbered *int-type int-number*

The parameters ***int-type*** and ***int-number*** specify the interface whose IP address the router uses while generating and processing packets—for example, routing updates—on the unnumbered interface. The referenced interface must be in the up state and assigned a valid IP address; it cannot be another unnumbered interface. Listing 2-6 gives an example of how the **ip unnumbered** command is used, whereby a loopback interface is created, and configuration of the serial interface refers to it.

```
R1#conf t
Enter configuration commands, one per line.  End with CNTL/Z.
R1(config)#int lo0
R1(config-if)#
%LINEPROTO-5-UPDOWN: Line protocol on Interface Loopback0, changed state to up
%LINK-3-UPDOWN: Interface Loopback0, changed state to up
R1(config-if)#ip address 20.1.1.2 255.255.255.0
R1(config-if)#int ser 0
R1(config-if)#ip unnumbered lo0
R1(config-if)#^Z
R1#
R1#show ip int ser 0
Serial0 is up, line protocol is up
  Interface is unnumbered. Using address of Loopback0 (20.1.1.2)
  Broadcast address is 255.255.255.255
  Peer address is 20.1.1.1
  MTU is 1500 bytes
R1#
```

Listing 2-6. *Using unnumbered IP interfaces*

The command **interface loopback 0** creates the loopback interface itself. Because the state of the loopback interfaces does not depend on the state of any physical interface, the loopback interfaces never go down unless the administrator uses an explicit **shutdown** interface command. Therefore, administrators tend to reference loopback interfaces rather than physical ones if the router has more than one WAN interface.

The **ip unnumbered** command can be used only for point-to-point interfaces or subinterfaces. Whether an interface is point-to-point is determined by the type of data link encapsulation (see Chapter 4). The command is not applicable to LAN or point-to-multipoint WAN interfaces; separate IP addresses must be assigned to them.

If a subnet of 0 needs to be used, the following Cisco IOS command needs to be entered in the global configuration mode:

ip subnet-zero

This command lets the administrator assign IP addresses, using all 0s combination in the subnet portion.

The **ip subnet-zero** command also enables processing of routing updates containing information about zero subnets (considered in more detail in Chapter 3).

Listing 2-7 shows an example of using the **ip subnet-zero** command.

```
R1#conf t
Enter configuration commands, one per line.  End with CNTL/Z.
R1(config)#int lo0
R1(config-if)#ip addr 50.0.0.1 255.255.255.0
Bad mask /24 for address 50.0.0.1
R1(config-if)#ex
R1(config)#ip subnet-zero
R1(config)#int lo0
R1(config-if)#ip addr 50.0.0.1 255.255.255.0
R1(config-if)#^Z
R1#
```

Listing 2-7. *Using the* ip subnet-zero *command*

As you can see, IOS does not permit the use of the all-0s combination for the subnet portion of IP addresses, by default. The **ip subnet-zero** command disables this check.

Cisco routers can handle all types of IP broadcasts, old and new styles, although they
generate the local broadcast as 255.255.255.255, by default. To change the default value
on an interface in order to meet the requirements of legacy IP hosts, use the following
command:

ip broadcast-address [*ip-address*]

Note that even if the broadcast address on an interface is changed using this command,
Cisco routers still accept all types of IP broadcasts on the interface.

Listing 2-8 shows how the **ip broadcast-address** command is used to change the destination address used for RIP broadcasts on an Ethernet interface. Although the broadcast
address is the default (255.255.255.255), it shows up in the debug output. After the
address has been changed, RIP updates are sent with the destination address set to local
broadcast; see the second debug output.

```
R1#
R1#debug ip rip
RIP protocol debugging is on
R1#
*Mar 10 21:56:12.684:RIP: sending v1 update to 255.255.255.255 via Ethernet0
(10.0.1.167)
...
R1#
R1#conf t
Enter configuration commands, one per line.  End with CNTL/Z.
R1(config)#int eth 0
R1(config-if)#ip broadcast-address 10.0.1.255
```

```
R1(config-if)#^Z
R1#
*Mar 10 21:56:39.520:RIP: sending v1 update to 10.0.1.255 via Ethernet0 (10.0.1.167)
...
R1#
```

Listing 2-8. *Changing the broadcast address*

When it receives a packet with the destination IP address set to a directed subnet broadcast—the host portion is set to all 1s—for a remote subnet, a router forwards the packet as a normal unicast submission. The router connected to the subnet where the packet is directed may send this packet to all nodes on the segment by using the data link layer broadcast transmission. However, this detail of the router's behavior has been used in a number of denial-of-service (DoS) attacks, and a common practice is to disable processing of directed broadcast packets. The following interface configuration command can be used to control whether directed subnet broadcast submissions should be translated to data link broadcasts or dropped:

ip directed-broadcast [*access-list*]

If an access list is specified, only packets matching the statements in the list are translated; all other packets are dropped. Before IOS v12.0, directed broadcast translation was enabled by default. However, as a protective measure against DoS attacks, many administrators disabled this command on all interfaces. Starting with IOS v12.0, directed broadcast processing is disabled, by default.

2.7 Frequently Asked Questions

Q: **My ISP gave me a class C network. Should I use classical subnetting or VLSM to address my networks and point-to-point links?**

A: It is recommended that you use VLSM. Note that it requires more up-to-date protocols, such as RIPv2, EIGRP, or OSPF, on all the routers in your network; static routes is another option, of course. Classical subnetting is now considered wasteful. However, it can be used with older routing protocols, such as RIP.

Q: **I want to use VLSM in my network, but some of the hosts inside my network have rather old TCP/IP stack implementations. Might they experience some problems in a VLSM environment?**

A: When you configure an IP host, you always specify the IP address, the address mask, and the IP address of the default gateway. It is the default gateway (router) that must be able to work in the VLSM environment. Variable-length subnet masks are transparent for end hosts.

Q: **What are the alternatives to using unnumbered interfaces?**

A: Instead of using unnumbered interfaces, you could number the WAN links, using IP addresses from private address ranges, described in [RFC1918]. You should not use this solution if your routing protocol is RIPv1 or IGRP, because these protocols belong to the classful routing protocol group and will lose subnet information on the major network boundaries. If you use classless routing, this solution is a good alternative, as it will allow you to number the WAN links with specific addresses. There are also some limitations, however. Because private addresses cannot be announced to the Internet, you will be able to ping the WAN links only from within your network. The same can be said about using the Traceroute utility. Also, please make sure that you do not announce your private addresses to the Internet. If you want your links to be numbered using the public IP addresses, it is a good idea to use the 31-bit mask on the point-to-point interfaces. See [RFC3021] for more information.

Q: **If I use private IP addresses for my WAN links, will I still be able to go to the Internet through them?**

A: Yes, you will be able to have Internet access. Remember that transit routers do not change the addresses in the headers of forwarded packets. Therefore, as soon as the routers have required routing information about public networks, explicit or default routes, packets will be forwarded properly.

Q: **If I decide to use the all-0s combination in the subnet portion of network addresses, will I have to change the configuration of all the routers in my network?**

A: The answer depends on the type of routing protocol you use. If it is a classful protocol (RIP and IGRP), you will have to add the **ip subnet-zero** command in every router within the major network to which the zero subnet belongs. This is to allow the routers to install zero-subnet routes in the routing tables. If you use classless routing protocols, such as RIPv2, OSPF, and EIGRP, you will need to add this command only on the routers attached to that zero subnet.

2.8 References

[RFC791] J. Postel, "Internet Protocol. DARPA Internet Program. Protocol Specification," RFC 791, September 1981, http://www.ietf.org/rfc/rfc791.txt.

[RFC950] J. Mogul and J. Postel, "Internet Standard Subnetting Procedure," RFC 950, August 1985, http://www.ietf.org/rfc/rfc950.txt.

[RFC1519] V. Fuller, T. Li, J. Yu, and K. Varadhan, "Classless Inter-Domain Routing (CIDR): an Address Assignment and Aggregation Strategy," RFC 1519, September 1993, http://www.ietf.org/rfc/rfc1519.txt.

[RFC1812] F. Baker, "Requirements for IP Version 4 Routers," RFC 1812, June 1995, http://www.ietf.org/rfc/rfc1812.txt.

[RFC1918] Y. Rekhter et al., "Address Allocation for Private Internets," RFC 1918, February 1996, http://www.ietf.org/rfc/rfc1918.txt.

[RFC2644] D. Senie, "Changing the Default for Directed Broadcasts in Routers," RFC 2644, August 1999, http://www.ietf.org/rfc/rfc264412.txt.

[RFC3021] A. Retana, R. White, V. Fuller, and D. McPherson, "Using 31-Bit Prefixes on IPv4 Point-to-Point Links," RFC 3021, December 2000, http://www.ietf.org/rfc/rfc3021.txt.

Chapter Three

Routing and Forwarding Processes

This chapter covers generic questions about the routing and forwarding processes. Operation of datagram networks, basics of routing table construction and packet-forwarding processes, and details of router operation in classful and classless environments are discussed.

For a long time, the term *routing* has been used interchangeably with the term *forwarding*. However, it is common today to differentiate these two notions.

In this book, as well as in the industry, the term *routing* is used to describe the functionality performed by the control software of the routers. This includes routing table maintenance, processing of static routes, dynamic routing protocols, and so on. The term *forwarding* is used to refer to the process of moving transit packets from one interface to another. The forwarding process includes looking through the forwarding table, making the forwarding decision, and sending the packet out of an interface. It is essential to understand the difference between the two processes, and this book emphasizes this in several places. This chapter discusses the concepts of both routing and forwarding processes.

3.1 Packet-Switched Technologies

The two main types of packet-switched technologies used in networks today are *virtual-circuit* (VC) and *datagram* networks. The difference between the two is in the data-delivery mechanism used on the network layer. Both types belong to the packet-switching group of telecommunication technologies, so the intermediate network devices decide where to send the packets carrying user data. The criteria taken into consideration while making this decision, as well as the procedures performed by the hosts and intermediate devices, depend on the type of the network.

Networks that use the virtual-circuit strategy can be compared to common circuit-switching telephone networks. When users of a telephone network need to communicate information—a voice or fax message—they explicitly establish a connection with the remote end by dialing a number. The network reacts by selecting and connecting the circuits, routing the call and allocating available resources for the connection. When the connection is established, it is used for the information transfer. When data is sent through the connection, the network does not perform any additional routing tasks for this connection, because the data flows along an already defined path.

Operation of VC-oriented packet-switching networks is similar. When one host needs to send some data to another, a connection through the network is opened before the transmission starts. In opening the connection, the source device specifies the called address—similar to dialing a telephone number—which is used by the network to route the call and to allocate bandwidth. When the network receives the call request, the network devices consult their *routing tables* to determine how the call-establishment request should be directed. The routing table is used only during the call setup. As the call traverses the network, the intermediate network devices create virtual circuits on the physical links and update their *switching tables*. The entries in the switching tables contain information about the virtual-circuit cross-connections. This information is used during data transfer. After the connection is established, the two hosts do not specify source or destination addresses in the data packets but rather include the identifier of the virtual circuit. This identifier is used to index within the switching table and to find the outbound interface and the new VC identifier. If either side decides to disconnect, it sends an explicit command to the network device it is connected to, which in turn requests other devices along the connection to release the resources.

Datagram networks operate on a different concept, which can be compared to that of the postal service. People sending letters to each other don't have to establish a connection beforehand. They simply provide proper address information and drop the letter at their local post office. The post office sends the letter to another post office closer to the destination. The letter traverses a set of post offices until it reaches the one local to the addressee.

In a datagram network, a host constructs a packet that includes the source and destination addresses. The packet is sent to the nearest network device, which in turn passes it to another device, closer to the destination. When it receives the packet, a network device performs a *routing decision*, also called a *forwarding decision*, based on the destination address of the packet and the contents of its routing table. The decision is made for every packet in every intermediate device.

This is the main difference between a datagram network and a virtual-circuit network. Devices in VC-oriented networks have to route only one packet per connection, the call setup; all other packets that belong to the same VC are switched using the switching table. Datagram network devices have to route every packet; each network device looks up its routing table and decides where to send the packet.

Both technologies have their pros and cons. For example, in virtual-circuit network devices, the code responsible for data transfer is very simple and efficient. Using only the switching table, it needs fewer CPU and RAM read cycles for data processing than do datagram network devices. At the same time, rerouting of already established connections, necessary in case of a topology change, can be a problem in virtual-circuit networks. Datagram networks adapt much faster, as every packet is routed at each hop. The adaptation, or convergence, time depends on how long it takes to propagate correct routing information. In most situations, it depends on the convergence time of the dynamic routing protocol used in the network. With modern protocols, such as OSPF and EIGRP, this time can be measured in seconds.

3.2 Router Operation Overview

As you know, every IP host in a network is normally configured with not only its own IP address and mask but also the IP address of the default gateway (see Figure 3-1). If the host needs to send an IP packet to a destination address that does not belong to a subnet the host is directly attached to, the host passes the packet to the default gateway (router).

A common misunderstanding is how the address of the default gateway is used. People tend to incorrectly think that when a packet is sent to the default router, the host sets the destination address in the IP packet to the configured default router address. However, the router would then consider the packet addressed to itself and would not forward it any further. Why configure the default gateway's IP address, then? The answer is that the host uses the *Address Resolution Protocol* (ARP) to find the *Media Access Control* (MAC) address of the specified router. Having acquired the router's MAC address, the host sends the packets directly to it as data link unicast submissions.

What happens when a router receives a packet on one of its interfaces? The first thing to remember is that normally, routers do not check the source IP address of the packet when it is received. It seems obvious. However, people are sometimes very surprised when they see, for example, packets coming from an interface attached to subnet 195.100.10.0 with the source address set to, say, 130.10.86.15.

As we will see in Chapter 5, however, Cisco routers can be explicitly configured to perform so-called unicast Reverse-Path Forwarding (RPF) check, whereby the router does verify the source address in the packets to prevent denial-of-service attacks.

Routers never change the source and the destination addresses in IP packets, except for *Network Address Translation* (NAT), which is not considered in this book. Routers send packets to each other by setting correct data link layer addresses—for example, MAC addresses for Ethernet or *Data Link Connection Identifier* (DLCI) for Frame Relay—in the data link frames or just pushing them through point-to-point links, using associated encapsulation mechanisms. If they changed the source and destination IP addresses, routers would lose information about where the packets were coming from

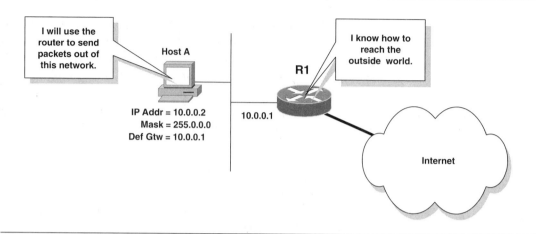

Figure 3-1. *Use of default gateway*

and going to. In our example, a packet with a source address of 130.10.86.15 could be originated by a host outside the network and forwarded by another router on subnet 195.100.10.0. The intermediate routers won't change the packet's IP addresses but instead just pass the packet to the next closest neighbor toward the destination address.

When a packet is received, the router checks its validity and determines whether the packet must be delivered locally—it is addressed to the router itself—or forwarded further. If the packet must be forwarded, the router makes the routing decision and determines the outbound interface and the IP address of the router that should be the next hop in the path, if the destination network is not directly attached.

Consider a simple example. Suppose that a router is connected to two networks—10.0.0.0 and 20.0.0.0—as illustrated in Figure 3-2. Host A on the first segment sends an IP packet to host B on the second segment. Host A passes the packet to the router by specifying the router's MAC address as the destination address in the Ethernet frame. (The destination IP address is the IP address of B.)

When it receives the frame, R1 examines the IP packet and uses its routing table to decide where to forward the packet. The table contains information in the form "to reach hosts on network N, use interface X and next hop Y." Such a combination of routing parameters is called a *route*. How does the router know where the networks are, though?

Part of every router's configuration task is assignment of IP addresses to the router's interfaces. A router therefore functions like a normal IP host on each network to which it is connected. Even if it never originated IP packets itself, a router would still need this information to answer the ARP requests sent by end nodes while trying to find the MAC address of the default router or by neighboring routers looking for the MAC address of the next hop.

Because a router's interfaces are configured with IP addresses and corresponding address masks, the router can derive information about the networks connected to its

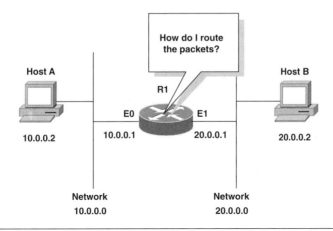

Figure 3-2. *Two segments connected by a router*

interfaces by applying address masks to the associated addresses. That is the way routers obtain their startup information about directly connected networks and put this information into the routing tables. In our example, the routing table of R1 would look like the following:

```
Network 10.0.0.0 is directly connected to interface Ethernet 0
Network 20.0.0.0 is directly connected to interface Ethernet 1
```

This table contains enough information to route the packet from host A to host B. The router just takes the destination address from the IP packet header and looks through the table. Having found the information about network 20.0.0.0, the router understands that the packet destined for a host on this network should be delivered on interface Ethernet 1. The decision is made. Now the router has to encapsulate the IP packet into an Ethernet frame and send it to host B. If this is the first time the router is sending a packet to this host, the router sends an ARP request, asking for B's MAC address. Otherwise, the router uses its ARP cache. This example is quite simple, as both networks are directly connected.

Now look at a network constructed of several routers (Figure 3-3). Every router in the network has information only about directly attached networks:

- R1:

```
Network 10.0.0.0 is directly connected to the interface Ethernet 0
Network 20.0.0.0 is directly connected to the interface Ethernet 1
```

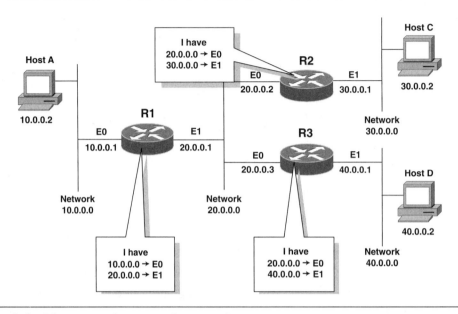

Figure 3-3. *More complex routed network*

- R2:

```
Network 20.0.0.0 is directly connected to the interface Ethernet 0
Network 30.0.0.0 is directly connected to the interface Ethernet 1
```

- R3:

```
Network 20.0.0.0 is directly connected to the interface Ethernet 0
Network 40.0.0.0 is directly connected to the interface Ethernet 1
```

Now host A from network 10.0.0.0 sends an IP packet to host C on network 30.0.0.0. When it receives the packet, R1 cannot make the forwarding decision, because it has no information about destination network 30.0.0.0. R1 will drop the packet and send an ICMP "Destination Unreachable" message to host A. What information would R1 need in its routing table to successfully route the packet to host C? There should obviously be a line saying that network 30.0.0.0 is reachable via router R2. The routing table of R1 would have to look like the following.

```
Network 10.0.0.0 is directly connected to the interface Ethernet 0
Network 20.0.0.0 is directly connected to the interface Ethernet 1
Network 30.0.0.0 is accessible via 20.0.0.2
```

With this information, the router would make its forwarding decision as follows.

1. The packet is destined to host 30.0.0.2 (host C).
2. Look through the routing table for information about address 30.0.0.2.
3. Address 30.0.0.2 belongs to network 30.0.0.0 that is accessible via host 20.0.0.2.
4. Look through the routing table for information about address 20.0.0.2.
5. Network 20.0.0.2 belongs to network 20.0.0.0 that is directly connected to interface Ethernet 1.
6. Send the packet through the Ethernet 1 interface, using R2's MAC address as the destination MAC address.

As you see, the router performs recursive table lookup, trying to find a route to the next-hop address, specified in the last route in the table. If there were another router, R4, on network 30.0.0.0 and connected to network 50.0.0.0, router R1 would have the following routing table:

```
Network 10.0.0.0 is directly connected to the interface Ethernet 0
Network 20.0.0.0 is directly connected to the interface Ethernet 1
Network 30.0.0.0 is accessible via 20.0.0.2
Network 50.0.0.0 is accessible via 30.0.0.5        (router R4's IP address)
```

The steps taken by the router in this case would be the same: "Find information about the destination network; if it goes through another network, find information about that one, too." The router would continue looking through the table recursively until it found a reference to a router's address that belonged to a directly connected network or it realized that there was no route for the address.

Following are some rules of thumb about routing in datagram networks. (IP networks belong to the datagram network group.) Knowing these basic principles is required for network maintenance and troubleshooting.

- *Every router makes its decision alone, based on the information it has in its own routing table.* When making the routing decision, a router can use only information in its own routing table. There is no way for a router to check whether its neighbors are going to make a consistent decision. Routers route packets according to the information they have in the routing tables at a particular instance. When it forwards a packet to the next router, a router assumes that the next router will do the same: make its decision according to the information in its own routing table. Only consistent routing information can guarantee a consistent forwarding decision throughout the network.

- *The fact that one router has certain information in its routing table does not mean that other routers have the same information.* Even if the first-hop router—the router nearest to the source—has required information about a remote network, other routers on the way to the destination may have no information about it. Therefore, even if the first-hop router forwards a packet successfully, the next router may drop the packet if it doesn't have enough routing information to forward it.

- *Routing information about a path from one network to another does not provide routing information about the reverse, or return, path.* Even though all routers along the way to a destination have information about the destination network, the remote routers may have no information about how to route packets coming back. In the example, if host C on network 30.0.0.0 sent a reply to host A on network 10.0.0.0, router R2 would need additional information about how to reach network 10.0.0.0. If it had no information about this network, R2 would have to drop the packet.

According to these rules, the administrator needs to make sure that all routers in a network have adequate and consistent information about every network that might be involved in the communication process.

Lack of routing information about a destination network is not the only reason for a router to drop a packet. A router can also drop packets because of output queue overflow or because of a lack of CPU time needed for the router to take packets out of the input queues. A packet is also dropped when the value of its *Time-to-Live* (TTL) field reaches 0; each router decrements it by 1. This is a protective measure introduced to make sure that even in the presence of temporary or permanent routing loops, the network does not accumulate—forward endlessly—packets destined for the networks for which the loops are experienced. Another reason for a packet drop is inability to fragment an IP packet while trying to send it through one of the router's interfaces.

Normally, every router's interface is assigned a value that specifies the maximum size of a data block that can be sent over it. This value is called *maximum transmission unit* (MTU) and is usually specific for a given media type. For example, the default MTU for Ethernet and serial interfaces in Cisco routers is 1,500 bytes; for the 16Mbps Token Ring, it is 8,136 bytes. When it is about to send an IP packet over an interface, a router checks whether the packet fits into the interface MTU. If the packet is bigger than the MTU, the router breaks the packet into pieces that fit into it and sends them as separate IP packets. This process is called *IP packet fragmentation*. Routers can fragment an IP packet if necessary unless it has the *do not fragment* (DF) bit set in the header. When this bit is set and a router sees that the packet must be fragmented, the router drops the packet and sends an ICMP "Destination Unreachable" message with the code field set to "Fragmentation needed and DF set" to the originator.

The difference between an IP packet and an IP datagram is that hosts always send datagrams, which can be fragmented into several IP packets. Therefore, any IP packet can be either a whole IP datagram or a fragment of it. IP packets can be further fragmented if they need to be sent over a link with even smaller MTUs.

If a datagram is fragmented while going through the network, the receiving host performs IP datagram reassembly. Routers do not reassemble IP datagrams from IP packets not destined for themselves, for several reasons. First, it would add extra delays in routing: A router would have to wait until all fragments of a given datagram came to it. Second, the router would need to store all fragments of all datagrams before reassembly. (Imagine an Internet core router doing this.) Third, and maybe most important, because routers perform load sharing—send packets to the same destination along parallel paths—and because IP packets are sometimes dropped on their way through the network, a router may never receive all fragments of a datagram.

3.3 Routing Information Sources

In Figure 3-3, which shows three routers connecting four networks, router R1 would need additional information to be able to route to network 30.0.0.0. A line in R1's routing table would say that the network is accessible via router R2. How does this piece of information get into the routing table?

Routing information can get into the routing table in only two ways. As in any computer, information in a router can be either entered manually or gathered automatically. The administrator can investigate the network, sketch the topology, formalize the information—that is, represent it in the form "For router R1, network N2 is accessible via router R3"—and feed it to every router in the network. This is what happened at the beginning of the network world: Administrators used to watch the networks and edit the routing tables manually whenever the topology changed. This type of routing information, provided and entered into routers by administrators, is called *static*. Static routes reflect the administrators' knowledge of the topology and the policy they want to apply to the traffic going to a certain destination.

The drawbacks of static routing are obvious. Static routing generally cannot adapt to changes in topology or to load and error rates of channels. To have this adaptation, administrators would need to constantly keep an eye on the network and change the routing tables in real time. It may not seem difficult for a network with five routers, but imagine what would happen if this technique were used to manage a network consisting of hundreds of routers and channels connecting them. It would be impossible. This is the reason *dynamic routing protocols*—automatic distributed network discovery and route calculation algorithms—were proposed, designed, and implemented.

The function of dynamic routing protocols is to exchange information about the networks routers know how to reach. Routing protocols provide routers with real-time information about where the networks are, which path is better for accessing a given network, which parallel paths can be used to balance the load among multiple channels, and so on. If routers have this information, they can maintain adequate routing tables.

3.4 Static Routing

Although dynamic routing protocols are widely used now, many networks still use static routing. It is effective when networks have stable topology and don't need real-time adaptation. In static routing, the administrator configures routers with all the information necessary for successful packet forwarding. The administrator constructs the routing table in every router by putting in the entries for every network that could be a destination.

In connecting a branch office to the central site, for example, static routing does everything needed for hosts on the central and remote networks to communicate (Figure 3-4). The administrator can just add static routes to the routers in the central and the remote offices, saying that respective networks are accessible via the corresponding routers. This arrangement doesn't demand a dynamic routing protocol, as neither site cares about the specific subnets behind the routers and there's no redundancy in the topology. Router R1 needs to know only that it must send packets to router R2 to reach any host in the remote office, no matter what IP subnet the host is in. R2, in turn, needs to know only that all hosts in the central office's network can be reached via router R1. Note, however, that if more routers were in the central or the remote network, they would also need to be configured with corresponding static routes.

The next example, closer to real life, is a hub-and-spoke topology, with multiple remote branches connected to the central site, which is connected to another, newly acquired company's network (see Figure 3-5). The addressing scheme used in this example is a bit more realistic: Remote offices are assigned subnet numbers from major network 10.0.0.0. The central site also contains subnet 10.9.0.0, to which the global resources are connected.

As you see in Figure 3-5, every router is configured with static routes that define which router should be used as the next hop to move the packet to the destination network. The routers in the remote offices have information that their local subnets are reachable via the interfaces connected to them and that all other parts of network 10.0.0.0 can be accessed via router R1. This route is called a *summary route*. Use of a summary route means that it doesn't matter which specific subnets are there, and packets destined for any subnet of the major network can be sent through router R1. The same principle works for other major networks—in this case, network 30.0.0.0. Routers can have only summary routes for them.

Let's take a more careful look at the routes to network 30.0.0.0 in R2 and R1. Both routers have routes to it, illustrating the first and second routing rules given in Section 3.2. Every router along the path to a destination must have adequate routing information. Router R0 in network 30.0.0.0 demonstrates the third rule: Every router must have infor-

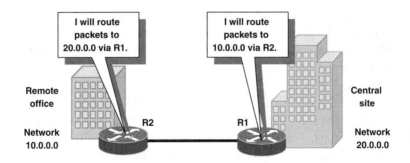

Figure 3-4. *Use of static routes—simple example*

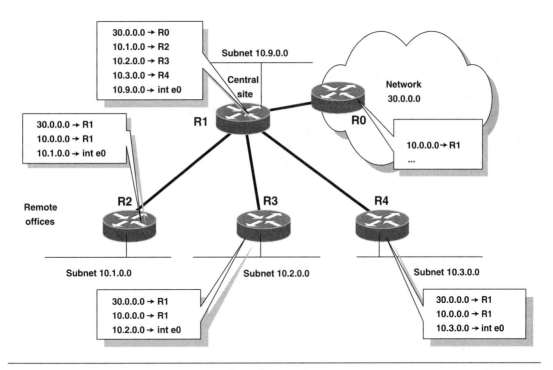

Figure 3-5. *Static routes—hub-and-spoke topology*

mation about the return path. For this reason, a static route to major network 10.0.0.0 was added to R0's routing table. Without it, R0 would drop the packets going back from 30.0.0.0.

In general, when configuring a static route, the administrator explicitly or implicitly specifies the next-hop address and the outgoing interface to be used to reach a certain network. If a static route is configured specifying only the address of the next router, this is the next hop, configured explicitly, and the outgoing interface is determined by the recursive routing table lookup operation. If a static route points to a certain router's interface, the interface is explicitly specified, and another step is taken to find the next-hop address (see Chapter 4).

As you can see, the larger the network, the more difficult it is to control. The administrator must be very careful while configuring static routes, as it is easy to create a routing loop. This can happen because when a static route is configured, there is no way for the router to check and see whether the destination network is really behind the specified next hop. Dynamic routing is not a panacea for this problem—it can also experience temporary routing loops in transition periods—but dynamic routing protocols are based on the algorithms that guarantee convergence of the network within a finite period of time.

3.5 Dynamic Routing

You already know that dynamic routing protocols are a means of exchanging routing information between routers. Thousands of complex networks run different types of routing protocols. The best-known example of such a network is the Internet, a community of independent providers, customer networks, and *Internet exchanges* (IXs), each having its own set of routers, which share common traffic policies and administration (Figure 3-6). Such a set of routers, controlled by a single organization or provider, is usually called an *autonomous system* (AS). This term is widely used in the Internet community.

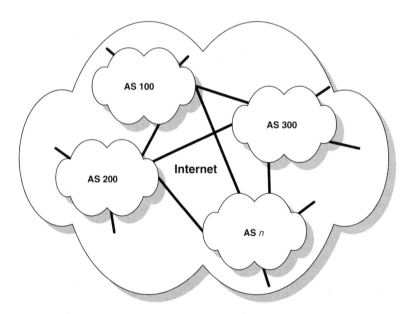

Figure 3-6. *The Internet, a group of autonomous systems*

The term *routing domain* is frequently confused with the term autonomous system. A routing domain is a set of routers running a single dynamic routing protocol, such as RIP, OSPF, or IGRP. An autonomous system may consist of many routing domains, each running its own protocol, and still be a single entity to the outside world, as shown in Figure 3-7.

All routing protocols can be classified as *interior gateway protocols* (IGPs) or *exterior gateway protocols* (EGPs). IGPs run inside an autonomous system and perform so-called *intra-domain routing* functions. This set of protocols consists of RIP v1/v2, IGRP, OSPF, EIGRP, integrated IS-IS, and some other, rarely used ones. EGPs run between autonomous systems. The set of EGPs includes two protocols—EGP and BGP. BGP version 4 is now the de facto standard for inter-AS routing, also called *inter-domain routing*. The main difference between the IGPs and EGPs is in the goals the two types are designed to achieve. IGPs are implemented to provide fast convergence within ASs, whereas EGPs are designed to share network reachability information—which networks are in which ASs—and to permit application of routing policies, influencing the results of the local and remote best-path selection algorithms. This book describes intra-domain routing via the most widely used IGPs—RIP, IGRP, OSPF, and EIGRP. (Inter-domain routing is not considered here, as this topic deserves a separate book.)

All routing protocols share the same basic concept: They exchange messages containing information about the networks routers know about. These messages are called *routing updates*. Every routing protocol has its own format for routing updates and its own

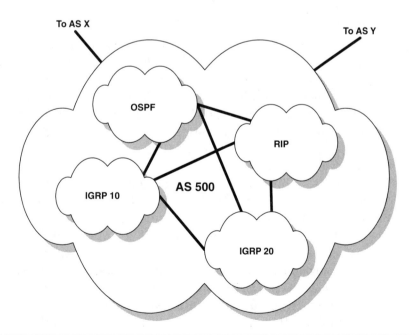

Figure 3-7. *Autonomous systems—a set of routing domains*

algorithm for exchanging and analyzing them. Routing updates contain information about one or many remote networks that the sending router has information about. While sending information about a network in an update, routing protocols supply additional information that can be used to understand how far the network is from the advertising router and how optimal the route is. Based on this information, routers calculate *metrics* for the routes and use those metrics to characterize the quality of routes and to perform route comparison. Different routing protocols use different information for metric calculation. The simplest example is RIP, which uses the number of hops. More sophisticated protocols, such as IGRP and EIGRP, use a set of parameters, such as minimum path bandwidth, maximum path delay, and so on.

When it receives a dynamic routing update about a remote network, a router selects the best routes—one or many—to the destination, based on the metrics associated with the routes. Having chosen the best route, the router can determine the two parameters for the routing table entries: the outbound interface and the next-hop address. In the simplest case, the outgoing interface is the one the routing update was received on, and the next-hop address is the address of the router that sent the update. Some protocols include the next-hop address in the routing update, and this address can be different from that of the advertising router. Also, link state protocols such as OSPF, do not care about the interface the update is received on. They calculate the routes on the basis of the network topology information.

3.6 Default Routing

In some situations, it is not desirable for all routers to have complete routing information. For example, in Figure 3-8, router R1 should know only about subnets 10.1.0.0–10.3.0.0; if it is sending a packet somewhere else—the Internet or another company's network—it sends it via router Rc, which has a full routing table. The routing decision for router R1 would then be, "If I don't have information about a destination network in my routing table, I use the route to Rc." This type of routing information is called a *default route*. "Default" means that the route is used only if there is no more specific information about the destination network a packet is going to.

Use of default routes simplifies network management, as it saves a router from having to know all networks and makes it possible for routers to reference a "smarter guy" that can do the work. Default routes are widely used in real networks.

Like any other route, default routes can be either static or dynamic. The administrator can configure a static default route manually, saying, "For all other destinations, use router Rx." In case of a dynamically propagated default route, the administrator configures a router to originate it and say, "Everyone around, use me to reach any network you don't know about." After receiving such a routing update, other routers install the default route in their routing tables; the administrator doesn't need to configure it manually (Figure 3-9).

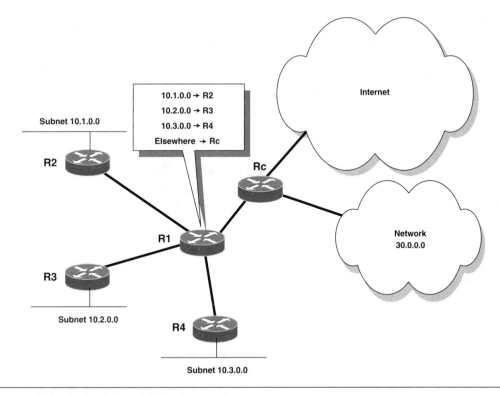

Figure 3-8. *Principle of default routing*

A default route is usually represented as a pseudonetwork with all 0s in the address and mask parts, that is, 0.0.0.0 0.0.0.0 or 0.0.0.0/0. Most dynamic protocols use this convention to provide default routing information. IGRP, however, has its own method, considered in Chapter 8.

Default routes are similar to summary routes. A summary route to a major network hides all details of that network, saying, "Want to reach someone in this network? Go this way!" A default route hides all details about all networks, saying, "Want to reach someone somewhere? Come on over here!" The way routers treat summary and default routes, as well as the algorithm of router operations, depends on the kind of environment—classful or classless—the routers work in. The following sections cover the basic forwarding algorithm and the details of the routing table lookup performed in classful and classless modes.

3.7 Basic Forwarding Algorithm

This section provides an overview of the forwarding algorithm performed by the router when it is clear that the packet is not destined for the router itself and should be delivered to a remote network. The algorithm uses the following data structures:

- *Packet:* the IP packet being forwarded. Each packet has fields described in Chapter 2. In particular, the forwarding algorithm uses such fields as Destination Address and Time-To-Live (TTL).

- *Interface:* the network attachment description. Various characteristics are associated with each interface, including the following, which are considered interesting from the forwarding perspective:

  - *Type*—Can be point-to-point, point-to-multipoint, or broadcast, depending on the type of encapsulation. For example, PPP and High-Level Data Link Control (HDLC) interfaces are point-to-point; Frame Relay and X.25 interfaces are point-to-multipoint; Ethernet and Token Ring interfaces are broadcast.

  - *State*—Operational status—up or down—of the interface. The state of the interface is determined by the status of the physical and the data link layer protocols.

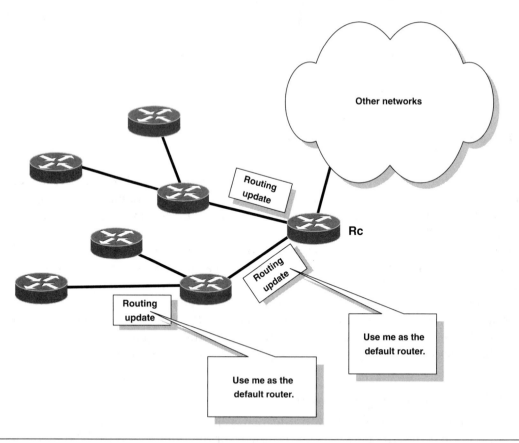

Figure 3-9. *Dynamic propagation of a default route*

- *IP status*—Flag specifying whether IP processing is enabled on the interface.

- *IP unnumbered*—Flag indicating that the interface—point-to-point—is configured as unnumbered.

- *Reference interface*—Interface whose IP address should be used when the packets are generated for the unnumbered interface.

- *IP address*—Address assigned to the interface.

- *Address mask*—Mask configured together with the IP address to specify the border between the network and hosts parts of the address.

- *Routing table*—Collection of *routing entries* (routes). The following parameters are associated with each entry:

  - *Network prefix*—IP prefix—in the form of the prefix value and its length, or a network address and a route mask—that describes a collection of destinations. For example, 192.0.0.0/8, or 192.0.0.0 255.0.0.0, describes all IP hosts that are assigned IP addresses starting with 192, such as 192.1.1.1 or 192.200.150.129.

  - *Default candidate*—Flag indicating that the route should be considered a candidate for becoming the default route

  - *Paths*—Collection of next-hop structures, each corresponding to a distinct path to the destination through the network. The following parameters are associated with each path, and at least one of the two must be present.

    - *Outbound interface*—The interface that should be used to forward packets to the collection of destinations described by the route. If the path does not specify the interface, the route is considered *recursive*.

    - *Intermediate address*—If the path specifies the interface, this is the next-hop address that should be used to find out the data link layer details. If the path does not specify the interface, this is the address that should be used for the next iteration of the recursive routing table lookup operation.

The following algorithm is an outline of functionality performed by the routers. The packet is assumed to have passed initial checks: the sanity check (basic IP header validity verification), the inbound packet filtering policy, the TTL field check, and so on. These checks and the forwarding algorithm are discussed in more detail in Chapter 5.

1. Set the next-hop address to the destination address in the packet.
2. Perform recursive routing table lookup operation as follows.
   a. Find the route for the current next-hop address in the routing table.

   b. If a route is found and it specifies the intermediate address, set the next-hop address to the address in the route.

   c. If the route is found and it does not specify the interface, loop back to step 2.a.

3. If the recursive route lookup did not succeed—no matching route was found or a route could not be resolved—send an ICMP "Destination Unreachable, Host Unreachable" message to the packet originator, using the source IP address in the packet as the destination IP address in the ICMP message, and drop the packet.

4. Otherwise, if the current value of the next-hop address equals the prefix value of the found route, set the next-hop address back to the destination IP address in the packet.

5. Pass the packet to the packet-delivery function. Provide the interface in the route and the current next-hop address as the arguments.

The algorithm is pretty simple. First, the routing table is searched for a route that can be used to route to the destination IP address in the packet. (The routing table lookup algorithm is discussed later.) If a route is found and it specifies only an interface—describes a directly connected network—the packet is sent out of the specified interface, using the destination IP address in the packet as the next-hop address. If the route specifies both the address and the interface—this is how IGP routes are installed—the packet is sent out of the interface to the next-hop router corresponding to the address in the route. If the route is recursive—only the intermediate address is specified—the intermediate address becomes the current next-hop route, and a routing table lookup operation is performed again.

The check in step 4 needs more explanation. That check is required when the routing table contains information similar to that shown in the following example:

```
10.0.0.0 is accessible via 20.1.1.0
20.1.1.0 is directly connected to the interface Ethernet 1
```

The recursive route to network 10.0.0.0 specifies a subnet address (20.1.1.0) as the intermediate address. Without the check, the subnet address would be used as the next-hop address. The check makes sure that the destination address in the packet is used as the next-hop address in this situation.

The packet-delivery procedure is initiated by the forwarding algorithm and receives the packet, the outbound interface, and the next-hop IP address as the arguments from it. Following is the outline of the steps taken by the packet-delivery process.

1. If the interface state is down or IP processing is not enabled on the interface, send an ICMP "Destination Unreachable, Host Unreachable" message to the source host, and stop processing the packet.

A route in the routing table can reference an interface in down state while the routing table is converging—it takes time to remove invalid routes—or because a static route through an interface was configured to be never removed from the routing table (see Chapter 6).

2. If the interface type is point-to-point, pass the packet directly to the packet encapsulation procedure specific to the interface. There is no need to look up data link layer details for point-to-point interfaces. They are either not necessary (such as HDLC or PPP encapsulation) or statically configured for the interface, such as, a point-to-point Frame Relay interface.

3. Otherwise, if the interface type is point-to-multipoint, perform the following steps.
   a. Search the map table associated with the interface, using the next-hop address as the search parameter.
   b. If no map for the next-hop address is found, log an encapsulation failure, send an ICMP "Destination Unreachable, Host Unreachable" message to the source host, and stop processing the packet,
   c. Otherwise, pass the packet to the packet encapsulation procedure specific to the interface, and pass the located map table entry as a parameter; it will be used to construct the data link layer frame for the packet.

4. Otherwise, if the interface type is broadcast, perform the following steps.
   a. Search the ARP cache for the MAC address corresponding to the next-hop address and outbound interface.
   b. If no ARP entry is found, log an encapsulation failure, send an ARP request message for the next-hop address, send an ICMP "Destination Unreachable, Host Unreachable" message to the source host, and drop the packet.

Note that the router does not wait for the ARP reply message to come in and does not queue the packet.

   c. Otherwise, pass the packet to the packet encapsulation procedure specific to the interface, providing the found ARP entry as a parameter; it will be used to construct the data link layer frame for the packet.

As you can see, the data link parameters vary by type of interface. Point-to-point interfaces require very little additional work. Point-to-multipoint links, such as Frame Relay or X.25, require the DLCI or X.121, which should be used to reach a specific next-hop router. The mapping between the next-hop addresses and the data link layer details is usually configured manually by the administrator (see Chapter 5 for details). Broadcast interfaces require knowledge of the next-hop router's MAC address that is discovered using ARP. Also note that the interface MTU check and the IP packet fragmentation functionality are performed by the packet encapsulation function.

3.8 Classful Routing Operations

Before we proceed to the principles of classful IP routing, an important detail about routing table entries needs to be discussed. The routing table structure defined in the previous section specified that each route describes a set of destinations in the form of a network prefix with its value and length. However, all examples given before showed routes in the routing tables just as network addresses (10.0.0.0) instead of as network prefixes (10.0.0.0/8). Indeed, when they install routes in the routing table, Cisco routers provide the corresponding route mask as well. This discussion of the idea behind the route mask was intentionally delayed until the topic of routing table lookup functionality. For better understanding of why routing table entries need masks, let's consider several examples.

Suppose that a summary route to major network 10.0.0.0 with mask 255.0.0.0 and a route to subnet 10.0.0.0 255.255.0.0 (zero subnet) are installed in the routing table as shown in the following example. Note that if routes did not have associated masks, these two routes would be indistinguishable.

```
10.0.0.0/8      — via 10.2.0.1
10.0.0.0/16     — via 10.2.0.3
```

The number after / in the routes represents the number of significant bits in the prefix value; the number is equal to the number of bits in the route mask. So, /8 implies a mask of 255.0.0.0, and /16 means a mask of 255.255.0.0. The route mask specifies the portion of the route's network address that must be compared with the destination address in the packet. A route is declared matching a destination address if the bits in the address corresponding to the bits set to 1 in the route mask are equal to the bits in the same positions in the route's prefix value. In our example, both routes would match address 10.0.0.15 because the 10.0.0.0/8 route matches the first octet of the address, and the 10.0.0.0/16 route matches the first two octets of it. In this situation, 10.0.0.0/8 is said to be a less specific route, and 10.0.0.0/16 is said to be a more specific one. When multiple matching routes are available to the same destination, routers choose the longest matching route to forward the packets. So, for a packet to IP address 10.0.0.15, the 10.0.0.0/16 route would be used. The other route, 10.0.0.0/8, would be used to forward packets to all other, unknown subnets of major network 10.0.0.0. This is an example of a so-called *network default route*.

Now let's move on to the classful routing topic. The principles of classful addressing discussed in Chapter 2 state that the whole major network must use a single subnet mask. Moreover, the routing protocols designed for classful environments do not send the route masks in their updates. The route mask is determined on the basis of the address masks configured on the interfaces on which the updates are received. Indeed, routers do not have any other source of information about the subnet mask used on remote subnets. Let's see how dynamic routing protocols work in a classful environment.

An update message of a classful protocol can carry routes of the following types.

- Host routes
- Subnet routes
- Network routes
- Default routes

Consider two routers connected to subnets of the same major network—R1 to 10.1.0.0, 10.2.0.0 and 10.3.0.0 and R2 to 10.3.0.0, 10.4.0.0, and 10.5.0.0 (see Figure 3-10). The subnet mask used on the interfaces of the routers is 255.255.0.0. When it receives the update from router R2 about subnets 10.4.0.0 and 10.5.0.0, router R1 installs the routes to these subnets in the routing table with the subnet mask taken from its own interface connected to subnet 10.3.0.0, that is, mask 255.255.0.0. Provided that all hosts and routers in major network 10.0.0.0 use this subnet mask—a basic rule of classful addressing—this approach works.

Now imagine that R2 is connected to another major network, say, 20.0.0.0, which uses a different subnet mask—255.255.255.0. One of R2's interfaces is attached to subnet 20.1.1.0. If R2 sent information about this subnet to R1, R1 would make a wrong decision about the route mask. It would use its own, 255.255.0.0, and it would see that the network address is 20.1.0.0 and that the host part of the route is 0.0.1.0. If it saw that the host part was not all zeros, R1 would assume that the route was a host route and would insert it with the route mask of 255.255.255.255, which is wrong.

To prevent this misunderstanding, routers connected to multiple major networks do not send subnet information about one major network into another. Instead, they send summary network routes. The receiving routers are supposed to install these routes in the routing tables with the default class address masks. A route from any major network with a nonzero host part of the address is considered a host route. (Some implementations ignore host routes coming from remote major networks.)

The behavior when subnet routing information is not propagated from one major network to another is called *automatic route summarization*. It has its own pros and cons.

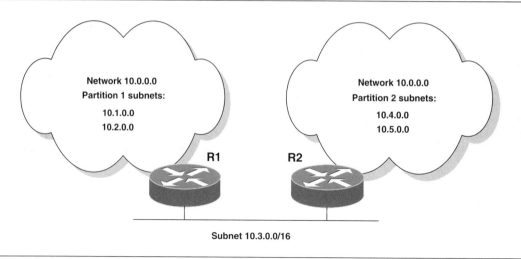

Figure 3-10. *Example of classful routing*

On the one hand, autosummarization decreases the size of the routing tables. On the other hand, it can cause routing problems when *discontiguous networks* are used. For example, consider a situation in which major network 10.0.0.0 is geographically divided by major network 20.0.0.0 (Figure 3-11). The border router R1 sends only a summary route, 10.0.0.0, to routers in major network 20.0.0.0. Border router R2 does the same. So, the router in major network 20.0.0.0 has no information about subnets of network 10.0.0.0 and hence cannot properly route packets going there. In the worst case, routers inside major network 20.0.0.0 choose only the best route to network 10.0.0.0 and install it. This leads to a situation in which a router can see only one partition of the network and cannot send packets to the other. In the best case, when the routers have routes with equal metrics, the routers use both and load-balance the traffic between them. This is still not good, as packets can be sent in a wrong direction. In both cases, the routing is not functional.

Another interesting subject is how the routing table lookup operation is performed when routers are working in a classful environment. The algorithm follows.

1. If the routing table contains a route to a destination in the major network that the destination address belongs to, including a route to the major network itself, perform the following steps.

   a. Look up the longest matching route limiting the set of routes to those describing the destinations in that major network.

   b. If no route is found, do not consider the supernet routes or the default route; indicate a route lookup failure, and stop the algorithm.

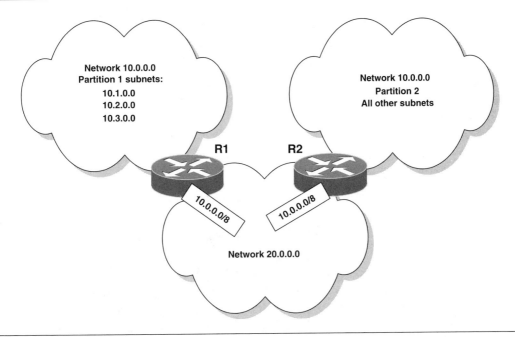

Figure 3-11. *Classful routing when one major network is split by another*

2. Otherwise, look up the best matching route among the supernet routes. If a route is found and it is not a route to pseudonetwork 0.0.0.0, use the route for packet forwarding.

3. Otherwise, if the default route is available, use it to forward the packet.

4. Otherwise (no matching route and no default route is available), indicate a route lookup failure.

The behavior of the lookup algorithm depends on the result of the first step. If the router has any route for a network in the destination major network—that is, the router is assumed to have attachments to the major network, the only routes considered are those describing address ranges in the same major network: subnet and network default routes. If no route belongs to the destination major net, a simple best-matching route is chosen. Note that the default route is used only if the router is not attached to the destination major network. (We discuss the reason for this later in this section.)

The following example illustrates how the routing table lookup algorithm works. Suppose that a router needs to forward a packet with the destination address 20.1.2.3. The routing table contains the following routes:

```
1: Network 10.0.0.0/8 is directly connected to the interface Ethernet 0
2: Network 20.0.0.0/8 is accessible via 10.1.1.1
```

```
3: Subnet   20.1.1.0/24 is directly connected to the interface Ethernet 1
4: Subnet   20.1.2.0/24 is accessible via 10.1.1.2
```

Following is the log of the steps taken by the algorithm.

1. The destination address is 20.1.2.3, and the destination major network is 20.0.0.0.

2. The router has routes in the destination major network—routes 2, 3, and 4—so the algorithm branches to step 1.a.

3. All routes in major network 20.0.0.0 are processed as follows.

   a. Route 2—20.0.0.0/8. The route's mask is applied to the destination address, which gives 20.0.0.0. This value is the same as the network address part of the route, so the route matches. So far, this route is the best, but the router proceeds to the next route, as there may be better ones.

   b. Route 3—20.1.1.0/24. The binary AND between the route mask and the destination address results in 20.1.2.0, which is different from this route's network address (20.1.1.0). This route does not match, so it is skipped.

   c. Route 4—20.1.2.0/24. The result of 20.1.2.3 AND 255.255.255.0 is 20.1.2.0, which is equal to the network address portion of the route. The current best route is route 2 (20.0.0.0/8). The route mask of route 4 (255.255.255.0) is longer than that of route 2 (255.0.0.0), so 20.1.2.0/24 is better and is selected as the current best route.

   d. Because no other routes are in the routing table belonging to the destination major network, the algorithm stops, and the 20.1.2.0/24 route is considered the best.

Consider a situation in which a router has somewhat different routing information, the presence of the default route:

```
1: Network 10.0.0.0/8 is directly connected to the interface Ethernet 0
2: Subnet   20.1.1.0/24 is directly connected to the interface Ethernet 1
3: Subnet   20.1.3.0/24 is accessible via 10.1.1.2
4: Network 0.0.0.0/0 is accessible via 10.1.1.3 (Default route)
```

The router finds out that the destination (20.1.2.3) belongs to the same major network but cannot find a matching route. Now, because the destination address is in the same major network as the router, the algorithm does not try to find a default route and the route lookup fails, causing the packet to be dropped.

The idea behind treating the default route this way in classful routing is that if a router does not know about some subnet of a "known" major network—the administrator didn't configure a static route or a routing protocol didn't send any information about it—it considers this subnet either nonexistent or down. If the packet were destined for another major network that the router is not connected to, it would take the default route and send the packet to the corresponding router (10.1.1.3).

For better understanding, let's consider another example (Figure 3-12). Routers R1 and R2 are boundary routers. Router R1 has announced the summary route to its major network (10.0.0.0) to R2, as has R2 (route 20.0.0.0 in R1's routing table). Now assume that the administrator of network 10.0.0.0 configured a default route pointing to R2. Consider a situation in which a station from network 20.0.0.0 sends an IP packet with the destination address 10.4.1.1. R2 routes the packet to R1. Looking through the routing table, R1 does not find a route to the destination subnet. Assume that R1 takes the default route, sending the packet back to R2, which in turn sends it to R1 again. The packet is looped until the TTL field in the header reaches 0 and the packet is dropped by one of the routers.

In other words, because a default route is used to describe destinations in other networks, sending a packet along a default route is equivalent to sending a packet in the direction of the exit from the local major network and, finally, out of it. Because major

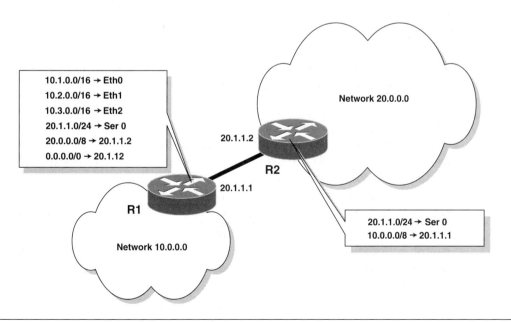

Figure 3-12. *Use of default in classful routing*

networks must be contiguous in classful routing, forwarding a packet out of its destination major network doesn't make much sense and leads to routing loops because routers in other major networks believe that a given subnet can be found in the major network the subnet belongs to.

This concept also applies to the *supernet routes:* routes installed in the routing table with route masks shorter than the default class masks. The only difference is that a supernet route aggregates information about several major networks, whereas the default route aggregates information about the rest of the world.

A router's behavior in a classful environment can be summarized as follows:

- Classful routing protocols do not include subnet masks in routing updates.

- Classful routing protocols hide subnet information from other major networks by announcing only summary network routes into them.

- Classful routing protocols can announce host routes, which are used when hosts do not reside on the same segment as the rest of the subnet.

- Each classful router can have the following types of routing information in its table:

  - *Host routes*—Routes received with nonzero host address parts and implicitly assigned the network mask of 255.255.255.255 or static routes with explicitly configured masks.

  - *Subnet routes*—Routes to subnets within the major network to which a router has an attachment. These routes are inserted into the routing table with subnet masks on the interface the update is received from used as route masks, unless it is a static route and was configured with different subnet mask.

  - *Network summary routes*—Routes to other major networks. These routes are inserted into the routing table with the default classful address mask (without subnets) and represent other major networks if they are provided by routing protocols. This type of route can also be used to represent the rest of the local major network (the network default route). Such a route must be statically configured by the administrator.

  - *Default routes*—Either a 0.0.0.0/0 route, which is marked as default by the router automatically, or other routes to any networks explicitly marked as default by the administrator or a routing protocol (see Chapter 4 for a detailed explanation).

- While routing packets, routers pay attention to whether the destination major network is local (some of its subnets are directly connected).

- If the destination major network is local, the router needs to have either a host route with a /32 mask or an explicit route to the subnet or a summary network route describing the rest of the local major network. If this condition is not met, the packet is dropped, and the default and supernet routes are not considered.

- If the destination major network is not local, the routing table lookup algorithm is changed. The router looks for the best-matching route, paying attention to the length of the route masks; supernet routes may be taken. If no match was found, the router checks the default route. If there's no default route, the packet is dropped.

Following are some problems that can be seen in classful environments.

- Variable-length subnet masks cannot be used, as routing updates do not contain route masks.

- Automatic summarization to classful networks prevents use of noncontiguous addressing plans, such as private IP addresses for WAN links.

- Use of default routes is limited, which can be a problem in very large networks because the only type of summarized route that can be distributed within one major network by routing protocols is the default. This occurs because if the routing protocol sends a network summary route for a local major network, this route is considered an update for zero subnet, not a network summary. So, every router must have either a full routing table or a network summary route representing the rest of the local major network configured manually.

These problems are addressed by the classless routing approach, discussed in the next section.

3.9 Classless Routing Operations

Let's try to understand what enhancements should be made to the routing process and routing protocols to guarantee normal routing of classless addressing schemes. Because classless routing assumes use of VLSMs, routes in the routing updates should be augmented with route masks. Once this condition has been met, the problem with mandatory summarization is automatically canceled; even if information about subnets is sent into another major network, the routers have explicit information about the corresponding route mask in the update. This is not enough, however.

Even though automatic route summarization can cause problems, the technique in general is necessary to scale the networks. Without route summarization, every router would have to know about every prefix in the network. One of the problems that stimulated deployment of CIDR in the Internet was the growing size of the routing tables in the backbone routers. At that time, every backbone router had to know every major network in the Internet, and because the number of networks connected to the Internet grew at an exponential rate, the growth of the routing table size followed the same trend. There had to be a method that would stop this. *Route aggregation,* a part of CIDR, is a technique similar to classful summarization and allows routes to be aggregated at an arbitrary boundary and hence permits aggregation of major networks. Arbitrary aggregation also helps reduce the size of routing tables within major networks.

The principle of route aggregation states that routes to specific subnets or networks can be represented by a smaller number of aggregate routes. The route masks of the aggregate routes do not need to equal the default classful mask or the subnet mask used in the major network. To illustrate this, consider an example in which a network is geographically split in three parts (Figure 3-13).

The first remote site is assigned subnets 10.1.1.0–10.1.14.0; the second one uses subnets 10.1.17.0–10.1.30.0. All other subnets are located in the central site. The classful routing approach requires either a full routing table or network default routes on each router in this network. With classless routing, another method can be used.

Look at the first three address bytes of the subnets in remote site 1; the third byte is represented in binary notation in Table 3-1. Only the four lowest-order bits change in the third byte; the highest-order four bits do not. This means that all subnets in the site do not have to be announced, provided that all outside routers know that subnets with the four highest-order bits in the third byte, set to 0, and the first two bytes, set to 10 and 1, can be reached via router R1. This can be achieved by propagating only an aggregate route, 10.1.0.0/20, to R2 and R3. In this case, the route represents not a real subnet but a group of subnets. The routing tables in the routers could be as shown in Figure 3-14.

Note that networks in remote site 2 are also represented by an aggregate route: 10.1.16.0/20. Another interesting detail is that all subnets in the central site are described in R1 and R3 via a network summary route. Also, pay attention to the fact that router R3 has two routes with the same address parts but different route masks. Because the routing table lookup algorithm selects the most specific—the longest matching—route for the destination address, routing is unambiguous. This rule can be demonstrated by the forwarding decision that router R3 makes.

Suppose that R3 receives a packet destined for address 10.1.2.10. The router starts looking through the routing table. In its first iteration, the best route it finds is 10.1.0.0/16, but when R3 looks at the second one—10.1.0.0/20—it finds that this route also matches and has a longer route mask. So, route 10.1.0.0/20 is selected as the best and the packet is forwarded to R1. If it had to route a packet destined for one of the subnets within the central site, R3 would see that the second route doesn't match, and the first one would remain the best.

The same principle works in aggregating routes describing classful networks. Consider an example of a small Internet provider that is given eight class C networks,

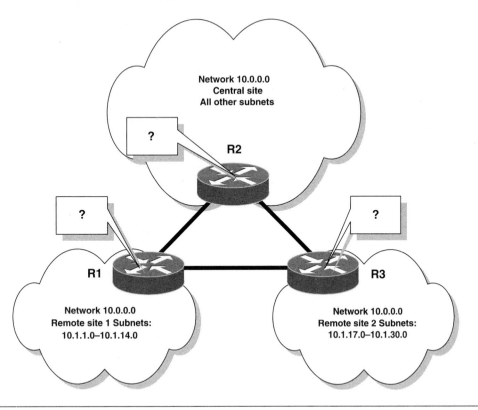

Figure 3-13. *Classless routing—a sample network*

Table 3-1. *Aggregation of Subnet Routes*

Subnet	First Byte	Second Byte	Third Byte	Fourth Byte
10.1.1.0	10	1	0000 0001	0
10.1.2.0	10	1	0000 0010	0
10.1.3.0	10	1	0000 0011	0
10.1.4.0	10	1	0000 0100	0
....				
10.1.14.0	10	1	0000 1110	0

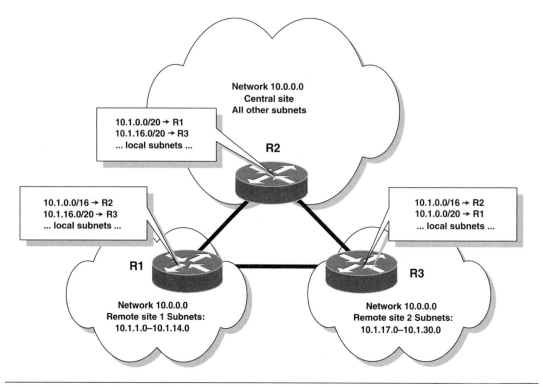

Figure 3-14. *Classless routing—route aggregation*

190.150.16.0–190.150.23.0. The method used to aggregate subnet routes is used to aggregate class C networks to a supernet (Table 3-2). Note that only the three rightmost bits change. This means that all these networks can be announced with one aggregate route, 190.150.16.0/21, so we have only one route instead of eight. Note that this aggregate route uses an arbitrary address mask, which is shorter than the default classful mask. This makes it a supernet route in contrast to a subnet route having the mask longer than the default. Note that supernet routes could not be used with classful routing protocols, because routes in the updates are not accompanied by the route masks. It is the route mask announced in the updates that allows classless routing protocols to announce supernet routes or arbitrary aggregate routes in general.

In classful routing, default routes are used very carefully. Classless routing principles state that default routes must be taken every time a router doesn't know where to route the packet. This is easily understood because in classless routing, there are no classes and therefore no major networks. In classless routing, the whole network address is not divided into network, subnet, and host portions but rather is considered as a combination of a network prefix and a host part, where the network prefix is derived by using the mask of a given route. A router looks through the routing table for a route whose net-

Table 3-2. *Building a Supernet Route*

Network	First Byte	Second Byte	Third Byte	Fourth Byte
190.150.16.0	190	150	00010 000	0
190.150.17.0	190	150	00010 001	0
190.150.18.0	190	150	00010 010	0
190.150.19.0	190	150	00010 011	0
....				
190.150.23.0	190	150	00010 111	0

work prefix matches the destination address best, that is, the longest matching route. If no matching route is available, the default route is used.

This treatment of the default route seems to be acceptable, unless we recall why classful routing restricted use of the default route. This restriction prevents routing loops caused by sending packets out of the local major network if they are destined for one of its unknown subnets. Consider the same network similar to the one in the previous example, but assume that it uses default routes instead of network summary routes (see Figure 3-15).

Suppose that router R2 receives a packet with destination address 10.1.2.15 and that subnet 10.1.2.0 is down. Router R2 follows the aggregate route 10.1.0.0/20 and forwards the packet to R1. R1 does not have information about subnet 10.1.2.0 (because it is down), takes the least specific route in the routing table—the default route (0.0.0.0/0)—and sends the packet back to R2. The routers keep ping-ponging until the packet's TTL field is decreased to zero, when the packet is dropped. This situation represents the simplest two-hop routing loop.

To remedy this problem, classless routing requires that every router that announces an aggregate route drops a received packet if it's destined for one of the aggregated networks and the router has no information about the destination. In our example, when router R1 receives the packet from R2 and sees that it has no information about the destination subnet in the routing table, it must drop it. Analyzing which routes have been announced could be time consuming, and in any case, the aggregate route in R2 could be configured statically, so R1 would never know about it. This is why so-called discard routes are installed in the routers, announcing aggregates (R2 in the example). While looking for a route in the table, routers should consider the discard route as a normal one, but packet delivery along such a route must result in a packet drop. It may seem that having a route like 10.1.0.0/20–>Discard on R1 would cause the router to drop every

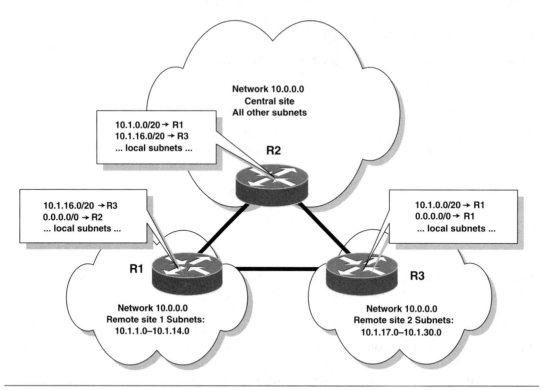

Figure 3-15. *Use of default route in classless routing*

packet that matches this route, but this is not what happens. Remember that the best-matching route is always picked up. So if the router has a more specific route to the destination, it will route the packet properly; only if the destination is not explicitly listed in the routing table will the router take the discard route and drop the packet.

The algorithm of the classless routing table lookup operation is really simple—look up the longest matching route in the routing table; if no matching route is available, use the default route. (If the default route is announced as 0.0.0.0/0, the last step is not needed, as this route matches all addresses.) As we will see in the following chapters, the exact details of the router operation are slightly different, but the behavior follows the principles described here.

Chapter Four

Routing Table Maintenance

This chapter presents the details of the routing table structure in Cisco routers, essential information that you will need throughout the rest of the book. The first section describes the sources providing Cisco routers with routing information. The second section explains in detail how the routing table is constructed and updated in routers. The last section contains answers to the most frequently asked questions about routing table maintenance.

4.1 Routing Information Sources

As explained before, when a router forwards packets, it uses its routing table to find the output interface and the next-hop router address. Cisco routers construct their routing tables by using the following three types of routes:

- Routes describing directly attached networks
- Statically configured routes
- Routes provided by dynamic routing protocols

The routing table usually contains routes from multiple sources. For easy identification of routes from specific sources, each route installed in the routing table is displayed with a corresponding source code shown in the leftmost column of the **show ip route** command's output (Listing 4-1). Every potential route source has its own code. The code legend is given at the beginning of the output.

```
R1# show ip route
Codes: C - connected, S - static, I - IGRP, R - RIP, M - mobile, B - BGP
       D - EIGRP, EX - EIGRP external, O - OSPF, IA - OSPF inter area
```

```
N1 - OSPF NSSA external type 1, N2 - OSPF NSSA external type 2
E1 - OSPF external type 1, E2 - OSPF external type 2, E - EGP
i - IS-IS, L1 - IS-IS level-1, L2 - IS-IS level-2, * - candidate default
U - per-user static route, o - ODR

Gateway of last resort is not set

     20.0.0.0/8 is variably subnetted, 3 subnets, 2 masks
C       20.1.1.0/24 is directly connected, Serial0
I       20.1.3.0/24 [100/2600] via 20.1.1.1, 00:00:06, Serial0
C       20.1.2.0/27 is directly connected, Loopback0
I    10.0.0.0/8 [100/3100] via 20.1.1.1, 00:00:06, Serial0
     30.0.0.0/24 is subnetted, 1 subnets
C       30.0.0.0 is directly connected, Ethernet0
S    200.0.0.0/8 is directly connected, Serial0
R1#
```

Listing 4-1. *Sample routing table*

Figure 4-1 shows the relationship among the route sources, the routing table, and the forwarding engine. (It does not illustrate how dynamic routing protocols acquire routes from the routing table for distribution, though.)

The forwarding engine does not directly communicate with dynamic routing protocols or any other route source; it uses the routes installed by those sources in the routing table. Also note that dynamic routing protocols do not forward packets, which is commonly misunderstood.

Before proceeding to the subsections that discuss the details of specific route source types, two terms that are used throughout this book need to be clarified: directly attached networks and directly connected routes. There is a big difference between the two.

Directly attached networks are major networks or subnets connected to a router's interfaces and known to the router from assigned IP addresses and corresponding subnet masks. These routes are always displayed with the C (connected) code in the output of the **show ip route** command (see Listing 4-1). In this book, we call these routes *interface routes,* or *connected routes.* We also refer to the source of these routes as *Connected.*

Directly connected routes reference only interfaces without next-hop addresses; that is, this term indicates the amount of next-hop information rather than the route source. Such routes can be identified by the is directly connected to phrase in the routing table (see Listing 4-1 again). The only two sources that can supply directly connected routes are Connected, providing routes to directly attached networks, and Static. Whether a route is directly connected or not is important for the forwarding engine, as explained in Chapter 5.

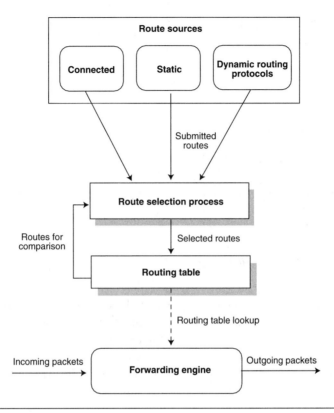

Figure 4-1. *Routing information flow*

In fact, PPP normally also installs a directly connected host route to the remote device's address, but it is not considered to be a route source, as this route shows up as Connected in the routing table.

4.1.1 Directly Attached Networks and Interface Routes

Routes to directly attached networks are derived from the IP addresses and associated address masks when the administrator configured them on the interfaces. Assume that a router with an Ethernet and a Serial interface is configured using the following commands:

```
interface Ethernet0
ip address 25.1.1.1 255.255.255.0 secondary
ip address 10.0.1.167 255.255.255.0
!
interface Serial0
ip address 20.2.1.2 255.255.255.0
```

The routing table produced by this configuration, displayed using the **show ip route** command, is given in Listing 4-2.

```
R1#show ip rou
Codes: C - connected, S - static, I - IGRP, R - RIP, M - mobile, B - BGP
...
Gateway of last resort is not set

     20.0.0.0/24 is subnetted, 1 subnets
C       20.2.1.0 is directly connected, Serial0
     25.0.0.0/24 is subnetted, 1 subnets
C       25.1.1.0 is directly connected, Ethernet0
     10.0.0.0/24 is subnetted, 1 subnets
C       10.0.1.0 is directly connected, Ethernet0
R1#
```

Listing 4-2. *Routing table with interface routes*

The routing table contains three routes to directly attached networks—indicated by the C code, one for interface Serial0 and two for interface Ethernet0. Without secondary addresses, every interface would have exactly one associated connected route in the routing table. However, because a secondary address is assigned to Ethernet0, subnet 25.1.1.0 is also present in the routing table. Basically, each **ip address** interface configuration command, with or without the secondary keyword, results in a connected route in the routing table.

Connected routes are calculated by applying the subnet masks to the IP addresses on the interfaces. These routes, one for each subnet assigned to the interface, are installed in and removed from the routing table whenever an IP-enabled interface goes up or down.

No connected routes are installed for unnumbered IP interfaces. Indeed, the whole reason of unnumbered point-to-point interfaces is to assign no subnets to them.

The debug output in Listing 4-3 illustrates how IOS installs routes to directly attached subnets 20.1.1.0 (primary) and 30.1.1.0 (secondary) when interface Serial0 goes up.

```
R1#conf t
Enter configuration commands, one per line.  End with CNTL/Z.
R1(config)#int s0
R1(config-if)#no shut
R1(config-if)#^Z
R1#
*Mar 21 02:35:35.932: %SYS-5-CONFIG_I: Configured from console by console
```

```
*Mar 21 02:35:37.888: %LINK-3-UPDOWN: Interface Serial0, changed state to up
*Mar 21 02:35:37.924: RT: add 20.1.1.0/24 via 0.0.0.0, connected metric [0/0]
*Mar 21 02:35:37.928: %LINEPROTO-5-UPDOWN: Line protocol on Interface Serial0,
changed state to up
*Mar 21 02:35:37.944: RT: add 30.1.1.0/24 via 0.0.0.0, connected metric [0/0]
*Mar 21 02:35:37.948: RT: interface Serial0 added to routing table
R1#
```

Listing 4-3. *Debug: addition of interface routes*

Let's consider some more interesting examples. In Figure 4-2, Ethernet segments are connected to routers R1 and R2. Ethernet0 interfaces of the routers are assigned IP subnets as indicated. R1's configuration is the same as the one given at the beginning of the section, except that subnet 25.1.1.0 has been removed from it. Router R2 has similar settings.

Because the type of encapsulation for serial interfaces hasn't been explicitly specified, routers run Cisco HDLC, Cisco's proprietary data link protocol based on standard HDLC. Now the encapsulation is changed to PPP for Serial0 in both routers; only R1's log is given.

```
R1#conf t
Enter configuration commands, one per line.  End with CNTL/Z.
R1(config)#int ser 0
R1(config-if)#enc ppp
R1(config-if)#^Z
R1#
```

Listing 4-4 shows the routing table of R1 after interface Serial0 has changed its state to up.

```
R1#show ip rou
Codes: C - connected, S - static, I - IGRP, R - RIP, M - mobile, B - BGP
...
Gateway of last resort is not set
```

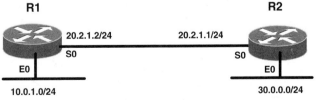

Figure 4-2. *Sample connection scheme*

```
        20.0.0.0/8 is variably subnetted, 2 subnets, 2 masks
C          20.2.1.1/32 is directly connected, Serial0
C          20.2.1.0/24 is directly connected, Serial0
        10.0.0.0/24 is subnetted, 1 subnets
C          10.0.1.0 is directly connected, Ethernet0
R1#
```

Listing 4-4. *Results of changing serial encapsulation to PPP*

Note that the routing table contains an additional host route—20.2.1.1/32—that is displayed as directly connected to Serial0. This host route is installed in the routing table by PPP. The reason for this lies in PPP itself.

Although Cisco HDLC assumes that both ends of a link are in the same subnet, even as small as /31, this is not necessary for PPP. PPP was developed to allow remote sites to negotiate IP addresses on each side of the link. In general, the two addresses on a link can be from different subnets if a source—a routing protocol, the administrator, or the data link protocol like PPP—provides routing information to ensure correct packet forwarding. And this is exactly what PPP does: It installs a host route to the remote device into the routing table by default to make the forwarding engine choose the proper interface when forwarding packets to the remote end's address. This behavior can be turned off by the **no peer neighbor-route** interface configuration command.

Consider an example in which the configuration of routers R1 and R2 is changed to the following. (Note the presence of the **ip unnumbered** interface configuration command.) R1:

```
interface Ethernet0
ip address 10.0.1.167 255.255.255.0
!
interface Serial0
ip unnumbered Ethernet0
encapsulation ppp
```

R2:

```
interface Ethernet0
ip address 30.0.0.1 255.255.255.0
!
interface Serial0
ip unnumbered Ethernet0
encapsulation ppp
```

The **ip unnumbered** command enables IP processing on a given interface without assigning an IP address. Hence, we can expect no route pointing to the Serial0 interface to be installed in the routing table. Nevertheless, look at R1's routing table, shown in Listing 4-5.

```
R1#show ip rou
Codes: C - connected, S - static, I - IGRP, R - RIP, M - mobile, B - BGP
...
Gateway of last resort is not set

     10.0.0.0/24 is subnetted, 1 subnets
C       10.0.1.0 is directly connected, Ethernet0
     30.0.0.0/32 is subnetted, 1 subnets
C       30.0.0.1 is directly connected, Serial0
R1#
```

Listing 4-5. *Routing table with* **ip unnumbered** *used*

You can see that a host route to 30.0.0.1—the IP address of R2's Ethernet0 interface—is now in R1's routing table and points to interface Serial0 because interface Serial0 of R2 is using the IP address of Ethernet0 (see Listing 4-6). While establishing the data link connection, PPP installs this information in the routing table. The routing table of R2 contains the same type of information about R1's Serial0 interface.

```
R2#show int s0
Serial0 is up, line protocol is up
  Hardware is HD64570
  Interface is unnumbered.  Using address of Ethernet0 (30.0.0.1)
  MTU 1500 bytes, BW 1544 Kbit, DLY 20000 usec, rely 255/255, load 1/255
  Encapsulation PPP, loopback not set, keepalive set (10 sec)
...
```

Listing 4-6. *Output of the* **show interface** *command when* **ip unnumbered** *is used*

Because PPP is the only data link protocol that installs routes into the routing table, we can expect that changing the type of encapsulation back to Cisco HDLC, along with the use of the **ip unnumbered** command, would clear the routing entry for the remote router's address. Listing 4-7 proves that it does.

```
R1#conf t
Enter configuration commands, one per line.  End with CNTL/Z.
R1(config)#int s0
R1(config-if)#encapsulation hdlc
R1(config-if)#^Z
```

```
R1#
R1#show ip route
Codes: C - connected, S - static, I - IGRP, R - RIP, M - mobile, B - BGP
...
Gateway of last resort is not set

     10.0.0.0/24 is subnetted, 1 subnets
C        10.0.1.0 is directly connected, Ethernet0
R1#
R1# show int s0
Serial0 is up, line protocol is up
  Hardware is HD64570
  Interface is unnumbered.  Using address of Ethernet0 (10.0.1.167)
  MTU 1500 bytes, BW 1544 Kbit, DLY 20000 usec, rely 255/255, load 1/255
  Encapsulation HDLC, loopback not set, keepalive set (10 sec)
...
```

Listing 4-7. *Using* ip unnumbered *with Cisco HDLC encapsulation*

When two routers are connected with a numbered point-to-point link, each router will have in its routing table an entry corresponding to the assigned subnet, so the remote router's IP address is reachable via this route. If this link is reconfigured to be unnumbered with Cisco HDLC encapsulation, the entry will be removed from the routing table.

A very interesting question is how the routers know the addresses and networks on the remote side of the link. The answer is proper routing information. If the administrator configures a static route to a remote network referencing an unnumbered interface, or if a dynamic routing protocol installs routes through this interface, the router will have enough information to successfully forward transit packets through the unnumbered link.

4.1.2 Static Routes

Chapter 6 is dedicated to the details of using static routes in IP networks. Here, only a brief explanation of static routes is given.

Static routes are configured in Cisco IOS with the following global configuration command:

ip route *prefix mask* {*address* | *interface* [*address*]} [*distance*] [**permanent**]

where **prefix** is the destination network address and **mask** is the route mask used to put the configured route into the routing table. The next parameter in the line is either the intermediate network address or an interface. Thus, in Cisco routers, static routes pointing to the interfaces can be configured. These routes are considered directly connected. The next optional argument, **distance**, defines the administrative distance value for the route. The administrative distance is considered in Section 4.2.3. The last optional keyword,

permanent, can be added to the command to instruct the router to leave the route in the routing table even when the referenced interface goes down or there's no route to the intermediate network address.

To illustrate the use of static routes, configuration of router R1 is changed back to

```
interface Ethernet0
ip address 10.0.1.167 255.255.255.0
!
interface Serial0
ip address 20.2.1.2 255.255.255.0
encapsulation ppp
```

Configuration of R2 is changed back to

```
interface Ethernet0
ip address 30.0.0.1 255.255.255.0
!
interface Serial0
ip address 20.2.1.1 255.255.255.0
encapsulation ppp
```

Finally, a static route is added on R1. This static route provides information that network 30.0.0.0, attached to R2's Ethernet0 interface, is accessible for R1 via the IP address of R2's Serial0 interface, as shown in Listing 4-8.

```
R1#conf t
Enter configuration commands, one per line.  End with CNTL/Z.
R1(config)#ip route 30.0.0.0 255.255.255.0 20.2.1.1
R1(config)#^Z
R1#
```

Listing 4-8. *Configuring a static route*

Take a look at the routing table of R1 (Listing 4-9).

```
R1#show ip rou
...
     20.0.0.0/8 is variably subnetted, 2 subnets, 2 masks
C        20.2.1.1/32 is directly connected, Serial0
C        20.2.1.0/24 is directly connected, Serial0
```

```
         10.0.0.0/24 is subnetted, 1 subnets
C           10.0.1.0 is directly connected, Ethernet0
         30.0.0.0/24 is subnetted, 1 subnets
S           30.0.0.0 [1/0] via 20.2.1.1
R1#
```

Listing 4-9. *Static route in the routing table*

Now the static route appears in the routing table and is marked with an S (static) code. The next time it receives a packet destined for subnet 30.0.0.0, router R1 will forward the packet to 20.2.1.1 through the interface Serial0. Let's test it with Ping (Listing 4-10).

```
R1#ping 30.0.0.1

Type escape sequence to abort.
Sending 5, 100-byte ICMP Echos to 30.0.0.1, timeout is 2 seconds:
!!!!!
Success rate is 100 percent (5/5), round-trip min/avg/max = 28/31/32 ms
R1#
```

Listing 4-10. *Testing connectivity with Ping*

Whenever a router originates a packet—for example, an ICMP Echo request, it by default uses as the source address the address of the interface nearest to the destination.

According to the rule, R1 uses the address of its Serial0 interface (20.2.1.2) for Ping. For R2, this address is directly connected (see Listing 4-11), so it needs no additional information to route the Echo replies back to R1.

```
R2#show ip rou
Codes: C - connected, S - static, I - IGRP, R - RIP, M - mobile, B - BGP
...
Gateway of last resort is not set

     20.0.0.0/8 is variably subnetted, 2 subnets, 2 masks
C        20.2.1.2/32 is directly connected, Serial0
C        20.2.1.0/24 is directly connected, Serial0
     30.0.0.0/24 is subnetted, 1 subnets
C        30.0.0.0 is directly connected, Ethernet0
```

Listing 4-11. *Routing table of R2*

Cisco routers support static routes configured over remote networks. The intermediate network address specified in a static route does not have to belong to a directly connected network. A route to the intermediate network address can be installed in the routing table by any route source—connected, static, or a dynamic routing protocol.

Before installing the static routes configured over intermediate network addresses in the routing table, the router checks whether the intermediate address can be resolved. If it is currently not resolvable, the route is not installed. However, it is not lost but remains in the router's memory until the routing table contains information allowing the route to be resolved and installed.

For example, static route on R1 is configured as shown in Listing 4-12.

```
R1#conf t
Enter configuration commands, one per line.  End with CNTL/Z.
R1(config)#
R1(config)#no ip route 30.0.0.0 255.255.255.0 20.2.1.1
R1(config)#ip route 55.0.0.0 255.0.0.0 30.1.1.1
R1(config)#^Z
R1#
```

Listing 4-12. *Configuring a static route over a remote intermediate address*

Looking at R1's routing table (Listing 4-13), we can see that the static route is not installed. The reason is that the routing table does not contain a route that could be used to resolve the intermediate address—30.1.1.1—specified in the static route.

```
R1#show ip rou
Codes: C - connected, S - static, I - IGRP, R - RIP, M - mobile, B - BGP
...
Gateway of last resort is not set

     20.0.0.0/24 is subnetted, 2 subnets
C       20.1.1.0 is directly connected, Serial1
C       20.2.1.0 is directly connected, Serial0
     10.0.0.0/24 is subnetted, 1 subnets
C       10.0.1.0 is directly connected, Ethernet0
R1#
```

Listing 4-13. *Routing table of R1*

To make things work, another static route, covering major network 30.0.0.0, is added (Listing 4-14).

```
R1#conf t
Enter configuration commands, one per line.  End with CNTL/Z.
R1(config)#ip route 30.0.0.0 255.0.0.0 ser 0
R1(config)#^Z
R1#
```

Listing 4-14. *Static route to resolve the pending one*

Because this route can be used to resolve the first static route's intermediate address (30.1.1.1), both routes appear in the routing table (Listing 4-15).

```
R1#show ip rou
...
Gateway of last resort is not set

S    55.0.0.0/8 [1/0] via 30.1.1.1
     20.0.0.0/24 is subnetted, 2 subnets
C       20.1.1.0 is directly connected, Serial1
C       20.2.1.0 is directly connected, Serial0
     10.0.0.0/24 is subnetted, 1 subnets
C       10.0.1.0 is directly connected, Ethernet0
S    30.0.0.0/8 is directly connected, Serial0
R1#
```

Listing 4-15. *Installation of a static route with nondirectly connected intermediate address*

More details of static route processing are given in Section 4.2.10.

4.1.3 Dynamic Routes

Cisco IOS supports numerous dynamic routing protocols, each of which is represented by a software module functioning inside the router. Routing protocol modules, such as RIP or OSPF, running inside neighboring routers exchange routing information and submit routes for installation in the routing tables. This section contains basic information about dynamic routing protocols required to understand the topics described in the following chapters. The process of cooperation between the routing protocol modules and the routing table maintenance module is discussed in Section 4.2.9.

Routing protocols in Cisco routers are configured with at least two commands. The first one starts an instance of the corresponding dynamic routing protocol in the router:

router *protocol [process-ID]*

The second one specifies which interfaces will participate in the routing protocol being configured and which directly attached networks the router will announce to its neighbors:

network *network-number*

In RIP, IGRP, and EIGPR, the network number specified in a **network** command must be a major network to which the router is directly connected with one or more of its interfaces. OSPF and EIGRP use a slightly different version, considered in the chapters describing specific routing protocols.

> Even though this book does not describe IS-IS and BGP, it is important to note that the **network** command is not used in IS-IS and has a different meaning in BGP.

To briefly illustrate how dynamic routing protocols provide the routing table with routes, the static routes configured before are removed, and RIP is started in both routers:

```
R1#
R1#conf t
Enter configuration commands, one per line.  End with CNTL/Z.
R1(config)#no ip route 30.0.0.0 255.0.0.0 ser 0
R1(config)#no ip route 55.0.0.0 255.0.0.0 30.1.1.1
R1(config)#router rip
R1(config-router)#network 10.0.0.0
R1(config-router)#network 20.0.0.0
R1(config-router)#^Z
R1#
```

```
R2#conf t
Enter configuration commands, one per line.  End with CNTL/Z.
R2(config)#router rip
R2(config-router)#network 30.0.0.0
R2(config-router)#network 20.0.0.0
R2(config-router)#^Z
R2#
```

Look at the routing tables of R1 and R2 given in Listings 4-16 and 4-17.

```
R1#show ip rou
...
     20.0.0.0/8 is variably subnetted, 2 subnets, 2 masks
C        20.2.1.1/32 is directly connected, Serial0
C        20.2.1.0/24 is directly connected, Serial0
     10.0.0.0/24 is subnetted, 1 subnets
C        10.0.1.0 is directly connected, Ethernet0
R     30.0.0.0/8 [120/1] via 20.2.1.1, 00:00:03, Serial0
R1#
```

Listing 4-16. *R1's routing table with a RIP-learned route*

```
R2#show ip rou
...

     20.0.0.0/8 is variably subnetted, 2 subnets, 2 masks
C        20.2.1.2/32 is directly connected, Serial0
C        20.2.1.0/24 is directly connected, Serial0
R     10.0.0.0/8 [120/1] via 20.2.1.2, 00:00:25, Serial0
     30.0.0.0/24 is subnetted, 1 subnets
C        30.0.0.0 is directly connected, Ethernet0
R2#
```

Listing 4-17. *R2's routing table with a RIP-learned route*

Thanks to the dynamic routing protocol, static routes do not have to be entered; everything is done by RIP. Note that the routes supplied by RIP are marked with the R origin code. The output also shows the values of the route's administrative distance (120) and metric (1), discussed in Section 4.2.

The beauty of dynamic routing is that the administrator does not have to think through the forwarding paths to each potential destination network and configure them on each transit router. Dynamic routing algorithms investigate the network topology and distribute network reachability information with minimal human intervention.

4.1.4 Comparison of the Route Sources

Cisco IOS supports three general types of routes according to the amount of routing information provided:

- Routes that reference only interfaces (see Listing 4-18)
- Routes that reference only intermediate addresses (see Listing 4-19)
- Routes that reference both interfaces and intermediate addresses (Listing 4-20)

```
C        30.0.0.0/24 is directly connected, Ethernet0
S        200.0.0.0/8 is directly connected, Serial0
```

Listing 4-18. *Interface-only routes*

```
S     55.0.0.0/8 [1/0] via 30.1.1.1
S     10.0.0.0/8 [1/0] via 30.0.0.3
```

Listing 4-19. *Intermediate address routes*

```
I        20.1.3.0/24 [100/2600] via 20.1.1.1, 00:00:06, Serial0
I        10.0.0.0/8 [100/3100] via 20.1.1.1, 00:00:06, Serial0
S        10.0.0.0/8 [1/0] via 30.0.0.2, Ethernet0
```

Listing 4-20. *Interface and next-hop routes*

The algorithm performed by the forwarding engine while routing packets along different types of routes varies, depending on the type of route, described in more detail in Chapter 5.

Different route sources supply different types of routes to the routing table. Routes derived from the interface addresses always reference only interfaces. Static routes can be of any of three types. Routes supplied by the interior dynamic routing protocols reference both the interfaces and intermediate addresses, whereas BGP provides only the latter.

This difference among connected, static, and dynamic routes leads to a difference in the information every type of route needs to have in the routing table prior to installation. Clearly, the only information interface routes, originated by the connected route source, need to have is that the interfaces they reference are up and IP-enabled. Such routes do not rely on other routes in the routing table, because they refer to the interfaces rather than to next-hop addresses.

Because routes provided by IGPs include the interfaces and intermediate addresses, these routes also depend only on interfaces. When an interface is referenced in a route, no recursive lookup is performed for the intermediate address, and it is used only to find the data link layer details.

The situation is different for static routes. The intermediate network address of a static route, which doesn't reference an interface, must be resolved via another route—connected, static, or dynamic. Whatever the source is, when a route that can be used to resolve the intermediate address of a static route appears in the routing table, the corresponding static route must also be installed, and vice versa. Whenever a route disappears, all routes resolved by it are removed from the routing table, provided that no other route can be used for intermediate address resolution. The next section contains information about how this is done, as well as other details of the routing table maintenance process.

4.2 Routing Table Maintenance

The routing table contains the data on which the forwarding decision is based, so routing table maintenance is definitely one of the really important tasks for any router implementation. Cisco routers are no exception.

The most frequently asked questions about the routing table are, What happens when an interface goes down? How are the static routes processed? How many parallel routes can I have? This section contains answers, discussing the details of how Cisco IOS stores and manipulates the routes.

4.2.1 Representation of Routing Information and Interfaces

The structure used in the previous chapter, to store the routing information, included all parameters of a route: the address range covered by the route, outgoing interface, address of the next-hop router, and so on. Cisco IOS uses an approach that is a bit different. Instead of using a single block for everything, the data is split into two parts. The first part contains such parameters as covered address range, route source, and administrative distance (considered later). This part is called the *prefix descriptor* throughout the book. The second part contains the information needed to forward the packets: output interface, intermediate network address, and route metric. This part is called the *path descriptor*.

Every address range in the routing table is represented by a prefix descriptor, whereas routing details of the routes covering an address range are represented by corresponding path descriptors. Each prefix descriptor can have one or many path descriptors linked to it. If a prefix descriptor has several path descriptors—the route source supplied more than one route to the network—the destination network can be reached via several paths and the forwarding engine will distribute traffic among them.

In Cisco IOS, a maximum of six path descriptors can be linked to one prefix descriptor. Therefore, the maximum number of parallel routes to one destination that Cisco routers can support is also six. By default, all dynamic routing protocols supply not more than four routes per destination to the routing table. BGP is an exception, as it is limited to one route by default. The number of routes installed by the dynamic route sources can be changed by using the **maximum-paths** router configuration command, discussed in Chapter 7.

> The maximum number of paths has been changed to eight in IOS versions 12.0(14)S, 12.0(14)ST, and 12.0(14)SC. Note that all other IOS branches still have the old limit.

Another type of data structure is used in IOS to store information about interfaces. This is the *interface descriptor block* (IDB). Every physical or logical interface in a Cisco router has an interface descriptor instance. Interface descriptors are also used for internal system entities not really connected with interfaces. Interface descriptors contain such information as encapsulation type, address of the interface input buffer pool, reference to the output queue structure, pointers to the functions of the interface drivers—software modules that communicate with the controllers—and so on.

The interface descriptor information can be displayed by using the **show interface** command. Apart from general information, every network protocol links a block of specific information to the interface descriptor whenever processing of this protocol is enabled. This information can be seen by using appropriate commands in form **show** *protocol* **interface**, such as **show ip interface**.

Discussion of the pseudocode type definition of the data structures mentioned in this chapter is given after the description of the routing table structure in the following subsections. More detailed discussion of the interface descriptor structure appears in Chapter 5 in the description of the packet delivery procedure.

4.2.2 Routing Table Structure

Cisco routers do not store the routes as a flat database, as was assumed in the earlier discussion of general routing principles. Instead, the routing table is a hierarchical structure used to speed up the lookup process while locating routes and forwarding packets. The routing table hierarchy in Cisco IOS, originally implemented with the classful routing scheme in mind, includes several levels. The first level consists of two hash tables: the table of major network prefix descriptors and the table of supernet prefix descriptors. The second level incorporates the subnets of a given major network, represented with subnet prefix descriptors. All subnets are linked to the corresponding major network prefix descriptor through a subnet table. The third level contains the path descriptors storing the information about the outgoing interfaces—the fourth level—and the next-hop addresses. The same routing table structure is used in both classful and classless routing. As you will see in Chapter 5, even though this multilevel hierarchy was initially oriented to classful addressing, it still speeds up the lookup process while performing classless routing.

The structure of the routing table is illustrated in Figure 4-3. First, a default route pointer contains a reference to a route used as the default route. This pointer saves the forwarding engine and the dynamic routing protocols from an extra job of looking through the routing table and searching for the so-called candidate-default marked routes (considered in Section 4.2.13). The major network routes in the first level can be either ultimate or parent. Parent network prefix descriptors have several references to the level 2 routes, describing subnets of a given major network. Subnet and supernet routes are always ultimate. Only ultimate prefix descriptors have a path descriptor list.

The routing table hierarchy can be viewed with the **show ip route** command, as illustrated by Figure 4-4. Network routes 20.0.0.0/24, 10.0.0.0/8, and 30.0.0.0/24 belong to the first level of hierarchy. Note that 20.0.0.0 and 30.0.0.0 have subnet routes linked, so they are parent rather than ultimate prefix descriptors and function as placeholders for ultimate subnet prefix descriptors.

The subnet mask displayed with the parent network route is not the real subnet mask stored in the route entry but rather is the mask used for all subnets in the network. The subnet mask is not shown for each subnet only when all child routes have the same mask; that is, VLSM is not used. If more than one subnet mask is used in a major network, each subnet route is augmented with a specific route mask, and the major network is shown with the classful mask.

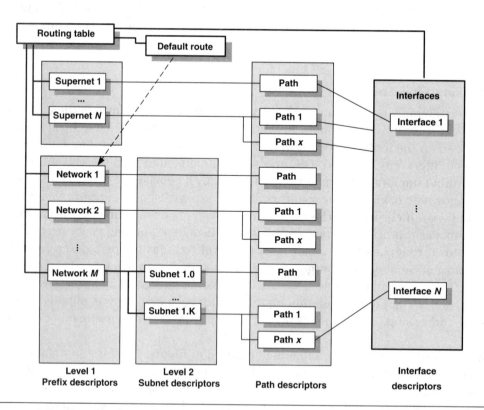

Figure 4-3. *Levels of routing table hierarchy*

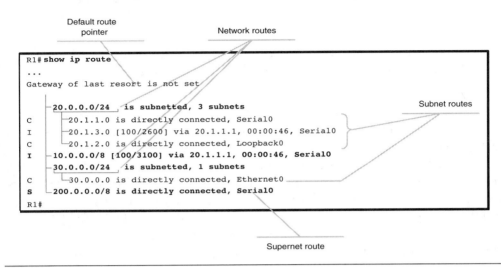

Figure 4-4. *Identifying routes in output of the* **show ip route** *command*

The network route 10.0.0.0 was learned via IGRP and has a linked path descriptor. It is an ultimate network route. No subnet route is linked to this route, because IGRP is a classful routing protocol and does not propagate subnet information across the major network boundaries, and no static routes were configured to subnets of this major network. The supernet static route to 200.0.0.0/8 is also an ultimate route with a path descriptor. Because its route mask is shorter than the default classful route mask, this route belongs to the first level.

Now consider the pseudocode type definition of the TPrefixDescr type used to store the information about a routing entry (Listing 4-21).

```
typedef struct PrefixDescr{        // Network Descriptor Block
      TFlag             Ultimate;    // 1 - Ultimate, 0 - Parent
      TIPAddress        Network;
      TMask             Mask;
      TFlag             Default;     // Marked as a candidate default
      TProto         *  Source;      // The source of the route,
      TFlag             Connected;   // "Directly connected" flag
      u_char            AD;
      u_int             Metric;
      u_char            NumOfPaths;
      TTime             LastUpdated;
      TIPAddress        LastUpdAddr; // Need it when in holddown
      TInterfaceDescr * LastUpdInt;  // Need it when in holddown
      void           *  Pointer;     // reference to Path or NetworkInfo
```

```
       struct PathDescr *  ActivePath;    // the path to use
       //...
} TPrefixDescr;
```

Listing 4-21. *Pseudocode: TPrefixDescr structured type definition*

Note that the `Source` field has been changed. Now it is a pointer to an instance of the TProto type, the protocol descriptor used to store information about the route sources (described later).

The TPrefixDescr type contains no information about the intermediate address and the output interfaces, because this information is stored in the path descriptors. The `Pointer` field is used to store the address of the first path descriptor in the list, provided that the `Ultimate` field equals 1. If `Ultimate` is 0, the `Pointer` field points to an instance of the TNetworkInfo type (considered later), which contains general information about a given major network and the pointer to the first entry in the list of subnets.

The log given in Listing 4-22 shows the correspondence between the data structures and the **show ip route** command output.

```
R1#show ip route 20.1.1.0
Routing entry for 20.1.1.0/24
  Known via "connected", distance 0, metric 0 (connected)
  Redistributing via igrp 100, ospf 100
  Advertised by igrp 100
  Routing Descriptor Blocks:
  *directly connected, via Serial0
    Route metric is 0, traffic share count is 1
```

Listing 4-22. *Prefix descriptor fields displayed by the* **show ip route** *command*

The highlighted lines display the information from the TPrefixDescr structure of the route. The rest of the output contains the information held by this route's path descriptor. The pseudocode type definition for the TPathDescr structure is shown in Listing 4-23.

```
typedef struct PathDescr{       // Path Descriptor
    TIPAddress       Intermediate;   // 0.0.0.0 if not specified
    TinterfaceDescr * Interface;     // Out.Int, Null if none
    u_int            Metric;         // Route metric, 0 for statics
    TFlag            Connected;      // "Directly connected" flag
    TFlag            Permanent;      // "Permanent" route
    char             ShareCount;     // Traffic share count
    char             ShareValue;
    TIPAddress       Originator;     // Who sent this route for RPs
    TTime            LastUpdated;
```

```
    struct PathDescr * Next;        // next path in list, Null if last
    // ...
} TPathDescr;
```

Listing 4-23. *TPathDescr structured type definition*

The `Intermediate` field of the TPathDescr structure specifies the network address the forwarding engine must use while routing the packets. The `Interface` field in turn specifies the output interface.

Recall that every routing protocol specifies the quality of routes by supplying the route metrics. This information is stored in every path descriptor in the `Metric` field. Note that the prefix descriptor data structure also has a field with the same name. The value of the prefix descriptor's `Metric` field is the minimum of the `Metric` field values found in the linked path descriptors.

Dynamic routing protocols are able to install multiple routes to the same destination as long as all the routes have the same metric and this metric is the best of those of all routes available. As always, there's an exception: Two routing protocols—IGRP and EIGRP—can supply several routes to the same destination with unequal metrics, using the variance parameter to determine the range of valid metric values. This is why one prefix descriptor can have path descriptors with different metric values. Section 4.2.3 discusses how this information is analyzed by the routing table maintenance process, or RT process, that is responsible for the proper structure of the routing table.

The `Connected` field flags whether the path descriptor references only an interface and, consequently, whether the path descriptor and the prefix descriptor must be considered as directly connected. (The prefix descriptor structure also has a `Connected` field.) The path descriptor's `Connected` field is consulted by the forwarding engine while looking up an appropriate route for a packet's destination address. Once it has found a directly connected route, the lookup function stops recursive lookup iterations.

The `ShareCount` field contains the number of packets or flows—depending on the switching mode, as described in Chapter 5—that must be sent along a given path descriptor before taking the next path descriptor in the list. The `ShareCount` and the `ShareValue` fields in the path descriptor, as well as the prefix descriptor's `ActivePath` field, are used for load sharing when a prefix descriptor has more than one path descriptor in the path descriptor list.

The `Originator` field is used to store the IP address of the router that sent an update about the network described in the prefix descriptor. Because a router can receive multiple updates about the same network from different neighbors with the same metric, the prefix descriptor can have several path descriptors, each for one routing update originator.

The `LastUpdated` field is a timestamp, updated when the router receives an update about a given address range from another router. This timer is consulted by the RT process while serving routes learned via distance-vector protocols (RIP and IGRP).

The `Next` field contains the pointer to the next path descriptor in the list. If the current path descriptor is the last one, the `Next` field has the value of NULL.

Listing 4-24 gives the psuedocode type definition for the network information element, used to store the parameters of the child route entries for a parent network route.

```
typedef struct {          // General information about a major network
    u_int        Subnets;      // Number of subnets
    u_int        Masks;        // Number of subnet masks
    u_int        Connections;  // Number of connected routes
    TPrefixDescr * Pointer;    // Reference to the first subnet
} TNetworkInfo;
```

Listing 4-24. *The TNetworkInfo structured type definition*

The `Subnets` field is a counter of subnets linked to the parent prefix descriptor. The `Masks` field counts the number of subnet masks used in the network. If the value of this field is greater than 1, the network is subnetted, using the VLSM technique. The number of child routes marked as "directly connected" is stored in the `Connections` field. The `Pointer` field contains the reference to the subnets hash table containing subnet routes. Note that the TNetworkInfo structure has no `Next` field, as there can be only one instance of it per network parent route.

The contents of the TNetworkInfo record can be displayed by the **show ip route** command with the major network address specified (Listing 4-25).

```
R1#show ip route 20.0.0.0
Routing entry for 20.0.0.0/24, 3 known subnets
  Attached (2 connections)
  Redistributing via igrp 100

C       20.1.1.0 is directly connected, Serial0
I       20.1.3.0 [100/2600] via 20.1.1.1, 00:00:35, Serial0
C       20.1.2.0 is directly connected, Loopback0
R1#
```

Listing 4-25. **TNetworkInfo** *fields displayed by the* **show ip route** *command*

Listing 4-26 shows the results of changing the subnet mask on the interface Loopback0 to make it different from that used in the rest of the major network 20.0.0.0.

```
R1#conf t
Enter configuration commands, one per line.  End with CNTL/Z.
```

```
R1(config)#int lo0
R1(config-if)#ip addr 20.1.2.1 255.255.255.224
R1(config-if)#^Z
R1#
R1#show ip rou
...
Gateway of last resort is not set

      20.0.0.0/8 is variably subnetted, 3 subnets, 2 masks
C        20.1.1.0/24 is directly connected, Serial0
I        20.1.3.0/24 [100/2600] via 20.1.1.1, 00:00:06, Serial0
C        20.1.2.0/27 is directly connected, Loopback0
I     10.0.0.0/8 [100/3100] via 20.1.1.1, 00:00:06, Serial0
      30.0.0.0/24 is subnetted, 1 subnets
C        30.0.0.0 is directly connected, Ethernet0
S     200.0.0.0/8 is directly connected, Serial0
R1#
R1#show ip route 20.0.0.0
Routing entry for 20.0.0.0/8, 3 known subnets
  Attached (2 connections)
  Variably subnetted with 2 masks
  Redistributing via igrp 100

C        20.1.1.0/24 is directly connected, Serial0
I        20.1.3.0/24 [100/2600] via 20.1.1.1, 00:00:46, Serial0
C        20.1.2.0/27 is directly connected, Loopback0
R1#
```

Listing 4-26. *Subnet mask information when VLSM is used*

Note that the parent network route is now shown as variably subnetted and that the route mask augments every subnet route. Also, the route mask of the network route is the default classful route mask. Every time it adds or deletes a subnet route in the routing table, a router checks the presence and the correctness of the parent network route. Installation of the first subnet route in a given major network leads to the installation of the corresponding parent network route, to which the subnet route is linked. When the last subnet route is deleted and unlinked from the parent network route, the parent network route is also deleted from the routing table. This way, Cisco routers keep their routing tables structured.

To completely understand how the elements of the routing table are linked, consider Figure 4-5. It contains data structures for the first five routes of the show ip route output in the previous example.

The routing table contains two first-level routes: one for major network 20.0.0.0 and one for network 10.0.0.0. The first network route has three subnet routes in the list; the second route has a directly linked path descriptor.

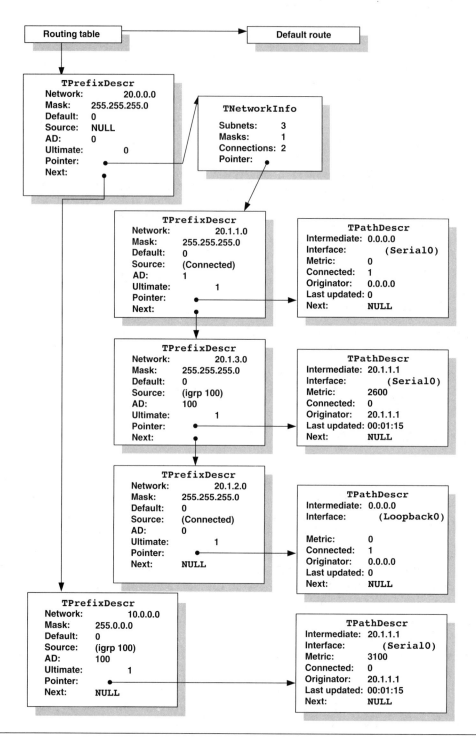

Figure 4-5. *Data structures' layouts for sample routing table*

If multiple routes to the same destination were available, Figure 4-5 would show multiple path descriptors linked to a single prefix descriptor.

Figure 4-3 illustrates the process of the routing table composition in the output of the **debug ip routing** command. An IP address is assigned to one of R1's interfaces, and then the interface is shut down. Note how network route 40.0.0.0 is deleted after the subnet route is deleted.

```
R1#debug ip routing
IP routing debugging is on
R1#conf t
Enter configuration commands, one per line.  End with CNTL/Z.
R1(config)#int lo1
R1(config-if)#
%LINEPROTO-5-UPDOWN: Line protocol on Interface Loopback1, changed state to up
%LINK-3-UPDOWN: Interface Loopback1, changed state to up
R1(config-if)#ip address 40.1.1.1 255.255.255.0
R1(config-if)#
*Mar  4 22:40:34.328: RT: add 40.1.1.0/24 via 0.0.0.0, connected metric [0/0]
*Mar  4 22:40:34.336: RT: interface Loopback1 added to routing table
R1(config-if)#
R1(config-if)#shutdown
R1(config-if)#
*Mar  4 22:40:43.416: RT: interface Loopback1 removed from routing table
*Mar  4 22:40:43.416: RT: del 40.1.1.0/24 via 0.0.0.0, connected metric [0/0]
*Mar  4 22:40:43.420: RT: delete subnet route to 40.1.1.0/24
*Mar  4 22:40:43.424: RT: delete network route to 40.0.0.0
%LINEPROTO-5-UPDOWN: Line protocol on Interface Loopback1, changed state to down
%LINK-5-CHANGED: Interface Loopback1, changed state to administratively down
R1(config-if)#^Z
R1#
```

Listing 4-27. *Deletion of network parent route after the last subnet route has been removed*

As shown in Figure 4-3, any ultimate route in the routing table can have several linked path descriptors. Listing 4-28 shows a sample routing table with three path descriptors linked to one prefix descriptor.

```
R1#show ip rou
...
Gateway of last resort is not set

     20.0.0.0/8 is variably subnetted, 2 subnets, 2 masks
```

```
C       20.1.1.0/24 is directly connected, Serial0
C       20.1.2.0/27 is directly connected, Loopback0
S     10.0.0.0/8 [1/0] via 30.0.0.3
                [1/0] via 30.0.0.2, Ethernet0
                [1/0] via 20.1.1.1, Serial0
      30.0.0.0/24 is subnetted, 1 subnets
C       30.0.0.0 is directly connected, Ethernet0
R1#
```

Listing 4-28. *Multiple path descriptors representing parallel routes*

You can see that one route entry has three routing descriptor blocks, which are shown in the output as corresponding to one primary line. The routing table in the example is constructed on the basis of the interface addresses and the static routes configured, as shown in Listing 4-29.

```
R1#conf t
Enter configuration commands, one per line.  End with CNTL/Z.
R1(config)#ip route 10.0.0.0 255.0.0.0 30.0.0.3
R1(config)#ip route 10.0.0.0 255.0.0.0 Ethernet 30.0.0.2
R1(config)#ip route 10.0.0.0 255.0.0.0 Serial 0 20.1.1.1
R1(config)#
```

Listing 4-29. *Configuring parallel static routes*

The Static route source supplies three routes to the RT process. These three routes are installed in the routing table as one prefix descriptor and three path descriptors—one for each static route—linked to it.

You can take a more detailed look at the path descriptors by using the **show ip route 10.0.0.0** command, output of which is given in Listing 4-30.

```
R1#show ip route 10.0.0.0
Routing entry for 10.0.0.0/8
  Known via "static", distance 1, metric 0
  Routing Descriptor Blocks:
  *30.0.0.3
    Route metric is 0, traffic share count is 1
  30.0.0.2, via Ethernet0
    Route metric is 0, traffic share count is 1
  20.1.1.1, via Serial0
    Route metric is 0, traffic share count is 1

R1#
```

Listing 4-30. *Path descriptor fields displayed by the* **show ip route** *command*

Note that the interface of the first path descriptor is not specified but that the interfaces of the other two path descriptors are. This means that when using the first path descriptor to route packets, the forwarding engine performs another routing table lookup to find a route to the intermediate address 30.0.0.3. (It will be directly connected to route 30.0.0.0/24 in this example.) The purpose of recursive lookup is to find the output interface, which is not specified in the path descriptor (see Chapter 5 for more details).

As mentioned before, Cisco IOS performs traffic sharing among several path descriptors of a prefix descriptor. The path descriptor that will be used to forward the next packet is marked with an asterisk (*) at the left when displayed with the **show ip route** *route-address* command. The proportion of traffic sent over each path descriptor is determined by the traffic share count (ShareCount field in path descriptor), which equals 1 in case of equal-cost load sharing.

Now consider the pseudocode of a function that accepts routes and maintains proper routing table structure. Assume that the routes passed to this function are already checked and approved for installation; the function that does this is explained in Section 4.2.6. Assume also that the function is always given ultimate routes to install. The parameter TheRoute is supposed to have valid values of the fields Network, Mask, Source, Connected, AD, and Metric. Listing 4-31 displays the pseudocode of the route installation function.

```
TRoutingTable TheRoutingTable;                    //The routing table

void RouteInstall(TPrefixDescr *TheRoute, TPathDescr* Path)
{
TPrefixDescr        Majornet;
TPrefixDescr        *Route;
TPrefixDescr        *Network;

Major(TheRoute->Network, &Majornet);

TheRoute->Ultimate = 1;

Route = FindRoute(TheRoute);
if (Route) {
    CheckPath(Route, Path);
}
else {
 switch (GetEntryType(TheRoute)){
  case etSupernet:
      AddToChain(&TheRoutingTable.Supernets, TheRoute, Path);
      break;
  case etNetwork:
      Network = FindInChain(TheRoutingTable.Majornets, &Majornet, 0);
      //try to locate the network parent route
      if (!Network){
```

```
              AddToChain(&TheRoutingTable.Majornets, TheRoute, Path);
              //no subnets
           }
        else AddSubnet(Network, TheRoute, Path);
        //consider it subnet
        break;
    case etSubnet:
        Network = FindInChain(TheRoutingTable.Majornets, &Majornet, 0);
        //try to locate the network route
        if (!Network){
            Network = CreateNetwork(TheRoute);
            Route = FindInChain(TheRoutingTable.Majornets, &Majornet, 1);
            //try to locate an ultimate network route
            if (Route){
              TNetworkInfo * NInfo = (TNetworkInfo*)Network->Pointer;
              UnlinkFromChain(&TheRoutingTable.Majornets, Route);
              LinkToChain(&NInfo->Pointer, Route);
              CountSubnet(Network, Route);
            }
        }
        AddSubnet(Network, TheRoute, Path);
        break;
    default:;
    }
 }
}
```

Listing 4-31. *Pseudocode:* `RouteInstall()` *function*

First take a look at the description of the functions used in the code of
`RouteInstall()`.

- `Major()` computes the major network route, based on the address passed as the
  parameter, and copies the result to a TPrefixDescr instance referenced by the
  `Route` argument.

- `GetEntryType()` returns the type of the route—etSupernet, etNetwork, or
  etSubnet—based on its `Network` and `Mask` fields.

- `FindInChain()` looks through a chain of prefix descriptors—supernets, major
  networks, or subnets—specified by the `Chain` argument, trying to find a route
  with the network and route mask equal to those in `TheRoute` parameter and with
  the `Ultimate` field equal to the `IsUltimate` argument. If the lookup is successful,
  the reference to the found route is returned; otherwise, the returned value is
  NULL.

- `FindRoute()` calls `FindInChain()`, looking for a route with specific parameters in
  the routing table.

- `FreeRoute()` frees the memory allocated for a prefix descriptor.

- `AddToChain()` adds a prefix descriptor, referenced by `TheRoute` argument, to a chain of prefix descriptors pointed by the `Chain` argument and also passes the information to the path descriptor–checking function `CheckPath()`.

- `CheckPath()` links the new path descriptor to the prefix descriptor if the path descriptor is totally new or updates the path descriptor information if it is already linked.

- `AddSubnet()` links a subnet route to the network prefix descriptor and updates the corresponding counters (discussed a bit later).

- `CreateNetwork()` adds a parent network route to which the subnets are linked.

- `UnlinkFromChain()` removes a route from a chain of prefix descriptors.

The algorithm performed by the `RouteInstall()` function is as follows.

1. Obtain the major network route for the route to be installed.

2. Find in the routing table a route that covers the same address range as the route being processed.

3. If such a route is already present, the new route's path descriptor is passed for processing by the `CheckPath()` function, which is supposed to make the decision whether to link the new path descriptor to the existing route.

4. If a route was not found, which means that a new one should be installed, the list of actions depends on the type of network entry being added.

   a. If it's a supernet route, the code just adds it to the chain of first-level prefix descriptors by calling the `AddToChain()` function, which in turn links the new prefix descriptor to the chain and passes the path descriptor to the `CheckPath()` function.

   b. If the entry is a network type, the code first tries to locate the parent network route, which may already have subnets of the same major network in the table. If such a parent route exists, the new ultimate network route is linked as a subnet by calling the `AddSubnet()` function. If the major network has no parent network route, the new network route is installed in the first level of the routing table hierarchy.

   c. If the new route is a subnet, the function must either locate an existing network parent prefix descriptor or create a new one. When creating a new parent node, the code looks through the first-level routing entries again for an ultimate major network route entry, which may have been installed before. If an ultimate major network route entry exists, it is unlinked from the first-level prefix descriptor table and linked to the newly created parent network entry as a subnet. After an existing parent network node has been found or a new one has been created, the new subnet is linked to it.

Now consider the pseudocode of the `CheckPath()` used by `RouteInstall()` (Listing 4-32).

```
void CheckPath(TPrefixDescr *TheRoute, TPathDescr *NewPath)
{
 TPathDescr **Pointer = (TPathDescr**) &TheRoute->Pointer;
 u_char NumOfRoutes = 0;

 for(;(*Pointer);Pointer = &(*Pointer)->Next){
   NumOfRoutes++;

   if (((*Pointer)->Intermediate == NewPath->Intermediate) &&
      ((*Pointer)->Interface == NewPath->Interface)) {

      (*Pointer)->LastUpdated = get_time(); //It's just been updated
      TheRoute->LastUpdates   = get_time();
      TheRoute->LastUpdAddr = NewPath->Intermediate;
      TheRoute->LastUpdInt  = NewPath->Interface;
      if ((*Pointer)!=NewPath)FreePath(NewPath);
      return;          //We already have similar or the same Path
   }
 }

 //This is a new Path
 //Check how many paths we have
 if (NumOfRoutes==MAX_PATHS){
    FreePath(NewPath);
    return;                   //We do not support more than 6 Paths
 }

 //Link the new one
 (*Pointer) = NewPath;
 NewPath->ShareValue = NewPath->ShareCount;

 //Update the TPrefixDescr info
 if (NewPath->Connected)
    TheRoute->Connected = 1;

 if (NumOfRoutes == 0)
    TheRoute->ActivePath = NewPath;

 if ((NumOfRoutes == 0) || (NewPath->Metric < TheRoute->Metric))
    TheRoute->Metric = NewPath->Metric;
}
```

Listing 4-32. *Pseudocode:* `CheckPath()` *function*

The function first looks through all path descriptors linked to a given route and checks whether there is the same path descriptor or a path descriptor with equal parameters in the list. If there's a path descriptor with equal parameters, the function updates the `LastUpdated` field, releases the new path descriptor—there's no need to keep two equal path descriptors—and returns. If the new path descriptor is considered to be unique and addition of it does not exceed the maximum (six) number of path descriptors allowed, the new path descriptor is linked to the route. If the path descriptor being processed carries the `Connected` flag, the same flag is set in the route's prefix descriptor. If the added path descriptor is the first for this route or its metric is better than that in the prefix descriptor, the metric value of the path descriptor is copied to the prefix descriptor's `Metric` field.

Consider some examples of how the `RouteInstall()` function operates and manages the routing table structure. The routing table shown in Listing 4-33 has a parent network prefix descriptor that describes major network 40.0.0.0 and one subnet route to 40.1.0.0/16.

```
R1#show ip rou
...
Gateway of last resort is not set

     40.0.0.0/16 is subnetted, 1 subnets
S       40.1.0.0 [1/0] via 30.0.0.3, Ethernet0
     30.0.0.0/24 is subnetted, 1 subnets
C       30.0.0.0 is directly connected, Ethernet0
R1#
```

Listing 4-33. *Sample routing table*

Then another static route covering the whole major network is added, as shown in Listing 4-34.

```
R1#conf t
Enter configuration commands, one per line.  End with CNTL/Z.
R1(config)#ip route 40.0.0.0 255.0.0.0 Eth 0 30.0.0.2
R1(config)#
R1#
*Mar  7 02:18:10.291: RT: network 40.0.0.0 is now variably masked
*Mar  7 02:18:10.295: RT: add 40.0.0.0/8 via 30.0.0.2, static metric [1/0]
R1#
```

Listing 4-34. *Configuring the summary network static route*

Look at the result. Because a parent network route already covers the same major network, the new static route is not installed in the first level but is linked to the parent route as if it were a subnet one (Listing 4-35).

```
R1#show ip route
...
Gateway of last resort is not set

     40.0.0.0/8 is variably subnetted, 2 subnets, 2 masks
S        40.0.0.0/8 [1/0] via 30.0.0.2, Ethernet0
S        40.1.0.0/16 [1/0] via 30.0.0.3, Ethernet0
     30.0.0.0/24 is subnetted, 1 subnets
C        30.0.0.0 is directly connected, Ethernet0
R1#
```

Listing 4-35. *Resulting routing table*

As you will see in Chapter 5, the location of a route in the routing table is very important when the routing table is being searched during packet forwarding. Once a parent network route is created, all routes covering destinations in the corresponding major network must be installed in the routing table as the parent route's child entries in order to guarantee proper route lookup.

Here is another illustration of this rule. The routing table has an ultimate network route, 40.0.0.0/8, configured manually by the administrator (Listing 4-36). Because the route mask is the default classful route mask—the route is not a subnet—the parent network route is not created, and the route is linked to the first level.

```
R1#show ip rou
...
Gateway of last resort is not set

S    40.0.0.0/8 [1/0] via 30.0.0.2, Ethernet0
     30.0.0.0/24 is subnetted, 1 subnets
C        30.0.0.0 is directly connected, Ethernet0
R1#
```

Listing 4-36. *Sample routing table with an ultimate network route*

Now a subnet route 40.1.0.0 is added. Because the route mask is longer than the major network's route mask—the route is to a subnet—the network parent route is created. All routes belonging to the major network, 40.0.0.0, are linked to the parent routing entry, including the ultimate network route in the first-level route table (Listing 4-37).

```
R1#conf t
Enter configuration commands, one per line.  End with CNTL/Z.
R1(config)#ip route 40.1.0.0 255.255.0.0 Eth 0 30.0.0.3
R1(config)#
```

```
R1#
*Mar  7 02:18:10.291: RT: network 40.0.0.0 is now variably masked
*Mar  7 02:18:10.295: RT: add 40.1.0.0/16 via 30.0.0.3, static metric [1/0]
R1#
R1#show ip route
...
Gateway of last resort is not set

     40.0.0.0/8 is variably subnetted, 2 subnets, 2 masks
S        40.0.0.0/8 [1/0] via 30.0.0.2, Ethernet0
S        40.1.0.0/16 [1/0] via 30.0.0.3, Ethernet0
     30.0.0.0/24 is subnetted, 1 subnets
C        30.0.0.0 is directly connected, Ethernet0
R1#
```

Listing 4-37. *Addition of a subnet route in the presence of the ultimate network route*

Now look at the function dedicated to route deletion. Consider the pseudocode given in Listing 4-38.

```
int RouteRemove(TPrefixDescr *TheRoute, TPathDescr * ThePath)
{
TPrefixDescr        Majornet;
TPrefixDescr       *Route;
TPrefixDescr       *Network;

Major(TheRoute->Network, &Majornet);

Route = FindRoute(TheRoute);
if (Route==NULL) return 0; //Not found

switch (GetEntryType(TheRoute)){
  case etSupernet:
            if (DeletePath(Route, ThePath)){
                InvalidateRoute(Route, &TheRoutingTable.Supernets);
                return 1;
            }
            break;
  case etNetwork:
            Network = FindInChain(TheRoutingTable.Majornets,
                            &Majornet, 0);
            //try to locate the network parent route
            if (DeletePath(Route, ThePath)) {
                if (!Network)        //It was an ultimate node
                  InvalidateRoute(Route, &TheRoutingTable.Majornets);
                //no subnets
                else DelSubnet(Network, Route); // Delete a subnet
```

```
                        return 1;
                }
                break;
    case etSubnet:
                Network = FindInChain(TheRoutingTable.Majornets,
                                      &Majornet, 0);
                //try to locate the network route
                if (!Network) return 0; //Error
                if (DeletePath(Route, ThePath)){
                    DelSubnet(Network, Route);
                    return 1;
                }
                break;
    default:;
    }
    return 0;
}
```

Listing 4-38. *Pseudocode:* `RouteRemove()` *function*

The function is supposed to return 0 if the route just removed was not the last, that is, other path descriptors are linked to the same prefix descriptor. If deletion of the specified path descriptor results in removal of the prefix descriptor it was linked to, the return value must be 1. Route removal itself is done as follows.

1. The `RouteRemove` function tries to locate the route to be removed by calling the `FindRoute()` function.

2. If the route does not exist in the routing table, the function returns.

3. If the route exists and is a supernet, the code unlinks the path descriptor from the route by calling the `DeletePath()` function and invalidates the prefix descriptor if the path descriptor was the last one, indicated by a nonzero value returned by the `DeletePath()` function.

4. If the route type is the `etNetwork`, it can be either in the first-level table or linked to the parent network route. This is why the function first tries to locate the parent route. If it is found and the path descriptor just deleted is the last—the path descriptor list is free—the route is removed as a subnet by calling the `DelSubnet()` function. If there is no parent network route, the route being deleted is passed for processing to the `InvalidateRoute()` function, which can either delete the prefix descriptor from the route chain or change its state if the prefix descriptor was supplied by a distance-vector protocol (discussed in later chapters).

5. If instructed to delete a subnet route, the function always tries to find the network parent route. The path descriptor is unlinked and the route is deleted, if necessary, by calling the `DelSubnet()` function.

The `DelSubnet()` function decreases the number of subnets linked to the parent route. If the subnet route to be deleted carries the `Connected` flag, the number of connections is also decreased. Then the route is processed by the `InvalidateRoute()` function. If the route has been deleted, it may be that the only route linked to the parent is an ultimate network route, which should be moved back to the major network route chain. Then the code checks whether the parent network route has any subnet routes. If there are no subnets, the parent route is also deleted from the major network route chain. If some subnet routes are still left, the function makes sure that the `Masks` counter in the network information structure contains adequate information.

A summary of the process follows.

- The routing table is a hierarchical structure that consists of the following two main levels: first-level prefix descriptor tables, including supernet and major network hash tables, and second-level prefix descriptors: subnet routes for given major networks.

- The first-level major network prefix descriptors can be either ultimate or parent, whereas the supernet prefix descriptors are always ultimate.

- The network parent prefix descriptors do not have any directly linked path descriptors; instead, they have a set of subnet routes, each an ultimate one that has at least one path descriptor.

- Ultimate prefix descriptors are used for packet forwarding and have not less than one and not more than six linked path descriptors.

- Each path descriptor has information about the intermediate network address, outgoing interface (optional), and other parameters used for packet forwarding.

- All subnet routes are always linked to corresponding parent network routes that are created when the first route with the subnet mask longer than the default classful mask is passed for installation into the routing table.

- Ultimate major network routes are installed in the first level, provided that there is no parent network route for the major network this route covers.

- Once the parent network route is created because of installation of a subnet route, the ultimate network route for a given major network is also moved to the second level, linked as a subnet route to the parent network route.

- In addition to the list of routes, the routing table structure also holds a pointer to a route selected as the default.

4.2.3 Route Source Selection

The concept of administrative distance and route source selection is a fundamental idea in route manipulation in Cisco IOS. Routes can come into the routing table from different sources at the same time. For example, a router can run several dynamic routing protocols simultaneously with no problem unless routes from different sources cover the same address range. Imagine a router that gets information about a network X from two different routing protocols—RIP and OSPF. The router cannot choose between them by comparing metrics, as the metrics have different significance in each protocol. For instance, in RIP, a route with metric 16 is considered infinitely remote and unreachable, whereas in OSPF, a route with the same metric can become the best. Because different protocols have different metric scales, some other tiebreaker must let the router choose among the route sources. Cisco routers use the term *administrative distance* (AD) as this tiebreaker. The administrative distance specifies the level of trust for a given route source. The lower the AD value, the more the corresponding source is "trusted."

Every route source is described using a *protocol descriptor*, which contains information about a given route source. Listing 4-39 displays the beginning of the protocol descriptor structure pseudocode definition; additional fields are presented in Chapter 7.

```
// TProto.Type (route source) values:
#define RS_CONNECTED 0x0100
#define RS_STATIC    0x0200
#define RS_DYNAMIC   0x0300
#define RS_DV        0x1000 + RS_DYNAMIC
#define RS_RIP       0x0001 + RS_DV
#define RS_IGRP      0x0002 + RS_DV
#define RS_OSPF      0x0003 + RS_DYNAMIC
#define RS_EIGRP     0x0004 + RS_DYNAMIC
#define RS_ISIS      0x0005 + RS_DYNAMIC
#define RS_EGP       0x0006 + RS_DYNAMIC
#define RS_BGP       0x0007 + RS_DYNAMIC

typedef struct Proto{            // Protocol Descriptor Block
   u_int      Type;              // RS_XXXXX pattern
   text       Name;              // The name of the process
   u_char     Distance;          // Administrative distance
   // ...
   struct Proto * Next;          // Link to the next Proto
} TProto;
```

Listing 4-39. *Pseudocode: TProto structured type definition*

Default AD values are assigned to each route source. (For static routes and dynamic routing protocols, the AD value is configurable and discussed in corresponding chapters.) For example, routes to directly attached networks are inserted into the routing table with an AD of 0, whereas the static routes are assigned an AD of 1. Table 4-1 shows default values of AD for each route source.

Table 4-1. *Default AD Values for Route Sources*

Route Source	Default AD Value
Connected interface	0
Static route	1
Mobile IP	3
Enhanced IGRP summary route	5
External BGP	20
Internal Enhanced IGRP	90
IGRP	100
OSPF	110
IS-IS	115
RIP	120
EGP	140
ODR	160
External Enhanced IGRP	170
Internal and local BGP	200
Nontrusted	255

As you can see, the third type route source—dynamic routing protocols—is enhanced, and every routing protocol is assigned its own AD value. Also, a route assigned the AD of 255 never gets into the routing table.

The way AD works can be understood as an additional level of route selection before installing the routes in the routing table. Figure 4-6 illustrates the process of route selection performed by the RT process. The idea behind this operation is that the RT process accepts routes from several sources. Some sources, such as Static or BGP, first validate their routes to see whether the routes are eligible to be installed in the routing table, that is, whether the referenced interface is up or the intermediate address is resolvable. For other sources, this check is not necessary. For example, OSPF will never try to install a route through an interface that does not have an active OSPF adjacency.

When a route is passed to the RT process, the router uses the following logic.

1. Check whether the routing table already has a route to the same network.
2. If no route is found, install the new route.
3. If an existing route is found, compare the AD and metric values of the old and new routes as follows.

a. If the AD of the new route is different from the AD of the route in the table, the route with the lower AD value is preferred. If the new route is chosen, all paths in the old route are removed, the new path is installed, and the associated AD and metric values of the route are changed accordingly. Otherwise— the already installed route has a better AD value—the new route is not installed, but the router saves information about the protocol that submitted the new route for installation in the prefix descriptor and sends a query to the protocol when a backup route is needed.

b. If the AD values of the routes are equal and both routes were submitted by the same process, the new route is processed according to the rules of distance-vector protocols (see Chapter 8).

c. If the AD values are equal but the routes are from different sources, the behavior depends on whether the routes are submitted by processes of the same type. If they are, the metrics of the routes are compared as if the routes were from the same protocol. If metrics are the same, the route from the process with the lower process number wins. If the routes are from different sources, the new route is ignored. (Note that this check is implemented for EIGRP routes only. All other routes are treated as from different protocols, so the old route is left in the routing table.)

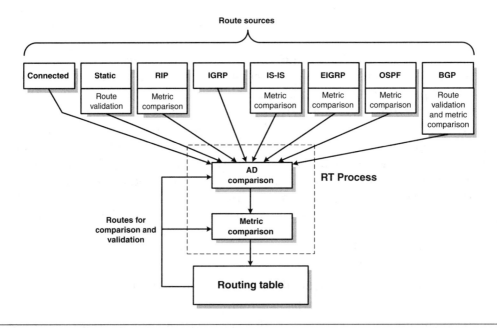

Figure 4-6. *Routing information flow with AD comparison*

IGRP does not select best routes before passing them to the RT process. The RT process selects the best route and maintains the timers for routes from IGRP. RIP used to have the same behavior, but it was changed with introduction of RIP demand circuit extensions that required RIP to have its own routing database. Implementations of more recent protocols, such as OSPF and EIGRP, do not and cannot rely on the RT process; they perform the entire route processing independently. With older protocols, the only role of the RT process is routing table management. We get back to this question in later chapters.

To understand the meaning of AD comparison, consider the following example. A router accepts routing information as follows:

Networks known as connected:	10.1.0.0, 10.2.0.0
Networks known from static routes:	10.3.0.0, 10.4.0.0
Networks known from RIP:	10.2.0.0, 10.3.0.0, 10.4.0.0, 10.5.0.0, 10.6.0.0, 10.7.0.0
Networks known from OSPF:	10.4.0.0, 10.5.0.0, 10.7.0.0

The route maintenance process receives all these routes one by one for installation. The RT process selects routes with the best AD values. The final routing table contains routes from the following sources:

Network 10.1.0.0—Connected	(no other sources)
Network 10.2.0.0—Connected	(Connected < RIP)
Network 10.3.0.0—Static	(Static < RIP)
Network 10.4.0.0—Static	(Static < OSPF < RIP)
Network 10.5.0.0—OSPF	(OSPF < RIP)
Network 10.6.0.0—RIP	(no other sources)
Network 10.7.0.0—OSPF	(OSPF < RIP)

To formalize the process of route selection, a function is included that compares two routes and identifies the better of the two (Listing 4-40).

```
#define cmBetter 1
#define cmWorse -1
#define cmEqual 0
```

```
int CompareRoutes(TPrefixDescr * Route1, TPrefixDescr * Route2)
{
 if (Route1->AD < Route2->AD) return cmBetter;
 if (Route1->AD > Route2->AD) return cmWorse;
 if (Route1->Source == Route2->Source)
  {
     if (Route1->Metric < Route2->Metric) return cmBetter;
     if (Route1->Metric > Route2->Metric) return cmWorse;
  }
 return cmEqual;
}
```

Listing 4-40. *Pseudocode:* `CompareRoutes()` *function*

This route-comparison function is applied only to the routes covering exactly the same address blocks. There is no competition between two or more routes if the address blocks they cover are different. The `CompareRoutes()` function accepts two routes as arguments and compares them. If the administrative distance values of the routes are different, the route with the lower AD is considered better. If the AD values are the same and routes are from the same process, the one with the better (lower) metric is preferred. Otherwise, the routes are reported to be equal, and the tiebreaking rules described earlier are used.

The route sources must have a way to supply their routes to the RT process for further processing and possible installation. The function the route sources call whenever they have a route is `RouteUpdate()`, the pseudocode of which is given in Listing 4-41.

```
int RouteUpdate(TPrefixDescr * TheRoute, TPathDescr * ThePath)
{
 TPrefixDescr    * Route;
 int        Result;

 if (TheRoute->AD == 255) return 0;
 // Routes with this AD are never installed

 if (!PathValid(ThePath, NULL)) return 0;
 //sorry, cannot install if unresolved

 Route = FindRoute(&TheRoutingTable.Routes, TheRoute, 1);
 //Try to find a route to the same destination

 if (!Route) {
   RouteInstall(TheRoute, ThePath);
   return 1;
 }

 TheRoute->Metric = ThePath->Metric;
 Result = CompareRoutes(TheRoute, Route);
 switch (Result) {
```

```
    case cmWorse:    // Save info for backup route query
                     return 0;
    case cmEqual:    if (Route->Source == TheRoute->Source) {
                         CheckPath(Route, ThePath); //Install another Path;
                         FreeRoute(TheRoute);    //and free new Route
                         return 1;
                     }
                     // EIGRP checks skipped...
                     return 0;
    case cmBetter:   ChangeRoute(Route, TheRoute, ThePath);
                     return 1;
  }
}
```

Listing 4-41. *Pseudocode:* `RouteUpdate()` *function*

The function accepts a prefix descriptor and the corresponding path descriptor as the arguments. The returned value is 0 (Boolean false) if the new prefix descriptor/path descriptor pair is not installed by the function. If the function successfully processes the route, the returned code is 1 (Boolean true).

Here is a description of the pseudocode. First, the value of the administrative distance is checked. If the AD is 255, the route is not processed and the function returns, as no route with this value of AD must get into the routing table. The function then checks whether the path descriptor is valid, using the `PathValid()` function, defined later (Listing 4-50). If the path descriptor is not resolvable, the function fails to install the route. After all prerequisites are met, the code calls the `FindRoute()` function, trying to find a route to the same destination the new one covers. If no route is found, the new route is passed for installation to the `RouteInstall()` function. If an already installed route is found in the routing table, the new route is compared to it, using the `CompareRoutes()` function. If the new route is less preferred than the already existing one, the new route is skipped. If the routes are equal and are from the same route source, the new path descriptor is passed for further processing to the `CheckPath()` function. If the sources are different—this can happen in transition states when a route source is configured with a new AD value but its old routes are still in the routing table—or the new route is better, the `ChangeRoute()` function is called, and both routes and the new path descriptor are passed as the parameters. The code of the `ChangeRoute()` function is given in Listing 4-42.

```
void ChangeRoute(TPrefixDescr *OldRoute, TPrefixDescr *NewRoute, TPathDescr *NewPath)
{
 FreeAllPaths(OldRoute);
 OldRoute->Source    = NewRoute->Source;
 OldRoute->Connected = NewRoute->Connected;
 OldRoute->AD        = NewRoute->AD;
 OldRoute->Metric    = NewRoute->Metric;
```

```
CheckPath(OldRoute, NewPath);
FreeRoute(NewRoute);
}
```

Listing 4-42. *Pseudocode:* `ChangeRoute()` *function*

The task of this function is to change the properties of a route, including linked path descriptors, to those of the new route. The code first releases all path descriptors of the old route. The attributes of the new route are copied to the fields of the old one. Then the path descriptor passed to the function is linked to the route's prefix descriptor by calling the `CheckPath()` function.

A demonstration of how a static route with the AD value of 10 is installed in the routing table is shown in Listing 4-43.

```
R1#conf t
Enter configuration commands, one per line.  End with CNTL/Z.
R1(config)#
R1(config)#ip route 20.1.3.0 255.255.255.0 Ser 0 20.1.1.1 10
R1(config)#
*Mar  1 05:17:43.838: RT: add 20.1.3.0/24 via 20.1.1.1, static metric [10/0]
R1(config)#^Z
R1#
R1#show ip rou
...
Gateway of last resort is not set

     20.0.0.0/24 is subnetted, 2 subnets
C       20.1.1.0 is directly connected, Serial0
S       20.1.3.0 [10/0] via 20.1.1.1, Serial0
     30.0.0.0/24 is subnetted, 1 subnets
C       30.0.0.0 is directly connected, Ethernet0
R1#
```

Listing 4-43. *Static route with changed AD value*

The route is successfully installed in the routing table. Now a competing static route covering the same destination but with a different AD value is added (Listing 4-44).

```
R1#conf t
Enter configuration commands, one per line.  End with CNTL/Z.
R1(config)#ip route 20.1.3.0 255.255.255.0 Eth 0 30.0.0.2 5
R1(config)#
*Mar  1 05:20:07.690: RT: closer admin distance for 20.1.3.0, flushing 1 routes
*Mar  1 05:20:07.690: RT: add 20.1.3.0/24 via 30.0.0.2, static metric [5/0]
```

```
R1(config)#^Z
R1#show ip rou
...
Gateway of last resort is not set

     20.0.0.0/24 is subnetted, 2 subnets
C       20.1.1.0 is directly connected, Serial0
S       20.1.3.0 [5/0] via 30.0.0.2, Ethernet0
     30.0.0.0/24 is subnetted, 1 subnets
C       30.0.0.0 is directly connected, Ethernet0
R1#
```

Listing 4-44. *Competing static route*

The first route is removed from the routing table, and the new one is installed because the AD value of the new route is better: [5/0] in Listing 4-44. If the second route is deleted because Ethernet0 goes down or the administrator removes the route from configuration, the RT process will request route sources, including Static, for a backup route, and the first static route will be installed again, as there will be no valid competing route with better AD value (Listing 4-45).

```
R1#conf t
Enter configuration commands, one per line.  End with CNTL/Z.
R1(config)#no ip route 20.1.3.0 255.255.255.0 Eth 0 30.0.0.2 5
R1(config)#
*Mar  1 05:23:21.010: RT: del 20.1.3.0/24 via 30.0.0.2, static metric [5/0]
*Mar  1 05:23:21.014: RT: delete subnet route to 20.1.3.0/24
*Mar  1 05:23:21.018: RT: add 20.1.3.0/24 via 20.1.1.1, static metric [10/0]
R1(config)#^Z
R1#
R1#show ip rou
...
Gateway of last resort is not set

     20.0.0.0/24 is subnetted, 2 subnets
C       20.1.1.0 is directly connected, Serial0
S       20.1.3.0 [10/0] via 20.1.1.1, Serial0
     30.0.0.0/24 is subnetted, 1 subnets
C       30.0.0.0 is directly connected, Ethernet0
R1#
```

Listing 4-45. *Installation of pending static route*

If two routes are compared and the AD values are the same, the ordinary metric value comes into play. The route with the best (lower) metric wins. Consider the following example. The routing table contains an IGRP-learned route as shown in Listing 4-46.

```
R1#show ip rou
...
Gateway of last resort is not set

     20.0.0.0/24 is subnetted, 2 subnets
C       20.1.1.0 is directly connected, Serial0
I       20.1.3.0 [100/2566] via 20.1.1.1, 00:00:04, Serial0
     30.0.0.0/24 is subnetted, 1 subnets
C       30.0.0.0 is directly connected, Ethernet0
R1#
```

Listing 4-46. *Sample routing table with IGRP-learned route*

Note the value of the AD (100) and of the metric (2566) provided by the IGRP process. A static route is configured that covers the same address range and that has the same administrative distance. Because all static routes are always installed with a metric of 0, this new route replaces the IGRP one (Listing 4-47).

```
R1#conf t
Enter configuration commands, one per line.  End with CNTL/Z.
R1(config)#ip route 20.1.3.0 255.255.255.0 Eth 0 30.0.0.2 100
R1(config)#
*Mar  1 05:33:48.586: RT: del 20.1.3.0/24 via 20.1.1.1, static metric [100/2566]
*Mar  1 05:33:48.590: RT: add 20.1.3.0/24 via 30.0.0.2, static metric [100/0]
R1(config)#^Z
R1#
R1#show ip rou
...
Gateway of last resort is not set

     20.0.0.0/24 is subnetted, 2 subnets
C       20.1.1.0 is directly connected, Serial0
S       20.1.3.0 [100/0] via 20.1.1.1, Serial0
     30.0.0.0/24 is subnetted, 1 subnets
C       30.0.0.0 is directly connected, Ethernet0
R1#
```

Listing 4-47. *Static route with AD value equal to IGRP's*

Of course, configuration of static routes with AD value equal to that of an other route source doesn't make sense in real life and is used only to demonstrate the way the RT process handles the routes. A more realistic example would be a change of the metric in case of dynamic routing protocols. Look at the log shown in Listing 4-48.

```
R1#show int s0
Serial0 is up, line protocol is up
  Hardware is HD64570
  Internet address is 20.1.1.2/24
  MTU 1500 bytes, BW 128 Kbit, DLY 20000 usec, rely 255/255, load 1/255
...
R1#show int s1
Serial1 is up, line protocol is up
  Hardware is HD64570
  Internet address is 20.1.2.2/24
  MTU 1500 bytes, BW 64 Kbit, DLY 20000 usec, rely 255/255, load 1/255
...
R1#show ip route
...
Gateway of last resort is not set

     20.0.0.0/24 is subnetted, 2 subnets
C       20.1.1.0 is directly connected, Serial0
C       20.1.2.0 is directly connected, Serial1
I       20.1.3.0 [100/80625] via 20.1.1.1, 00:00:12, Serial0
     30.0.0.0/24 is subnetted, 1 subnets
C       30.0.0.0 is directly connected, Ethernet0
R1#
R1#conf t
Enter configuration commands, one per line.  End with CNTL/Z.
R1(config)#int s1
R1(config-if)#bandwidth 256
R1(config-if)#^Z
R1#
*Mar 1 05:41:29.246:RT: del 20.1.3.0/24 via 20.1.1.1, igrp metric [100/80625]
*Mar 1 05:41:29.246:RT: add 20.1.3.0/24 via 20.1.2.1, igrp metric [100/41562]
R1#show ip route igrp
I       20.1.3.0 [100/41562] via 20.1.2.1, Serial1
R1#
```

Listing 4-48. *Change of IGRP route metric*

Initially, the bandwidth parameter was set to 128Kbps for the Serial0 interface and to 64Kbps for the Serial1 interface. Based on these values and parameters in the routing update, IGRP calculated the metric for the best route to subnet 20.1.3.0/24 through interface Serial0 (80625). The value of bandwidth on Serial1 was changed to 256Kbps to make IGRP prefer the route through this interface. Next time IGRP receives an update from its neighbor 20.1.2.1 on the Serial1 interface and passes the route to the RT process, the RT process removes the old best path and installs the route through Serial1 because the new route has a better (lower) metric value.

Information explained in this section can be summarized as follows.

- Routers can have competing routes, that is, routes covering the same address ranges and originated by different route sources.
- The route metrics cannot be used to choose between the routes from different route sources, as different sources have incompatible metric scales.
- Administrative distance is the parameter used to discriminate between route sources; the lower the AD value, the more trustable the source.
- Every route source is assigned the default AD value; this parameter is configurable.
- Every route is accompanied by the AD value set to the route source's AD value.
- The RT process accepts one route at a time for processing. The AD and metric values of the new route are compared with those of already installed route(s) covering the same destination.
- If the AD value of the new route is better than that of the old one, the new route replaces the old one.
- If the AD value of the new route is worse, the old route stays in the routing table.
- If the AD values of the two routes are equal and the routes are from the same source, the route with the better route metric wins (see Chapter 8 for more details).
- If both the ADs and the metric values of the routes are equal and the routes are from the same source, the path descriptor of the new route is added to the path descriptor list of the route in the routing table, provided that the routes are from the same sources; if the sources are different, the old route stays in the table. (EIGRP routes are a special case.)
- Whenever a route with a better AD value is deleted from the routing table owing to the unresolvability of the intermediate network address or because the referenced interface is down, other, competing routes covering the same address range but with worse AD values can go into the routing table. This is ensured by the mechanisms described in Section 4.2.5.

The steps of route manipulation described in this section take place whenever the RT process is passed some routing information for processing. The following sections describe a set of events that lead to changes in the routing table, as well as the details of processing different types of routing information.

4.2.4 Routing Table Initialization

When the administrator turns on a Cisco router, it reads its start-up configuration file. Cisco routers represent configuration in plaintext form, and it is processed exactly as if the commands were typed in from an ASCII terminal using the **configure terminal** command.

While processing the configuration file, a router may encounter the following commands that can change the state of the routing table:

- **[no] shutdown**, used to administratively bring the interface down or up
- **[no] ip address**, used to assign or to deassign the primary or secondary addresses to an interface
- **[no] ip unnumbered**, used to enable or to disable IP processing without assigning a separate IP address to an interface
- **[no] ip route**, used to add or to delete a static route
- **[no] ip routing**, used to turn on and off IP routing in the router; when IP routing is off, the router stops maintaining the routing table
- **[no] ip default-network**, used to mark or to unmark a route as a candidate default
- **[no] router *protocol***, used to start or to stop a dynamic routing protocol

Cisco routers install and remove routes asynchronously, calling appropriate RT process functions as needed.

4.2.5 Asynchronous Table Maintenance

Like any asynchronous process, routing table maintenance can be described as a list of events and corresponding actions. Following are the events that the RT process can receive and on which it must react.

- *Interface going up* happens when the data link layer protocol declares the interface up. The data link layer is started on an interface if it is up both physically and administratively, that is, not disabled by a **shutdown** command. Whether the interface is considered operational from the IP routing perspective depends on whether IP processing is enabled on it. Processing of this event must include installation of the routes derived from the interface's primary and secondary IP addresses, static routes directly referencing the interface, and other routes that can be resolved over routes referencing the interface. The processing function should also notify all dynamic routing protocols about the event.
- *Interface going down* happens when the data link protocol of an interface is going down because of an administrative action, such as **shutdown** interface command, physical state transition, or a communication problem. If IP processing is enabled on the interface, it becomes inoperational from the IP routing perspective. Processing of this event must include removal of the routes derived from the interface's primary and secondary IP addresses, routes directly referencing the interface, and those resolved over the deleted ones. The process must also notify the dynamic routing protocols about the event.

- *IP processing enabled on an interface* is caused by applying an **ip address** or an **ip unnumbered** command to the interface's configuration. Whether IP considers this interface operational depends on the state of the data link layer protocol. The processing of this event should be the same as when an IP-enabled interface is going up.

- *IP processing disabled on an interface* can be caused by taking off the command that was used to enable IP processing, either **ip address** or **ip unnumbered**. In any case, the interface must be considered inoperational, and processing must be just the same as for the event of an IP-enabled interface going down.

- *Secondary IP address added to an interface* occurs when an **ip address secondary** command was configured on an interface. This event should be processed only if the state of the data link protocol running on the interface is up. The processing function must install the route derived from the new secondary address and static routes resolvable through the new route.

- *Secondary IP address deleted from an interface* occurs when an **ip address secondary** command was removed from an interface's configuration. The event should be processed only if the state of the data link layer protocol is up. The processing function must remove the route derived from the deleted secondary address and any routes that become unresolvable because of this action.

- *Route installation is requested by a route source.* A routing protocol has a new route or the administrator has configured a new static route, using the **ip route** command; the new route is passed for further processing. A general AD and metric value check must be done before installation. The process must ensure that static routes resolvable via the newly installed routes are also installed in the routing table.

- *Route deletion is requested by a route source.* A routing protocol asks to invalidate a route or the administrator has deleted a route, using the **no ip route** command. The routing table must be consulted to find whether the route is in it. If the route is present, it must be removed. The process must ensure that any static routes that become unresolvable after deletion of the route are removed from the routing table as well. All route sources must be requested for a backup route to the same destination.

- *Route was marked as candidate default.* This happens when the parser has processed an **ip default-network** command and the specified route is found and marked as candidate, a route specified in this command has just been installed in the routing table and marked as candidate, or a route has been installed in the routing table and automatically marked as candidate because it is a route to network 0.0.0.0/0 or because the dynamic routing protocol—for example, IGRP or EIGRP—requested so. The algorithm should consider all candidates and select the actual default.

- *Default route has been deleted from the routing table.* The algorithm should consider all candidates and select the new default, if any.

The algorithm of the routing table maintenance process must be sophisticated enough to handle some complicated situations. Consider the following analysis.

Addition of any route to the routing table can lead to the following consequences.

1. Some competing routes, covering the same address block, can be replaced by the new one.
2. If no route was covering the same address block, some previously not installed routes can become resolvable and must be installed, which in turn may lead to installation of other routes, and so on.
3. Some newly installed routes may be marked as candidate defaults, and an actual default route must be recalculated.
4. If there was no default route before, some routes can become resolvable and should be installed.

Deletion of any route from the routing table can lead to the following consequences.

1. Some competing routes may have a chance to get into the routing table.
2. If no routes are competing, some routes, referencing the deleted one, can become unresolvable and must be deleted.
3. The deleted route and those that referenced it might have been the default or candidates, so an actual default must be recalculated.
4. If, after deleting the routes, no candidate defaults were left, other routes can become unresolvable and must also be deleted.

Obviously, some events can be recursive. For example, the installation of a route may lead to the installation of other routes, which may lead to the appearance of the default route, which may lead to the installation of other routes, and so on.

Think how you would implement the routing table maintenance process. The straightforward approach, making use of recursive route processing, is not a good idea. Imagine a situation in which addition of an RIP-learned route leads to processing of all other routes, followed by selection of the default route and a recursive route processing. The router would spend a considerable amount of CPU time only on route processing.

To understand how the routing table maintenance process works, remember the route source comparison in the previous section. The conclusion was that all IGP-supplied routes reference specific interfaces, which means that they do not rely on the presence of other routes in the routing table. This really simplifies the problem, as the installation of a route sourced by a dynamic routing protocol cannot lead to the installation of other dynamic routes. (This is true for IGP not for BGP, as BGP installs routes with intermediate addresses only; BGP is not considered in this book.)

Because routes derived from the interface addresses also don't rely on other routes, the only route source that must be taken care of is Static. Only static routes can rely on the existence of other routes, which in turn can be static, dynamic, or derived from interface addresses. Consequently, only static routes must be reexamined periodically to check that they reflect the changes made to the routing table by dynamic routing protocols. Processing static routes every time a dynamic route is added or deleted wouldn't be smart, as this too would take much CPU time. Instead, this process is scheduled in IOS once a minute and on such events as the change of an interface state.

Another issue is the installation of alternative routes from other sources after deleting a route from the routing table. As you will see in later chapters, some distance-vector protocols periodically supply all their routes to the RT process. So, for example, if an IGRP-learned route is deleted and RIP can provide an alternative one, the latter will be installed next time RIP receives an update and passes the routing information to the RT process by calling the `RouteUpdate()` function.

OSPF, IS-IS, EIGRP, and BGP call this function only when there is a change in the network topology; these protocols must be explicitly requested for a backup route to the same destination covered by the deleted one. This is why the `RouteRemove()` function is not called directly; instead, when a route needs to be removed from the routing table by its source or by the RT process, the `RouteDelete()` function is invoked. Listing 4-49 gives the pseudocode definition of this function.

```
void RouteDelete(TPrefixDescr * TheRoute, TPathDescr * ThePath)
{
   if (!RouteRemove(TheRoute, ThePath)) return;
   RequestBackup(TheRoute, ThePath);
   //...code skipped
}
```

Listing 4-49. *Pseudocode:* `RouteDelete()` *function*

The `RouteDelete()` function checks whether deletion of the path descriptor resulted in deletion of the prefix descriptor to which the path descriptor was linked. If the prefix descriptor was deleted, which is indicated by a nonzero value returned by the `RouteRemove()` function, the `RequestBackup()` function, which requests alternative routes from all route sources, is called. If any of the requested processes can provide the RT process with a backup route to the same destination, they will do so, using the `RouteUpdate()` function.

Remember that static routes are not examined at the moment of a dynamic route deletion; instead, the static route processing algorithm is called once a minute. The

Connected route source is also not included when backup routes are requested, as routes derived from interface addresses are always installed with an AD of **0** and cannot be overridden.

The `RouteUpdate()` and the `RouteDelete()` functions are those called while processing the events listed at the beginning of this subsection. The following subsections describe how Cisco IOS treats each event, as well as the details of the static route processing algorithm.

4.2.6 Route Resolvability

Before installation of a route in the routing table, the router checks whether the route is valid, that is, whether the route is resolvable, as shown in the pseudocode of the `RouteUpdate()` function in Listing 4-41. An unresolvable route prevents the forwarding engine from normal routing and other competing valid routes from being installed. The resolvability condition is defined as follows.

1. A route, Rte1, referencing only the intermediate network address, is considered resolvable if the routing table contains at least one resolvable route, Rte2, that matches Rte1's intermediate network address and is not recursively resolved directly or indirectly through Rte1. If multiple matching routes are available, the most specific route much be chosen.

2. Routes referencing interfaces with or without intermediate addresses are considered resolvable if the state of the referenced interface is up and IP processing is enabled on this interface.

Sentence 1 in this definition is obviously recursive and implies that a route via an intermediate address can be resolved over another route of the same type. Sentence 2 defines the condition of the exit from such a recursion: Every route that does not reference an interface must finally be resolved via a route with an interface descriptor reference in the corresponding path descriptor.

Look at the sentence 1 again. Note the "not recursively resolved" specification in it. This part of the resolvability condition implies that the route being checked (Rte1) cannot be used to resolve its own intermediate address or the intermediate address of any route explicitly or implicitly used to resolve Rte1's intermediate address.

Consider an example with the following three static routes:

Rte1: ip route 10.1.0.0 255.255.0.0 20.1.1.1

Rte2: ip route 20.1.0.0 255.255.0.0 30.1.1.1

Rte3: ip route 30.1.0.0 255.255.0.0 10.1.1.1

Here, Rte1's intermediate address is resolved via route Rte2, Rte2's intermediate address is resolved via Rte3, and Rte3's intermediate address is resolved via Rte1. Rte1 and two other routes cannot be considered resolvable. In this case, Rte2 is said to resolve Rte1's intermediate address explicitly, and Rte3 is said to resolve it implicitly. Route Rte1 cannot be installed or kept in the routing table, because the presence of such a route would lead to endless recursion of the route lookup operation during packet forwarding. (The route lookup function in IOS, discussed in Chapter 5, is designed not to loop even in the described situation.) Listing 4-50 shows the pseudocode of the PathValid() function, which checks resolvability of a given path descriptor.

```
int PathValid(TPathDescr * ThePath, TPrefixDescr * TstRoute)
{
TPrefixDescr      * ChkRoute;
TPathDescr       * ChkPath;
TIPAddress    Intermediate;

if (ThePath->Interface){              //it's a route referencing int.
   if ((ThePath->Interface->Flags & IF_STATE_UP) &&
       (ThePath->Interface->Flags & IF_IP_ENABLED))
         return 1;
   else return 0;
}

if (ThePath->Intermediate == 0) return 0;
// No interface, no address -- error

// Now check the Intermediate address
Intermediate = ThePath->Intermediate;
ChkRoute = LookUp(Intermediate, 0);  // Classful RT lookup
if (ChkRoute == NULL) return 0;
if (SameRanges(ChkRoute,TstRoute)) return 0; // Recursion error
if (ChkRoute->Flags & Route_GARBAGE) return 0; // Don't consider
if (TstRoute==NULL) TstRoute=ChkRoute;

ChkPath = (TPathDescr *) ChkRoute->Pointer;
for(;ChkPath;ChkPath = ChkPath->Next){
   if (PathValid(ChkPath, TstRoute)) return 1;
}
return 0; //No valid Path was found, will be deleted
}
```

Listing 4-50. *Pseudocode:* PathValid() *function*

The function is given two parameters: the path descriptor for checking and a prefix descriptor. The passed prefix descriptor is used to prevent endless recursion. Normally, it is the prefix descriptor to which the corresponding path descriptor is or must be linked. Here's how the pseudocode works.

The function begins by checking whether the path descriptor references an interface. If it does and the interface is up and able to process IP traffic, the path descriptor is considered resolvable. If the path descriptor does not have an interface reference, the code checks the resolvability of the intermediate network address. A classful routing table lookup function is used for this purpose. If the lookup function returns a NULL pointer, meaning that the routing table contains no route that can be used to resolve the intermediate address, the path descriptor is considered not resolvable.

If the lookup function returns a nonzero pointer, the code checks whether the referenced prefix descriptor is equal to the prefix descriptor passed to the function as the TstRoute parameter. If it is, the function detects recursive routes and considers the path descriptor unresolvable. Otherwise, the code tries to find at least one resolvable path descriptor among those linked to the prefix descriptor returned by the lookup function. Note that the function calls itself for this purpose and passes the TstRoute parameter to prevent endless recursion.

The `PathValid()` function is used in many routing table maintenance procedures, described in the following subsections. The main one is the `ValidateRT()` function, called on such events as an interface up or down transition. The pseudocode of this function and the functions it calls are given in Listing 4-51.

```
void ValidateRT()
{
 ValidateRoutes(TheRoutingTable.Majornets);
 ValidateRoutes(TheRoutingTable.Supernets);
}

void ValidateRoutes(TPrefixDescr * RouteChain)
{
 TPrefixDescr       * TheRoute = RouteChain;
 TPrefixDescr       * Next;
 TNetworkInfo * NInfo;

 for(;TheRoute;) {
    Next = NextRoute(TheRoute);   //The route can be deleted, so we save it
    if (TheRoute->Ultimate) ValidateRoute(TheRoute);
    else {
     NInfo = (TNetworkInfo*)TheRoute->Pointer;
     ValidateRoutes(NInfo->Pointer);
     }
    TheRoute = Next;
 }
}

void ValidateRoute(TPrefixDescr * TheRoute)
{
 TPathDescr    * ThePath = (TPathDescr*) TheRoute->Pointer;
 TPathDescr    * Next;
```

```
for(;;){
  Next = ThePath->Next;
  if ((TheRoute->Source == &proto_STATIC)){
     if (ThePath->Interface)
        if ((!ThePath->Permanent) && (!PathValid(ThePath, TheRoute)))
           RouteDelete(TheRoute, ThePath);
  }else
  // Routes not referencing interfaces are processed
  // by ProcessStatics() and by BGP
  if (TheRoute->Source != &proto_CONNECTED){ // It's a dynamic route
     if (!PathValid(ThePath, TheRoute))
        InvalidateDynamic(TheRoute, ThePath);
  }
  if (Next == NULL) break;
  ThePath = Next;
  }
}
```

Listing 4-51. *Pseudocode: routing table validation functions*

The goal of the ValidateRT() function is to delete all unresolvable routes. The route processing is performed by the two functions ValidateRoutes() and ValidateRoute(). The ValidateRoutes() function goes through the prefix descriptor chain; considers subnet routes linked to the parent network prefix descriptors, if necessary; and passes the prefix descriptors one by one to the ValidateRoute() function, which in turn checks every path descriptor in a given prefix descriptor calling the PathValid() function.

If a path descriptor is not valid, it can be either flushed from the routing table, if these routes are not dynamic, or processed by InvalidateDynamic(), a special function, that performs route management for distance-vector protocols (considered in future chapters). Note that static routes configured as permanent are not deleted even if they are unresolvable.

4.2.7 Change of an Interface State

When one of a router's interfaces goes up or down, the router must correct its routing table. Furthermore, all routing protocols must be informed about this event to be able to correct their internal databases or to send updates informing neighbors about the topology change.

The actions taken on these two events—an interface coming up and an interface going down—are different. On receiving a signal about an interface going up, the router:

1. Determines whether IP processing is enabled on the interface; if not, the router skips the interface

2. Adds the routes derived from the interface's IP addresses if the interface has one or more **ip address** commands configured

3. Schedules static route processing

4. Informs the dynamic routing protocols enabled on the interface about the event

First, the address-derived routes are installed if the interface is configured with the **ip address** command. (Note that if IP processing is enabled on a WAN interface by using the **ip unnumbered** command, no interface route is added.) The static route processing algorithm is invoked to give the static routes a chance to get into the routing table. If some static routes reference the interface or their intermediate addresses are resolvable over the interface's connected routes, they are installed. The last thing that is done is notification of the dynamic routing protocols currently running in the router. These protocols perform their own checks to find out whether the interface should participate in the process. If it should, a routing protocol takes specific typical steps. For example, OSPF tries to find neighbors and to build adjacencies on this interface, whereas the distance-vector protocols just send routing updates and listen for incoming ones. If a dynamic routing protocol learns new routes from the newly added interface, the routes are added, using the `RouteUpdate()` function. The pseudocode of the function called when an IP-enabled interface has gone up is depicted in Listing 4-52.

```
void IPinterfaceUp(TInterfaceDescr * TheInt)
  {
TSecIPAddr *SecAddr = TheInt->Secondary;

if (!(TheInt->Flags & IF_IP_UNNUM)) {
  ConnectedAdd(TheInt->Addr & TheInt->Mask, TheInt->Mask, TheInt);

  for(;SecAddr;SecAddr=SecAddr->Next)
   ConnectedAdd(SecAddr->Addr & SecAddr->Mask, SecAddr->Mask,
            TheInt);
}

ProcessStatics();
InformIntUp(TheInt); //Inform dynamic routing protocols
}
```

Listing 4-52. *Pseudocode:* `IPinterfaceUp()` *function*

When an interface goes down, the RT process has to check all routes installed in the routing table. The actions taken on this event are as follows.

1. Delete all routes derived from the IP addresses of this interface, requesting the backup routes that may come up.

2. Validate the routing table by calling the `ValidateRT()` function.

3. Inform every active dynamic-routing protocol about the state of the interface.

4. Run the static route processing algorithm to let the static routes, which are not in the routing table because they do not have the best AD value, be installed in case the routes they were overridden by are now unresolvable and gone.

Step 1 is simple and easy to understand. Step 2 takes care of every route in the routing table, no matter whether its source is static or dynamic. Note that in the first three steps, routes are deleted by using the `RouteDelete()` function; that is, the backup routes are requested from the alternative sources. Step 3 sends signals to every routing protocol currently running in the router. Exact actions taken by specific routing protocols are described in other chapters of this book.

What is important to know right now is that all routes that were known over the interface are considered inaccessible, and all neighbors are notified about this. Step 4 makes sure that pending backup static routes have a chance to get into the table. That is, if some routes to a specific destination were deleted after the interface went down, other static routes to the same destination but with higher AD value and pointing to other interfaces or intermediate addresses can be installed. The pseudocode of the `IPinterfaceDown()` function is presented in Listing 4-53.

```
void IPinterfaceDown(TInterfaceDescr * TheInt)
{
 TSecIPAddr *SecAddr = TheInt->Secondary;

 if (!(TheInt->Flags & IF_IP_UNNUM)) {
  ConnectedDel(TheInt->Addr & TheInt->Mask, TheInt->Mask, TheInt);

  for(;SecAddr;SecAddr=SecAddr->Next)
    ConnectedDel(SecAddr->Addr & SecAddr->Mask, SecAddr->Mask, TheInt);
 }

 ValidateRT();
 ProcessStatics();
 InformIntDown(TheInt);
}
```

Listing 4-53. *Pseudocode:* `IPinterfaceDown()` *function*

Listing 4-54 shows an example in which interface Serial0 is shut down and this event is processed by IOS.

```
R1#show ip rou
...
Gateway of last resort is not set

    20.0.0.0/8 is variably subnetted, 2 subnets, 2 masks
C       20.2.1.1/32 is directly connected, Serial0
C       20.2.1.0/24 is directly connected, Serial0
    10.0.0.0/24 is subnetted, 1 subnets
C       10.0.1.0 is directly connected, Ethernet0
    30.0.0.0/24 is subnetted, 1 subnets
O       30.0.0.0 [110/74] via 20.2.1.1, 00:00:05, Serial0
R1#conf t
Enter configuration commands, one per line.  End with CNTL/Z.
R1(config)#ip route 30.0.0.0 255.255.255.0 10.0.1.2 115
R1(config)#int s0
R1(config-if)#shut
R1(config-if)#
R1#
%SYS-5-CONFIG_I: Configured from console by console
...
*Mar  5 10:20:39.317: RT: delete route to 30.0.0.0 via 20.2.1.1, Serial0
*Mar  5 10:20:39.321: RT: no routes to 30.0.0.0, flushing
*Mar  5 10:20:39.321: RT: add 30.0.0.0/24 via 10.0.1.2, static metric [115/0]
%LINEPROTO-5-UPDOWN: Line protocol on Interface Serial0, changed state to down
%LINK-5-CHANGED: Interface Serial0, changed state to administratively down
R1#
```

Listing 4-54. *Processing of interface-down transition*

The routing table initially contains an OSPF-learned route to subnet 30.0.0.0/24. The static route is configured to the same destination but with higher (worse) administrative distance. When interface Serial0 goes down, the OSPF-learned route is removed, and the backup static route is installed.

4.2.8 Change of Interface Address

When an interface is assigned the primary IP address by using the **ip address** command, IP processing is implicitly enabled on the interface. The functions ifSetPrimaryIP() and ifDelPrimaryIP() are called by the parser when it processes the **ip address** and the **no ip address** commands. The pseudocode of the function ifSetPrimaryIP() is given in Listing 4-55.

```
void ifSetPrimaryIP(TInterfaceDescr * TheInt, TIPAddress TheAddr,
                    TMask TheMask)
```

```
{
if (!IPaddrSanityCheck(TheAddr, TheMask)) return;

if ((TheInt->Flags & IF_IP_ENABLED) &&
    (!(TheInt->Flags & IF_IP_UNNUM))){
    if ((TheInt->Addr == TheAddr) && (TheInt->Mask == TheMask)) return;
    ConnectedDel(TheInt->Addr & TheInt->Mask, TheInt->Mask, TheInt);
}

TheInt->Addr = TheAddr;
TheInt->Mask = TheMask;

TheInt->Flags |= IF_IP_ENABLED;
if (TheInt->Flags & IF_STATE_UP) IPinterfaceUp(TheInt);
}
```

Listing 4-55. *Pseudocode:* `ifSetPrimaryIP()` *function*

The function first checks the validity of the IP address. If the IP address is valid, the function checks whether the address and the mask being set are the same as those already assigned to the interface. If they are, the function returns. If the address or the mask is different, the route derived from the old interface address is deleted from the routing table. Then the interface address is set to the new one; the IF_IP_ENABLED flag is set to 1; and, if the interface state is up, the IPinterfaceUp() considered in the previous section is called.

The function ifDelPrimaryIP() is given in Listing 4-56. This function first checks whether all secondary addresses were deleted prior to deleting the primary one. If this condition is not met, the router refuses to unset the primary IP address. If no secondary address is assigned to the interface, the code deletes the route derived from the interface address and calls route validation and static processing functions. Then the function calls the IPinterfaceDown() function, which, among other things, notifies the dynamic routing protocols.

```
void ifDelPrimaryIP(TInterfaceDescr * TheInt, TIPAddress TheAddr,
                    TMask TheMask)
{
if (TheInt->Secondary) return;
//Must delete secondary before deleting primary

ConnectedDel(TheInt->Addr & TheInt->Mask, TheInt->Mask, TheInt);

TheInt->Flags &= !IF_IP_ENABLED;
IPinterfaceDown(TheInt);
}
```

Listing 4-56. *Pseudocode:* `ifDelPrimaryDel()` *function*

Secondary IP addresses can be added or deleted to the interfaces by using the **ip address secondary** and the **no ip address secondary** commands. When the parser encounters them, it calls the functions `ifAddSecondaryIP()` and `ifDelSecondaryIP()`. The first function, the pseudocode of which is given in Listing 4-57, checks whether IP processing is enabled on the interface and looks through all secondary IP addresses assigned to the interface, avoiding duplications. If the address passed as the argument is unique and correct, it is linked to the list of secondary addresses, and the corresponding interface route is installed in the routing table.

```
void ifAddSecondaryIP(TInterfaceDescr * TheInt, TIPAddress TheAddr,
                      TMask TheMask)
{
 TSecIPAddr  *SecAddr =  TheInt->Secondary;
 TSecIPAddr **Pointer = &TheInt->Secondary;

 if (!(TheInt->Flags & IF_IP_ENABLED)) return;
    //Cannot add address without it
 if (TheInt->Flags & IF_IP_UNNUM) return; //No secondary without primary
 if (!IPaddrSanityCheck(TheAddr, TheMask)) return;
 if ((TheInt->Addr == TheAddr) && (TheInt->Mask == TheMask)) return;

 for(;SecAddr;SecAddr=SecAddr->Next)
    if ((SecAddr->Addr == TheAddr) &&
        (SecAddr->Mask == TheMask)) return;

 for(;(*Pointer);Pointer = &(*Pointer)->Next); //find the last secondary

 SecAddr = malloc(sizeof(TSecIPAddr));
 SecAddr->Addr = TheAddr;
 SecAddr->Mask = TheMask;
 SecAddr->Next = NULL;
 (*Pointer) = SecAddr; //Link the new one

 ConnectedAdd(TheAddr & TheMask, TheMask, TheInt);
}
```

Listing 4-57. *Pseudocode:* `ifAddSecondaryIP()` *function*

When a secondary route is deleted from an interface, the function `ifDelSecondaryIP()` unlinks the address from the list and deletes the corresponding route from the routing table, as shown in Listing 4-58.

```
void ifDelSecondaryIP(TInterfaceDescr * TheInt, TIPAddress TheAddr,
                      TMask TheMask)
{
 TSecIPAddr  *SecAddr;
```

```
TSecIPAddr **Pointer = &TheInt->Secondary;

if (!(TheInt->Flags & IF_IP_ENABLED)) return;
    //Cannot delete an address witout it
if (TheInt->Secondary==NULL) return;//No secondary

for(;(*Pointer);Pointer = &(*Pointer)->Next)
    if (((*Pointer)->Addr == TheAddr) &&
        ((*Pointer)->Mask == TheMask)) break;

if ((*Pointer)==NULL) return; //Not found

SecAddr = *Pointer;
(*Pointer) = (*Pointer)->Next; //Unlink the secondary

ConnectedDel(TheAddr & TheMask, TheMask, TheInt);
free(SecAddr);
}
```

Listing 4-58. *Pseudocode:* `ifDelSecondaryIP()` *function*

4.2.9 Dynamic Route Processing

As previously mentioned, when it processes the **router** *protocol* command, a router's command parser starts the software module corresponding to a specific dynamic routing protocol. A router can have several dynamic routing processes running simultaneously. Each of them can provide the operating system with information about new or dead routes. Every time it has a change in routing information, a routing protocol reports the news to the RT process via the `RouteUpdate()` and the `RouteDelete()` functions. Installing dynamic routes is easier than installing static routes. All that's important are the AD and the metric values; dynamic routes directly reference interfaces and specify the next-hop router address as additional information, so they don't rely on other routes; again, BGP is an exception. The `RouteUpdate()` function removes the routes overridden by the new route, provided that there were some routes to the same destination but with worse AD value.

When a dynamic route is deleted by using the `RouteDelete()` function, the backup routes to the same destination are requested from other route sources. Consider Listing 4-59, in which a route learned from IGRP is deleted and a backup OSPF route is installed.

```
R1#show ip rou
...
Gateway of last resort is not set

     20.0.0.0/8 is variably subnetted, 2 subnets, 2 masks
C       20.1.1.0/24 is directly connected, Serial0
C       20.1.1.1/32 is directly connected, Serial0
I     200.2.2.0/24 [100/158350] via 20.1.1.1, Serial0
     22.0.0.0/8 is variably subnetted, 2 subnets, 2 masks
```

```
I        22.0.0.0/8 [100/158350] via 20.1.1.1, Serial0
O E2     22.22.22.0/24 [110/10] via 20.1.1.1, Serial0
      30.0.0.0/24 is subnetted, 1 subnets
C        30.0.0.0 is directly connected, Ethernet0
R1#
R1#conf t
Enter configuration commands, one per line.  End with CNTL/Z.
R1(config)#no router igrp 100
R1(config)#^Z
R1#
*Mar  1 02:38:35.607: RT: delete route to 200.2.2.0/24
*Mar  1 02:38:35.611: RT: delete route to 22.0.0.0/8
*Mar  1 02:38:35.755: RT: add 200.2.2.0/24 via 20.1.1.1, ospf metric [110/10]
R1#
%SYS-5-CONFIG_I: Configured from console by console
R1#
```

Listing 4-59. *Installation of backup OSPF route*

The routing table maintenance module manages the routes from the distance-vector routing protocols. As you will see in Chapters 8 and 9, RIP and IGRP use a group of special timers, such as *invalid* and *holddown,* as a means of identifying unreachable networks or neighboring routers and protecting the network from inconsistent routing information. Historically, Cisco IOS has been implemented in such a way that all timer logic for distance-vector protocols is performed in the RT process. Details on specific routing protocols are provided in later chapters; here, a simple example illustrates this process.

Listing 4-60 shows the initial routing table of router R1 to subnet 10.32.0.0.

```
R1#show ip rout
...
R        10.32.0.0 [120/1] via 10.1.2.2, 00:00:05, Serial0
                   [120/1] via 10.1.1.1, 00:00:05, Serial1
...
R1#
```

Listing 4-60. *Initial routing table of R1 containing RIP route*

The router has two path descriptors and is splitting the traffic between them. Now one of R1's neighbors—10.1.1.1—loses its route to this subnet and informs R1 about it. Listing 4-61 shows how R1's RT process reacts to this event.

```
*Mar 25 00:52:58.128: RIP: received v2 update from 10.1.1.1 on Serial1
*Mar 25 00:52:58.132:      10.1.3.0/24 -> 0.0.0.0 in 1 hops
*Mar 25 00:52:58.132:      10.1.2.0/24 -> 0.0.0.0 in 2 hops
```

```
*Mar 25 00:52:58.136:       10.32.0.0/24 -> in 0 hops (inaccessible)
*Mar 25 00:52:58.140: RT: delete route to 10.32.0.0 via 10.1.1.1, rip metric [120/1]
*Mar 25 00:52:58.140:       1.0.0.0/8 -> 0.0.0.0 in 1 hops
```

Listing 4-61. *Loss of the first RIP route*

The process deletes one of the path descriptors. Because it still has a route to the subnet, R1 doesn't inform its neighbors about the event. Upstream routers do not need to know how R1 will route packets; they must just know that R1 can route packets to this destination. Now the second neighbor of R1 loses its route to the subnet and sends an update to R1. Because R1 has no path descriptors to the destination, the RT process puts the prefix descriptor into the holddown state, starts the holddown timer, and signals the RIP process to send an update to the neighbors (Listing 4-62).

```
*Mar 25 00:53:54.452: RIP: received v2 update from 10.1.2.2 on Serial0
*Mar 25 00:53:54.456:       10.1.3.0/24 -> 0.0.0.0 in 1 hops
*Mar 25 00:53:54.456:       10.1.1.0/24 -> 0.0.0.0 in 2 hops
*Mar 25 00:53:54.460:       10.32.0.0/24 -> in 0 hops (inaccessible)
*Mar 25 00:53:54.460: RT: delete route to 10.32.0.0 via 10.1.2.2, rip metric [120/1]
*Mar 25 00:53:54.464: RT: no routes to 10.32.0.0, entering holddown
*Mar 25 00:53:54.468:       1.0.0.0/8 -> 0.0.0.0 in 1 hops
```

Listing 4-62. *Loss of the last RIP route*

4.2.10 Static Route Processing

Every time an interface goes up or down, the static route processing algorithm is called to check for static routes that must be either deleted or installed. This algorithm is called by Cisco IOS every minute to reflect the changes in static and dynamic routes.

To understand how static routes are processed, you must first know what happens when the administrator adds or deletes a static route. It is clear that the router must store all configured static routes, no matter which of them are installed and which are not, as some routes are not installed at the time they are configured but could be installed later, when they become resolvable or win the AD competition. Cisco IOS stores configured static routes grouped by the destination prefix—route address and mask portions—and ordered, using the administrative distance as the parameter. This ordering allows the router to find a backup static route more quickly and also makes the static route installation process more optimal; the function begins with the routes with better AD value for each destination prefix. If a route is valid for installation, static routes to the same destination and with worse AD values are not considered.

When it has processed an **ip route** command, the parser calls the StaticAdd() function (Listing 4-63).

```
void StaticAdd(TIPAddress Network, TMask Mask, TInterfaceDescr * Interface,
               TIPAddress Intermediate, u_char AD)
{
  TPrefixDescr * Route;
  TPathDescr * Path;

  Route = NewRoute();
  Path  = NewPath();
  // 1. Initialize Route variable with Network, Mask and AD values
  // 2. Initialize Path variable with Interface, Intermediate and AD values
  // 3. Add the route to the list of static routes:
  Proto_AddRoute(&proto_STATIC, Route, Path);

  // 4. Try installing it:
  RouteUpdate(Route, Path);

  // 5. Schedule ProcessStatic() in 5 seconds
}
```

Listing 4-63. *Pseudocode:* `StaticAdd()` *function*

On processing the "no" form of the same command, used to delete a static route, the pseudocode given in Listing 4-64 is executed.

```
void StaticDel(TIPAddress Network, TMask Mask, TInterfaceDescr * Interface,
               TIPAddress Intermediate, u_char AD)
{
  TPrefixDescr * Route;
  TPathDescr * Path;

  Route = NewRoute();
  Path  = NewPath();
  // 1. Initialize Route variable with Network, Mask and AD values
  // 2. Initialize Path variable with Interface, Intermediate and AD values
  // 3. Delete the route from the list of static routes:
  Proto_DelRoute(&proto_STATIC, Route, Path);

  // 4. Delete the route from the routing table:
  RouteDelete(Route, Path);
}
```

Listing 4-64. *Pseudocode:* `StaticDel()` *function*

If you look at these two functions, you can see that whenever a static route is added, all other static routes are also processed in five seconds. When a static route is deleted, `ProcessStatics()` is not called. Instead, IOS relies on the per minute static route check.

In Cisco IOS version 12.0, static route processing is scheduled in one second after a static route has been added or removed by the administrator.

What does the function implementing the static route processing algorithm do? First, we need to understand that some static routes in the routing table can be invalid. That is, they can reference inactive interfaces or the intermediate network addresses that are unresolvable. The algorithm must be smart enough to be able to find the invalid static routes and delete them from the routing table, as well as to install the static routes that are valid. The whole algorithm can be logically split into two parts: deletion of unresolvable routes and installation of resolvable ones.

Considering the first part of the static route processing function—the part supposed to delete unresolvable routes—note that all routes, including static routes, that reference inactive interfaces are removed by the `ValidateRT()` function called by the `IPinterfaceDown()` function when an interface goes down. This simplifies the algorithm a bit because we need to process only static routes with no interface descriptor references in the path descriptor. Because static routes can be resolved over other static routes, the algorithm cannot just go through all static routes in the routing table one time and delete all unresolvable routes. Because deletion of some static routes can lead to unresolvability of others, the algorithm must iterate until all static routes in the routing table are resolvable. The logic of this part of the function can be described as follows.

1. In the routing table, go through every static route and, if it is unresolvable, remove it from the routing table.

2. If unresolvable routes are found, go to step 1; otherwise, return.

The pseudocode of this algorithm is given in Listing 4-65. Note that `AllStaticRoutes` in this example is used to store all static routes that the administrator has configured.

```
void CheckInvalidStatics()
{
 int Found;
 TPrefixDescr * Entry, * Route;

 do {
  Found = 0;
  for every Entry in AllStaticRoutes {
    Route = FindRoute(Entry);
    for every Path in Entry->Paths
      if (Path->Installed && !PathValid(Path, Route)){
       RouteDelete(Route, Path->Reference);
       Found = 1;
      }
  }
```

```
} while (Found);
}
```

Listing 4-65. *Pseudocode:* `CheckInvalidStatics()` *function*

After all unresolvable static routes are removed, it is safe to check pending static routes. If some of the routes have become resolvable, the function must install them. The algorithm in this case is not as simple as it may seem. It cannot just go through the list of static routes configured in the router and pass them one by one to the `RouteAdd()` procedure for further checking and AD comparison, because some routes that go earlier in the configuration can reference those appearing later. In this case, such routes are not installed, because at the time they are considered, the referenced ones are not yet in the table. The algorithm must install static routes incrementally. The human-language description of the algorithm follows.

1. Let StaticRoutes be the set of all static routes configured in the routing table.
2. For every destination prefix in the StaticRoutes set, perform the following steps.
    a. Go through every route in the list and find a resolvable route.
    b. If no resolvable route is found, proceed to the next destination prefix—go to step 2.e.
    c. If the route is not yet installed, install it in the routing table.
    d. Save the route's AD value in the BestAD variable.
    e. Take the next route in the list. If there are no more routes for the given destination, go to step 2.
    f. If the route's AD value is the same as the BestAD and it is resolvable, install the route and go to step 2.e.
    g. If the route's AD value is greater than BestAD, proceed to the next destination prefix (go to step 2); otherwise, the route is unresolvable, so go to step 2.e.
3. If no route is installed in step 2, return; otherwise, loop to step 2.

After performing step 2.e, the algorithm cannot encounter a route with AD value better than the BestAD, because routes are ordered by the AD value. The pseudocode for this algorithm is presented in Listing 4-66.

```
void CheckResolvableStatics()
{
 int Found;
 TPrefixDescr * Entry, * Route;
 u_char BestAD;
```

```
do {
  Found = 0;
  for every Entry in AllStaticRoutes {
    Route = FindRoute(Entry);
    BestAD = 255;
    for every Path in Entry->Paths {
      if (Path->AD > BestAD) continue;
      if (!Path->Installed && PathValid(Path, Route)){
        RouteUpdate(Entry, Path);
        if (!PathValid(Path, Route)) {
         RouteDelete(Route, Path);
         continue;
        }
        Found = 1;
        BestAD = Path->AD;
      }
    }
  } while (Found);
}
```

Listing 4-66. *Pseudocode:* `CheckResolvableStatics()` *function*

After installing a route, the algorithm checks its resolvability again. If the route's intermediate address is resolved via the default, installation of the new route can lead to unresolvability of the intermediate address. Listing 4-67 shows the pseudocode of a simplified version of the `ProcessStatics()` function, which calls the functions described in Listings 4-65 and 4-66.

```
void ProcessStatics()
 {
CheckInvalidStatics();
CheckResolvableStatics();
}
```

Listing 4-67. *Pseudocode:* `ProcessStatics()` *function*

How the static route installation process works in a Cisco router is shown in the following examples. First, look at the routing table shown in Listing 4-68.

```
R1#show ip rou
Codes: C - connected, S - static, I - IGRP, R - RIP, M - mobile, B - BGP
...
Gateway of last resort is not set

     20.0.0.0/24 is subnetted, 1 subnets
C       20.1.1.0 is directly connected, Serial1
```

```
       10.0.0.0/24 is subnetted, 1 subnets
C         10.0.1.0 is directly connected, Ethernet0
```

Listing 4-68. *Initial routing table*

Note that the Serial0 interface is disabled. Now static routes are configured as shown in Listing 4-69.

```
R1#conf t
Enter configuration commands, one per line.  End with CNTL/Z.
R1(config)#ip route 60.0.0.0 255.255.255.0 30.10.0.1
R1(config)#ip route 30.0.0.0 255.0.0.0 Ser 0
R1(config)#
```

Listing 4-69. *Configuring static routes*

The routes are not installed in the routing table, because the first one cannot be resolved and the second, which resolves the first, references an inactive interface. Now interface Serial0 is brought up, with the results shown in Listing 4-70.

```
R1(config)#int s0
R1(config-if)#no shutdown
R1(config-if)#
%LINK-3-UPDOWN: Interface Serial0, changed state to up
R1(config-if)#
Jun 30 21:44:38.353: RT: add 30.0.0.1/32 via 0.0.0.0, connected metric [0/0]
Jun 30 21:44:38.361: RT: network 30.0.0.0 is now variably masked
Jun 30 21:44:38.361: RT: add 30.0.0.0/8 via 0.0.0.0, static metric [1/0]
Jun 30 21:44:38.365: RT: add 60.0.0.0/24 via 30.10.0.1, static metric [1/0]
R1(config-if)#
%LINEPROTO-5-UPDOWN: Line protocol on Interface Serial0, changed state to up
R1(config-if)#^Z
%SYS-5-CONFIG_I: Configured from console by console
R1#show ip rou
Codes: C - connected, S - static, I - IGRP, R - RIP, M - mobile, B - BGP
...
Gateway of last resort is not set

     20.0.0.0/24 is subnetted, 1 subnets
C         20.1.1.0 is directly connected, Serial1
     10.0.0.0/24 is subnetted, 1 subnets
C         10.0.1.0 is directly connected, Ethernet0
     60.0.0.0/24 is subnetted, 1 subnets
S         60.0.0.0 [1/0] via 30.10.0.1
     30.0.0.0/8 is variably subnetted, 2 subnets, 2 masks
S         30.0.0.0/8 is directly connected, Serial0
```

```
C       30.0.0.1/32 is directly connected, Serial0
R1#
```

Listing 4-70. *Installation of pending static routes*

The routes are installed because the route to network 30.0.0.0/8 has become resolvable—Serial0 is up—and can be used to resolve the route to 60.0.0.0/24.

Now take a look at how static routes are deleted from the routing table. First, two static routes are added; the first will reference the second. The routes are installed instantly, but if the second route is deleted, the first one will be deleted only when the static processing algorithm is scheduled again (Listing 4-71).

```
R1#conf t
Enter configuration commands, one per line.  End with CNTL/Z.
R1(config)#ip route 60.0.0.0 255.0.0.0 50.1.1.1
R1(config)#ip route 50.0.0.0 255.0.0.0 10.0.1.2
R1(config)#
*Mar  2 11:18:49.207: RT: add 50.0.0.0/8 via 10.0.1.2, static metric [1/0]
*Mar  2 11:18:49.215: RT: add 60.0.0.0/8 via 50.1.1.1, static metric [1/0]
R1(config)#no ip route 50.0.0.0 255.0.0.0 10.0.1.2
R1(config)#
*Mar  2 11:18:56.111: RT: del 50.0.0.0 via 10.0.1.2, static metric [1/0]
*Mar  2 11:18:56.115: RT: delete network route to 50.0.0.0
R1(config)#
*Mar  2 11:19:41.607: RT: del 60.0.0.0 via 50.1.1.1, static metric [1/0]
*Mar  2 11:19:41.607: RT: delete network route to 60.0.0.0
R1(config)#
```

Listing 4-71. *Deletion of unresolvable static routes*

The algorithm in Listing 4-66 takes care of recursive routes. It does not install the routes resolved via each other. For example, using the routing table in Listing 4-72 and configuring the static routes as shown in Listing 4-73, the algorithm will not install these routes, because neither of them can be resolved via the routes already in the routing table.

```
R1#show ip rou
...
Gateway of last resort is not set

     20.0.0.0/8 is variably subnetted, 3 subnets, 2 masks
C       20.1.1.0/24 is directly connected, Serial1
C       20.2.1.1/32 is directly connected, Serial0
C       20.2.1.0/24 is directly connected, Serial0
```

```
        10.0.0.0/24 is subnetted, 1 subnets
C          10.0.1.0 is directly connected, Ethernet0
R1#
```

Listing 4-72. *Initial routing table*

```
R1#conf t
Enter configuration commands, one per line.  End with CNTL/Z.
R1(config)#ip route 50.0.0.0 255.0.0.0 60.1.1.1
R1(config)#ip route 60.0.0.0 255.0.0.0 50.1.1.1
R1(config)#^Z
R1#
```

Listing 4-73. *Configuration of recursive static routes*

The pseudocode of the static route processing algorithm is rather simplified to make what happens inside the router easier to understand. Actual static route processing is much more sophisticated and performs other types of checking before installing the routes into the routing table. For example, Cisco routers do not install a new route describing a destination network if this route is resolved via an installed route already covering this destination. So if you have the routing table shown in Listing 4-74 and configure a static route with the command **ip route 30.1.0.0 255.255.0.0 30.2.0.0**, the route will not be installed, because the destination it describes is already covered with the highlighted static route, and the new route is resolved via this route.

```
R1#show ip rou
...
Gateway of last resort is not set

        20.0.0.0/8 is variably subnetted, 3 subnets, 2 masks
C          20.1.1.0/24 is directly connected, Serial1
C          20.2.1.1/32 is directly connected, Serial0
C          20.2.1.0/24 is directly connected, Serial0
        10.0.0.0/24 is subnetted, 1 subnets
C          10.0.1.0 is directly connected, Ethernet0
S       30.0.0.0/8 [1/0] via 10.0.1.2
R1#
```

Listing 4-74. *Routing table containing summary network route*

The idea is to keep the routing table as small as possible and to avoid odd lookup iterations when routing packets.

Figure 4-7 illustrates the principle of this rule. You can see that static route 1 covers address range A1. Static route 2 covers address range A2, a subrange of A1. Because it is

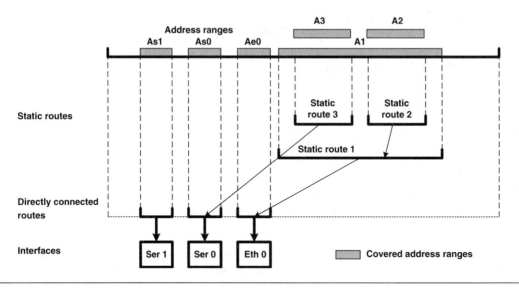

Figure 4-7. *Coverage of static routes' address ranges*

itself resolved via static route 1, inserting static route 2 adds no valuable information for the router, as static route 1 can work for this destination range quite well. When a static route is resolved via another route, as is static route 3, even though range A3 is a sub-range of A1, this route must be installed, as it is resolved via a different interface route, which will lead to routing packets destined for this subrange via another interface.

The algorithm performs this check only if both the new static route and the resolving route are configured over an intermediate network address, not an interface. The reason for this behavior is twofold. First, if a new route is configured over an interface, not the intermediate address, the route no longer references any other static route. Second, if the resolving route is configured over an interface and the new static route is not installed, the router will use the destination address in the packet as the next-hop address, which will end up causing a lot of ARP traffic. Instead, the router performs only a partial check to see whether the new route's intermediate address would be resolved via the route itself. If so, the new route is not installed. Otherwise, the route is installed even if the resolving route covers the new route's prefix. See Listing 4-75.

```
R1#conf t
Enter configuration commands, one per line.  End with CNTL/Z.
R1(config)#ip route 30.0.0.0 255.0.0.0 Ser 0
R1(config)#
*Mar  4 04:47:20.644: RT: add 30.0.0.0/8 via 0.0.0.0, static metric [1/0]
R1(config)#ip route 30.1.0.0 255.255.0.0 30.2.0.0
*Mar  4 04:47:30.952: RT: network 30.0.0.0 is now variably masked
```

```
*Mar  4 04:47:30.952: RT: add 30.1.0.0/16 via 30.2.0.0, static metric [1/0]
R1(config)#^Z
%SYS-5-CONFIG_I: Configured from console by console
R1#show ip rou
Codes: C - connected, S - static, I - IGRP, R - RIP, M - mobile, B - BGP
...
Gateway of last resort is not set

     20.0.0.0/8 is variably subnetted, 3 subnets, 2 masks
C       20.1.1.0/24 is directly connected, Serial1
C       20.2.1.1/32 is directly connected, Serial0
C       20.2.1.0/24 is directly connected, Serial0
     10.0.0.0/24 is subnetted, 1 subnets
C       10.0.1.0 is directly connected, Ethernet0
     30.0.0.0/8 is variably subnetted, 2 subnets, 2 masks
S       30.0.0.0/8 is directly connected, Serial0
S       30.1.0.0/16 [1/0] via 30.2.0.0
R1#
```

Listing 4-75. *More specific static route resolved via less specific static route*

This case is shown in Figure 4-8. Because it is configured via the interface Serial0, static route 1 is considered connected, and the sanity check is not performed when the second static route is installed.

A very important detail about the sanity check and route installation is that if a new route is not installed, because of the reason described in the preceding paragraphs, another route covering the same address range and with worse AD value may already be present in the routing table and will not be substituted. Figure 4-9 represents this situation.

The old route, static or dynamic, covering address range A2 points to a network directly connected to interface Serial0. If a new static route is now configured that covers the same A2 range and points to route 1—it too can be static or dynamic—the new route will not be installed and the old one will not be substituted, although the old route has a higher AD value. If the idea is to make the router route the packets destined to A2 via the same path as the whole A1 range, static route 2 must be configured over the corresponding interface.

The following example demonstrates how the sanity check works and how it can be overridden, using static routes over an interface. Consider the routing table shown in the Listing 4-76.

```
R1#show ip rou
...
Gateway of last resort is not set

     20.0.0.0/8 is variably subnetted, 3 subnets, 2 masks
C       20.1.1.0/24 is directly connected, Serial1
C       20.2.1.1/32 is directly connected, Serial0
```

```
C        20.2.1.0/24 is directly connected, Serial0
       10.0.0.0/24 is subnetted, 1 subnets
C        10.0.1.0 is directly connected, Ethernet0
       30.0.0.0/8 is variably subnetted, 2 subnets, 2 masks
S        30.0.0.0/8 [1/0] via 10.0.1.2
S        30.1.0.0/16 [50/0] via 20.2.1.1
```

Listing 4-76. *Initial routing table with static routes*

Note that the static route to subnet 30.1.0.0 was configured with an AD value of 50, which is worse than the default of 1. Now an administratively better route is configured to the same subnet (Listing 4-77).

```
R1#conf t
Enter configuration commands, one per line.  End with CNTL/Z.
R1(config)#ip route 30.1.0.0 255.255.0.0 30.0.0.0
R1(config)#^Z
R1#show ip rou
...
       30.0.0.0/8 is variably subnetted, 2 subnets, 2 masks
S        30.0.0.0/8 [1/0] via 10.0.1.2
S        30.1.0.0/16 [50/0] via 20.2.1.1
```

Listing 4-77. *Static route not installed, because of the sanity check*

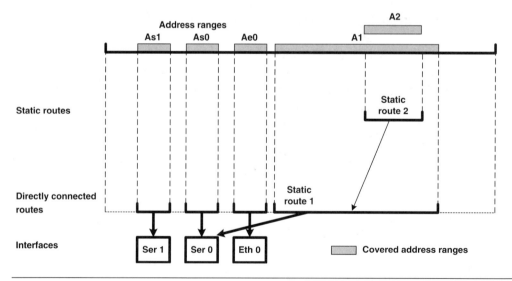

Figure 4-8. *Directly connected static route*

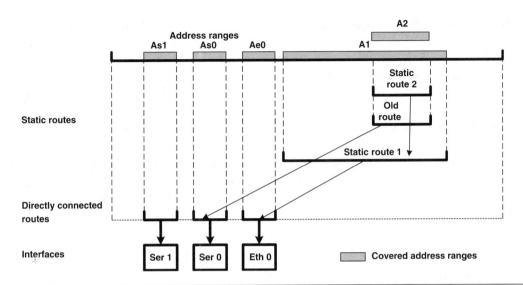

Figure 4-9. *Another static route address range coverage*

The route is not inserted, because of the sanity check.

Listing 4-78 shows the route configured over an interface.

```
R1#conf t
Enter configuration commands, one per line.  End with CNTL/Z.
R1(config)#no ip route 30.1.0.0 255.255.0.0 30.0.0.0
R1(config)#ip route 30.1.0.0 255.255.0.0 Eth0 10.0.1.2
R1(config)#
*Mar  9 03:26:29.599: RT: closer admin distance for 30.1.0.0, flushing 1 routes
*Mar  9 03:26:29.599: RT: add 30.1.0.0/16 via 10.0.1.2, static metric [1/0]
R1(config)#^Z
%SYS-5-CONFIG_I: Configured from console by consoleo

R1#show ip rou
...
Gateway of last resort is not set
...
     10.0.0.0/24 is subnetted, 1 subnets
C       10.0.1.0 is directly connected, Ethernet0
     30.0.0.0/8 is variably subnetted, 2 subnets, 2 masks
S       30.0.0.0/8 [1/0] via 10.0.1.2
S       30.1.0.0/16 [1/0] via 10.0.1.2, Ethernet0
R1#
```

Listing 4-78. *Installation of directly connected static route*

This time it works, but it is not an ideal path. You might want to use a static route to subnet 30.1.0.0 over an intermediate address resolved over a dynamic route. In this case, the new static route would always follow the dynamic route, and forwarding would always be correct, at least as correct as the dynamic routing protocol. To achieve these results, you could filter out an unwanted route if it were a dynamic one or delete it manually if it were static.

Another interesting case is when the 0.0.0.0/0 default route is used to resolve the new static route. The rules are the same as with the network summary route used in the previous example. If the intermediate address of a new route is resolved via the static default and this default is configured over a next hop rather than an interface, the new route is not installed (see Listing 4-79), because the default ensures routing to a subrange in the same direction anyway.

```
R1#conf t
Enter configuration commands, one per line.  End with CNTL/Z.
R1(config)#ip route 0.0.0.0 0.0.0.0 20.2.1.1
*Mar  4 04:54:03.536: RT: add 0.0.0.0/0 via 20.2.1.1, static metric [1/0]
*Mar  4 04:54:03.564: RT: default path is now 0.0.0.0 via 20.2.1.1
*Mar  4 04:54:03.564: RT: new default network 0.0.0.0
R1(config)#ip route 30.1.0.0 255.255.0.0 1.1.1.1
R1(config)#^Z
R1#show ip rou
Codes: C - connected, S - static, I - IGRP, R - RIP, M - mobile, B - BGP
...
Gateway of last resort is 20.2.1.1 to network 0.0.0.0

     20.0.0.0/8 is variably subnetted, 3 subnets, 2 masks
C       20.1.1.0/24 is directly connected, Serial1
C       20.2.1.1/32 is directly connected, Serial0
C       20.2.1.0/24 is directly connected, Serial0
     10.0.0.0/24 is subnetted, 1 subnets
C       10.0.1.0 is directly connected, Ethernet0
S*   0.0.0.0/0 [1/0] via 20.2.1.1
R1#
```

Listing 4-79. *Static route resolved over default*

The address range coverage in this case is illustrated in Figure 4-10. As shown in the figure, the static default covers all possible addresses; it was put under connected routes because the default route is considered only if no more specific route matches a given destination address. Because static route 2 covers only a subrange of the range covered by the static default and because static default was configured via an intermediate network address, the new static route—to network 30.1.0.0/16—is not installed. The same static route is installed if the default route is configured over an interface, as it is considered a directly connected interface (Listing 4-80).

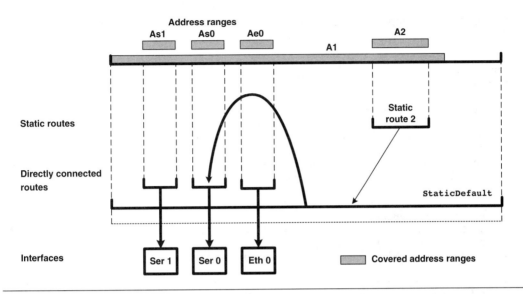

Figure 4-10. *Address range coverage for static route resolved via default*

```
R1#show ip rou
Codes: C - connected, S - static, I - IGRP, R - RIP, M - mobile, B - BGP
...
Gateway of last resort is 0.0.0.0 to network 0.0.0.0

     20.0.0.0/8 is variably subnetted, 3 subnets, 2 masks
C       20.1.1.0/24 is directly connected, Serial1
C       20.2.1.1/32 is directly connected, Serial0
C       20.2.1.0/24 is directly connected, Serial0
     10.0.0.0/24 is subnetted, 1 subnets
C       10.0.1.0 is directly connected, Ethernet0
     30.0.0.0/16 is subnetted, 1 subnets
S       30.1.0.0 [1/0] via 1.1.1.1
S*   0.0.0.0/0 is directly connected, Serial0
R1#
```

Listing 4-80. *Static route resolved via default over interface*

When the RT process checks resolvability of static routes configured via intermediate
network addresses, it uses a classful routing table lookup procedure. This implies that
the intermediate address of a static route is not resolved over the default route if the
routing table contains at least one route to a subnet of the major network to which
the intermediate address belongs. This rule is further restricted for static default
routes: The intermediate address of a static default route can never be resolved via
another default route. Otherwise, installation of the static default route could affect
resolvability of its own intermediate address.

The following example illustrates this rule. The routing table is shown in Listing 4-81.

```
R1#show ip rou
Codes: C - connected, S - static, I - IGRP, R - RIP, M - mobile, B - BGP
...
Gateway of last resort is 10.0.1.2 to network 0.0.0.0

     20.0.0.0/8 is variably subnetted, 3 subnets, 2 masks
C       20.1.1.0/24 is directly connected, Serial1
C       20.2.1.1/32 is directly connected, Serial0
C       20.2.1.0/24 is directly connected, Serial0
     10.0.0.0/24 is subnetted, 1 subnets
C       10.0.1.0 is directly connected, Ethernet0
     30.0.0.0/16 is subnetted, 2 subnets
S       30.2.0.0 is directly connected, Serial0
S       30.1.0.0 is directly connected, Serial1
S*  0.0.0.0/0 is directly connected, Ethernet0
R1#
```

Listing 4-81. *Initial routing table with default and subnet routes*

Now a static route to the major network 40.0.0.0 is configured (Listing 4-82).

```
R1#conf t
Enter configuration commands, one per line.  End with CNTL/Z.
R1(config)#ip route 40.0.0.0 255.0.0.0 30.2.0.0
R1(config)#
*Mar  5 02:58:22.003: RT: add 40.0.0.0/8 via 30.2.0.0, static metric [1/0]
R1(config)#
```

Listing 4-82. *Configuration of static route resolved over subnet route*

The static route is successfully installed because it can be resolved via the static route pointing to interface Serial0. If the interface is now taken down, simulating a link failure, the route will go out of the routing table; when it is checking resolvability of the intermediate address, the RT process does not take the default, as this check is performed in classful mode, even if **ip classless** is configured. See Listing 4-83.

```
R1(config)#
R1(config)#int s0
R1(config-if)#shut
R1(config-if)#
*Mar  5 03:03:36.083: RT: interface Serial0 removed from routing table
*Mar  5 03:03:36.083: RT: del 20.2.1.0/24 via 0.0.0.0, connected metric [0/0]
*Mar  5 03:03:36.087: RT: Serial0 peer adjust
```

```
*Mar  5 03:03:36.087: RT: delete subnet route to 20.2.1.0/24
*Mar  5 03:03:36.115: RT: delete route to 20.2.1.1 via 0.0.0.0, Serial0
*Mar  5 03:03:36.115: RT: Serial0 peer adjust
*Mar  5 03:03:36.115: RT: no routes to 20.2.1.1, flushing
*Mar  5 03:03:36.171: RT: delete route to 30.2.0.0 via 0.0.0.0, Serial0
*Mar  5 03:03:36.171: RT: no routes to 30.2.0.0, flushing
*Mar  5 03:03:36.251: RT: del 40.0.0.0 via 30.2.0.0, static metric [1/0]
*Mar  5 03:03:36.255: RT: delete network route to 40.0.0.0
%LINEPROTO-5-UPDOWN: Line protocol on Interface Serial0, changed state to down
%LINK-5-CHANGED: Interface Serial0, changed state to administratively down
R1(config-if)#
```

Listing 4-83. *Deletion of static route caused by classful route lookup*

The route will not appear in the routing table until the corresponding interface (Serial0) comes up or the routing table has no routes to the subnets of major network 30.0.0.0. Removing the static route to subnet 30.1.0.0 or downing the interface Serial1 can satisfy the last condition. When the RT process schedules the `ProcessStatic()` function again, the route is installed (Listing 4-84).

```
R1(config)#int s1
R1(config-if)#shut
R1(config-if)#
*Mar  5 03:11:09.603: RT: interface Serial1 removed from routing table
*Mar  5 03:11:09.603: RT: del 20.1.1.0/24 via 0.0.0.0, connected metric [0/0]
*Mar  5 03:11:09.607: RT: delete subnet route to 20.1.1.0/24
*Mar  5 03:11:09.607: RT: delete network route to 20.0.0.0
*Mar  5 03:11:09.683: RT: delete route to 30.1.0.0 via 0.0.0.0, Serial1
*Mar  5 03:11:09.687: RT: no routes to 30.1.0.0, flushing
*Mar  5 03:11:09.687: RT: delete network route to 30.0.0.0
*Mar  5 03:11:09.767: RT: add 40.0.0.0/8 via 30.2.0.0, static metric [1/0]
%LINEPROTO-5-UPDOWN: Line protocol on Interface Serial1, changed state to down
%LINK-5-CHANGED: Interface Serial1, changed state to administratively down
R1(config-if)#
```

Listing 4-84. *Installation of the route after the last subnet route is gone*

Another interesting example is when installation of the new static route affects resolvability of its own intermediate network address or intermediate addresses specified in other routes. Consider the routing table in Listing 4-85.

```
R1#show ip rou

...

Gateway of last resort is 10.1.2.2 to network 0.0.0.0
```

```
         10.0.0.0/24 is subnetted, 4 subnets
C           10.10.0.0 is directly connected, Serial2
C           10.14.0.0 is directly connected, Ethernet0
C           10.1.2.0 is directly connected, Serial0
C           10.1.1.0 is directly connected, Serial1
S*       0.0.0.0/0 is directly connected, Serial0
R1#
```

Listing 4-85. *Initial routing table with default*

Now a static route is added to subnet 20.1.0.0/16 via the intermediate address from the same major network (Listing 4-86).

```
R1#conf t
Enter configuration commands, one per line.  End with CNTL/Z.
R1(config)#ip route 20.1.0.0 255.255.0.0 20.2.0.2
R1(config)#
*Mar  2 04:03:38.909: RT: add 20.1.0.0/16 via 20.2.0.2, static metric [1/0]
R1(config)#^Z
R1#show ip route
...
Gateway of last resort is 0.0.0.0 to network 0.0.0.0

         20.0.0.0/16 is subnetted, 1 subnets
S           20.1.0.0 [1/0] via 20.2.0.2
         10.0.0.0/24 is subnetted, 4 subnets
C           10.10.0.0 is directly connected, Serial2
C           10.14.0.0 is directly connected, Ethernet0
C           10.1.2.0 is directly connected, Serial0
C           10.1.1.0 is directly connected, Serial1
S*       0.0.0.0/0 is directly connected, Serial0
R1#
```

Listing 4-86. *Installation of static route leading to its unresolvability*

At the moment of route installation, the route's intermediate address is resolvable via the default. But once it is installed, the classful routing table lookup function used to resolve the intermediate address cannot consider supernet and default routes, because the routing table contains a subnet route for the major network to which the intermediate address belongs. So the intermediate address becomes unresolvable, and the next time period static route processing is scheduled, the static route will be finally deleted (Listing 4-87).

```
*Mar  2 04:03:58.817: RT: del 20.1.0.0/16 via 20.2.0.2, static metric [1/0]
*Mar  2 04:03:58.821: RT: delete subnet route to 20.1.0.0/16
*Mar  2 04:03:58.821: RT: delete network route to 20.0.0.0
```

```
*Mar  2 04:03:58.849: RT: add 20.1.0.0/16 via 20.2.0.2, static metric [1/0]
*Mar  2 04:03:58.865: RT: del 20.1.0.0/16 via 20.2.0.2, static metric [1/0]
*Mar  2 04:03:58.869: RT: delete subnet route to 20.1.0.0/16
*Mar  2 04:03:58.873: RT: delete network route to 20.0.0.0
```

Listing 4-87. *Recurrent static route installation and deletion*

This situation—consequent route installation and deletion—repeats every minute, as shown in Listing 4-88. This instability can involve other static routes, resolved via the route in question. A way to get rid of it is to configure static routes via interfaces with intermediate addresses (considered in Chapter 6).

```
*Mar  2 04:04:58.913: RT: add 20.1.0.0/16 via 20.2.0.2, static metric [1/0]
*Mar  2 04:04:58.929: RT: del 20.1.0.0/16 via 20.2.0.2, static metric [1/0]
*Mar  2 04:04:58.933: RT: delete subnet route to 20.1.0.0/16
*Mar  2 04:04:58.937: RT: delete network route to 20.0.0.0
*Mar  2 04:04:58.969: RT: add 20.1.0.0/16 via 20.2.0.2, static metric [1/0]
*Mar  2 04:04:58.973: RT: del 20.1.0.0/16 via 20.2.0.2, static metric [1/0]
*Mar  2 04:04:58.977: RT: delete subnet route to 20.1.0.0/16
*Mar  2 04:04:58.981: RT: delete network route to 20.0.0.0
*Mar  2 04:05:59.021: RT: add 20.1.0.0/16 via 20.2.0.2, static metric [1/0]
*Mar  2 04:05:59.033: RT: del 20.1.0.0/16 via 20.2.0.2, static metric [1/0]
*Mar  2 04:05:59.033: RT: delete subnet route to 20.1.0.0/16
*Mar  2 04:05:59.037: RT: delete network route to 20.0.0.0
*Mar  2 04:05:59.069: RT: add 20.1.0.0/16 via 20.2.0.2, static metric [1/0]
*Mar  2 04:05:59.073: RT: del 20.1.0.0/16 via 20.2.0.2, static metric [1/0]
*Mar  2 04:05:59.077: RT: delete subnet route to 20.1.0.0/16
*Mar  2 04:05:59.081: RT: delete network route to 20.0.0.0
```

Listing 4-88. *Recurrent route installation and deletion in per minute check*

The idea behind classful lookup while resolving the intermediate addresses of the static route is easily understood. If it were done in classless mode and the default were present, no backup static routes with higher AD value would be able to make it into the routing table, as any static route even referencing a nonexistent network could be resolved. (Backup static routes are discussed in more detail in Chapter 6.)

Now consider some basic examples of cooperation between static and dynamic routing. As mentioned before, when a static route is configured over an intermediate network address, any route in the routing table—static or dynamic—can be used to resolve the intermediate address. The RT process invokes the static route processing function every minute to install or to remove static routes according to the dynamically changing routing table.

The following example shows how addition of an OSPF route leads to installation of a static route when the `ProcessStatic()` procedure is run once again. OSPF is started on routers R1 and R2. R2 reports a route to its loopback interface with address 55.55.55.1; as the static route referenced it as an intermediate network address, the static route is added to the routing table by the RT process when it looks through the static routes (Listing 4-89). Note how much time elapsed between the two events.

```
R1#conf t
Enter configuration commands, one per line.  End with CNTL/Z.
R1(config)#ip route 60.0.0.0 255.255.255.0 55.55.55.1
R1(config)#
*Mar  2 11:29:55.363: RT: add 55.55.55.1/32 via 20.2.1.1, ospf metric [110/65]
R1(config)#
*Mar  2 11:30:41.859: RT: add 60.0.0.0/24 via 55.55.55.1, static metric [1/0]
R1(config)#
```

Listing 4-89. *Installation of a dynamic route followed by installation of a static route*

The process of a dynamic route deletion is just the same. The route is removed from the table, and all static routes are processed the next time the algorithm is scheduled (Listing 4-90).

```
R1#
*Mar  2 11:39:29.107: RT: del 55.55.55.1/32 via 20.2.1.1, ospf metric [110/65]
*Mar  2 11:39:29.111: RT: delete subnet route to 55.55.55.1/32
*Mar  2 11:39:29.111: RT: delete network route to 55.0.0.0
R1#
*Mar  2 11:39:42.119: RT: del 60.0.0.0/24 via 55.55.55.1, static metric [1/0]
*Mar  2 11:39:42.119: RT: delete subnet route to 60.0.0.0/24
*Mar  2 11:39:42.123: RT: delete network route to 60.0.0.0
R1#
```

Listing 4-90. *Deletion of a dynamic route followed by deletion of a static route*

4.2.11 Manual Routing Table Clearance

The administrator can remove specific or all routes from the routing table at any time, forcing the router to recalculate affected routes. The command used for this purpose has the following syntax:

clear ip route {*destination* [*mask*] | * }

If only the destination address is entered, without the subnet mask, the router looks up the routing table for the best route to the specified destination.

If a route is found, it is deleted from the routing table, and every route source is queried for a backup route to the same destination.

To illustrate how this process works, **debug ip routing** and **debug ip ospf spf** are enabled (Listing 4-91).

```
R1#show ip rou
...
Gateway of last resort is not set

     20.0.0.0/8 is variably subnetted, 3 subnets, 2 masks
O        20.2.2.0/24 [110/128] via 20.2.1.1, 01:20:04, Serial0
C        20.2.1.1/32 is directly connected, Serial0
C        20.2.1.0/24 is directly connected, Serial0
     10.0.0.0/24 is subnetted, 1 subnets
C        10.0.1.0 is directly connected, Ethernet0
     30.0.0.0/8 is variably subnetted, 2 subnets, 2 masks
O E2     30.0.0.0/8 [110/20] via 20.2.1.1, 00:00:17, Serial0
30.0.0.0/24 [110/74] via 20.2.1.1, 00:02:29, Serial0
R1#clear ip rou 30.0.0.0
R1#
*Mar  6 09:35:54.375: RT: del 30.0.0.0/24 via 20.2.1.1, ospf metric [110/74]
*Mar  6 09:35:54.375: RT: delete subnet route to 30.0.0.0/24
*Mar  6 09:35:54.379: RT: delete network route to 30.0.0.0
*Mar  6 09:35:54.383: RT: add 30.0.0.0/24 via 20.2.1.1, ospf metric [110/74]
*Mar  6 09:35:54.387: OSPF: Added backup Network Route to 30.0.0.0
     Metric: 74, Next Hop: 20.2.1.1
R1#
```

Listing 4-91. *Example of the* **clear ip route** *command*

If both the destination address and the subnet mask are entered, the router tries to find a route that exactly matches specific parameters. Only if one or more is found is deletion done and the route sources signaled (Listing 4-92).

```
R1#clear ip rou 30.0.0.0 255.0.0.0
R1#
*Mar  6 09:39:38.495: RT: del 30.0.0.0/8 via 20.2.1.1, ospf metric [110/20]
*Mar  6 09:39:38.499: RT: delete subnet route to 30.0.0.0/8
*Mar  6 09:39:38.503: OSPF: Service partial SPF 0/1/0
*Mar  6 09:39:38.507: OSPF: Start partial processing Type 5 External LSA 30.0.0.0,
mask 255.0.0.0, adv 20.2.1.1, age 93, seq 0x80000001, metric 20, metric-type 2
*Mar  6 09:39:38.507:    Add better path to LSA ID 30.0.0.0, gateway 20.2.1.1, dist 20
*Mar  6 09:39:38.511:    Add path: next-hop 20.2.1.1, interface Serial0
```

```
*Mar  6 09:39:38.515: OSPF: delete lsa id 30.0.0.0, type 5, adv rtr 20.2.1.1 from
delete list
*Mar  6 09:39:38.515: RT: network 30.0.0.0 is now variably masked
*Mar  6 09:39:38.519: RT: add 30.0.0.0/8 via 20.2.1.1, ospf metric [110/20]
*Mar  6 09:39:38.523:    Add External Route to 30.0.0.0. Metric: 20, Next Hop:
20.2.1.1
*Mar  6 09:39:38.523: OSPF: insert route list LS ID 30.0.0.0, type 5, adv rtr
20.2.1.1
R1#
```

Listing 4-92. *The* **clear ip route** *command used with route mask*

If an asterisk is specified as the argument for the command, all routes are deleted from the routing table, connected and static routes are processed, and all routing protocols are sent the initialization signal. Different routing protocols do different things on receiving this signal. RIP, for example, sends general requests through all interfaces on which it is enabled, whereas OSPF just recalculates all routes, using its own database, and does not send any messages to the neighbors. The chapters of this book describing specific routing protocols discuss the behavior of each protocol on different types of events. Listing 4-93 shows a truncated version of the log taken after issuing a **clear ip route*** command.

```
R1#clear ip route *
R1#
*Mar  6 09:44:16.315: RT: Serial0 peer adjust
*Mar  6 09:44:16.319: RT: Serial0 peer adjust
*Mar  6 09:44:16.427: RT: add 20.2.1.1/32 via 0.0.0.0, connected metric [0/0]
*Mar  6 09:44:16.463: RT: add 10.0.1.0/24 via 0.0.0.0, connected metric [0/0]
*Mar  6 09:44:16.499: RT: network 20.0.0.0 is now variably masked
*Mar  6 09:44:16.503: RT: add 20.2.1.0/24 via 0.0.0.0, connected metric [0/0]
*Mar  6 09:44:16.511: RT: interface Serial0 added to routing table
*Mar  6 09:44:16.547: OSPF: running SPF for area 0
*Mar  6 09:44:16.547: OSPF: Initializing to run spf
...
*Mar  6 09:44:16.623: RT: add 20.2.2.0/24 via 20.2.1.1, ospf metric [110/128]
*Mar  6 09:44:16.623: OSPF: Add Network Route to 20.2.2.0 Mask /24. Metric: 128, Next
...
*Mar  6 09:44:16.631: RT: add 30.0.0.0/24 via 20.2.1.1, ospf metric [110/74]
*Mar  6 09:44:16.635: OSPF: Add Network Route to 30.0.0.0 Mask /24. Metric: 74, Next
Hop: 20.2.1.1
...
*Mar  6 09:44:16.659: RT: network 30.0.0.0 is now variably masked
*Mar  6 09:44:16.663: RT: add 30.0.0.0/8 via 20.2.1.1, ospf metric [110/20]
*Mar  6 09:44:16.667:    Add External Route to 30.0.0.0. Metric: 20, Next Hop:
20.2.1.1
*Mar  6 09:44:16.667: OSPF: insert route list LS ID 30.0.0.0, type 5, adv rtr
```

```
20.2.1.1
*Mar  6 09:44:16.671: OSPF: ex_delete_old_routes
*Mar  6 09:44:16.671: OSPF: Started Building Type 7 External Routes
*Mar  6 09:44:16.675: OSPF: ex_delete_old_routes
R1#
```

Listing 4-93. *Using the* **clear ip route*** *command to delete all routes and to build the routing table from scratch*

When the **clear ip route** command is used, static routes configured with the permanent keyword are also deleted. Furthermore, such static routes are checked for resolvability again and are not installed if they are not resolvable. The **permanent** keyword works only when resolvability of already installed routes is verified. It is not taken into consideration during initial route installation, so before a **permanent** static route stays in the routing table forever—or until the **clear ip route** command is issued—it must pass the resolvability check and get in the table.

4.2.12 Defining Default Routes

Principles of default routing were considered in Chapter 3. Cisco routers support default routes in several implementations. Default routes can be of any type—interface, static, or dynamic. In Cisco routers, any route to a major network or the pseudonetwork 0.0.0.0 that is in the routing table can be used as the default. Whenever the router has no specific route that matches the destination address, the lookup function chooses the default route, taking the state of the **ip classless** command into consideration, as described in Chapter 5.

Cisco IOS uses the idea of *candidate default* routes: One or more routes are marked manually or automatically as candidates, and the real default route is chosen from among them. The administrator has three options for specifing the candidates:

1. Static or dynamic route to the pseudonetwork 0.0.0.0/0 route
2. Route to a major network manually marked as a candidate with an **ip default-network** command
3. Dynamic route marked as a candidate by the routing protocol while passing it to the routing table maintenance process

The first option is the most widely used. You may have seen such a line in the router configuration files:

ip route 0.0.0.0 0.0.0.0 *interface next-hop-addr*

When a route with the address and mask set to all 0s is passed for installation into the routing table, the router automatically marks it as candidate, no matter whether the route is static or dynamic.

The second option allows the administrator to tell the router that a route must be marked as a candidate default whenever it is installed in the active routing table. The command to do this is

ip default-network *netAddr*

This command is usually very confusing. First, it is very often mixed up with the **ip default-gateway** command.

The **ip default-gateway** command is used only when the router is not performing any IP routing—**no ip routing** is configured or the router is running the boot image—and is operating in the IP host mode. This command sets the address of the default router, that is, the router that is used to send packets destined for networks not attached directly. When the router is doing IP routing, this command does not influence the default route selection process and is ignored.

Second, there can be two types of network addresses passed as the *netAddr* parameter: a subnet address and a major network address.

If a subnet address is specified, the router automatically installs a static summary network route via the specified subnet, as shown in Listing 4-94. Such a route cannot be removed from the routing table by using the **no ip default-network** command; the administrator must instead use the **no ip route** command as if the route were configured manually.

```
R1#show ip rou
...
Gateway of last resort is not set

     10.0.0.0/24 is subnetted, 2 subnets
C       10.1.2.0 is directly connected, Serial0
C       10.1.1.0 is directly connected, Ethernet0
R1#conf t
Enter configuration commands, one per line.  End with CNTL/Z.
R1(config)#ip default-network 10.1.2.0
R1(config)#^Z
```

```
R1#
*Mar  2 21:25:07.684: RT: network 10.0.0.0 is now variably masked
*Mar  2 21:25:07.684: RT: add 10.0.0.0/8 via 10.1.2.0, static metric [1/0]
R1#show ip rou
...
Gateway of last resort is not set

     10.0.0.0/8 is variably subnetted, 3 subnets, 2 masks
C       10.1.2.0/24 is directly connected, Serial0
S       10.0.0.0/8 [1/0] via 10.1.2.0
C       10.1.1.0/24 is directly connected, Ethernet0
R1#
```

Listing 4-94. *Default network route configured using the* **ip default-network** *command*

If a major network address is specified as the parameter, the router marks both parent and ultimate prefix descriptors as candidates. Treatment of candidate-marked prefix descriptors varies, depending on the prefix descriptor type: parent or ultimate. If the prefix descriptor is ultimate, meaning that the router received the route to a major network from another router and thus does not have active attachments to the network, the prefix descriptor will be considered when selecting the default, that is, will function as a pure candidate default (Listing 4-95).

```
R1#show ip rou
...
Gateway of last resort is not set

R    20.0.0.0/8 [120/1] via 10.1.2.2, Serial0
     10.0.0.0/24 is subnetted, 3 subnets
C       10.1.2.0 is directly connected, Serial0
C       10.1.1.0 is directly connected, Ethernet0
R       10.64.0.0 [120/1] via 10.1.2.2, Serial0
R1#conf t
Enter configuration commands, one per line.  End with CNTL/Z.
R1(config)#ip default-network 20.0.0.0
R1(config)#
*Mar  2 22:15:52.864: RT: 20.0.0.0 is now exterior
*Mar  2 22:15:52.884: RT: default path is now 20.0.0.0 via 10.1.2.2
*Mar  2 22:15:52.884: RT: new default network 20.0.0.0
R1(config)#^Z
R1#show ip rou
...
Gateway of last resort is 10.1.2.2 to network 20.0.0.0

R*   20.0.0.0/8 [120/1] via 10.1.2.2, Serial0
     10.0.0.0/24 is subnetted, 3 subnets
C       10.1.2.0 is directly connected, Serial0
C       10.1.1.0 is directly connected, Ethernet0
```

```
R        10.64.0.0 [120/1] via 10.1.2.2, Serial0
R1#
```

Listing 4-95. *Network marked as candidate default, using the* **ip default-network** *command*

If the prefix descriptor is a parent, which means that the router is attached to the major network and has routes to its subnets, the prefix descriptor is not considered a candidate default on the router in question. The major network, described by a candidate-marked prefix descriptor, is marked as external when included as a summary network route into the routing updates of IGRP and EIGRP, instructing neighboring routers to mark the route as candidate (Listing 4-96). RIP, in turn, sends the default route (0.0.0.0/0) to its neighbors whenever a candidate-marked route is in the routing table.

```
R1#show ip route
...
Gateway of last resort is not set

R     20.0.0.0/8 [120/1] via 10.1.2.2, Serial0
      10.0.0.0/24 is subnetted, 3 subnets
C        10.1.2.0 is directly connected, Serial0
C        10.1.1.0 is directly connected, Ethernet0
R        10.64.0.0 [120/1] via 10.1.2.2, Serial0
R1#conf t
Enter configuration commands, one per line.  End with CNTL/Z.
R1(config)#ip default-network 10.0.0.0
R1(config)#
*Mar  2 22:17:53.820: RT: 10.0.0.0 is now exterior
R1(config)#^Z
R1#
R1#show ip rou
...
Gateway of last resort is not set

R     20.0.0.0/8 [120/1] via 10.1.2.2, Serial0
      *10.0.0.0/24 is subnetted, 3 subnets
C        10.1.2.0 is directly connected, Serial0
C        10.1.1.0 is directly connected, Ethernet0
R        10.64.0.0 [120/1] via 10.1.2.2, Serial0
R1#
```

Listing 4-96. *Local major network marked as external, using the* **ip default-network** *command*

The network address specified in the **ip default-network** command must exactly match the route the administrator wants to mark. Also, because no route mask information can be specified, zero subnets are considered major network addresses.

The third way of providing the candidates for the default route involves dynamic propagation of the default route throughout the network. Different protocols use different methods to do this. For example, RIP and OSPF just send the 0.0.0.0/0 route—in fact, RIP v1 does not include the subnet masks in its updates, so it just sends a route with the address set to all 0s—to the neighbors, and when other routers receive the update and hand the 0.0.0.0/0 route to the RT process, the latter automatically marks it as a candidate default.

IGRP uses a different approach for dynamic propagation of the default route. IGRP includes summary routes to major networks marked by the **ip default-network** command in a special "external" portion of the update. As stated before, when it installs such a route into the routing table, an IGRP process marks it as a candidate. The route to the pseudonetwork 0.0.0.0/0 cannot be used inside an IGRP domain to propagate the default. EIGRP can use both of the discussed methods—the administrator can either make it mark some advertised routes as external or inject a 0.0.0.0/0 route into an EIGRP domain.

> Using the **ip default-network** command with EIGRP is not recommended, unless this command is already used for IGRP.

4.2.13 Default Route Selection

From potentially multiple default candidate routes, the router needs to choose one that will be used as the actual default route. The algorithm that performs selection of the default route takes into consideration two parameters of the candidate routes: administrative distance and the metric supplied by the route sources. First, the routes with the lowest AD value are chosen from the set of all candidates. If more than one is left, the metric is used as the tiebreaker. If more than one route is left after this check, the first route is selected.

The default selection process is run once per minute, after processing of the static routes, to reflect the changes in the routing table made by the dynamic routing protocols. It is also executed on the following events.

- The **[no] ip default-network** command is entered to add or to delete a candidate default.
- A route specified in an **ip default-network** command is added or removed from the routing table.
- A route to pseudonetwork 0.0.0.0/0 is added to the routing table.
- A static route is added and no default route has yet been selected.
- A route, static or dynamic, is deleted and it is the current default route.
- A **clear ip route** command is issued.

Events such as interface state transition and manual table clearance do not explicitly affect this process. When proper routes are added or deleted after one of these events, however, the default route is reselected.

The following examples should clarify selection of the default route. Listing 4-97 shows how the static route describing the pseudonetwork 0.0.0.0/0 is marked as a candidate for default.

```
R1#show ip rou
...
Gateway of last resort is not set
     20.0.0.0/8 is variably subnetted, 3 subnets, 2 masks
     20.2.2.0/24 [110/128] via 20.2.1.1, 00:22:56, Serial0
C        20.2.1.1/32 is directly connected, Serial0
C        20.2.1.0/24 is directly connected, Serial0
     10.0.0.0/24 is subnetted, 1 subnets
C        10.0.1.0 is directly connected, Ethernet0
     30.0.0.0/24 is subnetted, 1 subnets
     30.0.0.0 [110/74] via 20.2.1.1, 00:22:56, Serial0

R1#conf t
Enter configuration commands, one per line.  End with CNTL/Z.
R1(config)#ip route 0.0.0.0 0.0.0.0 Ser 0
R1(config)#
*Mar  6 10:33:15.323: RT: add 0.0.0.0/0 via 0.0.0.0, static metric [1/0]
*Mar  6 10:33:15.347: RT: default path is now 0.0.0.0 via 0.0.0.0
*Mar  6 10:33:15.347: RT: new default network 0.0.0.0
R1(config)#^Z
R1#show ip rou
Codes: C - connected, S - static, I - IGRP, R - RIP, M - mobile, B - BGP
       D - EIGRP, EX - EIGRP external, O - OSPF, IA - OSPF inter area
       N1 - OSPF NSSA external type 1, N2 - OSPF NSSA external type 2
       E1 - OSPF external type 1, E2 - OSPF external type 2, E - EGP
       i - IS-IS, L1 - IS-IS level-1, L2 - IS-IS level-2, * - candidate default
       U - per-user static route, o - ODR

Gateway of last resort is 0.0.0.0 to network 0.0.0.0

     20.0.0.0/8 is variably subnetted, 3 subnets, 2 masks
O        20.2.2.0/24 [110/128] via 20.2.1.1, 00:23:11, Serial0
C        20.2.1.1/32 is directly connected, Serial0
C        20.2.1.0/24 is directly connected, Serial0
O    10.0.0.0/24 is subnetted, 1 subnets
C        10.0.1.0 is directly connected, Ethernet0
     30.0.0.0/24 is subnetted, 1 subnets
O        30.0.0.0 [110/74] via 20.2.1.1, 00:23:12, Serial0
S*   0.0.0.0/0 is directly connected, Serial0
R1#
%SYS-5-CONFIG_I: Configured from console by console
R1#
```

Listing 4-97. *Configuring static candidate default route*

Note that the asterisk (*) at the left of the static route highlights the routes used as the candidates for the default. Because the static route to the 0.0.0.0/0 network is the only candidate, it is selected as the default, indicated by the line beginning with "Gateway of last resort is . . . ."

If two static routes are being considered as candidate defaults, the first available one is selected, provided that the default AD value has not been changed. In the example in Listing 4-98, we add another static route and mark it as candidate default via an **ip default-network** command.

```
R1#show ip rou
...
Gateway of last resort is 0.0.0.0 to network 0.0.0.0

     20.0.0.0/8 is variably subnetted, 2 subnets, 2 masks
C        20.2.1.1/32 is directly connected, Serial0
C        20.2.1.0/24 is directly connected, Serial0
     10.0.0.0/24 is subnetted, 1 subnets
C        10.0.1.0 is directly connected, Ethernet0
S*   0.0.0.0/0 is directly connected, Serial0
R1#
R1#conf t
Enter configuration commands, one per line.  End with CNTL/Z.
R1(config)#ip route 50.0.0.0 255.0.0.0 20.2.1.1
R1(config)#
*Mar  6 11:07:46.355: RT: add 50.0.0.0/8 via 20.2.1.1, static metric [1/0]
R1(config)#ip default-network 50.0.0.0
R1(config)#
*Mar  6 11:08:09.731: RT: 50.0.0.0 is now exterior
*Mar  6 11:08:09.751: RT: default path is now 50.0.0.0 via 20.2.1.1
*Mar  6 11:08:09.755: RT: new default network 50.0.0.0
R1(config)#^Z
R1#
R1#show ip rou
...
Gateway of last resort is 20.2.1.1 to network 50.0.0.0

S*   50.0.0.0/8 [1/0] via 20.2.1.1
     20.0.0.0/8 is variably subnetted, 2 subnets, 2 masks
C        20.2.1.1/32 is directly connected, Serial0
C        20.2.1.0/24 is directly connected, Serial0
     10.0.0.0/24 is subnetted, 1 subnets
C        10.0.1.0 is directly connected, Ethernet0
S*   0.0.0.0/0 is directly connected, Serial0
R1#
```

Listing 4-98. *The first route chosen as default between two equal candidates*

Note that even though two routes are marked as candidates, only one is selected as the default route. The gateway of last resort is 20.2.1.1 on the path to network 50.0.0.0, whereas in the previous example, the gateway was 0.0.0.0 because the static default was configured pointing to an interface: The route did not reference any intermediate network address.

> Make sure that you are not confused here. Even though the network prefix of the second candidate route is not 0.0.0.0/0, it has been selected as the default. When forwarding transit packets, the router will use this route as the default regardless of whether the packet's destination address matches the route's prefix.

When a router has several candidates for default with different administrative distance values, the router selects the one with the lowest value as default. For example, if an OSPF route and an RIP route are marked as candidates, the OSPF route will be chosen (Listing 4-99).

```
R1#conf t
Enter configuration commands, one per line.  End with CNTL/Z.
R1(config)#ip default-network 50.0.0.0
*Mar  6 11:38:13.103: RT: 50.0.0.0 is now exterior
*Mar  6 11:38:13.127: RT: default path is now 50.0.0.0 via 20.1.1.2
*Mar  6 11:38:13.127: RT: new default network 50.0.0.0
R1(config)#ip default-network 30.0.0.0
R1(config)#
*Mar  6 11:38:18.475: RT: 30.0.0.0 is now exterior
*Mar  6 11:38:18.487: RT: default path is now 30.0.0.0 via 20.2.1.1
*Mar  6 11:38:18.487: RT: new default network 30.0.0.0
R1(config)#^Z
R1#
%SYS-5-CONFIG_I: Configured from console by console
R1#show ip rou
...
Gateway of last resort is 20.2.1.1 to network 30.0.0.0

R*    50.0.0.0/8 [120/1] via 20.1.1.2, 00:00:25, Serial1
      20.0.0.0/8 is variably subnetted, 3 subnets, 2 masks
C        20.1.1.0/24 is directly connected, Serial1
C        20.2.1.1/32 is directly connected, Serial0
C        20.2.1.0/24 is directly connected, Serial0
      10.0.0.0/24 is subnetted, 1 subnets
C        10.0.1.0 is directly connected, Ethernet0
      30.0.0.0/24 is subnetted, 1 subnets
O*       30.0.0.0 [110/74] via 20.2.1.1, 00:00:37, Serial0
R1#
```

Listing 4-99. *Candidate with the lower AD value is chosen as the default*

If a router has two or more networks marked as candidates for default and the routes describing them are of the same administrative distance, the router chooses the one with the lowest metric. Listing 4-100 shows how the router selects the default route between two OSPF routes.

```
R1#conf t
Enter configuration commands, one per line.  End with CNTL/Z.
R1(config)#ip default-network 30.0.0.0
R1(config)#
*Mar  9 01:35:37.787: RT: 30.0.0.0 is now exterior
*Mar  9 01:35:37.803: RT: default path is now 30.0.0.0 via 20.2.1.1
*Mar  9 01:35:37.803: RT: new default network 30.0.0.0
R1(config)#ip default-network 40.0.0.0
R1(config)#
*Mar  9 01:35:43.035: RT: 40.0.0.0 is now exterior
*Mar  9 01:35:43.051: RT: default path is now 40.0.0.0 via 20.2.1.1
*Mar  9 01:35:43.051: RT: new default network 40.0.0.0
R1(config)#^Z
%SYS-5-CONFIG_I: Configured from console by console
R1#show ip rou
...
Gateway of last resort is 20.2.1.1 to network 40.0.0.0

     20.0.0.0/8 is variably subnetted, 4 subnets, 2 masks
O       20.2.2.0/24 [110/128] via 20.2.1.1, 00:13:02, Serial0
C       20.1.1.0/24 is directly connected, Serial1
C       20.2.1.1/32 is directly connected, Serial0
C       20.2.1.0/24 is directly connected, Serial0
O*E2 40.0.0.0/8 [110/20] via 20.2.1.1, 00:13:02, Serial0
O*E2 30.0.0.0/8 [110/65] via 20.2.1.1, 00:13:02, Serial0
R1#
```

Listing 4-100. *Candidate with better metric is chosen as default*

4.3 Summary

Table 4-2 summarizes all routing table maintenance details presented in this chapter.

4.4 Frequently Asked Questions

Q: **Do routing protocols really not forward IP packets? I've heard that IGRP and EIGRP can forward packets among multiple paths, sharing the traffic according to the metrics of the routes, and that the RFC describing OSPF includes sections dedicated to packet forwarding.**

A: The job of dynamic routing protocols is providing the routing table with routes to remote destinations, not forwarding the packets. Packet forwarding is the task of the forwarding engine, which does not interact with routing protocols directly but

Table 4-2. *Events and Actions in Routing Table Maintenance Process*

Events	Actions
ip address entered	Add the interface to the set of active IP interfaces.
	Add corresponding interface route.
	Inform every dynamic routing protocol.
	Process static routes.
	Recalculate the default.
ip unnumbered entered	Add the interface to the set of active IP interfaces.
	Inform every dynamic routing protocol.
	Process static routes.
	Recalculate the default.
no ip address or **no ip unnumbered** entered	Delete all routes derived from the IP addresses of this interface, if applicable.
	Check every route in the routing table.
	Inform every active dynamic routing protocol about the state of the interface.
	Process static routes, taking care of default.
Interface goes up	See processing of the **ip address** and the **ip unnumbered** commands.
Interface goes down	See processing of the **no ip address** and the **no ip unnumbered** commands.
Static route added	Add the route to the list of static routes.
	Pass the route for installation in the routing table.
	If installed, schedule static-route processing routine.
Static route deleted	Delete the route from the list of static routes.
	Delete the route from the routing table and request the backup from all route sources.
	Schedule static-route processing routine (only if IOS 12.0).
Dynamic route added	Pass the route for installation in the routing table.
Dynamic route deleted	Delete the route from the routing table and request the backup from all route sources.
clear ip route *NetAddr* entered	Find the route best matching **NetAddr**.
	Remove the route; request the route to the same address range from all route sources.
clear ip route * entered	Clear the routing table.
	Process connected and static routes.
	Send "initialization" messages to every routing protocol.
	Recalculate the default.
Every minute	Check routes in the routing table.
	Process static routes.
	Select the default.

looks up an appropriate route in the routing table. In Cisco IOS, all route sources, including static and dynamic routing protocols, can install multiple routes with the same metric to a destination network. IGRP and EIGRP can install routes with different metrics, thus making it possible for the forwarding engine to split traffic among multiple path descriptors in accordance with the metrics (discussed in Chapter 5). In RFC 2328, the OSPF specification, Section 11.1 is dedicated to routing table lookup, but this does not make an OSPF process in a router perform the functions of the forwarding engine. The purpose of Section 11.1 is to instruct the protocol implementers how the routing information that OSPF provides to the routing table should be used properly to achieve correct routing in a classless environment.

Q: **How do an address mask, a route mask, and a subnet mask differ?**

A: An address mask is the mask specified in addition to the IP address when configuring interfaces of hosts and routers. An address mask can be equal to or longer than the default classful mask. When it is longer—contains more bits set to 1—than the default classful mask, an address mask becomes a subnet mask. A route mask is the address mask used for the routes in the routing table. A route mask can be a default classful mask, a subnet mask, or a supernet mask—when the mask is shorter than the default classful mask. Different route sources find the route masks by using different methods. For example, the Connected route source installs interface routes, using the address mask on the interface as the route mask. The route mask for static routes is configured manually by the administrator. The route mask for the dynamic routes is either taken directly from the routing update—classless routing protocols—or is assigned the value of the address mask configured on the interface on which the update is received—classful routing protocols—as described in the chapters on specific routing protocols.

Q: **Cisco routers provide an alternative to secondary addresses in IPX (Internet Packet Exchange) networks on Ethernet links: subinterfaces. Why can't I use this feature for IP?**

A: The nature of secondary addresses is different for IP and IPX. Primary and secondary networks in IPX use different encapsulation types; in IP, all attached networks—primary and secondary—are accessible via one type of encapsulation (Ethernet II). When subinterfaces are configured for an IPX-enabled Ethernet interface, different types of encapsulation are used for different subinterfaces—for example, Ethernet II for the first subinterface, IEEE 802.2 for the second, and so on—thus reflecting the ability of the data link layer to distinguish different types of data flows. Because Cisco routers support only one type of IP encapsulation on Ethernet interfaces, subinterfaces are not an option.

Q: **Why is no route to the peer router installed when Cisco HDLC is used on a serial interface, but with PPP it is?**

A: Unlike PPP, the Cisco HDLC protocol does not perform any negotiation when the link is going up. Cisco HDLC specification includes the rules of packet framing and keep-alive packet exchange but does not specify a method for the peers to exchange information. Therefore, a router has no way of knowing the IP address of its peer.

Q: **When I configure a dynamic routing protocol—for example, IGRP—on a router connected to major network X, should I include a "network" statement for major network Y if I want to have routes to it in my routing table?**

A: You must include a "network" statement for major network Y only if your router has active attachments to it or one of its subnets. If your router is not connected to this major network, you must not configure this command for network Y. Information about network Y will be sent by the routers connected to it.

Q: **Why is Cisco IOS routing information split into two separate structures—prefix descriptors and path descriptors?**

A: This makes support of parallel routes algorithmically easier; the route lookup function finds the best-matching prefix descriptor and selects the path descriptor to use for forwarding the given packet, taking into consideration traffic-sharing parameters (details appear in Chapter 5).

Q: **If every interface and subinterface has a corresponding interface descriptor in a Cisco router, is the number of interface descriptors limited, and how many interfaces and subinterfaces in total can I have in one router?**

A: The number of interface descriptors is limited in Cisco IOS. In IOS versions 11.3 and earlier, the maximum number of interface descriptors is 300 unless you use an ISP (Internet service provider)-specific 11.1CC or 11.1CA IOS train. In version 12.0, the number of interface descriptors is platform specific. For most models, it is still 300; for Cisco 3600 series, 800; for Cisco AS5300, 700; for Cisco AS5800 and Cisco 7200, 3,000. For RSP-based models (Cisco 7000, 7500), 1,000. In IOS version 12.0, you can use a hidden **show idb** command to see how many interface descriptors are allocated and what they are used for.

Q: **What is the maximum size of the routing table in Cisco IOS?**

A: The size of the routing table in Cisco IOS is limited only by the amount of available RAM.

Q: **In which level of the routing table is the 0.0.0.0/0 route placed?**

A: The 0.0.0.0/0 route is always placed in the supernet route list, so it appears after major networks in the output of the **show ip route** command.

Q: **When different subnet masks are used in one major network, the routing table contains an explicit note about it. Does the note mean that the router changes its operation when VLSM is used?**

A: The behavior of the forwarding engine basically remains unchanged. The only difference is in the route lookup function; when all subnet masks are the same, the "first match" subnet lookup is used, whereas with VLSM, the "best match" strategy is used. You should be aware that classful routing protocols cannot work in a VLSM environment. Information about subnets with one subnet mask will not be sent over interfaces configured with another subnet mask. To achieve full connectivity, you should use classless routing protocols.

Q: **Is it possible to have parallel routes coming from different route sources?**

A: No, parallel routes must have the same (best) metric, or, in the case of IGRP and EIGRP, the metric must be not worse than the best metric multiplied by the variance parameter. Because different route sources have different metric scales and meaning, one destination network may be covered by routes from a single route source only. Furthermore, by default, all route sources have different values of the administrative distance, so routes with better AD value will replace routes to the same destination with worse AD. Therefore, metrics of the routes originated by different sources will not normally be compared. However, even if two routes have the same metric and the same AD value but are sourced by different protocol descriptors, they will not be installed together. The new route will override the route in the routing table in this case.

Q: **I heard that static routes configured via next hops are by default assigned an AD of 1, whereas the static routes configured via interfaces are assigned an AD of 0 because they are considered directly connected routes. Is that true?**

A: That is not true and, in fact, is a common misunderstanding. All static routes, no matter what routing information they contain, are assigned an AD of 1 by default. Moreover, no route source except Connected can supply routes with an AD of 0 to the routing table. In fact, static routes configured over interfaces only—no intermediate network addresses—are considered directly connected, but this doesn't make them interface routes.

Q: **When do I want to assign an AD of 255 (nontrusted) to a route source?**

A: You would typically want to assign this value to a route or a whole route source if you don't want some routes to appear in the routing table. For example, your router is running RIP and you don't want to install routes announced by a specific host. You assign all routes coming from the nontrusted host an AD of 255, thus effectively filtering them out. (Details of configuration will be given in later chapters.)

Q: **In the pseudocode of the `PathValid()` function, why is the classful lookup used for intermediate address resolution?**

A: If the function used the classless lookup function and the routing table contained a default route, any intermediate address would always be resolvable. Consequently, the route would never be deleted from the routing table.

Chapter Five

Packet Forwarding

This chapter presents the process of packet forwarding in Cisco routers. The chapter provides information on IP input packet processing, IP packet forwarding, and IP packet delivery, including the details of normal destination-based routing, policy routing, access control lists, and other techniques used in Cisco IOS.

5.1 Overview of IP Forwarding

Let's first go through a brief overview of the forwarding process to understand the path taken by transit IP packets inside a router. As in any generic router, packets processed by Cisco IOS go from the physical layer up to the network layer, where the forwarding decision is made, and then back to the physical layer of the output interface, as shown in Figure 5-1.

Packet forwarding includes the following key actions:

- Data link layer frame validation: basic frame length and FCS verification, as well as the frame sanity checks

- Network-layer protocol demultiplexing: determination of the upper protocol that needs to receive encapsulated data and queuing the frame contents for it

- IP packet validation: basic IP header verification

- Local or remote delivery decision: determining whether the packet should be forwarded or received by the router itself

- Forwarding decision: routing table lookup

- Data link parameter mapping: determination of data link parameters, based on the outbound interface and the next-hop address

- Data link frame construction: packet encapsulation

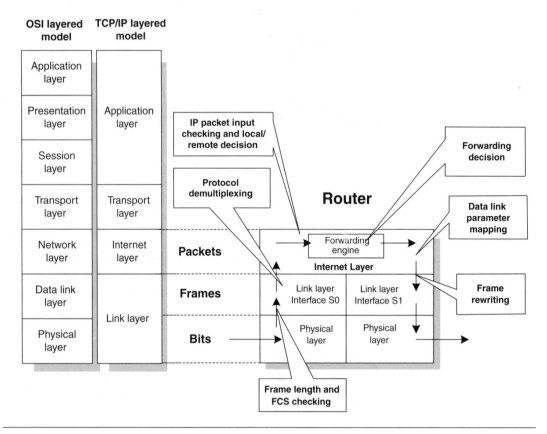

Figure 5-1. *Routing operation*

These actions are carried out in different parts of the hardware and software of a Cisco router. Figure 5-2 shows how the various components of Cisco routers cooperate while packets are being forwarded.

When it receives a frame from the media, an *input/output controller* (I/O controller) puts the received frame into its receive (RX) ring to be able to start receiving the next frame and sends an *interrupt request* (IRQ) to the CPU. The interrupt-handling routine, which is part of the Cisco IOS kernel, takes care of the frame by taking the buffer out of the controller's RX ring, performing basic packet verification, and placing it in the software *IP processing queue*. Further packet processing is done by a scheduled *IP switching process*.

The details of memory and buffer management vary by platform. For example, in the Cisco 2500 series, all frames are stored in shared memory (SRAM), which is accessible by the CPU and I/O controllers, and no copy of the frame is made. In the Cisco 7500 series, when it needs to be processed by the route switch processor (RSP), a packet is moved from packet memory into main memory.

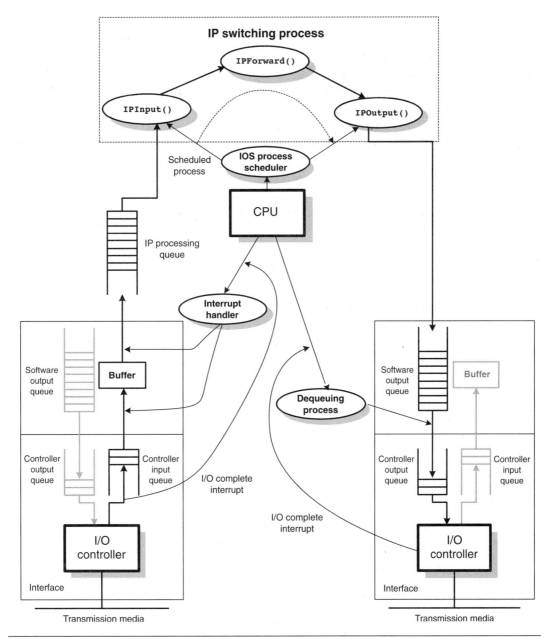

Figure 5-2. *Packet flows in Cisco routers*

A quite interesting fact is that even though the output of the **show interface** command includes the term "input queue" (see Listing 5-1), no per interface queue or *first-in-first-out* (FIFO) structure is maintained for the incoming packets. Instead, on all interfaces, arriving packets are put on protocol-specific processing queues, such as the IP processing queue, the IPX processing queue, and so on. However, each interface is limited in the number of packets it can hold on the queue simultaneously. The counter is incremented every time a buffer is placed in a packet-processing queue and decreased when the router is finished processing the corresponding packet; that is, the buffer has been assigned to an interface's output queue or passed to another process when local delivery is in effect. So, the momentary value of the input queue's depth and its limit as shown in the output of the **show interface** command are just the current number of buffers that the interface has put on the common queues and the maximum number of buffers that it can potentially put there.

If the number of packets that an interface has put on the processing queues reaches the limit, the router starts dropping packets arriving on that interface: The drop counter will increase. This usually indicates a performance problem on platforms with centralized architecture—all tasks, including packet forwarding, are performed by a single CPU—when the CPU does not have enough cycles to handle the packets. When an interface starts dropping packets, the router throttles the interface—stops listening to the incoming packets—for one second as a protective measure.

```
R1>show int e0
Ethernet0 is up, line protocol is up
  Hardware is Lance, address is 00e0.1e68.9fa0 (bia 00e0.1e68.9fa0)
  Internet address is 1.1.1.1/24
  MTU 1500 bytes, BW 10000 Kbit, DLY 1000 usec, rely 255/255, load 1/255
  Encapsulation ARPA, loopback not set, keepalive set (10 sec)
  ARP type: ARPA, ARP Timeout 04:00:00
  Last input 00:00:00, output 00:00:00, output hang never
  Last clearing of "show interface" counters never
  Queueing strategy: fifo
  Output queue 0/40, 0 drops; input queue 0/75, 0 drops
  5 minute input rate 0 bits/sec, 1 packets/sec
  5 minute output rate 9000 bits/sec, 2 packets/sec
     170112 packets input, 12232047 bytes, 0 no buffer
     Received 164913 broadcasts, 0 runts, 0 giants, 0 throttles
     0 input errors, 0 CRC, 0 frame, 0 overrun, 0 ignored, 0 abort
     0 input packets with dribble condition detected
     201623 packets output, 115300507 bytes, 0 underruns
     0 output errors, 0 collisions, 7 interface resets
     0 babbles, 0 late collision, 8 deferred
     0 lost carrier, 0 no carrier
     0 output buffer failures, 0 output buffers swapped out
R1>
```

Listing 5-1. *The* **show interface** *command output*

This type of forwarding, when the interrupt handler just stores the packets for the forwarding process, is called *process switching*. Other types of packet forwarding used in Cisco routers are discussed later in this chapter.

After the IP switching process has looked through the routing table, determined the output interface for the packet, and found the data link parameters—MAC address or DLCI, for example—it changes the frame and checks the *interface output queue*. If the interface queue is empty and the controller's transmit (TX) ring has some free space, the buffer is submitted directly to the controller; otherwise, it is enqueued into the interface output queue.

Cisco routers do not discard the frame the packet is received in; instead, this information is kept along with the packet in the buffer, as the router needs the data link information at every step of processing. The packets are really decapsulated only when they are locally delivered—destined for the router itself—and the application does not need the data link information, as when the packet is part of a TCP segment.

Although the IP processing queue works in simple FIFO mode, the router can use more advanced methods for output queuing, such as *weighted fair queuing* (WFQ), *custom queuing* (CQ), or *priority queuing* (PQ). This is why the output queues are handled by specific routines, which are given the control on an "I/O completion" interrupt and scheduled by the IOS kernel. This dequeuing process analyzes the interface's output queue according to the queuing policy, identifies the frames containing the packets to be sent first, and moves them to the controller's TX ring. In some cases, when the output interface uses a nontrivial type of encapsulation, such as X.25, the frames can be processed more after dequeuing from the interface output queue and before being submitted to the controller's queue.

Because this book is not dedicated to the techniques of queuing and quality of service (QOS), it does not cover the methods of configuring various queuing mechanisms here. For more information on this subject, refer to [Vegesna].

5.2 Packet Input

When traversing networks, IP packets are not transmitted as is. Instead, they are always encapsulated into some type of frame, depending on the encapsulation method used on corresponding links. On Ethernet media, for example, IP packets are carried in Ethernet II or IEEE 802.3 frames; on Token Ring segments, packets are encapsulated in IEEE 802.5 frames with 802.2 headers. On WAN links, packets are wrapped in frames of a particular WAN protocol, such as PPP, Frame Relay, or Cisco-proprietary HDLC. Figure 5-3 illustrates how IP packets are encapsulated into Ethernet II and PPP frames.

When a router's interface receives a frame, the controller first checks it for validity, looking at the frame's length, calculating and verifying the *frame check sequence* (FCS),

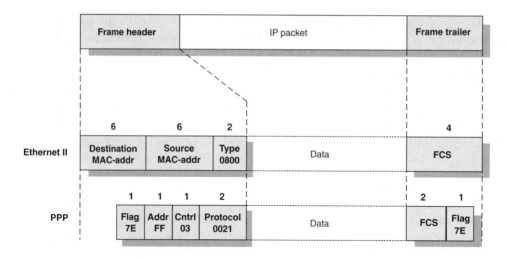

Figure 5-3. *Packet encapsulation*

and so on. If the frame is valid and the packet has been received on a LAN interface, on which all stations receive a frame while it's being sent, the controller determines whether the frame was destined for the router by analyzing the destination MAC address. If the destination MAC address is not the active MAC address of the controller and is not a broadcast address (all Fs) and also is not the address of a multicast group the router currently participates in, the frame is ignored. In point-to-point WAN protocols that don't use the address field—the destination MAC address always contains the same value—this check is not performed. In point-to-multipoint protocols, such as X.25, Frame Relay, and asynchronous transfer mode (ATM), the virtual-connection validity check is performed to verify whether the referenced connection exists.

After finishing the frame examination, the controller hands the frame to the interrupt handler, as described in the previous section. The interrupt handler routine takes the buffer with the frame from the controller's RX ring and determines the network-layer protocol—IP, IPX, or AppleTalk—by looking at the Protocol field of the frame. Every type of encapsulation has its own values for network protocols. For example, the IP identifier for Ethernet v2 is the hexadecimal value 0800; for PPP, it is 0021. After the protocol type is determined, the pointer to the packet buffer is inserted into the corresponding protocol processing queue, which from here on we assume is IP. Note that this is when the interface's input queue counter is incremented. At this point, the interrupt handler returns control to the operating system, and all further processing is done by the IP switching process. The following parameters are associated with each queued packet:

■   Length of the frame's data field, that is, the length of the data being passed to the network layer.

- Identifier of the interface from which the packet or, initially, the frame was received, that is, a pointer to the corresponding interface descriptor.

- Type of the link-layer destination address: unicast, multicast, or broadcast. (For some link-layer protocols, only the unicast value is available, as in PPP or X.25.)

When CPU control is passed to the IP switching process, this process dequeues the packets from the IP processing queue and passes them for processing to the IpInput() function (see Listing 5-2).

```
void IpInput(TMemBuf * TheBuf)
{
  TIPheader * Header = (TIPheader *) TheBuf->Packet;

  if (!IpSanityCheck(TheBuf)) return;

  if (!CheckInpACL(TheBuf->RcvInt, TheBuf)) return;

  if (!CheckRPF(TheBuf->RcvInt, TheBuf)) return;

  if (IpForUs(TheBuf->Packet)) {
     IpLocal(TheBuf);
     return;
  }

  if (flags & IP_FORWARDING)
      IpForward(TheBuf);
  else DropPacket(TheBuf);
}
```

Listing 5-2. *Pseudocode:* IpInput() *function*

The first step this function takes is packet validation. The IP verification process includes the following checks, described in [RFC1812].

- The total data length passed by the link layer must not be less than the minimum legal length of an IP packet; that is, it must be greater than or equal to 20 bytes.

- The IP packet checksum must be calculated and compared to the value of the corresponding field in the header.

- The IP version field in the header is checked. The current IP version is 4, so if this value is not 4, the packet is dropped.

- The value of the IP header length field is checked. It must be at least 5, as the minimum length of the IP header is 20 bytes and the value of this field is treated as the number of 32-bit (4-byte) words.

- The value of the IP total length field is checked. It must not be less than the length of the packet's header; that is, it must be greater than 4 multiplied by the IP header length. The multiplier with the value 4 is used because the total IP packet length is measured in bytes, whereas the header length is measured in 4-byte words.

If any of these conditions is not met, the packet is silently discarded, or ignored without sending any notification to the packet originator. Otherwise, if the inbound interface is configured with an inbound *access control list* (ACL), the packet is checked against it. ACLs are a means of traffic filtration and can be used as both input and output on a per interface basis. Because the output interface is not known until the forwarding decision is made, the IpInput() function checks only the inbound ACL.

Listing 5-3 gives you an example of an access list configuration. This access list permits only incoming TELNET and FTP (File Transfer Protocol) connections on interface Serial0.

```
interface serial0
 ip access-group 101 in
 !
access-list 101 permit tcp any any eq 23
access-list 101 permit tcp ant any eq 20
access-list 101 permit tcp ant any eq 21
```

Listing 5-3. *ACL configuration example*

Listing 5-4 shows the pseudocode of functions CheckInpACL() and CheckACL(), which process the received packet against an access list.

```
int CheckACL(TIPacl * TheACL, TMemBuf * TheBuf)
{
 TIPheader    * Header = (TIPheader *) TheBuf->Packet;

 if (TheACL == NULL) return 1;

 if (IPdeniedByACL(TheACL, TheBuf)){
     SendICMP(Header->SourceAddr, ICMP_UNREACHABLE, ICMP_CODE_ADMIN);
     DropPacket(TheBuf);
     return 0;
 }
 return 1;
}

int CheckInpACL(TInterfaceDescr * TheInt, TMemBuf * TheBuf)
{
```

```
if (TheInt->IpInpACL == 0) return 1;

return CheckACL(FindACL(TheInt->IpInpACL), TheBuf);
}
```

Listing 5-4. *Pseudocode: ACL checking functions*

The interface descriptor of the input interface contains the identifiers of ACL structures for both input and output. If the IpInpACL field is 0—the input access list was not specified for the given interface—CheckInpACL() returns 1, meaning that the packet can be further processed. If the ACL identifier is nonzero, the CheckInpACL() function finds the pointer to the ACL record and passes it as a parameter for CheckACL(). If the ACL with the specified ID cannot be found, indicated by a NULL pointer returned from FindACL(), the CheckACL() function returns 1 as if no access list were on the interface. Otherwise, the packet is compared against the access list records by the IPdeniedByACL() function, which returns 1 if the packet should be denied and 0 if the packet can be further processed. When input ACLs are being considered, packet-processing permission is equal to permission to route or locally deliver the packet.

> In Cisco IOS, if no line of an access list matches the packet, the packet is denied; that is, each access list contains an implicit **deny-any** line at the end. Consequently, the default logic of an access list is to permit something and deny everything else. To invert the logic, the access list must be configured with an explicit **permit-any** command as the last line.

If a packet is not allowed by the access list, the router sends an ICMP "Destination Unreachable" message with the code value set to Administratively Prohibited to the packet source.

> The ICMP "Destination Unreachable" message will not be sent out of the input interface if it is configured with a **no ip unreachable** interface command. In addition, the rate at which the router generates these ICMP messages is limited to two packets per second, by default. The rate-limiting parameters can be adjusted by using the **ip icmp rate-limit unreachable** global configuration command.

Next, the router checks whether it is configured to perform unicast RPF verification for the incoming interface, using the **ip verify unicast reverse-path interface** command. If it is, the router performs routing table lookup for the *source* IP address in the packet and checks whether it is resolvable through the interface on which the packet has been received. If the result of this comparison is negative, the packet is silently ignored by the router.

The unicast RPF (Reverse Path Forwarding) verification is usually enabled by ISPs as a measure against packet-spoofing attacks. Note that this check may cause valid packets to be dropped if routing in the network is asymmetric, that is, if the route from network A to network B is not topologically identical to the route from network B to network A.

If the packet passes all the checks, its destination IP address is examined by the IpForUs() function. The router determines whether the packet should be forwarded by calling IpForward() or whether it is for the router itself and hence must be queued for local processing. This decision is made by comparing the destination address with that of every IP-enabled interface of the router running IP and with the addresses of IP multicast groups the router has joined.

5.3 Forwarding Engine

The next step in packet processing is routing table lookup. The purpose of this operation is to find the route along which the packet must be forwarded. Having found a route, the router identifies the two parameters that determine the path of the packet through the network: the output interface and the address of the next-hop node.

The pseudocode in Listing 5-5 represents the algorithm performed by the forwarding engine. Note that the code incorporates policy routing functions.

```
void IpForward(TMemBuf * TheBuf)
{
  TIPheader    * Header = (TIPheader *)TheBuf->Packet;
  TPrefixDescr * Route;
  TPathDescr   * Path;
  TIPAddress     PrevHop, NextHop, DefNextHop;
  TInterfaceDescr  * Interface, * DefInterface;


  if (—Header->TTL == 0){
     if (Header->FragOffs == 0)
        SendICMP(Header->SourceAddr, ICMP_TTL, 0);
     DropPacket(TheBuf);
  }

  PrevHop    = NextHop = Header->DestAddr;
  Interface  = DefInterface = NULL;
  DefNextHop = 0;

  if (TheBuf->RcvInt->IPFlags & IF_IP_POLICY_ROUTING)
     IpPolicyRoute(TheBuf, &Interface, &NextHop,
                   &DefInterface, &DefNextHop);
```

```
if (Interface==NULL){

    IpRTLookup(&NextHop, &Interface, &PrevHop);

    /* If we didn't succeed in normal routing, we try
     * Default next-hop and interface from policy routing
     * if they are set.
     */

    if ((Interface==NULL) && DefNextHop) {

        PrevHop = NextHop = DefNextHop;
        IpRTLookup(&NextHop, &Interface, &PrevHop);
    }

    if ((Interface==NULL) && DefInterface) {

        Interface = DefInterface;
        PrevHop   = NextHop = Header->DestAddr;
    }
}

if (Interface == NULL){
    if (Header->FragOffs == 0)
        SendICMP(Header->SourceAddr, ICMP_UNREACHABLE, ICMP_CODE_HOST);
    DropPacket(TheBuf);
    return;
}

if (!CheckOutACL(Interface, TheBuf)) return;

if (NextHop == 0){ //It's a directly connected route
    if (PrevHop != Route->Network)
        NextHop = PrevHop;
    else NextHop = Header->DestAddr;
}

if ((TheBuf->RcvInt == Interface)&&
    ((Header->SourceAddr && Interface->Mask)==
     (Interface->Addr && Interface->Mask)) &&
    (Header->FragOffs == 0) &&
    (Interface->IPFlags & IF_IP_ICMP_REDIRECT))
    SendICMPredirect(TheBuf, NextHop);

if (Interface->Flags & IF_DIALER){
    DialerProcess(TheBuf, Interface, NextHop);
    return;
}

IpOutput(TheBuf, Interface, NextHop);
}
```

Listing 5-5. *Pseudocode:* `IpForward()` *function*

The function processes the packet as follows.

1. The TTL field in the header is decremented and checked to see whether the packet must be dropped. If TTL becomes 0, the function sends an ICMP "Time Exceeded" message and discards the packet. This check is done before all others because there's no need to spend any time on the packet if it is going to be discarded.

2. If the packet's TTL is okay and policy routing has been configured on the interface, the function calls the policy routing engine, function `IpPolicyRoute()`, which can potentially set the output interface, next-hop address, default interface, and default next-hop address, based on the routing policy configured by the administrator. (Policy routing is described in more detail in Section 5.3.2.)

3. If the policy routing engine does not set the output interface, normal routing is performed by calling the `IpRTLookup()` function, which finds the interface and the next-hop address by recursive lookup through the routing table (considered later).

4. If normal routing does not succeed—no route is found—the function checks the default interface and default next-hop values that the policy routing engine may have set. Note that these default values are considered only when normal routing fails.

It doesn't matter what kind of routing—policy or normal—succeeds; the main goal is to finally determine the output interface over which the packet will be forwarded.

5. If the interface cannot be found—there's no route to be used—the function drops the packet and sends an ICMP "Destination Unreachable" message with Host Unreachable code to the source.

6. If the output interface is found, the packet is checked against the outbound ACL by calling the `CheckOutACL()` function, which is analogous to `CheckInACL()`.

7. If the packet is not denied by the ACL, the function checks whether the next-hop address is known.

8. If the address is not known—no intermediate address in the path was found during the routing table lookup—the function sets it to either the destination IP address in the packet's header or the value of the intermediate network address of the route, considered just before the final route. The last option is used when the route matching the packet's destination address—let's call it Rte1—does not reference an interface in the currently active path and the intermediate network address must be resolved over another route, which we'll call Rte2. In this case, the intermediate address in Rte2's path can, in turn, be set to 0 (unspecified),

and the router should use the intermediate address of Rte1's path as the next-hop address.

9. When both the output interface and the next-hop address are determined, the function checks whether the packet is going to be sent over the same interface on which it was received. If it is and the source IP address belongs to an address space assigned to the interface—the originating host is directly accessible—the router sends an ICMP "Redirect" message, saying that the destination may be reached via a closer router on the same media. Note that the packet is not dropped in this situation but is still forwarded to the other router or host.

10. Now the function verifies whether the dialer is enabled on the interface. (The dialer is enabled by default on ISDN interfaces and can be manually enabled on serial interfaces by using the **dialer in-band** interface command.) If the dialer is enabled, the packet is submitted to the dialer process, which is supposed to establish a dial-up connection if necessary and call the IpOutput() function itself. If the dialer is not active on the output interface, the forwarding procedure calls the IpOutput() function directly, with the output interface and the address of the next-hop passed as arguments.

5.3.1 Route Lookup

Let's take a closer look at some functions called from IpForward(). The first one is IpRTLookup(), which finds a route for the packet's destination address. The pseudocode of the function is presented in Listing 5-6.

```
void IpRTLookup(TIPAddress * NextHop, TInterfaceDescr ** Interface,
                TIPAddress * PrevHop)
{
 TPrefixDescr * Route, * FirstRoute;
 TPathDescr    * Path;

    // The first lookup considering the IPClassless
    FirstRoute = Route = LookUp(*NextHop, flags & IP_CLASSLESS);

    if (Route) GetNextHop(Route, Interface, NextHop);

    //On error--Int = NULL, NextHop = 0;

    // If route is not Connected — recursive classful lookup

    for(;Route && (*NextHop) && (!(*Interface));){

        *PrevHop = *NextHop;
        Route = LookUp(*NextHop, 0);
        if (Route) {
```

```
        if (Route==FirstRoute){ //recursion error
            *Interface = NULL;
            return;
        }
        GetNextHop(Route, Interface, NextHop);
    }
  }
}
```

Listing 5-6. *Pseudocode:* `IpRTLookup()` *function*

The function uses the `NextHop` argument as a parameter and returns three values: the final next-hop IP address, the output interface, and the next-hop address of the previous route.

The `NextHop` argument is supposed to be initially set to the destination address of the packet being forwarded: the `NextHop` variable in the `IpForward()` function. The function will change the value of this variable while performing the recursive route lookup in the "for" cycle. At the beginning of each step of the recursive routing table lookup, the value of the current next-hop address is saved in the `PrevHop` variable in order to save the intermediate network address of the route considered in the previous iteration. The algorithm implemented in the `IpRTLookup()` function is as follows.

1. Find a route matching the packet's destination address.

2. If the route's active path contains a reference to an interface, the algorithm stops.

3. Otherwise, consider the active path's intermediate address as the next-hop address for the next routing table lookup iteration, and return to step 1.

Note that the `IP_CLASSLESS` flag, indicating the state of the **ip classless** command, is passed to the `LookUp()` function only when finding the first matching route. All recursive route lookups are performed in classful mode; otherwise, presence of a default route in the routing table would lead to resolvability of any—even an invalid—intermediate address of any path. The function also includes checking against recursive loops. The route found by the first lookup operation is saved in the `FirstRoute` variable. If the Route variable gets the same value as `FirstRoute` in any recursive lookup iteration, a loop is detected, and the function returns `NULL` in the `Interface` parameter, indicating that no route was found.

The route lookup operation, as a means of finding a proper prefix descriptor, is decoupled from the path lookup, which is used to find the output interface and the next-hop address. Corresponding functions—`LookUp()` and `GetNextHop()`—are considered later. The pseudocode of the `LookUp()` function is depicted in Listing 5-7.

```
TPrefixDescr * LookUp(TIPAddress Addr, int IPClassless)
{
 TPrefixDescr * Route;

 Route = NetLookup(Addr);
 if (Route){
     if (Rroute->Ultimate) return Route;
     Route = SubnetLookup(Route, Addr);    //look through subnets
     if (Rroute || (!IPClassless)) return Route;
 }
 Route = SupernetLookup(Addr);
 if ((!Route) ||
     ((Route->Network == 0) &&
     (Route->Mask == 0) && TheRoutingTable.Default))
     Route = TheRoutingTable.Default; //NULL if no default
 return Route;
}
```

Listing 5-7. *Pseudocode:* LookUp() *function*

The LookUp() function is given two arguments: the IP address for which a route must be found and the flag specifying which kind of lookup operation should be performed: classless or classful.

The function starts with finding a network route, ultimate or parent, that matches the address passed as an argument. If a matching network route is found and is ultimate—there are no more specific matching routes—this route is returned as the result. If the network route is a parent, the subnet routes are looked through to find the best-matching one. If a matching subnet route is found, it is returned; otherwise, the code checks the mode of operation. If classful IP routing is active, the function returns NULL; in classless mode, the function proceeds to supernets and default routes.

> When the **ip classless** command is inactive on the router—classful routing is in effect—the routing table lookup function does not consider supernet and default routes once it has determined that there is a parent network route for the destination major network, meaning that the router knows about at least one subnet of the destination major network. Only children routes are considered. The router considers supernets and the default route only if there's no matching route in the major network route list.

> When **ip classless** is enabled, the code finds the best-matching route among subnet, network, and supernet routes or takes the default if no matching route is found.

If no matching route is found or if the matching route describes the pseudonetwork 0.0.0.0/0, used by protocols other than IGRP to describe the default route, the code returns the actual default route, which is not necessarily a 0.0.0.0/0 route. If a 0.0.0.0/0 route is present in the routing table but the actual default is different, the 0.0.0.0/0 route is not considered matching; otherwise, it would match every address, and any manipulations with default candidates would be meaningless. For example, an RIP-learned default route would always be taken even if the actual default had a better administrative distance. The 0.0.0.0/0 route is automatically marked as a candidate default, but it may or may not be used for default routing, depending on whether it is selected as the actual default.

When a route is found and returned to the `IpRTLookup()` function, the latter calls the `GetNextHop()` function, which looks through the paths linked to the route's prefix descriptor and finds the output interface and the next-hop address. In the pseudocode of the `GetNextHop()` function given in Listing 5-8, the function first checks the flags of the prefix descriptor. If the prefix descriptor is in the hold-down or the garbage state—because RIP or IGRP has lost its last route to the network—and has no paths linked to it, the function sets the output interface and the next-hop address to the interface and address from which the update was received last.

```
void GetNextHop(TPrefixDescr * Route, TInterfaceDescr ** Interface,
                TIPAddress * NextHop)
{
 TPathDescr * Path = (TPathDescr*)Route->ActivePath;
 TPathDescr * ActivePath = Path;

 if (Route->Flags & (ROUTE_HOLDDOWN + ROUTE_GARBAGE)){
    *Interface = Route->LastUpdInt;
    *NextHop   = Route->LastUpdAddr;
    return;
 }

 if (—Path->ShareValue == 0){
    Path->ShareValue = Path->ShareCount;
    for(;Path->Next != Route->ActivePath;){
        if (Path->Next == NULL) Path = (TPathDescr*) Route->Pointer;
        if (Path->ShareCount){ //we can have it 0 with [E]IGRP
           if (Path->Interface == NULL) break;
           if ((Path->Interface->Flags & IF_STATE_UP)&&
               (Path->Interface->Flags & IF_IP_ENABLED))
              break;
        }
    }
    Route->ActivePath = Path;
 }
 *Interface = ActivePath->Interface;
```

```
*NextHop    = ActivePath->Intermediate;
 return;
}
```

Listing 5-8. *Pseudocode:* `GetNextHop()` *function*

If the prefix descriptor is normal, the code selects the path, trying to balance the load among multiple paths if more than one is available. The amount of traffic each path accepts is determined by the `ShareCount` field. After the current path is used `ShareCount` times to route packets, the next path in the list becomes active, accepting the next portion of traffic. Note that the `ShareCount` value is set by the route source and in most cases is equal to 1 for all paths. Routes learned via IGRP and EIGRP are an exception if the variance parameter is greater than 1. (See Chapters 8 and 10 for more information on IGRP and EIGRP.) In this case, the two protocols are allowed to install parallel routes (multiple paths) with unequal metrics. The `ShareCount` field of each path is assigned a value in inverse proportion to the value of metric in this case; the better the metric, the more the `ShareCount` value, and consequently the more traffic is forwarded via the path.

The `GetNextHop()` function implements the described algorithm by managing the `ShareValue` field in each path and the `ActivePath` field in the prefix descriptor. The `ShareValue` field is assigned the value of `ShareCount` during path installation and is decreased each time the path is used. When `ShareValue` reaches 0, it is reinitialized with the `ShareCount` value, and the `ActivePath` field of the prefix descriptor is set to the address of the next path in the list.

5.3.2 Policy Routing

As shown in the pseudocode of the `IpForward()` function (Listing 5-5), Cisco routers can be configured to perform so-called *policy routing*. Policy routing is a technique that allows the administrator to instruct the router to forward packets according to a configured policy rather than according to the contents of the routing table and the packet's destination address. This gives the administrator more control on the paths of the traffic flows.

When policy routing is configured, the packets can be sent to a specific interface or next-hop address, based on the following conditions:

- Input interface: the interface from which the packet was received
- Conformance to an access list, which in turn can analyze a wide range of network-, transport-, and application-layer parameters: source and destination addresses, TOS (Type of Service) and IP precedence values, transport protocol, application port, and so on
- Packet length

Policy routing is configured by using *route maps,* or sequential configuration structures, each having a number of **match** and **set** clauses considered by the router one by one. Match clauses are used to identify the packets, using the conditions in the preceding list. Set clauses are used to specify how the packet must be forwarded. The following parameters can be set for each packet to influence the behavior of the forwarding engine:

- Output interface: an interface on which the packet must be sent
- Next-hop address: an address that must be used by the forwarding engine instead of the packet's destination address to perform routing table lookup
- Default next-hop address: an address that must be used by the forwarding engine if normal destination-based routing fails to find a route
- Default output interface: an interface that should be used to send the packet if normal routing fails
- IP TOS and Precedence values in the packet's header

An example of a route map is given in Listing 5-9.

```
interface ethernet 0
 ip address 150.50.55.1 255.255.255.0
 ip policy route-map Policy
!
route-map Policy 10
 match ip address 101
 set ip next-hop 10.1.1.2
!
route-map Policy 20
 match ip address 102
 set ip next-hop 10.1.2.2
!
access-list 101 permit ip 150.10.1.0 0.0.0.255 any
access-list 102 permit ip 150.20.1.0 0.0.0.255 any
```

Listing 5-9. *Example of policy routing configuration*

Note the two route map structures with the same name but different sequence numbers. The router processes the packets against the route maps according to the sequence numbers in the route map statements. The first route map's **match** statement refers to access list 101, which permits the packets coming from subnet 150.10.1.0/24. The **set** clause specifies the next-hop address—10.1.1.2, which is the address of another router. The route map entry number 20 directs all packets originated by hosts on subnet 150.20.1.0/24 to router 10.1.2.2. This example demonstrates how routing based on source address can be achieved with policy routing.

Policy route maps can be applied to incoming and locally originated traffic. For incoming traffic, an interface command, **ip policy route-map**, must be configured as shown in Listing 5-9. The code checks all traffic coming through the interface against the route map and tries to perform policy routing. If policy routing fails, normal forwarding is used. If it is necessary to perform policy routing on locally originated traffic, such as outgoing TELNET sessions, the administrator can configure the **ip local policy route-map** global configuration command, as shown in Listing 5-10.

```
! send outgoing telnet packets according to my policy
ip local policy route-map LocalPolicy
!
route-map LocalPolicy 10
 match ip address 101
 set interface Serial 0
!
access-list 101 permit tcp any any eq telnet
```

Listing 5-10. *Policy routing on locally originated traffic*

To understand how policy routing cooperates with a normal forwarding session, look at the partial pseudocode of the `IpForward()` function in Listing 5-11.

```
void IpForward(TMemBuf * TheBuf)
{

  //... skipped code here! ...

  PrevHop   = NextHop = Header->DestAddr;
  Interface = DefInterface = NULL;
  DefNextHop = 0;

  if (TheBuf->RcvInt->IPFlags & IF_IP_POLICY_ROUTING)
      IpPolicyRoute(TheBuf, &Interface, &NextHop,
                    &DefInterface, &DefNextHop);

  if (Interface==NULL){

    IpRTLookup(&NextHop, &Interface, &PrevHop);

    /* If we didn't succeed in normal routing, we try
     * Default next-hop and interface from policy routing
     * if they are set.
     */

    if ((Interface==NULL) && DefNextHop) {
       PrevHop = NextHop = DefNextHop;
```

```
        IpRTLookup(&NextHop, &Interface, &PrevHop);
    }

    if ((Interface==NULL) && DefInterface) {
       Interface = DefInterface;
       PrevHop   = NextHop = Header->DestAddr;
    }
 }

// ... skipped code here! ...
```

Listing 5-11. *Pseudocode: Part of* `IpForward()` *function relevant to policy routing*

If the interface on which the packet has been received is configured with a policy route map, the code lets the `IpPolicyRoute()` function set the outgoing interface, next-hop address, default interface, and default next-hop address. If the outgoing interface is known after policy routing—either a **set interface** clause was used or a **set ip next-hop** clause was used and the next-hop address was successfully resolved—the code does not perform normal routing. If the interface is still unknown—because the next-hop address is not resolvable or the interface referenced in the route map is not operational—normal destination-based routing is done by calling the `IpRTLookup()` function. If normal routing fails—no route is found to the destination—the code checks whether the default next-hop address or the default interface was set by policy routing. If so, the code tries to use them.

Now consider the pseudocode of the `IpPolicyRoute()` function (Listing 5-12).

```
TInterfaceDescr * IpPolicyInt, * IpPolicyDefInt;
TIPAddress        IpPolicyNh ,   IpPolicyDefNh;

void IpPolicyRoute(TMemBuf   *TheBuf, TInterfaceDescr ** Interface,
                   TIPAddress *NextHop, TInterfaceDescr **DefInterface,
                   TIPAddress *DefNextHop)
{
 TIPAddress PR_NextHop, PR_PrevHop;
 TInterfaceDescr      *PR_Int;

 IpPolicyInt = IpPolicyDefInt = *DefInterface = PR_Int = NULL;
 IpPolicyNh  = IpPolicyDefNh  = *DefNextHop   = PR_NextHop =
 PR_PrevHop = 0;

 if (!RM_Process(TheBuf, TheBuf->RcvInt->PolicyRMap))
    return;

 if (IpPolicyNh) {
    PR_NextHop = IpPolicyNh;
    IpRTLookup(&PR_NextHop, &PR_Int, &PR_PrevHop);
```

```
    if (PR_Int) {
       *Interface = PR_Int;
       *NextHop   = PR_NextHop;
       return;
    }
}

if ((IpPolicyInt)&&
    (IpPolicyInt->Flags & IF_STATE_UP)&&
    (IpPolicyInt->Flags & IF_IP_ENABLED)) {
   *Interface = IpPolicyInt;
   return;
}

*DefNextHop = IpPolicyDefNh;
*DefInterface = IpPolicyDefInt;

}
```

Listing 5-12. *Pseudocode:* `IpPolicyRoute()` *function*

The function is called with five parameters—the pointer to the buffer holding the packet and four pointers to the variables of the forwarding engine that policy routing may or may not change. The function starts with variable initialization. Then the packet is passed for processing to the route map software module, the `RM_Process()` function. This function checks **match** sentences; if the packet matches, it processes the **set** clauses, which can set `IpPolicy()` variables to certain values. If the packet doesn't match any route map, indicated by 0 returned from `RM_Process()`, the policy routing function returns. Otherwise, the code analyzes the parameters, which could be set via the route maps, in the following order.

1. First, the next-hop address is checked for resolvability; the next-hop address must be resolvable via a directly connected route. If the address is resolvable, the code sets output interface and next-hop parameters for the forwarding engine and returns.

2. If the next-hop address is not set, the output interface variable (`IpPolicyInt`) is checked. If it is set and the corresponding interface is operational, the code assigns its value to the corresponding forwarding engine's variable and returns; the next-hop address is not changed and remains equal to the packet's destination address.

3. If neither parameter is set or if both of them are not applicable, the code checks for the default values (`IpPolicyDefNh` and `IpPolicyDefInt`) and reports them to the forwarding engine.

In addition to forcing traffic to go along specific paths, policy routing can be used to change IP TOS and Precedence fields that are considered by the output queuing algorithms, such as WFQ or *WRED* (weighted random early detection). The administrator can mark certain types of packets, determined by access lists, with certain values of these fields in the routers at the entrance to the network (*ingress routers*). The transit routers in the network will treat such packets according to the values, giving them more or less bandwidth or higher or lower priority when sending them out of an interface. (The interface must be configured with the proper queuing technique.) For more information on QOS techniques, refer to [Vegesna].

5.4 Packet Delivery

To understand the packet-delivery process, it is helpful to know something about the types of network interfaces used in Cisco routers. The behavior of the process varies, depending on which interface type the packet is delivered on.

5.4.1 Network Interface Types

From the standpoint of the packet-delivery process, all interfaces are one of three types: *point-to-point* (interfaces to links connecting only two nodes); *point-to-multipoint* (interfaces to networks permitting one-to-many connections); and *broadcast* (interfaces to networks permitting any-to-any connectivity with broadcast capabilities). LAN interfaces, including Ethernet, FastEthernet, Token Ring, and FDDI (Fiber Distributed Data Interface) are always considered *broadcast*, regardless of the type of IP data link encapsulation on them. On a broadcast media, when a station sends a frame, all stations on the segment receive it (Figure 5-4). After analyzing the destination address, each station determines whether the frame was destined for it. All stations can be addressed at once with the broadcast destination MAC address.

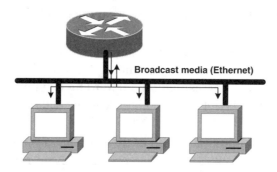

Figure 5-4. *Frame transmission on broadcast segment*

The group of WAN interfaces includes, but is not limited to, the following:

- Asynchronous serial
- Synchronous serial
- Low-speed serial
- High-speed serial interface (HSSI)
- Channelized E1
- Channelized T1
- ISDN BRI
- ISDN multiple BRI
- ISDN PRI
- ATM
- Packet OC-3

Depending on the encapsulation type used for a given interface, it is considered either *point-to-point* or *point-to-multipoint*. For example, interfaces with encapsulation SLIP (Serial Line IP), PPP, HDLC, and LAPB (Link Access Procedure Balanced) are considered point-to-point. Use of Frame Relay and X.25 encapsulations changes the type of the primary interface to point-to-multipoint because one interface can be used to reach several destinations via virtual circuits, as shown in Figure 5-5.

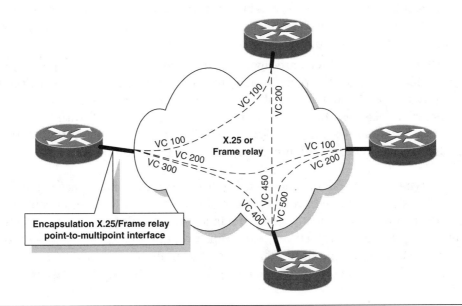

Figure 5-5. *Frame Relay cloud*

The group of logical interfaces—those not directly corresponding to physical connections—includes *loopback, null, tunnel, multilink, dialer, virtual-access,* and *virtual-async* interfaces. Following is a brief summary of functionality specific to each type of interface.

- Loopback, a software-only interface, is always up—unless shut down administratively—because it does not correspond to any physical interface. Loopback interfaces are always considered point-to-point interfaces. All packets routed through a loopback interface are internally looped back to the router. However, loopback interfaces are most frequently used for their stable operational state.

- Null is a software-only interface. When a packet is routed via this interface, the router drops the packet. This method is used as an effective alternative to ACLs and in some other situations, considered later.

- Tunnel, another software interface, does, unlike loopback and null interfaces, represent connectivity between routers. Each tunnel interface represents a pipe created using IP tunneling methods, such as *generic routing encapsulation* (GRE) or IP-in-IP. Network-layer protocols can be enabled on a tunnel interface, which will result in the packets' being encapsulated into general IP packets and transported by the IP network. Depending on the configuration of a tunnel interface, it can be considered either a point-to-point or a point-to-multipoint interface.

- Multilink, a logical interface, represents a group of point-to-point links bundled using the *multilink PPP* mechanism.

- Dialer, a logical interface, is used to abstract the dialing logic and configuration for a number of physical interfaces. When a call must be placed via a dialer interface, the next unused physical interface associated with the dialer is chosen.

- Virtual-access interfaces are dynamic instances of the point-to-point interface described as virtual-template, which are used for such purposes as multilink PPP configuration. Virtual-async interfaces are also dynamically created and deleted whenever a user establishes a remote connection (PPP, SLIP) with a router over a virtual terminal session, such as TELNET or PAD. To enable this feature, the administrator has to configure the **vty-async** command on the router.

Another type of a logical interface is the *subinterface.* Subinterfaces can be created for a given physical interface to represent the ability of data link layer encapsulation to segregate distinct data flows, using special techniques. For example, a Frame Relay interface can have multiple subinterfaces, each representing a single VC or group of VCs. Subinterfaces can be either point-to-point or point-to-multipoint, depending on the topology and the configuration commands used when the subinterfaces are created.

From the IP routing perspective, subinterfaces are not any different from primary interfaces. Each can be assigned an IP address. Both subinterfaces and the primary interface or only subinterfaces can be used at the same time. The principles of these two possible variants are illustrated in Figure 5-6. In the first case, the primary interface and the subinterfaces are all assigned IP addresses and masks, so they all are used for routing. The configuration in this case could be as follows:

```
interface serial 0
 encapsulation frame-relay
 ! the encapsulation type implicitly makes this interface multipoint
 ip address 10.9.1.1 255.255.255.0
 frame-relay map ip 10.9.1.2 51
 frame-relay map ip 10.9.1.3 52
!
interface serial 0.1 point-to-point
 frame-relay interface-dlci 100
 ip address 10.9.2.1 255.255.255.0
!
interface serial 0.2 multipoint
 ip address 10.9.3.1 255.255.255.0
 frame-relay map ip 10.9.3.2 61
 frame-relay map ip 10.9.3.3 62
 frame-relay map ip 10.9.3.4 63
```

Look at the configuration commands for the primary interface. You can see encapsulation set to Frame Relay, assigned IP address-mask pair, and two **frame-relay map** statements that are used to build the map table. This table is referenced by the packet-delivery functions (described later) to know which *data link connection identifier* (DLCI) to use while sending packets to a specified next-hop address—that is, which virtual connection the packets should be sent through. The process of looking through the map table (described later) is very similar to the process of ARP resolution.

Look at the configuration of the primary interface again. DLCIs 51 and 52 are logically grouped into one IP subnet: 10.9.1.0/24. Other DLCIs are used in the configuration of subinterfaces. DLCI 100 is dedicated to a point-to-point subinterface, Serial0.1, and we don't need any map statements in it, as the packet-delivery process knows that only one peer is accessible through this interface, as the interface is the point-to-point. Subinterface Serial0.2 was created as point-to-multipoint, grouping DLCIs 61–63 into another distinct IP subnet:10.9.3.0/24. It means that the encapsulation functions must have information to map the next-hop IP address to an appropriate DLCI value. That's why **frame-relay map** statements are included here.

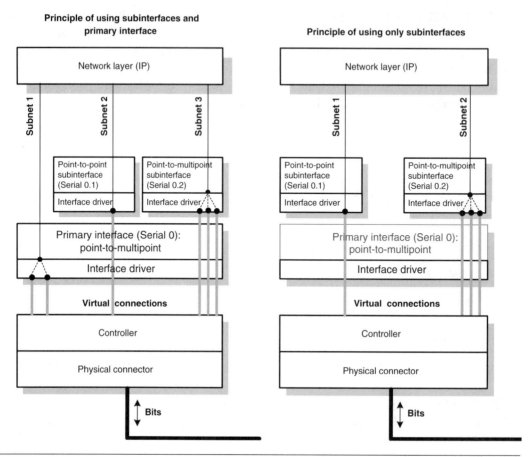

Figure 5-6. *Point-to-point and multipoint subinterfaces*

The right-hand part of Figure 5-6 shows that the primary interface is grayed out. You can also see that there's no line with the label "subnet" going from the network layer to the primary interface. The reason is that no IP address is assigned to the physical interface, and it is used only for encapsulation. In this case, configuration could be as follows:

```
interface serial 0
 encapsulation frame-relay
 no ip address
!
interface serial 0.1 point-to-point
 frame-relay interface-dlci 100
 ip address 10.9.2.1 255.255.255.252
!
interface serial 0.2 multipoint
```

```
ip address 10.9.3.1 255.255.255.0
frame-relay map ip 10.9.3.2 61
frame-relay map ip 10.9.3.3 62
frame-relay map ip 10.9.3.4 63
```

After this configuration is applied to a router, the routing table will not contain routes referencing the primary interface, because IP processing is not enabled on it. At the same time, both subinterfaces will be seen as normal network interfaces in the router and will be referenced in routes.

5.4.2 General Packet-Delivery Functionality

Consider the pseudocode of the `IpOutput()` function given in Listing 5-13. This function is responsible for general packet-delivery functionality.

```
void IpOutput(TMemBuf * TheBuf, TInterfaceDescr * TheInt,
              TIPAddress NextHop)
{
 TDLdetail * LinkDetail;
 TIPheader * Header = (TIPheader *) TheBuf->Packet;

 if (((TheInt->Flags & IF_STATE_UP)==0) ||
     ((TheInt->Flags & IF_IP_ENABLED)==0)) {
     SendICMP(Header->SourceAddr,
              ICMP_UNREACHABLE,
              ICMP_CODE_HOST);
     DropPacket(TheBuf);
     return;
 }

 switch (TheInt->Flags & IF_TYPE) {
  case IF_TYPE_PTP:
                 if (TheInt->Flags & IF_SUBINT) {
                    LinkDetail = MapTableLookUp(TheInt, 0);
                    if (LinkDetail == NULL){
                       SendICMP(Header->SourceAddr,
                                ICMP_UNREACHABLE,
                                ICMP_CODE_HOST);
                       DropPacket(TheBuf);
                    }
                 }else LinkDetail = NULL;

                 IpSend(TheBuf, TheInt, LinkDetail);
                 break;
  case IF_TYPE_PTMP:
                 LinkDetail = MapTableLookUp(TheInt, NextHop);
                 if (LinkDetail == NULL){
                    SendICMP(Header->SourceAddr,
```

```
                              ICMP_UNREACHABLE,
                              ICMP_CODE_HOST);
                    DropPacket(TheBuf);
                }
                else IpSend(TheBuf, TheInt, LinkDetail);
                break;
        case IF_TYPE_BCAST:
                LinkDetail = ARPLookUp(TheInt, NextHop);
                if (LinkDetail == NULL){
                    SendICMP(Header->SourceAddr,
                              ICMP_UNREACHABLE,
                              ICMP_CODE_HOST);
                    DropPacket(TheBuf);
                }
                else IpSend(TheBuf, TheInt, LinkDetail);
    }
}
```

Listing 5-13. *Pseudocode:* IpOutput() *function*

The function begins by checking the state of the interface over which the packet must be delivered. If the state of the interface is down, indicated by the IF_STATE_UP flag's being 0, or if IP processing is not enabled on it—the IF_IP_ENABLED flag is off—the packet is dropped, and an ICMP "Destination Unreachable" message is sent to the source. Note that a situation in which the IpOutput() function detects an inactive output interface can be seen either in a transient period, when routes over such an interface are not yet removed from the routing table, or when permanent static routes are configured. (Permanent static routes are not removed from the routing table after initial installation unless the **clear ip route** command is used.)

Specific actions performed by the IpOutput() function depend on the type of the interface: point-to-point, point-to-multipoint, or broadcast. These actions are discussed in the following subsections.

Every thread of the switch statement in the IpOutput() function ends with a call of IpSend(). This function performs data link frame construction, based on the details found by the IpOutput() function; encapsulates the IP packet in the frame; and enqueues it for transmission on the output interface.

5.4.2.1 Packet Delivery on Broadcast Interfaces

When an IP packet must be sent on a broadcast segment, the frame must be filled in with the proper data link layer address information: the source and the destination MAC addresses. The source address in the outgoing frame is set to the address of the router's physical interface, whereas the destination address must be discovered on the basis of the network layer's next-hop information passed from the forwarding engine.

Certain protocols, such as IPX or DECnet, allow a router to obtain the MAC address of the next-hop router or the host by converting the network-layer address. In IPX, for example, the MAC address will be the host portion of the whole IPX address. In the TCP/IP suite, the MAC address cannot be algorithmically obtained from a unicast IP address. Instead, a separate protocol, called *Address Resolution Protocol* (ARP), is used to accomplish this functionality.

> Unlike unicast IP addresses, link-local multicast IP addresses are mapped to MAC multicast addresses algorithmically "by placing the low-order 23-bits of the IP address into the low-order 23 bits of the Ethernet multicast address 01-00-5E-00-00-00 (hex)," as specified in [RFC1112].

When a router needs to send a packet over a broadcast media, it doesn't at first know the MAC address of the next-hop machine. To obtain this information, the router sends an ARP request in a frame with the destination address set to the broadcast value: all 1s. This request contains the IP address to be resolved. When it receives the request, a station with the specified IP address or a router having a route to this address sends its MAC address in an ARP reply packet. The ARP reply message is encapsulated into a frame with the destination MAC address set to the address of the requesting host, which is obtained from the frame in which the ARP request was transmitted.

> When a router replies to an ARP request for an IP address that does not belong to it but for which the router has a route in the routing table, the router is said to perform proxy ARP functionality. This feature is helpful in multiple situations, including those in which legacy hosts run old IP software that does not support IP subnets. Another example is when a router should attract traffic destined for a particular host—for instance, a router is terminating dial-up connections and dialing hosts are assigned IP addresses from one of the router's directly connected subnets. It is recommended that proxy ARP functionality be disabled by using the **no ip proxy-arp** command, unless it is required.

On reception of the ARP reply, the router stores the information in the ARP cache table so that the information can be used the next time a packet to the same host needs to be delivered. Each ARP entry contains the following main fields: reference to the interface, IP address, MAC address, timer containing the age of the entry, and flags specifying whether the state of the entry is complete, expired, and so on. Note that every ARP entry is associated with an interface because when routing information changes, the same IP address may become reachable via a different interface, and the MAC address used on the previous interface will not be eligible.

In Cisco IOS, the ARP is implemented in such a way that when initial packets arrive with the destination IP address for which there is no ARP entry, the packets are dropped. This approach saves the packet-delivery processes from waiting until the MAC address is determined, that is, waiting for an ARP reply, which may potentially never be received, thus not stopping other packets from flowing through the interface.

The pseudocode in Listing 5-14 illustrates the details of ARP operation.

```
TDLdetail * ARPLookUp(TInterfaceDescr * TheInt, TIPAddress NextHop)
{
 TDLdetail *MAC;

 MAC = ARPTableLookUp(TheInt, NextHop);
 if (MAC) return MAC;

 ARPCreateIncompleteEntry(TheInt, NextHop);
 ARPSendRequest(TheInt, NextHop);
 return NULL;
}
```

Listing 5-14. *Pseudocode:* ARPLookUp() *function*

The first time it is called for a given IP address, the ARPLookUp() function creates an "incomplete" entry in the ARP table, enqueues a request by calling the ARPSendRequest() function, and returns NULL as the result. Note that the function does not wait for the reply to come; it just informs the calling function that the data link details were not found. If a reply to the ARP request ever comes, it is processed asynchronously. The processing function fills in the fields in the ARP entry, previously created as incomplete, and the next time a packet arrives destined for the same destination, this entry is used.

> Note that loss of initial packets in a data flow does not cause much harm. TCP-based applications will benefit from TCP retransmission of the data when the network fails to deliver it. Applications sending data via UDP (User Datagram Protocol) or directly through IP are always designed with an assumption that data may be dropped and need to be retransmitted.

The log in Listing 5-15 shows how the ARP mechanism works in IOS.

```
R1#debug arp
ARP packet debugging is on
R1#debug ip routing
IP packet debugging is on
R1#term mon
R1#show arp
Protocol  Address          Age (min)  Hardware Addr   Type    Interface
Internet  22.22.22.22          -      00e0.1e68.4219  ARPA    Ethernet0
Internet  10.0.1.67            0      00e0.1455.4ca0  ARPA    Ethernet0
```

```
Internet   10.0.1.166              -    00e0.1e68.4219   ARPA    Ethernet0
Internet   200.2.2.2               -    00e0.1e68.4219   ARPA    Ethernet0
R1#
R1#ping 10.0.1.39

Type escape sequence to abort.
Sending 5, 100-byte ICMP Echos to 10.0.1.39, timeout is 2 seconds:
.!!!!
Success rate is 80 percent (4/5), round-trip min/avg/max = 4/4/4 ms
R1#
*Mar 1 00:01:34.127:IP:s=10.0.1.166 (local), d=10.0.1.39 (Ethernet0), len 100, sending
*Mar 1 00:01:34.131:IP ARP: creating incomplete entry for IP address: 10.0.1.39
*Mar 1 00:01:34.135:IP ARP: sent req src 10.0.1.166 00e0.1e68.4219,
             dst 10.0.1.39 0000.0000.0000 Ethernet0
*Mar 1 00:01:34.139:IP:s=10.0.1.166 (local), d=10.0.1.39 (Ethernet0), len 100,
encapsulation failed
*Mar 1 00:01:34.155:IP ARP:rcvd rep src 10.0.1.39 0800.207c.d6c0, dst 10.0.1.166
Ethernet0
*Mar 1 00:01:36.131:IP:s=10.0.1.166 (local), d=10.0.1.39 (Ethernet0), len 100, sending
*Mar 1 00:01:36.135:IP:s=10.0.1.39 (Ethernet0), d=10.0.1.166 (Ethernet0), len 100,
rcvd 3
...
R1#
```

Listing 5-15. *ARP debugging output*

Note that an encapsulation failed condition is met for the first packet because of the absence of the ARP information for the 10.0.1.39 IP address. As an ARP reply is received before sending the next packets, all of them are successfully delivered.

Look in the log at the output of the **show arp** command, which contains the Age column. This column shows the time in minutes elapsed from the moment of an ARP entry insertion. This counter is not zeroed when the ARP entry is used by the packet-delivery process but rather times out after four hours by default. Incomplete entries are stored in the ARP table for one minute.

The entries in the ARP table are periodically processed by the ARP aging process. The remaining lifetime is calculated for each entry. If the remaining lifetime is less than one minute, the entry is refreshed by sending an ARP request for the IP address in the entry on the associated interface. If the remaining time is over, the ARP entry is removed.

```
R1#
*Mar 1 00:18:04.559:IP ARP:sent req src 10.0.1.166 00e0.1e68.4219,
        dst 10.0.1.39 0800.207c.d6c0 Ethernet0
*Mar 1 00:18:04.571:IP ARP:rcvd rep src 10.0.1.39 0800.207c.d6c0, dst 10.0.1.166
Ethernet0
*Mar 1 00:18:04.575:IP ARP:creating entry for IP address: 10.0.1.39, hw:
0800.207c.d6c0
R1#
```

Note that no ARP request is sent when an "incomplete" ARP entry is deleted.

When the destination MAC address has been determined by the ARP lookup function, the frame is constructed according to the MAC-level information and queued for delivery through the output interface by calling the `IpSend()` function. Note that FIFO is the recommended queuing mechanism on LAN interfaces, as use of other, more sophisticated algorithms would only add unnecessary delays.

5.4.2.2 Packet Delivery on Point-to-Point Interfaces

From the point of view of the packet-delivery process, point-to-point interfaces and subinterfaces are the simplest case. In case of a point-to-point primary interface, data link parameters are not necessary—for example, the interface's encapsulation is PPP—and the `IpOutput()` function does not perform any map table lookup but just passes the packet for encapsulation to the `IpSend()` function. (Listing 5-16 shows the relevant part of the `IpOutput()` function.) If the interface is a point-to-point Frame Relay subinterface, the data link parameters are statically preassigned by the administrator—for example, a specific DLCI—and the function calls the map table lookup function with the next-hop address set to 0, meaning that it needs to know data link parameters for the subinterface as a whole.

```
void IpOutput(TMemBuf * TheBuf, TInterfaceDescr * TheInt,
             TIPAddress NextHop)
{
 ...

 switch (TheInt->Flags & IF_TYPE) {
  case IF_TYPE_PTP:   if (TheInt->Flags & IF_SUBINT) {
                         LinkDetail = MapTableLookUp(TheInt, 0);
                         if (LinkDetail == NULL){
                           if (Header->FragOffs == 0)
                             SendICMP(Header->SourceAddr,
                                      ICMP_UNREACHABLE,
                                      ICMP_CODE_HOST);
                           DropPacket(TheBuf);
                         }
                      }else LinkDetail = NULL;

                      IpSend (TheBuf, TheInt, LinkDetail);
                      break;
 ...
```

Listing 5-16. *Pseudocode: Part of the* `IpOutput()` *function for point-to-point interfaces*

An example of how point-to-point subinterfaces are configured follows:

```
interface Serial0
 encapsulation frame-relay IETF
 no ip address
!
interface Serial0.1 point-to-point
 ip address 10.1.1.1 255.255.255.0
 frame-relay interface-dlci 18
!
```

Consider the output of the **show frame-relay map** command in Listing 5-17.

```
R4#show frame-relay map
Serial0.1 (up): point-to-point dlci, dlci 18(0x12,0x420), broadcast
         status defined, active
R4#
```

Listing 5-17. *Output of the* **show frame-relay map** *command for point-to-point subinterface*

Note that the map entry created for the point-to-point subinterface does not contain any next-hop address, as the router doesn't need to know it when routing over point-to-point interfaces.

5.4.2.3 Packet Delivery on Point-to-Multipoint Interfaces

When a packet is delivered on a point-to-multipoint interface or subinterface, the router needs to know, for each specific next-hop address, the data link parameters, which can be passed from the forwarding engine. These details are specified in the map tables, which the administrator constructs manually, using such commands as **x25 map** or **frame-relay map**, considered earlier, or by an automatic mechanism, such as *Inverse ARP* for Frame Relay. To obtain the data link layer details, the IpOutput() function calls the MapTableLookup() function, as shown in Listing 5-18, which contains the corresponding part of the IpOutput() function.

```
...

case IF_TYPE_PTMP:  LinkDetail = MapTableLookUp(TheInt, NextHop);
                    if (LinkDetail == NULL){
                        if (Header->FragOffs == 0)
```

```
        SendICMP(Header->SourceAddr,
                ICMP_UNREACHABLE,
                ICMP_CODE_HOST);
    DropPacket(TheBuf);
}
else IpSend(TheBuf, TheInt, LinkDetail);
break;
```

...

Listing 5-18. *Part of the* `IpOutput()` *function for multipoint interfaces*

If the map table contains no entry for a given next-hop address, the router drops the packet and sends an ICMP "Destination Unreachable" message with the code Host Unreachable.

The information in the map table must correlate with the information in the routing table. The administrator should clearly understand which values the next-hop parameter may be assigned when the router is delivering packets along certain types of routes. There are several important details here.

Suppose that a router has a Frame Relay interface terminating five VCs to remote offices. The administrator configures the central router as follows:

```
interface serial 0
 encapsulation frame-relay
 ip address 10.1.1.1 255.255.255.0
 frame-relay map ip 10.1.1.2 102
 frame-relay map ip 10.1.1.3 103
 frame-relay map ip 10.1.1.4 104
 frame-relay map ip 10.1.1.5 105
 frame-relay map ip 10.1.1.6 106
!
ip route 10.1.2.0 255.255.255.0 serial 0
ip route 10.1.3.0 255.255.255.0 serial 0
ip route 10.1.4.0 255.255.255.0 serial 0
ip route 10.1.5.0 255.255.255.0 serial 0
ip route 10.1.6.0 255.255.255.0 serial 0
```

At first sight, the configuration seems to be reasonable: The administrator enabled Frame Relay encapsulation, enabled IP processing on the interface, provided Frame Relay maps for every neighbor router, and configured static routes for remote subnets over the Frame Relay interface. However, if the administrator tries to ping a host on a remote subnet from the central site, ICMP "Destination Unreachable" messages will appear on the screen. To understand why this happens, let's consider what the router does.

Assume that the central router has received or generated—it is not critical in this example—a packet with the destination IP address 10.1.2.10. The router looks through the routing table and finds the first static route as the only matching one. Then the `IpOutput()` function is called. The question is what parameters is it given. The output interface is definitely Serial0, as specified in the static route, but what about the next-hop address? The static route used to route the packet does not specify it, and this means that the router will use the destination IP address in the packet as the next-hop address. So far so good. Now the `IpOutput()` function calls the `MapTableLookup()` function to find DLCI for the next-hop address. Because there is no map entry for address 10.1.2.10, the router drops the packet and sends an ICMP message to the originator.

In this example, there are theoretically two ways to make the network work. The first is to configure a Frame Relay map for every possible destination address on the Serial0 interface. Clearly, this way is not the best, as the number of possible destinations can be very large, so the method is not scalable. The second way is to make the router use specific next-hop addresses when routing packets to certain subnets. The next-hop addresses in this case must be the addresses of the neighboring routers via which the subnets are accessible. To achieve this, we must change the static routes as follows:

```
ip route 10.1.2.0 255.255.255.0 serial 0 10.1.1.2
ip route 10.1.3.0 255.255.255.0 serial 0 10.1.1.3
ip route 10.1.4.0 255.255.255.0 serial 0 10.1.1.4
ip route 10.1.5.0 255.255.255.0 serial 0 10.1.1.5
ip route 10.1.6.0 255.255.255.0 serial 0 10.1.1.6
```

Now the routes have explicit next-hop addresses, which the router will use for map table lookup.

In Cisco IOS, the map tables for given encapsulation methods can be viewed with the **show *encapsulation* map** command, where *encapsulation* is the name of the data link layer protocol. Sample output of the **show frame-relay map** command is given in Listing 5-19.

```
r4#show frame map
Serial2 (up): ip 10.10.7.3 dlci 18(0x12,0x420), static,
            CISCO, status deleted
Serial2 (up): ip 10.10.7.1 dlci 17(0x11,0x410), dynamic,
            broadcast,, status defined, active
r4#
```

Listing 5-19. *Output of the* **show frame-relay map** *command for multipoint interfaces*

In this example, the Frame Relay map table has two entries, both of which correspond to interface Serial2. The first map refers to DLCI 18, known from a static **frame-relay map** configuration command; hence the word static in the output. The second map refers to DLCI 17, installed dynamically by InverseARP. Note the state of the Permanent Virtual Circuit (PVC): DLCI 17 is in deleted status, meaning that the Frame Relay switch doesn't know about it; DLCI 18 is active and can be used for data transmission. The broadcast keyword shown in the second entry means that when it generates a broadcast or a multi-cast packet for interface Serial2, the router will replicate the packet and send its replica through DLCI 17. Dynamic frame relay map entries are always installed with a broadcast flag, whereas static entries must be explicitly configured with trailing **broadcast** keyword in the **frame-relay map** clause.

5.4.2.4 Packet Delivery on Dialer-Enabled Interfaces

As described earlier in this chapter, when being forwarded on a dialer-enabled inter-face, a packet is passed to the `DialerProcess()` function, which is supposed to take specific actions and call the `IpOutput()` function itself. This subsection describes the `DialerProcess()` function.

Dialer is enabled by default on ISDN (integrated services digital network) interfaces because dialing functionality is native for them: Before transferring data, the end devices connected to an ISDN network have to establish a connection to a specific destination. This is analogous to a PSTN (public switched telephone network), whereby a person has to dial a number in order to speak to someone.

Both synchronous and asynchronous serial interfaces can also be configured to support dial-on-demand routing. The **dialer in-band** interface command is used for this purpose. Note that whenever dialer is enabled on an interface, the interface state changes to "up (spoofing)." This means that the interface is logically up and can be used to forward packets over it, but the device driver is aware that the physical—in case of serial inter-faces—or data link—in case of ISDN interfaces—connection is yet to be established. The reason the dialer-enabled interfaces are in this state is simple to understand: The router cannot set up a connection on an interface until at least one packet is routed through it and considered interesting, or eligible to trigger establishment of the connection and keep it active. At the same time, packets may be routed to a specific interface only if there are routes in the routing table referencing it, and the routes are not eligible to be in the routing table until the interface is up, that is, until the connection is established. The router breaks this tie by allowing the IP level to consider the interface up while it is, in fact, down.

Let's now turn to the pseudocode of related functions. First, recall that the `Dialer Process()` function is called only when the dialer is enabled on the interface, so a dialer data block must be linked to the interface descriptor, which the `DialerProcess()` function finds with the `FindDialerData()` function. Some of the fields are shown in Listing 5-20.

```
typedef struct DialerData {
  u_int        Flags;
  TTime        IdleTime;
  TTime        FastIdleTime;
  TDialerMap  *MapTable;
  TDialerList *DialerList;
  TCallData   *ActiveCall;
  TQueue      *Queue;
  //... other fields
} TDialerData;
```

Listing 5-20. *Pseudocode: Dialer control block data structure*

Listing 5-21 gives the pseudocode of the `DialerProcess()` function, which clarifies how dialer establishes connections and treats them.

```
void DialerProcess(TMemBuf * TheBuf, TInterfaceDescr * TheInt,
                   TIPAddress NextHop)
{
TIPheader    * Header = (TIPheader *) TheBuf->Packet;
TDialerData  * DialerData;
char         * DialNum;
TFlag          Interesting;

DialerData = FindDialerData(TheInt);
if (DialerData==NULL) return; //error

Interesting = DialerList(DialerData, TheBuf);

if ((DialerData->ActiveCall == NULL) ||
    (DialerData->ActiveCall->NextHop != NextHop)) {
   // A call to this neighbor is not yet established

   if (Interesting) {

      if (DialerData->ActiveCall) {
         // The int is already busy with another call

         if (! (DialerData->Flags & DIALER_FAST_IDLE))
            StartFastIdleTimer(DialerData);
         DropPacket(TheBuf);
         return;
      }

      DialNum = DialerMapLookUp(DialerData->MapTable, NextHop);
      if (DialNum) {
         DialerInitCall(TheInt, DialNum);
         if (DialerData->Queue) DialerEnqueue(DialerData, TheBuf);
      } else {
```

```
            if (Header->FragOffs == 0)
                SendICMP(Header->SourceAddr, ICMP_UNREACHABLE,
                    ICMP_CODE_HOST);
            DropPacket(TheBuf);
        }
        return;
    }
    //The packet is not interesting and no connection
    DropPacket(TheBuf);
}else {
    // The call to this direction is already active

    if (!(DialerData->ActiveCall->Flags & CALL_CONNECTED)) {
        if (DialerData->Queue) DialerEnqueue(DialerData, TheBuf);
        else DropPacket(TheBuf);
        return;
    }

    if (Interesting) ClearIdleTimers(DialerData->ActiveCall);
    IpOutput(TheBuf, TheInt, NextHop);
}
}
```

Listing 5-21. *Pseudocode:* `DialerProcess()` *function*

The first step the `DialerProcess()` function takes is to identify whether the packet being forwarded over the interface is interesting. The router considers the packet interesting if it meets the criteria defined by the administrator through specific configuration commands. The dialer establishes a call only when it sees an interesting packet going by. An already established call is disconnected if no interesting traffic is seen going out of the interface during a predefined period of time, determined by the Idle and FastIdle timers, considered later.

The means of identifying interesting traffic is dialer lists, an example of which follows. In this example, all IP and AppleTalk packets are considered interesting.

```
dialer-list 1 protocol ip permit
dialer-list 1 protocol apple-talk permit
```

Dialer lists used in real router configurations are usually more sophisticated and identify traffic of specific applications instead of a protocol suite as a whole. Refer to [DIAL] for more information.

After the `Interesting` flag is set, the function checks whether the dialer has already established a call in the direction the packet must be sent. If the call is not yet established—there is no active call at all or it leads to a different next-hop router—and the packet is not interesting, the function drops it. If the packet is interesting and the interface is currently connected to a different next-hop device, the function starts, if it hasn't already been started, the `FastIdle` timer. This timer allows the dialer to disconnect the current call more quickly than usual if concurrent interesting traffic going in another direction is present. Concurrent interesting traffic can appear if a single interface is configured to establish connections to multiple locations, that is, if there are dialer maps with different phone numbers. If no concurrent traffic is present, the legacy `Idle` timer is consulted to find out when to tear the connection down.

If the interface is not occupied, the function determines the number to dial, using the `DialerMapTableLookUp()` function, which looks through the set of dialer maps configured on the interface and searches for the map entry matching the next-hop address. If such an entry is found, the code initiates the call and enqueues the packet in the dialer queue if the administrator has configured it by using the **dialer hold-queue** command. (The dialer queue is off by default.) If no map entry is found for the next-hop address, the router sends an ICMP "Destination Unreachable" message with the code set to Host Unreachable and drops the packet.

If the dialer's active call is to the next-hop router that the packet must be sent to, the function checks whether this call is fully established. If it is not, the router either enqueues the packet into the dialer queue—if the queue is configured—or drops the packet. If the call is already established, the router calls the `IpOutput()` function to send the packet out of the interface and clears the idle timers if the packet is classified as interesting.

In several lines of the `DialerProcess()` function, the code checks whether the dialer queue is configured and stores the outgoing packet in it. The purpose of the dialer queue is to hold the packets while the call is being established. Stored packets are sent out of the interface when the connection is successfully set up. The pseudocode of the `DialerOnConnect()` function illustrates this (Listing 5-22).

```
void DialerOnConnect(TInterfaceDescr * TheInt)
{
  TDialerData   * DialerData;

  DialerData = FindDialerData(TheInt);

  DialerData->ActiveCall->Flags |= CALL_CONNECTED;

  if ((DialerData->Queue) && (DialerData->Queue->Size))
      DialerDequeue(DialerData, TheInt);
}
```

Listing 5-22. *Pseudocode:* `DialerOnConnect()` *function*

Note that an interface has only one dialer queue, so only packets traveling along the currently active call are preserved. If the dialer is busy setting up a connection to one next-hop router, packets that should be sent to another are dropped.

Consider the sample dialer configuration given in Listing 5-23.

```
isdn switch-type basic-dms100
!
interface ethernet0
 ip address 10.1.1.1 255.255.255.0
!
interface bri0
 ip unnumbered ethernet0
 encapsulation ppp
 dialer-group 1
 dialer hold-queue 10
 dialer map ip 10.2.1.1 7773355
 dialer map ip 10.3.1.1 7773377
!
dialer-list 1 list 101
!
access-list 101 permit tcp any any eq telnet
access-list 101 permit tcp any any eq ftp
access-list 101 permit tcp any any eq smtp
!
ip route 10.2.1.0 255.255.255.0 bri0 10.2.1.1
ip route 10.3.1.0 255.255.255.0 bri0 10.3.1.1
```

Listing 5-23. *Sample dialer configuration*

First, the type of the ISDN switch is specified; without this command, ISDN dialing will not work. The Ethernet interface is configured with an IP address belonging to a local IP subnet. The router needs to be configured to provide dial-up connectivity to remote subnets 10.2.1.0/24 and 10.3.1.0/24. IP processing on the BRI0 interface is enabled by the **ip unnumbered** interface configuration command, which saves IP addresses. All remote routers are configured in the same manner.

Now the router has to decide to route packets destined for remote subnets via interface BRI0 and with a specific next-hop address, which will be used to determine the called-side phone number. Static routes are used for this purpose.

The next step is to define which packets to consider interesting for establishing the connection and keeping it active. A dialer list is created to do this; in the example, it is dialer list 1, which uses access list 101, permitting TELNET, FTP, and SMTP (Simple Mail Transfer Protocol) traffic. This list is tied to the interface, using the **dialer-group 1** command.

Subsequent dialer-map sentences define which phone numbers to dial when forwarding traffic via specific next-hop addresses. The dialer hold queue is also configured to store initial packets while the connection is being established. Without this queue, packets that trigger the connection would be dropped.

5.4.2.5 Packet Delivery on Tunnel Interfaces

Tunnel interfaces are logical IP pipes, providing virtual-link functionality through IP networks. Network-layer packets sent over tunnel interfaces are encapsulated in IP packets. Usually, tunnel interfaces operate in point-to-point mode; that is, a single tunnel is established between two IP routers that perform packet encapsulation and decapsulation. IP tunnels using the Cisco GRE encapsulation type, described in [RFC1701], can be configured to work in point-to-multipoint mode, using the *Next-Hop Resolution Protocol* (NHRP). For more information on multipoint tunnel interfaces, please refer to [IPCONF]. This book describes only point-to-point tunnel interfaces.

Before proceeding to packet-delivery functionality, consider how routers process packets received on a tunnel interface. Figure 5-7 illustrates how network-layer packets are encapsulated in IP packets. When it receives a frame containing an IP packet, the router calls the `IpInput()` function, as discussed earlier. If the packet's destination address is not equal to the address of one of the router's interfaces, the packet is forwarded by the forwarding engine. Intermediate routers do not know that IP packets carry encapsulated information from other network-layer protocols, including IP; they just forward them as transit traffic. At the router terminating the tunnel, the destination IP address of the transporting packet will be equal to one of the router's own addresses and will be passed for local delivery. The protocol number in the IP packet header—for example, 47 for Cisco GRE or 94 for IP-in-IP—lets the router know that the received packet contains an encapsulated packet. Once the protocol type has been determined, the packet is passed to a corresponding software module—in this example, it is the GRE or the IP-in-IP decapsulation process—for further processing. This module analyzes the header of the tunneling protocol, identifies the type of the packet encapsulated, strips off the tunneling header, and passes the encapsulated packet to the packet-input function of the corresponding protocol. In the case of IP packets sent over a GRE tunnel, decapsulated IP packets are passed to the `IpInput()` function. The packet-input function processes the decapsulated packet just as if it were received from a physical interface.

Packet delivery on tunnel interfaces comprises the following steps:

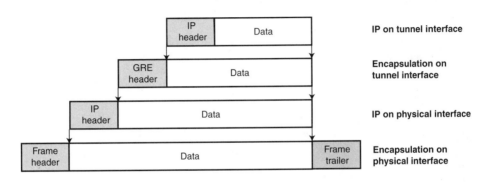

Figure 5-7. *Encapsulation of packets sent over tunnel interfaces*

1. Creating the tunnel header and attaching it to the packet being delivered
2. Creating an IP packet with the source and the destination address set to the tunnel source and the tunnel destination configured by the administrator on the tunnel interface, as well as the protocol type set to the registered number of the corresponding tunneling protocol (47 for GRE)
3. Sending the packet being delivered with prepended tunnel header as the data portion of the IP packet created in step 2

Note that the process of sending locally originated traffic includes routing table lookup, determination of the output interface, encapsulation of the packet into a data link frame, and other operations.

Configuration of tunnel interfaces in Cisco IOS is simple. The administrator needs to complete the following steps.

1. Create the tunnel interface, using the **interface tunnel *int-num*** global configuration command.
2. Specify the IP address of the remote side of the tunnel, using the **tunnel destination** interface configuration command.
3. Optionally, specify the IP address to use as the source address in IP packets carrying tunneled traffic, using the **tunnel source** interface configuration command. (Instead of an IP address, the administrator can specify an interface.) By default, the address of the interface nearest the tunnel destination address is used as the source.
4. Specify the method of tunneling, using the **tunnel mode** interface configuration command; by default, GRE encapsulation is used.
5. Enable processing of IP and other network protocols on the tunnel interface by assigning it an IP address or using the IP unnumbered feature.

The configuration in Listing 5-24 illustrates the process of tunnel interface configuration.

```
interface ethernet0
 ip address 10.1.1.1 255.255.255.0
!
interface serial0
 ! Public Internet Address
 ip address local-public-ip-addr 255.255.255.252
!
interface tunnel0
 tunnel source serial0
 tunnel destination remote-public-ip-addr
 tunnel mode ipip
 ip address 10.1.20.1 255.255.255.252
!
```

```
router eigrp 100
 network 10.0.0.0
!
ip route 0.0.0.0 0.0.0.0 serial0
```

Listing 5-24. *Sample tunnel interface configuration*

In this example, the router is connected to an ISP with its Serial0 interface, so a public IP address is assigned to this interface. Interface Ethernet0 is connected to a segment of a company's LAN. The IP tunnel established on the router is terminated on another router connected to a LAN segment of another office of the company. The tunnel is used to merge the company's LANs, which are assigned private IP addresses, using connections to ISPs. Note that EIGRP is run through the tunnel to exchange routing information between the sites.

5.4.2.6 Packet Delivery on Loopback Interfaces

In Cisco routers, the administrator can create loopback interfaces that are software-only and never go down unless an explicit **shutdown** interface command is issued. A loopback interface is created when an **interface loopback** *number* command is issued. As with an interface to a real network, a loopback interface can be assigned an IP address. All IP packets with the destination address set to the address of a loopback interface will be locally processed by the router.

> Unlike UNIX loopback interfaces, which are usually assigned a special IP address, 127.0.0.1, Cisco loopback interfaces can be assigned any valid IP address.

Although loopback interfaces are used for various purposes, such as for OSPF or BGP router ID determination, the main idea behind them is to have interfaces that never go down. A TCP connection for a BGP session, for example, that uses IP addresses of loopback interfaces will stay up until all paths between the routers become inaccessible.

Packet delivery on loopback interfaces does not presume any kind of data link framing, because loopback interfaces do not have associated I/O controllers. Note that if a packet is being delivered on a loopback interface, the destination address of the packet is not one of the router's interface addresses, as in this case the packet would have been queued for local processing by the `IpInput()` function. Listing 5-25 gives the pseudocode of the loopback interface packet-delivery function.

```
void LoopbackSendPacket(TInterfaceDescr * TheInt, void * ThePacket)
{
 TIPheader * Header = (TIPheader *) ThePacket;

 if (TheBuf->RcvInt == TheInt){
    DropPacket(TheBuf);
```

```
    return;
}


TheBuf->RcvInt = TheInt;
IpEnqueue(TheBuf); //insert into IP processing queue
}
```

Listing 5-25. *Pseudocode:* `LoopbackSendPacket()` *function*

Packets delivered on loopback interfaces are enqueued back to the IP processing queue. However, to avoid endless loops of these packets, packets that have already been looped back to the router are never looped again.

> Some administrators configure static routes pointing to a loopback interface as a method of traffic filtering or as a means of black-hole route configuration. This is not a good idea, as packets are sent to a loopback interface, come back from it, and then go to it again. Although Cisco routers detect this type of internal packet looping, it still eats CPU cycles. On Cisco 7500 and GSR platforms, such configuration causes traffic to go to the RSP/GRP and then to be process switched. The best way to configure black-hole routes is to reference interface Null0.

5.4.2.7 Packet Delivery on Null Interface

A Cisco router can have only one Null interface, namely, Null0. This special type of interface drops all packets delivered on it. This functionality is used for two main purposes: as a means of traffic filtering and as a means of avoiding packet loops in classless routing with route aggregation. Later chapters of this book contain examples for both variants. This subsection describes how traffic is processed when delivered on the Null interface.

In Listing 5-26, all packets forwarded to the Null interface are unconditionally dropped. If the interface configuration contains the **ip unreachables** command, indicated by the IF_IP_ICMP_UNREACH flag, the router sends an ICMP "Destination Unreachable" message with the code Host Unreachable before dropping the packet.

```
void NullSendPacket(TInterfaceDescr * TheInt, void * ThePacket)
{
 TIPheader * Header = (TIPheader *) ThePacket;

 if (TheInt->IPFlags & IF_IP_ICMP_UNREACH)
    SendICMP(Header->SourceAddr, ICMP_UNREACHABLE, ICMP_CODE_HOST);

 DropPacket(ThePacket);
}
```

Listing 5-26. *Pseudocode:* `NullSendPacket()` *function*

5.5 Forwarding Methods in Cisco IOS

The process of IP forwarding described in previous sections is called *process switching*. Process switching implies that IP packet forwarding is done by a process that receives CPU control from the scheduler, listed as IP input in the output of the **show processes** command, rather than by an interrupt-handling function. The scheduler switches to this process when it sees some data on the IP processing queue. This method is analogous to the one used in early implementations of IP forwarding in UNIX operating systems.

> Multitasking operating systems, such as UNIX, usually have several execution levels, such as the interrupt level, where hardware and software interrupts are processed, and the OS kernel level, where most critical tasks are performed. Processes not related to the operating system itself, such as network service daemons or user applications, are run at the process level. Each process is given a time slice by the process scheduler, which is part of the operating system. If several processes need to gain control simultaneously, the scheduler gives it to the process with highest priority.

The term *process switching* is used in Cisco technology not only to specify the method of IP forwarding but also to differentiate among the several ways packets can be processed in Cisco IOS. For instance, when a special feature, such as WFQ or *Real-Time Protocol* header compression, is said to be process switched, it means that the feature is implemented at the process level.

In addition to the process-switching path, which is the base switching path, Cisco IOS supports several alternative and improved switching technologies, as follows:

- *Fast switching*—Forwarding packets at the interrupt level, using the cache entries created by the IP switching process.

- *Autonomous* and *SSE switching*—Technology that speeds up the switching process on Cisco 7000 models by using such hardware accelerators as the Switch Processor in autonomous switching or the Silicon Switching Engine in SSE switching.

- *Optimum switching*—Optimized version of fast switching on Cisco 7500 models; more efficient cache structure and cache lookup are used.

- *Distributed switching*—Distributed version of fast switching offloads the main CPU by means of intelligent interface processors with their own CPUs.

- *Cisco Express Forwarding* (CEF)—A forwarding method using a resolved and very well optimized version of the routing table. The packet-switching performance is very high because of the speed of the routing table lookup operations, lack of recursive lookups, and precomputed frame headers. A distributed version of CEF (dCEF) is also supported; this technology is used in Cisco *Gigabit Switch Router* (GSR) platform.

- *NetFlow switching*—An enhanced switching method developed to remedy some disadvantages of legacy fast switching. NetFlow is used as a technique augmenting other switching methods for traffic statistics and feature acceleration.

- *Tag switching*—A Cisco proprietary implementation of *Multiprotocol Label Switching* (MPLS), a technique intended to introduce forwarding hierarchy and to allow explicit traffic engineering by means of VC-like packet switching. MPLS is a public standard developed by the IETF (Internet Engineering Task Force). See [RFC3031] for more information on MPLS.

Table 5-1 shows the switching methods supported on various platforms.

When introduced into Cisco IOS, a new feature is first implemented at the process level because process-level routines are more or less platform independent, whereas other data-processing paths require either platform-specific or low-level coding. In addition, process-switched functions are much easier to debug because they don't need to be real-time-oriented, as do those carried out at the interrupt level.

Why so many switching methods? Why not just go with process switching? We could, if we were not interested in router performance. The main problem with process switching is that the structure of the main routing table in Cisco IOS is not very optimal for fast forwarding—although very convenient for routing-protocol operations—and that the packet-processing flow includes too many steps. Consider the following rough outline of events when a packet is received and forwarded by the IP switching process.

1. The I/O controller buffers the frame and sends an IRQ to the CPU.

2. The CPU interrupts the currently running process, changes the execution context, and passes control to the interrupt handler.

3. The interrupt handler takes the buffer from the controller, performs basic checks of the frame, identifies the network protocol, stores the buffer in the corresponding processing queue, and returns control to the interrupted code.

4. The CPU gives control back to the interrupted process.

5. The next time it checks the queue of the pending processes, the IOS scheduler changes the execution context and gives control to the IP switching process, which takes the buffer out of the queue.

6. The IP switching process performs such functions as `IpInput()`, `IpForward()`, and `IpOutput()` and checks the state of the interface output queue. If it is free and the output controller's TX queue is not full, the buffer is submitted directly to the controller; otherwise, it is enqueued into the interface output queue.

7. If the packet has been enqueued into the interface output queue, the router waits for an interrupt from the controller and submits the buffer on it.

In multitasking operating systems, a very expensive task is changing the execution context, whether it is a software or hardware interrupt or process scheduling. The reason

Table 5-1. *Switching Methods in Cisco Routers*

Platform	Process	Fast	Autonomous/ SSE	Optimum	Distributed	NetFlow	Tag	CEF/ dCEF
1600	Yes	Yes	No	No	No	No	No	No
2500	Yes	Yes	No	No	No	No	No	No
2600	Yes	Yes	No	No	No	No	No	Yes
3600	Yes	Yes	No	No	No	No	No	Yes
4x00	Yes	Yes	No	No	No	No	No	Yes
7000	Yes	Yes	Yes	No	Yes[1]	Yes	Yes	Yes
7000-RSP	Yes	Yes	No	Yes	Yes	Yes	Yes	Yes
7200	Yes	Yes	No	No	No	Yes	Yes	Yes
7500	Yes	Yes	No	Yes	Yes	Yes	Yes	Yes
GSR	No[2]	No	No	No	Yes	No	Yes	Yes

[1]Distributed switching on Cisco 7000 routers require an RSP and VIP cards to be installed.

[2]On Cisco GSRs, only distributed CEF switching is supported; GSRs do not process switch packets.

is when control is given to another task, a huge number of instructions are carried out to preserve all registers, load the new task's context, and so on. In addition, the CPU memory cache is most probably invalidated. Because of the significant overhead, forwarding packets at the interrupt level when they have just been received might sound reasonable, but the functions used at the process level cannot be just cut and pasted into the code of the interrupt handler. The interrupt handling routines are a special type of code, which needs to be very fast and compact in order to minimize the possibility of nested and lost interrupts, as well as to leave enough time for other tasks. To achieve these characteristics, interrupt handlers are usually coded in a low-level programming language, such as assembler. In addition, performance is increased through use of sophisticated data-processing methods that store and find information more efficiently: information caching, hash functions, radix trees, and so on.

5.5.1 Fast Switching

The fast switching code is carried out at the interrupt level. The switching is fast not only because the packets don't have to wait for the IP switching process to be scheduled but also because the data structure and lookup mechanisms are much more optimized.

When performing fast switching, the router does not look into the routing table to find the output interface and next-hop address for a given destination but instead uses a forwarding decision cache, which is created at the process level. When the first packet to a specific destination address is process switched, the IP switching process creates a cache entry containing the destination IP prefix, the output interface, and data link parameters for the frame in which the packet must be encapsulated; that is, the switching process caches its forwarding decision. All subsequent packets to the same destination are switched at the interrupt level, using this cache entry.

> Note that when fast switching, the router does not perform recursive route lookups, because once a cache entry has been created, the output interface and the data link parameters for the destination are already known.

Only if there is no cache entry for a given destination address is the packet enqueued for process switching, as shown in Figure 5-8.

> An IP route cache entry is created only when the **ip route cache** command is not disabled on the interface over which the packet is forwarded in the process-switching path.

The IP route cache entries are organized so that lookup operations take as little time as possible. The time reduction is achieved by using a special data structure: a *radix tree*. The principles of radix tree data sorting and lookup mechanisms are described in [Knuth] and [Sedgewick], but the basic idea is that a binary tree is created. Each vertex of the tree can be either transit or leaf. Each generic radix tree vertex contains the following information:

- The position of the bit in the destination address to be checked
- A left-branch pointer to a vertex that should be taken if the value of the bit is 0
- A right-branch pointer to a vertex that should be taken if the value of the bit is 1
- For leaf vertexes, the prefix—a network address and a route mask—to check

When route cache entries are installed, they are represented in the radix tree by corresponding leaf entries and transit entries leading to them. The algorithm of radix tree lookup is as follows:

1. Set the current vertex to the root of the tree.
2. If the current vertex is leaf, check whether the destination address in the packet matches the address in the cache entry; if it doesn't, there is a lookup failure.
3. If the current vertex is transit, check the value of the bit specified in the vertex. If the value is 0, branch to the left vertex. Otherwise, branch to the right vertex.
4. Loop to step 2.

Note that when traversing through the tree, the code doesn't perform address match checking; instead, single-bit testing operations are performed. Because the tree is built so that only significant bits are checked, the code needs to check the matching condition only when it has reached a leaf entry. If the destination address doesn't match the prefix

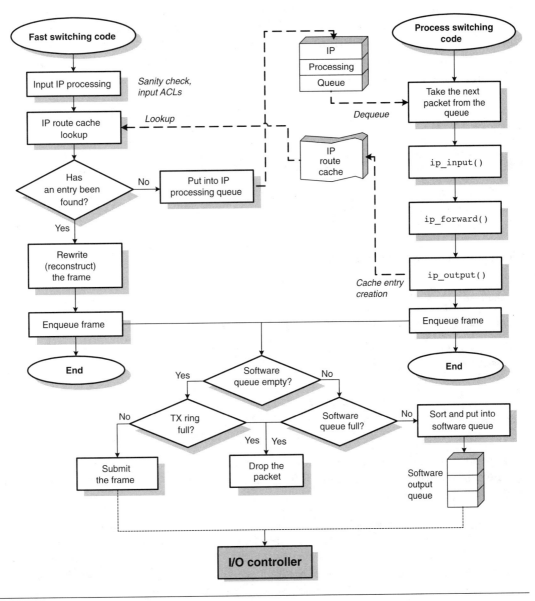

Figure 5-8. *Cooperation between fast and process-switching code*

in the tree entry, it is a route with the same combination of bits at certain positions but not the one to use for forwarding to a specific address. Because all route cache entries are stored in a radix tree structure, the router needs to do, in the worst case, 32 lookups instead of N, where N is the number of entries in case of a linear table.

The prefix provided with a cache entry depends on the information contained in the routing table. Generally, an entry is installed with the route mask equal to the longest mask known within the destination major network. For example, if VLSM is used in a network and the router has the routes shown in Listing 5-27, the result of forwarding a packet with the destination IP address set to 30.0.5.1 will be installation of the cache entry highlighted in Listing 5-28.

```
r4#show ip rou
...
     30.0.0.0/8 is variably subnetted, 3 subnets, 2 masks
S        30.0.5.0/24 [1/0] via 10.10.6.1
S        30.0.2.0/24 is directly connected, Serial0
S        30.0.5.128/25 [1/0] via 10.10.6.1
...
r4#
```

Listing 5-27. *Sample routing table*

```
r4#show ip cache
...
Prefix/Length        Age        Interface      Next-hop
...
30.0.5.0/25          00:03:07   Serial1        10.10.5.2
30.0.5.128/25        00:33:19   Serial1        10.10.5.2
...
r4#
```

Listing 5-28. *Sample route cache entries*

This means that if the routing table contains a host route with /32 metric, the route cache will be full of entries each covering a single host in the major network to which the host route belongs.

> Host route cache entries are also installed when packets are forwarded along routes with several paths. These entries ensure that packets matching the same route go to the correct next-hop router. The same logic works when packets are forwarded along directly connected routes: Each host needs its own data link layer details, so the code installs /32 cache entries for each destination address.

The reason the code follows these mask-creation rules while installing cache entries is to speed up the lookup operation. When it reaches an ultimate node in the tree, the cache lookup code needs to check only whether the packet-destination address matches the associated prefix. The code never goes back to the root of the tree, because the tree never contains less specific matching routes.

In addition to performing high-speed IP forwarding, the fast switching code has many other features now implemented at the interrupt level: ACL checking, policy routing, IP multicast routing, IP broadcast flooding, and so on. If a specific feature is supported at the process level only—the list of such features changes every day—fast switching may have to be disabled by the **no ip route cache** configuration command on the output interface.

Sometimes, a certain feature is said to be half-fast switched. Examples are the fancy queuing techniques—WFQ, Priority Queuing (PQ), and Custom Queuing (CQ). *Half-fast switching* means that when one of these methods is enabled on the output interface, the fast switching code sends packets directly to the controller, provided that there is a space in its TX ring: that the link is not congested. If the controller's TX ring is full, the packet being fast switched is not dropped but is put into the output software queue of the interface to be submitted to the controller when there is available space in its TX queue, as shown in Figure 5-8.

For high-speed interfaces, the situation is different; FIFO queuing strategy is usually used on them. (Fancy queuing is not effective on high-speed interfaces, as it introduces unnecessary interpacket delays.) When FIFO is used on an interface and the fast switching code finds no free space in its TX queue, the packet is dropped. This behavior can be improved on Cisco 7000 and 7500 routers by using the **transmit-buffers backing-store** interface configuration command, described later.

In Cisco IOS, fast switching is enabled by default. However, fast switching over the same interface—when a packet leaves the router from the same interface through which it came in—is disabled by default because the fast switching code cannot generate the ICMP "Redirect" messages that are necessary in this situation. However, fast switching can be enabled even in this situation with the **ip route cache same-interface** configuration command. Be aware that the router will not send ICMP "Redirect" messages in this case.

The fast switching cache in IOS is dynamic; that is, cache entries are created and deleted on demand. Creation of an entry is always done when the first packet to a given destination is process switched and the **ip route cache** command is enabled on the output interface. A route cache entry can be deleted on the following events.

- A new cache entry needs to be created, but all memory allocated for the route cache is used. The oldest cache entry is deleted in favor of the new one.

- Some changes to the main routing table have been made. All cache entries that may be affected are invalidated.

- Every minute 5 percent of all cache entries are randomly invalidated. (The idea behind this random invalidation is to refresh all cache entries in 20 minutes.)

Invalidation of the route cache is controlled with a number of timers that prevent cache instability:

- *Minimum interval*—Minimum time from the moment an invalidation request has been sent and actual invalidation of the route cache. This timer is set to 2 seconds by default.

- *Maximum interval*—Maximum time from the moment an invalidation request has been sent and actual invalidation of route cache. This timer is set to 5 seconds by default.

- *Quiet interval*—Length of the quiet period. If no invalidation requests have been received during this period, the requests are processed; the default value for this interval is 3 seconds.

- *Threshold*—Maximum number of requests that can be ignored during the quiet period. The default is 0.

When a cache invalidation request is received, it is delayed for at least the *Minimum interval*. The subsequent requests are also queued and delayed. The invalidation requests are executed if the cache has been quiet—not more than *Threshold* invalidation requests have been enqueued—during the *Quiet* period or if a request has been waiting for more than the *Maximum* number of seconds. Cache invalidation timers can be configured by using the following global configuration command:

ip cache-invalidate-delay [*minimum maximum quiet threshold*]

Changing route cache invalidation timers is not recommended, as it can lead to high CPU utilization or slow cache table convergence if not used correctly.

The administrator can display the entries of the route cache by using the **show ip cache** command (Listing 5-29).

```
C7200>show ip cache verbose
IP routing cache 1370 entries, 249012 bytes
   2664438 adds, 2663068 invalidates, 0 refcounts
Minimum invalidation interval 2 seconds, maximum interval 5 seconds,
   quiet interval 3 seconds, threshold 0 requests
Invalidation rate 0 in last second, 0 in last 3 seconds

Prefix/Length         Age        Interface        Next-hop
4.0.0.0/8-8                 1d15h      ATM2/0.1          195.161.2.177
                      12   00030000AAAA030000000800
10.0.0.0/8-0               00:12:08   ATM2/0.1          195.161.2.177
```

```
                  12   00030000AAAA030000000800
12.11.149.0/25-8       00:45:55   ATM2/0.1        195.161.2.177
                  12   00030000AAAA030000000800
12.15.76.128/25-8      00:00:39   ATM2/0.1        195.161.2.177
                  12   00030000AAAA030000000800
12.19.241.0/25-8       00:00:57   ATM2/0.1        195.161.2.177
                  12   00030000AAAA030000000800
12.27.72.0/25-8        00:27:22   ATM2/0.1        195.161.2.177
                  12   00030000AAAA030000000800
24.1.119.0/24-19       00:17:27   ATM2/0.1        195.161.2.177
                  12   00030000AAAA030000000800
```

Listing 5-29. *Output of the* **show ip cache verbose** *command*

This command displays each entry of the cache. All cache records contain network prefix information, reference to the output interface, and the data link layer parameters in the form of a precomputed frame header and its length. The last three lines of the first part of the output show cache invalidation timers and statistics. The invalidation rate shown in the output can be used to identify excessive invalidation problems.

A hidden **show interface switching** command displays internal IOS packet and character counters for each protocol and each switching path (Listing 5-30).

```
C7200>show int atm2/0 switching
ATM2/0
          Throttle count        0
    Drops        RP             0          SP           0
  SPD Flushes    Fast           4          SSE          0
  SPD Aggress    Fast           0
  SPD Priority   Inputs         0          Drops        0

     Protocol       Path    Pkts In    Chars In   Pkts Out    Chars Out
        Other    Process          0           0    3269158    183047968
          Cache misses           0
                     Fast         0           0          0            0
                Auton/SSE         0           0          0            0
           IP    Process     943524   251116111    4875493    631832364
          Cache misses        1432
                     Fast  169681004  1894478551  103636125  3989279424
                Auton/SSE         0           0          0            0
  Trans. Bridge  Process    2665915   160741156      34750      5113588
          Cache misses           0
                     Fast  78147770   239873055  763706010  1118203814
                Auton/SSE         0           0          0            0
  Spanning Tree  Process     873715    52422900    3471912    163179678
          Cache misses           0
                     Fast         0           0          0            0
                Auton/SSE         0           0          0            0
          ARP    Process          0           0      22763      1361104
          Cache misses           0
                     Fast         0           0          0            0
```

```
            Auton/SSE        0         0         0         0
C7200>
```

Listing 5-30. *Output of the* **show interface switching** *command*

In this example, 944,524 packets were process switched, 169,681,004 packets were fast switched, the route cache lookup failed for 1,432 packets, which were finally process switched. A documented IOS command—**show interface stats**—shows summary counters for each switching path on each interface, as shown in Listing 5-31.

```
C7200>show int atm2/0 stat
ATM2/0
            Switching path    Pkts In    Chars In    Pkts Out    Chars Out
               Processor    10522542  1257774467    11674808    984591209
              Route cache  247848032  2149970553   867364202    821253732
                   Total   258370574  3407745020   879039010   1805844941
C7200>
```

Listing 5-31. *Output of the* **show interface stats** *command*

> Both the **show interface switching** and the **show interface stats** commands can be used only for the primary physical interfaces; subinterfaces cannot be referenced in them.

The fast switching path is platform independent and is used on all native Cisco routers from the Cisco 1600 to the Cisco 7500 series. At the same time, high-end Cisco routers support a large number of high-speed network interfaces and cannot use the "one CPU does all" concept. More sophisticated, hardware-oriented switching methods need to be implemented in such devices. The following subsections describe the switching paths implemented in the Cisco 7000, Cisco 7500, and Cisco GSR series.

5.5.2 Autonomous and SSE Switching

Autonomous and silicon switching methods are tightly tied to the architecture of the Cisco 7000 router model (see Figure 5-9). A Cisco 7000 router is based on CxBus, a bus with an effective data transfer speed of 533Mbps. All interfaces are implemented in the form of *interface processors* that are attached to the CxBus. Interface processors function as network controllers, supplying frames to the *switch processor* (SP) over CxBus. The SP communicates with the *route processor* (RP) via the system bus. The RP runs the IOS code and carries out such tasks as dynamic routing protocols, main routing table calculation and maintenance, and process and fast switching. The SP, in turn, uses a highly optimized version of microcode and performs autonomous switching. The SP is not engaged in tasks other than packet forwarding, but rather is a piece of equipment specifically dedicated to perform high-speed IP switching.

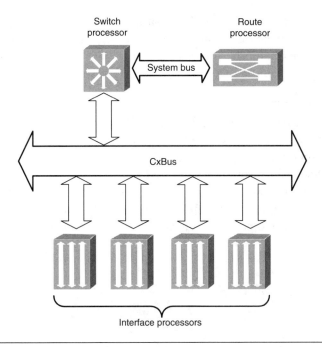

Figure 5-9. *Architecture of Cisco 7000 routers*

When it comes into an interface processor, a packet is copied to shared packet memory, also known as *MEMD* memory, on the SP via CxBus. The SP looks up the cache entry for the destination address in the packet. If an entry has been found, the packet is autonomous switched by the SP without interrupting the main CPU on the RP. If no entry is on the SP, it hands the packet to the RP for consequent fast or process switching. After the output interface has been identified, the frame is constructed in MEMD, and the SP sends a signal to the corresponding interface processor to take the frame.

Autonomous and silicon switching are platform-specific technologies and are used in Cisco 7000 routers only. Because this series has been made obsolete by Cisco 7500 and GSR series, autonomous and silicon switching paths are not considered in detail here.

5.5.3 Optimum Switching

Optimum switching is an optimized type of fast switching for IP. Optimization of data processing is made possible by the high-speed RISC processors and sophisticated hardware used in Cisco 7500 routers. A more efficient structure of the route cache and a faster cache lookup algorithm increase the fast switching performance.

On Cisco 7500 routers, optimum switching is enabled by default for the interfaces on which it is supported: serial interfaces with Cisco HDLC encapsulation, Ethernet,

FastEthernet, ATM, FDDI, and so on. To disable optimum switching (as a debugging action), the **no ip route-cache optimum** interface configuration command is used. When optimum switching is disabled, the router performs legacy fast switching.

5.5.4 Distributed Switching

Consider the architecture of Cisco 7500 routers (Figure 5-10). The Cisco 7505 router has one bus, called a *CyBUS;* Cisco 7507 and 7513 models have two buses, each providing a data transfer speed of 1Gbps. Instead of the separate RP and SP of the Cisco 7000 router, Cisco 7500-series routers use so-called *Route Switch Processors* (RSPs). Each 7500 router can have up to two RSPs, one functioning as the master and the other as the slave, or backup. A nonredundant configuration has only one RSP. The RSP functions as RP and SP, as well as a bridge between the two CyBUSes, if necessary.

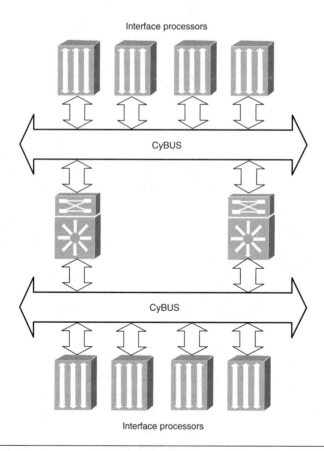

Figure 5-10. *Architecture of Cisco 7500 routers*

The interface processors used for Cisco 7000 routers are fully compatible with the Cisco 7500 series. A special type of interface processors, the so-called *Versatile Interface Processors* (VIPs), was introduced to achieve higher port density and modularity and faster packet processing in the Cisco 7000 and 7500 series. VIPs function as placeholders for the *Port Adapters* (PAs), which provide access to the network segments. Because VIP version 1 can work with both SP and RSP, it can be used in Cisco 7000 and Cisco 7500 routers.

The PAs used in VIPs can also be used in Cisco 7200 routers.

When legacy switching paths—process and fast switching—are used, a packet received by an interface processor is copied into MEMD memory on the RSP. The RSP makes the forwarding decision at either the interrupt—if there is a route cache entry—or the process level and signals the corresponding interface processor to take the frame from MEMD.

The process-switching performance of a Cisco 7500 router is much greater than that of a Cisco 7000 because of a faster CPU and because packets are processed by the RSP without the additional system bus transfers that occur in the Cisco 7000 between the SP and the RP.

Even though Cisco 7500 routers can use optimum switching to achieve higher throughput rates, this solution is not scalable, because everything is done by a single CPU of the master RSP. The CPU time is shared among multiple tasks, some of which, such as processing of BGP updates, can be time consuming. This approach leads to situations in which instability of the network topology affects the forwarding performance of the router. This problem becomes more serious in the context of the Internet core routers that have hundreds of simultaneous BGP sessions. The only scalable solution for this problem is to decouple the routing task—maintaining the routing table by means of the dynamic routing protocols—and the task of packet forwarding, or switching, and to implement them in separate hardware units with their own CPUs. This approach was taken to implement distributed switching.

Distributed switching is supported in version 2 (also called SVIP) and higher VIPs. Such VIPs require RSP in the router and hence cannot be used in Cisco 7000 routers. The VIPs have their own CPUs, RAM, and packet memory, and they run specialized IOS images. The architecture of VIP version 2 is depicted in Figure 5-11.

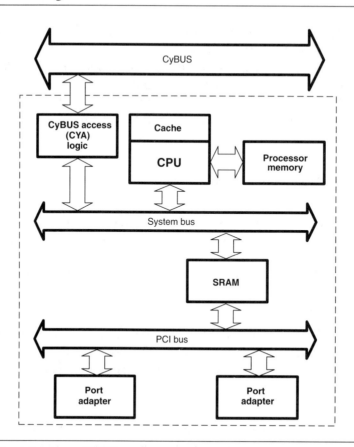

Figure 5-11. *Architecture of VIP*

When Distributed switching is used in a Cisco 7500 router, the RSP uploads the route cache and communicates changes in it to the VIPs. The flow of the packets in this situation is as follows.

1. A PA receives a frame and copies it into the shared memory (SRAM) of the VIP.

2. The PA notifies the VIP's CPU by sending it an IRQ.

3. The CPU processes the frame and performs fast switching, based on its local copy of the route cache provided by the RSP.

4. If a route cache entry for the packet is found, the VIP's CPU rewrites the frame with appropriate header information; if not, go to step 6.

5. If the output interface resides on the same VIP and the TX queue of the corresponding PA is not full, the frame is passed directly to the PA; if one of these conditions is not met, go to step 6.

6. The CPU commands the CyBUS access logic to transfer the frame into the MEMD of the RSP, which functions as a place for TX and RX queues of interface processors from the RSP's standpoint.

7. On completion of frame transfer, the CyBUS access logic notifies the VIP's CPU, and the CPU signals the RSP about the frame.

8. If the packet has not been distributed switched by the VIP, the RSP makes the forwarding decision, determines the output interface, and rewrites the frame; otherwise, the RSP skips this step.

9. The RSP signals the output interface processor. (The following steps are valid only for VIPs.)

10. The VIP's CPU instructs the CyBUS access logic to load the frame from MEMD into the local SRAM.

11. On completion of frame transfer, the CyBUS access logic notifies the VIP's CPU and processes the frame.

12. The CPU puts a pointer to the frame into the TX queue of the corresponding PA and notifies the PA that a new frame has been submitted.

13. The PA loads the frame from SRAM and transmits it on the line.

When packets are forwarded via the distributed switching path, the RSP does not spend its CPU time on packet processing but functions only as a bus arbiter for interprocessor communication. In the following cases, however, RSP is involved in packet processing, even if the receiving IP has a route cache entry for it.

- A packet must be forwarded out of a local PA—one residing on the same VIP—but its TX queue is full. In this situation, the packet is passed to the RSP in order to queue the packet and to share the available bandwidth according to the queuing strategy—WFQ, CQ, or PQ—used on the output interface.

- A packet must be sent via an interface processor, but the corresponding TX queue in MEMD is full, and the queuing strategy on the interface is other than FIFO; that is, a fancy queuing technique, such as WFQ or PQ, is used.

- The TX queue of the output interface is full and the queuing method is FIFO. Normally, the router would drop the packet, but if the **transmit-buffers backing-store** command is configured on the interface, the packet is copied into the Dynamic RAM (DRAM) of the RSP and is put into the outbound interface's software queue.

VIPs not only offload the packet forwarding task from the RSP but also carry out such functions as encryption, compression, queuing, IP multicasting, tunneling, fragmentation, access list checking, and so on. This method is called *Distributed Services;* it is supported on VIP2-50 cards.

5.5.5 Cisco Express Forwarding

Evolution of the Internet led to a requirement for the Internet core routers to support large routing tables and to provide high packet-switching speeds. Fast and optimum switching, used in Cisco routers, needed to be further improved to remedy the following disadvantages.

- Fast switching cache entries are created on demand, so one or several first packets need to be process switched. This is not scalable, as core routers in the Internet or a large corporate network have to process a considerable amount of traffic for which there are no cache entries, at the process level, spending CPU time on recursive route lookup. (All BGP routes specify only next-hop addresses, not interfaces.)

- Fast switching cache entries are destination based. This is also a scalability issue, as core routers need to process packets going to a large number of destination addresses, and the size of memory used to hold the route cache is limited. This causes cache memory overflow, resulting in permanent invalidation and creation of cache entries.

- The administrator has no flexibility in choosing techniques for load sharing among parallel routes. (Load-sharing techniques are described in Section 5.5.6.) If per packet load sharing is needed, the administrator has to disable all enhanced switching techniques and work with process switching, which results in performance degradation.

As a solution for these problems, Cisco developed a new switching method, named *Cisco Express Forwarding* (CEF), for IP. Initially implemented in IOS version 11.1CC, an ISP-oriented image, for high-end routers only, CEF is now supported on all Cisco router models, beginning with the Cisco 2600 series in IOS version 12.0. Moreover, Cisco GSR models can do only CEF; they support no process or fast switching.

CEF has the following basic characteristics.

- The CEF switching code uses the *Forwarding Information Base* (FIB), which is a forwarding table built using the information in the main routing table.

- FIB is a completely resolved, on all layers, version of the routing table, containing all routes present in the main routing table and incorporating the information held in prefix descriptors and paths.

- The FIB structure is optimized for high-speed lookups, using multiway tree structure (256-way MTrie).

- In contrast to fast switching cache tables, which are packet driven, FIB is totally event driven. That is, FIB always contains all routes and is kept synchronized with the main routing table.

- Depending on how many paths were in the original prefix descriptor, each FIB entry contains one or more links to the entries in the *Adjacency Table*, each link storing frame headers, all necessary data link layer parameters for successful packet encapsulation, and output queuing parameters.

- CEF is performed at the interrupt execution level.

- CEF supports two load-sharing methods, per packet and per destination, described in Section 5.6. Per destination load sharing in CEF is not the same as in fast switching, because both source and destination IP addresses are used in CEF as stream identifiers instead of just the destination address, as is the case in fast switching.

- CEF load-sharing behavior can be chosen by an explicit configuration command.

The major difference between CEF and other enhanced packet-switching methods is that CEF is not cache based. That is, FIB is not a cache of the decisions made at the process level. It is built using many sources, the routing table being the main one. The scheme of cooperation among CEF, fast switching, and process-switching code is shown in Figure 5-12.

When a CEF-capable router receives a packet, the code tries to forward it, using FIB. If no appropriate FIB entry is found, CEF drops the packet.

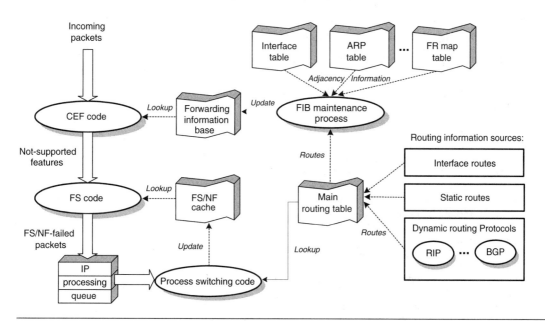

Figure 5-12. *Cooperation of CEF and switching-methods code*

Note that CEF operation is not affected by the **ip classless** command. CEF always forwards packets, using the longest matching route; that is, the FIB lookup operation is always classless.

If a feature or encapsulation is not supported in CEF, the code passes the packet to the next switching level (fast switching), which also tries to switch the packet by using its cache. If it cannot be switched at the interrupt level, the packet is placed into the IP processing queue.

CEF fails to switch packets only because of unsupported features or in transition periods when some routes are not yet resolved or some data link layer parameters are not yet known.

Let's consider the structure of the forwarding information base. Every FIB entry contains the following information:

- Destination network parameters: network address, route mask length, the route source, and so on—in short, all the parameters in a prefix descriptor
- Links to next-hop information structures, analogous to paths
- In each next-hop information structure, a pointer to an adjacency table entry corresponding to the next-hop address on a given interface
- Load distribution parameters (see Section 5.5.6)

Listing 5-32 shows a sample output of the **show ip cef** command and contains information for an entry in FIB.

```
C7200#show ip cef 10.1.0.0 internal
10.1.0.0/16, version 375 per-destination sharing
0 packets, 0 bytes
 via 11.1.0.1, Fddi3/0/0, 0 dependencies
  traffic share 2, current path
  next-hop 11.1.0.1, Fddi3/0/0
  valid adjacency
 via 12.1.0.1, POS9/0/0, 0 dependencies
  traffic share 2
  next-hop 12.1.0.1, POS9/0/0
  valid adjacency
 via 13.1.0.1, Hssi8/0/0, 0 dependencies
  traffic share 1
  next-hop 13.1.0.1, Hssi8/0/0
  valid adjacency
 ...
```

```
0 packets, 0 bytes switched through the prefix
Load distribution: 0 1 2 0 1 2 0 1 2 0 1 0 1 0 1 0 (refcount 1)
...
C7200#
```

Listing 5-32. *Output of the* **show ip cef internal** *command for multiple paths*

The FIB is created as follows.

1. When CEF is enabled, all routes in the routing table are passed to the FIB mainte-nance process that creates FIB entries, based on received prefix descriptors and paths. Each ultimate prefix descriptor will have a corresponding FIB entry; each path will have a corresponding path structure linked to the FIB entry.

2. Unresolved paths—those referring to intermediate addresses only, such as BGP routes—are processed by a special CEF process that runs every minute. This process walks through each FIB entry and tries to resolve unresolved paths.

3. When the contents of the main routing table change, the FIB maintenance process is notified and changes affected FIB entries according to the new routing information.

FIB entries are stored in a structure called a 256-way MTrie. At each lookup opera-tion, a whole byte of the destination IP address can be analyzed, so it takes only a maxi-mum of four lookups to find a route for a specific destination. Special *receive FIB entries* are installed for the IP addresses to which the router itself is listening: for exam-ple, the addresses assigned to the router interfaces. Packets with destination addresses matching receive entries are queued for local delivery.

The adjacency table contains information necessary for encapsulation of the packets that must be sent to given next-hop network devices. Each adjacency entry stores pre-computed frame headers used when forwarding a packet along an FIB entry referencing the corresponding adjacency entry. Listing 5-33 contains the output of a **show adjacency** command, displaying adjacency information for next-hop routers on the interface.

```
C7200#show adj FastEthernet2/0 det
Protocol Interface            Address
IP       FastEthernet2/0      10.0.1.11(5)
                              0 packets, 0 bytes
                              00900C82C3FF
                              00500B685C380800
                              ARP         03:44:37
IP       FastEthernet2/0      10.0.1.24(5)
                              0 packets, 0 bytes
                              0000C066039C
                              00500B685C380800
```

```
                                    ARP          03:58:12
IP         FastEthernet2/0          10.0.1.41(5)
                                    190 packets, 10640 bytes
                                    080020888552
                                    00500B685C380800
                                    ARP          03:45:37
IP         FastEthernet2/0          10.0.1.39(5)
                                    0 packets, 0 bytes
                                    0800207CD6C0
                                    00500B685C380800
                                    ARP          03:58:37
...
```

Listing 5-33. *Output of the* **show adjacency detail** *command*

Adjacencies can be of the following types:

- *Cached adjacency*—Installed for next-hop router addresses; created every time a route with an intermediate network address is installed in the routing table and the FIB

- *Glean adjacency*—Installed for directly attached networks; when packets are forwarded to such a network, the adjacency database is gleaned for a specific host-route adjacency

- *Host-route adjacency*—Installed, for instance, by ARP when packets are delivered to hosts on a directly attached network; also automatically installed for serial links running PPP

These adjacencies are said to be normal. Some special types of adjacencies are used to instruct CEF's forwarding process that the packets must be processed in an unusual way:

- *Punt adjacency*—Installed for the features that are not yet supported in CEF code, such as IP options, multilink PPP, and source route bridging

- *Drop adjacency*—Used for the routes referencing Null interface; packets forwarded over such an adjacency are dropped by the router

- *Incomplete adjacency*—State indicating that an adjacency is not operational, as when an interface has gone down

CEF is the most powerful switching method implemented in Cisco IOS. This is the method used in Cisco GSR routers, which perform FIB lookup by using specialized hardware on the line cards. The control card on a GSR—*gigabit route processor* (GRP)—practically does not participate in packet forwarding. Instead, it is dedicated for the CPU-intensive routing functionality.

CEF configuration is very straightforward. The router has to be configured with the following global configuration command:

ip cef [**distributed**]

The **distributed** keyword specifies that the line cards of the router should perform independent packet forwarding, using a copy of FIB downloaded from the central module (RSP or GRP). Once the **ip cef** command has been entered, all interfaces are automatically configured to perform CEF switching. CEF switching can be explicitly disabled on a particular interface by using the **no ip route-cache cef** interface command.

5.5.6 NetFlow Switching

NetFlow switching is a technique that was initially designed as an improvement on fast switching and was intended to resolve a number of problems specific to fast switching.

- Fast switching is destination based, whereas more sophisticated methods need to be flow oriented; the fast switching cache contains only the destination IP prefix, so the fast switching code does not differentiate between separate traffic streams to a single destination.
- Processing of packets against access control lists and other features requiring thorough packet examination, such as policy-based routing, affects router performance, even when performed in the fast switching mode, because every packet undergoes full classification process multiple times.
- Network traffic accounting must automatically distinguish specific types of traffic; fast switching code does not perform any type of traffic accounting.

Before discussing the NetFlow switching functionality, a traffic flow should be defined.

A traffic flow is a unidirectional sequence of packets with identical source and destination network addresses, as well as other network- and transport-level parameters, specific to a given protocol stack, received by a router with an interpacket delay not greater than a reasonable predefined value.

In IP, the network-layer parameters include the TOS byte in the IP header; the transport-layer parameters include the protocol ID—found in the IP header—and source and destination ports, found in the transport header. The definition specifies that a received packet is associated with a traffic flow if the following conditions are met.

- The source and destination addresses in the packet are equal to the addresses specific for a given flow.

- The value of the TOS field in the packet is equal to the value specific for the flow.

- The ID of the transport protocol shows that the packet carries a segment of the same transport protocol as the protocol of previously received packets of the flow.

- The source and destination ports in the transport-layer segment are the same as the ports specific for the flow.

- The packet being processed is received before the flow is declared inactive—because no packets belonging to the flow are received within a period of time—and the corresponding entry is deleted.

Introduction of NetFlow switching affected packet processing in IOS as follows.

- A flow cache entry is created for each data flow. When it is received by the router and needs to be forwarded, a packet is associated with a flow cache entry. Flow entries are organized in a hash table. The hash value is calculated over the flow-determining parameters.

- Only the first packet in a flow goes through all processing steps—inbound ACLs, policy-based routing, outbound ACLs, traffic sorting for output queuing, and so on. All subsequent packets belonging to the flow are processed according to the cache entry, which consolidates the information on how the packets belonging to the flow should be treated.

- NetFlow switching performance is not affected by the ACLs, as subsequent packets are not explicitly checked against them.

- The traffic-accounting task is consolidated with the switching task. Accounting information is held in the corresponding flow cache entry and is updated every time a packet belonging to the flow is switched by the router. These statistics can be automatically reported to external accounting servers.

The flow cache entries are created similarly to route cache entries in the case of fast switching. When the first packet in the flow is switched, a flow cache entry is created. While the packet is being further processed, the cache entry is updated to include such information as whether the packets belonging to the flow should be forwarded or dropped—if an ACL denies the first packet—how it should be queued, and so on. All subsequent processing and accounting of the packets within the flow is done according to cached information.

Note that even if the first packet is denied by an inbound access list, a flow entry is created to speed up processing—dropping—of subsequent packets.

Before CEF was introduced in IOS in version 12.0, the NetFlow mechanism used to affect the switching path. Specifically, each flow cache entry contained a reference to a route cache entry, so when a new packet belonging to an existing flow was received, the packet was forwarded, using information from the flow entry, which allowed the administrator to deploy per flow traffic load sharing. With introduction of CEF, NetFlow functionality was changed. Now the NetFlow cache is used only to accelerate feature processing and to collect statistical information about switched traffic. The forwarding table lookup is performed for every switched packet.

NetFlow switching can be configured only on Cisco 7200 and 7500 series, using the **ip route-cache flow** interface command. NetFlow switching is not enabled by default and must be configured explicitly; you must disable optimum switching before you can configure NetFlow switching. Note that when NetFlow switching is enabled, the router will still perform its forwarding decision, using fast switching or CEF to forward packets. Consequently, both fast-switching cache or CEF, and NetFlow switching cache structures are maintained.

The NetFlow cache entries can be displayed by using the **show ip cache flow** command, as illustrated in Listing 5-34. Note that IOS automatically identifies the applications that generate the flows, such as FTP, WWW (World Wide Web), and SMTP.

```
C7200>show ip cache flow
IP packet size distribution (939208131 total packets):
   1-32   64   96  128  160  192  224  256  288  320  352  384  416  448  480
   .000 .550 .049 .008 .007 .008 .021 .005 .005 .009 .008 .011 .012 .013 .010

   512  544  576 1024 1536 2048 2560 3072 3584 4096 4608
   .006 .006 .069 .023 .171 .000 .000 .000 .000 .000 .000

IP Flow Switching Cache, 4456448 bytes
  283 active, 65253 inactive, 130817658 added
  1013138503 ager polls, 0 flow alloc failures
  last clearing of statistics never
Protocol         Total  Flows  Packets Bytes  Packets Active(Sec) Idle(Sec)
--------         Flows  /Sec   /Flow  /Pkt    /Sec   /Flow      /Flow
TCP-Telnet        9080   0.0      25   127      0.1   18.2       12.7
TCP-FTP         406618   0.1      19    64      3.6    6.8        6.6
TCP-FTPD        287983   0.1      21   628      2.8    6.0        3.1
TCP-WWW      114164937  52.5       6   400    357.8    4.6        4.3
TCP-SMTP       2247465   1.0      13   340     13.7    5.0        4.8
TCP-X               42   0.0      39   216      0.0    4.6        7.3
TCP-BGP          59483   0.0      13    41      0.3   26.5       15.6
TCP-NNTP         21630   0.0     168   901      1.6   24.0       13.5
TCP-Frag          1622   0.0       4   292      0.0    4.7       15.7
```

```
TCP-other        3541468    1.6          10   424     16.7       3.2        8.8
UDP-DNS          2736159    1.2           1   114      1.8       1.3       15.7
UDP-NTP           839731    0.3           1    77      0.3       0.0       15.6
UDP-TFTP              29    0.0           2    62      0.0       5.0       15.4
UDP-Frag           10964    0.0          42    65      0.2      37.6       15.6
UDP-other        4162634    1.9           9   180     17.8       2.9       15.6
ICMP             2209497    1.0           5    86      5.4      10.3       15.6
GRE               118009    0.0         173   210      9.4      22.3       15.5
IP-other               3    0.0           1    42      0.0       0.0       15.9
Total:         130817354   60.1           7   380    432.1       4.6        5.4

SrcIf          SrcIPaddress     DstIf         DstIPaddress      Pr  SrcP DstP  Pkts
Fa1/0.18       212.111.64.70    Local         212.111.64.240    06  0684 0017   101
BV3            212.111.64.138   AT2/0.1       212.44.64.106     06  0050 04FE     2
BV3            212.111.64.138   AT2/0.1       212.44.64.106     06  0050 04FF     2
BV3            212.111.64.138   AT2/0.1       212.44.64.106     06  0050 04FB     2
Se3/0          212.111.64.202   BV3           212.111.64.135    01  0000 0303     1
Se3/0          195.218.138.28   BV1           194.85.159.2      11  06C5 0035     7
AT2/0.1        194.42.224.130   BV3           212.111.64.132    11  A41B 0035     1
BV3            212.111.64.132   Null          194.42.224.130    11  0035 A41B     1
BV3            212.111.64.138   AT2/0.1       212.44.64.106     06  0050 0502     2
```

Listing 5-34. *Output of the* **show ip cache flow** *command*

By default, the NetFlow cache can contain up to 65,536 entries. This limit can be changed to a value in the range 1,024 to 524,288 using the **ip flow-cache entries** global configuration command. Cisco documentation does not recommend changing this parameter, but in a big network, core routers may need more than the default number of flow entries.

> Each flow entry is about 64 bytes of memory, so to maintain the default number of flow entries, about 4MB of DRAM are necessary on the router. Having 128K entries on a router would require 8MB of free memory.

The NetFlow cache is intelligently maintained so that free entries can always be found when a new flow enters the router. Every time a new flow entry is created, the code checks the number of remaining free entries. If there are a very small number of them, the NetFlow cache aging process tries to free 30 entries, using more aggressive timeout. If, after creation of the new flow, only one free entry is found, NetFlow frees 30 entries, regardless of their age, to ensure that there are always enough entries for new flows.

ISPs use Cisco NetFlow technology for accounting and statistics. The data structures maintained by NetFlow provide detailed information about transit traffic. This information may be exported to an external statistics collection server (FlowCollector). For more information on NetFlow data export, refer to the description on the Cisco Web site [NetFlow].

5.6 Load Sharing in Cisco IOS

Cisco IOS supports several load-sharing techniques, each used on different OSI model layers and with different forwarding methods. Some of the techniques, such as multilink PPP or Cisco ISDN B-channel aggregation, operate on the data link layer and are not considered in this book. This chapter describes only the network-layer methods that allow splitting the load among multiple paths. All these methods require more than one route to a single destination to be installed into the routing table, achieved by either static route configuration or use of dynamic routing protocols. (Refer to Chapter 4 for more information on the routing table structure.) Table 5-2 summarizes the information on these techniques.

If only static routes can or should be configured, the administrator must provide more than one static route describing the same destination prefix with different routing parameters: intermediate network address and output interface. An example of such a configuration is given in Listing 5-35.

```
R1#conf t
R1(config)#ip route 50.0.0.0 255.0.0.0 Ser 0
R1(config)#ip route 50.0.0.0 255.0.0.0 Ser 1
R1(config)#ip route 50.0.0.0 255.0.0.0 Ser 2
R1(config)#^Z
R1#show ip route
...
Gateway of last resort is not set

S    50.0.0.0/8 [1/0] is directly connected, Serial0
                [1/0] is directly connected, Serial1
                [1/0] is directly connected, Serial2
...
R1#
```

Listing 5-35. *Configuring static routes for load sharing*

Table 5-2. *Load-Balancing Techniques in Cisco IOS*

Technique	Process Switching	Fast Switching	CEF
Per packet	Yes	No	Yes
Per destination	No	Yes	No
Per flow (with NetFlow)	No	Yes	Yes
Per source/destination	No	No	Yes

If dynamic routing protocols are used, corresponding routes are installed automatically, as shown in Listing 5-36.

```
R1#show ip rou
...
Gateway of last resort is not set

R    1.0.0.0/8 [120/1] via 10.14.0.2, 00:00:12, Ethernet0
                [120/1] via 10.1.2.2, 00:00:10, Serial0
                [120/1] via 10.1.1.1, 00:00:16, Serial1
...
```

Listing 5-36. *Routing table with dynamic parallel routes*

As mentioned in Chapter 4, the routing table can support as many as six parallel routes to a given destination. Dynamic routing protocols install only four parallel routes, by default, except for BGP, which installs only one. To change the number of parallel routes installed in the routing table by a dynamic routing protocol, the administrator can use the **maximum-paths** command in the routing protocol configuration mode, as shown in Listing 5-37.

```
R1#conf t
R1(config)#router ospf 100
R1(config-router)#maximum-paths 6
R1(config)#^Z
R1#
```

Listing 5-37. *Configuring routing protocols to allow parallel routes*

You cannot change the maximum number of parallel static routes installed in the routing table; the first six resolvable routes to a given destination are always installed.

5.6.1 Per Packet Load Sharing in Process-Switching Path

Consider how the router uses parallel routes to balance traffic among multiple available paths. Cisco IOS performs per packet load sharing when doing legacy process switching. The characteristics of this method follow.

1. There must be multiple parallel routes to a given destination for load sharing to take place, that is, more than one path must be linked to the corresponding prefix descriptor.

2. Each path is assigned a specific `ShareCount` value, which determines the number of packets to be switched along it before the next path is used.

3. `ShareCount` values are calculated based on the ratio of metrics in the paths. In most cases, only routes with identical metrics will be installed; hence, the `ShareCount` value will be 1 for all paths. If IGRP or EIGRP is used and configured with the variance parameter greater than 1, routes with different metrics can be installed; in this case, `ShareCount` values will be different for different paths, and this will affect the proportion of traffic forwarded along each path.

4. When packets are forwarded using a route with multiple paths, the next path becomes active after the currently active path has had its `ShareCount` number of packets.

Suppose that router R1 has the routing table shown in Listing 5-38.

```
R1#show ip route
...
S    1.0.0.0/8 [1/0] via 10.1.1.2, Ethernet0
               [1/0] via 10.1.2.2, Serial0
               [1/0] via 10.1.3.2, Serial1
...
R1#show ip route 1.0.0.0 255.0.0.0
Routing entry for 1.0.0.0/8
  Known via "static", distance 1, metric 0
  Routing Descriptor Blocks:
  * 10.1.1.2, via Ethernet0
      Route metric is 0, traffic share count is 1
    10.1.2.2, via Serial0
      Route metric is 0, traffic share count is 1
    10.2.2.2, via Serial1
      Route metric is 0, traffic share count is 1

R1#
```

Listing 5-38. *Static routes for equal-cost load balancing*

If the router receives five packets with destination addresses falling into the prefix 1.0.0.0/8 and fast switching has been disabled on Ethernet0, Serial0, and Serial1 interfaces by the **no ip route-cache** interface configuration command, all five packets will be process switched. The forwarding engine will use the three paths in round-robin fashion, forwarding a single packet along each path before switching to the next in the list. In the example, assuming that the first path was active initially, two packets will be forwarded along the first path, via 10.1.1.2 on Ethernet0; two packets over the second one, over the Serial0 interface; and one packet over the third.

A more interesting example is the routing table containing parallel routes with unequal metrics installed by EIGRP process with the variance parameter set to 2. Note that ShareCount values in corresponding paths are set in inverse proportion to their corresponding metrics. This setting balances the traffic among multiple paths according to the bandwidth available on each path. In this example, if the router receives the same five packets as it did in the previous example, each path will accept a number of packets corresponding to its ShareCount value.

Per packet load sharing is recommended when the traffic pattern consists of flows to a small number of the receiving hosts at a given moment. It also should be used when bandwidth and delay of the alternative paths are approximately the same. Otherwise, transport-level segments can arrive at the receiving host reordered—out of the initial sequence—and with considerable intersegment delays, which in turn can lead to performance degradation of the transport connections or excessive data retransmissions. When the number of the receiving hosts at a given moment is equal to or greater than the number of parallel paths, the per destination load-sharing technique is more appropriate. It allows packets going to a single destination—and, consequently, belonging to the same data stream—to be sent along the same path.

5.6.2 Per Destination Load Sharing in Fast Switching Path

Pure per destination load sharing is used when a router forwards the packet in the fast switching path. Fast switching code installs /32 cache entries whenever the prefix descriptor used for routing has multiple paths to make sure that each destination is forwarded along its own path.

As you know, before any packet is fast switched, a packet to the same destination IP address must be process switched so that a route cache entry is created. Because the route cache entries contain all the information about the outgoing interface and the data link layer parameters, all packets to the same destination are forwarded over the same path. The reason is that the fast switching code does not know the exact information in the routing table, and this is the process-switching path where alternative paths can be selected and used.

For better understanding of per destination load sharing in the fast switching path, consider an example in which a router needs to process a sequence of packets with the destination addresses given in Table 5-3. Assuming that the router's routing table contains the routes shown in Listing 5-38, the following sequence of events will happen.

1. On reception of the first packet, the router checks its route cache and, having found no matching entry, passes the packet to the process level, where it is processed as follows.

Table 5-3. *Destination IP Addresses in Processed Packets*

Packet Number	Destination IP Address
1	1.1.1.1
2	1.1.1.1
3	1.1.1.2
4	1.1.1.3
5	1.1.1.2

  a. In the process-switching path, the router looks through the routing table, finds the route to prefix 1.0.0.0/8, selects the currently active path—for simplicity, assume that this is the first path—and moves the `ActivePath` pointer to the next path in the list.

  b. When it has completed encapsulation of the packet for delivery on the output interface, the router creates a route cache entry, containing 1.1.1.1/32 as the prefix, Ethernet0 as the output interface, and calculated frame header for the next hop, 10.14.0.2.

2. On reception of the second packet, the router finds a route cache entry for address 1.1.1.1 and thus forwards the packet along the same path as the first one—over the Ethernet0 interface to the next-hop router, 10.14.0.2.

3. Packet 3 is received. Because no route cache entry has been created for this destination address, the router passes the packet to the process-switching path, where the routing table is looked up again. The same route, covering 1.0.0.0/8, is found, and the second path is used to route the packet. (Thus, a packet with a destination address other than that of the first packet but still falling into the same prefix is forwarded along another path.) A new route cache entry is created for IP address 1.1.1.2.

4. Packet 4 is processed the same way as packet 3. Because no cache entry is found, the packet is process switched along the next path in the list, and a cache entry is created.

5. Packet 5 is forwarded at the fast switching level, using the cache entry created in step 5 for packet 3.

Note that in these events, the source address in the packets doesn't really matter, because neither the forwarding engine nor the fast switching code cares about it, and the forwarding decision is based solely on the destination IP address.

5.6.3 Load Sharing in Cisco Express Forwarding

Two load-sharing techniques are available in CEF: per packet and per source/destination. The per packet load-sharing mode uses the same approach as in process switching. The per source/destination method, called per destination in Cisco documentation, is totally new and was not previously implemented in Cisco IOS.

As we saw in Section 5.5.5, FIB entries are similar to the prefix descriptors used in the main routing table. This sounds as if only per packet load sharing can be implemented without such additional information as that used in NetFlow switching. Fortunately, it is not quite so.

Each entry in the forwarding information base is accompanied by load-distribution information, which is an array of 16 elements, each containing the index of a path linked to the FIB entry. When a packet must be forwarded using the per source/destination load-sharing method, a 4-bit hash value is calculated, with source and destination IP addresses fed as input to the hash function. This 4-bit value is used as the index in the load-distribution array while deciding which path to use. When per packet load balancing is in effect, the method of path selection is similar to the one used in process switching: a field (RefCount) in each FIB entry is the index of the current path and is incremented after a path has been used. The array itself is prepared when a prefix is installed into FIB and corrected every time a path is added to or removed from the corresponding FIB entry.

Consider two examples of how FIB entries are created for equal- and unequal-cost load balancing. Listing 5-39 contains the output of **show ip route** and **show ip cef internal** commands, showing routing table and FIB entries for parallel static routes. Because static routes are always installed with a metric of 0, the traffic share count values are equal and set to 1. This is why the load-distribution array contains the same number of 0 and 1 indexes: 0 is the index of the first path and 1 is the index of the second path in the FIB entry.

```
C7200#show ip route 50.0.0.0 255.0.0.0
Routing entry for 50.0.0.0/8
  Known via "static", distance 1, metric 0
  Routing Descriptor Blocks:
  * 10.0.1.194, via FastEthernet2/0
      Route metric is 0, traffic share count is 1
    10.0.1.241, via FastEthernet2/0
      Route metric is 0, traffic share count is 1

C7200#
C7200#show ip cef 50.0.0.0 internal
50.0.0.0/8, version 102, per-destination sharing
0 packets, 0 bytes
  has tag information: local tag 30
  via 10.0.1.194, FastEthernet2/0, 0 dependencies
    traffic share 1
      next-hop 10.0.1.194, FastEthernet2/0
```

```
    valid adjacency
via 10.0.1.241, FastEthernet2/0, 0 dependencies
  traffic share 1
  next-hop 10.0.1.241, FastEthernet2/0
  valid adjacency

0 packets, 0 bytes switched through the prefix
Load distribution: 0 1 0 1 0 1 0 1 0 1 0 1 0 1 0 1 (refcount 1)

Hash  OK  Interface        Address        Packets  Tags imposed
1     Y   FastEthernet2/0  10.0.1.194           0  none
2     Y   FastEthernet2/0  10.0.1.241           0  none
3     Y   FastEthernet2/0  10.0.1.194           0  none
4     Y   FastEthernet2/0  10.0.1.241           0  none
5     Y   FastEthernet2/0  10.0.1.194           0  none
6     Y   FastEthernet2/0  10.0.1.241           0  none
7     Y   FastEthernet2/0  10.0.1.194           0  none
8     Y   FastEthernet2/0  10.0.1.241           0  none
9     Y   FastEthernet2/0  10.0.1.194           0  none
10    Y   FastEthernet2/0  10.0.1.241           0  none
11    Y   FastEthernet2/0  10.0.1.194           0  none
12    Y   FastEthernet2/0  10.0.1.241           0  none
13    Y   FastEthernet2/0  10.0.1.194           0  none
14    Y   FastEthernet2/0  10.0.1.241           0  none
15    Y   FastEthernet2/0  10.0.1.194           0  none
16    Y   FastEthernet2/0  10.0.1.241           0  none
C7200#
```

Listing 5-39. *Routing table and FIB entries for load balancing*

In Listing 5-40, EIGRP is configured with the variance parameter set to 6 and installs two parallel routes with unequal metrics to the same destination in the routing table. Traffic share counts are in inverse proportion to the metric values in this case.

```
C7200#show ip route 100.0.0.0 255.0.0.0
Routing entry for 100.0.0.0/8
  Known via "eigrp 100", distance 90, metric 258048, type internal
  Redistributing via eigrp 100
  Last update from 90.1.1.2 on ATM1/0.3, 00:00:14 ago
  Routing Descriptor Blocks:
  * 80.1.1.2, from 80.1.1.2, 00:00:14 ago, via ATM1/0.2
      Route metric is 258048, traffic share count is 3
      Total delay is 5080 microseconds, minimum bandwidth is 20000 Kbit
      Reliability 255/255, minimum MTU 1514 bytes
      Loading 1/255, Hops 1
    90.1.1.2, from 90.1.1.2, 00:00:14 ago, via ATM1/0.3
      Route metric is 770048, traffic share count is 1
      Total delay is 5080 microseconds, minimum bandwidth is 4000 Kbit
```

```
          Reliability 255/255, minimum MTU 1514 bytes
          Loading 1/255, Hops 1

C7200#show ip cef 100.0.0.0 255.0.0.0 internal
100.0.0.0/8, version 194, per-destination sharing
0 packets, 0 bytes
   has tag information: local tag 33
   via 80.1.1.2, ATM1/0.2, 0 dependencies
     traffic share 3
     next-hop 80.1.1.2, ATM1/0.2
     valid adjacency
   via 90.1.1.2, ATM1/0.3, 0 dependencies
     traffic share 1
     next-hop 90.1.1.2, ATM1/0.3
     valid adjacency

   0 packets, 0 bytes switched through the prefix
   Load distribution: 0 1 0 1 0 1 0 1 0 0 0 0 0 0 0 0 (refcount 1)

   Hash   OK   Interface         Address        Packets   Tags imposed
   1      Y    ATM1/0.2          point2point          0    none
   2      Y    ATM1/0.3          point2point          0    none
   3      Y    ATM1/0.2          point2point          0    none
   4      Y    ATM1/0.3          point2point          0    none
   5      Y    ATM1/0.2          point2point          0    none
   6      Y    ATM1/0.3          point2point          0    none
   7      Y    ATM1/0.2          point2point          0    none
   8      Y    ATM1/0.3          point2point          0    none
   9      Y    ATM1/0.2          point2point          0    none
   10     Y    ATM1/0.2          point2point          0    none
   11     Y    ATM1/0.2          point2point          0    none
   12     Y    ATM1/0.2          point2point          0    none
   13     Y    ATM1/0.2          point2point          0    none
   14     Y    ATM1/0.2          point2point          0    none
   15     Y    ATM1/0.2          point2point          0    none
   16     Y    ATM1/0.2          point2point          0    none
C7200#
```

Listing 5-40. *Routing table and FIB entries for unequal-cost load sharing*

By default, CEF performs per destination load sharing. The following interface configuration command instructs the router to perform per packet load sharing when forwarding packets out of the specified interface:

ip load-sharing { **per-destination** | **per-packet** }

Load-sharing flags are set on the FIB entries when path structures are added to or deleted from them. For per packet load balancing to be enabled on an FIB entry, all paths linked to it need to refer to the interface with per packet load sharing enabled. If the entry references an unresolved path or a path through an interface with per destination load sharing, all packets forwarded along this FIB entry will be processed using the default—per destination—load-sharing algorithm.

5.7 Summary

- IP packet forwarding entails three steps: reception of IP packets, forwarding decision, and outbound-interface packet delivery. IP input processing includes packet verification and local/remote delivery decision. If the packet needs to be locally delivered, it is queued for further processing by corresponding processes running on the router itself. Otherwise, the packet is passed to the forwarding engine that performs routing table lookup and finds out the outbound interface and the IP address of the next-hop router. If the router is configured with policy-based routing, its forwarding decision follows the set of rules, or policies, configured by the administrator. The packet is then passed to the packet-delivery functions, which find data link layer details, based on the next-hop router address; perform encapsulation of the packet; and enqueue it for further transmission.

- Cisco IOS supports a number of forwarding techniques, or packet-switching methods. Process switching, the legacy method initially implemented in Cisco routers, implies that packets are queued by the interrupt-processing functions and are processed later by a scheduled process, using the main routing table. This method is known to be slow. Fast switching is a cache-based method that increases packet-forwarding performance via caching of the forwarding decisions made at the process level and using the cache entries later in the interrupt-level functions to forward received packets without involving a scheduled process. CEF, the most powerful switching method in Cisco IOS, is not cache based, so it does not experience the scalability issues of fast switching. CEF switching is based on the forwarding table (FIB) constructed using the information in the routing table but is intensively optimized for high-performance packet forwarding: A maximum of four indexing operations are necessary to find the best-matching route. FIB contains all routes present in the routing table in a resolved form, so the router does not have to perform recursive routing table lookup when forwarding transit packets. A number of platform-specific forwarding methods are also available on various Cisco platforms.

- Status of the **ip classless** command affects the way routing table lookup is performed when packets are forwarded. When classless lookup is used, the router looks for the longest matching route—which can be a supernet route even if a subnet of the destination major network is known—or uses the default route if no matching route is found. With classful lookup, the router looks at supernet routes and the default only if it does not have any routes to subnets in the destination major network. CEF forwarding is always performed in the classless mode.

- Packets may be routed along routes with no reference to an interface. In such cases, the router performs recursive routing table lookup to find the outbound interface.

- Support for multiple routes to the same destination allows the forwarding engine in Cisco routers to perform load sharing among multiple paths.

5.8 Frequently Asked Questions

Q: **Is it possible to configure a Cisco router to perform forwarding based on source addresses?**

A: Cisco routers will not perform routing table lookup using the source address but can be configured with policy-based routing that is used to forward packets using arbitrary rules, such as incoming interface or the source IP address.

Q: **Is it possible to have multiple routing and forwarding tables in Cisco IOS and assign them to different interfaces?**

A: Yes, Cisco IOS supports the notion of *virtual routing and forwarding* instances (VRFs). Each interface can be assigned to its VRF. Each VRF has its routing and forwarding tables. Operation of the routing protocols is also changed to honor VRFs. See [MPLS-VPN] for more information.

Q: **I need to load share among multiple paths in my network. Is my only choice to disable fast switching and go with process switching?**

A: Process switching is one option. However, if your router supports CEF forwarding, it is recommended to use CEF with per packet load sharing to accomplish this in order to avoid high CPU load.

Q: **Is it possible to perform load sharing of traffic when it is forwarded along the default route?**

A: Yes. Packet forwarding along the default route is the same as along any matching route. Even though the output of the **show ip route** command displays parameters of only one path in the prefix descriptor, all paths are used.

Q: **What is the difference between the route cache that is used for fast switching and the FIB used in CEF?**

A: First, a fast switching data entry is a cache of the decision made during the process-level switching, whereas FIB is a lightweight, very well optimized copy of the main routing table and contains all routes that the routing table has. In addition, the route cache structure is organized as radix tree, whereas FIB structure is based on 256-way tree. FIB is not updated as packets are switched; the route cache is.

Q: **If I need to enable CEF switching on a production router, should I expect any disruption in packet forwarding performed by the router?**

A: Yes. If the routing table contains recursive routes, such as BGP routes, packet forwarding along these routes will be disrupted for several seconds until the FIB maintenance process resolves all recursive routes. In most situations, this disruption is negligible. However, it is still a good idea to enable CEF during the maintenance window. Note that disabling CEF does not have the same effect, as the router can switch to another switching method instantaneously.

5.9 References

[DIAL] "Cisco IOS Dial Services Configuration Guide," http://www.cisco.com/univercd/cc/td/doc/product/software/ios121/121cgcr/dialts_c/index.htm.

[IPCONF] "Cisco IP Addressing Configuration," http://www.cisco.com/univercd/cc/td/doc/product/software/ios121/121cgcr/ip_c/ipcprt1/1cdipadr.htm.

[Knuth] D. Knuth, *The Art of Computer Programming*, Reading, MA: Addison-Wesley, 1998.

[MPLS-VPN] http://www.cisco.com/univercd/cc/td/doc/product/software/ios120/120newft/120t/ 120t5/vpn.htm.

[NetFlow] http://www.cisco.com/warp/public/cc/pd/iosw/ioft/neflct/tech/ napps_wp. htm.

[RFC1112] S. Deering, "Host Extensions for IP Multicasting," STD 5, RFC 1112, May 1988.

[RFC 1812] F. Baker, "Requirements for IP Version 4 Routers," RFC 1812, June 1995.

[RFC 1701] S. Hanks, T. Li, D. Farinacci, and P. Traina, "Generic Routing Encapsulation," RFC 1701, October 1994.

[RFC 3031] E. Rosen, A. Viswanathan, and R. Callon, "Multiprotocol Label Switching Architecture," RFC 3031, January 2001.

[Sedgewick] Robert Sedgewick, *Algorithms in C++: Fundamentals, Data Structures, Sorting, Searching*, Reading, MA: Addison-Wesley, 1998.

[Vegesna] Srinivas Vegesna, *IP Quality of Service (Cisco Networking Fundamentals*, Indianapolis, IN: Cisco Press, 2001.

Chapter Six

Static Routes

Although most, if not all, of today's IP networks run dynamic routing protocols, static routing is still widely deployed, mostly because static routes allow administrators to change traffic flow trajectories and to apply arbitrary routing policies. Static routing can be used as a complementary technique when the router's forwarding decision needs to be affected without changes to the configuration of the dynamic routing protocols. Static routes are also used when dynamic routing is not necessary or not desirable because of the network topology, bandwidth constraints, or security reasons.

This chapter gives an in-depth explanation of static routing in Cisco IOS. Such details as forwarding along various types of static routes, altering administrative distance values, and providing default routing information are included. A thorough understanding of static routing is essential for successful network administration. Improper use of static routes can easily lead to routing loops and link bandwidth exhaustion. On the other hand, static routes become a useful tool for a well-educated administrator.

6.1 Static Routes in Cisco Routers

As discussed in previous chapters, static routes in Cisco IOS can be of the following three types, referencing

- Only interfaces
- Only intermediate network addresses
- Both interfaces and next-hop addresses

Unlike UNIX, in which the intermediate network address must belong to a directly attached subnet and thus be the next-hop address, Cisco IOS allows intermediate network addresses to be resolvable via any route in the routing table, no matter which source provides it. Chapter 4 contains information on resolvability and internal maintenance of static routes. Here, we explore the differences among the types of static routes from the network administrator's point of view.

If you revisit the logic of the forwarding engine in Cisco routers, you can see that when a packet is routed along a route referencing only an interface, the packet's destination address is used as the next-hop address. This is done just the same way as when a packet is delivered to a host on a directly attached subnet: The forwarding engine finds the interface route, takes the destination address as the next hop, and passes this information to the packet-delivery procedure. The packet-delivery code uses ARP or map tables to find data link layer details corresponding to the next-hop address. The same process is performed when a static route is configured with interface only. So, is this good or bad?

On the one hand, the next-hop address sometimes is not necessary at all. Consider a router with a serial point-to-point interface. If it is necessary to instruct the router to forward all packets destined for a specific subnet through this interface, the administrator can configure a static route specifying the corresponding interface only, as shown in the following example. In this case, the next-hop address is never used by the packet-delivery procedure, as it is not needed, anyway, and it doesn't really matter whether it is equal to the address of the router on the other end of the link.

```
interface serial0
 description Link to Remote Subnet 10.2.0.0/16
 ip address 10.1.1.1 255.255.255.252
!
ip route 10.2.0.0 255.255.0.0 serial0
```

A completely different behavior is seen when the interface referenced in a route is multipoint or broadcast. Consider the sample topology in Figure 6-1. Router R1 is configured with a static route specifying only the output interface and no next-hop address. When R1 receives packets going to subnet 10.1.3.0/24, it follows the static route and uses the destination addresses found in the packets as the next-hop ones. This results in a large number of ARP requests sent on the Ethernet segment and the size of the ARP cache table growing proportionally. Nevertheless, such a scheme will work, as router R2 is smart enough to function as a proxy ARP server—unless it is disabled with a **no ip proxy-arp** interface configuration command—and replies with its own MAC address to ARP requests from R1.

Another example of incorrect use of static routes in a Frame Relay environment was given in Section 5.4.2.3. In that case, the forwarding engine used the destination IP addresses in the packets to look through the Frame Relay map table. As no matching entry was found—the map statements were configured for the next-hop addresses corre-

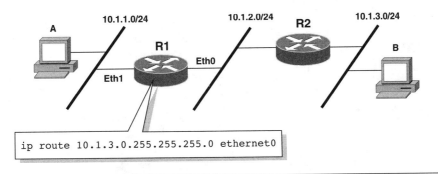

Figure 6-1. *Using static routes via broadcast interfaces*

sponding to remote routers, not hosts on remote subnets—the majority of packets were dropped. The same problem can show up if static routes referencing only interfaces are used for Dial-on-Demand Routing (DDR): The dialer maps contain the addresses of remote routers, whereas actual next-hop addresses used by the forwarding engine are the destination addresses from the packets.

So, how should the static routes be configured to function as expected? Consider the following rule of thumb.

> Use static routes over interfaces only if the corresponding interface is point-to-point, that is, if encapsulation is HDLC, SLIP, PPP, or LAPB or is a point-to-point subinterface. Otherwise, always configure static routes with both the output interface and the next-hop address.

What about static routes referencing only intermediate network address? In short, try to avoid using them. The reason is that these static routes are not bound to any interface, rely on intermediate address resolvability, and thus converge more slowly. They can also create unexpected routing loops.

For example, in Figure 6-2, router R1 has a connection to an ISP via interface Serial0 and a connection to a remote office via interface Serial1. The administrator configures R1 with a static default route via Serial0 and a static route to the remote subnet via the address of router R2. When interface Serial1 is up, the intermediate network address of the static route to the remote subnet is resolved via the interface route to subnet 10.1.1.0/30, so all traffic destined to 10.1.2.0/24 is forwarded via the appropriate interface. When Serial1 goes down, the interface route to 10.1.1.0/30 is removed, but the static route to the remote subnet is still in the routing table because its intermediate address can be resolved via the static default route. All packets coming from the ISP and destined for subnet 10.1.2.0/24 are forwarded back to the ISP and then back to R1. So, we have a loop.

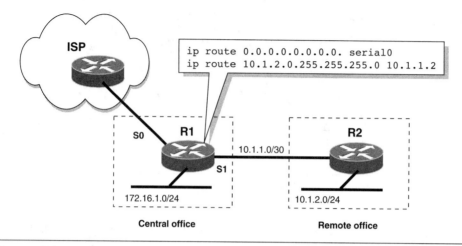

Figure 6-2. *Problems with static routes via intermediate network address*

In order to protect the network in the example from experiencing packet loops, R1 should be configured with a summary route via interface Null0, considered later in the chapter. This route should cover all destinations in the central and remote offices but on the other hand should be as specific as possible to prevent blackholing of traffic going to other subnets of the same summary.

6.2 Backup Static Routes

Static routes in Cisco IOS are by default installed with an administrative distance value of 1. A common misunderstanding is that static routes configured via interfaces are installed with an AD of 0, like interface routes. This is not true. No routing source except Connected can install routes with this AD. The reason for this misunderstanding is that static routes over interfaces are treated as directly connected routes, but that doesn't make them have an AD of 0.

Altering the value of the AD in static routes is used to configure backup static routes, also known as floating static routes, that get installed only when the primary static or dynamic route is removed from the routing table. For example, in Figure 6-3, R1 is connected to two remote offices that themselves are connected. R1 should be configured so that it normally uses Serial0 to reach networks in remote office 1 and Serial1 to reach networks in remote office 2. If one of the links fails, the router should use the remaining link to reach both locations.

To achieve the described functionality, the administrator configures R1 with the following static routes:

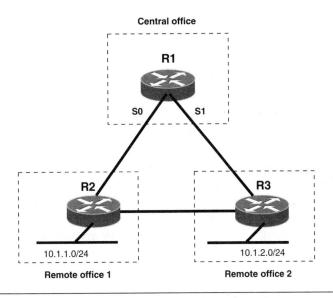

Figure 6-3. *Sample topology for backup static routes*

```
ip route 10.1.1.0 255.255.255.0 serial0
ip route 10.1.1.0 255.255.255.0 serial1 5
ip route 10.1.2.0 255.255.255.0 serial1
ip route 10.1.2.0 255.255.255.0 serial0 5
```

Note that two static routes are provided for each network: one with the default AD of 1 and one with an AD of 5. As a result, static routes with default AD values are used as the primary ones, and secondary routes appear in the routing table only when the interfaces referenced in the primary routes go down. See Listing 6-1 for an example.

```
R1#
06:31:18: %LINK-3-UPDOWN: Interface Serial0, changed state to down
06:31:18: RT: interface Serial0 removed from routing table
06:31:18: RT: delete route to 10.1.1.0 via 0.0.0.0, Serial0
06:31:18: RT: no routes to 10.1.1.0, flushing
06:31:18: RT: add 10.1.1.0/24 via 0.0.0.0, static metric [5/0]
06:31:19: %LINEPROTO-5-UPDOWN: Line protocol on Interface Serial0, changed state to
down
R1#
06:33:07: %LINK-3-UPDOWN: Interface Serial0, changed state to up
06:33:07: RT: closer admin distance for 10.1.1.0, flushing 1 routes
```

```
06:33:07: RT: add 10.1.1.0/24 via 0.0.0.0, static metric [1/0]
06:33:08: %LINEPROTO-5-UPDOWN: Line protocol on Interface Serial0, changed state to up
R1#
```

Listing 6-1. *Installation and removal of a backup static route*

Static routes can also be used in conjunction with dynamic routing protocols. In this case, a static route can be either primary or backup. If a static route should be preferable to a route supplied by a dynamic routing protocol, the administrator does not need to change the default administrative distance, because its default AD value is always better than the default AD value of any routing protocol. While the static route is in the routing table, the corresponding dynamic route is not active—is not in the routing table—but once the static route is deleted because the referenced interface is down or an intermediate network address becomes unresolvable, the dynamic route is installed in the routing table.

> Be careful when overriding a dynamic route with a static one, as you can create a routing loop if the router to which the traffic is forwarded along the static route uses a dynamic route pointing back to the router where the static route is configured.

If the static route is configured as a backup for a dynamic one, the administrator needs to alter the value of the static route's administrative distance to be worse than the administrative distance of the corresponding dynamic routing protocol. For example, if a dynamic route is provided by OSPF, whose default AD is 110, the static route must be configured with an AD greater than 110. This will make the static route appear in the routing table only if OSPF deletes its route. Listing 6-2 illustrates how a static route backs up an OSPF route to subnet 10.1.1.0/24 when the static route is withdrawn by the originating router.

```
R1#show ip route
...
Gateway of last resort is not set

    10.0.0.0/8 is variably subnetted, 2 subnets, 2 masks
O      10.1.1.0/24 [110/65] via 10.1.0.1, Serial0
C      10.100.1.1/32 is directly connected, Loopback0
R1#conf t
Enter configuration commands, one per line. End with CNTL/Z.
R1(config)#ip route 10.1.1.0 255.255.255.0 serial 1 115
R1(config)#^Z
R1#
```

```
06:40:30: RT: del 10.1.1.0/24 via 10.1.0.1, ospf metric [110/65]
06:40:30: RT: delete subnet route to 10.1.1.0/24
06:40:30: RT: add 10.1.1.0/24 via 0.0.0.0, static metric [115/0]
R1#
```

Listing 6-2. *Static route backing up a dynamic OSPF one*

6.3 Using Static Routes in NBMA and Dial-Up Environments

In non-broadcaset multi-access (NBMA)—Frame Relay, ATM, or X.25—and dial-up—ISDN or PSTN—environments, when available bandwidth is limited, use of static routes can be an effective alternative to dynamic routing protocols. Following the basic rules given in Chapter 3, static routes must be configured on all routers within the network and must cover all potential destinations. The best type of static route to be used in this situation is a static route referencing both the output interface and the next-hop address.

> In dial-up and NBMA environments with manually configured map entries, the next-hop addresses in the static routes are significant only within the router. These addresses are used only as unique tokens to find the proper map entry and do not need to correspond to the real network addresses of the remote routers.

This note means that if static routes are configured with both output interfaces and next-hop addresses, the next-hop addresses do not need to correspond to the actual IP addresses of the next-hop routers, as they are used locally to look through the corresponding map tables. For example, in Figure 6-4, router R1 is attached to an ISDN cloud and uses it to reach three other routers. From the network layer's standpoint, the ISDN cloud is one IP subnet, 10.1.1.0/24.

R1 is configured as follows:

```
hostname R1
!
interface bri0
 ip address 10.1.1.1 255.255.255.0
 dialer map ip 1.1.1.2 name R2 5557722
 dialer map ip 1.1.1.3 name R3 5557733
 dialer map ip 1.1.1.4 name R4 5557744
 dialer-group 1
!
dialer-list 1 protocol ip permit
!
ip route 10.1.2.0 255.255.255.0 bri0 1.1.1.2
ip route 10.1.3.0 255.255.255.0 bri0 1.1.1.3
ip route 10.1.4.0 255.255.255.0 bri0 1.1.1.4
```

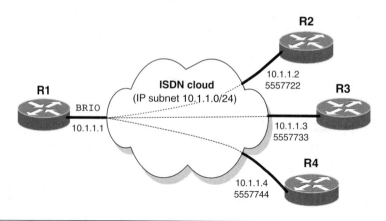

Figure 6-4. *Use of static routes in dial-up environment*

Note that next-hop addresses in static routes are not real, but this scheme works fine, as addresses used in static routes match the addresses configured in the dialer map entries and the routers have no way to check the remote interface addresses. Changing the encapsulation method on the BRI interface from HDLC to PPP breaks this example, however, because the routers start checking whether the configuration of the remote devices matches the locally configured map statements.

6.4 Default Routes

Static routes can be used to supply the default route to the routing table. In Chapter 4, it was noted that every time a route to pseudonetwork 0.0.0.0/0 is installed into the routing table, that route is automatically marked as a candidate default. Because the default values of the metric and the AD for static routes are 0 and 1, a static default route will most probably become the real default (see Listing 6-3).

```
R1#show ip route
...
Gateway of last resort is not set

   10.0.0.0/8 is variably subnetted, 2 subnets, 2 masks
S     10.1.1.0/24 is directly connected, Serial1
C     10.100.1.1/32 is directly connected, Loopback0
R1#conf t
Enter configuration commands, one per line. End with CNTL/Z.
```

```
R1(config)#ip route 0.0.0.0 0.0.0.0 ser1
R1(config)#
06:44:31: RT: add 0.0.0.0/0 via 0.0.0.0, static metric [1/0]
06:44:31: RT: default path is now 0.0.0.0 via 0.0.0.0
06:44:31: RT: new default network 0.0.0.0
R1(config)#^Z
R1#show ip route
...
Gateway of last resort is 0.0.0.0 to network 0.0.0.0

    10.0.0.0/8 is variably subnetted, 2 subnets, 2 masks
S     10.1.1.0/24 is directly connected, Serial1
C     10.100.1.1/32 is directly connected, Loopback0
S*  0.0.0.0/0 is directly connected, Serial1
R1#
```

Listing 6-3. *Configuring default route, using a static route to pseudonetwork 0.0.0.0*

Another way to configure a static default route is to mark a static route to a major network as a candidate default, using the **ip default-network** global configuration command, as illustrated in Listing 6-4. This method can be used when the administrator wants to tie the presence of the default route to availability of a specific major network.

```
R1#show ip route
...
Gateway of last resort is not set

    10.0.0.0/8 is variably subnetted, 2 subnets, 2 masks
S     10.1.1.0/24 is directly connected, Serial1
C     10.100.1.1/32 is directly connected, Loopback0
R1#conf t
Enter configuration commands, one per line. End with CNTL/Z.
R1(config)#ip route 20.0.0.0 255.0.0.0 serial1 10.1.2.1
06:50:40: RT: add 20.0.0.0/8 via 10.1.2.1, static metric [1/0]
R1(config)#ip default-network 20.0.0.0
R1(config)#^Z
R1#
06:50:46: RT: 20.0.0.0 is now exterior
06:50:46: RT: default path is now 20.0.0.0 via 10.1.2.1
06:50:46: RT: new default network 20.0.0.0
R1#show ip route
...
Gateway of last resort is 10.1.2.1 to network 20.0.0.0

S*  20.0.0.0/8 [1/0] via 10.1.2.1, Serial1
    10.0.0.0/8 is variably subnetted, 2 subnets, 2 masks
```

```
S    10.1.1.0/24 is directly connected, Serial1
C    10.100.1.1/32 is directly connected, Loopback0
R1#
```

Listing 6-4. *Configuring the default route, using the static route and the* **ip default-network** *command*

Note that the static route must be configured with a next-hop address in this case; otherwise, it will not be considered as a candidate default but only as an exterior route.

It is always a good idea to configure static default routes with the output interface specified, as it allows skipping recursive routing table lookups during packet forwarding and improves the stability of the routing table. The next-hop address is also desirable, as it saves the network from excessive ARP traffic on broadcast segments.

6.5 Routing Loops and Discard Routes

When used incorrectly, static routes can lead to routing loops if packets going from one router to another are forwarded back to the first router. Let's consider several scenarios in which such loops are created, with explanations of why this happens and how to configure routers correctly.

Figure 6-5 shows a sample network, with router R1 located in the central office and connected to R2 and R3, which are in corresponding remote offices. Routers R2 and R3 also have a link between them. R1 is configured with static routes to remote subnets 10.1.2.0/24 and 10.1.3.0/24 via corresponding interfaces. Static routes to the remote subnets are also provided to R2 and R3. In addition, R2 and R3 are configured with default routes, the primary one via Serial0 and a backup via Serial1. The idea behind this configuration is to make R2 and R3 use the primary link to R1 for routing to unknown destinations, most probably located in the central office or in the Internet, in normal circumstances and to switch to backup links through the other remote office in case of a failure.

R1 is configured with two routes for each remote subnet, with the primary route through the direct link and a secondary one through the link to the other remote office, as follows:

```
hostname R1
!
interface ethernet0
 ip address 10.1.1.0 255.255.255.0
!
interface ethernet1
 ip address 10.2.1.0 255.255.255.0
!
interface serial0
```

```
 description Link to Office 1
 ip unnumbered ethernet0
!
interface serial1
 description Link to Office 2
 ip unnumbered ethernet0
!
ip route 10.1.2.0 255.255.255.0 serial0
ip route 10.1.2.0 255.255.255.0 serial0 5
ip route 10.1.3.0 255.255.255.0 serial1
ip route 10.1.3.0 255.255.255.0 serial1 5
```

The configuration of routers R2 follows:

```
hostname R2
!
interface ethernet0
 ip address 10.1.2.0 255.255.255.0
!
interface serial 0
 description Link to Central office
 ip unnumbered ethernet0
!
interface serial 1
```

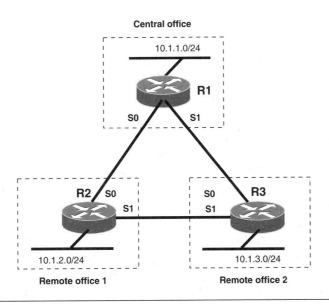

Figure 6-5. *Sample topology for routing loops with static routes*

```
description Link to Office 2
ip unnumbered ethernet0
!
ip classless
!
ip route 10.1.3.0 255.255.255.0 serial1
ip route 0.0.0.0 0.0.0.0 serial0
ip route 0.0.0.0 0.0.0.0 serial 1 5
```

The configuration of R3 follows:

```
hostname R3
!
interface ethernet0
 ip address 10.1.3.0 255.255.255.0
!
interface serial 0
 description Link to Central office
 ip unnumbered ethernet0
!
interface serial 1
 description Link to Office 1
 ip unnumbered ethernet0
!
ip classless
!
ip route 10.1.2.0 255.255.255.0 serial1
ip route 0.0.0.0 0.0.0.0 serial0
ip route 0.0.0.0 0.0.0.0 serial 1 5
```

Note that the **ip classless** command is necessary for R2 and R3. Otherwise, packets going to unknown subnets of a local major network would be dropped instead of being forwarded along the default route through interface Serial0.

All routers work correctly while all links are operational. However, when it loses its connectivity with R1, R2 removes the primary default route from its routing table and installs the backup via R3. Everything is still okay, as R3 uses its primary default to R1 for unknown destinations. If we now consider the possibility of a link failure between R3 and R1, we can see that a loop is formed between R2 and R3 because both routers use their backup static defaults, pointing to each other.

In the described scenario, there is no way to correctly configure backup default routes on both R2 and R3 without losing some level of redundancy. The reason is that static routing cannot check whether a network is actually accessible via a specified interface. The workaround here could be to configure no backup default route on either R2 or R3, but the best way would be to run a dynamic routing protocol, described in later chapters. Dynamic routing is definitely the right choice for complex networks with a high level of redundancy and a large number of alternative paths.

More interesting examples of routing loops can be seen when route summarization is used. In Figure 6-6, router R1 belongs to the network in the central office, and R2 serves a remote one. R2 has several LAN segments assigned subnets of major network 192.168.1.0 and one unnumbered point-to-point serial link to R1. Note that major network 192.168.1.0 is assigned to the remote office, and so R1 is configured with a summary route to 192.168.1.0/24 via interface Serial0. R2 is configured with a static default route via its interface, Serial0, to provide connectivity to external networks. Everything seems to be normal, and it does work fine while we're considering packets destined to existing subnets in the remote site. However, if R1 receives a packet with the destination IP address set to 192.168.1.254, R1 follows the summary network route and forwards the packet to R2. R2 in turn does not have an explicit route to the destination subnet and, because **ip classless** is enabled on it, forwards the packet back to R1 along the default route.

The administrator could remedy this problem by turning off the **ip classless** command on R2. This would make R2 drop packets going to unknown subnets. This method cannot always be used, though, because a router can have subnets of some major networks not directly connected to it, and it can be desirable to rely on default routing in order to reach them. To fix this problem, R2 must be configured with a static discard route corresponding to the summary route in R1's routing table, as shown in the following example. If it receives a packet for which it has a route more specific than the discard aggregate, R2 forwards the packet, using the more specific route. Otherwise, the discard route is used and the packet is dropped.

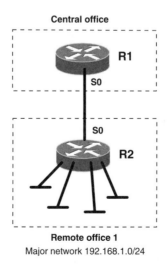

Figure 6-6. *Sample topology for static discard routes*

```
hostname R2
!
interface ethernet0
 description LAN1
 ip address 192.168.1.1 255.255.255.224
...
interface ethernet6
 description LAN6
 ip address 192.168.1.161 255.255.255.224
!
interface loopback0
 description Placeholder of IP address
 ip address 192.168.1.2 255.255.255.255
!
interface serial0
 description Uplink to the Central Site
 ip unnumbered loopback0
!
ip classless
!
ip route 0.0.0.0 0.0.0.0 serial0
!
! Discard route to prevent routing loops
ip route 192.168.1.0 255.255.255.0 null0
```

Configuring discard routes is the only way to prevent routing loops when several major networks are summarized into a supernet. In our example, R1 would have an aggregate supernet route covering all major networks accessible via R2:

```
hostname R1
!
interface ethernet0
 description LAN
 ip address 10.1.1.1 255.255.255.0
!
interface loopback0
 description Placeholder of IP address
 ip address 10.10.10.1 255.255.255.255
!
interface serial0
 description Link to Remote Site 1
 ip unnumbered loopback0
!
ip route 192.168.0.0 255.255.0.0 serial0
```

R2, however, could have these major networks used on LAN interfaces and the supernet discard route configured as static, as follows:

```
hostname R2
!
interface ethernet0
 description LAN1
 ip address 192.168.1.1 255.255.255.0
...
interface ethernet6
 description LAN6
 ip address 192.168.6.0 255.255.255.0
!
interface loopback0
 description Placeholder of IP address
 ip address 192.168.7.1 255.255.255.0
!
interface serial0
 description Uplink to the Central Site
 ip unnumbered loopback0
!
ip classless
!
ip route 0.0.0.0 0.0.0.0 serial0
!
! Discard route to prevent routing loops
ip route 192.168.0.0 255.255.0.0 null0
```

Without a discard route, if R1 forwards to R2 a packet destined for a major network covered by the supernet route in R1's routing table but not known by R2, R2 forwards the packet back to R1, regardless of the state of **ip classless**.

6.6 Implementation Scenarios

Several scenarios described in the following subsections give you practical examples of static routing. Although this book cannot cover all possible situations when static routes can be used, the examples given here cover the most common scenarios. In complex networks, you will most probably want to use dynamic routing protocols, as static routing is not scalable and has significant administrative overhead.

6.6.1 ISP and a Customer

When a corporate network is connected to an ISP via a single link, it is usually not necessary to run a dynamic routing protocol between the ISP and the customer. Consider the example in Figure 6-7, which shows a small company connected to an ISP through a serial link. The company's network consists of two sites—the central office and a remote office—connected by routers R2 and R3. For the sake of this discussion, all IP addresses assigned to network devices and hosts are taken from the private address range—

172.16.30.0/24. In reality, the ISP gives a prefix covering a range of public IP addresses to the customer.

Consider configuration of the ISP's router R1; only the relevant part of the configuration is given:

```
hostname R1
!
interface serial0
 description Link to Customer C1
 ip unnumbered loopback0
!
ip route 172.16.30.0 255.255.255.0 serial0
```

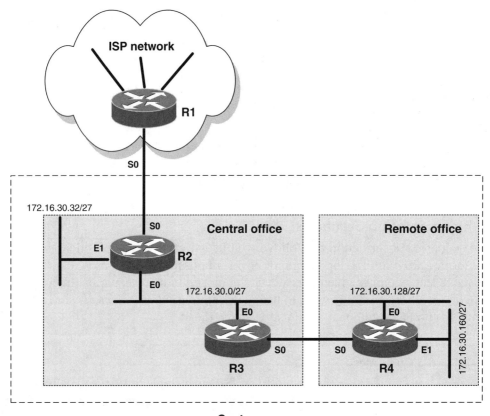

Figure 6-7. *Sample corporate network connected to an ISP*

The interface Serial0 is not assigned a separate IP address. Instead, the **ip unnumbered** command is used to preserve IP addresses for LAN segments and real hosts. Note that the static route to the customer's network does not reference a next-hop address, because the link is point-to-point, and the next-hop address is ignored by the forwarding engine, anyway.

> Even if the interface is configured with **ip unnumbered**, a static route via an intermediate IP address can still be used. However, this approach would require configuration of another static route, giving the router knowledge of how this address can be reached:
>
> **ip route 172.16.30.0 255.255.255.0 1.1.1.1**
> **ip route 1.1.1.1 255.255.255.255 serial0**
>
> Note that this configuration does not give any benefits but only leads to odd routing table lookups when forwarding packets.

The static route covers the whole address range allocated for the customer and not separate subnets. This reduces the size of the routing table and the router's configuration. Another interesting detail is that the static route to the customer's network will most probably be redistributed into a dynamic routing protocol running in the ISP's network so that other routers in the network know how to reach the customer's addresses. This is also necessary for BGP-enabled routers, because BGP must see a route in the routing table before advertising it outside.

Let's now look at the configuration of the customer router:

```
hostname R2
!
interface ethernet0
 description LAN 1st Floor
 ip address 172.16.30.1 255.255.255.224
!
interface ethernet1
 description LAN 2nd Floor
 ip address 172.16.30.33 255.255.255.224
!
interface serial0
 description Link to ISP
 ip unnumbered ethernet0
!
ip classless
```

```
ip route 0.0.0.0 0.0.0.0 serial0
ip route 172.16.30.0 255.255.255.0 nul0
ip route 172.16.30.128 255.255.255.224 ethernet0 172.16.30.2
ip route 172.16.30.160 255.255.255.224 ethernet0 172.16.30.2
```

IP processing on the Serial0 interface is enabled by the **ip unnumbered** command. A static default route is configured over this interface to provide a path to unknown destinations. In order to provide successful routing to unknown subnets of the major networks, which the customer's address space belongs to, the router is configured with the **ip classless** command, which takes effect when the router forwards a packet destined for subnets of major network 172.16.0.0 that are assigned to other clients of the same or a different ISP (see Chapter 5 for more details on **ip classless**). Note again that in this example, we use networks 172.16.0.0 to 172.31.0.0, which belong to the private address range and are not used in the Internet. In reality, such a customer would be assigned public addresses by its ISP.

Configuration of R2 includes a discard route covering the whole address range assigned to the customer network. The discard route prevents routing loops, as described in Section 5.6.

R2 is configured with two static routes covering subnets of the company's remote site. These routes reference both output interfaces and next-hop addresses, in order to avoid excessive ARP traffic on the LAN segment between R2 and R3.

Now look at the R3 configuration, which connects the central and remote offices:

```
hostname R3
!
interface ethernet0
 description LAN 1st Floor
 ip address 172.16.30.2 255.255.255.224
!
interface serial0
 description Link to Remote Site
 ip unnumbered ethernet0
!
ip classless
ip route 0.0.0.0 0.0.0.0 ethernet0 172.16.30.1
ip route 172.16.30.128 255.255.255.224 serial0
ip route 172.16.30.160 255.255.255.224 serial0
```

The router is provided with static routes to two remote subnets via the Serial0 interface. Subnet 172.16.30.32/27, attached to R2, is not covered by a separate static route, because **ip classless**, configured on R3, already allows it to use the static default route to reach unknown subnets of locally attached major networks.

The configuration of router R4, located at the remote site, is a bit simpler:

```
hostname R4
!
interface ethernet0
 description LAN Rooms 1-10
 ip address 172.16.30.129 255.255.255.224
!
interface ethernet1
 description LAN Rooms 11-15
 ip address 172.16.30.161 255.255.255.224
!
interface serial0
 description Link to Central Office
 ip unnumbered ethernet0
!
no ip classless
ip route 0.0.0.0 0.0.0.0 serial0
ip route 172.16.0.0 255.255.0.0 serial0
```

Note the **no ip classless** command in the router's configuration. This does not cause any routing problems, because R4 uses the summary network route, 172.16.0.0/16, when routing to unknown subnets of this major network and the default static route when routing to other unknown destinations. The routing table will also contain interface routes that are used to deliver packets on the LAN segments directly attached to the router.

Configuration of the routers in the described example provides loop-free behavior. Any packet for a subnet that falls into the address range assigned to the customer but does not exist will be dropped by router R2; a static discard route ensures this.

6.6.2 Central Office and Branch Offices (Partial Mesh)

The example described here illustrates how static routing can be used in complex networks with various types of primary and backup connections. The example is quite complex.

Consider the network topology shown in Figure 6-8. The company's network includes five sites: one central office site and four remote ones. Each remote site is assigned a separate subnet from major network 10.0.0.0/8; that is, the company uses private IP addressing. Every site is given an address space in the form 10.X.0.0/16, where X is the number of the site. Subnets 10.10.0.0/26 through 10.255.0.0/16 are assigned to the central site.

The routing policy in this sample network is as follows.

- The central office and remote sites 1, 2, and 3 are interconnected via a Frame Relay cloud; each remote site has a direct VC to the central site.

- Remote office 4 does not have direct connectivity to the central site but is connected to sites 2 and 3 via leased lines.

- Sites 2 and 3 must exchange a considerable amount of traffic; hence, they have a direct VC interconnecting them.

- All sites must use appropriate Frame Relay VCs to forward traffic local to the router at the other end of the VC. That is, central router R0 must use VCs to routers R1, R2, and R3 to reach destinations in corresponding sites; R2 must use VCs to R0 and R3 to reach destinations in the central office and remote site 3, respectively.

- VC from R0 to R2 can be used as the backup for direct VC from R0 to R3.

- VC from R3 to R2 can be used as the backup for direct VC from R3 to R0.

- R1 and R2 can use ISDN connections as the backup to reach the central site.

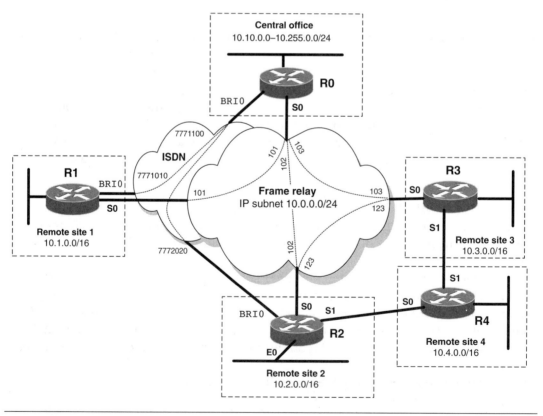

Figure 6-8. *Complex example of a corporate network with static routing*

- R0 can also use ISDN connections to reach sites 1 and 2 should the Frame Relay VCs fail.

- R4 should use the link to R3 as its primary connection to reach destinations in site 3 and the central office. The link from R4 to R2 must be used as the primary connection for destinations in site 2 and as the backup connection for destinations in site 2 and the central office.

Central router R0 is configured as follows. (Note that configuration of LAN interfaces is not included, as we're interested in routing to remote networks.)

```
hostname R0
!
! User database for CHAP authentication on BRI
username R1 password R0R1
username R2 password R0R2
!
interface loopback0
 description Placeholder of IP for FR
 ip address 10.0.0.100 255.255.255.255
!
interface serial0
 description Link to FR provider see subinterfaces
 encapsulation frame-relay
 frame-relay lmi-type ansi
 no ip address
 ! Note that we don't enable IP on this interface
!
interface serial0.1 point-to-point
 description VC to Site 1
 frame-relay interface-dlci 101
 ip unnumbered loopback0
!
interface serial0.2 point-to-point
 description VC to Site 2
 frame-relay interface-dlci 102
 ip unnumbered loopback0
!
interface serial0.3 point-to-point
 description VC to Site 3
 frame-relay interface-dlci 103
 ip unnumbered loopback0
!
interface bri0
 description Dial backup for FR VCs
 encapsulation ppp
 ppp authentication chap
 ip unnumbered loopback0
```

```
!
! IP next-hop addresses in the following map entries don't need to be real,
! they should just correspond to those used in static routes, but it's a good idea to make
! them correspond to real addresses
!
dialer map ip 10.0.0.1 name R1 7771010
dialer map ip 10.0.0.2 name R2 7772020
dialer load-threshold 50
dialer-group 1
!
dialer-list 1 protocol ip permit
!
! we do not have the default route
no ip classless
!
! Routes to Site 1
ip route 10.1.0.0 255.255.0.0 serial0.1
ip route 10.1.0.0 255.255.0.0 bri0 10.0.0.1 5
!
! Routes to Site 2
ip route 10.2.0.0 255.255.0.0 serial0.2
ip route 10.2.0.0 255.255.0.0 bri0 10.0.0.2 5
!
! Routes to Site 3
ip route 10.3.0.0 255.255.0.0 serial0.3
ip route 10.3.0.0 255.255.0.0 serial0.2 5
!
! Routes to Site 4
ip route 10.4.0.0 255.255.0.0 serial0.3
ip route 10.4.0.0 255.255.0.0 serial0.2 5
ip route 10.4.0.0 255.255.0.0 bri0 10.0.0.2 6
!
```

All subinterfaces are configured as point-to-point. Each subinterface terminates one Frame Relay PVC. IP processing is enabled on the subinterfaces, using the **ip unnumbered** command.

Primary and backup static routes are configured for each remote subnet. For example, three routes are provided for subnet 10.4.0.0/16, remote site 4: the primary route over subinterface Serial0.3, via remote site 3; and two backup routes over subinterface Serial0.2, via remote site 2, and over interface BRI0, also via remote site 2. The first backup static route is installed in the routing table only when the primary route is deleted: Subinterface Serial0.2 goes down owing to primary interface or PVC failure. The second backup route, via the BRI interface, in turn, is used only when both the primary and the first backup routes are not resolvable.

The configuration of router R1 follows:

```
hostname R1
!
! User database for CHAP authentication on BRI
username R0 password R0R1
!
interface loopback0
 description Placeholder of IP for FR
 ip address 10.0.0.1 255.255.255.255
!
interface serial0
 description Link to FR provider see subinterfaces
 encapsulation frame-relay
 frame-relay lmi-type ansi
 no ip address
 ! Note that we don't enable IP on this interface
!
interface serial0.1 point-to-point
 description VC to Central Site 1
 frame-relay interface-dlci 101
 ip unnumbered loopback0
!
interface bri0
 description Dial backup to Central Site
 encapsulation ppp
 ppp authentication chap
 ip unnumbered loopback0
 dialer map ip 10.0.0.100 name R0 7771100
 dialer load-threshold 50
 dialer-group 1
!
dialer-list 1 protocol ip permit
!
! follow the default for unknown subnets
ip classless
!
! The default route is enough, since we have ip classless on
ip route 0.0.0.0 0.0.0.0 serial0.1
ip route 0.0.0.0 0.0.0.0 bri0 10.0.0.100 5
```

Because site 1 can reach all remote networks only through the central site, router R1 is configured with two static default routes: the primary route through the Frame Relay cloud and a secondary route via the BRI interface. Because the **ip classless** command is configured, the router uses the configured default route to reach unknown subnets.

Now proceed to the configuration of router R2:

```
hostname R2
!
! User database for CHAP authentication on BRI
```

```
username R0 password R0R2
!
...
! Loopback, serial0, and BRI0 configuration commands are removed, see R1's configuration
!
interface serial1
 description Leased Line to Site 4
 ip unnumbered loopback0
!
! follow the default for unknown subnets
ip classless
!
! Route to Site 3
ip route 10.3.0.0.0 255.255.0.0 serial0.2
ip route 10.3.0.0.0 255.255.0.0 null0 5
!
! Route to Site4
ip route 10.4.0.0 255.255.0.0 serial1
ip route 10.4.0.0 255.255.0.0 null0 5
!
! Default route to all other subnets
ip route 0.0.0.0 0.0.0.0 serial0.1
ip route 0.0.0.0 0.0.0.0 bri0 5
```

R2 is configured with discard static routes that are installed when primary static routes go away. This definitely limits the set of alternative paths that could be used by the router. But without the discard routes, the network could experience routing loops when, for example, PVCs 103 and 123 fail. The reason is that R2 would forward all packets destined for site 3 to R0—following the default that is necessary to reach unknown subnets and external destinations—and R0 would forward them back to R2 along its backup static route.

Also note that the backup default route does not specify the next-hop address, although the output interface is configured with DDR (interface BRI0). The reason is that BRI0 is configured with the **dialer-string** command instead of a **dialer map** to indicate that the interface will always dial the same number, regardless of the next-hop address.

Consider the configuration of router R3, which has three connections: Frame Relay PVCs to R0 and R2 and a leased line to R4:

```
hostname R3
!
...
! Loopback, and serial0 configuration commands are removed, see R1's configuration
!
interface serial1
 description Leased Line to Site 4
```

```
 ip unnumbered loopback0
 !
 ! follow the default for unknown subnets
 ip classless
 !
 ! Route to Site 2
 ip route 10.2.0.0 255.255.0.0 serial0.2
 !
 ! Route to Site 4
 ip route 10.4.0.0 255.255.0.0 serial1
 ip route 10.4.0.0 255.255.0.0 serial0.2 5
 !
 ! Default route, covers Central Site, Site 1 and external destinations
 ip route 0.0.0.0 0.0.0.0 serial0.1
 ip route 0.0.0.0 0.0.0.0 serial0.2 5
```

Note that R3's configuration contains no backup static route to site 2. The router will use the default static route to forward packets to the central site even if its direct PVC to R2 fails.

The following configuration is applied to router R4 and is very simple:

```
 hostname R4
 !
 interface loopback0
  description Placeholder of IP for FR
  ip address 10.0.0.4 255.255.255.255
 !
 interface serial0
  description Leased Line to Site 2
  ip unnumbered loopback0
 !
 interface serial1
  description Leased Line to Site 3
  ip unnumbered loopback0
 !
 ! follow the default for unknown subnets
 ip classless
 !
 ! Default is enough
 ip route 0.0.0.0 0.0.0.0 serial1
 ip route 0.0.0.0 0.0.0.0 serial0 5
```

It is interesting to see how static routing in our example limits the set of alternative paths in favor of loop-free routing. The discussion also gives an idea of how difficult it is to use static routes to maintain networks of a considerable size.

6.7 Frequently Asked Questions

Q: **What is the purpose of configuring so-called static host routes?**

A: Static host routes are routes configured with the /32 route mask, using the following syntax:

ip route *host-address* **255.255.255.255 ...**

These routes are used to inform the router that a specific IP host must be reached via a path different from the subnet to which its IP address belongs. This type of route can be useful when, for example, it is necessary to take an IP address out of a connected subnet and give it to a remote router or a host reachable through a point-to-point link. In this case, your routing table will have routes similar to those shown in Figure 6-13.

```
R1#show ip route
...
C    10.1.1.0/24 is directly connected, Ethernet0
S    10.1.1.15/32 is directly connected, Serial0
R1#
```

Listing 6-5. *Example of a static host route*

Q: **How do I configure a static route that can monitor a remote link?**

A: In general, static routes cannot monitor the state of the links on remote routers. However, if a dynamic routing protocol is running in your network, you can configure a static route via the address of a remote subnet. The static route will be present in the routing table only if a dynamic route to the remote subnet also exists. Routing to the address range specified in the static route will be performed along the same path as to the remote subnet known via the dynamic routing protocol. This feature should be used with caution, because in some situations, described earlier in this chapter, an intermediate network address referenced in such a static route can be resolved via the default route, and this can lead to routing loops.

Q: **How do backup static routes and backup interfaces correlate?**

A: Cisco IOS includes the notion of a backup interface. The following interface configuration command can be used to inform the router about which interface must be activated when the one for which the command is configured goes down:

backup interface *type number*

Once this command is configured, the backup interface transitions to "standby" state, which is similar to state "administratively down." The backup interface stays in the standby state until the primary interface goes down. When this happens, the backup interface is activated. Backup static routes can be used together with backup interfaces. It is not necessary, but not prohibited, to alter the backup route's AD value if the route references the backup interface, because the route is installed in the routing table only when the primary interface goes down and the backup one goes up. Following is an example of a backup static route configured with a backup interface:

```
interface ethernet0
 description LAN segment
 ip address 10.0.0.1 255.255.255.0
!
interface serial0
 description Primary Link to Central Site via E1
 ip unnumbered ethernet0
 backup interface BRI0
 backup delay 0 0
!
interface BRI0
 description Backup Link to Central Site via ISDN Cloud
 ip unnumbered ethernet0
 dialer-string 5556677
 dialer-group 1
!
dialer-list 1 protocol ip permit
!
! Primary static route to Central Site subnet
ip route 10.1.0.0 255.255.0.0 serial0
! Backup static route to Central Site subnet
ip route 10.1.0.0 255.255.0.0 BRI0
```

Q: **Can backup static routes be used to provide dial backup?**

A: Yes, you can use backup static routes for dial backup. All you need to do is configure static routes and the dialing interface properly. A sample configuration follows:

```
interface ethernet0
 description LAN segment
 ip address 10.0.0.1 255.255.255.0
!
```

```
interface serial0
 description Primary Link to Central Site via E1
 ip unnumbered ethernet0
!
interface BRI0
 description Backup Link to Central Site via ISDN Cloud
 ip unnumbered ethernet0
 dialer-string 5556677
 dialer-group 1
!
dialer-list 1 protocol ip permit
!
! Primary static route to Central Site subnet
ip route 10.1.0.0 255.255.0.0 serial0
! Backup static route to Central Site subnet
ip route 10.1.0.0 255.255.0.0 BRI0 5
```

Note that no backup interface is configured for Serial0, but the router will not initiate dialing on the BRI0 interface until an interesting packet is forwarded through it. The forwarding engine, in turn, won't forward packets to BRI0 until a route in the routing table is referencing it, and the second (backup) static route will be installed only when the first static route goes away, when interface Serial0 goes down.

Q: **What is the preferred way to configure a static default route?**

A: The easiest, preferred way is to configure a static route to pseudonetwork 0.0.0.0/0 via both the interface and the next-hop address. This route will always function as expected and can be redistributed into almost all dynamic routing protocols, except IGRP as discussed in Chapter 8.

Q: **Is it possible to achieve load sharing with static routes?**

A: Yes, if you configure more than one static route covering exactly the same address range, up to six of them will be installed into the routing table. Transit and locally originated traffic will be distributed among them in equal proportions. See Section 5.6 for more details on load sharing in Cisco IOS.

Chapter Seven

Dynamic Routing Protocols
in Cisco IOS

This chapter discusses concepts that are common for all dynamic routing protocols in Cisco IOS. This includes commonalities in protocol operation, as well as operating system features that are applicable to all protocols discussed in later chapters.

7.1 Common Functionality of Dynamic Routing Protocols

Despite all the differences in routing protocols, such as underlying mathematical basis or transport protocols, several characteristics are common for all of them. The main one is obviously the objective. Routing protocols are implemented in routers to calculate routes to remote networks. Generally speaking, the two main tasks that any dynamic routing protocol must finally accomplish are to (1) discover remote networks reachable in the domain, and (2) associate discovered networks with correct neighboring routers, or neighbors. The first task provides reachability information that is used to construct the prefix descriptor part of a route. The second task provides information necessary to find the next-hop routers for each destination and to construct the path descriptor structures for the routes.

In order to achieve this, routing protocols perform, in one form or another, the following elementary tasks:

- Neighbor discovery
- Remote network discovery, with networks finally reachable via the neighbors
- Detection of unreachable neighbors
- Detection of unreachable networks
- Best-path selection

Later chapters provide detailed information on specific routing protocols, including the methods used to accomplish the aforementioned tasks. Here, only a brief description of the methods is given for each class of routing protocol.

Distance-vector protocols—RIP versions 1 and 2 and IGRP—perform neighbor and network discovery by periodically sending broadcast (RIPv1 and IGRP) or multicast (RIPv2) messages on all interfaces. These messages function as both neighbor announcements and network announcements. When router A receives from router B a message containing information about network *N*, router A installs in its routing table a route to network *N* via neighbor B.

Detection of unreachable neighbors and networks in distance-vector protocols is performed by using the route-expiration technique. Every route provided by a distance-vector protocol must be periodically updated in order to stay in the routing table. If the original *successor*—a neighbor residing closer to the destination and through which packet forwarding to this destination is performed—does not update a route by sending periodic messages during a predefined period of time, this neighbor is deemed to have no ability to route packets to that destination any more, and the route through it is removed. In addition to the timer-expiration method, routers using distance-vector protocols can send explicit withdraw messages, notifying neighbors that a network is not reachable through them any more and that alternative paths should be used, if possible.

Distance-vector routing protocols select best paths to remote networks by choosing the route with the lowest metric. The metric of a directly connected route is always 0; when a route is put into a message, its metric is recalculated—for example, incremented in the case of RIP—to include the information about the part of the path corresponding to the link from the announcing router to the receiving router.

In link-state routing protocols (OSPF and IS-IS), a different approach is used. Neighbor discovery, maintenance, and unreachable-neighbor detection are achieved through a special subprotocol, called *Hello*. Each router periodically sends a small hello message to its neighbors, identifying itself as operational. If such a message is not received in a reasonable amount of time, the corresponding neighbor is declared down.

Link-state protocols do not relay routing information as distance-vector protocols do. Instead, each router abstracts the piece of topology local to it and associates routing information with itself. This information is distributed to other routers in special messages using the *flooding algorithm*. Every router maintains a number of *link-state databases* (LSDBs), which are used to store the network topology. The algorithms for flooding and LSDB synchronization ensure that all routers keep their LSDBs synchronized with one another. LSDBs provide routers with information sufficient to reconstruct the network topology and to determine the best paths to all remote networks, based on the summary path costs, the sum of costs of all links that must be traversed in order to reach a specific network. When a specific link or a network attachment goes down, the router builds the new version of the corresponding topology data block containing the up-to-date information and floods it to all other routers. Remote routers recalculate the network topology and change their routing tables accordingly. Because topology information is flooded to all routers, link-state protocols are often called topology-broadcast-based protocols.

Enhanced IGRP, which is a hybrid protocol, also uses a version of the Hello subprotocol to maintain adjacencies, but the mathematical basis of it is not the same as that of the link-state protocols. EIGRP uses an improved distance-vector approach, developed by J. J. Garcia Luna Aceves, to achieve loop-free routing with improved convergence characteristics (see [EIGRP]).

7.2 Routing Protocol Configuration

All IP routing protocols in Cisco IOS must be explicitly configured to run, unlike IPX RIP, which is enabled by default, for example. Basic configuration steps, outlined in Chapter 4, include starting the protocol software module by using the **router** *protocol-name* configuration command and specifying the interfaces on which the protocol must operate, by using a number of **network** *network-address* statements. The following configuration example contains a very simple configuration of EIGRP. Of course, real router configurations require commands that are discussed in corresponding chapters of this book.

```
interface ethernet 0
 ip address 10.1.1.1 255.255.255.0
 !
interface ethernet 1
 ip address 20.1.1.1 255.255.255.0
 !
router eigrp 100
 network 10.0.0.0
 network 20.0.0.0
 !
```

It may be necessary to disable a routing protocol on a specific interface, even if that interface's IP address is covered by a **network** statement. For this purpose, the administrator can configure the routing protocol process with a **passive-interface** *interface-name* router configuration command. For distance-vector routing protocols, this command disables transmission of the protocol packets on that interface but does not disable processing of incoming protocol messages. This means that if at least one router is sending its routing updates on the connected segment, a distance-vector protocol can still install routes through the interface specified in a **passive-interface** command in the routing table. If it is necessary to disable installation of these routes, the administrator must either configure the **passive-interface** command on all other routers connected to the link or filter the incoming updates on the receiving router, using distribute lists, considered later in this section.

When used for link-state routing protocols, the **passive-interface** command disables generation and processing of protocol packets, including Hello packets, on the specified interface and thus effectively prevents the router from forming the adjacencies with other routers connected to the link. Consequently, link-state protocols do not install any routes through passive interfaces.

In some cases, it may be necessary to disable a routing protocol on most interfaces covered by the network commands. If a router has several interfaces connected to subnets of a single major network, but a routing protocol, such as IGRP, must be executed on a single one, it is more effective to use the **passive-interface default** command to disable the routing protocol on all interfaces and to then use the **no passive-interface** command to enable the routing protocol for some specific subnets. This situation is illustrated in the the following configuration:

```
interface ethernet 0
 ip address 10.1.1.1 255.255.255.0
!
interface ethernet 1
 ip address 10.1.2.1 255.255.255.0
!
interface ethernet 2
 ip address 10.1.3.1 255.255.255.0
!
interface ethernet 3
 ip address 10.1.4.1 255.255.255.0
!
interface ethernet 4
 ip address 10.1.5.1 255.255.255.0
!
interface ethernet 5
 ip address 10.1.6.1 255.255.255.0
!
router igrp 100
 network 10.0.0.0
 passive-interface default
 no passive-interface ethernet 0
!
```

The **passive-interface default** router configuration command is available starting with IOS version 12.0.

Most dynamic routing protocols—all IGPs—are designed to find neighboring routers dynamically. Nevertheless, sometimes it may be necessary to explicitly configure a routing protocol with the list of neighbors, as when a router should send routing updates to a single neighbor on a multiaccess segment or when a routing protocol should be prevented from broadcasting on an NBMA media (Frame Relay or an X.25 cloud).

In order to provide a routing protocol with the list of neighbor IP addresses, the administrator must use the **neighbor** *ip-address* router configuration command. In the following example, RIP is configured to send its updates to a single router on the Ethernet0 interface and to four remote routers reachable via a Frame Relay network:

```
interface ethernet0
 ip address 10.1.1.1 255.255.255.0
 !
interface serial0
 encapsulation frame-relay
 ip address 20.1.1.1 255.255.255.0
 frame-relay map ip 20.1.1.2 100
 frame-relay map ip 20.1.1.3 200
 frame-relay map ip 20.1.1.4 300
 frame-relay map ip 20.1.1.5 400
 !
router rip
 network 10.0.0.0
 network 20.0.0.0
 passive-interface ethernet 0
 passive-interface serial 0
 neighbor 10.1.1.5
 neighbor 20.1.1.2
 neighbor 20.1.1.3
 neighbor 20.1.1.4
 neighbor 20.1.1.5
 !
```

Note that in this example, the **passive-interface** command disables transmission of RIP broadcast updates, whereas the **neighbor** commands instruct RIP to send unicast updates to specified neighbors.

The next configuration example illustrates how the **frame-relay map** commands must be changed to ensure propagation of broadcast RIP updates through specific VCs without statically configured neighbors.

```
interface ethernet 0
 ip address 10.1.1.1 255.255.255.0
 !
interface serial 0
 encapsulation frame-relay
 ip address 20.1.1.1 255.255.255.0
 frame-relay map ip 20.1.1.2 100 broadcast
 frame-relay map ip 20.1.1.3 200 broadcast
```

```
frame-relay map ip 20.1.1.4 300 broadcast
frame-relay map ip 20.1.1.5 400 broadcast
!
router rip
 network 10.0.0.0
 network 20.0.0.0
 passive-interface ethernet 0
!
```

The **broadcast** keywords in the **frame-relay map** commands make the router replicate the broadcast messages generated by RIP for the serial interface—note that the **passive-interface** command for interface Serial0 has been removed—and send them through appropriate Frame Relay VCs.

Another technique common to all routing protocols is route filtering. Cisco routers can be configured to filter routes received or sent by the routing protocols. This is achieved through configuration of distribute lists. Distribute lists are direction specific. A routing protocol can be configured with a single distribute list in a single direction. The following types of distribute lists can be configured for a routing protocol:

- General inbound and outbound distribute lists
- Interface specific inbound and outbound distribute lists
- Outbound distribute lists used when routes from a particular route source are redistributed in the protocol (considered in Section 7.4)

General distribute lists are applied to all incoming and outgoing routing updates, depending on the direction of the configured distribute list. Interface-specific distribute lists are applied to the routing protocol messages coming from or going out of specific interfaces mentioned in the configuration. Source-specific distribute lists are used to filter redistributed routes when they are imported from the routing table by the announcing routing protocol.

Configuration of distribute lists is pretty simple. The administrator must configure a standard access list and reference it in a **distribute-list** statement of the configured routing protocol. The following example demonstrates how a routing protocol can be configured with general and interface-specific inbound and outbound distribute lists:

```
interface ethernet 0
 ip address 10.1.1.1 255.255.255.0
!
interface ethernet 1
 ip address 20.1.1.1 255.255.255.0
!
```

```
router igrp 100
 network 10.0.0.0
 network 20.0.0.0
 distribute-list 1 in ethernet 0
 distribute-list 2 out ethernet 0
 distribute-list 3 in
 distribute-list 4 out
 !
 access-list 1 permit 10.1.0.0 0.0.255.255        ! I want to know about 10.1.X.X subnets only
 access-list 1 deny any
 !
 access-list 2 deny 10.0.0.0 0.255.255.255        ! Don't announce 10.X.X.X subnets to net 20.0.0.0
 access-list 2 permit any
 !
 access-list 3 permit 10.0.0.0 0.255.255.255      ! Make sure I don't install routes to other major nets
 access-list 3 permit 20.0.0.0 0.255.255.255
 access-list 3 deny any
 !
 access-list 4 deny host 10.1.1.0                 ! Don't announce my private subnet
 access-list 4 permit any
```

The exact logic of distribute lists depends on the type of the routing protocol—distance vector or link state—and is considered in more detail in the corresponding chapters of the book.

Extended access lists can be used in distribute lists with some routing protocols to filter routes based on both prefix value and prefix length. Check the corresponding chapters for more information.

Every routing protocol has a default value of the administrative distance for the routes it installs in the routing table (see Chapter 4 for more information). This default value may be changed by using the **distance** *ad-value* router configuration command, the short form of the **distance** command. The same command, when used in the long form—**distance** *ad-value network wildcard-mask [access-list]*—can be used for more flexible AD assignment on a per route or per neighbor basis. The first two parameters are similar to the address and the wildcard portions of the access list entries and are used to identify routes based on the route's network part. The optional access list is applied to the IP address of the router that submitted the route and can be used to assign different AD values, based on the address of the reporting router. This useful feature can be used when, for example, the administrator does not trust all neighbors and the protocol itself does not allow for message authentication, such as RIP version 1. In this case, a configuration similar to the following could be used:

```
router rip
 network 10.0.0.0
 network 20.0.0.0
 distance 255 0.0.0.0 255.255.255.255 1
 !
access-list 1 permit host 10.1.1.2      ! Do not trust these hosts
access-list 1 permit host 10.1.1.3
access-list 1 permit host 20.1.1.2
access-list 1 permit host 20.1.1.3
```

In this example, the router is instructed to assign AD 255 to the routes that are received from routers 10.1.1.2, 10.1.1.3, 20.1.1.2, and 20.1.1.3. This will effectively filter out the routes received in the updates from these neighbors—an AD of 255 means that the route should never be installed—whereas the routes from other neighbors are installed in the routing table with the default AD value for RIP—120.

Note that there can be only one short-form **distance** sentence and multiple long-form sentences in a routing protocol configuration. If multiple long-form sentences are configured, they are considered in the same order as entered by the administrator.

7.3 Routing Protocol Data Structures

All routing protocol parameters configured by the administrator or set to their default values are stored in two types of data structures: protocol descriptors, containing general configuration information for a routing protocol; and instances of TRPInterfaceInfo, holding the interface-specific information for the protocol. Complete pseudocode type definition for protocol descriptor structure is given in Listing 7-1.

```
// TProto.Type values:
#define RS_DYNAMIC    0x0100
#define RS_DV         0x0200 + RS_DYNAMIC

#define RS_CONNECTED 0x0001
#define RS_STATIC     0x0002
#define RS_RIP        0x0003 + RS_DV
#define RS_IGRP       0x0004 + RS_DV
#define RS_OSPF       0x0005 + RS_DYNAMIC
#define RS_EIGRP      0x0006 + RS_DYNAMIC
#define RS_ISIS       0x0007 + RS_DYNAMIC
#define RS_EGP        0x0008 + RS_DYNAMIC
#define RS_BGP        0x0009 + RS_DYNAMIC
#define RS_MAX        0x0009

typedef struct Proto{           // Route source descriptor
        u_int         Type;
```

```
        u_int        ID;
        text         Code;              // Text source code;
        text         Name;              // The name of the process
        u_char       Distance;          // Administrative distance
        TprotoTimers *Timers;
        TEvVectors   *Vectors;
        TMetricInfo  *MetricInfo;
        TList        *Networks;
        TList        *Neighbors;
        TList        *RedistributedTo;  // Where to redistribute
        TList        *RedistributeFrom; // What to redistribute
        TList        *ADMaps;           // Distance maps
        u_int        DefaultMetric;
        u_int        DistributeListIn;
        u_int        DistributeListOut;
        u_int        OffsetIn;
        u_int        OffsetListIn;
        u_int        OffsetOut;
        u_int        OffsetListOut;
        u_char       DefaultOriginate;
        //...
} TProto;
```

Listing 7-1. *Pseudocode: Full definition of the* TProto *data structure*

The fields in the protocol descriptor data structure are used as follows:

- Type, the routing source type: Connected, Static, RIP, IGRP, and so on

- ID, the unique numeric identifier of a routing protocol process

- Code, the string used in the output of the **show ip route** command to mark routes installed by the corresponding route source

- Name, the full name of the source

- Distance, the default value of the administrative distance

- Timers, pointers to an instance of the TProtoTimers structure, which contains the information necessary for the RT process to maintain routes installed by the distance-vector protocols (see Chapter 8)

- MetricInfo, a pointer to an instance of the TMetricInfo structure, which provides generic information about route metrics used by the routing protocol, especially the infinity metric value

- Networks, a list of network elements that correspond to the **network** router configuration commands specified by the administrator

- Neighbors, a list of manually configured neighbors

- RedistributedTo and RedistributeFrom, fields that contain information about protocols that are interested in redistributing routes from the owner of the protocol descriptor and about sources the owner of the protocol descriptor itself is configured to redistribute

- `ADMaps`, a list containing information configured with the long form of the **distance** command

- `DefaultMetric`, the metric value used by the routing protocol for the routes redistributed from other sources when no source-specific metric is specified (discussed further in Section 7.4)

- `DistributeListIn` and `DistributeListOut`, fields that contain the identifiers of the general inbound and outbound distribute lists

- `OffsetIn`, `OffsetListIn`, `OffsetOut`, and `OffsetListOut`, fields that store information about inbound and outbound offset lists used to alter the route metric in updates of distance-vector routing protocols (see Chapter 8)

- `DefaultOriginate`, a flag that indicates whether the protocol should inject default routes into the routing domain

All dynamic route sources allocate and initialize protocol descriptors dynamically when corresponding processes are started. Two static protocol descriptors—Connected and Static—describe permanent route sources.

Cisco IOS also supports only one instance of RIP and BGP per router. In addition, the number of protocol descriptors in Cisco IOS is limited to 32. Because two descriptors are allocated for Connected and Static route sources on system startup, the number of dynamic routing processes is limited to 30 in the same router.

Whenever a routing protocol is enabled on an interface, an instance of the routing protocol interface data structure—`TRPInterfaceInfo`, shown in Listing 7-2—is linked to the `RPInfo` list of the corresponding interface descriptor.

```
typedef struct RPAuxInfo{ // Auxiliary protocol-specific interface info
   struct RIPInterfaceInfo   *RIPInfo;
   struct IGRPInterfaceInfo  *IGRPInfo;
   struct OSPFInterfaceInfo  *OSPFInfo;
   struct EIGRPInterfaceInfo *EIGRPInfo;
   struct ISISInterfaceInfo  *ISISInfo;
   //...
} TRPAuxInfo;


typedef struct RPInterfaceInfo{ // Routing Protocol Interface Info
   u_int         Type;          // Protocol Type
```

```
u_int         ID;                // Process ID
u_char        Passive;
u_char        SplitHorizons;
u_int         *DistributeListIn;
u_int         *DistributeListOut;
u_int         *OffsetListIn;
u_int         OffsetIn;
u_int         *OffsetListOut;
u_int         OffsetOut;
TRPAuxInfo    AuxInfo;
} TRPInterfaceInfo;
```

Listing 7-2. *Pseudocode: Definition of the* TRPInterfaceInfo *data structure*

When multiple routing protocols are enabled on the same interface, the RPInfo list contains more than one instance of TRPInterfaceInfo, each containing information specific to a particular routing protocol.

To illustrate how protocol descriptors and interface data structures are used, consider the pseudocode of the Proto_DistributeListOut() function (Listing 7-3). The function accepts the network portion of the route and the output interface as the arguments and returns 1 if the route to the specified network is not prohibited by the general or interface-specific outbound distribute list. The Proto_FindIntInfo() function used in the pseudocode locates the instance of TRPInterfaceInfo structure in the interface list. The function Proto_DistributeListIn()(Listing 7-4) returns 1 if the route to the specified network is not prohibited by the general or interface-specific inbound distribute list.

```
int Proto_DistributeListOut(TPROTO * TheProto, TIPAddress Network,
                            TInterfaceDescr * TheInt)
{
  TRPInterfaceInfo *IntInfo;

  if (TheProto->DistributeListOut &&
      IPdeniedByACL (TheProto->DistributeListOut, Network))
    return 0;

  IntInfo = Proto_FindIntInfo(TheProto, TheInt);
  if (IntInfo == NULL) return 1;

  if (IntInfo->DistributeListOut &&
      IPdeniedByACL (IntInfo->DistributeListOut, Network))
    return 0;
  return 1;
}
```

Listing 7-3. *Pseudocode: The function* Proto_DistributeListOut()

```
int Proto_DistributeListIn(TPROTO * TheProto, TIPAddress Network,
                           TInterfaceDescr * TheInt)
{
  TRPInterfaceInfo *IntInfo;

  IntInfo = Proto_FindIntInfo(TheProto, TheInt);
  if (IntInfo == NULL) return 1;

  if (IntInfo->DistributeListIn &&
      IPdeniedByACL (IntInfo->DistributeListIn, Network))
    return 0;

  if (TheProto->DistributeListIn &&
      IPdeniedByACL (TheProto->DistributeListIn, Network))
    return 0;

  return 1;
}
```

Listing 7-4. *Pseudocode: The function* `Proto_DistributeListIn()`

The pseudocode in Listing 7–5 contains the definition of the `TADInfo` data structure. This structure is used to store information configured with the long form of the **distance** command. Instances of this data structure are stored in the `ADMaps` field of the protocol descriptors.

```
typedef struct ADInfo {
    u_char      Distance;
    TIPAddress  Network;    // The network portion to test
    TIPAddress  Mask;       // The wildcard mask
    u_int       ACL;        // ACL to filter on per-router basis
} TADInfo;
```

Listing 7-5. *Pseudocode: Definition of the* `TADInfo` *data structure*

The function `Proto_ADForRoute()` (Listing 7-6) returns the AD value, based on the network portion of the route to be installed in the routing table and configuration of the routing protocol. It illustrates the logic performed by the routing protocols when multiple **distance** statements are configured.

```
u_char Proto_ADForRoute(TPROTO * TheProto, TIPAddress Network,
                        TIPAddress NextHop)
{
  TListNode * node;
```

```
   TADInfo * Info;

 FOR_EVERY(node, TheProto->ADMaps){
   if ((Info = node->data)==NULL)
      continue;

   if ((Network & ~Info->Mask)==Info->Network){
      if (Info->ACL &&
          IPdeniedByACL(Info->ACL, NextHop))
         continue;
      else
         return Info->Distance;
   }
 }

   return TheProto->Distance;
 }
```

Listing 7-6. *Pseudocode: The function* `Proto_ADForRoute()`

Essentially, the function goes through a set of instances of the TADInfo data structure—we assume that the instances are sorted so that more specific entries go first—and checks whether the network portion of the route matches the network and mask values specified in the long-form **distance** commands. If an entry matches, the function checks whether the next-hop address of the route is permitted by the access list specified in the command, if any. If no access list has been configured or the address is permitted, the AD value configured in the command is returned. Otherwise, the next entry is considered. If no entry matched the route, the function returns the AD value assigned to the protocol by default or using the short form of the **distance** command.

7.4 Route Redistribution

Information in the routing table can be provided by many sources. However, dynamic routing protocols normally do not take into consideration routes installed by other processes. For example, when it composes a message, also called a routing update, an RIP process searches the routing table for the directly connected routes, derived from the interface addresses or static, covered by its network configuration statements and the routes that the protocol installed itself: RIP routes. Routes are announced by RIP with the metric by one greater than the corresponding metric in the routing table. RIP just skips routes from other route sources by default. Nevertheless, in some situations, it may be necessary to inject routing information provided by one routing protocol into the messages of another. Consider an example.

Two companies are merging and both have their own corporate IP networks. Company A uses OSPF as the routing protocol and company B uses EIGRP. The two companies want to provide connectivity between the networks, and neither side is willing to reconfigure its routers in favor of the other routing protocol. In this situation, a border router can be placed between the routing domains. A subset of the router's interfaces is attached to the network of company A, and another subset is attached to the network of company B. The router is configured to participate in both the OSPF and EIGRP domains. However, this doesn't provide connectivity between the networks yet, because neither OSPF nor EIGRP advertises the routes of its counterpart. The routing protocols on the border router must be configured for route redistribution to make the things work. When configured to redistribute the routes of another route source, a routing protocol searches the routing table for the routes of the redistributed protocol while building the routing update and includes them in the message. The definition of route redistribution follows.

> Route redistribution is the process of adoption of routes from the routing table, performed by a dynamic routing protocol that is not the source of these routes.

Different protocols use different approaches for this purpose, but the main idea is the same. The redistributing protocol imports the routes installed in the routing table by the redistributed route source and injects them into its own domain. In the example of two corporate networks, the border router will announce EIGRP-learned routes into the OSPF and OSPF-learned routes into the EIGRP domain as external.

Redistribution is configured by using the **redistribute** router configuration command, as shown in the following example:

```
interface ethernet 0
 description Company A subnet 1
 ip address 10.1.1.1 255.255.255.0
!
interface ethernet 1
 description Company A subnet 2
 ip address 10.1.2.1 255.255.255.0
!
interface ethernet 2
 description Company B subnet 1
 ip address 20.1.1.1 255.255.255.0
!
interface ethernet 3
 description Company B subnet 2
 ip address 20.1.2.1 255.255.255.0
!
router ospf 10
 network 10.0.0.0 0.255.255.255 area 0
 redistribute eigrp 100 subnets
!
router eigrp 100
 network 20.0.0.0
```

```
redistribute ospf 10 match internal
default-metric 10000 10 255 1 1500
```

When RIP, IGRP, or EIGRP is configured to redistribute routes supplied by a different routing protocol, it is necessary to instruct the router about the metric parameters that should be used when redistributed routes are incorporated into the messages. RIP uses a hop count of 16 by default, thus making other routers treat redistributed routes as unreachable. IGRP and EIGRP do not redistribute routes if metric information is not specified. The **default-metric** router configuration command provides the seed metric information to the redistributing routing protocol, as shown in the previous configuration example. The value configured with this command is used for all redistributed routes. However, sometimes it is necessary to define different seed metrics for different types of redistributed routes. This can be done by using an extended syntax of the **redistribute** router configuration command, shown in the following example:

```
...
!
router eigrp 100
 network 20.0.0.0
 redistribute ospf 10 match internal metric 10000 10 255 1 1500
```

Here, the EIGRP process is configured to redistribute only internal OSPF routes—no external OSPF routes will be redistributed—and to announce them with specified bandwidth, delay, reliability, load, and MTU values.

When a routing protocol A is configured to redistribute routes from a routing protocol B, directly connected routes covered by the network statements of protocol B are also redistributed. Static routes are also redistributed automatically if they reference interfaces only—considered directly connected—and are covered by a network statement. Metric assignment for automatically redistributed static routes is performed as for the routes to directly connected networks.

Whenever a routing protocol is configured to redistribute routes from another routesource, an instance of the `TRedistributeInfo` data structure (Listing 7-7) is included in the `RedistributeFrom` list of the corresponding protocol descriptor. The `Proto_IsRedistributed()` function (Listing 7-8) illustrates how the router decides whether a route should be redistributed.

```
typedef struct RedistributeInfo{
        u_int  Type;
        u_int  ID;
```

```
        u_int  Metric;
        u_int  DistributeList;
        //...
} TRedistributeInfo;
```

Listing 7-7. *Pseudocode: Definition of the* TRedistributeInfo *data structure*

```
int Proto_IsRedistributed(TPROTO * TheProto, TPrefixDescr * Route)
{
TListNode         * node;
TRedistributeInfo * Info;
TPROTO            * Proto;
TPrefixDescr      * Copy;
int                 Permit;

/* first check whether it's a connected route covered by our
   own network clause
 */

if (Route->Connected) {

    if (Proto_CoveredByNetwork(TheProto, Route->Network))
      return 0;
      /* The route was announced by the protocol as internal */

    if (Proto_FindRedistributeInfo(TheProto, Route->Source->Type,
                          Route->Source->ID))
      if (Proto_RedistributeList(TheProto, Route))
        return 1; /* Explicitly redistributed */


    /* Now check if it's a connected route covered
       by a network clause of a redistributed protocol
     */

    FOR_EVERY(node, TheProto->RedistributeFrom){

      if ((Info = node->data)==NULL)
        continue;

      if ((Info->Type == RS_CONNECTED) ||
         (Info->Type == RS_STATIC))
        continue;

    Proto = Proto_Find(Info->Type, Info->ID);

      if (Proto_CoveredByNetwork(Proto, Route->Network)){

        Copy = CopyRoute(Route);
        Copy->Source = Proto;

        Permit = Proto_RedistributeList(TheProto, Copy);
```

```
        FreeRoute(Copy);

        if (Permit) return 1;
    }
  }

  return 0;
} /* Route->Connected */

if (Proto_FindRedistributeInfo(TheProto, Route->Source->Type,
                               Route->Source->ID))
    if (Proto_RedistributeList(TheProto, Route))
       return 1; /* Explicitly redistributed */

  return 0;
}
```

Listing 7-8. *Pseudocode: The function* `Proto_IsRedistributed()`

The logic implemented in this function is as follows.

1. If a route is directly connected, perform the following steps.
    a. If the route is covered by a network statement of the redistributing protocol, it is announced as internal to that protocol and is not redistributed.
    b. Otherwise, if an explicit **redistribute connected** or a **redistribute static** command is configured and the route is not filtered out by a corresponding distribute list, it is accepted for redistribution.
    c. Otherwise, if the route is covered by a **network** statement of a redistributed protocol and is not filtered by a distribute list specific for redistribution out of this protocol, the route is accepted for redistribution.
    d. Otherwise, the directly connected route is not redistributed.
2. If the route is not directly connected, it is redistributed only when there is a corresponding **redistribute** statement for the route source and the route is not filtered by a corresponding distribute list.

Note that according to this algorithm, a directly connected route can get redistributed via two paths—either explicitly via redistribution of the route source or implicitly via redistribution of a routing protocol that covers the route with one of the configured networks. For example, suppose that a router is running EIGRP and OSPF as shown in the following configuration:

```
interface ethernet 0
 ip address 10.1.1.1 255.255.255.0
```

```
!
interface ethernet 1
 ip address 20.1.1.1 255.255.255.0
!
router eigrp 100
 network 10.0.0.0
 default-metric 10000 10 255 1 1500
 redistribute ospf 100
!
router ospf 100
 network 20.0.0.0 0.255.255.255 area 0
!
```

The administrator configured EIGRP to redistribute OSPF routes, using a **redistribute ospf 100** command and did not configure redistribution of connected routes. However, because the route derived from the IP address of the Ethernet1 interface is covered by the network statement in OSPF, that route will also be redistributed.

Function `Proto_RedistributeMetric()`, displayed in Listing 7-9, returns the value of the metric that must used when the route passed as the argument is redistributed. Note that if no source-specific metric information is available—configured in the **redistribute** statement—the default metric value from the **default-metric** command is used. Functions used by IGRP and EIGRP to obtain the seed metric value are a bit different, because these protocols need to know a set of parameters to announce in the update instead of a single scalar value (see Chapters 8 and 10 for more details on IGRP and EIGRP).

```
u_int Proto_RedistributeMetric(TPROTO * TheProto, TPROTO * Source)
{
  TRedistributeInfo * Info;

  Info = Proto_FindRedistributeInfo(TheProto, Source->Type, Source->ID);
  if (Info)
     return Info->Metric;
  return TheProto->DefaultMetric;
}
```

Listing 7-9. *Pseudocode: The function* `Proto_RedistributeMetric()`

Besides the distribute lists, the administrator can control the route-redistribution process by using *route maps*. A route map is a set of numerated structures sharing the same name, as shown in the following syntax outline.

route-map *name* {**permit**|**deny**} *seq_num_1*
 match *condition*

match *condition2*
...
match *conditionN*
set *parameter value*
set *parameter2 value*
...
set *parameterN value*

route-map *name* {**permit**|**deny**} *seq_num_2*
  match *condition*
...
  set *parameter value*
...

Every structure contains a set of clauses of two types: **match** and **set**. The **match** clauses are used to identify the routes for which the **set** clauses must be executed. A route map structure itself can also be configured with either the **permit** or the **deny** keyword, specifying whether the routes identified by the **match** clause should be redistributed or omitted from redistribution. The route map structures are processed according to the sequence numbers specified in the **route-map** command. If a route satisfies the **match** criterion of a route map structure, the **set** clauses in the structure are executed, and no other structures are considered.

Following is the list of parameters that can be used in the **match** clause of a route map structure when used to control route redistribution.

- **as-path**, applicable for BGP routes only, identifies routes on the basis of the AS_PATH BGP route attribute.

- **community-list**, applicable for BGP routes only, identifies routes on the basis of the COMMUNITY BGP route attribute.

- **interface** allows for identification of routes on the basis of the interface they reference. If a route has multiple path descriptors, the interface specified in the first path descriptor should match the value in the route map.

- **ip address** identifies routes based on the network prefix; a standard or an extended access list number is used as the parameter.

- **ip next-hop** identifies routes on the basis of the next-hop address used in the route's path descriptor; in case of multiple path descriptors, the first path descriptor must use the address specified in the route map in order for the route to be accepted.

- **ip route-source** allows for identification of routes on the basis of the address of the router providing the route.

- **route-type** identifies routes on the basis of their types in OSPF, EIGRP, and BGP, such as internal and external routes in OSPF and EIGRP.

- **tag** identifies routes on the basis of the route tags. Not all routing protocols allow for tag assignment; for example, no tag can be announced in RIPv1 or IGRP routes.

Other attributes can be set when route maps are used for policy routing; see Chapter 6 for more details.

The following parameters can be used in the route map **set** clauses to change the parameters of announced routes:

- **as-path**, applicable only for BGP routes, changes the AS_PATH route attribute.

- **comm-list**, applicable only for BGP routes, allows restriction of the community values announced in the route; disallowed communities are removed.

- **community**, applicable only for BGP routes, sets specific community values in the routes.

- **dampening**, applicable only for BGP routes, sets BGP route flap dampening parameters.

- **level** specifies the level of the IS-IS area where redistributed routes should be announced.

- **local-preference**, applicable only for BGP routes, specifies the local-preference attribute of the BGP route.

- **metric** specifies the metric value announced in the redistributed route.

- **metric-type** specifies the type of route that must be generated: external type 1 or type 2 for OSPF and internal or external for IS-IS.

- **origin**, applicable only for BGP routes, sets the value of the BGP ORIGIN attribute.

- **tag** specifies the value that must be assigned to the `tag` field of the announced route and is valid only for RIPv2, OSPF, and EIGRP.

- **automatic-tag** specifies that the value of the tag of the BGP route installed in the routing table should be calculated automatically, based on the guidelines in [RFC1403].

- **weight**, applicable only for BGP routes, sets the weight route attribute that is local to the router.

The following configuration examples illustrate how route maps can be used to influence the process of route redistribution.

```
router ospf 100
 network 10.0.0.0 0.255.255.255 area 0
 redistribute static subnets route-map StaticToOSPF
!
route-map StaticToOSPF deny 10
 ! deny routes from major network 20.0.0.0
 match ip address 5
!
route-map StaticToOSPF permit 20
 ! For the route to subnet 10.1.1.0 set metric to be 50
 match ip address 6
 set metric 50
!
route-map StaticToOSPF permit 30
 ! For the route to subnet 30.5.1.0 set tag to value 1
 match ip address 7
 set tag 1
!
route-map StaticToOSPF permit 40
 ! Permit all other routes
 match ip address 8
!
access-list 5 permit 20.0.0.0 0.255.255.255
!
access-list 6 permit host 10.1.1.0
!
access-list 7 permit host 30.5.1.0
!
access-list 8 permit any
```

In this example, route map StaticToOSPF is used apply the following policy to redistributed routes.

- No routes to the subnets of major network 20.0.0.0 must be announced.
- When the route to subnet 10.1.1.0 is announced, the external metric of the generated OSPF route must be set to 50. (The same route may be announced by another OSPF router with a different metric.)
- The route to subnet 30.5.1.0 must be announced with the tag value 1 to instruct another OSPF router to redistribute the route to another routing protocol.
- All other routers should be announced by using the default values: as OSPF external type 2 routes with a metric value of 20 and zero route tag.

More information on route redistribution in specific routing protocols is given in corresponding chapters.

7.5 Events Processed by Routing Protocols

Routing protocols are said to be dynamic because they are supposed to react quickly to changes in the network topology. In order to meet this requirement, routing protocol processes need to accept and process the following events:

- *Routing protocol enabled on an interface*, generated when a new network statement is added to the configuration of a routing protocol and the statement covers the interface primary or secondary IP address. (The details of secondary subnet support vary by protocol.) The routing protocol is supposed to link all necessary interface-specific information to the corresponding instance of the `TRPInterfaceInfo` structure.

- *Routing protocol disabled on an interface*, generated when a network statement is removed from the configuration of a routing protocol and this protocol is disabled on an interface.

- *Interface-up transition*, generated when an interface on which the routing protocol is enabled changes its state to up. Each protocol takes specific actions, such as starting the Hello subprotocol or enabling message processing. Distance-vector protocols send a general request on the interface and schedule sending of triggered updates to all neighbors.

- *Interface-down transition*, generated when an interface on which the routing protocol is enabled changes its state to down. Processing of this event depends on the type of protocol; link-state protocols generate a special event for the interface state machine, whereas distance-vector protocols send triggered updates to all their neighbors.

- *Redistributed route added to the routing table*, happens when a route from a route source redistributed by the routing protocol is added to the routing table. Protocols are supposed to consider the new route and announce it to its neighbors if the route passes redistribution checks.

- *Redistributed route removed from the routing table*, happens when a route from a route source redistributed by the routing protocol is removed from the routing table. Redistributing protocols need to send an update to their neighbors. Pure distance-vector routing protocols (RIP and IGRP) historically do not process this event; instead, routes no longer available for redistribution just do not appear in the routing updates and time out naturally from neighbors' routing tables.

- *Backup route request*, happens when a route to a specific destination is removed from the routing table. If other sources tried to install routes to the same destination but their routes failed the AD comparison (see Chapter 4), each source receives a backup route request. A route source receiving this request is supposed to check whether a route to the same destination can be installed.

- *Routing protocol being stopped,* generated when the routing protocol is deconfigured by the administrator or when the router is instructed to restart. The routing protocol may take some specific actions, such as withdrawing announced routes. Routes installed by the routing protocol are automatically removed from the routing table.

The protocol descriptor data structure contains the `Events` field, which allows the dynamic routing protocols to process these events. This field points to an instance of a data structure, holding so-called `callback` function pointers. These callback functions are called by the RT process when specific events are experienced. Each dynamic protocol initializes the callback fields with the addresses of its own functions.

7.6 Summary

The information presented in this chapter can be summarized as follows.

1. Cisco routers can be configured to run more than one routing protocol simultaneously.

2. Configuration of all routing protocols in Cisco IOS is similar: The global command **router** *protocol-name [process-id]* is used to start a routing protocol, and a number of **network** *network-address* router configuration commands are used to specify participating interfaces. A routing protocol can be disabled on a given interface by using the **passive-interface** *interface-name* or the **passive-interface default** router configuration command.

3. Every route source is represented with an instance of the protocol descriptor structure. Protocol descriptors contain general protocol information, such as the default value of the administrative distance, configured networks, static neighbors, and information about redistributed routes.

4. Interface-specific protocol information is stored in a data block linked to the interface descriptor. Each routing protocol maintains its own block of data.

5. Routing information received and sent on the router's interfaces by a routing protocol can be controlled by using distribute lists.

6. The administrator can control the value of the administrative distance for installed routes on a per route or a per neighbor basis, using the long form of the **distance** router configuration command.

7. By default, routing protocols do not announce routes installed in the routing table by other sources, except for directly connected routes from the Connected or Static route source, covered by the network statements.

8. All routing protocols can be configured to perform route redistribution—importing routes from the routing table installed by other route sources. Distribute lists and route maps can be used to control the redistribution process. Configuration of the default metric is necessary in most cases.

9. All dynamic routing protocols interface with the operating system, using a set of functions for such tasks as routing table manipulation and IP packet transmission and a set of callback functions used to receive external events, such as interface-up or interface-down transition.

7.7 Frequently Asked Questions

Q: **Why can only a single RIP process be configured in Cisco routers, whereas EIGRP and OSPF allow for multiple instances?**

A: This is a historical fact rather than something driven by internal architecture. RIP was the first routing protocol implemented in Cisco IOS, and there seemed to be no reason for more than one instance, as RIP didn't differentiate between internal and external—redistributed—routes and had no idea about AS numbers and boundaries. In contrast, the next routing protocol—also distance-vector—implemented in IOS—IGRP—allowed for multiple instances. This was necessary because one of the IGRP design goals was to be able to interconnect multiple routing domains. In order to do so, the AS boundary router had to run several IGRP processes.

Q: **Why must the addresses specified in the network statements be major network addresses? What if I specify a subnet to enable a routing protocol on a smaller set of interfaces?**

A: Today, this is true only for RIP and IGRP because they are classful protocols, and are supposed to run on each subnet of a major network attached to the router. If a subnet is configured in a network statement of these two protocols—and in EIGRP, using old syntax—the router automatically truncates the address to the major network boundary. All other protocols have extended syntax for the **network** configuration command, allowing for better granularity in the definition of participating interfaces.

Q: **Why doesn't the passive-interface command, when used for distance-vector protocols, prevent the router from listening to incoming routing updates?**

A: For two reasons. First, this is the way distance-vector protocols, such as RIP, are supposed to work in so-called passive mode; hence the word *passive* in the command. The passive mode could potentially be used to listen to the wire and build the routing table but not announce anything, preventing transit traffic. Second, this is flexible. If reception of incoming updates was also prohibited, configuring an interface in a listen-only mode would require more configuration through distribute lists.

Q: **If I configure OSPF to redistribute RIP routes and an RIP route gets overriden by a static route, will OSPF still announce the route?**

A: No. Because an RIP route is no longer in the routing table, the static route will not be announced by OSPF unless explicitly configured to do so, using the **redistribute static** command.

References

[EIGRP] B. Albrightson, J. J. Garcia-Luna-Aceves, and J. Boyle, "EIGRP—A Fast Routing Protocol Based on Distance Vectors," *Proc. Networld/Interop 94*, Las Vegas, Nevada, May 1994.

[RFC1403] K. Varadhan, "BGP OSPF Interaction," RFC 1403, January 1993.

Chapter Eight

Distance-Vector Routing Protocols

In Chapter 8, we begin the book's descriptions of various dynamic routing protocols. This chapter discusses distance-vector routing protocols based on implementations of the distributed Bellman-Ford algorithm. After discussing the principles of distance-vector routing protocols, we consider two protocols:

- Routing Information Protocol (RIP), one of the oldest routing protocols in the Internet
- Interior Gateway Routing Protocol (IGRP), a proprietary Cisco routing protocol

8.1 Distance-Vector Principles

The mathematical basis of the distance-vector routing protocols is the distributed version of the Bellman-Ford algorithm, named after Bellman, the author of its original (centralized) version; and Ford, who first published the distributed version of the algorithm. A formal description of these two algorithms is given in Section 8.1.7, which you should read first if you would rather have a mathematical introduction.

Because of the simplicity of the Bellman-Ford algorithm, its implementations are very efficient and hence have been used widely in many areas of computer networks, including IP routing, as well as in IP RIP, IGRP, IPX RIP, AppleTalk RTMP, and others. Although it is easy to write an implementation of a distance-vector protocol, nothing is for free. Pure distance-vector protocols suffer from possible temporary routing loops; although additional remedies are introduced into the basic algorithm, these routing protocols can nonetheless have long convergence times in some situations.

8.1.1 Topology Discovery

Let's begin our exploration of how distance-vector protocols work by considering the process of routing information exchange in a sample network. Consider a full-mesh topology of three routers: R1, R2, and R3 (Figure 8-1). Each router is attached to a LAN segment—with subnets 10.1.1.0/24, 10.1.2.0/24, and 10.1.3.0/24, respectively—and has two unnumbered serial links to every other router. Initially, the routers have the following information in the routing tables:

```
R1:    10.1.1.0/24 is directly connected to interface Ethernet 0
```

```
R2:    10.1.2.0/24 is directly connected to interface Ethernet 0
```

```
R3:    10.1.3.0/24 is directly connected to interface Ethernet 0
```

Now let's identify what information the routers should exchange to ensure connectivity to every remote LAN segment. Clearly, it is enough for every router to tell the others about its own LAN segment: directly attached networks. Because routers are fully meshed, they do not need to distribute information about networks not attached directly. When the routers have exchanged routing information, their routing tables will contain the following information:

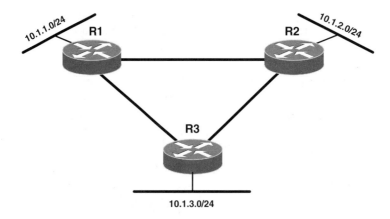

Figure 8-1. *Exchange of routing information in a full-mesh topology*

```
R1:    10.1.1.0/24 is directly connected to interface Ethernet 0
       10.1.2.0/24 is accessible via interface Serial 0, R2
       10.1.3.0/24 is accessible via interface Serial 1, R3


R2:    10.1.2.0/24 is directly connected to interface Ethernet 0
       10.1.1.0/24 is accessible via interface Serial 0, R1
       10.1.3.0/24 is accessible via interface Serial 1, R2


R3:    10.1.3.0/24 is directly connected to interface Ethernet 0
       10.1.1.0/24 is accessible via interface Serial 0, R1
       10.1.2.0/24 is accessible via interface Serial 1, R2
```

Now consider a more complex scenario (Figure 8-2). We have the same three routers, but they are not fully meshed now. R1 and R3 have a connection only to R2. In this situation, it is not enough to announce only directly connected networks, because R1 and R3 do not have a direct connection; thus, R1 has no opportunity to receive information about networks attached to R3 and vice versa. This problem can be solved if we allow R2 to relay information about networks that are not directly connected to it but have been announced to R2 by its neighbors. In this case, R2 would send routes known from R1 to R3 and routes known from R3 to R1, as shown in Figure 8-3.

So far, so good. Consider again the full-mesh topology in Figure 8-1. Now R3 receives routing information about 10.1.1.0 from two neighbors: R1, which knows about it directly; and R2, which knows about 10.1.1.0 via R1. Which of the two routes should R3

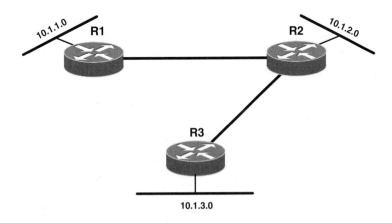

Figure 8-2. *Partial-mesh topology*

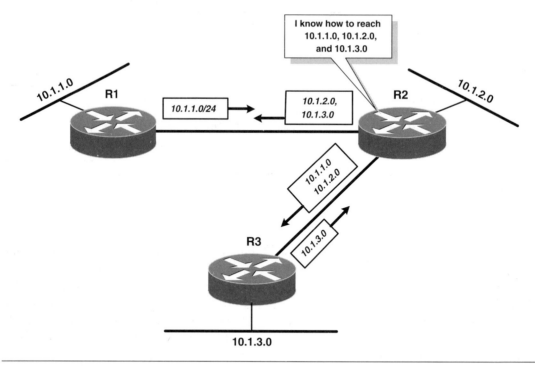

Figure 8-3. *R3 relaying routing information*

select? Obviously, R2 must install the shortest route in its routing table; otherwise, the routers could form a loop. But how does R2 know which route is better?

Each piece of routing information in distance-vector protocols is augmented with a path characteristic. Different implementations use different information for this purpose, but in the simplest case, such as RIP, this information is the number of hops that the route has traversed and, consequently, the number of hops that a packet must go through from the calculating router to the announced destination. For the metric to reflect the distance in hops, routers install routes to directly connected networks with metric 0 and increase the value of the metric when the corresponding route is put into a message to be sent to other routers. Each router installs in the routing table received routes with the metric from the received message and increases the metric when routes are sent to other routers. Therefore, the metric reflects the distance from the network in hops, and receiving routers select the routes with the fewest hops: the smallest metric value.

Another interesting detail is how messages containing routing information are sent to the neighbors. Because more than one neighbor may be on a given link in case of multi-access media and because information sent to different neighbors through the same interface is identical, sending a separate message to each neighbor is not efficient. Rather, it makes sense to use broadcasting or multicasting capabilities for these tasks.

Distance-vector protocols broadcast messages to all neighbors on a given link at once, even though they have no idea about what and how many routers are listening to them.

Now recall from Chapter 7 the list of main tasks performed by every routing protocol. Basic distance-vector functionality helps distance-vector protocols to find routes to remote destinations and to select the best path. What about other tasks, however? First, let's talk about neighbors.

Distance-vector routing protocols do not maintain formal relations with neighboring routers and do not store information about them in an explicit form, as do hybrid and link-state routing protocols. Nevertheless, routers still need to know about their neighbors because routes need to have next-hop addresses when installed in the routing table, and distance-vector protocols have to provide this information.

Imagine a router attached to an Ethernet segment and running an implementation of a distance-vector routing protocol. When sending a routing update to its neighbors, the router uses the corresponding network-layer protocol; thus, IP routing protocols send their messages in IP packets, IPX routing protocols use IPX packets, and so on. Each message is encapsulated into a packet, and the packet's header is filled in with the network address information. The destination network address is the broadcast or multicast address, but the source network address remains unicast and is set to the address of the interface through which the message is going to be sent. When neighboring routers receive the message, they extract the source IP address from the network-layer header and use that address as the next-hop address. This is how neighbors and networks are discovered in distance-vector protocols. Now what about determining unreachable networks and neighbors?

When a route supplied by a distance-vector protocol is put into the routing table, the route starts aging. When the route's age reaches a predefined value, specific to the protocol, the route is considered not valid any more and is removed from the routing table. It doesn't mean that in stable topology, routers have proper routing information only for a certain period. Every distance-vector router sends its routing updates periodically in order to refresh the routes in the neighbors' routing tables. If it has lost connectivity to a directly attached segment, a router purges the corresponding route by immediately sending an update specifying that the network is unreachable. When a neighboring router is no longer reachable because, for example, it has been turned off or has lost its network connection, distance-vector protocols do not know about this explicitly, as do link-state or hybrid routing protocols, but simply age out the routes supplied by this neighbor.

A simple formal description of the distance-vector routing algorithm follows.

1. Every router stores in the routing table all routes reported by its neighbors. Every route is augmented with the following information:

   a. Destination network address: network prefix, in the case of IP routing

   b. Route metric: cumulative cost to the network

    c. Network address of the neighbor that supplied the route

    d. Outgoing interface used for packet forwarding: the interface the update was received on

    e. Next-hop address: in most situations, the address of the neighbor that supplied the route

    f. Aging timer: used to remove from service routes not refreshed periodically by the originator

    g. Garbage collection timer: lets an invalid route stay in the routing table while neighbors are being notified

2. Every router periodically announces the contents of its routing table to its direct neighbors, modifying the attributes of the routes to reflect the cost of the output link.

3. When a routing update is received, every router processes each route record in the message, as follows.

    a. Look up a route to the same destination in the routing table.

    b. If there is no existing route and the new route is reachable, add the new route to the routing table, and perform the following actions on it.

        i.   Set the output interface to the interface on which the update was received.

        ii. Set the next-hop network address to the source address of the datagram containing the update.

        iii. Set the route metric to the value reported in the update.

        iv. Start the route age timer.

    c. If a route is found and the new route is received from the same neighbor as the already existing route, update the route metric to the value reported in the update, and restart the route age timer.

    d. If a route is found and the new route is received from a different neighbor, compare the metrics of the new and existing routes, and perform the following steps, depending on the result of the comparison.

        i.   If the metric of the new route is better—less—than the metric of the existing route, change the route metric, output interface, and next-hop address in favor of the new route, and restart the route age timer.

        ii. If the metric of the new route is worse—greater—than the metric of the existing route, ignore the new route.

        iii. If the metric of the new route is the same as the metric of the existing route, the implementation may add the route to the routing table, providing load balancing.

4. On expiration of the route age timer, mark the route as unreachable, and start the garbage collection timer. Routes in this state are included in the routing update messages as unreachable and are removed from the routing table only after the garbage collection timer has expired. Until then, these routes are used for packet forwarding. A better route to the same destination can override a route in the garbage collection state.

The algorithm provides basic distance-vector functionality and ensures that the network converges within a finite period of time. Although the distance-vector algorithm is easy to implement, distance-vector protocols have several problems, caused by the fact that every router has to trust its neighbors and has no way to verify the correctness of the advertised routes. A number of remedies have been introduced into the implementations of distance-vector protocols. We now turn to a description of these problems and the corresponding techniques used to solve them.

8.1.2 Counting-to-Infinity Problem

Consider the sample network in Figure 8-4. Assume that a distance-vector routing protocol is running in the network and that both routers announce the network attached directly to their LAN interfaces. After the initial exchange of routing updates, both routers know both networks and announce them to each other. Each router selects the route through its own interface, based on the metric comparison: 0 for connected routes versus 2 in a routing update. (In Cisco routers, the received route would fail the AD comparison.)

Now suppose that subnet 10.1.2.0, connected to R2, becomes unreachable. Having noticed that, R2 removes from the routing table the route to 10.1.2.0 and explicitly marks it as unreachable in the next periodic routing update. However, before R2 constructs and

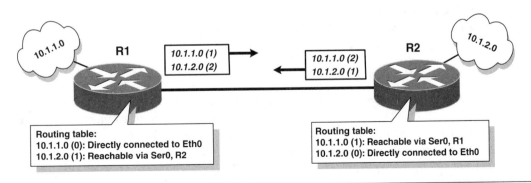

Figure 8-4. *Example of the counting problem*

sends its next routing update, R1 could send its own update, containing information that 10.1.2.0 is available via R1. Because it has no route to 10.1.2.0 in its routing table, R2 accepts information from R1 and installs the route through it. In its next routing update, R2 informs R1 that it can reach 10.1.2.0; R2's own route points back to R1. R1 accepts the new route and installs it, believing that R2 is updating the route it provided. Note that when routers send routing updates, they modify the route attributes to include the cost of the link on which the update is sent. The new metric calculated by a router receiving an update is greater than the metric in the sending router, so the route metric increases each time a router sends an update to the neighbor, and both routers believe that the information they receive is correct.

This behavior is known as "counting" and results in a routing loop. It is easy to see that the routes of R1 and R2 to network N point to each other, so if either of these two routers receives a packet destined for that network, the packet is forwarded from router to router until its TTL field reaches 0 and the packet is dropped. At first glance, it does not seem to be a problem. In reality, however, looping packets may lead to high CPU utilization and link congestion, which in turn may lead to drops of routing update packets and thus may significantly delay convergence of a distance-vector protocol.

Routing protocols based on the distance-vector algorithm limit the maximum number of hops a route can traverse in order to remedy the counting problem. In some protocols, such as RIP, this is achieved by setting the upper limit of the metric value. In this case, all values greater than the limit are considered "infinity," and networks announce with these metrics are considered infinitely remote and thus unreachable. RIP uses this approach by limiting the valid metric value—effectively, the hop count—to 15. The metric value of 16 is considered "infinity." In another distance-vector protocol—IGRP—the metric value is not limited; instead, routers explicitly include, among other route attributes, the hop count incremented by each router. IGRP does not allow a route to traverse more than 100 hops, by default. We will consider this method in more detail later, when RIP and IGRP are discussed.

The infinity metric value is also used to explicitly announce routes as unreachable. This is necessary when a router wants to withdraw a route from the network.

The following additions are made to the basic algorithm to introduce the "infinity" logic.

1. When an update message is being composed and a route's metric in the update is changed to reflect the cost of the output interface, the routers must not increase it beyond the infinity value; that is, the metric must be the minimum between the infinity value and the modified value.

2. When a route internally marked as unreachable is announced in a routing update, the route's metric must be set to infinity.

3. If, when processing an update message from another router, a route's metric is infinity, do the following.

a. If a route to the same destination exists and the message is received from the router that announced the currently installed route, mark the route as unreachable, and start the garbage collection timer.

b. Otherwise, if no route to the same destination exists or the message was received from a router other than the one that announced the currently used route, ignore the new route.

4. If the route metric is not infinity and an existing route is in the routing table, check whether the existing route is in the garbage collection state. If so, modify the route's metric, output interface, and the next-hop address in favor of the new route; stop the garbage collection timer; and start the route's age timer.

Although setting the infinity value does provide final convergence of a distance-vector protocol, it still takes a long time for the routers to agree on new routing information, using only this method. The problem described in the last example can be solved more quickly if the split-horizon technique is used.

8.1.3 Split Horizon

The split-horizon method is based on the observation that a router does not need to send information about a specific network to a neighbor that the router itself uses to reach this network. Apparently, the neighbor has a better metric for a route to the same destination and will ignore routes with higher metric values, anyway.

In the example with the routers used in the previous section, this rule instantly solves the counting problem. The loop is not formed, and the protocol does not count.

The split-horizon rule is defined as follows.

Split-horizon rule: When sending an update on a network interface, exclude the routes referencing this interface in the next-hop data structure (path descriptor).

It is interesting that the split-horizon rule does not say anything about neighbors; only interfaces are considered. Although it is obvious that each point-to-point interface corresponds to exactly one neighbor, this is not so for broadcast and point-to-multipoint links. Nevertheless, this rule works for these interfaces as well. Consider the sample network in Figure 8-5 for an explanation.

All three routers are connected to a common Ethernet segment. Because every router broadcasts its routing updates on the segment, no router need send the information about networks reachable through it. For instance, R2 sends its routing update on the Ethernet segment and includes information about network 10.1.2.0 connected to one of its interfaces. Both R1 and R3 receive this information and install proper routes via corresponding interfaces. It is now useless for R1 or R3 to send this route back to the same

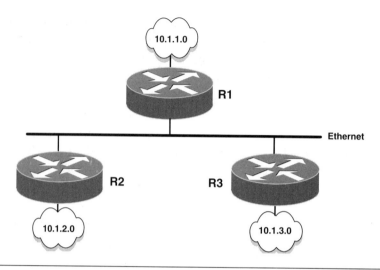

Figure 8-5. *Illustration of the split-horizon rule for LAN segments*

interface, because its metric can be only worse than the metric of routes already installed in the routing tables of their neighbors.

Another interesting detail is that the split-horizon rule works perfectly not only for routes installed by RIP but also for the routes derived from interface addresses, from the Connected route source. Figure 8-5 shows that there is no need for any of the routers to send one another information about the network assigned to the LAN segment itself, as this network is already covered by a Connected route, which cannot be overridden by any other.

The split-horizon rule may now seem to be enough to ensure robustness of a distance-vector protocol. In fact, this is not so. The split-horizon rule prevents loops involving only two neighboring routers. If the length of a loop is greater than one hop—more than two routers are involved—the split-horizon rule does not help. An example of such a situation is given in Figure 8-6.

Assume that routers initially converge on correct routing information. Now R3 loses its connection to subnet 10.1.3.0. R3 removes the route to it from the routing table and lists it as unreachable in the next periodic routing update.

Now suppose that R1 did not receive the message from R3 but that R2 did. R1 still believes that it can route to 10.1.3.0 through R3. After processing the message from R3, R2 marks the route to 10.1.3.0 as unreachable and starts the garbage collection timer. However, the next time it receives a periodic update from R1, R2 changes the routing table entry in favor of the new, better route and advertises it in its message to R3. R3 installs a route to 10.1.3.0 via R2 and announces it to R1. The protocol starts counting again, and, as you can see, the split-horizon technique does not help to remedy this.

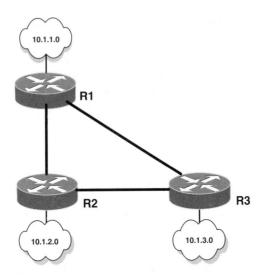

Figure 8-6. *Another example of counting*

It is, of course, understood that the protocol will not count forever. The infinity-metric value eventually makes all routers mark the route to 10.1.3.0 as unreachable, and the protocol converges. However, we again get transient routing loops, and it takes the protocol a long time to remove the invalid routes. The holddown timers, discussed next, provide a solution to transient routing loops.

8.1.4 Holddown Timers

The main idea behind holddown timers is to prevent the routing protocol from establishing loops during transition periods. The rule is simple: Once a route is marked as unreachable, it must stay in this state for a period of time assumed sufficient for all routers to receive new information about the unreachable network. In essence, we instruct the routers to let the rumors calm down and then to pick up the truth.

Formally, the basic distance-vector algorithm is changed as follows.

1. Whenever a route in the routing table is marked as unreachable, start the holddown timer instead of the garbage collection one.

2. When a routing update is received and an existing route is already in the routing table and is in the holddown state, ignore the new route.

3. On expiration of a route's holddown timer, start the garbage collection timer on it. Note that after the holddown timer has expired, the entry in the routing table can be updated with routes having a metric better than infinity.

Holddown timers not only save distance-vector routing protocols from transient routing loops but also improve behavior when some links in the network continuously go up and down, or flap. By applying the holddown timers, routers dampen unstable routes—routes to unstable networks—and thus give them a chance to stabilize.

An interesting question is whether the routes in the holddown state should be used for packet forwarding. On the one hand, such routes describe potentially unreachable destinations. On the other hand, the destination networks can become reachable while the route is in the holddown state, and routers cannot have any better routing information during transition periods. In practice, routes in the holddown state are used for packet forwarding. Clearly, use of these routes cannot lead to packet looping. In the worst case, packets are forwarded toward the router that was previously connected to the destination network, which drops them. In the best case, they are forwarded along a potentially suboptimal but valid path.

Although they seem to be a useful technique against transient routing loops, holddown timers have their disadvantages as well. When routers put an unreachable route into the holddown state, the network cannot converge on the alternative paths until the holddown timer expires for this route in all routers. Nevertheless, waiting for an alternative for a relatively short period of time is deemed to be better than having a routing loop that may introduce really unpleasant problems into the network or significantly delay convergence of the routing protocol.

In fact, the use of holddown timers was introduced by Cisco for its proprietary distance-vector protocol, IGRP, as discussed in Section 8.3, as an improvement on the basic distance-vector algorithm. The same method is used for RIP in Cisco IOS.

8.1.5 Triggered Updates

Up to this point, we have assumed that routers running distance-vector protocols sent only periodic updates. Although this is a very important part of the algorithm, convergence characteristics of distance-vector protocol implementations can be improved if we allow the algorithm to react more quickly to changes in the network topology by sending so-called *triggered updates*.

Triggered updates are the same as periodic updates, except for the following two details.

- Triggered updates are sent when a router sees a topology change or a change in the routing information; the router doesn't have to wait for the period timer.
- Triggered updates do not need to include complete routing information. Only modified routes can be sent.

In practice, routers send triggered updates when one of the following conditions is met.

- An interface transitions to the up or the down state.

- A route has entered or exited an unreachable state.

- A new route is installed in the routing table.

Triggered updates are processed by the receiving routers in the same way as periodic ones, so this method is transparent to the protocol implementations. However, a problem, such as a flapping interface, may arise when too many events are causing triggered updates to be sent. To ensure that triggered updates do not put too much load on the network, implementations usually limit the frequency of triggered-update generation.

8.1.6 Counting to Infinity Again

Although split horizons, triggered updates, and holddown timers decrease the probability of the counting problem, they do not guarantee that it never appears. A loop can be formed in the sample network depicted in Figure 8-6 even if all these methods are applied. For example, suppose that the path R2–R3 has a larger cost than the summary cost of the path R2–R1–R3, so R2 routes packets destined for 10.1.3.0 via R1. When it loses its connection to 10.1.2.0, R3 sends the routing update messages to R1 and R2. If we accept that both messages can be lost, neither R1 nor R2 will know that the network is down. When R2 sends its update to R3, R3 installs the new route because it does not have any existing route to the network in its routing table. In its next periodic update, R3 includes information about 10.1.3.0 and closes the loop.

This example illustrates that distance-vector protocols must have methods to limit the maximum number of hops that a route can traverse and hence prevent loops of updates. Defining the infinity value for the metric is one such method, and it is widely used in protocol implementations.

8.1.7 The Bellman-Ford Algorithm

We now describe and provide the pseudocode of the centralized version of the Bellman-Ford algorithm, as well as an explanation of how the distributed version is derived. The original algorithm has been modified slightly to reflect IP routing concepts. The input to the algorithm is three matrices, as defined in Listing 8-1.

```
#define MAX_RTR 100
#define MAX_NET 100
#define MAX_LNK 100
#define INFINITY 1000
#define NO_NEIGHBOR -1
#define NO_ROUTE -1

int Cost    [MAX_RTR][MAX_LNK]; /* Link costs */
```

```
int Neighbor[MAX_RTR][MAX_LNK]; /* Nbrs over links */
int Distance[MAX_RTR][MAX_NET]; /* Distances */
int Route   [MAX_RTR][MAX_NET]; /* Routes (output links) */
```

Listing 8-1. *Pseudocode: Input matrices for centralized Bellman-Ford algorithm*

The Cost matrix defines the costs of the links on corresponding routers; that is, Cost[r][l] is the cost of link l on router r. If a link does not exist or should not be considered, Cost[r][l] is set to INFINITY. The Neighbor matrix contains information about the neighbors reachable via the links described in the Cost matrix. If a link is stub, Neighbor[r][l] is set to the NO_NEIGHBOR constant. The Distance matrix contains distance values from any given router to any given network. If network n is unreachable for router r, Distance[r][n] is set to INFINITY. These three matrices are enough to represent a topology of a network with a single link characteristic.

The algorithm updates the Distance matrix and produces the Route matrix, which holds the identifiers of the links each router uses to reach each destination network. If no route from router r to network n is present, Route[r][n] is set to the NO_ROUTE constant.

The data structures are initialized as follows.

- The elements of the Cost and Neighbor matrices are assigned the values representing the link topology and link costs.

- For every network n directly connected to router r via link l, Distance[r][n] is set to 0, and Route[r][n] is set to l.

The pseudocode of the algorithm is presented in Listing 8-2.

```
void BellmanFordCentralized()
{
 int router, dest, link, distance, neighbor;
 int changed;
 int iterations = 0;

 InitMatrices();

#define LINK_EXISTS (Cost[router][link]!=INFINITY)

 do {
   iterations++;
   printf("——Iteration %d——\n", iterations);

   changed = 0;

   /* For all routers */
   for(router = 0; router < NumOfRouters; router++)
```

```
    /* For all router's links */
    for(link = 0; (link < NumOfLinks) && LINK_EXISTS; link++)
    {
        neighbor = Neighbor[router][link];
        if (neighbor == NO_NEIGHBOR)
            continue; /* Stub link */

        /* For all destinations */
        for(dest = 0; dest < NumOfDests; dest++)
        {
            distance = Cost[router][link] + Distance[neighbor][dest];

            if (distance < Distance[router][dest]) {
                printf("Found better path for router %d to "
                       "destination %d\n", router, dest);
                printf("The new cost is %d, via link %d\n\n",
                       distance, link);

                Distance[router][dest] = distance;
                Route[router][dest] = link;
                changed = 1;
            } /* if better distance */
        } /* for all destinations */
    }/* for all links */
} while (changed);

printf("Total number of iterations: %d\n", iterations);
PrintResults();
}
```

Listing 8-2. *Pseudocode: Centralized version of the Bellman-Ford algorithm*

The human-language description of the algorithm is defined as follows.

1. For every router, consider every link of the router and try to find a better way through it to all destinations. If the sum of the link cost and the distance from the neighbor reachable through this link to a destination is better, or less, than the router's current distance to that destination, update the distance value, and use the new neighbor to forward the packets in that direction.

2. If any element of the Distance matrix has changed, loop to step 1. Otherwise, the computation is complete and the algorithm stops.

Looking at the algorithm, we can see that it finds the routing tables of all routers in the network. Clearly, this is not necessary in IP networks, as all a router needs to know is its own routing table, represented in the form of remote networks with associated next-hop routers. Let's try to modify the centralized version of the algorithm to get the distributed version.

First, the outer for cycle can be removed from the algorithm; there is no reason to calculate routing tables of other routers. Now we can see that we use only one row of the `Route` matrix during the calculation, so it can easily be transformed into an array: sort of a simplified routing table, whereby `Route[n]` gives the link to use when routing to destination n. The same is valid for the `Cost` and `Neighbor` matrices: The calculating router considers only its own links. However, the router would need to use more than one row in the `Distance` matrix because it still needs to know the distances that other routers have. We can see, though, that the `Distance` matrix is used to obtain only two types of distances: the router's own distances to remote networks and the distances of the router's direct neighbors. Therefore, the only information necessary for successful route calculation is the cost of the router's links, the router's own current distances, and the distances the router's direct neighbors have.

Apparently, the last piece of information, which we can call a vector of distances, or a distance vector, is the only data routers should exchange, and they can do it in a neighbor-to-neighbor manner, which is important. However, this is not enough for the distributed version to work. Recall that the centralized version iterates until the routing tables of all routers calm down. We can use the observation that algorithm calculations performed after no changes in the routing table have been seen do not introduce any new changes. If we make sure that every router runs the distributed version of the algorithm periodically, the protocol will converge within a finite period of time, provided that there are no more changes in the topology. This algorithmic model is exactly what distance-vector routing protocols use.

8.2 Routing Information Protocol

8.2.1 Basic Description and History

Routing Information Protocol (RIP) is one of the oldest IGPs used in the Internet and is still working on routers and hosts today. It was initially implemented in the Berkeley UNIX routed program. In fact, IP RIP was derived from RIP developed by Xerox for its XNS protocol stack.

Because IP RIP is extremely simple to implement, owing to its distance-vector nature, it has been widely deployed in IP networks. Practically every router vendor supports this protocol. Moreover, some types of routers and IP hosts support *only* RIP as a dynamic routing protocol.

There are two versions of RIP for IP version 4 today. The first version, documented in 1980s but developed even earlier, is an example of a purely classful routing protocol. Specified in [RFC1058] by Charles Hedrick, this version does not support CIDR and uses IP broadcasts to announce routing information. Version 2, an extension to the base RIP, includes classless routing support, route tagging, and message authentication and uses IP multicasts to limit the number of IP hosts processing RIP routing updates. RIP version 2 was defined in [RFC1723] by Gary Malkin in 1994. The main characteristics of RIP versions 1 and 2, including Cisco implementation details, are given in Table 8-1.

RIP has also been extended to support IPv6, so-called RIPng. Algorithmically, this is essentially the same protocol, but the message format was redefined to support IPv6 prefixes. [RFC2080], by Gary Malkin and Robert Minnear, defines RIPng.

Next, we provide functional descriptions of RIP version 1. We return to RIPv2 in Section 8.2.7, after we have explored basic RIP functionality.

8.2.2 Configuration Parameters

Before proceeding to the algorithms of Cisco RIP implementation, let's identify the type of information involved in RIP operation and how that information can be configured. In addition to the parameters described in Chapter 7, RIP uses some additional interface-specific and global attributes. Listing 8-3 defines RIP's interface information block.

```
/* RIP interface information */

#define RIP_RECEIVE_VER_1 0x01
#define RIP_RECEIVE_VER_2 0x02
#define RIP_SEND_VER_1    0x04
#define RIP_SEND_VER_2    0x08

#define RIP_AUTH_NONE 0
#define RIP_AUTH_TEXT 1
#define RIP_AUTH_MD5  2

typedef struct RIPInterfaceInfo{
  u_char   VersionFlags;
  u_char   AuthType;
} TRIPInterfaceInfo;
```

Listing 8-3. *Pseudocode: RIP interface-specific information*

The parameters in the RIP interface information block can be changed by using the following commands.

- The **ip rip send version** interface configuration command changes the version of RIP messages sent out of the interface. The router can send messages of version 1, version 2, or both.

- The **ip rip receive version** interface configuration command explicitly specifies the version of messages that are accepted on the interface. The router can accept messages of both RIP versions.

- The **ip rip authentication mode** interface configuration command sets the type of authentication used on the interface. Configurable modes are text and MD5 (message digest).

Another attribute affecting RIP operation is the IF_IP_SPLIT_HORIZON flag, which is set in the IPFlags field of the interface descriptor structure, as shown in the pseudocode of the ifRegister() function (Listing 8-4). This flag is called every time the interface descriptor for an interface is created or changed.

```
void ifRegister(TInterfaceDescr * TheInt)
{
#define ENC_IS_FR_SMDS(I) ( ((I->Flags & IF_ENC) == IF_ENC_FR) || \
                            ((I->Flags & IF_ENC) == IF_ENC_SMDS) )

   TheInt->Broadcast = SetIP(255,255,255,255);

   if (!CHECK_FLAG(TheInt->Flags, IF_SUBINT) &&
       ENC_IS_FR_SMDS(TheInt))

      UNSET_FLAG(TheInt->IPFlags, IF_IP_SPLIT_HORIZON);

   else if (CHECK_FLAG(TheInt->Flags, IF_SUBINT) &&
            ((TheInt->Flags & IF_TYPE) == IF_TYPE_PTMP) &&
            ENC_IS_FR_SMDS(TheInt->MainInt) )

      UNSET_FLAG(TheInt->IPFlags, IF_IP_SPLIT_HORIZON);
   else
      SET_FLAG(TheInt->IPFlags, IF_IP_SPLIT_HORIZON);

   list_add(InterfaceList, TheInt);
}
```

Listing 8-4. *Pseudocode: The function* ifRegister() *setting the split-horizon flag*

The split-horizon flag is enabled by default for all interfaces except physical interfaces using Frame Relay or Switched Multimegabit Data Service (SMDS) encapsulation and their multipoint subinterfaces. The state of this flag can be changed by using the **ip split-horizon** interface configuration command.

Cisco's implementation of RIP allows the administrator to control the process of metric modification. When a route is announced by RIP, its hop count is increased by default by 1. If it is necessary to further increase the metric of some routes when they are sent or received, the administrator can configure offset lists, specifying the number that must be added to the route metric, by using the **offset-list** *acl-name* {**in**|**out**} *offset* [*int-name*] router

Table 8-1. *General Characterics of RIP*

Protocol Characteristics	RIP
Algorithm type	Distance vector.
Metric type	Hop count: the number of routers a route has traversed.
Best-path selection	Distributed version of the Bellman-Ford algorithm.
Multipath support	Equal-cost multipath supported.
View of the network	Routers see network topology from their neighbors' perspective; no full topology information.
New-neighbor discovery	No explicit mechanism is provided. Formal connections are not formed between neighboring routers. Neighbors are discovered when they send routing update messages.
Unreachable-neighbor discovery	No explicit mechanism is provided. Routers stop routing through unreachable neighbors when routes supplied by these neighbors age out from the routing table.
New-route discovery	Every router sends to its neighbors routes to directly connected networks and routes received from other neighbors; that is, routing information is relayed. When constructing an update, the router increments the route's hop count to reflect the cost of the link through which the update is sent.
Unreachable-route discovery	Via either (1) an explicit message specifying the infinite distance—hop count equal to 16—to a network or (2) the route aging process
Periodic updates	Every router sends periodic updates every 30 seconds by default; the interval is randomized to avoid synchronization.
Event-driven updates	So-called triggered updates are sent by routers after a network topology change.
Transport protocol	RIP versions 1 and 2 use UDP; well-known port 520 is used as both source and destination to send the updates.
External routing information	External routes injected into an RIP domain are indistinguishable from native RIP routes.
Classful route summarization	RIPv1 performs classful route summarization, Cisco's implementation of RIPv2 also does this by default.
CIDR and route aggregation	RIPv1 is a classful routing protocol and hence does not send route masks in the updates, so it cannot be used for CIDR. RIPv2 is a classless protocol and supports VLSM and route aggregation.

configuration command. Offset lists can be applied to all incoming or outgoing updates, as well as to updates coming from or going out of specific interfaces; this method works for IGRP as well. Access lists are used in the offset lists as a means of identifying routes that need to be modified. Functions `Proto_OffsetListOut()` and `Proto_Offset ListIn()`, presented in Listing 8-5, alter the metric of the route according to the configuration of the offset lists. These functions are called from the RIP module before an update is sent.

```
void Proto_OffsetListOut(TProto * TheProto, TIPAddress Network,
                         TInterfaceDescr * TheInt, u_int * Metric)
{
  TRPInterfaceInfo *IntInfo;

  if (TheProto->OffsetOut)
    if (!TheProto->OffsetListOut ||
        !IPdeniedByACL (TheProto->OffsetListOut, Network))
      *Metric = MIN((*Metric) + TheProto->OffsetOut,
                    TheProto->MetricInfo->Infinity);


  IntInfo = Proto_FindIntInfo(TheProto, TheInt);
  if (IntInfo == NULL) return;

  if (IntInfo->OffsetOut)
    if (!IntInfo->OffsetListOut ||
        !IPdeniedByACL (IntInfo->OffsetListOut, Network))
      *Metric = MIN((*Metric) + TheProto->OffsetOut,
                    TheProto->MetricInfo->Infinity);

}


void Proto_OffsetListIn(TProto * TheProto, TIPAddress Network,
                        TInterfaceDescr * TheInt, u_int * Metric)
{
  TRPInterfaceInfo *IntInfo;

  IntInfo = Proto_FindIntInfo(TheProto, TheInt);
  if (IntInfo == NULL) return;

  if (IntInfo->OffsetIn)
    if (!IntInfo->OffsetListIn ||
        !IPdeniedByACL (IntInfo->OffsetListIn, Network))
      *Metric = MIN((*Metric) + TheProto->OffsetIn,
                    TheProto->MetricInfo->Infinity);

  if (TheProto->OffsetIn)
    if (!TheProto->OffsetListIn ||
        !IPdeniedByACL (TheProto->OffsetListIn, Network))
```

```
           *Metric = MIN((*Metric) + TheProto->OffsetIn,
                         TheProto->MetricInfo->Infinity);
}
```

Listing 8-5. *Pseudocode: Functions* `Proto_OffsetListIn()` *and* `Proto_OffsetListOut()`

RIP uses a number of timers, including the periodic-update timer, the route-invalidation timer, the route holddown timer, and the route flush (garbage collection) timer. All these timers have default values, but the administrator can change the values by using the **timers basic** router configuration command.

Before IOS version 12.0T, RIP did not use any kind of internal route database but operated on the main routing table, storing routes in it and announcing them directly from the routing table. Beginning with version 12.0T, which introduced RIP on-demand circuit support (see Section 8.2.8), RIP has its own routing information database, which can be displayed by using the **show ip rip database** command. However, because the main purpose for this database is to store routes received over the demand circuit and because the other part of RIP operation remains unchanged, it can be assumed that without demand links, RIP still operates on the main routing table.

> An interesting fact is that because RIP announces routes from the routing table, if it gets overridden by a route with a better AD value, an RIP route will not be known to other RIP routers any more and will age out from their routing tables, unless RIP is configured to redistribute the new route.

RIP configuration commands are explained in more detail in Section 8.2.9.

8.2.3 Message Format

RIP uses UDP and well-known port 520. All RIP messages are sent to this port; that is, the destination UDP port for all RIP messages must be 520. Otherwise, the messages would not be directed to the RIP process by the TCP/IP stack. Most RIP messages must be sent from the same port number; that is, the UDP source port in the messages must also be 520. Request messages, explained later, are an exception; they can be sent from any port. The format of the message RIP places inside a UDP datagram is shown in Figure 8-7. The pseudocode type definition for an RIP message is given in Listing 8-6.

```
#define AFI_NONE        0
#define AFI_IP          2

#define RIP_METRIC_INFINITY    16
```

```
typedef struct RIPEntry {
  u_int16_t  AFI;              /* Address Family Identifier. 2 for IP */
  u_int16_t  Reserved;         /* Must be zero */
  TIPAddress Network;          /* Destination address (prefix value) */
  u_int32_t  Reserved_[2];     /* Must be zero (8 bytes) */
  u_int32_t  Metric;           /* Metric (1..16) 16 is infinity*/

} TRIPEntry;

#define RIP_ENTRY_SIZE  sizeof (TRIPEntry)
#define RIP_MAX_ENTRIES 25

#define RIP_COMMAND_REQUEST    1       /* RIP request */
#define RIP_COMMAND_REPLY      2       /* RIP reply   */
#define RIP_COMMAND_MAX        2

#define RIP_VERSION_1          1
#define RIP_VERSION_2          2

typedef struct RIPMessage {
  u_char    Command;           /* Request/Reply       */
  u_char    Version;           /* RIP version (1 or 2) */
  u_int16_t Reserved;          /* Must be zero        */
  TRIPEntry Entries[RIP_MAX_ENTRIES];
                               /* Will be more in reality */
} TRIPMessage;

#define RIP_MSG_HEADER_SIZE    sizeof (u_char) +\
                               sizeof (u_char) +\
                               sizeof (u_int16_t)
```

Listing 8-6. *Pseudocode: Type definition for RIP message and entry*

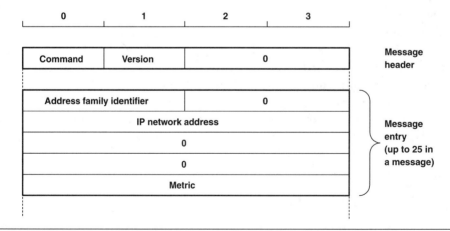

Figure 8-7. *Format of RIPv1 message*

The message contains a header and up to 25 routing information entries. The number of information entries is limited to keep the size of the message under 512 bytes so that hosts running older implementations of the TCP/IP stack can receive RIP messages.

The header contains three fields: a 1-byte `Command` field, a 1-byte `Version` field, and a 2-byte field reserved for future use. The `Version` field must contain 1 for RIP version 1 and 2 for RIP version 2. The `Command` field identifies the type of the message. The two types of standard messages used in today's implementations are Request—command code 1 and Reply—command code 2. (More command codes are used to support demand circuit extensions to RIP; see Section 8.2.8.) The rest of the message contains a number of routing information entries. The format of each entry for RIP version 1 is given in Listing 8-6; RIP version 2 is considered in Section 8.2.7.

The *address family identifier* (AFI) specifies the network protocol for which the routing information is included in the following fields. Initially, RIP was developed to allow distribution of routing information for several network protocols. However, IP RIP is not used by other protocols, so only the AFI of IP (value 2) is used in practice. Nevertheless, implementations are required to ignore routing information entries with unknown AFI values. Note that RIPv1 messages do not contain route masks, only network addresses. This detail identifies RIPv1 as a classful routing protocol.

The two types of RIP messages are used for different purposes. The majority of traffic generated by RIP, Reply messages, is used for periodic and triggered updates, as well as for the messages sent in reply to Requests messages, which are a means of routing information inquiry. Routers send requests on all interfaces when an RIP processes starts. Routers do this to obtain routing information before the neighbors' periodic timers trigger updates and to start routing packets as soon as possible. Request messages are also sent when an RIP-enabled interface goes up.

Reply messages always include routing information entries from the router's routing table; Request messages may contain a query for the whole routing table—a *general request*—or a number of requests about specific networks that the sender would like to know about—a *specific request*. The general request includes exactly one routing entry. The AFI value for this entry is set to 0, and the metric value is set to infinity (16). By convention, when it is the only one in an RIP Request message, such an entry is considered an inquiry for the whole routing table. A router receiving a general request must reply to it by sending a Reply message built the same way as when a periodic update is prepared (see Section 8.2.6).

When a specific request is received, it contains one or more routing information entries. The processing router is supposed to consider these entries one by one and to fill in the metric fields. If a route to a specified network is found in the router's routing table, the metric from the found route is put into the Reply message. Otherwise, the router puts the infinity value in the `metric` field. When all entries in the request have been processed, the router sends information back to the requesting router's IP address and UDP port.

Specific requests are normally not used in router operation. They are supposed to be used for debugging and network monitoring, when it is necessary to know what routes routers have for specific networks.

Periodic RIP updates, sent in RIP Reply messages, are constructed for and sent on all interfaces. The destination IP address is set to the local broadcast address (255.255.255.255 by default), except when updates must be sent to statically configured neighbors. The source address in the IP packets containing a UDP datagram carrying an RIP message is set to the IP address of the interface for which the update is prepared.

> If an interface is configured with secondary IP addresses belonging to different major networks, RIP sends one update for each major network over the interface, using appropriate source addresses. The reason is that RIP is supposed to summarize subnet information on the network boundaries, so routes sent to subnets of different major networks will be different. However, it is not necessary to send an update to each secondary subnet, because Cisco's RIP accepts and processes a received RIP message if it was sent by a neighbor belonging to any of the primary or secondary subnets assigned to the interface.

8.2.4 Input Processing

When the RIP process is started, the router starts listening on UDP port 520. When an RIP message is received on this port, the router performs the algorithm illustrated with the pseudocode in Listing 8-7. Note that real implementations must convert specific fields from machine-independent—the most-significant octet first—to machine-specific formats, using functions similar to the `ntohX()` group in the UNIX socket library. These function calls are omitted from the pseudocode for simplicity, and fields in processed messages are assumed to be in the machine-specific format.

```
void IPRIPReceive (TRIPMessage * msg, int msg_len, TIPAddress from,
                   TInterfaceDescr *from_if, TPort from_port)
{
  if (!IPRIPMsgSanityCheck (msg, from_if)) {
    IPRIPIgnoreMsg (msg);
    return;
  }

  switch (msg->Command) {
   case RIP_COMMAND_REQUEST:
      IPRIPProcessRequest (msg, msg_len, from, from_if, from_port);
      break;
   case RIP_COMMAND_REPLY  :
      IPRIPProcessReply (msg, msg_len, from, from_if, from_port);
      break;
```

```
    default:;
    }
}
```

Listing 8-7. *Pseudocode: The function* `IPRIPReceive()`

Before an RIP message is processed, its sanity is checked by the `IPRIPMsgSanityCheck` function, shown in Listing 8-8.

```
int IPRIPMsgSanityCheck (TRIPMessage * msg, TInterfaceDescr * from_if)
{
  if (! IPRIPIfActive(from_if, NULL))
     return 0;

  if (msg->Version == 0)
     return 0;
  else if (msg->Version == 1) {
     if (msg->Reserved)
        return 0;
     else
        return 1;
  }
  else return 1;
}
```

Listing 8-8. *Pseudocode: The function* `IPRIPMsgSanityCheck()`

If the message was received on an interface where RIP is not enabled by a **network** command, the message is ignored. It is also ignored if the version set in the message header is 0, because it is a message from RIP's predecessor, which used machine-specific messages. If the version is 1, the reserved fields are checked to be 0. If the version is higher, the RIP version 1 code considered in this section ignores the reserved fields.

Further message processing depends on the message type. RIP Request messages are processed by the `IPRIPProcessRequest()` function, and RIP Reply messages are processed by `IPRIPProcessReply()`. The pseudocode for the `IPRIPProcessRequest()` function is given in Listing 8-9.

```
void IPRIPProcessRequest (TRIPMessage *msg, int msg_len, TIPAddress from,
                          TInterfaceDescr *from_if, TPort from_port)
{
  int entry_counter, i;
  TPrefixDescr * route;
```

```
entry_counter = (msg_len - RIP_MSG_HEADER_SIZE) / RIP_ENTRY_SIZE;

if (entry_counter == 0) return;

/* Check general request */

if ((entry_counter == 1) &&
    (msg->Entries[0].AFI == AFI_NONE) &&
    (msg->Entries[0].Metric == RIP_METRIC_INFINITY)) {

    IPRIPScheduleReply (RIP_REPLY_SOLICITED, from, from_port);
    return;
}

/* Specific requests are processed right away
   Note that we don't care about split-horizon
   and classful route summarization here.
 */

for (i = 0; i < entry_counter; i++) {

    route = LookUp (msg->Entries[i].Network, 1);

    if (!route || route->Source != &ProtoRIP)
        msg->Entries[i].Metric = RIP_METRIC_INFINITY;
    else
        msg->Entries[i].Metric = route->Metric;
}

msg->Command = RIP_COMMAND_REPLY;
IPRIPSendMessage (msg, entry_counter, NULL, 0, from, from_port);
}
```

Listing 8-9. *Pseudocode: The function* `IPRIPProcessRequest()`

The request-processing routine can receive both general and specific types of requests. In any case, if the Request message contains no entries, no reply is sent, and the received message is ignored. If the message is a general request, the function schedules a reply to the requesting host. Note that routes sent in reply to general requests are subject to split-horizon and classful route summarization (see Section 8.26).

If the received message is a specific request, entries in the message are processed sequentially. The most specific route to the destination in the message entry is looked up. If a route is found, the message entry's Metric field is filled in with the metric value from the route. Otherwise, the infinity value (16) is entered. When all entries have been processed, the received message is used to send the reply.

Processing of RIP Reply messages does not depend on whether they were generated in response to a request or owing to expiration of a periodic timer. The pseudocode of the `IPRIPProcessReply()` function is given in Listing 8-10.

```
void IPRIPProcessReply    (TRIPMessage *msg, int msg_len, TIPAddress from,
                           TInterfaceDescr *from_if, TPort from_port)
{

#define ENTRY_NETWORK msg->Entries[i].Network
#define ENTRY_METRIC  msg->Entries[i].Metric

  int entry_counter, i;
  TIPAddress mask;
  TPrefixDescr * Route;
  TPathDescr * Path;

  entry_counter = (msg_len - RIP_MSG_HEADER_SIZE) / RIP_ENTRY_SIZE;

  if (entry_counter == 0) return;

  if (! IPRIPSanityReply (msg, msg_len, from, from_if, from_port)) {
     IPRIPIgnoreMsg (msg);
     return;
  }

  for (i = 0; i < entry_counter; i++) {

     if (!IPRIPSanityEntry (& msg->Entries[i], RIP_VERSION_1))
        continue;

     if (!IPRIPShouldAccept (& msg->Entries[i], from_if))
        continue;

     Proto_OffsetListIn (&ProtoRIP, ENTRY_NETWORK, from_if,
                    (u_int *) &ENTRY_METRIC);

     mask = IPRIPGetMask(& msg->Entries[i], from_if);

     if ((ENTRY_NETWORK & ~mask) == ~mask) /* Broadcast */
        continue; /* ignore such entry */

     if (ENTRY_NETWORK & ~mask ) /* Host route */
        mask = SetIP (255, 255, 255, 255);

     if (IPZeroSubnet(ENTRY_NETWORK, mask) &&
          !CHECK_FLAG(flags, IP_SUBNET_ZERO))
        continue;

     Route = NewRoute();
     Path = NewPath();
     IPRIPComposeRoute(&msg->Entries[i], mask, from, from_if,
                    Route, Path);
     RouteUpdate(Route, Path);
  }
}
```

Listing 8-10. *Pseudocode: The function* `IPRIPProcessReply()`

The function first checks whether the message contains at least one entry. If the message has no entries, it is ignored. Otherwise, the message is checked by the `IPRIPSanityReply()` function (Listing 8-11).

```
int IPRIPSanityReply (TRIPMessage *msg, int msg_len, TIPAddress from,
                      TInterfaceDescr *from_if, TPort from_port)
{
  TSecIPAddr * SecAddr;

  if (from_port != RIP_UDP_PORT)
    return 0;

  if ((from & from_if->Mask) == (from_if->Addr & from_if->Mask))
    return 1;
  else for(SecAddr=from_if->Secondary; SecAddr; SecAddr = SecAddr->Next)
         if ((from & SecAddr->Mask) == (SecAddr->Addr & SecAddr->Mask))
            return 1;
  return 0;
}
```

Listing 8-11. *Pseudocode: The function* `IPRIPSanityReply()`

For an RIP message to be approved, it must be sent from UDP port 520. This check ensures that the message is not sent from a process started by a nonprivileged user on a UNIX host, as this port can be used only by applications executed by a user with system administrator privileges. Another condition is that the message must have been sent by a host on a directly connected primary or secondary network. This is a very important condition, as RIP uses a distance-vector approach, relying on incremental metric computation.

> The check of the source UDP port was included in the algorithm to provide some protection from intruder attacks. Today, when anyone can install an implementation of UNIX on a PC and get administrator privileges, this check does not add real security any more but just ensures correct operation of other routers.

After the Reply message has been validated, all entries in the message are processed as follows.

1. The entry itself is validated. (The pseudocode for the `IPRIPSanityEntry()` function is given in Listing 8-12.)

2. Inbound distribute lists are checked in the `IPRIPShouldAccept()` function, which just calls `Proto_DistributeListIn()`. If the route is filtered out, the algorithm proceeds to the next entry.

3. Inbound offset lists are applied to the metric in the `Proto_OffsetListIn()` function.

4. The route mask is determined by the `IPRIPGetMask()` function (considered later). If the destination address in the entry belongs to the same major network as the primary address of the interface the message was received on, the subnet mask configured on the interface is used as the route mask. If the major networks are different, the default classful mask is used.

5. The network address in the entry is checked to be a directed subnet broadcast or an all-subnet broadcast. If the destination is one of these broadcast addresses, the entry is skipped.

6. If the address is not a broadcast but the host bits are nonzero, the mask is changed to the value 255.255.255.255; that is, the entry is processed as a route to a specific host.

7. If the route derived from the received entry describes a subnet with all 0s in the subnet portion and the **ip subnet-zero** command is not configured, the entry is ignored.

8. A new prefix/path descriptor pair is constructed in the `IPRIPComposeRoute()` function and submitted to the RT process, using the `RouteUpdate()` function. (The full version of this function is considered later in this section.)

Now let's look at the functions called while RIP message entries are being processed. First, the `IPRIPSanityEntry()` is considered.

```
int IPRIPSanityEntry (TRIPEntry *entry, u_char version)
{
  if (entry->Metric > RIP_METRIC_INFINITY)
    return 0;

  if (entry->AFI != AFI_IP)
    return 0;

  /* If it's the loopback net—fail */
  if ((entry->Network & SetIP(255,0,0,0)) == SetIP(127,0,0,0))
    return 0;

  /* If it's net 0, but not the default—fail */
  if ( (entry->Network & SetIP(255,0,0,0) == 0) &&
       (entry->Network != 0))
    return 0;
```

```
   /* If it's class D or E—fail */
   if ((entry->Network & SetIP(255,0,0,0)) > SetIP(223,0,0,0))
      return 0;

   /* If it's broadcast—fail */
   if (entry->Network == SetIP (255,255,255,255))
      return 0;

   if ((version== RIP_VERSION_1) &&
      ( entry->Reserved || entry->Reserved_[0] || entry->Reserved_[1]))
      return 0;

   return 1;
}
```

Listing 8-12. *Pseudocode: The function* IPRIPSanityEntry()

The function reports the entry to be invalid if any of the following conditions is met.

- The metric in the entry has a value greater than infinity.
- The AFI does not correspond to the IP stack.
- The network reported in the entry is the loopback network: The first byte has the value 127.
- The network portion of the address is 0, but some other bits are set; this is not the default route.
- The network address is local IP broadcast (255.255.255.255).
- The version of the message is 1 and a reserved field contains a nonzero value.

The next function is IPRIPGetMask()(Listing 8-13).

```
TIPAddress IPRIPGetMask (TRIPEntry * entry, TInterfaceDescr * ifp)
{
TPrefixDescr if_net, entry_net;
 TSecIPAddr  *SecAddr;

 Major (entry->Network, &entry_net);

 Major (ifp->Addr, &if_net);

 if (entry_net.Network == if_net.Network)   /* Same major network ? */
    return ifp->Mask;   /* Yes — use subnet mask from int */
 else if (ifp->Secondary)

   for(SecAddr = ifp->Secondary; SecAddr; SecAddr = SecAddr->Next){

     Major (SecAddr->Addr, &if_net);
```

```
      if (entry_net.Network == if_net.Network)
         return SecAddr->Mask;
   }

 else
   return entry_net.Mask;
}
```

Listing 8-13. *Pseudocode: The function* IPRIPGetMask()

The route mask is determined as follows. If the network reported in the route belongs to the same major network as one of the interfaces assigned subnets—primary or secondary—the route mask is the same as the subnet mask of the interface's address. Otherwise, the classful default address mask is used.

The IPRIPComposeRoute() function, given in Listing 8-14, fills in the fields in the prefix descriptor and the path descriptor passed as the arguments, based on the information in the RIP message entry.

```
void IPRIPComposeRoute(TRIPEntry *Entry, TIPAddress mask,
                   TIPAddress from, TInterfaceDescr * from_if,
                   TPrefixDescr * Route, TPathDescr *Path)
{
  Route->Ultimate = 1;
  Route->Network  = Entry->Network;
  Route->Mask     = mask;
  Route->Source   = &ProtoRIP;
  Route->AD       = Proto_ADForRoute(&ProtoRIP, Entry->Network, from);
  Route->Metric   = Entry->Metric;

  Path->Intermediate = from;
  Path->Interface    = from_if;
  Path->Source       = &ProtoRIP;
  Path->AD           = Route->AD;
  Path->Metric       = Entry->Metric;
  Path->Tag          = 0;
  Path->ShareCount   = 1;
  Path->Originator   = from;
}
```

Listing 8-14. *Pseudocode: The function* IPRIPComposeRoute()

Note that the administrative distance for the route is determined by the Proto_AD ForRoute() function, discussed in Chapter 7, which takes into consideration the **distance** statements configured by the administrator for the routing protocol. The route metric is taken directly from the message entry.

When a route is composed, it is passed to the update version of the `RouteUpdate()` function. The full version of its pseudocode is given in Listing 8-15. Highlighted lines indicate new pieces of the code.

```
#define ROUTE_UNREACHABLE(R) (R->Metric >= \
                              R->Source->MetricInfo->Infinity)

int RouteUpdate(TPrefixDescr * TheRoute, TPathDescr * ThePath)
{
TPrefixDescr    * Route;
TPathDescr      * Path = NULL;
int        Result, i;

  if (TheRoute->AD == 255) return 0;
  // Routes with this AD are never installed

  Route = FindRoute(TheRoute);
  //Try to find a route to the same destination

  if (!PathValid(ThePath, Route)) return 0;

  if (!Route) {
     if (ROUTE_UNREACHABLE(ThePath))
        return 0;
     DebugTxt("Route not found, installing \n")
     RouteInstall(TheRoute, ThePath);
     return 1;
  }

  if (Route->Source == TheRoute->Source) {

     if (CHECK_FLAG(Route->Flags, ROUTE_HOLDDOWN))
       return 0;

     if (CHECK_FLAG(Route->Flags, ROUTE_GARBAGE) &&
         ROUTE_UNREACHABLE(TheRoute))
       return 0;

     // Find the Path through the same neighbor
     Path = (TPathDescr *) Route->Pointer;

     while (Path) {
       if (Path->Originator == ThePath->Originator)
          break;
       Path = Path->Next;
     };
  }

TheRoute->Metric = ThePath->Metric;
Result = CompareRoutes(TheRoute, Route);
switch (Result) {
```

```
case cmWorse:    if (Path) { //We have a route from the same nbr
                    if (Route->NumOfPaths > 1) {
                        DeletePath(Route, Path);
                        return 0;
                    }
                    else {
                        UpdatePathInfo (Path, ThePath);
                        Route->Metric = Path->Metric;

                        if (ROUTE_UNREACHABLE(Route))
                            RouteMetricUnreachable(Route);
                        else
                            ResetPathInvalidTimer(Path);

                        MarkRouteChanged(Route);
                        return 0;
                    }
                 }
                 else return 0;
                 break;

case cmEqual:    if (Route->Source == TheRoute->Source) {
                    CheckPath(Route, ThePath);
                    FreeRoute(TheRoute);
                    //Install another Path;
                    return 1;
                 }
                 //Fall down to cmBetter case
case cmBetter:   ChangeRoute(Route, TheRoute, ThePath);
                 MarkRouteChanged(Route);
                 return 1;
  }
}
```

Listing 8-15. *Pseudocode: Updated version of the function* `RouteUpdate()`

The new logic of the function conforms to the improved distance-vector algorithm of routing information update, presented in Section 8.1, and supports parallel routes to the same destination. Whenever an update is received and RIP submits a route for installation in the routing table, the following steps are performed.

1. If no route to the same destination exists and the metric of the new route is not equal to infinity, the new route is installed in the routing table.

2. If a route to the same destination is found and is from the same source as the update, the state of the existing route is verified.

3. If the old route is in the holddown state, the new route is unconditionally ignored, because no route in this state can be updated.

4. If it is in the garbage collection state, the old route cannot be updated by a route with infinite metric; there's no reason to update an unreachable route with another unreachable route.

5. If the old route is not in the holddown or the garbage collection state and the new route is worse than the old route, the algorithm checks whether this destination has more than one route to it.

6. If so, the path descriptor corresponding to the route from the neighbor that reported a worse metric is unlinked from the prefix descriptor; there are better routes, represented by other path descriptors.

7. If there is only one path descriptor, it is updated, the metric of the route is changed to the new value, and the function checks whether the new metric is infinity.

8. If the metric indicates that the route is now unreachable, the algorithm calls the `RouteMetricUnreachable()` function, described later in this section, to put the route into the holddown state.

9. Otherwise, the path descriptor's Invalid timer is reset. In any case, the route is marked as changed to let the triggered-update function know that the route should be included in the messages.

10. If the old and the new routes are the same, the new route is linked as a parallel-path descriptor, provided that the route sources of the new and already installed routes are the same.

11. If the new route is better than the old one, the route is changed in favor of the new route, the `ROUTE_GARBAGE` flag is cleared on it, and the route is marked as changed.

Note that when in the holddown state, a route is still used for packet forwarding—because the router has no better information—and included in RIP updates with a metric value of infinity. When put in the garbage collection state, a route is also sent in RIP messages with an infinite metric but is no longer used for packet forwarding.

The algorithm uses several timers. Each path descriptor has an Invalid timer. In addition, each prefix descriptor can be in one of the following states—valid, holddown (indicated by the `ROUTE_HOLDDOWN` flag), and garbage collection (indicated by the `ROUTE_GARBAGE` flag). A single timer is associated with every prefix descriptor. This timer is used to move the prefix descriptor to the garbage collection state after the holddown time has expired and to remove the route from the routing table when the garbage collection period is over.

Holddown timers in RIP are an extension used by Cisco IOS to prevent transient routing loops. This technique was imported from IGRP (described in Section 8.3). [RFC 1058] does not describe the holddown state; only the garbage collection state is discussed.

8.2.5 Event Processing

All events that are supposed to be processed by RIP can be characterized as internal or external. Internal events are those generated during normal RIP operation, not as reaction to any activities external to RIP. Expiration of the periodic-update timer and various route timers are examples of internal events. By contrast, external events are not generated by RIP itself but rather are reported to RIP to inform it about interface state change or route addition and removal.

8.2.5.1 Internal Events

Following is the list of internal RIP events. Each event is augmented with a description and a list of actions taken when the event is experienced.

> **Event:** Periodic-update timer expiration, triggered update, or reply to a general request
>
> **Event Description:** The RIP process must send a periodic or triggered update or a reply to a general request.
>
> **Action List:**
> - When the periodic-update timer expires, RIP restarts the timer and sends full updates through all RIP-enabled interfaces. The periodic-update timer is randomized to avoid synchronization of updates within a network; see [UpdSync] for more information on synchronization of routing updates.
> - When a triggered update must be sent, RIP sends only changed routes in the updates through all RIP-enabled interfaces. Subsequent triggered updates, if any, are sent not earlier than 1 to 5 seconds after the previous triggered update. The exact value of the delay is a random number. This delay is introduced to accumulate into a single update triggered updates that must be sent within a short period.
> - When a reply to a general request is sent, the update is built similarly to the periodic update but is sent to a single host as unicast.

Although the details of processing these three events are different, the event-processing routines for them call the same function—`IPRIPUpdate()`—that is described in Section 8.2.6.

Event: Expiration of the Invalid route timer

Event Description: A route in the routing table was not updated during the Invalid period.

Action List: Whenever the Invalid timer for a route expires, the `IPRouteInvalid-Timer()` function is called (see Listing 8-16).

```
void IPRouteInvalidTimer (TTimer * timer, TPathDescr * Path, u_long data)
{
 TPrefixDescr * Route = Path->Route;

 Path->Timer = NULL;

 if (Route == NULL) return;
 if (Route->NumOfPaths == 0) return;

 if (Route->NumOfPaths > 1)
    RouteRemove (Route, Path, 1);
 else if (Route->NumOfPaths == 1) {
    Route->Metric = Route->Source->MetricInfo->Infinity;
    RouteMetricUnreachable(Route);
 }
}
```

Listing 8-16. *Pseudocode: The function* `IPRouteInvalidTimer()`

If it is not the last one linked to the prefix descriptor, the expired path description is unlinked from the prefix descriptor, as the router can continue routing, using other valid path descriptors. When the route's last path descriptor expires, the `RouteMetricUnreachable()` function is called, as well as whenever a route is marked as unreachable in the `RouteUpdate()` function after the route's metric has been updated. The `RouteMetricUnreachable()` function saves the last-second routing information about the outgoing interface and the next-hop address in the prefix descriptor, releases the last path descriptor, and tries to move the route to the holddown state (see Listing 8-17) by calling the `DV_Holddown()` function.

```
void RouteMetricUnreachable (TPrefixDescr * TheRoute)
{
 TEntryType Type;
 TPathDescr * ThePath;

 if (TheRoute->Pointer){
    ThePath = (TPathDescr*) TheRoute->Pointer;
    TheRoute->LastUpdInt = ThePath->Interface;
    TheRoute->LastUpdAddr= ThePath->Intermediate;
```

```
      FreePath(TheRoute->Pointer);
      TheRoute->Pointer = NULL;
  }

  if ((TheRoute->Source->Type & RS_DV)==RS_DV)
      DV_Holddown(TheRoute);
  else
      RouteRemove(TheRoute, NULL, 1);
}
```

Listing 8-17. *Pseudocode: The function* `RouteMetricUnreachable()`

`DV_Holddown()`, given in Listing 8-18, checks the value of the holddown timer configured for the protocol. If the value is greater than 0, the route is put in the holddown state, and the holddown timer is started on it. Otherwise, the function tries to put the route in the garbage collection state, calling the `DV_Garbage()` function. The same function is used in `IPRouteHolddownTimer()`, called when a route's holddown timer expires.

Note that while in the holddown state, a route cannot be updated with any other route.

```
#define ROUTE_TIMER_HOLDDOWN(R) (R->Source->Timers->Holddown)

void DV_Holddown(TPrefixDescr* TheRoute)
{
  if (ROUTE_TIMER_HOLDDOWN(TheRoute)){
     if (TheRoute->Timer) StopTimer(TheRoute->Timer);
     TheRoute->Timer = StartTimer(ROUTE_TIMER_HOLDDOWN(TheRoute),
                                  (TTimerCallback)IPRouteHolddownTimer,
                                  TheRoute, 0);
     SET_FLAG(TheRoute->Flags, ROUTE_HOLDDOWN);
     MarkRouteChanged(TheRoute);
  }
  else {
   DV_Garbage(TheRoute);
   MarkRouteChanged(TheRoute);
  }
}
```

Listing 8-18. *Pseudocode: The* `DV_Holddown()` *function*

Event: Holddown route timer expiration

Event Description: A route in the routing table was in the holddown state for the holddown period.

Action List: The holddown timer is specific for a prefix descriptor. When the timer expires, RIP puts the prefix descriptor in the garbage collection state and starts the garbage collection timer. Note that while in the garbage collection state, the route can be updated with a better route. If this happens, the garbage collection timer is canceled.

The pseudocode of the `IPRouteHolddownTimer()` function, part of the routing table maintenance module, is given in Listing 8-19.

```
void IPRouteHolddownTimer (TTimer * timer, TPrefixDescr * Route, u_long data)
{
 DV_Garbage(Route);
}


#define ROUTE_TIMER_GARBAGE(R) (R->Source->Timers->Garbage)

void DV_Garbage(TPrefixDescr* TheRoute)
{
  if (ROUTE_TIMER_GARBAGE(TheRoute)){
    if (TheRoute->Timer) StopTimer(TheRoute->Timer);
    TheRoute->Timer = StartTimer(ROUTE_TIMER_GARBAGE(TheRoute),
                        (TTimerCallback)IPRouteGarbageTimer,
                        TheRoute, 0);
    UNSET_FLAG(TheRoute->Flags, ROUTE_HOLDDOWN);
    SET_FLAG(TheRoute->Flags, ROUTE_GARBAGE);
  }
  else RouteRemove(TheRoute, NULL, 1);
}
```

Listing 8-19. *Pseudocode: The functions* `IPRouteHolddownTimer()` *and* distance-vector_ Garbage()

The function checks the value of the protocol's garbage collection time interval, which can be configured with the **timers basic** router configuration command. If the value is not 0, the route is placed in the garbage collection state and the timer is started. If the garbage collection interval is 0, the route is removed from the routing table right away.

Event: Garbage collection route timer expiration

Event Description: A route in the routing table was in the garbage collection state during the garbage collection period and was not updated by a better route.

Action List: Expiration of the garbage collection timer for a prefix descriptor means that the route was not updated by any better route. Thus, no neighbor has reported the network with a metric better than infinity, the network cannot be considered reachable any more, and the corresponding route is removed from the routing table.

The pseudocode of the `IPRouteGarbageTimer()` function is presented in Listing 8-20.

```
void IPRouteGarbageTimer (TTimer * timer, TPrefixDescr * Route, u_long data)
{
 RouteRemove(Route, NULL, 1);
}
```

Listing 8-20. *Pseudocode: The function* `IPRouteGarbageTimer()`

In order to get a summarized view of how RIP routes are processed while in the routing table, consider the RIP route state machine shown in Figure 8-8. A formal definition of the route state machine follows.

An RIP route can be in one of the following states:

- *Nil*, a pseudostate indicating a nonexisting route to a specific destination. Transition from this state implies route installation. Transition to this state implies deletion of the route.

- *Valid*, whereby the metric of a route in this state is better than infinity, the corresponding path descriptor is regularly updated by the neighbor, and the route is used for packet forwarding.

- *Holddown*, the state in which the route is the only path to the destination and has the metric of infinity because a corresponding neighbor reported so or because the Invalid timer expired for the last route to the destination. The route is included in updates and is still used for packet forwarding. A route in this state cannot be updated by any route with a better metric, to prevent routing loops in transition periods.

- *Garbage collection*, the state in which a route has the metric of infinity. The route is included in updates but is not used for packet forwarding. However, routes in this state can be substituted by routes with a better metric. If a route in this state is not updated with a better one, the route is removed from the routing table after expiration of the garbage collection timer.

The following events are used in the description of the RIP route state machine.

- **evRefresh**, generated when the router receives an update for an already installed route. The update contains the same metric value as the route in the routing table.

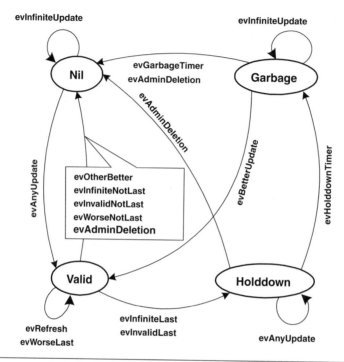

Figure 8-8. *RIP route state transition graph*

- **evBetterUpdate**, generated when an update for an already installed route is received. The new metric is better than the currently used one.

- **evOtherBetter**, generated when a better route to the same destination is received from a neighbor different from the originator of the route found in the routing table and experiencing this event.

- **evWorseLast**, generated when an update for a single, already installed route is received from the same neighbor. The new metric has greater value than the one currently used but it is better than infinity.

- **evWorseNotLast**, generated when an update for an already installed route is received from the same neighbor. There are multiple routes to the destination, and the new metric is worse than the one currently used.

- **evInfiniteUpdate**, generated when an update containing the infinity metric value is received for a route.

- **evInfiniteLast**, generated when **evInfiniteUpdate** happened for a route that is the only one to a destination.

- **evInfiniteNotLast**, generated when **evInfiniteUpdate** happened for a route that is not the only route to a destination.

- **evAnyUpdate**, a pseudoevent that describes "all other updates"; used to specify the events other than those explicitly listed in the diagram.

- **evInvalidLast**, generated when the Invalid timer expires for the route and it is the only one for the corresponding destination.

- **evInvalidNotLast**, generated when the Invalid timer expires for the route and it is not the only one for the corresponding destination.

- **evHolddownTimer**, generated when the holddown timer expires for the route.

- **evGarbageTimer**, generated when the garbage collection timer expires for the route.

- **evAdminDeletion**, generated when the administrator enters a command to delete the route from the routing table.

Table 8-2 contains the event-processing and state-transition logic. Note that processing of the **evAdminDeletion** event is not included, as it always results in route deletion.

When a route is changed, the algorithm is supposed to set the route's Change flag and to schedule a triggered update. Triggered-update generation is an internal RIP event.

8.2.5.2 External Events

External events are received by RIP through the callback functions defined in RIP's protocol descriptor. RIP needs to know when interfaces go up and down and when a route from a redistributed source gets installed in the routing table. The pseudocode of the interface event-processing function is given in Listing 8-21.

```
void IPRIPIntEventHandler(TInterfaceDescr * ifp, TIntEvent event)

{
 switch (event) {
  case ieUp      : IPRIPIfUp(ifp);
                   break;

  case ieDown    : IPRIPIfDown(ifp);
                   break;
  //...
 }
}
```

Listing 8-21. *Pseudocode: The function* `IPRIPIntEventHandler()`

Table 8-2. *RIP Route State Machine Definition*

Current State	Event	Next State
Nil	evInfiniteUpdate	Nil
	evAnyUpdate	Valid
Valid	evOtherBetter	Nil
	evInfiniteNotLast	Nil
	evInvalidNotLast	Nil
	evWorseNotLast	Nil
	evRefresh	Valid
	evWorseLast	Valid
	evInvalidLast	Holddown
	evInfiniteLast	Holddown
Holddown	evAnyUpdate	Holddown
	evHolddownTimer	Garbage collection
Garbage collection	evGarbageTimer	Nil
	evInfiniteUpdate	Garbage collection
	evBetterUpdate	Valid

A description of external events processed by RIP and their corresponding actions follows.

Event: Interface-up transition

Event Description: An RIP-enabled interface changes its state to up.

Action List: RIP reacts to this event by sending a general request on the interface added to the RIP domain and scheduling a triggered update. This update provides existing neighbors with information about the new directly connected network and delivers routing information in the router's routing table to the routers available through the new link. The pseudocode of the processing function is given in Listing 8-22.

```
void IPRIPIfUp(TInterfaceDescr * ifp)
{
  if (! IPRIPIfActive(ifp, NULL))
    return;
```

```
  IPRIPScheduleGeneralRequest(ifp);
  IPRIPScheduleTriggeredUpdate();
}
```

Listing 8-22. *Pseudocode: The function* `IPRIPIfUp()`

A general request is sent on an interface regardless of the state of the passive flag for it. The reason is that a general request is not an update but rather a request for updates.

Event: Interface-down transition

Event Description: An RIP-enabled interface changes its state to down.

Action List: When an RIP-enabled interface goes down, the routing table maintenance module removes directly connected routes referencing the interface from the routing table and puts all RIP-installed routes referencing this interface into the garbage collection state, provided that the value of the garbage collection interval is not 0; otherwise, the routes are removed from the routing table. This event also initiates generation of a triggered update for all interfaces; see Listing 8-23.

```
void IPRIPIfDown(TInterfaceDescr * ifp)
{
  if (! IPRIPIfActive(ifp, NULL))
    return;

  IPRIPSaveConnectedRoutes(ifp);
  IPRIPScheduleTriggeredUpdate();
}
```

Listing 8-23. *Pseudocode: The function* `IPRIPIfDown()`

Note that RIP saves routes derived from the primary and secondary IP addresses of the interface that is going down. This information is used by the message-composing function, which includes these routes with an infinity metric to notify the neighbors that these networks are not reachable any more.

Event: Installation of a redistributed route

Event Description: A route that must be redistributed to RIP is added to the routing table.

Action List: RIP reacts to this event by generating a triggered update that includes the new route.

Beginning with IOS version 12.0, which introduced RIP on-demand circuit extensions, RIP sends a triggered update only when a redistributed route is first installed into RIP's internal database.

Event: Removal of a redistributed route

Event Description: A route previously announced by RIP via redistribution has been deleted from the routing table.

Action List: RIP ignores this event. Subsequent periodic updates will not contain this route—as it was removed from the routing table—and corresponding routes in the neighbor's routing tables will age out.

Because RIP does not explicitly withdraw the routes in these situations, a temporary routing loop can be formed. Such a loop will be removed in several minutes when the route's metric reaches infinity.

8.2.6 Sending RIP Updates

We now consider how RIP messages are composed and sent over interfaces. But first, it must be noted that regardless of the type of the update that must be sent, the same function is called: IPRIPUpdate(), shown in Listing 8-24.

```
void IPRIPUpdate (int type, TIPAddress where, TPort where_port)
{
  TInterfaceDescr    * ifp;
  TPrefixDescr       * Route;
  TPathDescr         * Path;
  TRIPMessage   * msg;
  int                entry_count = 0;
  TListNode     * node;
  TList         * MajorNets = NULL;
  TSecIPAddr    * SecAddr;
  TIPAddress    * Neighbor;
  TIPAddress      Source, NextHop, PrevHop;
  TFlag           Passive;

  msg = IPRIPNewMessage ();

  switch (type)
  {
    case RIP_REPLY_SOLICITED:
      ip_rtlookup(&NextHop, &ifp, &PrevHop);
      if (ifp == NULL) return;

      IPRIPUpdateForIf (type, ifp, ifp->Addr, ifp->Broadcast,
```

```
                            msg, &entry_count);
      if (entry_count==0)
         break; /* Suppressing zero-update */
      IPRIPSendMessage (msg, entry_count, NULL, 0,
                           where, where_port);
      break;
   case RIP_REPLY_PERIODIC:
   case RIP_REPLY_TRIGGERED:
      FOR_EVERY(node, InterfaceList)
      {
         if ((ifp = node->data)==NULL) continue;
         if (!IPRIPIfActive (ifp, &Passive)) continue;
         if (Passive) continue;

         IPRIPUpdateForIf (type, ifp, ifp->Addr, ifp->Broadcast,
                           msg, &entry_count);
         if (entry_count)
            IPRIPSendMessage (msg, entry_count, ifp, ifp->Addr,
                              ifp->Broadcast, RIP_UDP_PORT);
         entry_count = 0;
         if (!CHECK_FLAG(ifp->Flags, IF_IP_UNNUM)){
            MajorNets = list_new();
            IPRIPAddServedNet(MajorNets, ifp->Addr);
            for(SecAddr=ifp->Secondary; SecAddr; SecAddr = SecAddr->Next){
               if (!IPRIPCoveredByNet(SecAddr->Addr)) continue;
               if (IPRIPNetServed(MajorNets, SecAddr->Addr)) continue;
                  /* This net is already served */

               IPRIPUpdateForIf (type, ifp, SecAddr->Addr,
                                 ifp->Broadcast, msg, &entry_count);
               if (entry_count)
                  IPRIPSendMessage (msg, entry_count, ifp, SecAddr->Addr,
                                    ifp->Broadcast, RIP_UDP_PORT);
               entry_count = 0;
               IPRIPAddServedNet(MajorNets, SecAddr->Addr);
            }
            list_free(MajorNets);
         } /* if not unnum*/
      } /* for all RIP-enabled interfaces*/

      /* Static neighbors now */
      FOR_EVERY(node, ProtoRIP.Neighbors){
         if ((Neighbor = node->data)==NULL)
            continue;
         Route = LookUp(*Neighbor, 0); /* Classful nbr lookup */

         /* Check nbr is reachable and directly connected */
         if ((Route == NULL) ||
             (Route->Source->Type != RS_CONNECTED))
            continue;
         GetNextHop(Route, &ifp, &NextHop);

         if ((ifp == NULL) ||
```

```
            !CHECK_FLAG(ifp->Flags, IF_STATE_UP))
         continue; /* Sanity Check*/

      /* Find correct source IP address */
      Source = IPRIPFindSource(ifp, Route);
      IPRIPUpdateForIf (type, ifp, Source, *Neighbor,
                     msg, &entry_count);
      if (entry_count)
         IPRIPSendMessage (msg, entry_count, ifp, Source,
                     *Neighbor, RIP_UDP_PORT);
      entry_count = 0;
   }
  break;
 default:;
}
IPRIPClearChangeFlag ();
IPRIPFreeMessage (msg);
}
```

Listing 8-24. *Pseudocode: The function* `IPRIPUpdate()`

The argument passed to `IPRIPUpdate()` indicates the type of the update to be sent. The value `RIP_REPLY_PERIODIC` is passed when the function is called, because of expiration of the periodic timer. The value `RIP_REPLY_TRIGGERED` is used when the function is supposed to send an incremental update. The value `RIP_REPLY_SOLICITED` indicates that the update must be sent to a particular host in response to a general request message. Note that `where` and `where_port` arguments are used only for the last type of updates.

The logic of the function depends on the type of the update to be sent. In any case, the message is prepared on a per interface basis by the `IPRIPUpdateForIf()` function. If the update is a reply to a general request, the `IPRIPUpdateForIf()` function is called only once for the interface through which the requesting router is available. For periodic and triggered updates, the function operates as follows.

1. For every RIP-enabled and not passive interface, perform the following steps.

   a. Create an RIP message for the primary subnet and send that message to the interface broadcast address, using the interface primary IP address as the source IP address.

   b. If secondary IP addresses are present, create one or many separate RIP messages if the major network of the secondary subnet is different from the major network of the primary address and for only one subnet per major network. When sending these messages, use the interface broadcast address. The source IP address must be set to the corresponding secondary IP address of the interface.

2. For every statically configured neighbor, do the following.

   a. Find the interface through which the neighbor can be accessed; make sure that the neighbor is directly reachable.

   b. Create a message for this interface and send it directly to the neighbor as a unicast packet.

After the messages on all interfaces have been sent, RIP goes through all its routes in the routing table and clears the ROUTE_CHANGED flag, which is set to mark a route as changed.

Now consider how the IPRIPUpdateForIf() function, shown in Listing 8-25, creates a message for an interface. All major network routes are considered sequentially, as follows.

1. If the current major network route is ultimate—used for packet forwarding itself—there are no subnets for this major network, and this is the major network route itself and should be included in the message. If the function is constructing a triggered update, the route is not announced if the ROUTE_CHANGED flag is not set on it. The route should also pass the distribute lists, the split-horizons rule, and other restrictions checked in the IPRIPShouldAnnounce() function, considered later. The major network route is also included in the RIP message if it is parent—contains children subnet routes—but covers a major network other than the one to which the current interface's IP address belongs. In this case, RIP announces only a summary network route—that's why we include the major network route in the message—and no subnet routes in this major network. The reason is that routers in other major networks will have no information on the subnet mask used in the network that the currently considered major network route covers.

2. If the interface's IP address belongs to the same major network and the major network route is not ultimate, all subnet routes are considered as follows.

   a. If a triggered update is being prepared, only routes with the ROUTE_CHANGED flag set are considered. If the flag is not set on the route, it is not included in the message.

   b. If a subnet route should be announced, RIP checks whether the route's mask equals the subnet mask of the interface, calling the IPRIPValidMask() function. If the masks are different, meaning that RIP is working in a VLSM environment, the route is not included in the message unless it is a host route.

   c. If these checks are passed, the route is added to the message. Function IPRIPAddSavedConnectedRoutes() adds the routes saved by the IPRIPIf Down() function, setting their metric to infinity. The IPRIPAnnounce Default() function checks whether the default route—route to pseudonetwork 0.0.0.0—must be sent in the update and adds an appropriate entry, if necessary. The pseudocode of the IPRIPAnnounceDefault() function is discussed later.

```
void IPRIPUpdateForIf (int type, TInterfaceDescr * ifp, TIPAddress source,
                       TIPAddress dest, TRIPMessage * msg,
                       int * entry_count)
{
#define ENTRY_NETWORK msg->Entries[*entry_count].Network
#define ENTRY_METRIC  msg->Entries[*entry_count].Metric

  TPrefixDescr Majornet, *Net, *Route;
  TNetworkInfo *NetInfo;

    Major(source, &Majornet);
    for (Net = TheRoutingTable.Majornets; Net; Net = Net->Next)
    {
      if ( (Net->Ultimate) || (Majornet.Network != Net->Network) ) {
        if ((type == RIP_REPLY_TRIGGERED) &&
             Net->Ultimate &&
             (Net->Source == &ProtoRIP) &&
             (!CHECK_FLAG(Net->Flags, ROUTE_CHANGED)))
          continue;
        if (IPRIPShouldAnnounce (Net, ifp))
        {
          IPRIPAddMsgEntry (msg, Net, entry_count);
          Proto_OffsetListOut(&ProtoRIP, ENTRY_NETWORK, ifp,
                              (u_int *) &ENTRY_METRIC);
          IPRIPCheckMessage (msg, entry_count, ifp, source, dest);
        }
        continue; /* Don't consider the subnets */
      }

      /* Since the majornet route is not ultimate
         it has subnets. Since interface is from the same
         majornet, we should announce the subnets.
      */

      NetInfo = (TNetworkInfo*)Net->Pointer;
      for (Route = NetInfo->Pointer; Route; Route = Route->Next)
      {
        if ((type == RIP_REPLY_TRIGGERED) &&
            (Route->Source == &ProtoRIP) &&
            (!CHECK_FLAG(Route->Flags, ROUTE_CHANGED)))
          continue;
        if (! IPRIPShouldAnnounce (Route, ifp))
          continue; /* Check filters and split-horizons */
        if (! IPRIPValidMask (Route, ifp))
          continue; /* Check subnet masks */
        IPRIPAddMsgEntry (msg, Route, entry_count);
        Proto_OffsetListOut(&ProtoRIP, ENTRY_NETWORK, ifp,
                            (u_int *) &ENTRY_METRIC);
        IPRIPCheckMessage (msg, entry_count, ifp, source, dest);
      } /* for all subnets*/
    } /* for all majornets*/
```

```
      IPRIPAddSavedConnectedRoutes(msg, entry_count, ifp, source, dest);

   if ( (type == RIP_REPLY_PERIODIC) || (type == RIP_REPLY_SOLICITED) ||
        (TheRoutingTable.Default &&
         (TheRoutingTable.Default->Source == &ProtoRIP) &&
         CHECK_FLAG(TheRoutingTable.Default->Flags, ROUTE_CHANGED) ) )
      IPRIPAnnounceDefault (msg, ifp, source, dest, entry_count);
}
```

Listing 8-25. *Pseudocode: The function* `IPRIPUpdateForIf()`

While a message is being constructed, every time the `IPRIPAddMsgEntry()` function is called to add a route to the update, the `IPRIPCheckMessage()` function is used to ensure that the message is sent out of the interface and that a new message is created when the number of entries reaches `MAX_RIP_ENTRIES` (25).

Listing 8-26 shows the pseudocode of the `IPRIPShouldAnnounce()` function, used in the `IPRIPUpdateForIf()` to check whether a route from the routing table should be announced in the RIP update.

```
int IPRIPShouldAnnounce (TPrefixDescr * Route, TInterfaceDescr *ifp)
{
 TPathDescr * Path;

/* If not RIP, or a connected covered by network,
   it must be expicily redistributed */

  if ( Route->Ultimate && (Route->Source != &ProtoRIP) &&
       !(Route->Connected && IPRIPCoveredByNet (Route->Network)) ) {
    if (!Proto_IsRedistributed (&ProtoRIP, Route))
      return 0;
    else if (!Proto_RedistributeList(&ProtoRIP, Route))
      return 0;
  }

  if (!Proto_DistributeListOut(&ProtoRIP, Route->Network, ifp))
    return 0;

  /* Check split-horizon */
  if ( (Route->Ultimate) &&
       (CHECK_FLAG(ifp->IPFlags, IF_IP_SPLIT_HORIZON)) )
    for (Path = (TPathDescr*) Route->Pointer; Path; Path = Path->Next)
     if ( (Path->Interface) && (Path->Interface == ifp) )
       return 0;

  return 1;
}
```

Listing 8-26. *Pseudocode: The function* `IPRIPShouldAnnounce()`

The function works as follows.

1. If the route is ultimate and installed by RIP or is a directly connected route supplied by either the Connected or the Static route sources, covered by one of the **network** statements in the configuration, it is allowed for further checks.

2. If the route is installed by another route source, RIP must be configured to redistribute this type of route, and the source-specific distribute list, if configured, must not filter it out. A parent route will be marked for redistribution into RIP when at least one child subnet route must be redistributed to RIP. This is done automatically by the routing table maintenance functions.

3. If the route passes these checks, the global and interface-specific distribute lists are checked by `Proto_DistributeListOut()`.

4. Finally, the split-horizon rule is applied to the route. If the route references the same interface as the one for which the update is being prepared, the route is not allowed to be sent.

Now consider the pseudocode of the `IPRIPAnnounceDefault()` function (Listing 8-27). This function checks whether the default route should be included in the update.

```
void IPRIPAnnounceDefault (TRIPMessage *msg, TInterfaceDescr *ifp,
                           TIPAddress source, TIPAddress dest,
                           int *index)
{
#define ENTRY_NETWORK msg->Entries[*index].Network
#define ENTRY_METRIC  msg->Entries[*index].Metric

  TPrefixDescr Default;

  Default.Source  = &ProtoRIP;
  Default.Network = 0;

  if (TheRoutingTable.Default)
  {
    if (TheRoutingTable.Default->Source == &ProtoRIP)
       Default.Metric = TheRoutingTable.Default->Metric;
    else
       Default.Metric = 0;

    Default.Ultimate = 1;

    /* Copy Paths for the split-horizons check */
    Default.Pointer = TheRoutingTable.Default->Pointer;

    if (IPRIPShouldAnnounce (&Default, ifp))
    {
      IPRIPAddMsgEntry (msg, &Default, index);
```

```
      Proto_OffsetListOut(&ProtoRIP, ENTRY_NETWORK, ifp,
                          (u_int *) &ENTRY_METRIC);
      IPRIPCheckMessage (msg, index, ifp, source, dest);
    }
  }
  else if (ProtoRIP.DefaultOriginate ||
            (TheRoutingTable.Externals &&
             TheRoutingTable.Externals->count))
  {
    Default.Metric = 0;
    Default.Ultimate = 0; /* Prevent split-horizons checking */

    /* Let distribute lists work */
    if (IPRIPShouldAnnounce (&Default, ifp))
    {
      IPRIPAddMsgEntry (msg, &Default, index);
      Proto_OffsetListOut(&ProtoRIP, ENTRY_NETWORK, ifp,
                          (u_int *) &ENTRY_METRIC);
      IPRIPCheckMessage (msg, index, ifp, source, dest);
    }
  }
}
```

Listing 8-27. *Pseudocode: The function* `IPRIPAnnounceDefault()`

RIP announces the default route as a route to pseudonetwork 0.0.0.0. The conditions for default-route announcement in Cisco RIP are as follows.

1. If the router has the active default route, RIP announces that route as well. If the default route in the routing table is provided by RIP, the default is announced as any other RIP route, and the metric is increased by 1. If the default route is installed by another route source, RIP announces the default route with metric 1. In any case, the split-horizon rule and distribute lists are applied.

2. If the router does not have the default route but has at least one route in the routing table marked as external—augmented with an asterisk in the output of the **show ip route** command—or the `DefaultOriginate` flag has been set by the **default-information originate** configuration command, RIP announces the default route with metric 1, and the split-horizon check is not performed. However, distribute lists can still be used to filter the default route out from the update.

3. Otherwise, no default route is announced: The `DefaultOriginate` flag is not set; the router has no default and no external routes.

The **default-information originate** command in RIP is used to enforce default-route announcement even if the router itself doesn't have the default route. This command is turned off by default.

Now let's see how an entry is added to the RIP message by the `IPRIPAddMsgEntry()` function (Listing 8-28).

```
void IPRIPAddMsgEntry (TRIPMessage *msg, TPrefixDescr * Route, int * index)
{
  u_int Metric;

  msg->Entries[*index].AFI     = AFI_IP;
  msg->Entries[*index].Network = Route->Network;

  if (!Route->Ultimate)
    Metric  = 1; // Summary route is always announced with metric 1
  else if (Route->Source == &ProtoRIP)
    Metric  = Route->Metric + 1;
  else if ((Route->Connected) || (Route->Source->Type == RS_STATIC))
    Metric  = 1;
  else if (Metric = Proto_RedistributeMetric(&ProtoRIP, Route->Source))
    ;
  else
    Metric  = ProtoRIP.MetricInfo->Infinity;

  if (Metric > ProtoRIP.MetricInfo->Infinity)
    Metric = ProtoRIP.MetricInfo->Infinity;

  msg->Entries[(*index)++].Metric = Metric;
}
```

Listing 8-28. *Pseudocode: The function* `IPRIPAddMsgEntry()`

The function sets the entry fields, based on the route from the routing table, as follows.

1. The AFI field of the message entry is set to the value AFI_IP to indicate the TCP/IP suite.

2. The `Network` field of the entry is set to the value of the network address of the route.

3. The `metric` field is set. Recall that the Cisco implementation of RIP increments the hop count when the update is sent, whereas other implementations may do this when the update is received.

   a. If the route is a network summary or references only an interface—a directly connected route—or is statically configured, the metric value is set to 1.

   b. Otherwise, if the source of the route is RIP itself, the metric value of the entry is set to one more than the value of the metric in the announced route.

   c. The metric value for redistributed routes is set, based on the **redistribute *source* metric *metric-value*** and the **default-metric** router configuration commands. This is done by the `Proto_RedistributeMetric()` function. If no metric value is available, RIP sets the infinity metric value (16) for the route.

Because RIP uses the metric of infinity for redistributed routes when no seed metric information is available, configuring the **default-metric** command or specifying the metric value in the **redistribute** statement is obligatory when redistribution is used. Otherwise, remote routers will ignore redistributed routes, and corresponding networks will not be reachable for users.

8.2.7 RIP version 2

RIP version 2 is an extension to RIP version 1 to support classless routing, route tagging, authentication, and multicast messages. Described in [RFC1723], RIP version 2 uses the same algorithm and mainly the same basic format as the first version; however, some fields that must be 0 for RIP version 1 are used to propagate additional information. The format of an RIP version 2 message is given in Figure 8-9. Listing 8-29 shows the pseudocode type definition for the message entry.

```
typedef struct RIP2Entry {
  u_int16_t  AFI;              /* Address Family Identifier. 2 for IP */
  u_int16_t  Tag;             /* Route tag */
  TIPAddress Network;         /* Destination address (prefix value) */
  TIPAddress Mask;            /* Route mask */
  TIPAddress NextHop;         /* Nexthop address*/
  u_int32_t  Metric;          /* Metric (1..16) 16 is infinity*/

} TRIP2Entry;
```

Listing 8-29. *Pseudocode: Type definition for TRIP2Entry*

The unused 16-bit field following the `AFI` field in the message entry is now used for the route tag. Tags are used to associate some implementation or administratively specific information with routes. Tags can be used, for example, to mark routes imported to RIP from other routing protocols and to prevent route redistribution loops. Also, every RIPv2 message entry carries the route mask information and the next-hop address. The route mask is necessary in VLSM and CIDR environments, in which subnet masks can be different for different subnets, and routes can be aggregated at any arbitrary boundary. The next-hop address is an advisory field used to achieve more efficient routing if the next-hop address in a route redistributed into RIP is reachable through the same interface to which RIP sends its update.

As you can see, RIPv2 does not have any authentication-specific fields in the message entry format. There is no such field in the message header, either. Instead, RIPv2 uses the

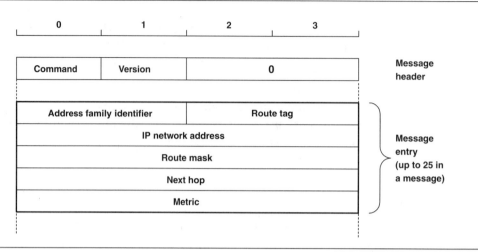

Figure 8-9. *Format of RIPv2 message entry*

same format of the message header as RIPv1, except that the Version field is set to 2. Nevertheless, RIPv2 supports authentication.

Recall that in RIPv1, a message is considered a general request if it contains exactly one entry and the entry fields contain specific values; see Section 8.2.3 for more details. A similar approach is used for authentication in RIPv2. If the very first entry in a message has 0xFFFF in the AFI field, the rest of the entry must be considered as an authentication subheader for the message (see Figure 8-10). In this case, an RIPv2 message can carry up to 24 routes instead of 25 when no authentication is used.

RIP version 2 also changed how RIP messages are sent. In RIP version 1, all messages are sent to the local broadcast address (255.255.255.255). In RIP version 2, all messages are sent to the multicast address 224.0.0.9. This is to ensure that only hosts interested in RIP messages have to receive and process them.

Now that a basic description of RIP version 2 has been given, let's proceed to the details. The following sections describe the changes that RIPv2 requires. Note, however, that event processing is not changed.

8.2.7.1 Changes to Input Processing

When routers run the RIP version 2, their input message processing is changed as follows.

- The router joins the IP multicast group used to exchange RIPv2 messages (224.0.0.9) on all RIP-enabled interfaces. Note that the router still processes messages sent to the local broadcast IP address (255.255.255.255) for backward compatibility with RIPv1.

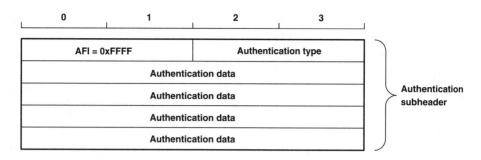

Figure 8-10. *Format of RIPv2 authentication subheader*

- If message authentication is disabled, the routers can receive and process messages of both RIP versions. It is assumed that received version 2 messages are not authenticated. Authenticated messages are discarded.

- If message authentication is enabled, the router processes RIPv1 messages. In version 2, messages are processed only if authenticated and only if they pass the authentication check.

- The administrator can explicitly disable or enable processing of messages of a specific version. The **ip rip receive version** interface configuration command is used for this purpose. If the version 2 authentication feature is used, it is highly recommended to disable processing of version 1 messages, using the **no ip rip receive version 1** interface configuration command.

- In response to a version 1 request, the router answers with a version 1 reply. If the router is configured to send only version 2 messages, no reply is sent to a version 1 request.

- When a reply message is processed, the route mask is not determined by the subnet mask of the interface on which the message has been received. Instead, the route mask is taken directly from the message entry. This allows version 2 to be used in VLSM environments.

8.2.7.2 Changes to Message Sending

Basic changes in message sending for version 2 are as follows.

- An interface can be configured to send messages of either version 1 or version 2 or both.

- If version 1 messages are sent on an interface, they are constructed according to the classful rules: Classful route summarization is performed, routes to subnets with one subnet mask are not sent to subnets with different subnet masks, and supernet routes are not announced.

- If version 2 messages are sent on an interface, they are constructed according to the following rules.

  - If message authentication is enabled, an authentication entry is included in every message as the first entry; see Section 8.2.9 for information on authentication configuration.

  - If automatic classful route summarization is enabled—it is enabled by default in Cisco IOS—messages sent to one major network do not contain subnet routes belonging to a different major network. Instead, a summary network route is announced. If automatic route summarization is disabled, using the **no auto-summary** router configuration command, subnet information is propagated across major network boundaries.

  - Every RIP route included in a message is augmented with its route mask and the route tag taken from the routing table. For directly connected routes announced in a version 2 message, the value of the route tag is 0 unless these routes are announced owing to route redistribution.

  - Redistributed routes also are augmented with the route mask and the route tag. Route tags can be assigned to the routes by the administrator through configuration of **route-map** statements, which are then used in the **redistribute** clause.

  - If the next-hop address of a redistributed route belongs to a network covered by RIP, the next hop in the RIP route is set to the value of the next hop of the redistributed route. Otherwise the next-hop field of the RIP route is set to 0.

8.2.8 RIP Demand Circuit Extensions

Distance-vector routing protocols require installed routes to be periodically refreshed. RIP sends periodic updates every 30 seconds by default. This may not be suitable for interfaces connected to circuit-oriented networks, such as ISDN, X.25, or Frame Relay, because periodic messages do not let the circuits go down. Specifying the packets of the routing protocols as not interesting in the configuration of the dialer or the circuit manager is not a solution, because once the circuit goes down, the routes over the corresponding interface are not updated, and they finally age out from the routing table. [RFC2091] describes triggered extensions to RIP to support demand circuit. Cisco routers support these extensions.

The demand circuit extensions are based on a simple idea, called "presumption of reachability," defined as follows.

If a node has been reached through a demand circuit at least once, it is deemed to be reachable—presumption of reachability—until explicit evidence proving the opposite is seen.

Routes received via regular interfaces are processed as in standard RIP, but routes received over demand circuit are processed differently. Instead of starting the Invalid timer for the route after its installation, these routes are frozen. Routers do not exchange standard RIP messages over demand circuit but use the following special new message types.

- Update Request (command code 9)
- Update Response (command code 10)
- Update Acknowledge (command code 11)

All messages exchanged by RIP over a demand circuit are acknowledged, so there is no need to repeatedly send the same information. After neighboring routers have informed each other about the routing information they have and this information has been acknowledged, no messages are sent over the demand circuit, allowing established circuits to be released. Any message that remains unacknowledged is retransmitted to the corresponding neighbor; a retransmission list is maintained for each neighbor. Routes received from the neighboring routers stay in the routing table until they are updated with better routes or removed. In the routing table, if any changes occur that must be communicated through a demand circuit, the router initiates a connection. If any neighboring router is reported to be unreachable by the data link layer software—an attempt to establish a connection to the router has been rejected by the network or the remote router—all routes through that neighbor start aging just like other RIP routes. This behavior can be understood as a reaction to explicit evidence proving that the remote node is not reachable. If it is not possible to reach the remote router during the Invalid interval, routes from this neighbor are put in the holddown state and are processed further, according to the route state machine described in Section 8.2.5.

It is interesting to see how demand circuit extensions handle alternative routes. In standard RIP, if the currently used route is removed or changes its metric, alternative routes get in the routing table because all RIP routers announce their routing information periodically. Therefore, if it is removed or its metric becomes worse, the currently best route is updated with a better route next time an update from the appropriate neighbor is received, which is why standard RIP stores only the best routes in the routing table. Now recall that periodic updates are not sent over the demand circuit. This means that RIP must have its internal routing information database where it can save the routes from all neighbors. Indeed, there is an internal RIP database.

Information stored in the RIP database includes routes to directly attached networks covered by the network statements in RIP configuration, RIP routes received over demand and regular links, automatically created network summary routes, and routes redistributed to RIP. Routes to directly connected networks reflect corresponding routes in the main routing table. The RIP database can contain two types of routes: permanent, for routes received over demand circuit; and temporary, for routes received over regular links. Temporary routes are aged according to standard RIP rules. Permanent routes start aging only after explicit evidence that the neighbor that supplied them is not reachable any more.

The RIP database contains all routes, regardless of whether they are best. All routes are sorted on a per destination basis. After some information in the database has changed, the new best route is selected for the attached destinations. If the new best route is an RIP route, it is installed in the routing table, possibly substituting for an already installed one. New routing information is also propagated to all neighbors in triggered updates. If new information must be sent to neighbors over demand circuit, the router initiates the necessary connections.

8.2.9 RIP Configuration

8.2.9.1 Configuration Commands

This section summarizes information on configuration commands used to start and to tune RIP processes in Cisco routers. For more detailed descriptions on configuration commands, see the official documentation from Cisco.

The global configuration command **router rip** is used to start the RIP process in a Cisco router. A router can have only one RIP process; hence, the command has no process identifier.

The router configuration command **network** *network-address* is used to specify the interfaces that should be included into the RIP domain. The *network-address* argument is a classful network address. If the subnet or the host portion of the address is nonzero, it is cleared, and the address is transformed to its classful form. Execution of this command enables RIP on the interfaces that have a primary or a secondary IP address covered by the configured network address. This command also defines which directly connected routes are announced in RIP messages. That is, if a directly connected route, configured statically or derived from the primary or a secondary interface IP address, is covered by one of the **network** commands, this route is announced in RIP messages.

When RIP is enabled on an interface, all updates are sent as IP broadcasts, multicasts in the case of RIPv2. The following router configuration command can be used to configure static neighbors that will receive unicast updates:

neighbor *ip-address*

Configured neighbors must be directly reachable through one of the networks directly connected to an RIP-enabled interface.

By default, when the RIP process is configured, only RIPv1 messages are sent on all interfaces, but both version 1 and version 2 messages are received. The following router configuration command can be used to change the version of the messages generated for the interfaces by default:

version {1|2}

If version 2 is configured, the router sends version 2 packets on all enabled interfaces unless the interface itself is explicitly configured with one of the following two interface configuration commands:

ip rip receive version [1] [2]
ip rip send version [1] [2]

The two commands set the version of RIP messages to be received and sent. Note that the router can simultaneously receive and send messages of both types on an interface.

Every IP-enabled interface is augmented with a flag specifying whether the split-horizon check should be performed when sending routing protocol updates on it. The following interface configuration command can be used to explicitly set this flag to a desired value:

ip split-horizon

By default, the split-horizon flag is set for all interfaces except physical interfaces with Frame Relay or SMDS encapsulation, as well as multipoint subinterfaces created for them. To disable the split-horizon check on an interface, use the **no ip split-horizon** form of this command. The **ip split-horizon** form enables the split-horizon check.

When operating in version 1 mode, RIP always performs automatic classful route summarization. This is necessary because version 1 messages do not contain route masks, so no subnet information can be propagated across major network boundaries. Version 2, as implemented in Cisco IOS, also performs this type of automatic route summarization. This is beneficial if no major network is divided by another major network, as summarized routes reduce the size of the routing table. The following router configuration command can be used to control classful route summarization when RIP works in version 2 mode:

auto-summary

In order to avoid problems with noncontiguous major networks, it is recommended that classful route summarization be disabled, using the **no auto-summary** form of this command when version 2 is used in CIDR environments. This command can be configured when RIP operates in version 1 mode but takes effect only when version 2 messages are prepared.

By default, RIP announces the default route whenever the router has an active default route in the routing table or at least one route is marked as external; see Section 8.2.6 for more details. The following router configuration command can be used to control origination of the default route:

default-information originate

If RIP is configured with this command, messages originated by RIP will always include the default route. The **no default-information originate** command sets the default RIP behavior for default route origination. Distribute lists can also be used in RIP to filter undesirable default routes.

The RIP best-path selection algorithm relies on hop-by-hop incrementing of the route metric. By default, RIP increments the metric by 1. However, it may be desirable to increment it by a larger number in order to reflect the different level of preference of different paths. The following router configuration command allows the administrator to instruct the router to increment the metric of a router when a message is received or about to be sent:

offset-list *acl-number* {**out** | **in**} *offset* [*interface-type interface-number*]

The *acl-number* sets the access list used to identify the routes to which the offset must be applied. If *acl-number* is 0, all routes are considered. The *offset* parameter is the value that must be added to the metric of the routes identified by the access list. If *offset* is 0, the metric is not changed. If the *interface-type* and *interface-number* parameters are specified, the offset list is applied only to the message received on or sent over a specific interface; otherwise, the offset list is applied to all incoming or outgoing messages.

RIP routers send periodic routing updates to one another to ensure consistency of the routing tables. The RIP route state machine also uses several timers. The following router configuration command controls them:

timers basic *update invalid holddown flush*

Description of the timers follows. For more information on the states of RIP routes, see Section 8.2.5.

- *Update* specifies the delay between periodic messages. The delay is also randomized to avoid synchronization. The default value is 30 seconds.

- *Invalid* specifies the number of seconds after which an unrefreshed route is declared invalid. The default value is three times the update interval, or 180 seconds. When a route is declared invalid, it is placed in the holddown state.

- *Holddown* specifies the number of seconds that a route must spend in the holddown state after expiration of the Invalid timer. The default value is three times the update interval, or 180 seconds.

- *Flush* specifies the number of seconds that a route must remain in the routing table in the garbage collection state after it exits the holddown state. The default value of this timer is four times the update interval, or 240 seconds. After a route's flush timer has expired, the route is removed from the routing table.

When configuring timers for distance-vector protocols, the invalid, holddown, and flush intervals should never be less than or equal to the update interval, because this would lead to persistent problems in the routing protocol. Owing to possible packet drops on the network links and dispersion introduced to the update interval in order to avoid synchronization of updates, the minimal safe value for the invalid, holddown, and flush intervals is three times the update interval. On the other hand, setting higher values for these timers leads to slower protocol convergence. The flush timer is an exception, because a route in the garbage collection state can be updated by any other route with a metric better than infinity; hence, it is safe for a route to stay in the garbage collection state longer than in other states.

All routers within the network must use identical timer settings to avoid persistent routing problems.

When creating a routing update, RIP includes only its own routes and directly connected routes covered by configured networks. This is the default behavior. However, external routing information, such as static routes or routes provided by other routing protocols, must sometimes be injected into an RIP domain. This may be achieved by route redistribution, configured using the following router configuration command.

redistribute *route-source* [*process-id*] [**metric** *metric-value*] [**route-map** *map-name*]

The syntax specified here is rather basic. A number of additional options control how routes from specific sources are redistributed. The ***route-source*** parameter is the name of the source, such as Connected, Static, or OSPF, whose routes must be redistributed by RIP from the routing table. Note that routes must be in the routing table before they appear in an RIP message. The ***process-id*** parameter is necessary if routes from a source that allows for multiple protocol instances are redistributed (OSPF is an example). The **metric** keyword allows the administrator to specify the value of the metric to be used as the seed value in the redistributed routes. If no metric value, is specified in the **redistribute** command, the default metric value, configured using the **default-metric** command, is taken. If the default metric command is not configured, RIP uses 1 for static and connected routes and infinity metric (16) for other routes. For more information on controlling route redistribution, see Chapter 7. For more information on route redistribution in RIP specifically, refer to Section 8.2.6.

Periodic updates sent by RIP can cause problems on demand circuit, as discussed in Section 8.2.8. To configure an interface to be treated as an RIP demand circuit, use the following interface configuration command.

ip rip demand-circuit

Note that Cisco IOS supports RIP demand circuit extensions on point-to-point interfaces only.

8.2.9.2 Configuration Examples

The configuration examples given here are based on the network topology described in Chapter 1, except that links between R1 and R2 and between R3 and R4 are now Ethernet segments. A loopback interface is configured in every router to simulate stub LAN segments connected to the routers. The loopback interfaces are assigned IP addresses in the form *N.N.N.N*/24, where *N* is the router's number. Figure 8-11 illustrates the topology. We

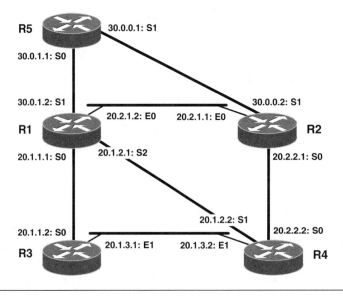

Figure 8-11. *Scheme of lab network for RIP examples*

start with a simple RIP configuration and modify it to achieve more optimal routing in the lab network.

The basic RIP configuration is simple: Just start RIP in the routers and let it run on all interfaces. Configurations for routers R1 and R4 follow.

- R1:

```
hostname R1
!
ip subnet-zero
!
interface Loopback0
 ip address 1.1.1.1 255.255.255.0
!
interface Ethernet0
 ip address 20.2.1.2 255.255.255.0
!
interface Serial0
 ip address 20.1.1.1 255.255.255.0
 bandwidth 64
!
interface Serial1
 ip address 30.0.1.2 255.255.255.0
 bandwidth 64
 clockrate 64000
!
interface Serial2
 ip address 20.1.2.1 255.255.255.0
 bandwidth 64
 clockrate 64000
!
router rip
 network 30.0.0.0
 network 20.0.0.0
 network 1.0.0.0
```

- R4:

```
hostname R4
!
ip subnet-zero
!
interface Loopback0
 ip address 4.4.4.4 255.255.255.0
!
interface Ethernet0
```

```
ip address 20.1.3.2 255.255.255.0
!
interface Serial0
ip address 20.2.2.2 255.255.255.0
bandwidth 64
no fair-queue
clockrate 64000
!
interface Serial1
ip address 20.1.2.2 255.255.255.0
bandwidth 64
!
router rip
 network 20.0.0.0
 network 4.0.0.0
```

Note that the **ip subnet-zero** command is configured on routers R1, R2, and R5 to enable configuration of interface IP addresses on R5 and R2 and to allow routes to subnet 30.0.0.0/24 to be installed in R1.

Although the configuration is simple, RIP does its job, finding the shortest paths and installing corresponding routes in the routing table. Listings 8-30, 8-31, and 8-32 illustrate routing tables constructed in routers R1, R2, and R4, respectively.

```
R1#sho ip route
...
Gateway of last resort is not set

     1.0.0.0/24 is subnetted, 1 subnets
C       1.1.1.0 is directly connected, Loopback0
R    2.0.0.0/8 [120/1] via 20.2.1.1, 00:00:11, Ethernet0
R    3.0.0.0/8 [120/1] via 20.1.1.2, 00:00:29, Serial0
R    4.0.0.0/8 [120/1] via 20.1.2.2, 00:00:20, Serial2
R    5.0.0.0/8 [120/1] via 30.0.1.1, 00:00:26, Serial1
     20.0.0.0/24 is subnetted, 5 subnets
R       20.2.2.0 [120/1] via 20.1.2.2, 00:00:20, Serial2
                 [120/1] via 20.2.1.1, 00:00:11, Ethernet0
C       20.1.1.0 is directly connected, Serial0
R       20.1.3.0 [120/1] via 20.1.1.2, 00:00:29, Serial0
                 [120/1] via 20.1.2.2, 00:00:20, Serial2
C       20.2.1.0 is directly connected, Ethernet0
C       20.1.2.0 is directly connected, Serial2
     30.0.0.0/24 is subnetted, 2 subnets
R       30.0.0.0 [120/1] via 30.0.1.1, 00:00:27, Serial1
C       30.0.1.0 is directly connected, Serial1
R1#
```

Listing 8-30. *RIP routes in routing table of R1*

```
R2#sho ip route
Codes: C - connected, S - static, I - IGRP, R - RIP, M - mobile, B - BGP
       D - EIGRP, EX - EIGRP external, O - OSPF, IA - OSPF inter area
       N1 - OSPF NSSA external type 1, N2 - OSPF NSSA external type 2
       E1 - OSPF external type 1, E2 - OSPF external type 2, E - EGP
       i - IS-IS, L1 - IS-IS level-1, L2 - IS-IS level-2, * - candidate default
       U - per-user static route, o - ODR

Gateway of last resort is not set

R    1.0.0.0/8 [120/1] via 20.2.1.2, 00:00:08, Ethernet0
     2.0.0.0/24 is subnetted, 1 subnets
C       2.2.2.0 is directly connected, Loopback0
R    3.0.0.0/8 [120/2] via 20.2.2.2, 00:00:17, Serial0
                [120/2] via 20.2.1.2, 00:00:09, Ethernet0
R    4.0.0.0/8 [120/1] via 20.2.2.2, 00:00:17, Serial0
R    5.0.0.0/8 [120/1] via 30.0.0.1, 00:00:22, Serial1
     20.0.0.0/24 is subnetted, 5 subnets
R       20.1.1.0 [120/1] via 20.2.1.2, 00:00:09, Ethernet0
C       20.2.2.0 is directly connected, Serial0
R       20.1.3.0 [120/1] via 20.2.2.2, 00:00:17, Serial0
R       20.1.2.0 [120/1] via 20.2.2.2, 00:00:17, Serial0
                 [120/1] via 20.2.1.2, 00:00:09, Ethernet0
C       20.2.1.0 is directly connected, Ethernet0
     30.0.0.0/24 is subnetted, 2 subnets
C       30.0.0.0 is directly connected, Serial1
R       30.0.1.0 [120/1] via 30.0.0.1, 00:00:22, Serial1
R2#
```

Listing 8-31. *RIP routes in routing table of R2*

```
R4#sho ip route
...
Gateway of last resort is not set

R    1.0.0.0/8 [120/1] via 20.1.2.1, 00:00:27, Serial1
R    2.0.0.0/8 [120/1] via 20.2.2.1, 00:00:26, Serial0
R    3.0.0.0/8 [120/1] via 20.1.3.1, 00:00:13, Ethernet0
     4.0.0.0/24 is subnetted, 1 subnets
C       4.4.4.0 is directly connected, Loopback0
R    5.0.0.0/8 [120/2] via 20.2.2.1, 00:00:26, Serial0
                [120/2] via 20.1.2.1, 00:00:28, Serial1
     20.0.0.0/24 is subnetted, 5 subnets
R       20.1.1.0 [120/1] via 20.1.2.1, 00:00:28, Serial1
                 [120/1] via 20.1.3.1, 00:00:13, Ethernet0
C       20.2.2.0 is directly connected, Serial0
C       20.1.3.0 is directly connected, Ethernet0
R       20.2.1.0 [120/1] via 20.1.2.1, 00:00:00, Serial1
                 [120/1] via 20.2.2.1, 00:00:26, Serial0
C       20.1.2.0 is directly connected, Serial1
```

```
R      30.0.0.0/8 [120/1] via 20.2.2.1, 00:00:26, Serial0
                  [120/1] via 20.1.2.1, 00:00:00, Serial1
R4#
```

Listing 8-32. *RIP routes in routing table of R4*

Look at the highlighted routes in Listing 8-32. Owing to classful route summarization, R4 cannot see subnets of major networks 5.0.0.0 and 30.0.0.0. Moreover, R4 splits the load between two parallel routes via interfaces Serial0 and Serial1. In real networks, this may lead to packet reordering, as RIP does not care about bandwidth and delay associated with the links.

The first problem can be solved by changing to RIP version 2. This is done easily by configuring the **version 2** command on every router. However, this is not enough, because version 2 also performs autosummarization by default and so must be disabled, using the **no auto-summary** router configuration command. When both commands have been entered and RIP has had enough time to remove old routes from the routing tables, routing tables converge on new information, as shown in Listings 8-33, 8-34, and 8-35.

```
R1#sho ip route
...
Gateway of last resort is not set

     1.0.0.0/24 is subnetted, 1 subnets
C       1.1.1.0 is directly connected, Loopback0
     2.0.0.0/24 is subnetted, 1 subnets
R       2.2.2.0 [120/1] via 20.2.1.1, 00:00:23, Ethernet0
     3.0.0.0/24 is subnetted, 1 subnets
R       3.3.3.0 [120/1] via 20.1.1.2, 00:00:14, Serial0
     4.0.0.0/24 is subnetted, 1 subnets
R       4.4.4.0 [120/1] via 20.1.2.2, 00:00:02, Serial2
     20.0.0.0/24 is subnetted, 5 subnets
R       20.2.2.0 [120/1] via 20.2.1.1, 00:00:23, Ethernet0
                 [120/1] via 20.1.2.2, 00:00:02, Serial2
C       20.1.1.0 is directly connected, Serial0
R       20.1.3.0 [120/1] via 20.1.2.2, 00:00:02, Serial2
                 [120/1] via 20.1.1.2, 00:00:14, Serial0
C       20.1.2.0 is directly connected, Serial2
C       20.2.1.0 is directly connected, Ethernet0
     5.0.0.0/24 is subnetted, 1 subnets
R       5.5.5.0 [120/1] via 30.0.1.1, 00:00:06, Serial1
     30.0.0.0/24 is subnetted, 2 subnets
R       30.0.0.0 [120/1] via 20.2.1.1, 00:00:25, Ethernet0
                 [120/1] via 30.0.1.1, 00:00:06, Serial1
C       30.0.1.0 is directly connected, Serial1
R1#
```

Listing 8-33. *RIP version 2 routing table of R1*

```
R2#sho ip route
...
Gateway of last resort is not set

     1.0.0.0/24 is subnetted, 1 subnets
R       1.1.1.0 [120/1] via 20.2.1.2, 00:00:21, Ethernet0
     2.0.0.0/24 is subnetted, 1 subnets
C       2.2.2.0 is directly connected, Loopback0
     3.0.0.0/24 is subnetted, 1 subnets
R       3.3.3.0 [120/2] via 20.2.2.2, 00:00:11, Serial0
                [120/2] via 20.2.1.2, 00:00:21, Ethernet0
     4.0.0.0/24 is subnetted, 1 subnets
R       4.4.4.0 [120/1] via 20.2.2.2, 00:00:11, Serial0
     20.0.0.0/24 is subnetted, 5 subnets
R       20.1.1.0 [120/1] via 20.2.1.2, 00:00:21, Ethernet0
C       20.2.2.0 is directly connected, Serial0
R       20.1.3.0 [120/1] via 20.2.2.2, 00:00:11, Serial0
R       20.1.2.0 [120/1] via 20.2.2.2, 00:00:12, Serial0
                 [120/1] via 20.2.1.2, 00:00:22, Ethernet0
C       20.2.1.0 is directly connected, Ethernet0
     5.0.0.0/24 is subnetted, 1 subnets
R       5.5.5.0 [120/1] via 30.0.0.1, 00:00:15, Serial1
     30.0.0.0/24 is subnetted, 2 subnets
C       30.0.0.0 is directly connected, Serial1
R       30.0.1.0 [120/1] via 20.2.1.2, 00:00:22, Ethernet0
                 [120/1] via 30.0.0.1, 00:00:15, Serial1
R2#
```

Listing 8-34. *RIP version 2 routing table of R2*

```
R4#sho ip route
...
Gateway of last resort is not set

     1.0.0.0/24 is subnetted, 1 subnets
R       1.1.1.0 [120/1] via 20.1.2.1, 00:00:18, Serial1
     2.0.0.0/24 is subnetted, 1 subnets
R       2.2.2.0 [120/1] via 20.2.2.1, 00:00:05, Serial0
     3.0.0.0/24 is subnetted, 1 subnets
R       3.3.3.0 [120/1] via 20.1.3.1, 00:00:19, Ethernet0
     4.0.0.0/24 is subnetted, 1 subnets
C       4.4.4.0 is directly connected, Loopback0
     20.0.0.0/24 is subnetted, 5 subnets
C       20.2.2.0 is directly connected, Serial0
R       20.1.1.0 [120/1] via 20.1.3.1, 00:00:19, Ethernet0
                 [120/1] via 20.1.2.1, 00:00:18, Serial1
C       20.1.3.0 is directly connected, Ethernet0
C       20.1.2.0 is directly connected, Serial1
R       20.2.1.0 [120/1] via 20.2.2.1, 00:00:06, Serial0
                 [120/1] via 20.1.2.1, 00:00:18, Serial1
     5.0.0.0/24 is subnetted, 1 subnets
```

```
R        5.5.5.0 [120/2] via 20.2.2.1, 00:00:06, Serial0
                 [120/2] via 20.1.2.1, 00:00:18, Serial1
      30.0.0.0/24 is subnetted, 2 subnets
R        30.0.0.0 [120/1] via 20.2.2.1, 00:00:06, Serial0
R        30.0.1.0 [120/1] via 20.1.2.1, 00:00:18, Serial1
R4#
```

Listing 8-35. *RIP version 2 routing table of R4*

However, routing is still not optimal: RIP does not take link characteristics, such as bandwidth or delay, into consideration; it counts only hops. Therefore, router R2, for example, has parallel routes to destination 20.1.2.0—highlighted in Listing 8-34—splitting the load equally between the Ethernet and serial links. This may lead to packet-reordering problems, as well as overloading of the serial link and underloading of the Ethernet link. Let's try to alter the simple configuration somehow to achieve better results.

We now want to affect RIP's shortest-path calculation and make it prefer Ethernet links rather than serial links. The most appropriate way to do this is to use *offset lists*. The question is how to configure them and on which routers.

Offset lists can be configured with two possible methods. One is configuring a uniform outbound offset list for every serial interface on all routers. Another method is configuring both inbound and outbound offset lists on a limited set of routers.

> In any case, the offsets applied to the messages crossing a link in different directions should modify route metrics equally to avoid asymmetric routing.

The first method, the preferred one, prevents configuration mistakes that can lead to routing loops and can be used in most cases when the administrator can reconfigure any routers in the RIP domain. If some routers are under administrative control of a different organization, the second method may be the only choice.

The configuration of all routers is changed to add an offset of 3 for each route going out of a serial interface. Configuration of routers R1, R2, and R4 follows.

- R1:

```
router rip
version 2
offset-list 0 out 3 Serial0
offset-list 0 out 3 Serial1
offset-list 0 out 3 Serial2
network 1.0.0.0
network 20.0.0.0
```

```
network 30.0.0.0
no auto-summary
```

- R2:

```
router rip
version 2
offset-list 0 out 3 Serial0
offset-list 0 out 3 Serial1
network 2.0.0.0
network 20.0.0.0
network 30.0.0.0
no auto-summary
```

- R4:

```
router rip
version 2
offset-list 0 out 3 Serial0
offset-list 0 out 3 Serial1
network 4.0.0.0
network 20.0.0.0
no auto-summary
```

The number of the access list specified as 0 in the **offset-list** command configured RIP to apply the offset to all routes going out specified interfaces. After RIP has converged on new routing information, R1, R2, and R4 have the routing tables shown in Listings 8-36, 8-37, and 8-38.

```
R1#sho ip route
...
Gateway of last resort is not set
     1.0.0.0/24 is subnetted, 1 subnets
C       1.1.1.0 is directly connected, Loopback0
     2.0.0.0/24 is subnetted, 1 subnets
R       2.2.2.0 [120/1] via 20.2.1.1, 00:00:09, Ethernet0
     3.0.0.0/24 is subnetted, 1 subnets
R       3.3.3.0 [120/4] via 20.1.1.2, 00:00:06, Serial0
     4.0.0.0/24 is subnetted, 1 subnets
R       4.4.4.0 [120/4] via 20.1.2.2, 00:00:12, Serial2
     20.0.0.0/24 is subnetted, 5 subnets
```

```
R       20.2.2.0 [120/1] via 20.2.1.1, 00:00:09, Ethernet0
C       20.1.1.0 is directly connected, Serial0
R       20.1.3.0 [120/4] via 20.1.2.2, 00:00:12, Serial2
                 [120/4] via 20.1.1.2, 00:00:06, Serial0
C       20.1.2.0 is directly connected, Serial2
C       20.2.1.0 is directly connected, Ethernet0
        5.0.0.0/24 is subnetted, 1 subnets
R       5.5.5.0 [120/4] via 30.0.1.1, 00:00:21, Serial1
        30.0.0.0/24 is subnetted, 2 subnets
R       30.0.0.0 [120/1] via 20.2.1.1, 00:00:11, Ethernet0
C       30.0.1.0 is directly connected, Serial1
R1#
```

Listing 8-36. *Routing table of R1 when offset lists are applied*

```
R2#sho ip route
...
Gateway of last resort is not set

        1.0.0.0/24 is subnetted, 1 subnets
R       1.1.1.0 [120/1] via 20.2.1.2, 00:00:06, Ethernet0
        2.0.0.0/24 is subnetted, 1 subnets
C       2.2.2.0 is directly connected, Loopback0
        3.0.0.0/24 is subnetted, 1 subnets
R       3.3.3.0 [120/5] via 20.2.2.2, 00:00:23, Serial0
                [120/5] via 20.2.1.2, 00:00:06, Ethernet0
        4.0.0.0/24 is subnetted, 1 subnets
R       4.4.4.0 [120/4] via 20.2.2.2, 00:00:23, Serial0
        20.0.0.0/24 is subnetted, 5 subnets
R       20.1.1.0 [120/1] via 20.2.1.2, 00:00:06, Ethernet0
C       20.2.2.0 is directly connected, Serial0
R       20.1.3.0 [120/4] via 20.2.2.2, 00:00:23, Serial0
R       20.1.2.0 [120/1] via 20.2.1.2, 00:00:06, Ethernet0
C       20.2.1.0 is directly connected, Ethernet0
        5.0.0.0/24 is subnetted, 1 subnets
R       5.5.5.0 [120/4] via 30.0.0.1, 00:00:04, Serial1
        30.0.0.0/24 is subnetted, 2 subnets
C       30.0.0.0 is directly connected, Serial1
R       30.0.1.0 [120/1] via 20.2.1.2, 00:00:07, Ethernet0
R2#
```

Listing 8-37. *Routing table of R2 when offset lists are applied*

```
R4#sho ip route
...
Gateway of last resort is not set

        1.0.0.0/24 is subnetted, 1 subnets
R       1.1.1.0 [120/4] via 20.1.2.1, 00:00:26, Serial1
```

```
         2.0.0.0/24 is subnetted, 1 subnets
R           2.2.2.0 [120/4] via 20.2.2.1, 00:00:15, Serial0
         3.0.0.0/24 is subnetted, 1 subnets
R           3.3.3.0 [120/1] via 20.1.3.1, 00:00:12, Ethernet0
         4.0.0.0/24 is subnetted, 1 subnets
C           4.4.4.0 is directly connected, Loopback0
         20.0.0.0/24 is subnetted, 5 subnets
R           20.1.1.0 [120/1] via 20.1.3.1, 00:00:12, Ethernet0
C           20.2.2.0 is directly connected, Serial0
C           20.1.3.0 is directly connected, Ethernet0
R           20.2.1.0 [120/4] via 20.2.2.1, 00:00:15, Serial0
                    [120/4] via 20.1.2.1, 00:00:27, Serial1
C           20.1.2.0 is directly connected, Serial1
         5.0.0.0/24 is subnetted, 1 subnets
R           5.5.5.0 [120/8] via 20.2.2.1, 00:00:15, Serial0
                    [120/8] via 20.1.2.1, 00:00:27, Serial1
         30.0.0.0/24 is subnetted, 2 subnets
R           30.0.0.0 [120/4] via 20.2.2.1, 00:00:15, Serial0
R           30.0.1.0 [120/4] via 20.1.2.1, 00:00:27, Serial1
R4#
```

Listing 8-38. *Routing table of R4 when offset lists are applied*

Note that R4 routes to subnet 20.1.1.0/24 through its Ethernet link only, not using the serial interface, as it did before. Similar changes occurred in the routing tables of other routers.

Continuing with our modification, let's imagine that our lab network is connected to two other networks—50.0.0.0 and 60.0.0.0—via router R5. R5 is configured with two static routes describing the external networks via interface Null0. This emulates a situation in which R5 is attached to the external networks and no dynamic routing protocol is used. Listing 8-39 illustrates the routing table of R5.

```
R5#sho ip rout
...
Gateway of last resort is not set

         1.0.0.0/24 is subnetted, 1 subnets
R           1.1.1.0 [120/4] via 30.0.1.2, 00:00:20, Serial0
         2.0.0.0/24 is subnetted, 1 subnets
R           2.2.2.0 [120/4] via 30.0.0.2, 00:00:19, Serial1
         3.0.0.0/24 is subnetted, 1 subnets
R           3.3.3.0 [120/8] via 30.0.1.2, 00:00:21, Serial0
         4.0.0.0/24 is subnetted, 1 subnets
R           4.4.4.0 [120/8] via 30.0.1.2, 00:00:21, Serial0
                    [120/8] via 30.0.0.2, 00:00:19, Serial1
         5.0.0.0/24 is subnetted, 1 subnets
C           5.5.5.0 is directly connected, Loopback0
         20.0.0.0/24 is subnetted, 5 subnets
```

```
R          20.1.1.0 [120/4] via 30.0.1.2, 00:00:21, Serial0
R          20.2.2.0 [120/4] via 30.0.0.2, 00:00:20, Serial1
R          20.1.3.0 [120/8] via 30.0.1.2, 00:00:21, Serial0
                    [120/8] via 30.0.0.2, 00:00:20, Serial1
R          20.2.1.0 [120/4] via 30.0.1.2, 00:00:21, Serial0
                    [120/4] via 30.0.0.2, 00:00:20, Serial1
R          20.1.2.0 [120/4] via 30.0.1.2, 00:00:21, Serial0
        30.0.0.0/24 is subnetted, 2 subnets
C          30.0.0.0 is directly connected, Serial1
C          30.0.1.0 is directly connected, Serial0
S       50.0.0.0/8 is directly connected, Null0
S       60.0.0.0/8 is directly connected, Null0
R5#
```

Listing 8-39. *Routing table of R5 with static routes*

Now we should instruct other routers to route all packets destined for networks 50.0.0.0 and 60.0.0.0 toward R5. This can be achieved if R5 announces the static routes via route redistribution. The configuration of R5 is changed as follows to fulfill the objective:

```
!
router rip
 version 2
 redistribute static
 offset-list 0 out 3 Serial0
 offset-list 0 out 3 Serial1
 network 30.0.0.0
 network 5.0.0.0
 no auto-summary
!
```

The output of the **debug ip rip command** enabled to ensure that RIP sends static routes in its updates, is shown in Listing 8-40. Note that even though the metric value hasn't been configured for redistributed routes, static routes are announced with metric 4. The reason is that static and connected routes are announced with metric 1 by default and because the offset list adds 3 to the metric when a route is sent out of interfaces Serial0 and Serial1.

```
R5#debug ip rip
RIP protocol debugging is on
R5#
RIP: sending v2 update to 224.0.0.9 via Serial0 (30.0.1.1)
      30.0.0.0/24 -> 0.0.0.0, metric 4, tag 0
```

```
    2.2.2.0/24 -> 0.0.0.0, metric 8, tag 0
    5.5.5.0/24 -> 0.0.0.0, metric 4, tag 0
    20.2.2.0/24 -> 0.0.0.0, metric 8, tag 0
    50.0.0.0/8 -> 0.0.0.0, metric 4, tag 0
    60.0.0.0/8 -> 0.0.0.0, metric 4, tag 0
RIP: sending v2 update to 224.0.0.9 via Serial1 (30.0.0.1)
    30.0.1.0/24 -> 0.0.0.0, metric 4, tag 0
    1.1.1.0/24 -> 0.0.0.0, metric 8, tag 0
    3.3.3.0/24 -> 0.0.0.0, metric 12, tag 0
    5.5.5.0/24 -> 0.0.0.0, metric 4, tag 0
    20.1.1.0/24 -> 0.0.0.0, metric 8, tag 0
    20.1.2.0/24 -> 0.0.0.0, metric 8, tag 0
    50.0.0.0/8 -> 0.0.0.0, metric 4, tag 0
    60.0.0.0/8 -> 0.0.0.0, metric 4, tag 0
```

Listing 8-40. *Debug output, showing redistributed static routes*

The following example illustrates redistribution of routes from other dynamic routing protocols to RIP. Static routes on R5 are removed, and the network topology is changed to allow R2 to communicate only with R5. R2 and R5 are configured with a very simple OSPF configuration that is used only to allow R5 to learn non-RIP routes from R2, which announces its loopback address, 2.2.2.2. The network topology is shown in Figure 8-12.

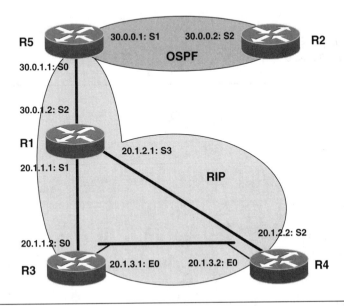

Figure 8-12. *Network topology for redistribution from OSPF to RIP*

R5 is configured to redistribute OSPF routes to RIP. The configuration of the routers is as follows:

- R2:

```
hostname R2
!
ip subnet-zero
!
interface Loopback0
 ip address 2.2.2.2 255.255.255.0
!
interface Ethernet0
 ip address 20.2.1.1 255.255.255.0
 shutdown
!
interface Serial0
 ip address 20.2.2.1 255.255.255.0
 bandwidth 64
 shutdown
!
interface Serial1
 ip address 30.0.0.2 255.255.255.0
 bandwidth 64
!
router ospf 1
 passive-interface lo0
 network 30.0.0.0 0.0.0.255 area 0
 network 2.2.2.2 0.0.0.0 area 0
!
```

- R5:

```
hostname R5
!
!
ip subnet-zero
!
interface Loopback0
 ip address 5.5.5.5 255.255.255.0
!
interface Ethernet0
 no ip address
 shutdown
!
interface Serial0
 ip address 30.0.1.1 255.255.255.0
 bandwidth 64
```

```
!
interface Serial1
 ip address 30.0.0.1 255.255.255.0
 bandwidth 64
 clockrate 64000
!
router ospf 1
 network 30.0.0.0 0.0.0.255 area 0
!
router rip
 version 2
 passive-interface serial 1
 redistribute ospf 1
 offset-list 0 out 3 Serial0
 offset-list 0 out 3 Serial1
 network 30.0.0.0
 network 5.0.0.0
 no auto-summary
!
```

After OSPF has established adjacencies and R5 and R2 have exchanged routing information, the routing table in R5 includes an OSPF route to R2's loopback address (Listing 8-41).

```
R5#sho ip route
...
Gateway of last resort is not set

     1.0.0.0/24 is subnetted, 1 subnets
R       1.1.1.0 [120/4] via 30.0.1.2, 00:00:06, Serial0
     2.0.0.0/32 is subnetted, 1 subnets
O       2.2.2.2 [110/1563] via 30.0.0.2, 00:00:57, Serial1
     3.0.0.0/24 is subnetted, 1 subnets
R       3.3.3.0 [120/8] via 30.0.1.2, 00:00:06, Serial0
     4.0.0.0/24 is subnetted, 1 subnets
R       4.4.4.0 [120/8] via 30.0.1.2, 00:00:06, Serial0
     5.0.0.0/24 is subnetted, 1 subnets
C       5.5.5.0 is directly connected, Loopback0
     20.0.0.0/24 is subnetted, 4 subnets
R       20.1.1.0 [120/4] via 30.0.1.2, 00:00:06, Serial0
R       20.1.3.0 [120/8] via 30.0.1.2, 00:00:06, Serial0
R       20.2.1.0 [120/4] via 30.0.1.2, 00:00:07, Serial0
R       20.1.2.0 [120/4] via 30.0.1.2, 00:00:07, Serial0
     30.0.0.0/24 is subnetted, 2 subnets
C       30.0.0.0 is directly connected, Serial1
C       30.0.1.0 is directly connected, Serial0
R5#
```

Listing 8-41. *OSPF route in R5's routing table*

The contents of RIP updates that R5 sends are shown in Listing 8-42.

```
R5#debug ip rip
RIP protocol debugging is on
R5#
RIP: sending v2 update to 224.0.0.9 via Serial0 (30.0.1.1)
      30.0.0.0/24 -> 0.0.0.0, metric 4, tag 0
      2.2.2.2/32 -> 0.0.0.0, metric 16, tag 0
      5.5.5.0/24 -> 0.0.0.0, metric 4, tag 0
```

Listing 8-42. *R5 sending redistributed route with infinity metric*

The metric sent for the route to 2.2.2.2/32 redistributed from OSPF is set to infinity (value 16) because the configuration of R5 does not explicitly specify the metric value. The problem is solved by configuring the **default-metric** command, as shown in the following configuration. (Note that we could also specify the metric value in the **redistribute** command.)

```
hostname R5
!
...
!
router rip
version 2
passive-interface serial 1
redistribute ospf 1
offset-list 0 out 3 Serial0
offset-list 0 out 3 Serial1
network 30.0.0.0
network 5.0.0.0
default-metric 5
no auto-summary
!
```

Now RIP sends the redistributed OSPF route correctly, setting the initial metric to 5 (Listing 8-43). Note that the offset list adds 3 to the metric value, so the route is sent with metric 8 to R1.

```
R5#debug ip rip
RIP protocol debugging is on
R5#
RIP: sending v2 update to 224.0.0.9 via Serial0 (30.0.1.1)
      30.0.0.0/24 -> 0.0.0.0, metric 4, tag 0
```

```
2.2.2.2/32 -> 0.0.0.0, metric 8, tag 0
5.5.5.0/24 -> 0.0.0.0, metric 4, tag 0
```

Listing 8-43. *R5 sending redistributed OSPF route correctly*

Other routers install this RIP route in their routing tables correctly (Listing 8-44).

```
R4#sho ip route
...
Gateway of last resort is not set

     1.0.0.0/24 is subnetted, 1 subnets
R       1.1.1.0 [120/4] via 20.1.2.1, 00:00:15, Serial1
     2.0.0.0/32 is subnetted, 1 subnets
R       2.2.2.2 [120/12] via 20.1.2.1, 00:00:15, Serial1
     3.0.0.0/24 is subnetted, 1 subnets
R       3.3.3.0 [120/1] via 20.1.3.1, 00:00:16, Ethernet0
     4.0.0.0/24 is subnetted, 1 subnets
C       4.4.4.0 is directly connected, Loopback0
     5.0.0.0/24 is subnetted, 1 subnets
R       5.5.5.0 [120/8] via 20.1.2.1, 00:00:15, Serial1
     20.0.0.0/24 is subnetted, 4 subnets
R       20.1.1.0 [120/1] via 20.1.3.1, 00:00:16, Ethernet0
C       20.1.3.0 is directly connected, Ethernet0
R       20.2.1.0 [120/4] via 20.1.2.1, 00:00:16, Serial1
C       20.1.2.0 is directly connected, Serial1
     30.0.0.0/24 is subnetted, 2 subnets
R       30.0.0.0 [120/8] via 20.1.2.1, 00:00:16, Serial1
R       30.0.1.0 [120/4] via 20.1.2.1, 00:00:16, Serial1
R4#
```

Listing 8-44. *Routing table of R4, containing route redistributed from OSPF by R5*

8.2.10 Summary

- Cisco IOS includes implementation of RIPv1, RIPv2, and demand circuit extensions.

- Only one RIP process can be in a router.

- RIP works directly on the routing table.

- RIPv1 is a classful routing protocol, broadcasting its messages every 30 seconds by default and running over UDP, port 520. RIPv1 does not send route masks in the updates and performs automatic route summarization on major network boundaries.

- RIPv2 is a classless version of RIP, supporting VLSM and arbitrary route aggregation—by explicitly specifying route masks in the updates—and using IP multicast instead of broadcast for message submission. Version 2 also performs automatic route summarization by default. However, this behavior can be turned off by using the **no auto-summary** command.

- RIP uses a number of techniques—including holddown timers, triggered updates, and split-horizon checking—to improve convergence characteristics. Split-horizon checking is enabled by default for all interfaces except those using Frame Relay or SMDS encapsulation. The state of the split-horizon flag can be changed by using the **ip split-horizon** interface configuration command.

- Basic configuration of RIP is simple. RIP is started with the **router rip** configuration command. Interfaces included in the RIP domain are identified by **network** statements.

- Distribute lists can be used to control information sent and received by RIP on the interfaces.

- By default, RIP increments the route metric by 1 when the route is put into an outgoing message. The route metrics can be increased to reflect the link preferences, using offset lists.

- RIP messages normally include routes installed by RIP itself and directly connected routes—static or derived from interface addresses—covered by **network** statements. RIP can be instructed to send routes from other route sources, using route redistribution: the **redistribute** router configuration command.

- Demand circuit extensions to RIP are implemented in Cisco IOS for point-to-point links.

Figure 8-13, a message-processing diagram for RIP, illustrates the most important logical processes performed when RIP messages are received or sent.

8.2.11 Frequently Asked Questions

Q: **Why does RIP use hop count as the route metric, and why is its maximum value limited to 15?**

A: When RIP was designed and implemented, dynamic routing protocols were not widely used. Instead, networks relied mostly on static routing. RIP, even with its hop-count metric—which seems very poor to us today—was quite a big improvement. Counting intermediate routers is the simplest method to measure the quality of routes. When similar types of links are used in the network, this method gives optimal results. As for the upper limit of the metric, RIP, as a distance-vector routing protocol, must limit the number of hops a route can traverse. Setting the infinity value for the metric is always a problem of choosing between wider

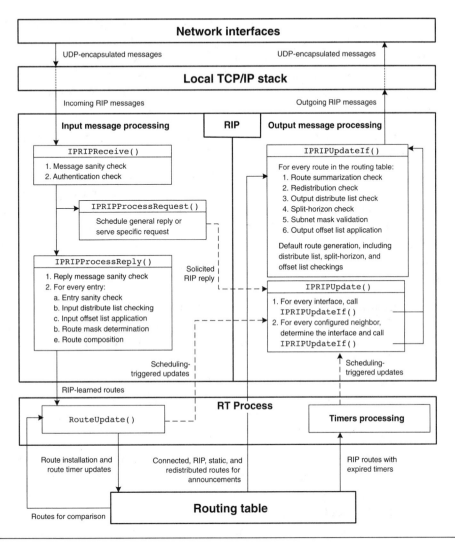

Figure 8-13. *RIP message processing*

networks and faster convergence when the protocol starts counting. When RIP was invented, it seemed unlikely to a have a network with the maximum diameter more than 15 routers, so 16 was chosen as the infinity value.

Q: **We use RIP in our network. Before we configured inbound access lists in one of our routers, everything was fine. However, the router can't see any routes from its neighbors now. Where is the problem?**

A: Inbound access lists filter all incoming packets, no matter whether they are destined for the router itself or must be forwarded. Outbound access lists, by contrast, do not filter locally originated packets. Make sure that you have a permit statement for RIP packets. Remember, RIP works over UDP port 520 and sends its updates as broadcasts (version 1) or as multicasts to address 224.0.0.9 (version 2).

Q: **Why does the output of the show running-config command show network 10.0.0.0 even if I enter a subnet address while configuring RIP?**

A: Routers expect a major network address to be specified in the network command for RIP, IGRP, and EIGRP. Whatever address is entered, the router transforms it to the major network address. Classful routing protocols are supposed to be run on every subnet, so this behavior decreases the number of mistakes caused by misconfiguration. Note that the OSPF **network** command allows the administrator to specify any network prefix. EIGRP has also been enhanced to include this feature.

Q: **I have problems running RIP on a set of routers interconnected through a Frame Relay cloud. When I enable RIP debugging, it shows that RIP messages are generated for the serial interface. However, remote routers do not receive anything.**

A: Most likely you have forgotten to specify the **broadcast** keyword in the **frame-relay map** statements. This keyword is necessary to allow the router to send broadcast and multicast messages generated for the interface along corresponding VCs. This is necessary for RIP messages as well.

Q: **I use the distance command to set the AD value to 130 for the routes received from a neighbor. If the neighbor sends a route with an RIP metric better than that of an already installed route, will this route update the routing table?**

A: Because you changed the AD of all routes coming from that neighbor to 130, they will be considered administratively worse than other RIP routes that have the default AD value (120). Therefore, even if routes with a better RIP metric are submitted for installation in the routing table, the routes with better AD value are preferred.

8.3 Interior Gateway Routing Protocol

We now turn to a Cisco proprietary routing protocol: Interior Gateway Routing Protocol (IGRP). This section provides detailed information on the theory of IGRP, as well as a description of the protocol's operation. Table 8-3 summarizes generic information about IGRP.

Table 8-3. *Characteristics of IGRP*

Protocol Characteristic	IGRP
Algorithm type	Distance vector
Metric type	Composite, calculated via a weighted function, based on a vector of path attributes: bandwidth, delay, reliability, and load
Best-path selection	Using distributed version of the Bellman-Ford algorithm
Multipath support	Equal-cost and unequal-cost multipath supported
View of the network	Routers see network topology from their neighbors' perspective; no full topology information
New-neighbor discovery	No explicit mechanism provided; formal connections not formed between neighboring routers; neighbors discovered when they send routing update messages
Unreachable-neighbor discovery	No mechanism is provided for this purpose. Routers stop routing through unreachable neighbors when routes supplied by these neighbors age out from the routing table.
New-route discovery	Routing information relayed; when constructing an update, router increments the route's hop count to reflect the cost of the link the update will be sent through
Unreachable-route discovery	Either via an explicit message specifying the infinite distance—delay attribute set to all binary 1s—to a network or via the route aging process
Periodic updates	Sent every 90 seconds by default by every router; interval randomized to avoid synchronization
Event-driven updates	Triggered updates sent by routers after a network topology change
Transport protocol	IGRP works directly over IP; the protocol ID is 9
External routing information	Indistinguishable from native IGRP routes
Classful route summarization	Yes
CIDR and route aggregation	No

8.3.1 Basic Description and History

IGRP, another member of the distance-vector group of routing protocols, was developed by Cisco Systems because RIP couldn't serve networks of a considerable size, and a more sophisticated substitution was in demand. While link-state protocols, such as OSPF, required a lot of effort to be implemented and the specifications were not yet mature, it seemed to be easier and faster to develop a distance-vector protocol with advanced characteristics.

The following requirements were set for the development of IGRP.

- The protocol must be able to choose the best path, based on link characteristics, such as available bandwidth, total delay, reliability, and load.
- There must be no practical limit for the number of hops a route traverses, unlike RIP, which limits the number of hops to 15.
- The protocol must be free of transient routing loops.

As was mentioned in the previous section, Cisco implemented holddown timers in IGRP as a method of avoiding transient routing loops. This was indeed an innovation, fulfilling the third requirement in the list. Another technique used in IGRP to prevent transient routing loops is route poisoning. When an IGRP update increases a route's metric by more than 10 percent or increases the route's hop count, IGRP believes that a routing loop has been established and poisons the suspected route by initiating the holddown procedure for it. This is much safer than allowing a potentially invalid route to be propagated through the network.

It was clear that the hop-count metric couldn't provide enough intelligence to take link characteristics into consideration while calculating the best path. The new protocol required something more sophisticated. A decision was made to pass a vector of characteristics, instead of only hop count as in RIP, along with every route in routing updates: effective path bandwidth, cumulative path delay, path reliability, and path load.

Effective bandwidth is the minimal bandwidth of all the network links the route has traversed. *Path delay* is the sum of the delays associated with the links comprising the path. *Path reliability* is the reliability of the least-reliable link along the path. Similarly, *path load* is the load of the most-occupied link in the path. Although all these attributes are relayed, with appropriate modifications, in IGRP updates, a scalar value is used as the metric when the best path is selected and installed in the routing table. This metric is calculated by using a weighting function.

Think how you would transform all the route attributes into a single value. First, the optimization criterion for each attribute must be understood. Clearly, the greater the path bandwidth and reliability, the better the path. At the same time, a better path assumes lower delay and load. It seems to be a bit difficult to optimize different parameters in different directions.

Think about the path bandwidth in a different way, though. Why do we prefer links with more bandwidth? We prefer them because they allow us to send more information, but what is the reason for this? Imagine two serial lines: one 64Kbps and one 2Mbps. How can the second line conduct more information? It can do so because its serialization delay is much smaller than the same characteristic of a 64Kbps link, so the router can send a lot more bits through this line during the same period: 2,048 kilobits per second versus 64 kilobits per second. This gives us an idea of how bandwidth can be introduced into the formula: We can use the inverse value.

Now we have bandwidth, which can be used as serialization delay, and delay. Is there any reason to have two delays in one formula? Yes. Imagine two T1 lines; a T1 line has a bandwidth of 1.5Mbps. One of the lines is satellite and the other is terrestrial. The serialization delay for both of them will be the same. However, the terrestrial link will be faster, because it has lower signal propagation delay than the satellite link (20 milliseconds versus 200 milliseconds). The path delay is the sum of signal propagation delays of all links. The lower it is, the better the path. Now we should incorporate both parameters into the formula, remembering that the route's metric must be smaller for the better route. The first approximation could be as follows:

$$M = Kb \times \frac{1}{Bandwidth} + Kd \times Delay$$

where Kb and Kd are the weights, $Bandwidth$ is the effective path bandwidth in bits per second, and $Delay$ is the accumulative path delay measured in microseconds.

This is not a very convenient formula, however, because the first item of the sum will always be less than 1, requiring Kb to be very large to make it comparable to the delay characteristic. To simplify the metric calculation, let's introduce a new variable, BW, which is calculated as follows:

$$BW = \frac{10^{10}}{Bandwidth}$$

Now the formula can be changed to

$$M = Kb \times BW + Kd \times Delay$$

This is good enough, but the metric doesn't take into consideration the other two path attributes: load and reliability. Both parameters are calculated as a fraction of 255; that is, 255 is 100 percent.

The path load parameter can be used to reflect available path bandwidth—in the inverse form again—as follows:

$$BWav = \frac{BW}{256 - Load}$$

We can easily introduce it into the formula:

$$M = Kb \times BW + Kab \times BWav + Kd \times Delay$$

That is,

$$M = Kb \times BW + Kab \times \frac{BW}{(256 - Load)} + Kd \times Delay$$

Note that because we have introduced available path bandwidth as a separate item of the sum, the formula is flexible enough to give more preference to the paths with more overall bandwidth or to the paths with more unused bandwidth, depending on the values of Kb and Kab.

The reliability path attribute gives us a probabilistic characteristic of the links comprising the path. The greater the value of the path reliability, the more the path should be preferred, and, consequently, the smaller the value returned by the formula should be. This could be easily implemented if we just divide the metric value by the value of reliability, but this does not give us control over how much the value of reliability should affect the metric value. In order to provide this control, two other weight coefficients are introduced, as follows:

$$M = \left[Kb \times BW + Kab \times \frac{BW}{(256-Load)} + Kd \times Delay \right] \times \frac{Kr1}{Reliability + Kr2}$$

Note that if $Kr1$ is 0—meaning that the administrator does not want path reliability to influence the metric—this multiplication is not performed.

We now have the formula used in IGRP for metric computation. After the names of coefficients are changed to conform to Cisco's convention, we have the following expression:

$$M = K1 \times BW + K2 \times \frac{BW}{(256-Load)} + K3 \times Delay$$

If K5 > 0, then

$$M = M \times \frac{K5}{Reliability + K4}$$

IGRP uses inverse bandwidth scaled by a factor of 10^{10}. The delay is measured in tens of milliseconds; that is, the total path delay is divided by 10. As mentioned, load and reliability are measured as a fraction of 255.

An important detail about IGRP and Cisco routers per se is that the bandwidth and delay parameters of an interface are static—they are not calculated by the routers but are assigned statically—whereas the load and reliability parameters are dynamic, calculated by the routers and reflecting the current state of the link.

To ensure correct calculation of the load and reliability parameters for the interfaces and, consequently, for IGRP routes, the administrator should configure real bandwidth values for the interfaces, using the **bandwidth** interface configuration command. Cisco routers default to 1.544Mbps—bandwidth of a T1 link—for all serial interfaces, regardless of the actual bandwidth.

The default values for the weight coefficients in IGRP are 1 for $K1$ and $K3$ and 0 for $K2$, $K4$, and $K5$. This disables IGRP's reaction on dynamic changes in link load and reliability but saves the routing protocol from oscillations.

The oscillations in IGRP can be experienced because when the new link, or a path, load value is announced in a periodic update, IGRP calculates new best routes that direct traffic along different trajectories, thus offloading the old path. When it accepts additional load, the new path becomes worse than the old one, and IGRP reacts by switching to the old path. This sequence of events is repetitive; IGRP can keep switching between the paths, thus causing instability in the network.

Changing the default values of $K2$, $K4$, and $K5$ is not recommended! However, the administrator may want to alter the values of $K1$ and $K3$, instructing IGRP to give greater preference to the paths with more bandwidth or to the paths with smaller signal propagation delay. In any case, all routers in a network must be consistent on the values of the weight coefficients. Otherwise, the network may experience permanent routing loops.

Note that the metric-calculation formula does not consider the hop count. Actually, this parameter is transmitted in IGRP messages but serves only as a method of avoiding routing loops. By default, the maximum hop count in IGRP is 100. If an update with a larger hop count is received, IGRP believes that a routing loop has formed, marks the route as unreachable, and puts it in the holddown state.

As explained earlier, RIP provides more than one route per destination network to the routing table. IGRP too supports multipath routes but extends the concept. The extension was introduced to remedy the main problem of the equal-cost multipath technique: underloading of paths that are correct but not best.

If a link that belongs to a nonbest path is not a part of a best path of another router in the network, the link is most probably underloaded. If none of the routers forwards the packets through such a link, the link is idling and its bandwidth is wasted. IGRP tries to remedy this problem by relaxing the route calculation algorithm: A route is installed in the routing table not only if its metric is best but also if its metric is "almost" as good as the metric of the best route. Definitely, that "almost" must be somehow quantified. IGRP uses the variance parameter for this purpose. If the metric of a route is not greater than the variance times the metric of the best route, the new route is also installed in the routing table. As explained in Chapters 4 and 5, when parallel routes with different metrics are installed in the routing table, the routes are assigned different load-sharing values. So the number of packets sent over a route is in inverse proportion to its metric: The lower the metric, the more packets the route accepts.

In Cisco IOS, both IGRP and EIGRP can provide routing information for unequal-cost multipath routing. Although this seems to be a great feature, it is always difficult to say how much the value of the variance parameter should be. If the variance is too small, some or all parallel routes may be omitted, because IGRP has a wide scale of metric values. If the variance is too big, neighboring routers might install routes pointing to each other. If the metric of a route is greater than the metric of the best route, we cannot guarantee that the neighbor that supplied this route does not use the calculating router as the next hop. Therefore, the default value of the variance parameter for IGRP and for EIGRP is 1, which limits IGRP to simple equal-cost multipath behavior.

Another interesting aspect of the approach used in IGRP is the way it provides default routing information. As you recall, RIP uses pseudonetwork 0.0.0.0 to announce the default route. The same approach is used in OSPF (see Chapter 9 for more details). This method is simple and effective. However, when several boundary routers announce this type of default route, selection of the default route often results in selection of the nearest boundary router. This means that the topology behind the boundary routers is hidden from all internal routers and that internal routers do not know whether the selected boundary router can send traffic to the outside world at any given moment.

IGRP uses another approach. Boundary routers announce one or more "exterior" networks in their updates. These networks do not belong to the autonomous system IGRP serves. Instead, they may be owned by an ISP or belong to one of the Internet exchange points. When they install routes to these exterior networks in the routing tables, internal IGRP routers automatically mark them as default candidates. The actual default is selected as described in Chapter 4, based on the administrative distances and metrics of the candidates. If one boundary router loses its connectivity with the outside world, internal IGRP routers automatically reselect the default, choosing the next-shortest path to the exterior network (see Figure 8-14).

This approach has some disadvantages, however. First, if all networks announced by IGRP as exterior become unreachable, internal routers will have no candidates for the default. This causes a loss of connectivity between the IGRP domain and other exterior networks that may be completely operational. Also, for IGRP routers to take advantage of choosing the most optimal default route, based on the routes to the exterior backbone, they must have the full IGRP metric information from the upstream routing domain. If this information is not conveyed and an exterior network is announced with a statically configured metric, internal IGRP routers will just select the closest exit point.

8.3.2 Protocol Parameters

Basic information involved in IGRP operation is essentially the same as for RIP. However, Cisco routers can run more than one instance of IGRP, so when an IGRP process is

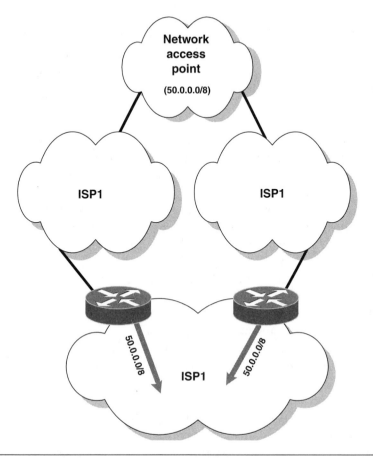

Figure 8-14. *Using external network for default routing IGRP*

started, the process identifier must be specified in the **router igrp** configuration command. Called an autonomous system number in official Cisco documentation, this number is used for two purposes: to identify specific instances of IGRP within a router and to make sure that IGRP processes belonging to different routing domains but having a common link do not exchange routing information. The process identifier is included in the IGRP messages but is not preserved when routing information is redistributed from one IGRP domain to another, so it serves only administrative purposes. One could hardly expect anything more sophisticated in this area, as IGRP is an intradomain routing protocol.

Another significant difference between IGRP and RIP is the value of the timers used by IGRP for periodic message transmissions and route management. By default, IGRP sends its updates every 90 seconds. A route is considered valid during 270 seconds without updates. The holddown timer is 280, and the garbage collection timer is 630 seconds. These values can be changed by using the same command as in RIP: **timers basic**.

Some additional parameters influence the way IGRP calculates metrics, installs routes, and maintains them. The most important configuration parameters for IGRP are the weight coefficients: $K1$, $K2$, $K3$, $K4$, and $K5$. The administrator can change the value of these parameters by using the **metric weights** router configuration command. Once again, changing the values of $K2$, $K4$, and $K5$ is discouraged, as doing so may lead to instability in the IGRP domain.

The **metric maximum-hops** router configuration command can be used to change the upper limit for the hop-count field in IGRP updates. The default value for this parameter is 100. IGRP uses this limitation to remove routing loops with very large diameters. Normally, such situations should never happen, because of the aggressive loop-avoidance mechanisms used in IGRP. Changing the value of this parameter is reasonable only in those rare situations when the maximum diameter of a network is larger than 100 hops.

IGRP uses holddown timers to avoid loops during transition periods. Although it increases robustness of the protocol, this technique does not let the routers quickly accept alternative routes when a currently used path is invalidated. To disable the hold-down feature, which is enabled by default, IGRP can be configured with the **no metric holddown** command. The route-poisoning technique ensures that circular routes are finally removed from the network if they appear.

IGRP can install parallel routes with unequal costs in the routing table. The variance parameter is used to determine the maximum value of metric that is considered acceptable for a route to be installed. The default value of this parameter is 1, meaning that IGRP defaults to equal-cost multipath. The value of the variance can be changed by using the **variance** *multiplier* router configuration command.

When parallel routes are installed, IGRP must properly set the share-count value for each path descriptor. If paths with unequal metrics are installed—the variance parameter has been configured with a value greater than 1—IGRP can either set the share-count fields in inverse proportion to the ratios of the metrics or instruct the forwarding engine to use only the routes with the best metric. In the second case, the share-count field is set to 0 for the worse-metric path descriptors and to 1 for path descriptors with the best metric. Therefore, the worse-metric path descriptors are used only for fast switchover when the primary paths are not available. To control which of these two load-distribution methods should be used, the administrator can configure IGRP with the **traffic-share balanced** or the **traffic-share min** command.

The method used in IGRP for default-route announcement requires boundary routers to send information about exterior networks in routing updates. The administrator can use the **default-information** configuration command to filter the exterior routes sent or received by the IGRP process. By default, IGRP sends and receives routes to exterior networks without any limitation. If the **no default-information in** command is configured, the router does not accept any routes to exterior networks. The **default-information in** *acl-name* command can be used to filter incoming routes to exterior networks. Similarly, the **no default-information out** and the **default-information out** *acl-name* commands control which routes to exterior networks are placed in outgoing updates.

When external routes are injected into an IGRP domain, the IGRP process must be explicitly configured with the seed metric parameters. This task is performed by using the **default-metric** *bandwidth delay reliability load mtu* router configuration command. It is not necessary to configure this command if connected or static routes are redistributed into IGRP.

8.3.3 Message Format

The IGRP process sends and receives its messages directly over IP, using protocol ID 9. Most of the messages are sent as IP local broadcasts, with destination IP address 255.255.255.255. However, when a message is sent to a statically configured neighbor or in reply to a request, the destination IP address is unicast. The source IP address is always unicast and equals one of the IP addresses of the interface over which the update is sent. The specific address used depends on whether the update is sent for the primary or one of the secondary subnets. The basic principles of setting the source and destination IP addresses in the IP packet carrying an IGRP message are the same as for RIP (see Section 8.1).

Every IGRP message starts with a standard header. The IGRP header is 12 bytes long and is structured as shown in Figure 8-15. The pseudocode type definition for the IGRP header is given in Listing 8-45.

```
#define IGRP_COMMAND_UPDATE     1        /* IGRP Update  */
#define IGRP_COMMAND_REQUEST    2        /* IGRP Request */
#define IGRP_COMMAND_MAX        2

#define IGRP_VERSION_1          1

typedef struct IGRPMessage {
  u_char     Version: 4;                 /* IGRP version      */
  u_char     OpCode : 4;                 /* Op. Code          */
  u_char     Edition;                    /* RT Edition Number */
  u_int16_t  ASystem;                    /* AS number         */
  u_int16_t  NumOfInterior;              /* # of subnets in message        */
  u_int16_t  NumOfSystem;                /* # of majornets in message      */
  u_int16_t  NumOfExterior;              /* # of exterior routes in message */
  u_int16_t  Checksum;                   /* Checksum of IGRP header and data */
  TIGRPEntry Entries[0];                 /* Actual IGRP entries */

} TIGRPMessage;


#define IGRP_MSG_HEADER_SIZE    sizeof(TIGRPMessage)
```

Listing 8-45. *Pseudocode type definition for IGRP header*

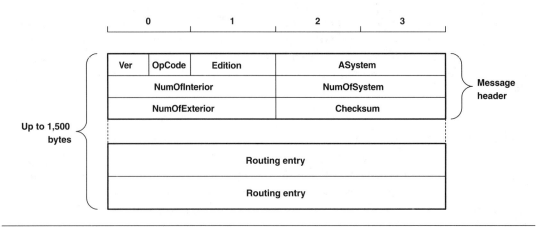

Figure 8-15. *IGRP message header*

The four-bit Version field always contains 1. Although EIGRP is sometimes called IGRP2, it uses protocol number 88 and a different message format, so this field of the IGRP header never has values other than 1.

The OpCode field can contain one of two values: 1 for an update or 2 for a request. Both types of messages are considered later.

The Edition field contains the serial number of the update. IGRP processes increment this number whenever they send a new update. The initial idea was to analyze this number while processing incoming messages and to ignore messages that had already been processed. However, this message-processing optimization has never been implemented. Although ignored during message processing, the Edition field is calculated and set correctly in outgoing messages.

The ASystem field of the IGRP header contains the process, or autonomous system, identifier configured when the IGRP process is started. An IGRP process is allowed to process messages from other routers only if they belong to the same routing domain, that is, if the value in the ASystem field matches the local setting. IGRP messages containing a different ASystem value are silently ignored.

The NumOfInterior, NumOfSystem, and NumOfExterior fields contain the number of subnets belonging to the local major network (interior routes), the number of summary routes to various major networks belonging to the same IGRP domain—or AS, in IGRP terms—and the number of routes to networks residing outside the routing domain. The routing information itself follows the Checksum field, which is calculated by using the same algorithm as for the standard IP packet checksum.

Now let's consider the two types of IGRP messages. An OpCode of 2 indicates that the IGRP message contains a request. IGRP requests contain no routing information, so only the Version, OpCode, and ASystem fields are set in the header. All other fields are zeroed. When it receives a Request, an IGRP process is expected to send to the originator an update message constructed the same way as when it is sent periodically, providing the other router with necessary routing information immediately.

IGRP updates, with an OpCode of 1, contain a number of routing information entries right after the IGRP header. The length of the message does not exceed 1,500 bytes. If more information needs to be sent, it is split into several messages. This is possible because IGRP is a distance-vector protocol, and routing information inside update messages is processed entry by entry.

The format of the entries containing routing information in IGRP messages is illustrated in Figure 8-16. The pseudocode type definition for the routing entry in IGRP is given in Listing 8-46.

```
typedef struct IGRPEntry {

    u_char      Number[3];        /* Network address          */
    u_char      Delay[3];         /* Cumulative path delay    */
    u_char      Bandwidth[3];     /* Effective path BW        */
    u_int16_t   MTU;              /* Minimum path MTU         */
    u_char      Reliability       /* Successful packet IO ratio  */
    u_char      Load;             /* Link load                */
    u_char      HopCount;         /* Number of hops           */

} TIGRPEntry;
```

Listing 8-46. *Pseudocode type definition of IGRP message entry*

The `Number` field contains three significant bytes of the address portion of the route. This may seem somewhat strange for an IP routing protocol, as IP addresses are four bytes long. However, this approach works. If the entry contains an interior route—a route to a subnet in the same major network as the receiving router—there is no reason to send the first byte of the address, because that byte will be the same as the first byte of the source address in the packet containing the IGRP message. If a network route, system or exterior, is announced, there is no need to send the last byte of the address, as that byte is always 0, anyway. The reason is that IGRP is a classful routing protocol and performs automatic route summarization on the major network boundaries. Therefore, in the case of an interior route, the `Number` field contains the last three bytes of the address. In both other cases, it contains the first three bytes of the update.

All other fields of the entry are self-explanatory and contain the attributes used to calculate the composite metric of the route. Note again that the `MTU` field has never been used in IGRP metric calculation and that the `HopCount` field is used only to stop the counting-to-infinity behavior.

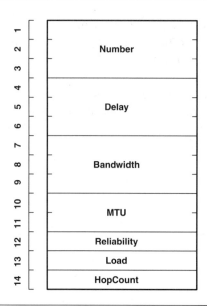

Figure 8-16. *IGRP message entry*

8.3.4 Input Processing

The basic functionality IGRP performs while processing received messages resembles that of RIP to a great extent. Refer to Section 8.1 for more details. Nevertheless, there are some differences.

First, IGRP alters the route attributes right after an update has been received, whereas RIP increases the hop count just before a message is sent. With RIP, it does not really matter whether the hop count is increased after a route is received or before it is sent to the neighbors. With IGRP, it is more accurate to do attribute alteration on the receiving side. Figure 8-17 shows why.

Routers R1 and R2 belong to different administrative domains and are connected with two lines: T1 and 64Kbps. Both lines are connected to the serial interfaces. Cisco IOS sets the bandwidth parameter to 1.544Mbps for both interfaces by default. Now suppose that the administrator of router R1 wants it to prefer the better link and configures the correct bandwidth value for the interface connected to the 64Kbps line. If route attribute alteration is done before the route is put in the outgoing message, R2's configuration needs to be changed to contain the correct value of the bandwidth attribute. Not very exciting. Now if the route attributes are altered when a route is received, R2 sends the route to N with the bandwidth parameter set to 10MBps (Ethernet connection), but R1 finds the minimum bandwidth for the route, taking its own configuration into consideration, and sets it to 64Kbps. This makes the route through the T1 line be more preferred. The new attributes for the routes are calculated as follows. (Note that the original values received in the update are also stored.)

```
Bandwidth  = min(Update->Bandwidth, Interface->Bandwidth);
Delay      = Update->Delay + Interface->Delay;
Reliability = min(Update->Reliability, Interface->Reliability);
Load       = max(Update->Load, Interface->Load);
```

So, the bandwidth associated with the route is calculated as the minimum between the bandwidth value received in the update and the value configured for the interface on which the update was received. Cumulative delay is calculated as the sum of received delay and the delay configured for the interface. Route reliability is the minimum between the received value and the value dynamically calculated for the interface. Load is the maximum between the received value and the current interface value (also a dynamic value). The new calculated parameters are used to calculate the composite metric for the route, as described in Section 8.3.1.

Another difference between RIP and IGRP is how the route is composed, based on the entry in the incoming message. For the interior routes that come first after the message header, the first byte of the address is taken from the source IP address of the packet that contains the IGRP message. The route mask is taken from the interface on which the message was received, as in RIP (see Section 8.1). For the system and the exterior network routes, the three bytes from the entry are used as the first three bytes of the address, whereas the fourth byte is simply set to 0. The route mask is set to the default classful mask used for the address specified in the entry. When exterior routes are submitted for installation in the routing table, the candidate default flag is automatically set on them so that the default route-selection logic considers them eligible to be the default.

As a distance-vector routing protocol, IGRP uses the same basic methods for routing-loop prevention and survival as RIP does: split horizons, holddown timers, and limiting the number of hops a route can traverse. As indicated in Section 8.3.1, the input-processing logic of IGRP also implements another technique to prevent loops. If the metric of an

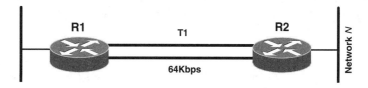

Figure 8-17. *Parallel links in IGRP*

updated route is greater than the old route's metric by 10 percent or more, IGRP considers this an indication of a routing loop, marks the route as unreachable, and triggers an update to "poison," or withdraw, the route in other routers.

8.3.5 Event Processing

IGRP's event-processing logic is very similar to RIP's for both internal and external events. As in RIP, IGRP performs classful route summarization on major network boundaries. The major difference with RIP is in the length of the update, Invalid, holddown, and garbage collection periods. IGRP-specific values for these timers are described in Section 8.3.2.

8.3.6 IGRP Configuration

Basic configuration of IGRP does not differ from that of RIP, except that the **router igrp** configuration command must be augmented with the process identifier. However, some differences arise in more complex situations.

First, IGRP is a purely classful routing protocol and does not have a classless counterpart. Consequently, IGRP does not send the route masks in its updates, and the automatic classful route summarization cannot be turned off. For this reason, IGRP cannot be used in classless environments with VLSM and arbitrary route summarization.

IGRP also has a unique mechanism for default-route origination through announcement of exterior networks. Understanding that IGRP marks exterior networks as candidate defaults when installing them in the routing table is the easy part. A more difficult question is how to make a router originate an update with a network announced as exterior.

The first step is to ensure that the route you want to be the candidate default for other routers is not a route to a subnet. Only summary network routes can be exterior. Summary network routes are announced in two situations: when the router has the network covered by a summary network route in its own routing table—the router does not know about the subnets of the network—and when the subnet routing information is summarized by the router when sending an update to the routers located in a different major network. To instruct the router that the corresponding summary network route must be placed in the exterior portion of the update, the administrator must configure the **ip default-network** global configuration command, specifying the major network address as the parameter.

> If a router that must announce the default route does not have a route to a remote major network, the administrator has to configure a static network summary route to a fake major network and to specify this network in the **ip default-network** command.

Although offset lists are not so important for IGRP, as the protocol takes the link parameters into consideration itself, the administrator may use the **offset-list** configuration command in IGRP. A detail to remember is that when an offset list is applied for IGRP, the offset value is added to the delay portion of the outgoing or incoming route, not the hop count as in RIP. No other route attributes, such as path bandwidth, reliability, or load, are changed.

Route redistribution into IGRP works the same way as for RIP. If connected or static routes are redistributed, it is not necessary to specify the metric parameters in configuration. IGRP uses interface parameters in these two cases; note that for redistributed static routes, load is always set to 1, and reliability is always set to 255. In all other cases—redistribution from dynamic route sources—it is necessary to configure the initial route attributes that IGRP should use when announcing redistributed routes. Unlike in RIP, which uses a scalar route metric, the administrator needs to specify a vector of parameters for IGRP, using the **default-metric** or the **redistribute** command.

Configuration examples for IGRP use the same network topology as in Listing 8-30. Every router is configured with a loopback interface to simulate stub LAN segments connected to the routers. The loopback interfaces are assigned IP addresses in the form *N.N.N.N*/24, where *N* is the number of the router.

8.3.6.1 Basic IGRP Configuration

To illustrate basic configuration of IGRP, we configure the routers in the lab as follows.

- R1:

```
!
hostname R1
!
router igrp 100
 network 1.0.0.0
 network 20.0.0.0
 network 30.0.0.0
!
```

- R2:

```
!
hostname R2
!
router igrp 100
 network 2.0.0.0
```

```
 network 20.0.0.0
 network 30.0.0.0
!
```

- R3:

```
!
hostname R3
!
router igrp 100
 network 3.0.0.0
 network 20.0.0.0
!
```

- R4:

```
!
hostname R4
!
router igrp 100
 network 4.0.0.0
 network 20.0.0.0
!
```

- R5:

```
!
hostname R5
!
!
router igrp 100
 network 5.0.0.0
 network 30.0.0.0
!
```

After IGRP has converged, the router's routing tables contain information about IP subnets in the attached major networks, as well as summary network routes to remote major networks. Listing 8-47 illustrates R5's routing table.

```
R5#sho ip route
...
Gateway of last resort is not set

I    1.0.0.0/8 [100/158750] via 30.0.1.2, 00:03:30, Serial0
I    2.0.0.0/8 [100/158750] via 30.0.0.2, 00:00:40, Serial1
I    3.0.0.0/8 [100/160750] via 30.0.1.2, 00:00:54, Serial0
I    4.0.0.0/8 [100/160750] via 30.0.0.2, 00:00:40, Serial1
                [100/160750] via 30.0.1.2, 00:00:54, Serial0
I    20.0.0.0/8 [100/158350] via 30.0.0.2, 00:00:40, Serial1
                [100/158350] via 30.0.1.2, 00:00:54, Serial0
     5.0.0.0/24 is subnetted, 1 subnets
C       5.5.5.0 is directly connected, Loopback0
     30.0.0.0/24 is subnetted, 2 subnets
C       30.0.0.0 is directly connected, Serial1
C       30.0.1.0 is directly connected, Serial0
R5#
```

Listing 8-47. *R5's routing table*

Listing 8-48 contains the output of the **show ip route** command taken from R4.

```
R4#sho ip route
...
Gateway of last resort is not set

I    1.0.0.0/8 [100/158750] via 20.1.2.1, 00:00:59, Serial1
I    2.0.0.0/8 [100/158750] via 20.2.2.1, 00:00:46, Serial0
I    3.0.0.0/8 [100/1600] via 20.1.3.1, 00:00:31, Ethernet0
     4.0.0.0/24 is subnetted, 1 subnets
C       4.4.4.0 is directly connected, Loopback0
     20.0.0.0/24 is subnetted, 5 subnets
I       20.1.1.0 [100/158350] via 20.1.3.1, 00:00:31, Ethernet0
C       20.2.2.0 is directly connected, Serial0
C       20.1.3.0 is directly connected, Ethernet0
I       20.2.1.0 [100/158350] via 20.2.2.1, 00:00:46, Serial0
                [100/158350] via 20.1.2.1, 00:01:00, Serial1
C       20.1.2.0 is directly connected, Serial1
I    5.0.0.0/8 [100/160750] via 20.2.2.1, 00:00:47, Serial0
                [100/160750] via 20.1.2.1, 00:01:00, Serial1
I    30.0.0.0/8 [100/160250] via 20.2.2.1, 00:00:47, Serial0
                [100/160250] via 20.1.2.1, 00:01:00, Serial1
R4#
```

Listing 8-48. *R4's routing table*

Listing 8-49 shows the details of the route to network 30.0.0.0/8.

```
R4#sho ip route 30.0.0.0
Routing entry for 30.0.0.0/8
  Known via "igrp 100", distance 100, metric 160250
  Redistributing via igrp 100
  Advertised by igrp 100 (self originated)
  Last update from 20.2.2.1 on Serial0, 00:01:09 ago
  Routing Descriptor Blocks:
  * 20.2.2.1, from 20.2.2.1, 00:01:09 ago, via Serial0
      Route metric is 160250, traffic share count is 1
      Total delay is 40000 microseconds, minimum bandwidth is 64 Kbit
      Reliability 255/255, minimum MTU 1500 bytes
      Loading 1/255, Hops 0
    20.1.2.1, from 20.1.2.1, 00:00:00 ago, via Serial1
      Route metric is 160250, traffic share count is 1
      Total delay is 40000 microseconds, minimum bandwidth is 64 Kbit
      Reliability 255/255, minimum MTU 1500 bytes
      Loading 1/255, Hops 0

R4#
```

Listing 8-49. *Details of route to 30.0.0.0/8*

To illustrate how IGRP selects the routes with more available bandwidth, let's change the bandwidth setting on the Serial1 interface (Listing 8-50).

```
R4#conf t
Enter configuration commands, one per line.  End with CNTL/Z.
R4(config)#int s1
R4(config-if)#bandwidth 62
R4(config-if)#^Z
R4#
```

Listing 8-50. *Changing the link bandwidth value*

After routers have converged on the new routing information, R4 routes to network 30.0.0.0/8 through a single interface (Listing 8-51).

```
R4#sho ip route
...
Gateway of last resort is not set

I    1.0.0.0/8 [100/158850] via 20.1.3.1, 00:00:08, Ethernet0
                [100/158850] via 20.2.2.1, 00:00:08, Serial0
```

```
I    2.0.0.0/8 [100/158750] via 20.2.2.1, 00:00:08, Serial0
I    3.0.0.0/8 [100/1600] via 20.1.3.1, 00:00:08, Ethernet0
     4.0.0.0/24 is subnetted, 1 subnets
C       4.4.4.0 is directly connected, Loopback0
     20.0.0.0/24 is subnetted, 5 subnets
I       20.1.1.0 [100/158350] via 20.1.3.1, 00:00:08, Ethernet0
C       20.2.2.0 is directly connected, Serial0
C       20.1.3.0 is directly connected, Ethernet0
I       20.2.1.0 [100/158350] via 20.2.2.1, 00:00:08, Serial0
C       20.1.2.0 is directly connected, Serial1
I    5.0.0.0/8 [100/160750] via 20.2.2.1, 00:00:08, Serial0
I    30.0.0.0/8 [100/160250] via 20.2.2.1, 00:00:08, Serial0
R4#
```

Listing 8-51. *R4's routing table after link bandwidth change*

8.3.6.2 Using Unequal-Cost Load Sharing

If the value of the variance parameter is changed to a value higher than 1, R4 will use the route with a worse metric as well. See Listing 8-52 for an example.

```
R4#sho ip route
...
Gateway of last resort is not set
...
I    30.0.0.0/8 [100/160250] via 20.2.2.1, 00:00:05, Serial0
                 [100/165290] via 20.1.2.1, 00:00:05, Serial1
R4#
```

Listing 8-52. *R4 using unequal-cost parallel routes*

Looking at the route (Listing 8-53), one can see that even though route metrics for two path descriptors are different, the traffic-share counts are the same. The reason is that metric ratio is less than 2:1.

```
R4#sho ip route 30.0.0.0
Routing entry for 30.0.0.0/8
  Known via "igrp 100", distance 100, metric 160250
  Redistributing via igrp 100
  Advertised by igrp 100 (self originated)
  Last update from 20.1.2.1 on Serial1, 00:00:27 ago
  Routing Descriptor Blocks:
  * 20.2.2.1, from 20.2.2.1, 00:00:27 ago, via Serial0
      Route metric is 160250, traffic share count is 1
      Total delay is 40000 microseconds, minimum bandwidth is 64 Kbit
      Reliability 255/255, minimum MTU 1500 bytes
      Loading 1/255, Hops 0
```

```
        20.1.2.1, from 20.1.2.1, 00:00:27 ago, via Serial1
          Route metric is 165290, traffic share count is 1
          Total delay is 40000 microseconds, minimum bandwidth is 62 Kbit
          Reliability 255/255, minimum MTU 1500 bytes
          Loading 1/255, Hops 0

R4#
```

Listing 8-53. *Equal traffic-share counts with different route metrics*

However, if we change the link bandwidth parameter of Serial1 to two times worse than that of Serial0, we can see how the traffic-share count changes and affects the load-sharing process (Listing 8-54).

```
R4#conf t
Enter configuration commands, one per line.   End with CNTL/Z.
R4(config)#int s1
R4(config-if)#bandwidth 32
R4(config-if)#^Z
R4#clear ip route *
R4#sho ip route
...
Gateway of last resort is not set
...
I    30.0.0.0/8 [100/160250] via 20.2.2.1, 00:00:00, Serial0
                [100/316500] via 20.1.2.1, 00:00:03, Serial1
R4#
R4#sho ip route 30.0.0.0
Routing entry for 30.0.0.0/8
  Known via "igrp 100", distance 100, metric 160250
  Redistributing via igrp 100
  Advertised by igrp 100 (self originated)
  Last update from 20.2.2.1 on Serial0, 00:00:12 ago
  Routing Descriptor Blocks:
  * 20.2.2.1, from 20.2.2.1, 00:00:12 ago, via Serial0
      Route metric is 160250, traffic share count is 2
      Total delay is 40000 microseconds, minimum bandwidth is 64 Kbit
      Reliability 255/255, minimum MTU 1500 bytes
      Loading 1/255, Hops 0
    20.1.2.1, from 20.1.2.1, 00:00:16 ago, via Serial1
      Route metric is 316500, traffic share count is 1
      Total delay is 40000 microseconds, minimum bandwidth is 32 Kbit
      Reliability 255/255, minimum MTU 1500 bytes
      Loading 1/255, Hops 0

R4#
```

Listing 8-54. *Different traffic-share counts*

Unequal-cost parallel paths provide two functions: bandwidth-aware load sharing and faster convergence via nonbest paths. In certain situations, it may be necessary to use worse routes only for the second purpose. In this case, the router must be configured as in Listing 8-55.

```
R4#conf t
Enter configuration commands, one per line.  End with CNTL/Z.
R4(config)#router igrp 100
R4(config-router)#traffic-share min across-interfaces
R4(config-router)#^Z
R4#
```

Listing 8-55. *Configuring R4 to use worse paths for backup only*

Note that the backup routes are not removed from the routing table. Instead, their traffic-share counters are assigned zero value to prevent any traffic from being forwarded over them (Listing 5-56).

```
R4#sho ip route 30.0.0.0
Routing entry for 30.0.0.0/8
  Known via "igrp 100", distance 100, metric 160250
  Redistributing via igrp 100
  Advertised by igrp 100 (self originated)
  Last update from 20.1.2.1 on Serial1, 00:00:09 ago
  Routing Descriptor Blocks:
  * 20.2.2.1, from 20.2.2.1, 00:00:09 ago, via Serial0
      Route metric is 160250, traffic share count is 1
      Total delay is 40000 microseconds, minimum bandwidth is 64 Kbit
      Reliability 255/255, minimum MTU 1500 bytes
      Loading 1/255, Hops 0
    20.1.2.1, from 20.1.2.1, 00:00:09 ago, via Serial1
      Route metric is 316500, traffic share count is 0
      Total delay is 40000 microseconds, minimum bandwidth is 32 Kbit
      Reliability 255/255, minimum MTU 1500 bytes
      Loading 1/255, Hops 0

R4#
```

Listing 8-56. *Zero traffic-share count of the backup route*

Let's now configure IGRP to propagate default-routing information. Remember that IGRP cannot carry the 0.0.0.0/0 route and must announce one or more networks as exterior. For this purpose, R1 is configured as shown in Listing 8-57.

```
R1#conf t
Enter configuration commands, one per line.  End with CNTL/Z.
R1(config)#ip default-network 1.0.0.0
R1(config)#^Z
R1#
```

Listing 8-57. *Configuring R1 to announce candidate default route in IGRP*

The result of this command is that the corresponding parent prefix descriptor is marked as exterior in the routing table (Listing 8-58).

```
R1#sho ip route
...
Gateway of last resort is not set

  *    1.0.0.0/24 is subnetted, 1 subnets
  C        1.1.1.0 is directly connected, Loopback0
...
R1#
```

Listing 8-58. *Major network marked as exterior in R1's routing table*

Note that the route to network 1.0.0.0/8 is marked as exterior only when it is sent as a network summary route to other major networks. Because this is true for all networks attached to R1, all routers in the lab network install this route as candidate default. See Listing 8-59.

```
R2#sho ip route
...
Gateway of last resort is 20.2.1.2 to network 1.0.0.0

I*    1.0.0.0/8 [100/1600] via 20.2.1.2, 00:00:07, Ethernet0
      2.0.0.0/24 is subnetted, 1 subnets
C        2.2.2.0 is directly connected, Loopback0
I     3.0.0.0/8 [100/158850] via 20.2.2.2, 00:00:08, Serial0
                 [100/158850] via 20.2.1.2, 00:00:07, Ethernet0
I     4.0.0.0/8 [100/158750] via 20.2.2.2, 00:00:08, Serial0
      20.0.0.0/24 is subnetted, 5 subnets
I        20.1.1.0 [100/158350] via 20.2.1.2, 00:00:07, Ethernet0
C        20.2.2.0 is directly connected, Serial0
I        20.1.3.0 [100/158350] via 20.2.2.2, 00:00:08, Serial0
I        20.1.2.0 [100/158350] via 20.2.1.2, 00:00:07, Ethernet0
C        20.2.1.0 is directly connected, Ethernet0
I     5.0.0.0/8 [100/158750] via 30.0.0.1, 00:00:02, Serial1
      30.0.0.0/24 is subnetted, 2 subnets
```

```
C        30.0.0.0 is directly connected, Serial1
I        30.0.1.0 [100/160250] via 30.0.0.1, 00:00:03, Serial1
R2#
```

Listing 8-59. *R2's routing table with candidate default installed by IGRP*

8.3.6.3 Redistributing to IGRP

To illustrate configuration of redistribution into IGRP, routers R5 and R2 are configured with OSPF to create routing domains with a topology similar to the one in Listing 8-41. R5 is also configured to redistribute OSPF routes to IGRP, as shown in Listing 8-60.

```
R5#conf t
Enter configuration commands, one per line.  End with CNTL/Z.
R5(config)#router igrp 100
R5(config-router)#redistribute ospf 1
R5(config-router)#^Z
R5#
```

Listing 8-60. *Configuring R5 to redistribute OSPF routes to IGRP*

Now look at the entry installed by OSPF in R5's routing table (Listing 8-61).

```
R5#sho ip route ospf
      2.0.0.0/8 is variably subnetted, 2 subnets, 2 masks
O        2.2.2.2/32 [110/1563] via 30.0.0.2, 00:01:49, Serial1
R5#sho ip route 2.2.2.2
Routing entry for 2.2.2.2/32
   Known via "ospf 1", distance 110, metric 1563, type intra area
   Redistributing via igrp 100, ospf 1
   Last update from 30.0.0.2 on Serial1, 00:01:52 ago
   Routing Descriptor Blocks:
   * 30.0.0.2, from 2.2.2.2, 00:01:52 ago, via Serial1
      Route metric is 1563, traffic share count is 1
R5#
```

Listing 8-61. *OSPF route not announced by IGRP*

Even though it is marked as redistributed by IGRP, the route is not marked as advertised by it. The reason is that the IGRP process was not configured with metric information necessary for it to announce redistributed routes.

When R5 is configured with a default metric information as shown in Listing 8-62, the route is finally announced through IGRP.

```
R5#conf t
Enter configuration commands, one per line.  End with CNTL/Z.
R5(config)#router igrp 100
R5(config-router)#default-metric 10000 10 255 1 1500
R5(config-router)#^Z
R5#
R5#clear ip route *
R5#sho ip route 2.2.2.2
Routing entry for 2.2.2.2/32
  Known via "ospf 1", distance 110, metric 1563, type intra area
  Redistributing via igrp 100, ospf 1
  Advertised by igrp 100
  Last update from 30.0.0.2 on Serial1, 00:00:13 ago
  Routing Descriptor Blocks:
  * 30.0.0.2, from 2.2.2.2, 00:00:13 ago, via Serial1
      Route metric is 1563, traffic share count is 1

R5#
```

Listing 8-62. *Configuring default metric information for IGRP to announce redistributed routes*

The routing table of R1 (Listing 8-63) shows that the route was not only announced but also summarized, as it covers a subnet and the message is sent to a different major network.

```
R1#sho ip route
...
Gateway of last resort is 30.0.1.1 to network 30.0.0.0

     1.0.0.0/24 is subnetted, 1 subnets
C       1.1.1.0 is directly connected, Loopback0
I    2.0.0.0/8 [100/158260] via 30.0.1.1, 00:00:35, Serial1
I    3.0.0.0/8 [100/158750] via 20.1.1.2, 00:00:31, Serial0
I    4.0.0.0/8 [100/158750] via 20.1.2.2, 00:00:24, Serial2
     20.0.0.0/24 is subnetted, 3 subnets
C       20.1.1.0 is directly connected, Serial0
I       20.1.3.0 [100/158350] via 20.1.1.2, 00:00:31, Serial0
                 [100/158350] via 20.1.2.2, 00:00:24, Serial2
C       20.1.2.0 is directly connected, Serial2
I    5.0.0.0/8 [100/158750] via 30.0.1.1, 00:00:35, Serial1
  *  30.0.0.0/24 is subnetted, 2 subnets
I*      30.0.0.0 [100/160250] via 30.0.1.1, 00:00:35, Serial1
C       30.0.1.0 is directly connected, Serial1
R1#
```

Listing 8-63. *Redistributed route in R1's routing table*

Recall that we have all major networks in the lab subnetted with subnet mask 255.255.255.0. Now R2 is configured with another subnet of the same major network but with a different subnet mask: 255.255.255.252, as shown in Listing 8-64.

```
R2#conf t
Enter configuration commands, one per line.  End with CNTL/Z.
R2(config)#int loopback1
R2(config-if)#ip addr 30.2.2.2 255.255.255.252
R2(config-if)#ip ospf network point-to-point
R2(config-if)#no shut
R2(config-if)#ex
R2(config)#router ospf 1
R2(config-router)#network 30.2.2.0 0.0.0.255 area 0
R2(config-router)#^Z
R2#
```

Listing 8-64. *Configuring a subnet with a different subnet mask on R2*

Listing 8-65 illustrates that the corresponding OSPF route is installed in R5's routing table and marked as advertised.

```
R5#sho ip route 30.2.2.0
Routing entry for 30.2.2.0/30
  Known via "ospf 1", distance 110, metric 1563, type intra area
  Redistributing via igrp 100, ospf 1
  Advertised by igrp 100
  Last update from 30.0.0.2 on Serial1, 00:00:30 ago
  Routing Descriptor Blocks:
  * 30.0.0.2, from 2.2.2.2, 00:00:30 ago, via Serial1
      Route metric is 1563, traffic share count is 1

R5#
```

Listing 8-65. *Corresponding route in R5's routing table*

However, if we look at the routing table of R1, we cannot see a route (see Listing 8-66 for an illustration).

```
R1#sho ip route
...
Gateway of last resort is 30.0.1.1 to network 5.0.0.0

     1.0.0.0/24 is subnetted, 1 subnets
```

```
C        1.1.1.0 is directly connected, Loopback0
I     2.0.0.0/8 [100/158260] via 30.0.1.1, 00:00:02, Serial1
I     3.0.0.0/8 [100/158750] via 20.1.1.2, 00:00:03, Serial0
I     4.0.0.0/8 [100/158750] via 20.1.2.2, 00:00:03, Serial2
      20.0.0.0/24 is subnetted, 3 subnets
C        20.1.1.0 is directly connected, Serial0
I        20.1.3.0 [100/158350] via 20.1.1.2, 00:00:03, Serial0
                  [100/158350] via 20.1.2.2, 00:00:03, Serial2
C        20.1.2.0 is directly connected, Serial2
I*    5.0.0.0/8 [100/158750] via 30.0.1.1, 00:00:02, Serial1
 *    30.0.0.0/24 is subnetted, 2 subnets
I*       30.0.0.0 [100/160250] via 30.0.1.1, 00:00:02, Serial1
C        30.0.1.0 is directly connected, Serial1
R1#
```

Listing 8-66. *R1 missing redistributed route*

The reason for this problem is that R5 does not announce the route, as its mask is longer than the one used in the major network where the route should be announced. To remedy this problem, we put the loopback interface on R2 into a separate area and configure a special command that instructs R2 to summarize this route to the required length when it is announced to other areas, including area 0, where other routers belong (see Listing 8-67). For more information on OSPF configuration, see Chapter 9.

```
R2#conf t
Enter configuration commands, one per line.  End with CNTL/Z.
R2(config)#router ospf 1
R2(config-router)#no network 30.2.2.0 0.0.0.255 area 0
R2(config-router)#network 30.2.2.0 0.0.0.255 area 1
R2(config-router)#area 1 range 30.2.2.0 255.255.255.0
R2(config-router)#^Z
R2#
```

Listing 8-67. *Configuring R2 to summarize redistributed subnet*

Listing 8-68 illustrates how the summarized route is installed as an OSPF interarea route in R5's routing table.

```
R5#sho ip route
...
Gateway of last resort is not set
...
      30.0.0.0/24 is subnetted, 3 subnets
O IA     30.2.2.0 [110/1563] via 30.0.0.2, 00:00:34, Serial1
C        30.0.0.0 is directly connected, Serial1
```

```
C       30.0.1.0 is directly connected, Serial0
R5#
```

Listing 8-68. *Summarized OSPF route in R5's routing table*

To make sure that the route is finally announced to IGRP domain, we check the contents of R1's routing table (Listing 8-69).

```
R1#sho ip route
...
Gateway of last resort is 30.0.1.1 to network 5.0.0.0
...
 *    30.0.0.0/24 is subnetted, 3 subnets
I        30.2.2.0 [100/158260] via 30.0.1.1, 00:00:20, Serial1
I*       30.0.0.0 [100/160250] via 30.0.1.1, 00:00:20, Serial1
C        30.0.1.0 is directly connected, Serial1
R1#
```

Listing 8-69. *R1's routing table containing redistributed route*

8.3.7 Summary

- IGRP is a Cisco-proprietary classful distance-vector routing protocol.
- The main differences between IGRP and RIPv1 are in route attributes and metric calculation, more aggressive loop-avoidance mechanisms in IGRP (route poisoning), and the unequal-cost multipath routing approach. All other mechanisms are the same.
- IGRP does not send the route metric in its updates. Instead, updates contain a vector of route attributes—path bandwidth, cumulative delay, path reliability, and load—that are altered by each router to reflect the actual path characteristics and used to calculate a composite metric through a weight function.
- Composite metrics allow IGRP to choose optimal paths in networks with diverse link characteristics, whereas RIP chooses the best paths, based on the hop count only.
- IGRP broadcasts its periodic updates every 90 seconds, whereas RIP does so every 30 seconds.
- By default, IGRP installs parallel routes only if they are the best and have the same metric, thus implementing the equal-cost multipath approach. However, the administrator can configure an IGRP process to allow installation of unequal-metric paths. This leads to load-balancing behavior proportional to the inverse ratio of route metrics, which may be useful in situations when the administrator wants to use multiple parallel paths even if they have different bandwidth and delay characteristics.

8.3.8 Frequently Asked Questions

Q: **Is IGRP implemented in routers of vendors other than Cisco?**

A: No. IGRP is a proprietary protocol, and some parts of the algorithms are patented by Cisco. No other vendors are known to support IGRP in their router software.

Q: **RIP uses the demand circuit approach to treat temporary connections more efficiently. Does IGRP have a similar technique?**

A: Yes. Cisco IOS provides a proprietary solution, called *snapshot routing*, for the distance-vector routing protocols. This approach allows the administrator to specify the length of active and passive periods. Routers do not exchange periodic-routing updates on the demand circuit during the passive periods and freeze routes through these circuits in the routing table. When an active period starts, routers confirm their current routing information through an exchange of routing updates. The efficiency is achieved by ensuring that the length of the passive period is much greater than that of the active period. See [SNAPSHOT] for more information on snapshot routing.

Q: **Even though EIGRP has not been considered in this chapter, what is the relationship between IGRP and EIGRP?**

A: IGRP and EIGRP have two similarities: their names and the method of metric calculation. The algorithm used in EIGRP is also based on the Bellman-Ford algorithm, used in pure distance-vector protocols but is far more complex. EIGRP calculates metrics very much as IGRP does but uses different scales for route attributes. All other characteristics are different. For example, EIGRP maintains formal connections with neighboring routers and keeps routing information in its own database, whereas IGRP does not do any of these things. See Chapter 9 for more information on EIGRP.

Q: **We are in the process of designing a new corporate network and are considering several routing protocols. RIP seems to be too simple and naive when it comes to the best-path calculation. Would you recommend IGRP as a good substitute for RIP?**

A: Yes and no. IGRP is definitely better than RIPv1 because of its more sophisticated metric-calculation algorithm and no hop-count limitation. However, IGRP is a classful routing protocol, so it cannot be used in VLSM environments, which is most likely the case for modern IP networks. On the other hand, RIPv2 nonetheless counts hops and has a maximum of 15 hops for the network diameter. If this is not an issue, meaning that all links in your network have almost identical characteristics, which seems unreal, and the network is small enough, RIPv2 is a better candidate. If network links are different but the addresses are laid out according to the classful rules, which too is unlikely, IGRP is a good choice.

Finally, if the network is going to use links of different natures and you are planning to use the address space efficiently or you do not want to face the slow convergence problem that is typical for distance-vector routing protocols, it is better to consider EIGRP or OSPF (see Chapters 9 and 10).

Q: **How can I influence the process of best-path selection in IGRP? I want IGRP to prefer some links over others even though they have the same bandwidth and delay characteristics.**

A: By default, IGRP takes into consideration only path bandwidth and cumulative path delay. In general, it is possible to change both bandwidth and delay characteristics of involved interfaces to control what routes IGRP chooses. However, changing the bandwidth parameter on an interface—setting it to an unreal value is not recommended—because it affects statistics calculation. It is more appropriate to change the setting of the interface delay.

Q: **IGRP is supposed to react to changes of the path bandwidth attribute. However, when I have changed the bandwidth parameter on an interface of a downstream router, the upstream routers didn't change their routing tables.**

A: First, make sure that the interface you reconfigured can be used to reach the network in question. Also, make sure that the path from that router to the upstream routers does not contain links with less bandwidth, because IGRP reports in its updates the minimum bandwidth seen for the links making up a path. Last, but not least, do not forget to wait for expiration of the periodic update timer in the routers (90 seconds, by default).

Q: **I am redistributing subnets of network 10.0.0.0 from OSPF to IGRP, but IGRP sends only a summary network route to its neighbors. Is this normal?**

A: Yes. Most probably, the portion of the network routed by IGRP uses IP addresses from a different major network. Because it is a classful routing protocol, IGRP assumes that different major networks can be subnetted by using different subnet masks. Both IGRP and RIP find the route mask by looking at the subnet mask of the interface on which the update is received, so the redistributing router cannot send subnet information from one major network to another and therefore performs automatic classful route summarization.

8.4 References

[RFC1058] C. Hedrick, "Routing Information Protocol," RFC 1058, June 1988, http://www.ietf.org/rfc/rfc1058.txt.

[RFC1723] G. Malkin, "RIP Version 2. Carrying Additional Information", RFC 1723, November 1994, http://www.ietf.org/rfc/rfc1723.txt.

[RFC2080] G. Malkin and R. Minnear, "RIPng for IPv6," RFC 2080, January 1997, http://www.ietf.org/rfc/rfc2080.txt.

[RFC2091] G. Meyer and S. Sherry, "Triggered Extensions to RIP to Support Demand Circuits," RFC 2091, January 1997, http://www.ietf.org/rfc/rfc2091.txt.

[SNAPSHOT] "Configuring Snapshot Routing," http://www.cisco.com/univercd/cc/td/doc/product/ software/ios121/121cgcr/dialns_c/dnsprt2/dcdnsnap.htm.

[UpdSync] S. Floyd and V. Jacobson, "The Synchronization of Periodic Routing Messages," SIGCOMM, 1993.

Chapter Nine

Link-State
Routing Protocols

This chapter discusses the group of protocols based on the *link-state* algorithm, also known as *topology broadcast*. The chapter begins with an introduction to the link-state routing algorithms. The major portion of the chapter covers one of the most widely deployed interior gateway protocols: OSPF.

9.1 Introduction to Link-State Routing

This section describes the algorithms used in link-state routing protocols: the topology abstraction mechanism, the flooding algorithm, and the Dijkstra algorithm for the shortest-path calculation. The section also compares the two link-state routing protocols available for IP today: OSPF and IS-IS.

9.1.1 Theoretical Basis

To understand the main principles of link-state routing, it is necessary to dispel a common belief that networks consist of IP subnets: that every link—point-to-point or LAN segment—is associated with some IP address information and every router has at least one IP address (Figure 9-1(a)). This association is so strong that most people cannot imagine a link or a router in an IP network that wouldn't be assigned an IP address. You need to drop that assumption.

Link-state routing protocols have a mathematical point of view on the network. For a link-state protocol, a network is nothing more than a graph. Vertices in the graph are routers and transit networks (LAN segments or WAN clouds), that is, entities that can be used to reach other entities (Figure 9-1(b)). Edges of the graph are links. This abstraction helps link-state protocols solve the main task: calculating routing information through calculation of shortest paths to all given vertices in a network.

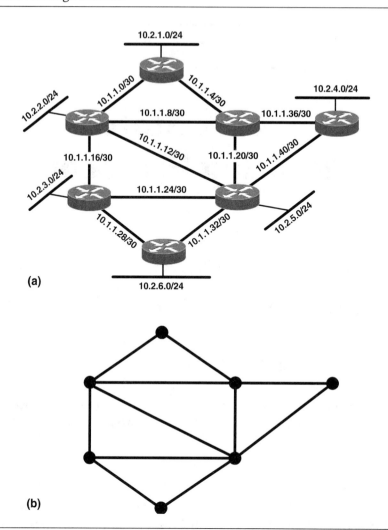

Figure 9-1. *(a) Traditional view of IP network; (b) IP network with routing information removed*

What is the benefit of representing a network as a graph? If it has complete information about network topology, every router can calculate the shortest paths to all destinations independently of other routers in the network. This is a huge improvement over the distance-vector concept. In distance-vector routing protocols, if one router in a network calculates a wrong route (see Chapter 8), all other routers accept this wrong information, calculate their own wrong routes, and distribute them to neighbors. In link-state routing, correctness of calculated routes depends only on the correctness of the topological information in the calculating router. Now we have another question: How do routers get correct topological information?

Every router participating in a link-state routing protocol announces its own piece of topology information to all other routers in the network: so-called topology broadcasting. Speaking plain English, routers would say something like this: "Hi, I'm router X, and I can reach router Y via a T1 link and router Z via a T3 link." Router Y in turn might say: "Hi, I'm router Y, and I can reach router X via a T1 link and router B via a 56Kbps link." Note that if two routers are connected with a common link, they both announce connectivity over it. The reason is that routers announce not physical links but rather connectivity to other routers through the links (see Figure 9-2). It does not make sense to announce a link if it does not provide connectivity.

So far so good. We have routers announcing topology information, which can be used to recreate the network topology graph. Using one of the shortest-path calculation algorithms—Bellman-Ford or Dijkstra, considered in Section 9.1.2—a router can find the best paths to other routers. What about IP networks, however?

In addition to topological information, every router announces network reachability information in the form of IP prefixes. Because prefixes are associated with graph vertices and do not provide connectivity to other vertices, they can be imagined as leaf entries in the graph, as shown in Figure 9-3.

Once it has calculated the *shortest-path tree* (SPT) over the topology graph, the router has a shortest path to every vertex in the graph, along with the associated cost and

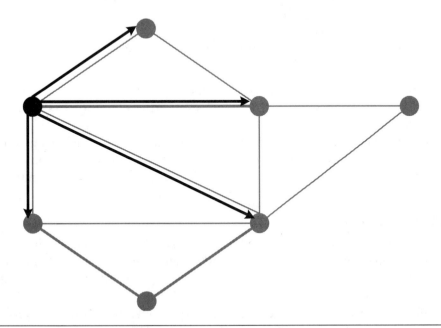

Figure 9-2. *Routers announcing topology information*

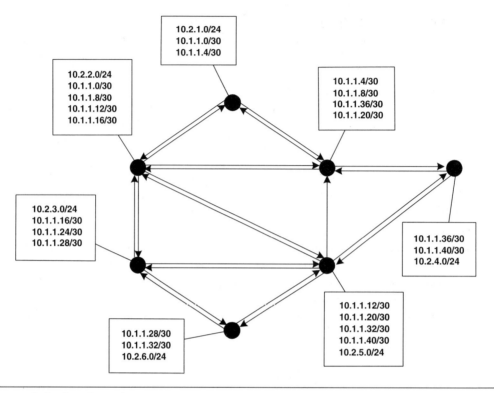

Figure 9-3. *Leaf entries representing IP routing information*

next-hop router, a process we will consider in more detail later. To find routes to advertised IP prefixes, the routers consider all reachable vertices and process the leaf entries associated with them.

Whenever the network topology changes, the routers noticing the change create new copies of their pieces of topology information and distribute them to all routers. Routers then recalculate the SPT, construct the new set of routes, and update their routing tables.

9.1.2 Dijkstra Algorithm

The SPT for a connectivity graph can be calculated by using a number of algorithms. The centralized version of the Bellman-Ford algorithm represented in Chapter 8 is one example. However, link-state routing protocols use a Dijkstra algorithm, which requires less memory and is faster.

The Dijkstra algorithm, invented by Edsger Wybe Dijkstra, is used in many areas of human activity requiring calculation of shortest routes. The algorithm allows calculation of the tree of shortest paths from a given vertex of a graph to all other vertices in the graph. The algorithm assumes that graph edges are unidirectional and are assigned positive costs that reflect link preferences. For example, with vertex A the root in Figure 9-4, Dijkstra will calculate the SPT depicted in Figure 9-5.

The concept behind the Dijkstra algorithm is amazingly simple, although people tend to think that it is difficult to understand. Look again at the sample topology graph in Figure 9-4. Assume that we need to find the shortest-path tree from vertex A to all other vertices. It is clear that we should do this gradually; that is, we should first find the shortest paths to the adjacent vertices and then proceed to others. Note that the shortest path

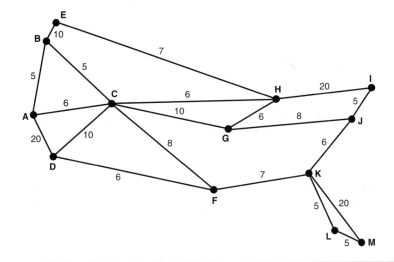

Figure 9-4. *Topology graph*

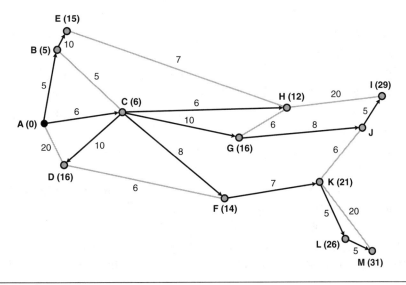

Figure 9-5. *SPT for the topology graph*

between two adjacent vertices is not necessarily the link between them. For example, the shortest path from A to D is through C. (This is the trick with SPT calculation.) At the same time, it is understood that among all adjacent vertices, there is one to which the shortest path is guaranteed to be the direct link from the root. This vertex is the one with the lowest cost (B, in our case). We can guarantee this because paths to B through other vertices would be worse: A path through C would have a cost greater than 6, whereas a path through D would have a cost greater than 20.

We now have link A–B in the SPT. However, it doesn't mean that the shortest paths to all other vertices would be through B. Links A–C and A–D are still candidates for the shortest-path tree; for example, the shortest path to C will be finally equal to A–C. However, all links to the vertices adjacent to B are also candidates. Fortunately, the same logic applies here: Among all candidate paths—paths from the root to the vertices adjacent to those already covered by the SPT—the one with the lowest summary cost is guaranteed to belong to the SPT, as other paths would give a worse cost to reach the same vertex. When such a path is identified, a corresponding link and vertex are added to the SPT, links to adjacent vertices become candidates, and the algorithm iterates until there are no more candidates.

The algorithm can be formalized as follows. Note that every vertex has an associated distance from the root—sum of link costs from the root to the vertex—and a list of predecessors, or vertices in the SPT that can potentially provide the shortest path to the vertex.

1. Clear the SPT and the candidate list.
2. Add the root vertex to the SPT with associated cost 0. (We don't have to cross any graph edge to reach ourselves.)
3. Consider every vertex W adjacent to the one just added to the SPT (vertex V).
    a. If W is already on the SPT (added in step 5 in a previous iteration), consider the next adjacent vertex.
    b. If W has no link back to V, consider the next adjacent vertex. (V may have no link to W during transition periods.)
    c. Calculate the cost, C, to vertex W as the sum of the cost associated with V and the cost of the edge from V to W.
    d. If W is not on the candidate list, set the cost associated with W to C and add W to the candidate list.
    e. If W is already in the candidate list, compare the associated cost C'—the cost calculated when W was added to the candidate list—with the newly calculated cost, C. If C is greater than C', loop to step 3.
    f. Otherwise, if cost C is smaller than C', set W's associated cost to C, clear W's list of predecessors, and add V to it: We found a better path to W through V.

    g. Otherwise (*C* is equal to *C'*), add V to W's list of predecessors: We found another shortest path to W.

4. If the candidate list is empty, the algorithm has finished.

5. Otherwise, among all the vertices in the candidate list, find vertex W that is closest to the root—has the least associated cost—add it to the SPT, and mark the links from the vertices listed in W's list of predecessors to W as belonging to the SPT.

6. Loop to step 3.

Consider the pseudocode for the Dijkstra algorithm (Listing 9-1). Note that the main function—`CalcDijkstra()`—is very short. Everything is done in a loop. Before the first iteration, a v variable, pointing to the vertex to be added to the SPT, is assigned the address of the root vertex corresponding to the calculating router. For every other iteration, the vertex to be added to the SPT is taken from the sorted list `CandidateList`. If this list is empty, v will have NULL value, and the function will leave the loop.

`AddVertexToSPT()` is the function in which the most interesting things are done. First, the vertex is removed from the candidate list and is then marked as belonging to the SPT so that other, alternative paths to it are not considered. The `MarkLinks()` function is called to mark links from v's parent vertices to v as belonging to the SPT. After that, all vertices adjacent to v are considered in the main for loop. Every vertex w is processed according to the algorithm.

```
typedef struct edge {          /* Graph edge structure */
    int     NbrID;             /* Neighbor ID */
    u_int   Cost;              /* Link cost */
    TFlag   InSPT;             /* Link is in shortest-path tree */
} TEdge;


#define MAX_EDGES    10
#define MAX_PARENTS  10

typedef struct vertex {        /* Graph vertex structure */
    int   ID;                  /* Vertex ID */
    int   EdgeCount;           /* Number of edges */
    TEdge Edges[MAX_EDGES];    /* Edges from the vertex */

    u_int Cost;                /* Cost from the root */
    TFlag InSPT;

    u_int ParCount;            /* Number of parent vertices */
    int   Parents[MAX_PARENTS];   /* Parent vertices */
} TVertex;
```

```
void AddVertexToSPT(TVertex * v)
{
  int      i;
  TVertex * w;
  u_int       d;

  /* Remove V from the candidate list */

  slist_del(CandidateList, v);
  v->InSPT = 1;

  if (v->Cost) /* It's not the root*/
     MarkLinks(v); /* Mark links from parents to V as in SPT */

  printf("Vertex %d added to the SPT, considering adjacent vertices\n",
         v->ID);

  /* Consider every vertex W adjacent to V
   * and add it to the candidate list
   */

  for(i = 0; i < v->EdqeCount; i++) {

     w = vertices[v->Edges[i].NbrID];

     printf(" Considering adjacent vertex %d\n", w->ID);

     if (w->InSPT) {
        printf("  It is already in the SPT, ignoring\n");
        continue;
     }

     if (!Backlink(w, v)) {
        printf("  No back link is found, ignoring ************\n");
        continue;
     }

     d = v->Cost + v->Edges[i].Cost;
     printf("  Cost to W through V: %d\n", d);

     if (w->Cost == 0) { /* W is not in the candidate list */

        printf("  W is not in candidate list yet, adding\n");
        w->Cost = d;
        slist_add(CandidateList, w, d);
        AddParent(w, v);
     }
     else if (w->Cost > d) {

        /* Change the cost and re-sort */
        printf("  New cost is better than old (%d), changing\n", w->Cost);
```

```
            slist_del(CandidateList, w);
            w->Cost = d;
            SetParent(w, v);
            slist_add(CandidateList, w, d);
        }
        else if (w->Cost == d) {

            printf("  New cost is the same, adding parent\n");
            AddParent(w, v);
        }
        else
            printf("  New cost is worse, ignoring this path\n");

    }
}


void CalcDijkstra()
{
  TVertex * v, *w;

  root->Cost = 0;

  printf("Starting Dijkstra\n");
  printf("————————————————————-\n");

  for(v = root; v ; v = slist_get_next(CandidateList)) {

    printf("Vertex %d is being added to the SPT\n", v->ID);
    AddVertexToSPT(v);

  }
}
```

Listing 9-1. *Pseudocode for Dijkstra algorithm*

9.1.3 Database Synchronization and Flooding Algorithm

Link-state routing protocols calculate the SPT and routing information by using the topology and routing data distributed by all routers in the network. As described before, every router announces its own piece of information, which we'll call a *link-state protocol data unit,* or LSPDU. Because all routers in a link-state domain must have an identical view of the network topology, the LSPDUs announced by routers must be distributed to all routers in the network. It is also understood that LSPDUs must be stored in a *link-state database* (LSDB) for use later, in the shortest-path tree calculation. In essence, to ensure convergence of a link-state routing protocol, all routers must be guaranteed to have up-to-date topology information within a finite period of time. Therefore, there must be a mechanism to distribute LSPDUs among participating routers reliably and quickly. This is what the flooding algorithm does.

Different link-state routing protocols use slightly different variations of the same flooding algorithm, so it makes sense to describe it in general. The flooding algorithm makes the following assumptions.

- Distributed information is represented in the form of LSPDUs, with the following information associated with each:
  - *Identifier*, an integer that unambiguously characterizes an LSPDU among others
  - *Sequence number*, an integer that specifies the version of the LSPDU; participating devices must increment the sequence number when the next version of an LSPDU is created
  - *Age*, an integer that reflects the number of seconds an LSPDU has been present in the link-state domain since its origination
  - *Checksum*, a checksum of the whole LSPDU except for the Age field
- Every participating device stores the LSPDUs in its LSDB and ensures that the Age fields of LSPDUs are maintained appropriately.
- LSPDUs must have a finite length of life, usually called MaxAge, to ensure cleaning of the LSDB when the originating router is no longer in the network.
- To flush an LSPDU from the domain, the originating router sets the Age field to the MaxAge value and floods it throughout the domain.

The goals of the flooding algorithm are as follows.

- The algorithm must guarantee that any given LSPDU is distributed to all routers within the link-state domain. If some of the LSPDUs to a given router cannot be delivered within a reasonable period of time, the flooding algorithm must signal the topology abstraction logic so that the corresponding router is removed from the topology view of the network. (If the remote router cannot process LSPDUs, it makes no sense to forward transit traffic through it.)
- The algorithm must guarantee removal of naturally or prematurely—and intentionally—aged LSPDUs.

The flooding algorithm performs asynchronous distribution of LSPDUs. Together with the initial LSDB synchronization process, it ensures consistency of LSDBs within time.

Initial LSDB synchronization is used by the routers to exchange LSDB contents when an adjacency is being brought up. As long as the neighbors have also synchronized their LSDBs with other routers, this process ensures that the newly connected router has the same information as all other routers in the network.

Asynchronous distribution of LSPDUs is necessary to guarantee that the LSDBs of all routers in the network are still synchronized when a new version of an LSPDU is originated after the initial LSDB synchronization process is over. These two mechanisms are mutually related and must be considered as two parts of the continuous LSDB synchronization process. For simplicity, we refer to this process as the flooding algorithm.

It is understood that for the flooding algorithm to work, the following requirements must be met.

- LSPDUs must be delivered from router to router in a reliable fashion.
- All routers must have a consistent approach to determine which copy of the same LSPDU is more recent.

The first requirement may be fulfilled only if routers acknowledge received LSPDUs and retransmit unacknowledged LSPDUs. Ideally, if some LSPDUs cannot be delivered to a router, it should be reported unreachable.

Determination of the more recent LSPDU is vital. All routers must agree on the method used to do this, and the method itself must be intelligent enough to ensure the correct result. At first appearance, it is not a difficult task at all: Just use the LSPDU sequence number field, as whenever a new version of the LSPDU is used, the next value of the sequence number is used. However, there may be more difficult situations, when, for example, a router reboots, loses track of the sequence number, and starts originating its LSPDUs by using the initial value. The problem is that earlier versions of the LSPDUs with the same or older sequence numbers may be in the LSDBs of other routers, so the sequence number does not help.

If the new sequence number is different, the originating router will receive LSPDUs that other routers believe are more recent and will install them in its LSDB. It is possible, however, that the router should not announce the LSPDUs it originated before the reload or that such LSPDUs should have different contents. To address this situation, whenever a self-originated LSPDU is installed in the LSDB, the router checks its contents. If the LSPDU should not be announced, it is flushed from the domain. If the contents of the LSPDU should be different, the router accepts the sequence number in the LSPDU and originates a new, correct version of it, incrementing the sequence number.

The real problem might appear when sequence numbers of the LSPDUs are equal after the reload. A decision could have been made to remove LSPDUs whenever the originating router becomes unreachable: The corresponding vertex is not covered by the SPT. This would introduce a number of disadvantages, though. The most considerable one is that in case of link or adjacency flapping, flooding storms might occur that would affect stability of the network. (Remember that to remove an LSPDU from a domain, a router must prematurely set its Age field to the value indicating the end of the LSPDU's life and reflood it.)

The real algorithm used to determine the more recent LSPDU follows. (The algorithm compares two LSPDUs: the newly received one and the one already in the LSDB.)

1. If the Sequence Number fields of LSPDUs contain different values, the LSPDU with the higher sequence number is more recent.

2. Otherwise, if the checksums of LSPDUs are different, the one having the larger checksum is considered more recent.

3. Otherwise, if the Age field of one of the LSPDUs contains the MaxAge value—the LSPDU is being prematurely flushed from the domain—that LSPDU is more recent.

4. Otherwise, if the Age fields of the LSPDUs differ by more than the MaxAgeDiff value, the LSPDU with the smaller Age is considered more recent.

5. Otherwise, the LSPDUs are considered identical.

This logic can be understood as follows. Whenever possible, the Sequence Number fields of the LSPDUs are used, because this is the simplest, most reliable way of determining which version of an LSPDU is more recent. Otherwise, if the Sequence Number fields have the same value, it is not so easy. One could potentially use the Age field to find the newer version. This method is not reliable, however, as routers may have inaccurate clocks or may have bugs in the code in charge of LSPDU aging. Also, as you will see later, the Age field of LSPDUs is incremented by every router when flooded throughout the domain, to avoid flooding loops. Therefore, when a router receives a copy of an LSPDU with the same sequence number that is already in the router's LSDB, the Age field cannot be reliably used. However, the routers try to understand whether the two instances are different, by checking the Checksum fields. If the values of the Checksum fields are different, the probability is very high that these are two different LSPDUs sharing the same sequence number. In this case, the LSPDU with the higher checksum value is considered to be more recent.

Note that higher checksum value does not necessarily mean that the LSPDU is newer. The probability is 50 percent that the older version of the LSPDU is selected as more recent. This is not a problem, however. The originating router will receive the old version of its LSPDU and will install it in its LSDB, overriding what it has just originated, as all routers use the same algorithm to determine the newer LSPDU. If the originating router sees that the newly installed self-originated LSPDU does not contain what the router is willing to advertise, the router will originate a new version of the LSPDU with the next Sequence Number value and flood it to all other routers. Because the sequence number will be different, all routers will agree on the same version of LSPDU.

Even if the Checksum fields of LSPDUs are equal, the two LSPDUs may not be identical, for the following reasons.

- The checksum does not cover the LSPDU Age field, which may contain a MaxAge value indicating that the LSPDU must be flushed from the domain.
- It is still possible, although unlikely, to have the same checksum value for two different data patterns.

So the algorithm checks the Age fields to see whether one of the LSPDUs contains the MaxAge value; if it does, this LSPDU is considered more recent. (This is essentially to support LSPDU flushing. Note that it is not necessary for the originating router to increment the Sequence Number field when flushing, as the LSPDU with MaxAge value of the Age field is a special case in the flooding algorithm.)

If none of the LSPDUs contains the MaxAge value in its Age field, the algorithm still tries to understand whether the LSPDUs are different, by comparing the Age fields. Because the value of the Age field does not reflect only the time the LSPDU has been stored in LSDB, Age fields are considered different only if they differ by a value larger than MaxAgeDiff; otherwise, the two LSPDUs are considered identical.

It is possible for the algorithm to result in a wrong decision, as only checksums, not complete data, are compared. So there is a possibility that when a router reboots, it originates an LSPDU with the sequence number equal to that of the LSPDU originated during the previous reincarnation, the contents of the LSPDU differ, but the Checksum is the same. If the new LSPDU is originated within the MaxAgeDiff period, other routers will not install the new LSPDU in their LSDBs and will not use the new information. This could be remedied if routers always compared the complete LSPDU data. But as probability of such a mistake is low, it was decided not to do complete data comparison. Instead, such malfunctions are addressed by periodic LSPDU reorigination: All LSPDUs in a link-state routing protocol must be periodically reoriginated and reflooded; usually, this period is on the order of hours. When an LSPDU is reoriginated, its sequence number is increased.

Let's consider how initial LSDB synchronization is performed. When it gets connected to a network—to one or more other routers—a router needs to learn the topology of that network and to advertise its own piece of topology information and information about the network behind it. To achieve this goal, as part of the adjacency establishment process, routers exchange database descriptions and request needed LSPDUs from each other. The nature of the process is very simple. Each router sends the headers of the LSPDUs in its LSDB to the neighbor. The receiving side looks up its LSDB and determines whether it needs to ask the neighbor for any LSPDUs. If any LSPDU needs to be received, a request is sent to the neighbor and the corresponding header is put on the neighbor's Request list. The router keeps asking the neighbor for required LSPDUs until it receives them all or the neighbor state goes down.

Once the initial database synchronization is complete, all routers need to do is make sure that all changes to the LSDB are propagated accordingly. Whenever a new LSPDU is installed in the LSDB of a router, the router floods it to all its neighbors by transmitting it through all interfaces except the one on which the new LSPDU was received and putting the LSPDU on corresponding retransmission lists. Because other routers are supposed to acknowledge new information, the router will keep sending the new LSPDU until it is acknowledged or the neighbor is reported to be down.

9.1.4 Calculating Routing Information

Routers running link-state protocols tie routing information as leaves to the vertices of the topology graph. After the Dijkstra algorithm has calculated the SPT, each vertex of the connectivity graph (represented with an LSPDU) is augmented with information about the cost to it from the root vertex and the list of parent vertices. This information can be easily used to calculate routes to remote networks. Indeed, the path to an IP prefix is the path to the vertex to which the corresponding leaf entry is attached.

If only one router is announcing an IP prefix, finding the best route is straightforward: Just follow the SPT to the corresponding vertex; find the nearest direct neighbor that leads to it, thus giving the next-hop information; and use the cost from the root plus the cost announced by the router as the route metric. (The metric is not even necessary in this situation, as the shortest path is already found.) If more than one router announces a given destination—for example, two routers announce the subnet assigned to a common point-to-point link—the best route among those available is selected, based on the route metric calculated as in the previous case. The route with the lowest metric value wins.

Algorithmically, the route calculation logic is as follows.

1. Run the Dijkstra algorithm over the topology graph.
2. Go through all the vertices that belong to the SPT—unreachable vertices do not—and consider every prefix announced in the corresponding LSPDU as follows.
    a. Calculate the cost, D, as the sum of the cost from the root to the considered vertex and the cost announced in the LSPDU for the destination.
    b. Look up in the routing table a route to the same destination.
    c. If there is no route, install a new one with route metric D and the appropriate next-hop address.
    d. Otherwise, if the metric of the existing route is equal to D, add another path (parallel routes are available).
    e. Otherwise, if the metric of the existing route is worse (greater) than D, substitute the route with the newly calculated one.

f.   Otherwise, if the metric of the existing route is lower than D, ignore the new route, and consider the next prefix in the LSPDU.

Because in most cases, only one router announces a given prefix, step 2 of the algorithm is usually not so time consuming.

9.1.5 Overview of Link-State Routing Protocols

The first link-state routing protocol was implemented and deployed in the ARPANET (Advanced Research Project Agency Network). This protocol was the predecessor for the link-state routing algorithms implemented later.

Later on, Digital Equipment Corporation proposed a link-state routing protocol for OSI networks. The IS-IS (Intermediate System–to–Intermediate System) protocol was designed as a purely OSI routing protocol but was later extended to carry IP routing information, called integrated IS-IS. This extension for IS-IS is currently standardized within the IETF by the corresponding working group; see [RFC1142] and [RFC1195]. The *NetWare Link Services Protocol* (NLSP) is also based on the IS-IS protocol. For more information on IS-IS, see [ISO10589], [RFC1195], and [RFC1142].

Another link-state routing protocol that was specifically designed for routing in IP networks is OSPF (Open Shortest Path First), developed by the OSPF working group in the IETF. This protocol, the next step in link-state routing, was positioned as an open-standard protocol from the very beginning.

Since we focus on OSPF in this book, without considering IS-IS, a brief comparison between the two protocols in given in Table 9-1.

9.2 Open Shortest Path First (OSPF)

This section describes the OSPF routing protocol in detail, as well as its implementation in Cisco routers and associated configuration commands. OSPF, developed and standardized within the IETF by the OSPF working group in 1987, is an open-standard IP routing protocol using the link-state routing technique. OSPF version 1, described in [RFC1131], was never used in production networks, because of a number of problems (see [JMOY] for more details) addressed in version 2, the version currently used in IP networks. The following RFCs describe OSPF and some of its extensions:

- The OSPFv2 protocol specification: [RFC2328]; previous versions: [RFC2178], [RFC1583], and [RFC1247])
- Management information base (MIB) for OSPFv2: [RFC1850]
- OSPF for IPv6 specification: [RFC2740]
- OSPF not-so-stubby area option: [RFC1587]

- OSPF on-demand circuit: [RFC1793]
- OSPF opaque LSA option: [RFC2370]
- Experience with the OSPF protocol: [RFC1246]

In addition to the base OSPF standard, these useful options allow for more optimal protocol operation and network design. Cisco routers support all the listed OSPF extensions.

9.2.1 Basic Characteristics

9.2.1.1 Subprotocols

The functionality of OSPF can be separated into the following subprocesses:

- Hello subprotocol
- Adjacency establishment
- LSA origination and flushing
- LSA flooding and LSDB maintenance
- Routing table calculation

OSPF uses the Hello subprotocol to discover neighbors and to ensure two-way connectivity between them. Every router periodically sends Hello packets on all its OSPF-enabled interfaces; each interface has an independent Hello timer. Other routers use these Hello packets as an indication that the sending router is alive. Every Hello packet contains a list the neighbors from which the sending router has seen a Hello packet. When it finds its own address in a Hello packet of a remote router, a receiving router can be sure that two-way connectivity is present. See Section 9.2.3.5 for more information on the Hello subprotocol.

Once it has discovered neighbors on an interface, a router must establish formal relationships with them to ensure that the LSDBs of the routers are synchronized before announcing the neighbors in its LSAs. These formal relationships with the neighbors are called *adjacencies* in OSPF.

The adjacency-establishment process is described using a neighbor *finite state machine* (FSM). Part of this process is database synchronization. See Section 9.2.3.8 for more information on adjacency establishment.

After it has established a full adjacency with a neighbor, a router announces this adjacency in its LSA, thus informing other routers about the new link in the network topology. When a piece of information in an LSA changes, the router originates—builds, installs in its LSDB, and floods to other neighbors—a new version of the LSA. If it does not want to originate an LSA, the originating router may flush it from the routing domain (see Section 9.2.3.11 for more details).

Table 9-1. *Comparison of IS-IS and OSPF*

Feature	IS-IS Implementation	OSPF Implementation
Transport protocol for Protocol Data Units	Link-layer 2 protocol	IP
PDU types	IS-IS uses *link-state PDUs* (LSPs). Each router announces one LSP, but each LSP has up to 256 fragments that are originated, stored, and flooded independently. All information announced by the routers is put into the LSP in the form of *type-length-value* triples (TLVs). There are only two types of LSPs—the node LSP announced by every router and the pseudonode LSP announced by the *designated IS* (DIS) to represent the topology of a broadcast segment.	Of the 11 *link-state advertisement* (LSA) types, only the first five are used by the base standard. Adjacency information and internal routes are announced in type 1 LSAs; LAN segments are represented by type 2 LSAs originated by *designated routers* (DRs). Inter-area routes are announced in type 3 LSAs. External destinations are announced by *AS boundary routers* (ASBRs) in type 5 LSAs. Routes to ASBRs in different areas are announced in type 4 LSAs.
LSPDU aging	LSPs are originated with some value in the Age field, and this value is decremented by routers while the LSP is in the LSDB or being flooded over network links. The LSP age cannot go below zero, and when it reaches this value, the router removes the LSP from LSDB. Each LSP must be refreshed every 15 minutes (by default), but this period may be manually configured to a larger value.	LSAs are originated with the Age field containing zero value. While an LSA is being flooded through the network, its Age field is incremented. It is also incremented every second while the LSA is stored in LSDB. The age of the LSA cannot go above 3,600 seconds. Then the LSA is removed from the LSDB. Every LSA must be refreshed at least every 30 minutes. If the DoNotAge OSPF extension is used, this period may be increased to infinity.
Topology abstraction	Topology is abstracted in terms of vertices representing routers and multiaccess networks, and edges representing adjacencies between the routers. An adjacency is announced in an LSP fragment as soon as two routers ensure two-way connectivity between each other.	Topology is abstracted practically in the same way as in IS-IS, but adjacencies are announced only after the neighbors have synchronized their LSDBs, to ensure that the router has all necessary information before it accepts transit traffic.
Flooding	LSPs are reliably flooded over all interfaces except for the one the LSP was received on. LSPs sent over LANs are not explicitly acknowledged by neighbors. Instead, the DIS constantly announces the summary of its database and other routers on the segment understand if they need to resend any LSP or request it from the DIS.	Transmitted LSAs are always acknowledged (explicitly or implicitly). On broadcast links, flooding is always done through the DR. The *backup DR* (BDR) is always ready to take over in case the DR fails to perform its duties.

Table 9-1. *continued*

Feature	IS-IS Implementation	OSPF Implementation
Costs and metrics	Standard IS-IS uses values from 1 to 32 to characterize link preferences. The whole path metric cannot exceed 1024. However, IS-IS was recently extended to introduce wider link costs and metric values through use of new-style TLVs [RFC2966].	OSPF uses 16 bits to announce link cost and 24 bits to announce the metric of inter-area and external routes. The maximum path cost is limited to 16,777,215 (hexadecimal FFFFFF).
Routing table calculation	Standard IS-IS uses optimized Dijkstra calculation that takes advantage of the fact that total path cost cannot exceed 1024. This simplifies sorting of the vertices in the candidate list. With introduction of new-style link costs, IS-IS routers need to use normal Dijkstra calculation with a different sorting method.	OSPF uses normal Dijkstra calculation.
Hierarchical routing	IS-IS allows for two levels of hierarchy. Each adjacency may belong to either level 1 (L1) or level 2 (L2). Any link may be used to establish adjacencies of both types simultaneously. Routers that have only L1 adjacencies are called L1 routers. Similarly, routers that maintain only L2 adjacencies are L2 routers. L1 routers know only the topology of their L1 areas. L2 routers know the topology of the L2 area. To distribute routing information between areas, L1L2 routers announce L1 prefixes in their L2 LSPs. Standard IS-IS does not allow for propagation of L2 prefixes into L1 areas. Instead, L1 areas rely on default routing through the nearest L1L2 router. L2 to L1 route leaking was recently implemented [RFC2966].	OSPF supports a two-level routing hierarchy. An OSPF routing domain may be split into a number of areas. If there is more than one area, one of them must be configured as the backbone (area 0). Routes internal to areas (intra-area routes) are announced to all other areas as inter-area. Inter-area routes from the backbone are reannounced by *area border routers* (ABRs) into other areas. Inter-area routes from other areas are not reannounced.
External routing	IS-IS allows for importing of external routing information through use of TLV 130. All L1L2 routers reannounce external routes to L2 in L2 LSP using TLV 130.	External routing information in OSPF is distributed in type 5 LSAs, which have a domainwide flooding scope to prevent duplication of LSAs by ABRs. Location of ASBRs (redistributing routers) is announced by ABRs across area borders in type 4 LSAs.

Flooding of LSAs in OSPF follows the basic rules described in Section 9.1.3. All routers send the new LSA out of all interfaces except the interface the LSA was received on. When other routers receive the new version of an LSA, they install it in their LSDBs and flood further to their neighbors.

When a new LSA is installed in the LSDB, the router may need to recalculate the routing table because the new LSA may contain a notification about some topology changes or changes in IP routing information. As in any link-state routing protocol, routing table calculation in OSPF is based on the Dijkstra algorithm (see Section 9.1.4 for more details).

9.2.1.2 Structure of OSPF Routing Domain

As a hierarchical routing protocol, OSPF can be used to build a multilevel routing domain, although it is not necessary, and an OSPF domain may be built as a flat network. Routing hierarchy in OSPF is achieved by dividing the whole domain into *areas*, or groups of routers and networks exchanging the topological and routing information; (see Figure 9-6 for an example).

The whole idea of hierarchical routing in OSPF is to hide the details of topology in one area from routers in other areas. OSPF does not propagate topological information across area borders; only routing information is conveyed, preferably in summarized form. Routers with more than one area attached are called *area border routers*, or ABRs.

An OSPF domain that contains more than one area must have an area 0, also called a *backbone area*, and all other areas must have physical or virtual connectivity to it. This allows for successful distribution of inter-area routing information among areas through the backbone. We consider inter-area routing and ABR functionality in more detail later.

In addition to inter-area routing information, OSPF can accept and distribute routing information from external sources, such as static routes, BGP, or other IGPs. Routers injecting external routing information into the domain are called *autonomous system boundary routers*, or ASBRs.

With regards to distribution of external routing information, all areas in OSPF can be divided into the following types:

- *Normal area:* Can accept external routing information from other areas. Normal areas can contain ASBRs and thus serve as transit areas for traffic destined for external destinations.

- *Stub area:* Cannot accept external routing information and cannot contain ASBRs. Routing to external destinations from a stub area is performed by using the default routes announced by the ABRs. Inter-area information may or may not be injected into stub areas, depending on the configuration of the ABRs.

- *Not-so-stubby area* (NSSA): Cannot accept external routing information from the backbone area but can contain ASBRs. NSSAs serve as diodes, allowing external information to flow from ASBRs to the backbone but not in the other direction. Inter-area routing information may or may not be injected into NSSAs, depending on the configuration of the ABRs.

In addition to ABR and ASBR, all routers in an OSPF domain may also be divided into the following types, depending on their location in an OSPF domain.

- *Internal router:* All interfaces of the router are assigned to one area.
- *Backbone router:* The router has at least one interface belonging to the backbone area.

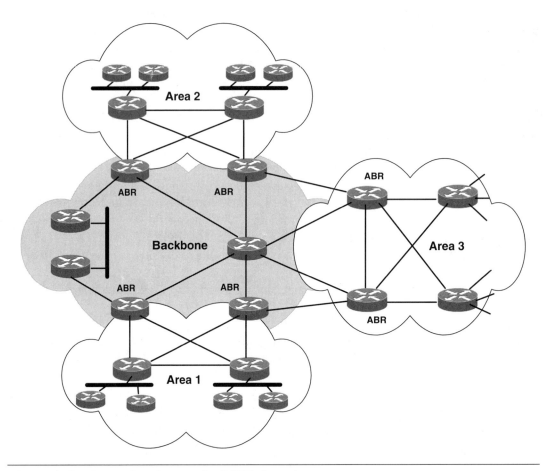

Figure 9-6. *Example of areas in OSPF domain*

For OSPF inter-area routing to work correctly, it is recommended that all ABRs also be backbone routers, that is, have a link belonging to the backbone.

9.2.1.3 Types of Routing within an OSPF Domain
OSPF may provide three types of routes to the routing table:

- *Intra-area route:* Route to a destination internal to a given area
- *Inter-area route:* Route to a destination in another area but still in the same OSPF domain
- *External route:* Route to a destination not internal to the OSPF domain

External routes are further divided into two types: external type 1 and external type 2. The difference between the two is that the metric announced by the ASBR—apparently, the metric imported from the other routing source—for a type 1 route is added to the cost of the path to the ASBR itself when the route metric is calculated. In the case of a type 2 external route, the metric of the route is considered to be the metric announced by the ASBR. The reason for having two types of external routes is that type 1 externals are used when the external metric has a scale similar to the OSPF metric—that is, it makes sense to add external and internal OSPF metrics—whereas type 2 externals are used when the external metric has more weight than the internal cost, as when the number of ASs in the BGP AS_PATH attribute is used as the announced metric.

If there is more than one route to the same destination within an OSPF domain, the route preference is defined as follows, regardless of the value of the route metric.

- Intra-area routes are preferred over inter-area and external routes.
- Inter-area routes are preferred over external routes.
- External type 1 routes are preferred over external type 2 routes.

If all available routes are of the same type, the best route, based on the route metric value, is chosen. When metrics are the same, parallel routes are installed in the routing table for intra-area and inter-area types. Among external routes, the route through the closest ASBR is preferred. (The more accurate path-preference algorithm is explained later.)

9.2.1.4 Route Aggregation
Route aggregation techniques in routing protocols in general and in OSPF in particular are the means of building scalable networks. Route aggregation allows the details of

topology and the underlying address structure to be hidden from different parts of a network and other networks.

OSPF allows route aggregation by

- ABRs, which can be configured to aggregate intra-area routes when announced as inter-area routes. Specifics are not announced if they are covered by an aggregate.
- ASBRs, which can be configured to announce an aggregate route instead of a set of specifics when external routing information is being injected.
- Translating NSSA ABRs. When external routing information is propagated from a not-so-stubby area to the backbone, that information can be aggregated one more time by the ABR connecting the NSSA to the backbone area.

Route aggregation on area borders is vital for large OSPF networks. Without route aggregation, a flap of every single subnet within an area is propagated throughout the whole OSPF domain as a change in an inter-area route. When route aggregation is configured in ABRs, changes in intra-area routing information are mostly hidden from other areas, because specific subnets are aggregated into less specific inter-area routes.

Aggregation of external routing information is possible when external routes are injected into the domain. Without the NSSA option, it is not possible to aggregate external routing information on area borders, as external routes are announced in LSAs that have domainwide flooding scope. NSSA routers use a different type of LSA to distribute external routing information within the NSSA itself. ABRs connecting the NSSA to the backbone area reannounce these external routes as normal to the rest of the OSPF network. Because new LSAs are created when NSSA-external routes are propagated to the backbone, it is possible to further aggregate these routes.

> A general rule for OSPF route aggregation is as follows. Routing information in OSPF can be aggregated only when a new LSA is originated, not when an LSA carrying the routing information is being flooded.

9.2.1.5 Convergence Characteristics

Convergence time in OSPF for the intra-area case is determined by the amount of time routers need to spend on

- Link-failure or neighbor-unreachability detection
- Origination of the new version of an LSA, including the MaxAge version if the LSA is being removed from the domain

- Flooding of the new version of the LSA to all routers
- SPF calculation on all routers

When inter-area routing is considered, installation or removal of a route in the routing table may trigger changes in LSAs. If this happens, the convergence time also includes the time for origination of the new versions of the LSAs and for flooding them through the domain, as well as the time necessary to calculate new inter-area routes in other areas.

Link failure in OSPF may be determined in two ways: from the data link layer or the physical layer—directly reported state change—or through the Hello subprotocol, when the neighbor is removed because the router hasn't heard anything from it during a certain period. The first method is faster: Once the carrier signal disappears for an interface—in the case of serial links, for example—the interface is reported to be down and OSPF is informed. If the data link layer protocol cannot be used for timely failure notification, the Hello subprotocol detects an inoperational adjacency within 40 seconds (configurable).

In most cases when there's more than one path between a pair of routers, it is enough to ensure that one of the neighbors detects the link failure quickly, as OSPF will not use a link to router R2 reported by router R1 if R2 does not report a back link to router R1.

LSA origination is a quick, simple process. According to the OSPF specification, any LSA may be originated not faster than once per MinLSInterval seconds. MinLSInterval is an architectural constant for OSPF and equals 1 second. Cisco routers honor this LSA origination pacing behavior.

The time necessary for LSA flooding is not constant but rather it is a function of multiple parameters, including but not limited to the number of LSAs to flood, the complexity of the network topology, the bandwidth and reliability of the network links, and the CPU power of the routers. The good news is that the flooding algorithm is really flooding. This means that even if it cannot be sent to a router using a direct link, an LSA will be delivered to the router through another link by another router—if, of course, there is a redundancy. If no retransmissions occur, the flooding time consists of the link delays and the processing overhead. If some OSPF packets get lost and routers start retransmitting, flooding time includes the retransmit interval (5 seconds).

The route calculation time should be considered as a sum of the delay from the moment when a new or new version of an LSA has been installed and the moment when the actual route calculation algorithm starts, plus the time necessary to perform the Dijkstra calculation and to change routing information. By default, the first component is 5 seconds. Cisco routers wait for 5 seconds before starting route calculation. This hold time helps avoid excessive route calculations in the case when the LSDB is updated frequently. The second component of the delay is the function of the number of routers and links in the networks, as well as the number of IP subnets announced. With a reasonable number—on the order of hundreds of routers in an area—and default timer configuration, OSPF should be able to converge within 10–20 seconds in one area after a single topology change, excluding the time necessary for detection of inactive neighbors.

It is possible to detect inactive neighbors in fewer than 40 seconds if all routers on the segment are configured with smaller Hello interval values. The SPF calculation delay may also be changed from 5 seconds to a lower value. This will provide faster network convergence in response to a single topology change but may put more load on the CPU if the network experiences some instability, such as a flapping link or route.

9.2.2 General Data Structures

Cisco OSPF implementation deals with the following data structures, which are generic for the OSPF protocol, but some implementation-specific details are also discussed. The *OSPF protocol global data structure*, represented by a special information block linked to the OSPF protocol descriptor, holds information global to the whole instance of OSPF in a router. There may be more than one instance of this data block in a router if more than one OSPF process is configured. Every time a **router ospf** *process-id* command is entered, a new OSPF information block is created. This data block contains the following main information, which can be shown by using the **show ip ospf** command:

- *Router-ID*, a configurable 32-bit number uniquely identifying the router within the OSPF domain. This number is used by the Hello protocol, during LSA origination, Dijkstra calculation, and other OSPF procedures.

- *List of areas*, a list of *area data structures* corresponding to each area the router is connected to.

- *Backbone area*, a pointer to the backbone area data structure, whose area ID is set to 0. This pointer is used by the router if it is performing ABR functionality.

- *External LSDB*, the database containing LSAs carrying external routing information, considered in more detail later.

- *Router routing table*, an internal OSPF structure containing entries that describe remote OSPF routers, or router routing entries. This information is used as an intermediate result for inter-area and external route calculation and contains routes to ABRs and ASBRs.

> Network routing entries are stored in the main routing table; OSPF does not have its own internal routing table.

- *Interface cost calculation flags*, configurable flags and variables used to automatically calculate link costs.

- *Default metric*, a configurable value of the metric used for route redistribution by default.

- *Default origination flags*, configurable flags specifying whether the router should inject the default route as an external LSA into the domain and associated parameters.

- *SPF wait and hold intervals*, configurable values specifying the amount of time that should elapse between the SPF calculation request and the Dijkstra calculation.

- *ABR/ASBR flags*, internally used flags indicating that the router is performing ABR or ASBR functions. The ABR flag is set when the router has more than one area attached and an active backbone connection. The ASBR flag is set when the router is configured to perform redistribution of external routing information.

To enable OSPF on a particular interface, the administrator needs to enter a **network** command covering that interface's primary IP address. A parameter to this command is the area number. Whenever OSPF is enabled on a new interface, the interface is assigned to a particular area, and a pointer to that interface's interface descriptor is put in the list of interfaces in that area. If, when OSPF is enabled on an interface, the referenced area does not exist, a new area data structure is created for the area. The area data structure contains the following information, also shown in the output of the **show ip ospf** command:

- *Area ID*, a 32-bit number uniquely identifying the area within the OSPF domain. The area ID is put into OSPF Hello packets. If neighboring routers do not agree on the area ID, they will not form adjacencies.

- *Stub area flag*, a flag specifying that the area does not accept external routing information and cannot contain an ASBR (see Section 9.2.5.5). Routers within the area must agree on the state of this flag. Otherwise, they will not form the adjacencies.

- *NSSA flag*, a flag specifying that the area does not accept external routing information from the backbone but can be used to inject external routes in the reverse direction (see Section 9.2.5.6 for information on not-so-stubby areas). All routers within the area must agree on the state of this flag to successfully form an adjacency.

- *No-summary flag*, a flag indicating that if the router is an ABR connecting a stub or an NSSA area to the backbone, the router should not inject any inter-area routes into this area except the default summary. This ABR-specific flag is not announced in any OSPF packets.

- *No-redistribution NSSA flag*, a flag used to instruct the router not to inject type 7 LSAs if the router is both ABR and ASBR for that not-so-stubby area and is configured to do route redistribution.

- *NSSA default origination flag*, a flag instructing the NSSA ABR to inject the type 7 default into the NSSA.

- *NSSA ABR translation flag*, a dynamic flag specifying whether the NSSA ABR is supposed to perform type 7–to–type 5 LSA translation.

- *Interface list*, a list of all interfaces belonging to the area.

- *List of area ranges*, a list of area ranges used if the router is an ABR to aggregate intra-area routing information when announcing it as inter-area to other areas.

- *Area LSDB*, the database of the LSAs that have area-local flooding scope. See Section 9.2.3.9 for more information on LSAs used for intra-area routing.

- *SPF calculation flags*, flags indicating that the Dijkstra algorithm should be recalculated as soon as possible. These flags are used internally.

- *Area candidate list*, a list of candidate vertices used internally during Dijkstra calculation for the area.

- *List of virtual links crossing this area*, a list of configured virtual links crossing the area. The state of the virtual links depends on connectivity inside the area. See Section 9.2.4.5 for more details.

Listing 9-2 shows output of the **show ip ospf** command, which can be used to display OSPF global and area-specific data structures.

```
R1#sho ip ospf
 Routing Process "ospf 1" with ID 1.1.1.1
 Supports only single TOS(TOS0) routes
 It is an area border and autonomous system boundary router
 Summary Link update interval is 00:30:00 and the update due in 00:17:38
 External Link update interval is 00:30:00 and the update due in 00:16:22
 Redistributing External Routes from,
 SPF schedule delay 5 secs, Hold time between two SPFs 10 secs
 Number of DCbitless external LSA 0
 Number of DoNotAge external LSA 0
 Number of areas in this router is 2. 1 normal 0 stub 1 nssa
    Area BACKBONE(0)
        Number of interfaces in this area is 2
        Area has no authentication
        SPF algorithm executed 32 times
        Area ranges are
           10.0.0.0/8 Active(0)
        Link State Update Interval is 00:30:00 and due in 00:17:37
        Link State Age Interval is 00:20:00 and due in 00:17:29
```

```
        Number of DCbitless LSA 0
        Number of indication LSA 0
        Number of DoNotAge LSA 0
    Area 1
        Number of interfaces in this area is 2
        It is a NSSA area
        Area has no authentication
        SPF algorithm executed 27 times
        Area ranges are
           30.0.0.0/8 Active(1)
        Link State Update Interval is 00:30:00 and due in 00:17:35
        Link State Age Interval is 00:20:00 and due in 00:17:29
        Router LSA rebuild timer due in 00:01:31
        Number of DCbitless LSA 0
        Number of indication LSA 0
        Number of DoNotAge LSA 0

R1#
```

Listing 9-2. *Output of the* **show ip ospf** *command*

Every interface on which OSPF is enabled has an instance of the OSPF interface data structure linked to a corresponding interface descriptor. The interface data structure contains the following information:

- *Interface type*, which may be one of the following: point-to-point, the default for serial interfaces; point-to-multipoint, which must be manually configured; broadcast, the default for LAN interfaces; nonbroadcast, the default for interfaces using NBMA encapsulation, such as X.25 or Frame Relay; virtual link, used to identify configured virtual links; or loopback, used for loopback interfaces.

- *State*, current FSM state of the interface; used in the adjacency establishment process (see Section 9.2.3.6) and when LSAs are originated (see Section 9.2.3.9); OSPF maintains an instance of the interface FSM for every interface.

- *Interface IP address*, used by the OSPF process as the source IP address for the packets sent over the interface and as the interface identifier during LSA origination. This is the primary IP address of the interface in Cisco IOS. Secondary IP addresses are not used to send OSPF packets, but associated subnets are announced in the router-LSA.

> Cisco routers need to agree on which IP network is the primary. Otherwise, they will not be able to establish OSPF adjacencies.

- *Interface mask*, the address mask associated with the primary IP address of the interface. This mask is used to validate incoming OSPF packets on LAN interfaces (see Section 9.2.3.3) and is also used as the route mask when a directly connected subnet is announced in the router-LSA.

- *Area,* a link to the area data structure to which the interface belongs. The OSPF process checks whether the area ID in the received packets matches the ID of the area associated with the receiving interface.

- *Hello interval,* the number of seconds between two consecutive Hello packets sent over the interface. This interval is announced by OSPF in Hello packets. Routers on a common segment must agree on the value of this interval. The default value for this interval is 10 seconds for LAN and 30 seconds for NBMA interfaces.

- *Dead interval,* the amount of time (in seconds) that is used to identify unreachable neighbors on this interface. If the router does not receive a Hello packet from a particular neighbor during this interval, the neighbor is declared down. The Dead interval is announced in Hello packets. Routers must agree on the value of this interval to successfully establish adjacencies. The default value for the Dead interval is four times the Hello interval.

- *Router priority,* an integer (0 to 255) used during the designated router election process (see Section 9.2.3.7 for more details). Router priority is announced in Hello packets.

- *Hello timer,* the periodic timer firing every Hello interval and causing the OSPF process to send a Hello packet over the interface. See Section 9.2.3.5 for more information on the Hello subprotocol.

- *Wait timer,* the timer started when an interface to a broadcast segment goes up and the interface FSM transitions to the Waiting state. Expiration of the timer causes the interface FSM to go out of the Waiting state. See Section 9.2.3.6 for more information about the interface FSM.

- *List of neighbors,* the linked list of neighbor data structures associated with the interface.

- *List of configured neighbors,* the linked list of manually configured neighbors. Manual neighbor configuration may be necessary when the media the interface is attached to does not provide broadcast capability, which prevents automatic neighbor discovery.

- *Designated router,* the interface IP address of the router that was designated for the segment connected to the interface. This address is announced in OSPF Hello packets.

- *Backup designated router,* the interface IP address of the router that was elected to be the designated router for the segment connected to the interface. This address is announced in OSPF Hello packets.

- *Interface cost,* an integer (0 to 65,535) defining the cost of sending packets over the interface. This value is used when adjacencies are announced in router-LSAs (see Section 9.2.3.9 for more details). The sum of link costs also constitutes the path cost used as the route metric by OSPF.

- *Retransmit interval,* the amount of time used for retransmit timers of the adjacencies belonging to the interface. The default value of this interval is 5 seconds.

- *Demand circuit flag,* the flag identifying the interface as the demand circuit, such as Dialer or BRI interfaces. See Section 9.2.7 for more details on OSPF demand circuit.

- *Authentication type,* the type of authentication algorithm used on this interface. It can be plaintext or MD5. See Section 9.2.9 for more information on how to configure OSPF authentication.

- *Authentication key,* the data used by the OSPF authentication procedure to generate and to validate authentication information for OSPF packets.

Values of the described fields of the OSPF interface data structure can be displayed by using the **show ip ospf interface** command (see Listing 9-3 for an example). Note that the Neighbor Count and the Adjacent neighbor count values differ. The reason is that not all OSPF conversations are progressed to adjacencies. Some of them can never develop, because there is no two-way communication between neighbors, and the remote router cannot see the Hello packets from the router on which the command is issued. On broadcast segments, a subset of OSPF conversations is explicitly held in a standby mode to minimize the flooding overhead between the neighbors. See Section 9.2.3.8 for more information.

```
R1#sho ip ospf int fddi4/0
Fddi4/0 is up, line protocol is up
  Internet Address 30.0.1.2/24, Area 1
  Process ID 1, Router ID 30.0.1.2, Network Type BROADCAST, Cost: 1
  Transmit Delay is 1 sec, State DR, Priority 1
  Designated Router (ID) 30.0.1.2, Interface address 30.0.1.2
  Backup Designated router (ID) 5.5.5.5, Interface address 30.0.1.1
  Timer intervals configured, Hello 10, Dead 40, Wait 40, Retransmit 5
    Hello due in 00:00:08
  Neighbor Count is 1, Adjacent neighbor count is 1
    Adjacent with neighbor 5.5.5.5  (Backup Designated Router)
R1#
```

Listing 9-3. *Output of the* **show ip ospf interface** *command*

When it receives a Hello packet from an unknown neighbor on an interface, a router creates an instance of the neighbor data structure for the neighbor and links it to the corresponding interface. Neighbor data structures are also created for manually configured neighbors. Each neighbor is identified either by the Router-ID—on point-to-point networks—or by the interface IP address—on broadcast, NBMA, and point-to-multipoint networks.

> Instances of the neighbor data structure should be considered informational blocks holding data necessary for the router to maintain adjacency with the neighbor. Some fields in this block describe the neighbor itself, whereas others are used locally to communicate with the neighbor and to perform such functions as database synchronization and flooding.

Each instance of the neighbor data structure contains the following fields:

- *Neighbor ID*, or Router-ID of the neighbor. This field is set to the value from the Hello packet when the neighbor data structure is created and every time a Hello packet is received.

- *Neighbor IP address*, the interface IP address of the neighbor. This address, learned through the Hello protocol or configured manually, is used as the destination address in the unicast packets sent directly to the neighbor.

- *Neighbor state* of the neighbor FSM, describing the functional state of the adjacency as considered by the local router itself. See Section 9.2.3.8 for more information on the adjacency establishment process.

- *Dead timer*, the timer rescheduled every time a Hello packet is received from the neighbor. Expiration of this timer indicates that the router has not received Hello packets from the neighbor during the Dead interval and that the neighbor must be reported down.

- *Retransmit timer*, the timer causing the router to retransmit LSAs from the neighbor's retransmit list. Acknowledged LSAs are removed from the list; periodic retransmission of unacknowledged LSAs ensures that LSAs are flooded reliably.

- *Poll timer*, the timer used to send Hellos to unreachable neighbors less frequently if they are supposed to be connected to an NBMA cloud.

- *DD retransmit timer*, the timer causing the router to retransmit the database description while synchronizing the LSDB (see Section 9.2.3.8 for details).

- *DD sequence number*, the sequence number chosen by the router for the neighbor and sent in database description packets.

- *Master/Slave flags*, flags defining the role of the router in the database-synchronization process.

- *Neighbor priority*, the interface priority associated with the neighbor. This value is used by the router during the process of DR and BDR election. For dynamically discovered neighbors, this value is taken from Hello packets received on the interface. For neighbors configured manually, the value of the neighbor's priority can be explicitly specified.

- *Neighbor's DR*, the IP address of the router elected as the DR by the neighbor. This address is taken from the Hello packet received from the neighbor.

- *Neighbor's BDR*, the IP address of the router elected as the BDR by the neighbor. This address also is taken from the Hello packet received from the neighbor.

- *Neighbor options*, the OSPF options announced by the neighbor. See Section 9.2.3.4 for details.

- *Neighbor cost*, usually the cost of the interface, but in the case of an NBMA cloud, when neighbors are configured manually, each neighbor may be configured with a different cost.

- *Hello suppression flag*, the flag indicating that the Hellos are suppressed on this link. Hello suppression is a part of demand circuit extension to OSPF. See Section 9.2.7 for more details.

- *Link-state retransmission list*, a list of pointers to LSAs that must be flooded to the neighbor and that were not acknowledged by it. LSAs are put on this link as part of the flooding procedure after being installed in the router's LSDB and are removed from it when they are acknowledged by the neighbor. See Section 9.2.3.11 for details.

- *Database summary list*, the list of LSA headers present in the router's LSDBs at the moment the adjacency has reached the state when database descriptions must be exchanged. The database summary is sent to the neighbor to describe the contents of the router's LSDB. The neighbor can then request LSAs that it needs to install.

- *Link-state request list*, the list of LSA headers that must be requested from the neighbor to synchronize LSDBs. The router puts items on this list after receiving and processing database description packets containing database summaries.

The contents of the OSPF neighbor data structure can be displayed by using the **show ip ospf neighbor** command (Listing 9-4).

```
R2#sho ip ospf ne

Neighbor ID     Pri   State              Dead Time   Address      Interface
N/A             0     ATTEMPT/DROTHER    00:01:39    10.1.1.4     Serial2/2
6.6.6.6         0     2WAY/DROTHER       00:01:45    10.1.1.6     Serial2/2
30.0.1.2        1     FULL/DR            00:01:57    10.1.1.1     Serial2/2
```

```
R2#sho ip ospf ne det
 Neighbor N/A, interface address 10.1.1.4
    In the area 0 via interface Serial2/2
    Neighbor priority is 0, State is ATTEMPT
    Poll interval 60
    Options 0
    Dead timer due in 00:01:37
 Neighbor 6.6.6.6, interface address 10.1.1.6
    In the area 0 via interface Serial2/2
    Neighbor priority is 0, State is 2WAY
    Poll interval 60
    Options 2
    Dead timer due in 00:01:43
 Neighbor 30.0.1.2, interface address 10.1.1.1
    In the area 0 via interface Serial2/2
    Neighbor priority is 1, State is FULL
    Poll interval 60
    Options 2
    Dead timer due in 00:01:54
R2#
```

Listing 9-4. *Output of* **show ip ospf neighbor** *command*

The data structures are used by the OSPF protocol to maintain adjacencies with the neighbors, to generate and flood LSAs, and to calculate routing information. Details of these processes follows.

9.2.3 Intra-Area Routing

OSPF provides routing information for destinations residing within the same area, in other areas, and outside the OSPF domain. The major part of OSPF functionality covers intra-area routing, which includes the adjacency-establishment process, topology abstraction, LSA generation, and LSA flooding and intra-area route calculation. All other parts of OSPF functionality rely on intra-area routing.

> Splitting OSPF domains into areas is not obligatory. If an OSPF domain is not split into areas, no routers will perform any type of inter-area functionality, and only intra-area—and, probably, AS-external—functions will be performed.

9.2.3.1 Overview of Intra-Area OSPF Functionality

Following are the main functions OSPF routers perform while participating in intra-area routing:

- Neighbor discovery

- Neighbor relationship maintenance
- Topology abstraction and distribution of routing information, including LSA origination
- LSDB synchronization via initial LSA exchange and asynchronous LSA flooding
- Routing table calculation

These functions are performed by the following OSPF subprocesses, whose cooperation is considered later.

- Interface maintenance
- Neighbor discovery and maintenance, including initial LSDB synchronization procedure
- LSA origination
- Asynchronous flooding
- Route calculation

All these functions, except for route calculation, imply exchange of protocol packets. Figure 9-7 outlines cooperation of OSPF subprocesses.

Neighbor discovery, as well as neighbor and interface maintenance, are tightly connected to the processing of Hello packets. By sending Hello packets, OSPF routers identify themselves on the network segments. By listening to Hello packets, OSPF routers discover their direct neighbors. Routers also use Hello packets to ensure two-way connectivity. Election of designated and backup designated routers is also based on the information provided in Hello packets. Results of the election are announced to all other routers in Hello packets as well. See Section 9.2.3.5 for more details on the Hello subprocess.

The neighbor maintenance process implements the OSPF's neighbor FSM (see Section 9.2.3.8), which includes initial LSDB synchronization. When two routers decide to form an adjacency, they send each other summaries of their LSDBs in the database description packets. Once they have a complete description of the peers' LSDBs, both routers exchange LSAs, using link-state request and link-state update packets.

Link-state update packets are also used by the flooding subprocess. The function of this subprocess is to ensure LSDB synchronization in the presence of asynchronous LSDB changes after initial synchronization of the neighbors. LSAs sent in link-state update packets are always acknowledged by the receiving router, using link-state acknowledgment packets. Reliability of OSPF flooding is ensured by periodic retransmission of unacknowledged LSAs.

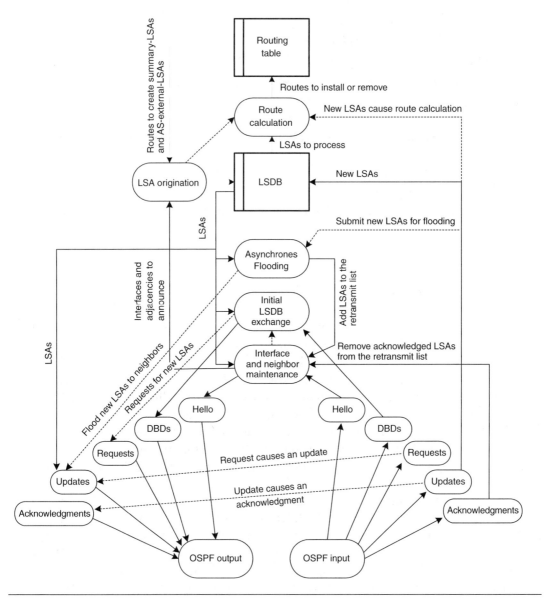

Figure 9-7. *Subprocesses within OSPF*

When new LSAs are installed into the LSDB, partial or full routing table calculation is scheduled. OSPF uses the Dijkstra algorithm to calculate the SPT over the topology graph. The algorithm then goes over all reachable vertices and considers announced IP prefixes, choosing the best, based on the summary path cost. See Section 9.2.3.12 for more details on intra-area route calculation in OSPF.

9.2.3.2 Types of Networks and Topology Abstraction

Although Cisco IOS has only four types of interfaces—point-to-point, multipoint, broadcast, and loopback—OSPF has its own network types. These network types affect the way OSPF routers exchange their packets, establish adjacencies, and represent the topology and routing information.

Point-to-Point Networks.   This network type is the default for physical point-to-point interfaces. All routers connected via point-to-point interfaces become adjacent. No DR/BDR election is performed for this type. Each router reports an adjacency to the corresponding neighbor in its router-LSA; thus, the topology graph will have two contradirectional links for each point-to-point network. The cost of adjacency is set to the interface output cost.

> The fact that every adjacency is announced by both routers is very important because neighbor FSMs on both ends of the link are asynchronous; whereas one router may think that the adjacency is already established, the other one may still be requesting LSAs to update its LSDB and thus not considering the adjacency to be fully established and not reporting it. To enforce this, the Dijkstra calculation does not consider any adjacencies that are not backed up with corresponding back links. This rule is generic for all types of networks and helps OSPF converge more quickly when, for example, one router loses its connection to a broadcast segment and reports this failure right away, whereas its neighbors need to wait for RouterDeadInterval seconds before they realize that the router is not reachable.

Each router also announces the IP subnet associated with the interface in its router-LSA, if such a subnet is assigned at all—the interface is not unnumbered. It is interesting that if no IP subnet is assigned to the interface, only adjacencies are reported; that is, the interface is represented only as a topological entity providing some sort of connectivity between routers, not as an IP subnet (see Figure 9-8).

> The OSPF standard contains two options that can be used to announce routing information on point-to-point links. The first option, considered legacy, instructs each router to announce a host route to the neighboring router's address. The second option allows routers to announce their own assigned subnets. Cisco routers use the second option; that is, they announce assigned subnets.

Broadcast Networks.   This is the default type for all LAN interfaces. This network type presumes broadcast capability of attached media and two-way connectivity between any pair of routers, which is very important. OSPF elects a DR and a BDR for every LAN seg-

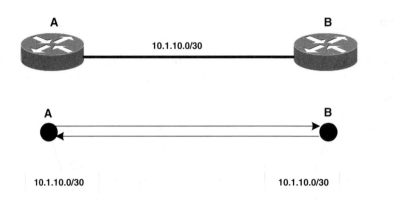

Figure 9-8. *Announcing topological and routing information for point-to-point networks*

ment. All nondesignated routers establish adjacencies only with the DR and the BDR. This allows for reduction of the number of adjacencies from $n*(n-1)$, where n is the number of routers on a segments, to $(n-2)*2+1$. This also reduces the number of adjacencies reported in router-LSAs and the complexity of the Dijkstra calculation.

Topology abstraction for broadcast networks is different from that for point-to-point links. Instead of having every router report every adjacent neighbor, the DR originates a network-LSA on behalf of the broadcast segment. The network-LSA represents the segment itself and lists all neighbors adjacent to the DR, as well as the DR itself. Also, the DR, as well as every router fully adjacent to it, reports a link to the segment referencing the network-LSA, with the cost equal to the interface output cost (Figure 9-9).

In the case of broadcast segments, routing information is announced in the network-LSAs. Routers do not include any IP reachability information in their router-LSAs for broadcast segments, except when no fully adjacent neighbor is yet known on the interface, and it is thus considered and announced as a stub subnet rather than as a transit segment.

NBMA Networks. This OSPF network type is used by default on interfaces configured with Frame Relay, SMDS, ATM, or ATM DXI as their encapsulation methods. OSPF NBMA mode is in fact an emulation of broadcast operation, with considerable optimization of protocol packet exchange rules. OSPF elects the DR and the BDR for NBMA clouds, so the mesh of VCs between neighboring routers is represented as effectively as in the case of broadcast networks, with a network-LSA originated by the DR.

NBMA mode is very effective in terms of amount of protocol traffic and LSA size. However, a very serious restriction must be met for the NBMA mode: All routers connected to the NBMA cloud must be able to reach one another directly. The reason is that OSPF installs routes to the networks reachable through the NBMA network, setting the

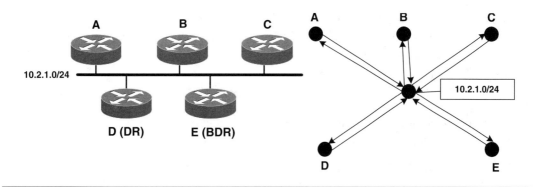

Figure 9-9. *Announcing topological and routing information for broadcast networks*

next hop to the interface IP address of the router that announced a remote network, not the DR. So, if a router can reach the DR and the BDR but cannot reach another router directly, OSPF will install the route in the routing table, but this route will not be used, as there will be no mapping between the next hop and a VC.

> If fully meshed topology of VCs is not available for the routers attached to an NBMA cloud, OSPF will not operate properly.

It is clear that this restriction cannot always be met. Two alternative methods can be used instead of NBMA mode when only a partial mesh of VCs is available.

- The first alternative is to create subinterfaces and to assign VCs to them. Point-to-point subinterfaces can be associated with a single VC only and are considered by OSPF as point-to-point networks. Multipoint subinterfaces are associated with a group of interfaces and are treated as NBMA networks by default. (This makes sense, as in most cases, partial-mesh topologies can be represented as a set of point-to-point subinterfaces and a number of multipoint subinterfaces associated with fully meshed regions.) The disadvantages of this method are configuration overhead and the need to assign a separate subnet to each subinterface, although point-to-point subinterfaces can be unnumbered.
- The second alternative, which can be used for both WAN interfaces and multipoint subinterfaces, is point-to-multipoint mode.

Point-to-Multipoint Networks.   Any OSPF-enabled WAN interface can be configured to operate in point-to-multipoint mode. After that, all adjacencies over this interface are treated as point-to-point. No DR or BDR is elected, and no network-LSA is originated.

Topological information is abstracted as if every adjacency were a point-to-point link; that is, every router reports connectivity to every adjacent router in its router-LSA. To distribute IP routing information, every router announces its own IP addresses, including secondary ones, as host routes in its router-LSA.

The point-to-multipoint method has the following advantages.

- Routers do not need to be connected in a fully meshed manner.
- A single subnet can still be assigned to the whole cloud.
- The topology of reported adjacencies reflects the topology of VCs within the cloud. Neighbors may be configured with different costs, so the paths through VCs are preferred—if other links in the paths do not prevent this, of course.

Note that all routers connected to the NBMA cloud must be configured to operate in point-to-multipoint mode. Otherwise, adjacencies between routers may not be formed.

Figure 9-10 illustrates how topological and routing information is announced in the case of a point-to-multipoint network.

Virtual Links.   Links of this type are used by OSPF internally for special adjacencies between ABRs (see Section 9.2.3.13 for details). No physical interface may be configured to operate in the mode. Virtual links are reported by OSPF routers only as topological entities; no routing information is associated with them or announced.

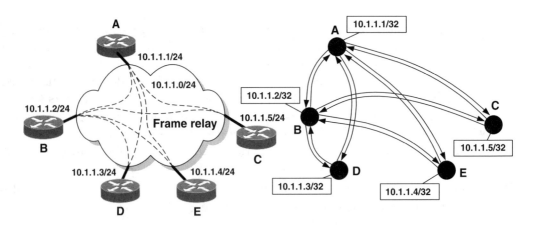

Figure 9-10. *Announcing topological and routing information for point-to-
       multipoint networks*

Interfaces in Loopback State. Although there is no separate loopback network type in OSPF, OSPF treats interfaces in this state in a special way. An interface can be in the loopback state because it is either a loopback interface in IOS or a physical interface that was looped back at the physical or logical level.

OSPF establishes no adjacencies over the interfaces in the Loopback state, as they do not provide connectivity to any other routers. However, it is still necessary to announce the interface's IP address, which can be used for testing purposes. To accomplish this, OSPF routers include in their router LSAs a host route to the IP address of every interface in Loopback state.

> Cisco routers can be configured to announce a route to the subnet assigned to a loopback interface instead of a host route to the interface IP address. See Section 9.2.9.3 for more information.

9.2.3.3 OSPF Transport Protocol and Packet Formats

Except for route calculation, all functions performed by OSPF imply exchange of protocol packets. OSPF runs directly over IP, using protocol ID 89. All OSPF packets start with a common 24-byte header, depicted in Figure 9-11. OSPF header fields are described as follows:

- Version, the OSPF version. The current version of OSPF for IPv4 is 2. OSPFv3 was designed to distribute IPv6 routing information.
- Type, the OSPF packet type. OSPFv2 uses five types of packets:
  - Type 1: *Hello*. Packets of this type are used for OSPF neighbor discovery and maintenance. See Section 9.2.3.5 for details.

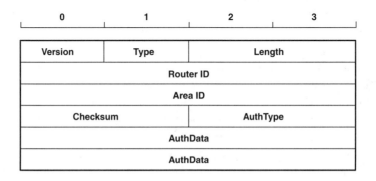

Figure 9-11. *OSPF packet header*

- Type 2: *Database description* (DBD). DBD packets are used during initial LSDB synchronization to exchange database summaries between the routers. See Section 9.2.3.8 for details.

- Type 3: *Link-state request*. Link-state requests are used during the initial LSDB synchronization process to request new LSAs from the neighboring router. See Section 9.2.3.8 for details.

- Type 4: *Link-state update*. Link-state update packets are used as a means of exchanging LSAs between the routers. See Section 9.2.3.8 for details.

- Type 5: *Link-state acknowledgment*. Packets of this type are used to acknowledge reception of an LSA. Use of acknowledgments ensures reliable flooding in OSPF.

- Length, the length of the OSPF packet, including the header.

- Router-ID, the ID of the sending router.

- Area ID, the ID of the area to which the outgoing interface of the sending router belongs. Each incoming OSPF packet is associated with a certain area, interface, and neighbor. Note that routers must agree on the area ID to form an adjacency over a link. Also note that this field is always set to 0 for the packets sent over the virtual links. See Section 9.2.4.5 for information on virtual links in OSPF.

- Checksum, the checksum calculated over the entire OSPF packet, using the standard IP checksum algorithm: "16-bit one's complement of one's complement sum of all 16-bit words in the packet," as stated in the standard. Note that the authentication field is not covered by the checksum.

- AuthType, the type of authentication—cleartext or MD5—used when the packet was created.

- AuthData, the data used by the authentication method identified by the AuthType field. The information in the AuthData field varies, depending on the method of authentication.

All OSPF packets are sent either as unicasts to the neighbors' addresses or as multicasts to one of the registered link-local IP multicast addresses: AllSPFRouters (224.0.0.5) and AllDRouters (224.0.0.6). The first multicast address is used to send OSPF packets to all OSPF routers connected to a link. The second addresses only the designated and backup designated routers of the LAN segment.

All OSPF routers listen for OSPF packets coming on OSPF-enabled interfaces to the AllSPFRouters address. If it was elected as the designated or the backup designated router, a router also starts listening to the address AllDRouters.

The OSPF standard does not specify any method for fragmenting transmitted information. Because OSPF works over IP, the standard IP fragmentation procedure is used if a large OSPF packet is sent. However, the standard recommends using packets no larger than the interface MTU size. When necessary and possible, information about LSAs should be split into several separate packets to keep them small. Cisco routers honor this recommendation.

When OSPF packets are submitted to the IP layer, the IP precedence field of the IP header is set to Internetwork Control, and the TOS field is set to Normal. Inside Cisco routers, OSPF packets have a higher priority than data packets when sent over an interface. This ensures that convergence of the router protocol is affected as little as possible by user data traffic.

All received OSPF packets are processed on the basis of their types. However, every router must first perform generic packet processing for every OSPF packet. It is understood that before an OSPF packet ever comes to the OSPF process, the IP packet it is encapsulated in must have passed all generic IP checks. The steps of OSPF generic input packet processing follow.

1. If OSPF is not enabled on the interface the packet was received on, the packet is dropped and a message is logged. This may happen, for example, when OSPF packets are received on an interface configured with a **passive-interface** command.

    In contrast with distance-vector protocols, the **passive-interface** command in OSPF prevents the router from both learning and announcing any routes through the interface.

2. If the length of the packet is smaller than that of the standard OSPF header or greater than the length reported in the IP header, the packet is dropped and a message is logged. If this error is ever seen, the IP or OSPF software has severe problems.

3. The OSPF packet checksum is verified. The checksum is calculated for the entire OSPF packet contents except for the Checksum and Authentication fields. If the calculated checksum value does not correspond to the received one, the packet is dropped and an error message is logged.

    If link-layer equipment (LAN or ATM switches) function properly, OSPF checksum errors should appear only in the case of damaged router memory; if an OSPF packet is corrupted somewhere in the media, the link-layer FCS should indicate the corruption with very high probability. However, in nearly all cases in which this error is seen, it actually does indicate problems with intermediate switches.

4. The OSPF version is verified. If the version specified in the packet is not 2, the packet is dropped and an error message is logged. It is practically impossible to see this message in live networks, as OSPFv1 was never used in production and is not supported by any vendor.

5. The area ID in the packet is verified. If the area ID received in the packet matches that of the interface, OSPF checks the source IP address of the packet. If the source address does not belong to the primary subnet assigned to the interface and the interface is not point-to-point, the packet is dropped. Routers must agree on the subnet in the case of broadcast of NBMA media, because routing information associated with these types of networks is announced only in the network-LSA.

6. If the area ID in the packet does not match that of the area the receiving interface belongs to, the only valid case is if the packet was sent over a virtual link (VL). If this is true, the area ID in the packet must be set to 0, indicating the backbone, and the Router-ID in the packet must match that configured for one of the VLs. If these conditions are met, the packet is associated with the corresponding VL from now on. If any of these conditions is not met, an error message is logged and the packet is dropped.

7. Authentication data is checked. If the authentication check fails, OSPF drops the packet and logs an error message.

If the packet goes through all the checks successfully, it is submitted for further processing to other subprocesses within OSPF, depending on the type of the packet.

9.2.3.4 Options Field

OSPF uses the Options field to exchange information about router capabilities. This field is present in OSPF Hello packets, DBD packets, and all LSAs. The semantics of the bits in the Options field vary, depending on the context. When used in Hello packets, this field allows OSPF routers to determine whether they can establish adjacencies with neighboring routers (used in the cases of stub areas and NSSA). Potentially, this field may also be used by routers to temporarily signal some events across a single link. The Options field in the DBD packets is used to permanently associate a capability with a specific neighbor. When used in the LSAs, this field allows the capabilities to be announced throughout the whole OSPF area or domain. Figure 9-12 illustrates the format of the Options field.

Figure 9-12. *OSPF Options field*

The functionality of the bits in the Options field is defined as follows:

- *E* (for external) *bit:* Used to announce the capability of processing AS-external-LSAs. Routers clear this bit if the corresponding area is configured as stub or NSSA.

- *MC bit:* Used by *multicast OSPF* (MOSPF) to announce the multicast capability of the router. Cisco IOS does not support MOSPF.

- *N/P bit:* Used in NSSA areas to make sure that routers agree on area configuration—when used as *N* bit in Hello and DBD packets—and to instruct NSSA ABRs whether a type 7 LSA should be translated—when used as the *P* bit in the LSAs. See Section 9.2.5.6 for more information.

- *DC bit:* Used in OSPF demand circuit extensions to negotiate Hello suppression on a link—when used in Hello packets—and to announce the capability of processing so-called DoNotAge (DNA) LSAs. See Section 9.2.7 for more information.

- *O bit:* Used to announce the capability of supporting opaque-LSAs used to distribute information via the OSPF flooding mechanism by some other applications.

Bits in the Options field are used for various purposes within OSPF. For routers to establish adjacencies, they must agree on bits E and N. All other bits may or may not be set, depending on routers' capabilities.

9.2.3.5 Hello Subprotocol
The Hello subprotocol is intended to perform the following tasks within OSPF:

- Provide a means for dynamic neighbor discovery
- Detect unreachable neighbors within a finite period of time
- Ensure two-way connectivity between neighbors
- Ensure correctness of basic interface parameters between the neighbors
- Provide information necessary for the election of designated and backup designated routers on a LAN segment

All OSPF Hello packets have the predefined format shown in Figure 9-13.

As with all OSPF packets, Hello packets start with the standard OSPF header. Descriptions of other fields in Hello packets follow.

- *Network mask* contains the address mask configured on the router's interface. Neighboring routers connected to a broadcast segment must agree on this value to form an adjacency.

OSPF requires identical subnet configuration from routers connected to a common LAN segment because IP routing information is announced in the network-LSA, not in the router-LSAs of the connected routers. If some routers have a different subnet configured for interfaces attached to the LAN segment, information about that subnet will be lost.

- *Hello interval* is the length, in seconds, of the period that routers wait before sending the next Hello packet. Routers must be configured with the same value to establish adjacencies.

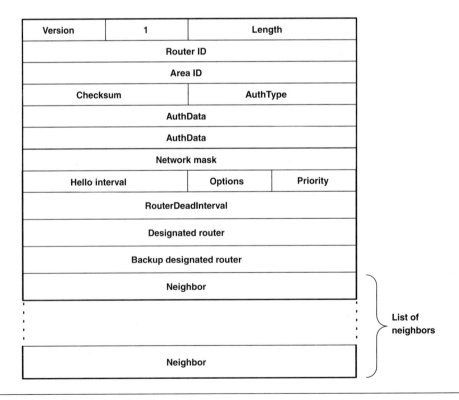

Figure 9-13. *OSPF Hello packet format*

- *Dead interval* is the length, in seconds, of the period that routers wait before declaring a neighbor unreachable if no Hello packet has been received from it. Routers must agree on the Dead interval value to establish adjacencies.

- *Options;* see Section 9.2.3.4 for information on the OSPF Options field.

- Priority, the router's priority influencing the results of the DR election process. Different routers may be configured with different values of priority.

- *Designated* and *backup designated router*, the interface IP address of the designated and backup designated routers that were elected by the sending router.

- *Neighbors*, the Router-IDs of the neighbors from which the sending router has received Hello packets.

Routers send Hello packets periodically on all OSPF-enabled interfaces. The default value of the Hello interval is 10 seconds for LAN segments and 30 seconds for NBMA clouds. When no Hello packet has been seen from a configured neighbor in the case of an NBMA cloud, Hello packets are sent every PollInterval seconds, which is two times the Hello interval for NBMA clouds (60 seconds).

In most cases, OSPF Hello packets are sent as multicasts to the AllSPFRouters IP address. Hello packets are sent as unicasts in only two cases: when the neighbor is configured manually, which can be the case when the router is connected to an NBMA cloud, or when the packet is sent over a virtual link.

OSPF routers use periodic transmission of Hello packets for dynamic neighbor discovery. All OSPF routers listen for incoming Hello packets. Whenever a Hello packet arrives that cannot be associated with an already known neighbor on that interface, a new neighbor data structure is created for the newly discovered neighbor, provided that the Hello packet is valid and that the neighbor is listed in the router's own Hello packets, thus informing the neighbor that it has been heard. (OSPF uses this feature to ensure two-way connectivity between neighbors.)

Dynamic neighbor discovery by means of OSPF Hello packets is intended for types of media that support broadcasts on the data link layer. This includes point-to-point links, as sending a broadcast over a point-to-point link is trivial and in fact is equal to sending a unicast.

When a router is connected to an NBMA cloud, two possible solutions can be used to make the Hello subprotocol work properly: broadcast emulation and manual neighbor configuration. In the first case, OSPF treats the interface as broadcast, so only one Hello packet is generated for a single interface. The data link layer module is then responsible for replication of the message for all possible receivers. A Frame Relay interface with Frame Relay maps configured as broadcast can be used as an example. In the second case, used when packet replication to all possible directions is not desirable, OSPF creates separate Hello packets for some listed neighbors and sends those packets as unicast to the corresponding IP addresses.

Hello packets in OSPF also carry the information necessary for DR election. In short, this process takes into consideration the priorities configured on the routers for the segment and Router-IDs as a tiebreaker. After the DR and the BDR are elected on a segment, routers establish adjacencies only with them (see Sections 9.2.3.7 and 9.2.3.8). Note that OSPF elects the DR and BDR for LAN segments and NBMA clouds, unless they are treated as point-to-multipoint links.

When neighbors are configured manually for an NBMA interface, the priority value can be specified for every neighbor. Usually, the priority is configured for the router's own interface. In the case of an NBMA interface, the idea behind configuration of the priority for the remote neighbors is to minimize Hello traffic between routers that will not establish adjacencies. As mentioned before, routers on broadcast and NBMA media establish adjacencies only with the DR and the BDR. It is a common practice to exclude some routers connected to an NBMA cloud from the DR election process by setting their priority to 0. This is usually done to restrict topology of OSPF data flows across the NBMA cloud. In general, Hello packets are exchanged only between eligible routers and between the DR, BDR, and all other routers, eligible or not.

The formal rules for sending Hello packets on different types of media are as follows.

- On broadcast segments and point-to-point links, Hello packets are sent every HelloInterval seconds—10 seconds by default—to the IP address AllSPFRouters (224.0.0.5).

- On virtual links, Hello packets are sent as unicasts every second directly to the address of the ABR terminating the other end of the virtual link.

- On point-to-multipoint networks, Cisco routers may operate in two modes: broadcast and nonbroadcast. In the first case, only one packet is generated for the whole interface, and the data link layer is responsible for replication of this packet. In the second case, neighbors are either configured manually or known via a dynamic protocol, such as Inverse ARP, and separate packets are sent to every neighbor.

- On NBMA networks, Hello packets are sent as follows.

  - If eligible to become the DR, the router starts sending Hello packets to all eligible neighbors: those with a specified priority greater than 0. Note that eligible routers are supposed to be configured with a full list of neighbors.

  - If it has been elected as the DR or the BDR for the segment, the router starts sending Hello packets to all configured neighbors, eligible or not. The reason is that the DR and the BDR must establish adjacencies with all reachable neighbors.

- If it is not eligible—its associated priority is 0—the router sends Hello packets only to the DR and the BDR. If the DR and the BDR are not yet known, the router does not send any Hello packets at all. The router also sends a Hello packet in reply to a Hello packet received from any eligible packet.

The described operation of the OSPF Hello subprotocol ensures that Hello packets are exchanged only between eligible routers when the DR and the BDR are not yet elected and then only between the DR and all neighbors and between the BDR and all neighbors. (No Hello packets are exchanged between ineligible neighbors, as they will not form adjacencies, anyway.)

OSPF routers start sending Hello packets whenever an OSPF-enabled interface goes up, except for ineligible routers, in the case of NBMA. Hello packets are sent as long as OSPF is enabled on the corresponding interface. This rule is used to identify unreachable neighbors; that is, if no Hello packet has been received from a neighbor during the RouterDeadInterval, the corresponding neighbor data structure is removed, and a new version of the router-LSA, one that does not list this adjacency, is created. This causes other routers to recalculate their SPTs, using alternative paths.

Processing of incoming Hello packets is very simple. Before Hello packets are processed, general OSPF packet-processing functions have already associated the entire OSPF packet with a specific interface. The following steps are then taken.

1. If the type of the receiving interface is not point-to-point, point-to-multipoint, or virtual link and if the network mask reported in the Hello packet is different from the mask configured on the receiving interface, the Hello packet is dropped.

    Network masks are not checked for point-to-point, point-to-multipoint, and virtual links, because OSPF does not assume that any subnets have to be assigned to them or, if assigned, that they must match on different sides of the link. This is safe because in all of these cases, routers announce connected subnets themselves, whereas in the case of LAN segments, the subnet is announced in the network-LSA, so all routers must agree on the subnet mask.

2. If the HelloInterval or the RouterDeadInterval received in the Hello packet does not match settings of the receiving interface, the Hello packet is dropped.

3. Configuration of the stub or NSSA area on the receiving interface is checked to match the parameters announced in the Hello packet: the E and N bits in the OSPF Options field.

4. The list of neighbors known on the interface is searched for an instance of the neighbor data structure corresponding to the router that sent the Hello packet being processed. On point-to-point links, neighbors are identified by the Router-ID; on all other types of interfaces, they are identified by the interface IP addresses. If no corresponding neighbor data structure is found, a new one is created.

5. HelloReceived for the corresponding neighbor state machine is generated; see Section 9.2.3.8 for more details on neighbor FSM.

6. The list of neighbors included in the Hello packet is examined. If the receiving router itself is in the list and the state of the neighbor FSM is lower than 2-Way, the 2-WayReceived event for the neighbor's FSM is generated. If the router is not listed and if the neighbor's FSM is in state 2-Way or higher, a 1-WayReceived event for the neighbor is generated, and processing of the Hello packet stopped.

7. Checks related to DR election are performed. These checks are considered in Section 9.2.3.7.

8. If the Hello packet was received from an eligible neighbor on an NBMA interface and the router itself is not eligible, a Hello packet is immediately sent in reply to the packet received.

9.2.3.6 Interface State Machine

For the router's forwarding component, any interface can be in only two states: up or down. In contrast, an interface in OSPF can be in different states, depending on the type of interface and logical events experienced by OSPF on that interface. First, let's get acquainted with interface states and events. Interface states correspond to the states of the interface FSM that may transition from one state to another. Depending on the state of the interface, OSPF will put different information into the router LSA (see Section 9.2.3.9 for details).

Any OSPF interface may be in one of the following states.

- *Down:* The interface is not operational. OSPF does not send or receive any packets on an interface in this state. This is the initial state for all OSPF-enabled interfaces.

- *Loopback:* The interface is operational but looped back on the physical or logical level and does not provide connectivity to any other hosts or routers.

Nevertheless, its associated IP address should be announced, as it may be used for testing purposes.

> OSPF-enabled loopback interfaces in Cisco routers are automatically put in the loopback state.

- *Point-to-point:* This is the most advanced state for any point-to-point interface. The point-to-point interface in this state is operational, as reported by the interface controller and the data link layer protocol and can be used to establish adjacencies.
- *Waiting:* This is the transitional state for LAN interfaces. In this state, the router sends Hello packets and listens for incoming Hello packets but does not elect the DR and the BDR and hence does not establish adjacencies over the interface. All interfaces are placed in this state whenever lower levels indicate that the interface is operational. The interface FSM may stay in this state for up to RouterDeadInterval seconds.
- *DR:* The interface is operational and the router has been elected the DR for the connected segment. When the interface FSM transitions to this state, the router establishes adjacencies with all neighbors on the segment. The router also originates a network-LSA on behalf of the connected segment.
- *Backup:* The interface is operational and the router has been elected the BDR for the connected segment. After the interface FSM has reached this state, the router establishes adjacencies with all other routers on the segment. Note that the router does not originate a network-LSA for the connected segment but includes a link to it in the router-LSA.
- *DROther:* The interface is operational, but as a result of the DR election process, the router has not been elected as the DR or the BDR. If the interface FSM reaches this state, the router establishes adjacencies only with the DR and the BDR. The router does not generate a network-LSA for the segment but includes a link to it in the router-LSA.

Note that states Waiting, DR, Backup, and DROther are valid only for broadcast and NBMA interfaces, that is, for interfaces that require the DR election process.

Following is a list of events the interface FSM can experience:

- InterfaceUp, generated when a signal from lower layers is received indicating that an interface has become operational. (The physical state of the interface is up and the state of the data link layer protocol also is up.)

- InterfaceDown, generated when the link-layer protocol or the interface controller signals that an interface has gone down. This event can be caused by physical problems in the transmission media or by problems at the data link layer, preventing data from being delivered over the interface.

- LoopInd, generated in response to a signal from lower-level protocols announcing that an interface has been looped back.

- UnloopInd, generated when the router receives a signal from lower-level protocols that the interface is not looped back.

- BackupSeen, generated for an interface in the Waiting state when, after a Hello packet has been received, it is certain that either a router is already the BDR on the segment or that no router is the BDR. In the first case, identified by the nonzero value of the BDR field in the Hello packet from the BDR itself, because a router is the BDR, the segment already has both DR and BDR. In the second case, identified by the nonzero value of the Designated Router field and zero value of the Backup Designated Router field in the Hello packet received from the DR, only one router was on the segment before the calculating router was attached to it, and that router was the DR for the segment.

- WaitTimer, indication that the Wait timer has expired while the interface was in the Wait state.

- NeighborChange, indication that the DR election algorithm needs to be rerun for the interface. Among the reasons for this event are changes in two-way connectivity with some of the neighbors and changes in some routers' opinion of the identity of the DR or BDR.

Table 9-2 defines the OSPF state machine as a set of actions performed in response to a certain event received when the interface FSM is in a particular state. As you can see, the interface FSM is simple. Each event is valid only for a specific subset of states. The diagram in Figure 9-14 helps to visualize the FSM.

9.2.3.7 Designated Router Election Algorithm

Election of the designated and backup designated routers has been referred to several times without details on how it is done. Let's explore this process.

The DR/BDR election process does not imply any type of negotiation between routers. The base principle of the algorithm is that if all routers follow the same logic, using the same input data, they will end up with the same results.

The input for the DR election algorithm is the information in the neighbor data structures—IP addresses of the designated and backup designated routers—associated with a particular interface. This information is taken from the Hello packets received on the interface. Hello packets, in turn, contain the information that the sending router believes

Table 9-2. *Interface FSM Definition*

Event	Current State	Action	Next State
InterfaceUp	Down	Start the Hello timer for the interface. If the network type is broadcast or NBMA, start the Wait timer. If there are any statically configured neighbors, generate the Start event for them.	Point-to-point for point-to-point, point-to-multipoint, and virtual links Waiting for NBMA and broadcast interfaces
	Other	None	No transition
InterfaceDown	Down	None	No transition
	Other	Set all fields of the interface data structure to initial values. Stop all interface timers. Inform neighbor FSM of the neighbors associated with the interface by generating the KillNbr event.	Down
LoopInd	Loopback	None	No transition
	Others	Same as when InterfaceDown is received.	Loopback
UnloopInd	Loopback	None	Down
	Others	None	No transition
BackupSeen	Waiting	Perform the DR election algorithm.	DR, Backup, or DROther, depending on the results of DR election
	Other	None	No transition
WaitTimer	Waiting	Perform the DR election algorithm.	DR, Backup, or DROther, depending on the results of DR election
	Other	None	No transition
NeighborChange	DR, Backup, DROther	Perform the DR election algorithm.	DR, Backup, or DROther, depending on the results of DR election
	Other	None	No transition

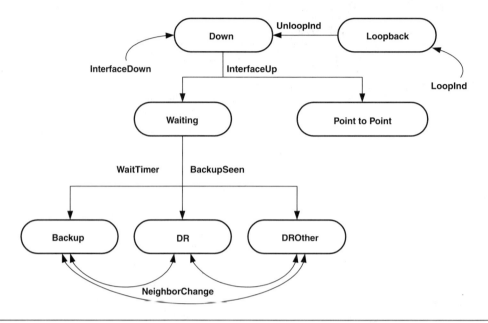

Figure 9-14. *OSPF interface FSM*

is correct. Because the algorithm takes this information into consideration and the results of the algorithm are announced in the DR and BDR Hello packet fields of Hello packets originated by the calculating router, all routers end up with the same decision.

The algorithm itself uses two procedures: BDR election and DR election. The backup designated router is elected as follows. Note that the algorithm stores the parameters of the currently best BDR for comparison with other neighbors.

1. Clear the parameters of the best BDR and consider all neighbors reachable through the interface, including the calculating router itself.

   a. If the state of the neighbor state machine is not 2-Way or higher, consider the next neighbor.

   b. If the value of the router priority in the corresponding neighbor data structure is 0—the router is not eligible to become the DR or the BDR—consider the next neighbor.

   c. If the neighbor declares itself the DR, skip this neighbor, as we're electing the backup designated router.

   d. Compare the currently best BDR and the neighbor.

      ■ If one of the routers declares itself to be the BDR but the other does not, set the best BDR to the neighbor that declares itself to be the BDR.

- Otherwise (both routers do or do not declare themselves to be the BDR), set the best BDR to the neighbor that has the highest value of the router priority field. If both routers have equal router priority, prefer the one with the highest Router-ID.

2. After all neighbors are considered, set the value of the BDR in the interface data structure to the interface IP address of the best BDR elected by the algorithm.

The designated router is elected similarly. The algorithm stores the parameters of the currently best DR for comparison with other neighbors.

1. Clear the parameters of the best DR and consider all neighbors reachable through the interface, including the calculating router itself.

   a. If the state of the neighbor state machine is not 2-Way or higher, consider the next neighbor.

   b. If the value of router priority in the corresponding neighbor data structure is 0—the router is not eligible to become the DR or the BDR—consider the next neighbor.

   c. Compare the currently best DR and the neighbor as follows.

   - If one of the routers declares itself to be the DR but the other does not, set the best DR to the neighbor that declares itself to be the BDR.

   - If both routers declare themselves to be the DR, set the best DR to the neighbor that has the highest value of the router priority field. If both routers have equal router priority, prefer the one with the highest Router-ID.

2. If, after all neighbors are considered, the best DR is still not known—no router declares itself to be the DR—set the DR field in the interface data structure to the value of the BDR field in it: stored during the BDR election stage. Otherwise, set it to the best DR elected by the algorithm.

The DR election algorithm operates as follows.

1. Elect the backup designated router for the interface.

2. Elect the designated router for the interface.

3. Repeat the calculations if the calculating router became the DR or the BDR after these calculations.

The last step of the algorithm is necessary so that no router is elected as both DR and BDR.

The reason for selecting the BDR before the DR is to ensure that the BDR takes over the DR responsibilities when the DR fails. Step 2 in the DR election stage ensures that the BDR is promoted to the DR status when the DR disappears. This step also makes it possible for the algorithm to result in the same router's being both the DR and the BDR. This can happen during transition periods when the BDR has not yet detected the absence of the DR but the calculating router has. The reason for additional calculation in step 3 is to ensure that the calculating router makes a consistent decision with other routers on the segment when the role of the calculating router changes as a result of the first round of calculations.

After the DR election algorithm is completed, the corresponding OSPF interface is placed in the DR, BDR, or DROther state, depending on which routers have become the DR and the BDR. Note again that when the state of a router's interface changes from or to DR or BDR, the router generates an AdjOK? event for all interface adjacencies. This event may cause some adjacencies to be dropped or promoted to the ExStart state. This is done to ensure that routers establish adjacencies only with the DR and the BDR on multiaccess segments.

9.2.3.8 Adjacencies and Neighbor State Machine

Adjacency is a key element in the OSPF protocol. Adjacencies in OSPF do not just reflect two-way connectivity between two routers, although an OSPF adjacency is always between two routers. Adjacency establishment implies database description exchange and database synchronization to ensure that neighboring routers have equal knowledge, and hence routes in the routing tables, before transit traffic is forwarded between them. Adjacencies are also used in OSPF to abstract network topology (see Section 9.2.3.9 for more details).

Every OSPF router represents its communications with other OSPF routers in the form of neighbor data structures, described in Section 9.2.2. Every neighbor can be in one of many states. Transitions between states are performed according to the received events and well-defined OSPF neighbor FSM.

First, consider the states of the OSPF neighbor FSM:

- *Down:* Initial state for any newly created neighbor. A neighbor FSM can also go to this state if the router has not received any Hello packet from the neighbor with the RouterDeadInterval or the data link layer module indicates that connectivity to the neighbor is not available anymore.
- *Attempt:* Transitional state for neighbors connected to an NBMA cloud. If a neighbor FSM is in this state, the router has not received anything from the neighbor but is trying to establish two-way communication with it.

- *Init:* State indicating that Hello packets were received from the neighbor but did not contain the ID of the receiving router, so no two-way connectivity is ensured, and adjacency establishment cannot proceed further. Normally, the FSM should get out of this state as soon as the router itself sends a Hello packet to the neighbor and sees its Router-ID in a Hello packet from the neighbor.

- *2-Way:* State in which two-way connectivity has been ensured with the neighbor by identifying the router's own ID in Hello packets received from the neighbor. An OSPF conversation can be "parked" in this state if both the neighbor and the router itself are neither the DR nor the BDR; that is, routers are not supposed to establish adjacencies with each other. If the router decides to establish an adjacency with the neighbor, the FSM goes to state ExStart.

In other words, it is normal to see that a router attached to a broadcast segment has multiple neighbors, but only two of them are in a state different from 2-Way.

- *ExStart:* State that starts the LSDB synchronization process between the neighbors. In this state, the routers decide which of them will be the master or the slave. Once this decision is made, the FSM transitions to the Exchange state. Formally, an OSPF session between two routers may be called an adjacency if the neighbor FSM is in ExStart or a higher state. Only OSPF conversations in state ExStart or higher—that is, only OSPF adjacencies—are used for asynchronous flooding of LSAs.

- *Exchange:* State in which routers exchange database description packets to inform one another about the contents of their LSDBs. When DBD packets are processed, routers form the link-state request lists that contain the headers of the LSAs to be requested from the neighbor. When they have finished exchanging DBDs, routers put the FSM into Loading or Full state, depending on whether anything is in the link-state request list.

- *Loading:* State in which an adjacency indicates that the router itself is requesting LSAs on its link-state request list from the neighbor. Once the router receives the last LSA it has on the request list, the FSM transitions to state Full.

- *Full:* FSM state indicating that the router has downloaded all LSAs from its neighbor and now can list the adjacency in its router-LSA. Neighbors whose FSM is in Full state are called fully adjacent.

OSPF announces an adjacency only when the FSM reaches Full state. In contrast, IS-IS announces adjacencies once two-way connectivity has been ensured.

Note that the process of adjacency establishment is asymmetric. This means that although a router on one end of the adjacency already has its FSM in state Full and lists it in its router-LSA, the other router may still have its FMS in the Loading state, requesting LSAs from the neighbor. Also note that OSPF does not use an adjacency in its route calculation unless there is an adjacency in the opposite direction. This means that a link between two routers is not used until both routers announce the adjacencies. However, counterdirectional adjacencies cannot be associated with each other in Dijkstra if more than one physical link is between routers. In this case, if one router announces n links to the other, it is enough that the other router announces a single adjacency back, for all n links to be used for forwarding in one direction.

Now consider the events that can be experienced by a neighbor FSM.

- **HelloReceived**, generated every time a Hello packet is received from the neighbor, regardless of the packet's contents.

- **Start**, generated for NBMA neighbors to indicate that the router should send periodic Hello packets to them.

- **2-WayReceived**, generated when the router receives a Hello packet from the neighbor and the packet lists the router itself; that is, two-way connectivity between neighbors is acknowledged.

- **NegotiationDone**, generated when the router receives the initial DBD packet for the neighbor in ExStart state, and the decision is made on which of the routers is master. This event causes the FSM to move to the Exchange state.

- **ExchangeDone**, indicates that the router has successfully exchanged all DBD packets with its neighbor while in the Exchange state.

- **BadLSReq**, indicates that the router has received a request for an LSA that is not in its LSDB. This is an indication of an error in the database exchange process.

- **LoadingDone**, indicates that while the neighbor FSM is in the Loading state, the link-state request list has become empty because the router has received the last LSA on the list either in reply to its request or via the asynchronous flooding process.

- **AdjOK?**, signals the router to check whether the adjacency should be maintained or established. The event is generated for all neighbors on broadcast and NBMA interfaces whenever the identity of the DR or the BDR changes.

- **SeqNumberMismatch**, error indication generated when the router receives from the neighbor a DBD packet with unexpected parameters, such as Sequence Number, Init bit, or Options field).

- **1-Way**, generated when the router receives a Hello packet from the neighbor and the packet does not list the router itself. This may happen when the neighbor does not receive Hello packets from the router and removes the neighbor data structure after the Dead timer has fired. This event always causes the FSM to move into Init state.

- **KillNbr**, generated when the interface hosting the adjacency is going down and the neighbor data structure must be freed.

- **InactivityTimer**, generated because of an expired inactivity timer for the neighbor. This event indicates that the router has not received any Hello packet from the neighbor within the RouterDeadInterval period, and the neighbor is declared down.

- **LLDown**, generated whenever the lower-level protocol, such as Frame Relay or X.25, sends a signal that the neighbor is not reachable anymore because, for example, the corresponding VC has gone down.

Table 9-3 contains the definition of the OSPF neighbor FSM. For each event, the processing actions and the next state are defined.

Before an OSPF adjacency is fully established, an OSPF session between two routers goes through two main stages: two-way connectivity and LSDB synchronization. For an OSPF session to reach the two-way state—that is, to reach state 2-Way or ExStart, the routers must have evidence that they both can hear each other. Reception of a Hello packet from a remote router indicates only that the router can hear from its neighbor, not that the neighbor can hear Hellos from the router. It would not be smart to start the LSDB synchronization process before both routers can be sure about two-way connectivity. Two-way connectivity is also very important for the DR election process, and this is why the DR election algorithm considers only neighbors in states 2-Way or higher.

Once two-way connectivity between neighbors has been established by using the Hello subprotocol, neighbors start the LSDB synchronization process. This process uses OSPF DBD packets. The format of an OSPF DBD packet is depicted in Figure 9-15. Following are the fields found in OSPF DBD packets.

- *Interface MTU:* The MTU of the interface on which the DBD packet is sent. This field is used by OSPF routers to detect MTU mismatch problems.

- *Options:* Optional capabilities field, as described in Section 9.2.3.4. OSPF announces the Options field in all its packets.

- *I (Init), M (More), and MS (Master) bits:* The I and MS bits are used during the initial negotiation process when one router is elected to be the master. The M bit is used to indicate whether the sending router has more DBD packets to send.

- *DD sequence number:* The sequence number of the database description packet. This field is used to reliably exchange DBD packets between routers.

- *LSA headers:* Headers of the LSAs in the LSDB being described. Each header contains enough information to uniquely identify an LSA.

Table 9-3. *Neighbor FSM Definition*

Event	Current State	Action	Next State
HelloReceived	Down	Start the inactivity timer for the neighbor.	Init
	Attempt	Restart the inactivity timer.	Init
	Init or greater	Restart the inactivity timer.	No transition
Start	Down	Send a Hello packet to the neighbor and start the inactivity timer for it.	Attempt
	Other	None	No transition
2-WayReceived	Init	If the adjacency should be formed with the neighbor, the FSM transitions to ExStart; otherwise, the next state is 2-Way.	ExStart or 2-Way
	Other	None	No transition
NegotiationDone	ExStart	Start sending DBD packets to the neighbor.	Exchange
	Other	None	No transition
ExchangeDone	Exchange	If the link-state request list is empty, the FSM transitions to state Full; otherwise, the FSM goes into state Loading, in which the router requests LSAs from the neighbor.	Loading or Full
	Other	None	No transition
BadLSReq	Exchange or greater	Clear all neighbor-associated lists and try to reestablish adjacency by transitioning to state ExStart.	ExStart
	Other	None	No transition
LoadingDone	Loading	None	Full
	Other	None	No transition
AdjOK?	2-Way	Check whether the adjacency should be established with the neighbor. If so, transition the FSM to ExStart. Otherwise, the adjacency stays in 2-Way.	ExStart or no transition

Table 9-3. *continued*

Event	Current State	Action	Next State
	ExStart or greater	Check whether the adjacency should still be maintained. If so, do nothing. Otherwise, the adjacency transitions to 2-Way.	2-Way or no transition
	Other	None	No transition
SeqNumberMismatch	Exchange or greater	Clear all neighbor-associated lists and try to reestablish adjacency by transitioning to state ExStart.	ExStart
	Other	None	No transition
1-Way	2-Way and greater	Clear all neighbor-associated lists.	Init
	Other	None	No transition
KillNbr	Any	Clear all neighbor-associated lists.	Down
InactivityTimer	Any	Clear all neighbor-associated lists.	Down
LLDown	Any	Clear all neighbor-associated lists.	Down

The process of LSDB synchronization consists of two steps: exchange of LSDB descriptions and asymmetric LSA download. OSPF neighbors do this to inform each other about the contents of LSDBs. Routers achieve this by reliably exchanging the database description. To ensure reliability, OSPF routers must account for two processes: DBD packet numbering and DBD packet acknowledgment. To successfully perform the acknowledgment function, routers must agree on packet sequence numbers. Instead of a separate sequence number for each direction used in TCP, OSPF uses one sequence number, thus simplifying the process and saving some space in DBD packets. One router sends a DBD packet with its sequence number, and the neighbor sends its own DBD packet back, quoting the received sequence number. When the router receives the reply and sees the sequence number it sent, the router considers this packet as an acknowledgment to the packet it sent and increments its sequence number. It is quite clear that for such a scheme to work, the routers must agree on which one will be incrementing the sequence number and which one will be quoting the received value. OSPF uses the concept of master and slave for this.

While in ExStart state, routers exchange initial DBD packets, negotiating who will be the master. Initially, before any DBD packets have been received, both routers send

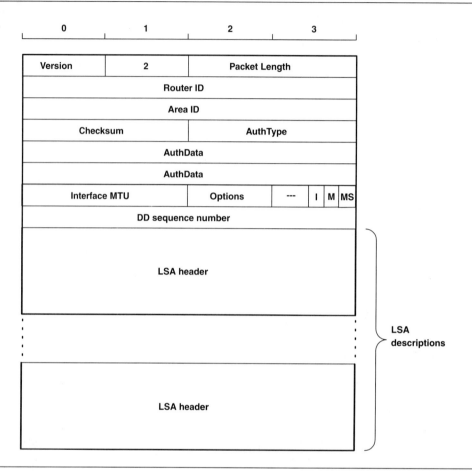

Figure 9-15. *OSPF DBD packet format*

empty DBD packets, setting all three control bits in them: I to indicate the beginning of the process, M to indicate that the packet is not the last, and MS to indicate that both of them can be the master. Routers also set the packet DD sequence number field according to their own values in the neighbor data structures, initialized to a random value when the new neighbor data structure is created. Routers negotiate the master/slave relationship as follows.

When the router with the higher Router-ID receives an initial DBD packet from its neighbor, the router does not agree with the contents, saying that the other router is the master, and discards the packet. When the router with the lower Router-ID receives the initial DBD packet, the router agrees with the contents of the received packet—and hence with the fact that the other router is the master—sets its master/slave bit to slave, accepts the DD sequence number from the packet, and transitions to state exchange, thus enabling transmission of the first noninitial DBD packet with the new DD sequence number. The router with the higher Router-ID receives this first noninitial DBD—now with the MS bit clear—sees that the other router agrees to be slave, and echoes the master's sequence number; it thus considers the packet as an acknowledgment that allows it to go to the exchange state as the master. Note that the master does not discard the contents of the first noninitial DBD packet from the slave but processes it as usual.

After both routers have agreed on the master and slave functionality, they exchange DBD packets, putting LSA headers in them. When a new DBD packet is received, the router looks through the LSA headers inside and identifies LSAs that are not in its LSDB or are different from its LSDB versions. If it is not in the router's LSDB or is more recent, the remote LSA adds an entry to the neighbor's link-state request list. If the local version of the LSA is more recent, the router does not perform any actions, as the neighbor is supposed to detect this itself by processing the database description packet received from the router.

Database description stops when both routers have sent and received acknowledgments for all their DBD packets—that is, when the routers have successfully sent complete database descriptions to each other.

> Note that the slave considers the process finished when it has sent an empty DBD packet in reply to the last DBD packet from the master. The master, in turn, considers the process finished when it receives the acknowledging DBD packet from the slave.

When either router determines the end of the process, that router looks at the contents of the link-state request list. If the router did not identify any new LSAs in the remote router's LSDB or they were already received while the DBD exchange process was going on—the list is empty—the neighbor FSM transitions directly to state Full. Otherwise, the neighbor FSM transitions to state Loading.

While in the Loading state, the router periodically sends link-state request packets, whose format is given in Figure 9-16, putting the LSA headers from its link-state request list inside the packets. The other router replies by sending the requested LSAs in the link-state update packets, considered in detail in Section 9.2.3.11. The LSAs received in the link-state update packets are processed as in the case of asynchronous flooding (refer to Section 9.2.3.11). If a link-state request packet refers to a nonexistent LSA, a BadLSReq event is generated for the neighbor, causing the adjacency to be reset and the LSDB synchronization process to be rerun. Note that this event should not occur with correct OSPF implementations.

When all LSAs on the neighbor's link-state request list have been received, a LoadingDone event is generated for the neighbor. This event causes the neighbor FSM to transition to state Full. Figure 9-17 illustrates the neighbor FSM in a graphical form.

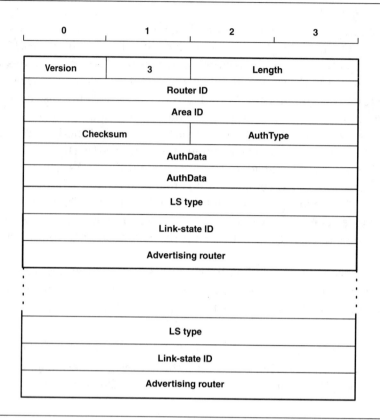

Figure 9-16. *Format of link-state request packet*

When a neighbor FSM transitions to or from state Full, the router originates a new version of the router-LSA and floods it to its neighbors, thus distributing new topological information.

9.2.3.9 OSPF Topology Abstraction and Types of LSAs

Topology abstraction in OSPF is one of the most important parts of the protocol, as topological information is used as input to the Dijkstra algorithm. OSPF represents intra-area network topology by using two types of LSAs: the router-LSA and the network-LSA. Before considering these LSAs, let's consider a generic LSA header (Figure 9-18).

All LSAs start with a standard header containing the following fields.

- *LSA age:* The number of seconds since the LSA was originated. This field is incremented while the LSA is stored in the routers' LSDBs, as well as when it is flooded through interfaces, incremented by InfTransDelay, which equals 1 by

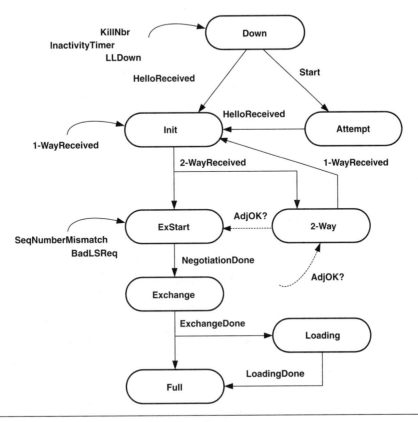

Figure 9-17. *OSPF neighbor state machine*

default. When an LSA's age reaches MaxAge (3,600 seconds), the LSA is flushed
from the domain and is removed from routers' LSDBs.

- *Options:* Optional capabilities, as described in Section 9.2.3.4.
- *LS type:* One of the following:
    - Type 1: Router-LSA, used to describe network topology and to propagate
      internal IP routing information.
    - Type 2: Network-LSA, used to represent the topology of multiaccess segments
      and to announce associated IP routing information.
    - Type 3: Summary-LSA, used to announce routing information between areas
      (see Section 9.2.4.2 for details).
    - Type 4: ASBR-summary-LSA, used to announce the location of ASBRs to
      remote areas (see Section 9.2.4.2).

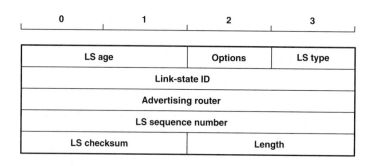

Figure 9-18. *Format of generic LSA header*

- Type 5: AS-external-LSA, used to propagate external routing information (see Section 9.2.5.2).

- Type 6: Group-membership-LSA, used by multicast OSPF to propagate information about IP multicast groups. Cisco does not implement MOSPF.

- Type 7: NSSA-external-LSA, used to propagate external routing information within not-so-stubby areas (see Section 9.2.5.6).

- Type 8: External-attribute-LSA, not standardized and not implemented by any vendor. This type was supposed to be used to propagate information associated with external routes announced in AS-external-LSAs, such as BGP attributes.

- Types 9, 10, and 11: Opaque-LSAs, used to propagate external information, using OSPF as a transport mechanism. See [RFC2370] for more information.

- *Link-state ID:* Field, together with the Advertising Router and LS type fields, used to uniquely identify the LSA in the LSDB. This field is also used to carry routing information. For example, in types 3, 5, and 7 LSAs, this field is set to the value of the IP prefix being announced, probably with some host bits set.

- *Advertising Router:* Router-ID of the router that originated the LSA.

- *LS sequence number:* Used to convey the LSA version.

- *LS checksum:* Fletcher checksum of the contents of the LSA; used to detect corruption of LSAs while they are being flooded or stored in routers' LSDBs.

- *Length:* The LSA length, in bytes

The router-LSA is the basic LSA that every OSPF router originates, provided that it has at least one fully adjacent neighbor or one route to announce. Figure 9-19 depicts the contents of the router-LSA. The Link-state ID of the router-LSA is always set to the router-ID of the originating router; thus, the router-LSA always has the same value in the

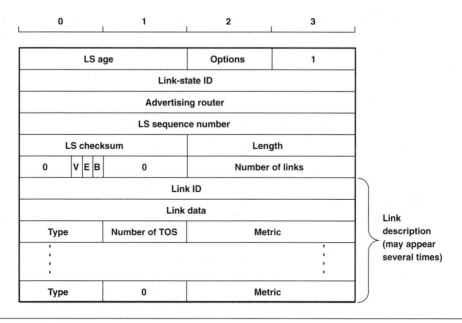

Figure 9-19. *Router-LSA format*

Link-state ID and Advertising Router fields. Each router-LSA has an Rtype field, the number of links, and actual link records.

The Rtype field contains the following bits:

- *B bit:* Set by the originating router when it is an ABR
- *E bit:* Set by the origination router when it is injecting AS-external-LSAs into the domain
- *V bit:* Set by the originating router when it has one or more fully adjacent virtual links with other ABRs
- *W bit:* Set when the originating router is a wildcard multicast server, used in MOSPF
- *Nt bit:* Set when the originating router is a NSSA ABR that is configured to always perform type 7–to–type 5 LSA translation (see Section 9.2.5.6).

Link records are generally used to describe a router's connections and internal IP routing information. Links are constructed of the following fields:

- *Link ID:* Identifies the entity to which the originating router is connected with the described link.

- *Link data:* Additional data carried in the link record for remote routers in calcu-lating the routing table. The contents depend on the link type and are described later in this section.

- *Link type:* The type of the link. OSPF currently supports the following four link types: type 1, point-to-point link to another router; type 2, link to a transit multi-access network; type 3, link to a stub network (used to announce internal IP rout-ing information); and type 4, virtual link to another ABR. Note that the links described here are informational records used for topology abstraction and rout-ing information announcement inside router-LSAs.

- *Number TOS:* The number of TOS metrics, except for the default metric, in the link. This field is left in the link format for backward compatibility with OSPFv1, which supported TOS routing; this field is always 0 in current OSPF implementa-tions.

- *Metric:* The cost associated with the announced link. This is the cost used in the Dijkstra algorithm to calculate the SPT.

The format of a network-LSA is depicted in Figure 9-20. The Link-state ID of the net-work-LSA is always set to the IP address of the designated router on the segment being described. (Note that the network-LSA is always originated by the DR.) The network-LSA carries the network mask, associated with the described segment and the list of attached routers—their Router-IDs. This list includes the DR itself.

OSPF topology representation is performed as follows. A router creates a router-LSA, setting the Link-state ID and the Advertising Router to its Router-ID. The router also puts into the router-LSA a number of link records, describing its adjacencies with other routers and associated IP prefixes. Note that only operational interfaces—interfaces in an OSPF state higher than Down—are considered.

For each operational point-to-point link, the OSPF router includes into its router-LSA two link records:

- A type 1 link to describe the adjacency to the other router on the link but only if the adjacency is in the Full state. The Link ID field is set to the Router-ID of the neighboring router. The Link Data field is set to the router's own interface IP address if the link is numbered, or it is set to the IfIndex value—an interface index used in SNMP protocol—associated with this interface if the link is unnum-bered. The link metric is set to the cost associated with the interface.

- A type 3 link to announce the IP prefix associated with the interface. This link record is not included if the point-to-point interface is unnumbered. The Link ID field is set to the value of the announced IP prefix. The Link Data field is set to the value of the network mask corresponding to the prefix length. The link metric

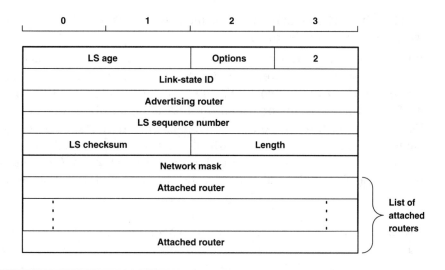

LS age		Options	2
Link-state ID			
Advertising router			
LS sequence number			
LS checksum		Length	
Network mask			
Attached router			
⋮		⋮	
Attached router			

List of attached routers

Figure 9-20. *Format of network-LSA*

is set to the cost associated with the interface. Note that a type 3 link is placed into the router-LSA regardless of the state of the adjacency crossing the link.

OSPF originally used another method to announce routing information associated with point-to-point links: Each router announced a type 3 link containing the IP address of the other router and the mask 255.255.255.255. This approach caused routers to install host routes to routers' interface addresses. The second option—announcing the associated IP subnet—was introduced later and is currently used by Cisco routers.

Effectively, each point-to-point link is represented as a set of counterdirectional adjacency announcements and leaf entries announcing associated IP prefixes.

For each multi-access—broadcast or NBMA—interface, the router performs the following steps.

1. If no fully adjacent neighbors are associated with the interface, only the associated IP prefix is announced. The router includes a type 3 link in its router-LSA for this purpose, as described in the case of a point-to-point link.

2. Otherwise, with at least one fully adjacent neighbor on the interface, the router includes a type 2 link in its router-LSA, describing a link to a transit network. The Link ID field of the link record is set to the IP address of the DR on the segment. The Link Data field is set to the router's own interface IP address. The link metric

is set to the cost associated with the interface. (This link is a reference to the network-LSA originated by the DR.)

3. If the router is the DR for the segment and at least one fully adjacent neighbor is on the interface, the router also originates a network-LSA for the segment. The Link-state ID of the network LSA is set to the IP address of the interface connected to the segment for which the LSA is being originated. The Advertising Router field is set to the router's Router-ID. The network mask field is set to the value corresponding to the length of the prefix associated with the segment. Finally, the router includes Router-IDs of all routers on the segment with which the route is fully adjacent. Note that the DR also includes its own Router-ID in this list.

LAN and NBMA networks are represented as a special vertex corresponding to the network itself (the network-LSA) and pairs of counterdirectional adjacency announcements between this vertex and vertices corresponding to the routers attached to the segment and fully adjacent to the segment's DR.

9.2.3.10 Origination of LSAs

The LSDB of any given OSPF router contains LSAs originated by the router itself, as well as LSAs originated by other routers. LSAs originated by the router itself are called *self-originated LSAs*.

A router may originate a new LSA or a new version of an existing LSA because of the following events.

> Note that here we discuss intra-area routing only. For the origination of LSAs involved in inter-area and external OSPF routing, see Sections 9.2.4.2 and 9.2.5.2.

- An interface changed its state to or from Down.
- A neighbor FSM transitioned to or from Full state.
- An interface output cost changed.
- The DR for an attached broadcast or NBMA segment changed.

A special case is when an LSA must be reoriginated even if its contents haven't changed, that is, when the age of a self-originated LSA reaches LSRefreshTime, or 1,800 seconds. As mentioned before, OSPF removes LSAs from the LSDB whenever its age reaches the MaxAge value. To make sure that routers do not remove valid LSAs from their LSDBs, originating routers reoriginate their LSAs every LSRefreshTime.

Whenever an OSPF router originates a new version of an LSA, the LSA's sequence number is incremented, its Age field is set to 0, and the LSA's checksum is recalculated.

> The first instance of any OSPF LSA is always originated with the sequence number equal to InitialSequenceNumber (0×80000001, or $-2^{31} + 1$). When successive versions of the LSA are originated, the sequence number is incremented by 1. When the sequence number reaches MaxSequenceNumber ($0 \times 7FFFFFFF$, or $2^{31} - 1$) and a new version of the LSA needs to be originated, the old version is flushed from the domain, and the new version is originated, using the InitialSequenceNumber value. Normally, this event will never be seen in real networks, as it takes more than a hundred years for an LSA to reach MaxSequenceNumber, even when a new version of the LSA is originated every second.

When a new LSA is originated, the router installs it into its own LSDB and submits it for flooding to its neighbors (see Section 9.2.3.11 for information on flooding in OSPF).

> The LSA origination rate is paced in OSPF. Any given LSA may not be reoriginated faster than once per MinLSInterval (5 seconds). This is to prevent flooding storms in unstable networks.

9.2.3.11 Flooding and LSDB Maintenance Procedures

The flooding algorithm ensures that all routers in an OSPF area agree on the information in their LSDBs within a finite period of time after the initial LSDB synchronization of neighbors has been performed. In short, flooding is the algorithm that ensures continual LSDB synchronization for adjacent routers.

> The same flooding algorithm is used by OSPF to flood type 5 LSAs throughout the OSPF domain, except for stub and not-so-stubby areas.

Sources of New Information.   LSAs are submitted for flooding right after they have been installed in the LSDB. Installation of a new LSA into the LSDB may occur either because the router itself has originated a new version of a self-originated LSA or because a new version of the LSA was received from another router in a link-state update packet.

Receiving the LSAs.   New LSAs are received from other routers in link-state update packets (see Figure 9-21 for the format). Every link-state update packet includes the number of LSAs and the actual LSA bodies.

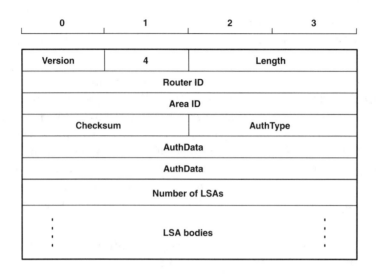

Figure 9-21. *Format of link-state update packet*

Before a received link-state update packet is processed, OSPF performs all steps required for general OSPF packet processing. The packet is also associated with a particular neighbor. Afterward, the packet is processed as follows.

1. If the FSM state of the neighbor that the packet is associated with is lesser than Exchange, silently drop the packet without further processing.

2. Otherwise, process every LSA within the link-state update packet as follows.

    a. Check whether the LSA is stored in the packet properly. If only part of the LSA is available, the packet was malformed, and the router logs an error message and discards the whole packet.

    b. Check the LSA data. If the LSA is malformed—for example, a router LSA does not contain all link records announced in its header—the LSA is ignored.

    c. Calculate the LSA checksum. If the calculated checksum and the checksum in the LSA body do not match—the LSA was corrupted—ignore this LSA and take the next LSA in the packet. (Ignored LSAs are not acknowledged and will be retransmitted by the sending router.)

    d. Check the type of the LSA. If the type of the LSA is not supported, ignore the LSA and take the next LSA in the packet. (Cisco routers support LSAs of types 1 through type 5, type 7, and types 9 through 11.)

e. If the type of the LSA is AS-external (type 5) and the area it was received from is stub or NSSA or if the type of the LSA is NSSA-external (type 7) and the area it was received from is not NSSA, discard the LSA.

f. Look up an instance of the LSA in the LSDB.

g. If the age of the LSA is MaxAge, no instance of the LSA is in the LSDB, and no neighbor is in the state Exchange or Loading in the same area—if the flooding scope of the LSA is areawide—or in any area—if the flooding scope is domain-wide—with FSM state Exchange or Loading, acknowledge the LSA by sending a link-state acknowledgment packet, considered later in this section, to the neighbor, discard the LSA, and consider the next LSA in the packet.

h. Otherwise, if no instance of the LSA is in the LSDB or if the received version of the LSA is more recent than the database copy, do the following.

    i. If the LSA was installed in the LSDB via flooding, not local origination, less than MinLSArrival seconds (1 second) ago, discard the LSA without acknowledging it. This check is done to prevent excessive load on the network because of frequent updates of an LSA.

    ii. Flood the LSA out to the neighboring routers. (The algorithm for selecting the interfaces to flood over is considered later in this section.)

    iii. Install the LSA in the LSDB, described later in this section. This step includes removing the new LSA from the link-state request lists of all neighbors within the flooding scope.

    iv. Acknowledge the LSA by sending the link-state acknowledgment packet to the neighbor, but do so only if the LSA has not already been flooded out of the same interface when the router itself is the DR for the segment. Note that Cisco routers always use delayed acknowledgments for all link types. This means that acknowledgments are grouped and sent in one link-state acknowledgment packet.

    v. If the installed LSA is self-originated, the router performs special actions, as described later in this section.

i. Otherwise, if there is a database copy of the LSA, the received version of the LSA is not more recent, and there is a corresponding LSA header in the neighbor's link-state request list, a BadLSReq event is generated for the neighbor FSM to indicate that there was an error in the database synchronization process.

j. Otherwise, if the received and the database versions of the LSA are equally recent, the received LSA may be either a duplicate or an implied acknowledgment if the router itself is not the DR but the other router is the DR on the segment and acknowledges the receipt of the LSA from the router implicitly by flooding it back to all OSPF routers through the same interface. The router performs the following steps.

    i.   If the received LSA is on the link-state retransmission list for the neighbor, the received LSA is considered an implied acknowledgment and is removed from the retransmission list.

    ii.   Otherwise, the LSA is a duplicate and should be acknowledged.

  k. Otherwise—the database copy is more recent—if the database copy of the LSA has its Age field equal to MaxAge and SequenceNumber equal to MaxSequence Number, the SequenceNumber of the LSA is wrapping; that is, the originating router has flushed the old version from the domain and is trying to install the new one, but the router itself cannot accept it, as not all its neighbors have acknowledged receipt of the old LSA with its Age field equal to MaxAge. In this situation, the received LSA is simply ignored without any acknowledgments, causing the sending router to retransmit the new version of the LSA again in the RxmtInterval period (5 seconds).

LSA Installation and SPF Scheduling.   When a new instance of an LSA is received or originated by an OSPF router, the instance is installed in the link-state database, probably overriding the old version of the LSA. The new LSA may carry some new topological or routing information, so the router may need to recalculate its routing table after the LSA is installed. To correctly detect whether this routing table recalculation is necessary, the router compares the old and the new versions of the LSA as follows.

1. Look up an instance of the LSA, using the LSA type, Link-state ID, and the Advertising Router fields as LSA identifiers, in the LSDB.

2. If no such instance exists, consider the new LSA different.

3. Otherwise, compare the old and the new instances of the LSA as follows:

  a. If the LSA is a summary-LSA, AS-external-LSA, or NSSA-external-LSA, compare the route masks in the LSA instances. If the route masks are different, consider the new LSA different. (This change will lead to removal of the route with the old mask and installation of the route with the new one.)

  b. Compare the LSA Options field. If the value of this field differs in the LSA instances being compared, consider the LSAs different. (Change in the Options bits is important for NSSA and demand circuit operation.)

  c. If the age of one of the LSAs is MaxAge but the age of the other is not, consider the new LSA different. (When the age of the LSA is MaxAge, the LSA is not considered during routing table calculation and is finally removed from the LSDB.)

d. If the lengths of the LSAs are different, consider the LSAs different.

e. Compare the contents of the LSAs. For example, for router-LSAs, the links records are compared; for network-LSAs, the lists of adjacent routers are checked; and so on.

If the LSAs are considered different after these checks, the router schedules appropriate SPF calculation. Note that routing table calculation in OSPF includes intra-area, inter-area, and AS-external parts. Changes in LSAs of different types may require different types of route recalculations. See Section 9.2.3.12 for details.

Flooding the LSA to Other Neighbors.   Whenever a new LSA is installed in the LSDB—because it was received from another router or was locally originated—the new LSA needs to be distributed to all other routers in the OSPF domain. OSPF does not try to send LSAs directly to all known routers in the domain; this approach would not work. Instead, OSPF relies on hop-by-hop flooding.

> The main principle of flooding is that once an LSA has been either reliably delivered to a router or locally originated, the router reliably sends the LSA to all other neighbors. Because all OSPF routers follow this rule, new LSAs are finally flooded to all reachable routers.

Formally, OSPF routers select interfaces over which to flood the new LSA. For all the interfaces within the flooding scope—all interfaces for type 5 and type 11 LSAs and interfaces within the same area for all other LSA types—the following steps are performed.

1. Consider the neighbors associated with the interface as follows.

    a. Check the state of the neighbor's FSM. If the state is ExStart or lesser, skip this neighbor. Until it is out of ExStart state, the neighbor's FSM cannot participate in asynchronous flooding.

    b. Otherwise, if the state is Exchange or Loading, look through the link-state request list and try to find an entry for the newly installed LSA in it. If there is such an entry and the new LSA is more recent, the router has requested or is about to request the same LSA from this neighbor while it was received from another neighbor. The LSA is removed from the link-state request list. If the list becomes empty at this time and the state of the neighbor is Loading, a LoadingDone event is generated for this neighbor's FSM.

    c. If the new LSA was received from this neighbor, skip it. LSAs must not be flooded back to the sending neighbors.

   d. Add the LSA to the neighbor's retransmission list. This will ensure that the LSA is finally delivered to the neighbor via periodic retransmission. The LSA is removed from the retransmit list when an acknowledgment is received from the neighbor.

2. If the LSA was not added to the retransmission list of any neighbor associated with this interface, skip this interface.

3. If the neighbor from which the new LSA was received is associated with this interface and the router itself is not the DR or the BDR for the segment, skip this interface. Non-DR routers flood LSAs only to the DR and the BDR. The DR and the BDR in turn make sure that the LSAs are successfully flooded to all other routers on the segment.

4. If the LSA was received on the same interface and the router itself is the BDR for the segment, skip this interface. The DR will multicast the LSA to all routers on the segment. Note, however, that the BDR still puts the LSA on the retransmission lists of corresponding neighbors, so if the DR fails to perform its duties, the BDR will retransmit the LSA to the neighbors even before the DR is determined to be down and reelected.

5. At this point, the LSA is sent over the interface in a link-state update packet. When the LSA is copied into the packet, its Age field is incremented by InfTransDelay (1 by default) to prevent endless flooding of LSAs in the case of software bugs. On broadcast interfaces, OSPF sends a single packet as a multicast. If the router itself is the DR or the BDR, the address AllSPFRouters is used; otherwise, the packet is sent to the AllDRouters address. For NBMA interfaces, a separate packet is sent as a unicast to each neighbor in state Exchange or higher.

Special Cases in Flooding Algorithm.   Most of the functionality performed by the flooding algorithm is rather generic for LSA types and situations. However, LSAs must be processed in an unusual way under certain conditions, as follows:

- Flooding of MaxAge LSAs: When an LSA with this value is received, the router gets an indication that the LSA is being flushed from the domain. The router cannot just remove the LSA from its LSDB right away but rather must make sure that all other routers also flush the LSA from their databases. Because of this requirement, OSPF routers process received MaxAge LSAs as follows. If no instance of MaxAge LSA is in the router's own LSDB and none of the neighbors is in state Exchange or Loading, the new LSA is acknowledged and discarded. Otherwise, the new LSA is installed into the router's database and is flooded to all other neighbors.

The reason for discarding the MaxAge LSAs in this case is that when an LSA's age reaches MaxAge naturally or as a result of the LSA flushing procedure, the LSA must finally be removed from the LSDBs of all routers. If the router receives a MaxAge LSA and it already has no copy of the LSA in the LSDB, there is no reason to install the LSA. The condition of no neighbors in state Exchange or Loading is to eliminate the situation whereby the router is establishing adjacencies with some neighbors and neighbors still have a copy of the LSA that is being flushed.

Next, the MaxAge LSA is removed from LSDB when the LSA is not in the retransmission list of any neighbor *and* none of the router's neighbors is in state Exchange or Loading.

- Receipt of self-originated LSAs: Normally, the router will not receive more recent self-originated LSAs. However, if the router reboots and loses track of the sequence numbers of its originated LSAs, it may receive LSAs that it originated before the reload, and these LSAs will be considered more recent and thus will be installed into the router's LSDB. In this situation, the router considers these LSAs and decides whether it wants to originate them anymore. If it does not, the router originates a new, correct version of the LSA, using the sequence number plus 1 of the received LSA.

LSA Aging, Periodic Checking, and Removal.   While LSAs are in the router's LSDB, a number of activities are performed on them by the OSPF process. First, all LSAs are aged. This means that the router keeps track of when the value of the Age field of a given LSA reaches MaxAge. When this happens, the LSA is put on the MaxAge list, which is checked periodically. The MaxAge list-checking procedure verifies the MaxAge LSA removal conditions, described earlier, and removes MaxAge LSAs from the LSDB, when possible.

Also, the router checks the checksums of LSAs whenever the age of an LSA reaches a multiple of CheckAge, every 10 minutes in Cisco OSPF implementation. If this check shows that an LSA has become invalid, because of memory corruption or software bugs, the router logs an error message.

OSPF routers perform reorigination of self-originated LSAs. When the Age of an LSA reaches LSRefreshTimer, the LSA is reoriginated with a new sequence number. This feature increases the protocol's robustness and ensures final convergence in case of bugs.

9.2.3.12 Routing Table Calculation
Intra-area route calculation in OSPF is based on the Dijkstra algorithm. However, intra-area route computation in OSPF does not consist only of the shortest-path computation

over the topology graph. The reason is that a single IP prefix can be announced by more than one router.

The intra-area routing table calculation algorithm includes two stages: calculation of the SPT and processing of stub links. The first stage is performed by OSPF routers to find the shortest paths from the vertex corresponding to the calculating router to all other vertices, as well as to update the routing table with IP prefixes associated with transit networks—LAN or NBMA segments. While performing this stage, OSPF considers router-LSAs and network-LSAs as vertex and link descriptions and ignores type 3 (intra-area prefix) link records. The algorithm performed by the routers directly corresponds to the Dijkstra algorithm, explained in Section 9.1.2. Formal specification of it can be found in [RFC2328].

When the first stage is complete, the calculating router walks through all vertices in the SPT and considers type 3 link records in corresponding router-LSAs as leaf entries in the tree. These link records represent IP prefixes associated with router interfaces. Among all available routes to the same destination—more than one router can announce the same prefix—OSPF chooses the route with the best metric, that is, the route through the path with the sum of transit link costs and the cost announced in the type 3 link record.

While intra-area route calculation is being performed, OSPF routers update entries in their router routing tables. Each entry in a router routing table describes an ABR or an ASBR. Routes in these tables can be either intra-area or inter-area. It is clear that routes to ABRs may be only intra-area, whereas routes to ASBRs can be either intra-area or inter-area, depending on whether the router is seen directly via the area topology or is announced by an ABR using an ASBR-summary-LSA (type 4 LSA). Processing of summary-LSAs is considered in Section 9.2.4.3. Entries in the router routing table are never used for packet forwarding. In fact, this table is internal to the OSPF process, and its entries are never propagated to the main routing table. However, entries in this table are used when intra-area and AS-external routes are calculated.

9.2.3.13 Frequently Asked Questions

Q: **Why does OSPF have so many LSA types?**

A: OSPF could potentially put all information that needs to be announced in the router-LSA. However, this method has several very serious disadvantages, one of which is the need to announce the whole contents of the LSA whenever a single element of information changes. This means considerable overhead when a single topology change occurs. Instead, OSPF splits different types of information into different LSA types. Each LSA lives its own life and can be updated or removed from the domain separately.

Q: **Does OSPF send periodic updates as RIP or IGRP do?**

A: Every 30 minutes, OSPF routers do update LSAs they have originated. However, this requirement was introduced into OSPF to improve protocol robustness; in distance-vector routing protocols, by contrast, periodic updates are essentially used as keep-alive messages. Periodic updates in OSPF do not trigger recalculation of the routing table. Also note that the periodic updates in OSPF are sent at a much lower rate than in RIP or IGRP.

Q: When originating a new LSA, a router needs to make sure that the LSA is installed in LSDBs of all routers in the area. Does the router send the new LSA directly to all known routers?

A: No. OSPF uses the flooding algorithm (see Section 9.2.3.11) to propagate new information through the network. This essentially means that the router sends the LSA to its neighboring routers, neighboring routers install it in the LSDB and send to all their neighbors, and so on. OSPF routers cannot send LSAs directly to all remote routers, for a number of reasons. First, it is wrong for a routing protocol to rely on correctness of its own routing information. Second, the nature of the protocol is dynamic; that is, some remote routers may not be known by the originating router when the new LSA is created.

Q: If OSPF adjacency is established over an unnumbered point-to-point link, how does the router send OSPF packets to the neighbor?

A: OSPF packets are always sent as multicast to the AllSPFRouters address over point-to-point links.

Q: What is the two-way connectivity check, and what is it used for?

A: The two-way connectivity check makes sure that both routers terminating the adjacency have consistent views on its state. OSPF abstracts the network topology in terms of vertices—routers or transit networks—and edges. Edges are the adjacencies every router has with its neighbors. Although each adjacency is between two routers, every router has its own view of the adjacency state. The same adjacency can be in different states on each side. Although one router can believe that the adjacency is in Full state, the other may still be loading LSAs from the neighbor and have the FSM in the Loading state. This means that neighbors have not yet synchronized their LSDBs. Another reason why one neighbor may report an adjacency whereas the other may not is the fact that one router has already determined that the neighbor is unreachable, whereas the other has not.

Q: Why did OSPF originally announce IP address of the remote neighbor in the case of a point-to-point link?

A: OSPF was designed with an assumption that IP subnets do not need to be assigned to point-to-point interfaces. This means that even though an IP address is assigned to an interface, the subnet mask is not configured for it, as the link connects only two routers, and each side may assign the IP address independently. In this case, routers consider IP addresses of the neighbors as addresses of attached hosts and announce them as host routes. However, a lot of networks are deployed with subnets assigned to point-to-point links, so an option was added to OSPF to allow both routers to announce the subnet itself. This method is used in Cisco IOS.

Q: **The DR election algorithm in OSPF is said to honor existing DR/BDR assignments. Can there be any situation in which a newly attached router takes over the DR or BDR responsibility?**

A: The DR election algorithm in OSPF is said to be nonpreemptive. However, it is also cooperative. This means that the algorithm is based on the assumption that all routers on a segment have the same input information and hence end up with the same results. The most important input information is the list of routers claiming to be the DR or the BDR. When a new router is attached to a segment and is eligible to become the DR, the DR election process is delayed until the router sees a hello from the BDR or one from the DR, indicating that no BDR is on the segment or a timer has expired. If for some reason the newly attached router cannot hear a Hello packet from the routers already on the segment, the router will end up promoting itself to the DR status. If other routers can hear the new router's Hello packets and the new router has a higher Router-ID than the current DR, the new router may preempt the DR functionality.

Q: **Does OSPF support QOS?**

A: OSPF does not support quality-of-service techniques. OSPF used to provide TOS-specific costs in its LSAs, which allowed routers to calculate separate routing tables for each TOS, but TOS support was removed from OSPF in [RFC2178] because no vendor implemented it.

Q: **What is the difference between the term autonomous system used in OSPF and the term OSPF routing domain?**

A: In the OSPF standard, autonomous system refers to the OSPF routing domain. BGP treats an autonomous system differently, however. From BGP's perspective, an AS can consist of more than one routing domain.

Q: **Do OSPF routers install routes to Router-IDs of the remote routers?**

A: No. An OSPF Router-ID may be equal to an IP address of the router but does not have to be. The Router-ID should be understood as a numeric identifier of every OSPF router, not as a source of routing information. However, if the Router-ID is derived from a loopback interface IP address and that interface is included in the corresponding OSPF process, such an address is announced by the router as a host route.

Q: Can I run more than instance of OSPF on the same interface?

A: No. OSPF packets do not contain a process ID field, so it wouldn't be possible to differentiate packets originated by different processes. In addition, Cisco routers do not allow the administrator to include a single interface in more than one OSPF process.

9.2.4 Inter-Area Routing

9.2.4.1 Introduction to Inter-Area Routing and ABR Functionality

As a hierarchical routing protocol, OSPF allows a routing domain to be split into subdomains, called areas. The main purpose of creating areas in an OSPF domain is scalability. Without areas, every router in the domain would be aware of every single link and router in the network, so whenever the topology of the domain changed, such as a link going up or down, all routers would need to recalculate their routing tables. With a large number of routers, links, and announced IP prefixes, this might put a significant load on the CPU.

If an OSPF domain is split into areas, routers see only the topology of the area they belong to. An exception is the ABRs. Because they are attached to more than one area, they see the topology of all areas they are attached to. When a Link state in one area changes, attached routers originate new versions of corresponding LSAs and flood them to their neighbors. Limitation of link-state change propagation is achieved by limitation of the LSA flooding scope. Most of the LSAs in base OSPF have areawide flooding scope. ABRs do not announce topological information between areas. Instead, only routing information is injected. For internal OSPF routers, inter-area routing information is represented as leaf nodes attached to ABR vertices in the topology graph.

The way OSPF distributes inter-area topology information is essentially a distance-vector technique. Area border routers calculate intra-area routes for directly attached areas and announce them to all other areas as inter-area. However, if the ABR announced only intra-area routes, all OSPF areas would need to be connected in a fully meshed topology, with each area having a connection to every other area. This is not possible to achieve in real networks. Instead, a special method is used to distribute inter-area routing information through the domain without having to struggle with the problems specific to distance-vector technologies. OSPF ABRs are allowed to announce inter-area routes but only those learned from the backbone area. This way, the backbone area serves as an inter-area routing information repository, and because inter-area routes are announced to it, OSPF is safe from inter-area routing loops.

Figure 9-22 illustrates the flow of routing information within an OSPF routing domain. Consider networks N and M, local to areas 1 and 2. ABRs connecting these areas to the backbone calculate their intra-area routes to these networks and install them in

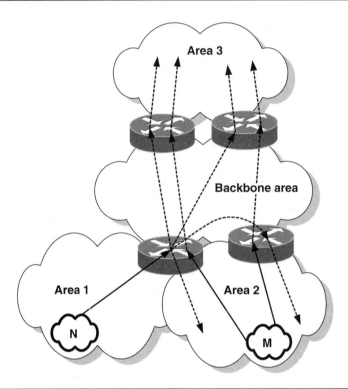

Figure 9-22. *Flow of routing information in OSPF domain*

their routing table. Then ABRs announce the intra-area routing information in their tables to all attached areas, including the backbone. All routers in the domain, including the ABRs, also calculate their inter-area routing information announced by the ABRs and install corresponding inter-area routes in their routing tables.

> ABRs are allowed to consider only inter-area routing information they receive from the backbone, and no other area. This implicitly means that all ABRs must have some connection to the backbone area for inter-area routing in OSPF to work correctly. Cisco implementation of OSPF allows ABRs without an active backbone connection to consider inter-area routing information from all attached areas. This topic is considered in detail in Section 9.2.4.6.

Distribution of inter-area routing information through the backbone area saves OSPF from routing loops but also introduces the possibility of connectivity problems if the backbone area is split into independent parts. In this case, routing between the areas connected to different parts of the split backbone is not possible, because inter-area routing information is not distributed via nonbackbone areas. The solution for this problem is to use virtual links through nonbackbone areas. Virtual links between ABRs are configured manually by the administrator. In fact, virtual links are just a specific type of adjacency that can cross more than one network link and always belong to the backbone area (even though they cross nonbackbone ones). Virtual links not only solve connectivity problems in the case of a backbone split but also help achieve more optimal inter-area routing in some cases. Virtual links are considered in detail in Section 9.2.4.5.

Route summarization is a very important technique that provides scalability to OSPF. Without route summarization, every intra-area route is announced as a single inter-area route into all other areas. This means that whenever there is a link flap, routers in other areas will need to recalculate their inter-area routing information; thus, topology changes in one area are not truly hidden from routers in other areas. If ABRs are configured to do route summarization, a block of specific intra-area routes is announced with a small set of aggregate routes. Because the state of a single, specific prefix does not define the state of the announced aggregate route, topology changes in areas are hidden from routers in other areas.

Inter-area route summarization in OSPF is not automatic. The administrator needs to configure the ABRs with a set of *area ranges*. Each area range is an IP prefix. When it announces intra-area routes associated with a specific area, an ABR looks through the list of address ranges configured for that area. If a specific intra-area route falls into a range, it is not announced; instead, an inter-area route with parameters exactly corresponding to those in the area range is advertised.

9.2.4.2 Distribution of Routing Information and Types of LSAs

OSPF distributes two types of routing information between areas: IP prefixes, associated with networks residing in specific areas, and the location of ASBRs. Two types of LSAs are used to achieve this:

- Summary-LSA (type 3), used to distribute inter-area IP routing information, possibly in a summarized form
- ASBR-summary-LSA (type 4), used to announce the location of ASBRs

Figure 9-23 illustrates the format of these LSAs, which are used to represent leaf entries linked to corresponding ABR vertices in the topology graph. The difference between the two is in the type field, the value placed into the Mask field, and the purpose of the LSA. In the case of summary-LSAs (type 3), the Mask field contains the route mask of the route being announced. In the case of ASBR-summary-LSA (type 4), this field is unused and is always 0.

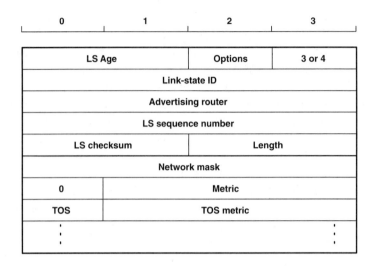

Figure 9-23. *Summary and ASBR-summary LSA format*

9.2.4.3 Inter-area Route Calculation

Summary-LSAs are processed by OSPF routers as follows. Note that the router has calculated its intra-area routes and—important!—has installed some entries in its router routing table before executing this algorithm.

1. Area border routers consider only summary-LSAs associated with the backbone area. Internal OSPF routers consider summary-LSAs of the attached area.

2. Process every summary and ASBR-summary-LSA in the corresponding area's LSDB as follows.

   a. If the LSA is originated by the calculating router, skip it.

   b. If the metric announced in the LSA equals LSInfinity, consider the associated network unreachable, and skip the LSA.

   c. If the LSA is a summary-LSA and the IP prefix announced by it exactly matches one of the active area ranges, skip the LSA. This is necessary to prevent inter-area routing loops when more than one ABR announces the same summary-LSA to the backbone.

   d. Look up the route to the router that originated the LSA in the router routing table. If there is no such route, ignore the LSA, as the originating router is not reachable. Otherwise, calculate the distance, D, to the destination announced in the LSA—remote network or ASBR—as the sum of the cost of the route to the ASBR and the cost announced in the LSA.

e. If the processed LSA is a summary-LSA, look up a route to the announced IP prefix in the routing table. If LSA is an ASBR-summary-LSA, look up an entry in the router routing table to the same ASBR as announced by the LSA.

f. If no route is found, add the new route to the routing table. The metric of the route is set to variable D. The next-hop structures are copied from the entry in the router routing table corresponding to the Advertising Router. The route type is set to inter-area.

g. If a route is found and it is an intra-area route, consider the next LSA in the LSDB. Intra-area routes are always preferred over inter-area ones.

h. If the type of the found route is inter-area, compare the metric of this route to variable D. If the new metric is better, overwrite the old route with the new one. If the new metric is worse, consider the next LSA. If the metrics are the same, install a parallel route to the same destination.

When it calculates inter-area routes and installs them in the routing table, a router uses next-hop structures associated with the announcing ABR; that is, inter-area route calculation depends on the results of the intra-area route calculation. If the announcing router is not reachable, routes corresponding to the summary-LSAs originated by it are not installed.

When ASBR-summary-LSAs are processed, routes to ASBRs are not installed in the primary routing table that can be shown with the show ip route command. Instead, a special internal OSPF routing table that can be shown with the show ip ospf border command is used.

9.2.4.4 Origination of Summary-LSAs

Origination of summary-LSAs by ABRs is performed as follows. After the ABR has calculated its routing table, including intra-area and inter-area route calculations, it goes through the main and the router routing tables and performs the following steps.

1. If the entry describes a router—that is, it is a router routing table entry—and the associated router is not an ASBR, skip the entry. (Only ASBR locations are announced to other areas.)

2. If the entry describes a network and the route type is external or if the route type is inter-area and is not associated with the backbone, skip the entry.

3. If the route metric is equal to or greater than LSInfinity, skip the entry.

4. If the entry describes a network and the route type is intra-area and falls into a range associated with the area the route belongs to, do not announce the route

but instead modify the area range data structure accordingly—the number of specific routes is incremented, and the minimal route metric is updated—so that the range itself is announced later.

5. If the route describes a router and it is not the best route to it—we can have more than one router to the same ABR or ASBR through different areas—consider the next entry. (As we are using a distance-vector algorithm, we should follow its rules: Announce only the information used by the router itself.)

6. If the route has passed all the checks, the ABR announces it to the attached areas as follows. For every attached area A, the following steps are performed.

   a. If the announced route is associated with area A, skip this area.

   b. If the route's next hops are resolvable through area A, skip this area. This check is targeted to the situations in which a backbone route is updated with a better inter-area route from a transit area.

   c. If the route type is inter-area and area A is the backbone, consider the next area. Inter-area routes are never announced to the backbone area.

   d. Otherwise, the destination should be announced to area A. If the destination is a network, originate a summary-LSA to area A, setting the Link-state ID to the value of the announced prefix—possibly setting some host bits if the prefixes with the same value but different lengths should be announced—the mask field to the corresponding route mask, and the cost to the value of the route metric.

   e. If the destination is the ASBR, originate an ASBR-summary-LSA to area A, setting the Link-state ID to the Router-ID of the announced ASBR, the mask field to 0, and the cost to the value of the route metric.

Originated summary-LSAs are flooded throughout the areas. Routers internal to the areas perform inter-area route calculation and install inter-area routes to the networks and ASBRs in their routing tables. Note again that routes to ASBRs are maintained in an internal OSPF routing table.

9.2.4.5 Virtual Links

As mentioned before, it is sometimes necessary to establish virtual adjacencies between OSPF ABRs. To establish virtual adjacencies, ABRs must be manually configured by the administrator with the parameters of the virtual links. The most important parameter of the virtual link is the Router-ID of the ABR that is terminating it in the same area.

Whereas normal adjacencies are established over a single physical interface—that is, they span only one link and are not routed through other routers—and the multicast capability of the attached media is used for neighbor discovery, virtual adjacencies span the whole area, always nonbackbone. OSPF packets belonging to virtual links are forwarded by internal routers; therefore, virtual adjacencies depend on intra-area routing. OSPF does not provide a mechanism to automatically provision topology of virtual links; instead, virtual links must be configured manually on the terminating ABRs. Note that a virtual adjacency and a virtual interface are two different things. A virtual interface is a useful abstraction. When the administrator configures a virtual link, an interface data structure is created in which two fields specific to virtual links are maintained: the Router-ID of the other ABR and the IP address that must be used to reach this ABR. The first parameter is configured manually when a virtual link is created. The second parameter is calculated dynamically when the router performs an intra-area routing table calculation for the area crossed by the virtual link, and the router-LSA originated by the ABR with the specified Router-ID is put on the SPT. (Areas used to establish virtual adjacencies between ABRs are called transit areas, as ABRs may route transit traffic through them.)

When an ABR configured with a virtual link notices that a corresponding ABR is reachable for the first time, the ABR generates an InterfaceUp event for the FSM associated with the virtual link. This event starts the hello sending process on the virtual link. Hellos sent over a virtual link are always sent as unicast to the precalculated router's address. When both routers identify reachability of each other, they form a virtual adjacency.

It must be emphasized that virtual links always belong to the backbone area. The cost associated with the virtual link equals the metric found in the router routing entry describing the ABR that terminates the virtual link. The state of the virtual link depends solely on the reachability of corresponding ABR.

Virtual adjacencies are announced by the area border routers in their router-LSAs, using type 4 link records. Note again that because virtual links always belong to the backbone area, virtual adjacencies are included in router-LSAs originated for the backbone area only. Other routers in the backbone area consider the virtual adjacency as a normal adjacency. The only detail that is different is that for a virtual link to be used, a virtual link in the opposite direction must be announced by the peer ABR.

Figure 9-24 illustrates how virtual links can be used to optimize inter-area routing in OSPF. ABRs A and B connect area 1 to the backbone. Note that the path between A and B through area 1 is preferable to the path in the backbone area because that path goes through higher-speed links. However, because they do not see the topology details of area 1, backbone routers do not use the fast path between A and B in their Dijkstra computation but prefer a slower path, using the backbone links. If configured between A and B through area 1, a virtual link will be announced to the backbone area and—important!— will be used by routers A and B themselves to calculate routes through the backbone area. Note that in this case, routes calculated through virtual links are associated with the backbone, whereas the next hops belong to the transit area.

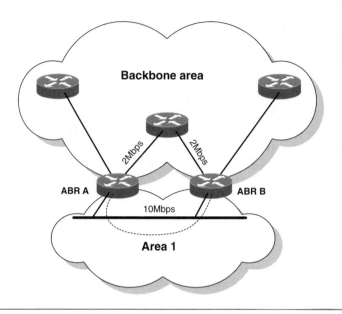

Figure 9-24. *Virtual links used to ensure optimal routing*

Another example illustrating how virtual links can be used is depicted in Figure 9-25. In this case, a network must be connected to an existing OSPF domain as area 2. Unfortunately, routers in this area do not have physical links to any backbone routers. If area 2 is attached to area 1 via router R1, R1 will not identify itself as an ABR by setting the B bit in its router-LSAs and will not inject inter-area routing information into areas. Even if R1 is configured with a fake backbone link—a loopback interface, for example—inter-area connectivity will not be complete, as R1 will not propagate inter-area routes from area 1 to area 2. The virtual link provides R1 with a backbone connection that is used to exchange backbone LSAs with R2.

> The ABR behavior described here is specific to Cisco's implementation of OSPF. The OSPF standard states that any router connected to more than one area is an ABR but limits ABRs to considering summary-LSAs received only from the backbone area.

9.2.4.6 Cisco ABR Behavior

The OSPF standard describes an ABR as a router connected to more than one area, regardless of whether the ABR is connected to the backbone. However, according to the OSPF specification, ABRs are restricted to considering summary-LSAs only from the backbone area to avoid loops of inter-area routing information. This means that if it has

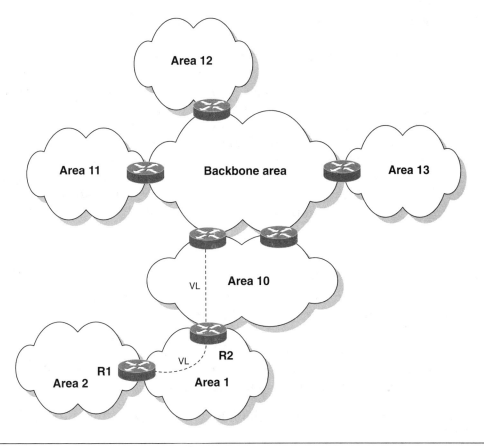

Figure 9-25. *Using virtual links to add area to OSPF domain*

no backbone area attachment, an ABR cannot route packets destined to networks residing in areas not directly attached to the ABR.

Cisco OSPF implementation is enhanced to address this problem. A router is considered to be an ABR—and hence the B bit is set in corresponding router-LSAs—only if it is attached to more than one area and has at least one interface in the backbone area in a state higher than Down. If the second condition is not met—no active OSPF interface is in the backbone area—but the router is attached to more than one area, the router is considered to be internal to all attached areas.

Inter-area route calculation is also modified. A router attached to more than one area considers only backbone summary-LSAs and only if it is an ABR and has at least one neighbor in the backbone. If the router is not an ABR or is an ABR but does not have a neighbor in the backbone area, the router considers summary-LSAs from all attached areas.

Origination of summary-LSAs is also modified. Inter-area routes are announced to other areas only if they are associated with the backbone area.

The described changes in OSPF ABR solve the problem illustrated by the following example. Router R1 in Figure 9-26 is attached to two nonbackbone areas and does not have any physical or virtual backbone connection. According to the OSPF standard, R1 would have only intra-area routes in its routing table and wouldn't be able to route to destinations in the backbone area and areas other than 3 and 4. With Cisco ABR behavior, R1 is allowed to consider summary-LSAs from both attached areas, as it does not consider itself an ABR. This rule relaxation causes R1 to install inter-area routes in its routing table through both attached areas. Note that if R1 is configured with a loopback interface and is assigned to the backbone area, R1 will provide a shortcut between attached areas—by announcing intra-area routes in summary-LSAs—and will consider summary-LSAs from the attached areas.

9.2.4.7 Frequently Asked Questions

Q: OSPF is a link-state routing protocol, but you say that it uses a distance-vector approach for inter-area routing. How can this be?

A: OSPF uses link-state principles only within the area. With inter-area routing, OSPF does not abstract inter-area topology and does not calculate any SPT. Instead, every ABR relays routing information pretty much like RIP or IGRP routers do. See Section 9.2.4.2 for more information.

Q: Why does the OSPF standard limit ABRs to considering only backbone summary-LSAs?

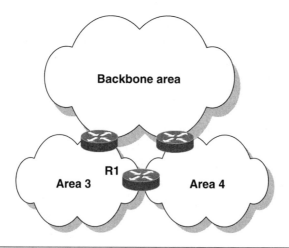

Figure 9-26. *Cisco ABR behavior*

A: If this limitation had not been introduced, ABRs would need to implement the techniques used in distance-vector protocols to stop routing loops. OSPF uses the backbone area as the central point of inter-area routing information distribution. Because of the limitation and because all areas should be physically or virtually connected to the backbone via ABRs, the flow of inter-area routing information follows a starlike topology: nonbackbone area, the backbone, and nonbackbone area.

Q: **Why is the Cisco OSPF ABR implementation not compatible with the OSPF standard?**

A: In fact, the two are compatible. Cisco ABR behavior works correctly in all cases covered by the standard ABR approach, and it also improves routing when an ABR does not have a backbone connection.

Q: **Can a virtual link cross more than one area?**

A: No. For a virtual link to go up, routers must be able to see one another via a common area. If you need to attach a nonbackbone area to another nonbackbone area connected to the backbone via a virtual link, you will need to configure a chain of virtual links, as shown in Figure 9-25.

Q: **Can OSPF inter-area routes be aggregated when announced from the backbone to nonbackbone areas?**

A: OSPF allows ABRs to aggregate only intra-area routing information when it is announced in summary-LSAs. So it is not possible to aggregate inter-area routes when they are announced to nonbackbone areas.

9.2.5 Routing to External Networks in OSPF

9.2.5.1 Introduction and Terminology

In the OSPF routing protocol, external routing information is announced in special AS-external-LSAs. This allows OSPF routers to distinguish between routes injected into the OSPF domain from an external source, such as static routes or routes from other OSPF domains or from BGP, and internal OSPF routing information. This differentiation ensures that if the same network is described by an internal—intra-area or inter-area—and an external route, the internal route is preferred. This logic is clear. If a network is known as both internal and external, either we have misconfigured IP addresses—the same IP prefix is used in different parts of the network—or an internal OSPF route was redistributed into another routing protocol and then injected back to the same OSPF domain. In either case, it is absolutely correct to prefer the internal route.

OSPF was designed with the assumption that routing information received from other autonomous systems via BGP would be injected as external into OSPF. So a lot of external routes were expected in OSPF domains. This is why external routing information is not propagated the same way as inter-area routing information.

When it has a route to inject into the OSPF domain, an ASBR originates an AS-external-LSA and floods it to its neighbors. LSAs of this type are flooded throughout the whole domain; that is, the flooding scope of AS-external-LSAs is domainwide versus areawide for all other LSA types. When routers in the same area with the ASBR calculate external routes announced by it, they perform an algorithm that is very similar to the inter-area route computation algorithm. AS-external-LSAs are considered as leaf entries of the graph linked to the vertices corresponding to the announcing ASBRs. However, when routers in other areas receive AS-external-LSAs via domainwide flooding, install them in their LSDB, and calculate their routing tables, they cannot see the ASBR, as its router-LSA is not flooded outside the area it belongs to. To ensure that all routers in the domain know the location of ASBRs, area border routers announce this information in ASBR-summary-LSAs. These LSAs result in inter-area ASBR routes in the internal router routing tables. These areas are then used to calculate the actual cost to the external network.

> The difference between propagation of external routing information and inter-area routing information prevents multiple LSAs from being created for the same prefix when more than one ABR connects an area to the backbone

The OSPF standard introduces two types of external announcements: type 1 and type 2. The difference between the two is in the method by which the final route metric is calculated. Every AS-external-LSA contains a metric field. When an LSA is originated, the metric field is assigned the metric value of the route being redistributed. If a prefix is announced as external type 1, remote routers calculate the route metric as a sum of the metric announced in the LSA and OSPF path cost to the ASBR. If type 2 advertisement is used, the metric equals the value announced in the LSA. Type 1 advertisements handle cases in which the metric of the external routing protocol is comparable to the OSPF path cost, such as RIP routes or routes from another OSPF domain, and type 2 advertisements handle cases in which the metrics are not comparable, such as routes redistributed from BGP.

> Cisco routers use external type 2 announcements by default.

In the OSPF protocol, LSAs may be modified only by the originating routers. Because AS-external-LSAs are flooded throughout the whole domain and are not relayed by the ABRs as summary-LSAs, for example, aggregation of external routing information in

OSPF is by default possible only once, when the AS-external-LSA is created by the ASBR. (See Section 9.2.5.6 for information on how not-so-stubby areas can be used to summarize external information more than one time.)

9.2.5.2 Distribution of Routing Information and Types of LSA

OSPF ASBRs announce external routing information in AS-external-LSAs. In particular, each AS-external-LSA carries exactly one external route. The format of LSAs of this type is shown in Figure 9-27.

The Link-state ID of the LSA is set to the value of the announced IP prefix. The Advertising Router can set some host bits if several prefixes with the same value but different lengths need to be announced when VLSM is used in the network. The network mask field is set to the corresponding route mask value. The E bit is set to 0 if the prefix is announced as external type 1 and to 1 if it is announced as external type 2. Setting of the 24-bit metric field of the LSA depends on the configuration of the redistributing router and the redistributed route itself."

- If the originating ASBR is configured with the default metric, all AS-external-LSAs will contain the default metric value.
- The value of the metric field may be influenced by route maps.

If neither of these conditions is met, the value of the metric announced in the AS-external-LSA depends on the type of redistributed route: OSPF, BGP, Connected, or other.

- If the redistributed route is learned via another OSPF process, the metric field is set to the route metric value.
- AS-external-LSAs derived from BGP routes always contain the metric value 1.
- If it is a connected route derived from an address of an OSPF-enabled interface, the metric used in the LSA is set to the interface output cost value. Otherwise, the metric is set to 1.
- If the redistributed route does not match the preceding conditions, the metric field in the LSA is set to the value 20.

The LSA's tag field is included to carry an arbitrary value that can be used for administrative purposes, such as route filtering. Cisco routers set this field as follows.

1. If the route being announced is the default (0.0.0.0/0), the tag value is set to the OSPF process number.
2. Otherwise, the tag field is set to the tag value in the prefix descriptor describing the route being redistributed.

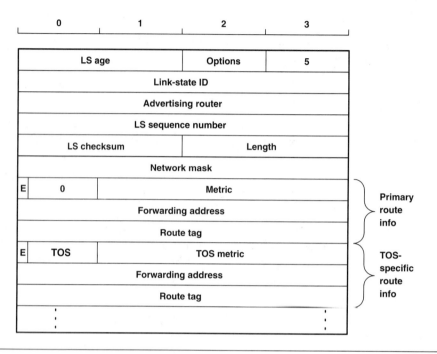

Figure 9-27. *Format of AS-external-LSA*

3. If the **redistribute** command was configured with the **tag** option, the tag value specified in the command overrides the value set in the preceding step.

4. Any value set in these steps can be overridden with a route map.

The forwarding address field in the LSA is used to eliminate an extra hop when an external route is received through an OSPF-enabled interface, as shown in Figure 9-28. In this example, the ASBR receives a BGP route from router R1 via an Ethernet segment to which OSPF router R2 is also attached. Now consider how routers R2, R3, and R4 would route to the external destination if the ASBR left the forwarding address as 0.0.0.0.

First, R2 would always forward packets to the ASBR instead of forwarding them directly to the BGP speaker. Also, R3 would always route through the low-speed path via the ASBR instead of the faster path via R2.

Formal rules for setting the forwarding address in the AS-external-LSA follow.

1. Among all the path descriptors of the redistributed routes, find the first one with the next-hop address that belongs to a directly connected route from an interface that meets the following criteria.

   ■ OSPF is enabled on this interface.

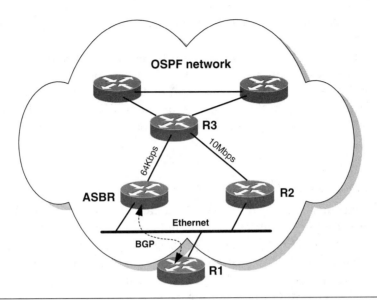

Figure 9-28. *Use of the forwarding address*

- The interface is not passive.
- The process ID of the OSPF instance running on the interface equals the ID of the redistributing process.
- The type of the interface is broadcast.
- The address is covered by a configured network statement.

2. If such a path descriptor is found, set the forwarding address in the LSA to the next-hop address in the path descriptor.

3. Otherwise, set the forwarding address field to 0.

9.2.5.3 Outline of ASBR Functionality

When a redistribute command is configured on an OSPF router, a special process, called OSPF scanner, is started in IOS. The purpose of this process is to ensure synchronization of the routing table—specifically, the routes to be redistributed—and self-originated AS-external-LSAs. This process walks through the routing table at 1-minute intervals and makes sure that the redistribution process is performed correctly.

However, the scanner is not the main part of the OSPF process involved in route redistribution. As discussed in Chapter 7, all redistributing routing processes in the Cisco IOS receive a callback whenever a route that should be redistributed is installed in the routing table or is removed from it. The OSPF process is no exception. The OSPF routing process receives these function calls and takes appropriate actions: LSA origination or flushing.

It is not enough for the ASBR to originate LSAs. As discussed in the next section, remote routers must have a corresponding entry in their router routing tables to install external routes derived from AS-external-LSAs announced by a particular router. To ensure that routers residing in the same area as the ASBR install such entries and that ABRs properly announce the ASBR location in ASBR-summary-LSAs, the ASBR sets the E bit in its router-LSA.

9.2.5.4 External Route Calculation

Calculation of external routes in OSPF is similar to inter-area routing calculation. Whereas inter-area route calculation is based on particular area-specific LSDBs, external route calculation considers the global, or process-specific, LSDB holding AS-external-LSAs. The calculation process proceeds as follows. Note that no AS-external-LSA is processed if the router is not attached to at least one normal—not stub and not NSSA—area, because stub areas cannot be used for transit traffic and NSSA areas are not supposed to be used to route traffic to destinations described in type 5 LSAs, which are not flooded within not-so-stubby areas.

For every AS-external-LSA, the following steps are performed.

1. If the LSA is originated by the calculating router itself, skip it, and consider the next LSA in the database.

2. If the LSA describes the default route and the router itself always originates a default—a **default-originate always** command is configured—skip the LSA. This is to prevent routing loops caused by the default originating router relying on a default route originated by another router in the domain.

3. If the metric reported in the AS-external-LSA equals LSInfinity or the age of the LSA equals MaxAge, discard the LSA.

4. The routing table is searched for a route to the destination described by the LSA. If a route is found and is installed by the same OSPF process and the route type is intra-area or inter-area, skip the LSA. (Internal OSPF routes are always preferred over external ones.)

5. The router routing table is searched for an entry describing the ASBR that originated the LSA. If no route is found, skip the LSA.

6. If the forwarding address in the LSA is nonzero, the router looks up a route to the forwarding address. If no such route exists or if the route is not OSPF intra-area or inter-area or connected or was installed in the routing table by a different OSPF process, discard the LSA.

7. Otherwise, the distance to the external network is calculated as follows.

   a. If the LSA describes a type 1 external destination, the route metric equals the sum of the metric announced in the LSA and the distance to the Advertising Router—if the forwarding address is zero—or to the forwarding address.

   b. If the LSA describes a type 2 destination, the route metric equals the metric announced in the LSA itself.

8. If the routing table contains an external OSPF route to the same destination installed by the same OSPF process, compare the new and the old routes as follows.

   a. If the old route is a type 1 route and the new route is a type 2, do not install the new route. Type 1 external routes are always preferred over type 2 external routes.

   b. Otherwise, if both routes are of the same type, the following rules apply.

      i. If the route metrics are different, install the route with the lower metric.

      ii. If the route metrics are equal and the route type is 2, install the route with the lower distance to the originating router or the forwarding address.

   c. If routes are still of equal preference, the new route is installed as a parallel route to the same destination.

9.2.5.5 Stub and Totally Stub Areas

So far, we have been considering normal OSPF areas: those capable of distributing external routing information. AS-external-LSAs originated anywhere in the OSPF domain are flooded to normal areas, so all routers in these areas install external routes in their routing table. In many cases, however, routers in some areas do not need external routing information. It is enough for them to have internal OSPF routes and route to external destinations, using a default route. This is the reason stub areas were introduced into the OSPF protocol.

When an area is configured as stub, no AS-external-LSAs are flooded into it. Flooding of these LSAs is stopped by ABRs connecting the stub area to the backbone. To ensure that routing to external destinations is successful, ABRs also originate special summary-LSAs into stub areas. These summary-LSAs carry the default route; that is, the Link-state ID and the mask are set to 0. ABRs still inject inter-area routing information into stub areas; internal routers have all intra-area and inter-area routes and an inter-area default for external destinations. However, if the LSDB size of routers internal to a stub area must be further minimized, stub area ABRs may be configured to inject only the default summary-LSAs. (Internal routers have only intra-area routes and an inter-area default in this case.) The area is called *totally stub* in this case.

All routers in the area must agree on area configuration to form the adjacency. If an area is configured to be normal in one router but stub in another one, these two routers will not establish the adjacency, because each will discard Hello packets from the other. Because routers in stub areas never flood type 5 LSAs to each other, ASBRs cannot reside in stub areas.

9.2.5.6 Not-So-Stubby Areas

Stub areas are ideal when an area neither has an ASBR nor needs to have external routing information, that is, when external routing information neither enters nor exits the area. *Not-so-stubby areas* (NSSAs) in turn, allow the area to provide the rest of the domain with external routing information but still not accept external routes from the backbone. This is achieved by introducing a new LSA type, NSSA-external-LSAs (type 7). Type 7 LSAs are flooded throughout the NSSA area but no farther and carry external routing information originated by ASBRs inside the NSSA. ABRs connecting the NSSA to the backbone translate type 7 LSAs into normal AS-external-LSAs with possible aggregation.

The NSSA approach is targeted to address situations described in the following two examples. The first example (Figure 9-29) illustrates a situation with a corporate OSPF backbone and a remote site running RIP. Before the remote site was connected to the backbone, area 1 used to be stub and accepted no AS-external-LSAs. Now that the routing information from the remote site needs to be announced to the rest of the OSPF backbone, the administrator would need to reconfigure the area to be normal, thus allowing, potentially, a huge amount of external routing information to be sent into it. The NSSA approach allows area 1 to inject external (RIP) routing information into the domain but still refrain from accepting AS-external-LSAs from outside.

Figure 9-30 illustrates an ISP network. Area 1 is a typical point-of-presence (POP) site. Access servers (titled as AS1…ASn) terminate numerous dial-up connections from customers. Customers are assigned IP addresses dynamically via PPP from a single pool of addresses configured on a DHCP (Dynamic Host Configuration Protocol) server—if the number of users is not very big—or from a pool specific to each access server. In the first case, if a normal area type is used, access servers will introduce a lot of external routes, each describing a host route to a single user. Under these conditions, the network will experience continual flooding activity, because every access server will originate or flush an AS-external-LSA every time a user connects to or disconnects from the server. In the second case, the situation is much better, as access servers may announce the whole address pool as a single IP prefix, so state changes of specific host routes are not reflected. Even in this case, however, it is a good idea to aggregate prefixes announced by access servers before propagating them to the backbone. The NSSA approach helps in both cases, as ABRs connecting the area to the backbone can be configured to aggregate routing information received from access servers before sending it to the backbone.

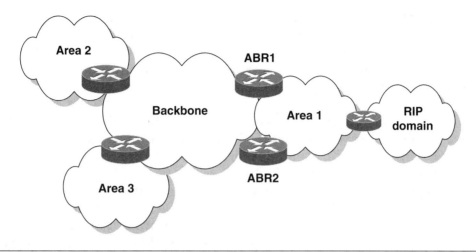

Figure 9-29. *NSSA used to import external routing information*

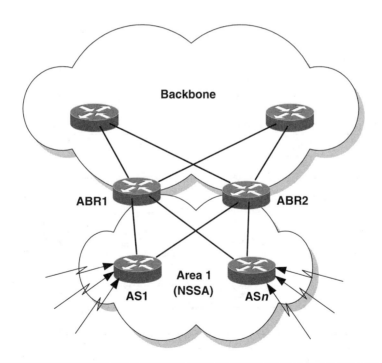

Figure 9-30. *NSSA used in ISP network*

The format of type 7 LSAs is depicted in Figure 9-31. The format is the same as for type 5 LSAs except for how the forwarding address field is set in type 7 LSAs. In type 5 LSAs, it is set when possible; in type 7 LSAs, it is always set. First, the originating router tries to set the forwarding address in the LSA as it does in the case of type 5 LSAs. If this is impossible, the forwarding address is set to the IP address of an OSPF-enabled interface.

Also, a new bit is introduced into the OSPF Options field. When used in Hello and DBD packets, this bit is called the N bit (for NSSA) and its use is similar to the E bit's: to ensure that all routers in the area agree on the NSSA setting. When used in type 7 LSAs, this bit is called the P (for propagate) bit, and is used to instruct NSSA ABRs whether the LSA should be translated into a type 5 LSA. When the router that originated a type 7 LSA is connected only to the NSSA itself, the P bit is set, and the LSA is propagated to the backbone. When, for example, the NSSA ABR also performs ASBR functionality and redistributes external routing information into both NSSA (as type 7 LSAs) and the backbone area (as type 5 LSAs), the P bits of LSAs originated for the NSSA are reset, thus preventing other NSSA ABRs from translating type 7 LSAs into type 5 ones.

Translation of type 7 LSAs into type 5 LSAs works as follows.

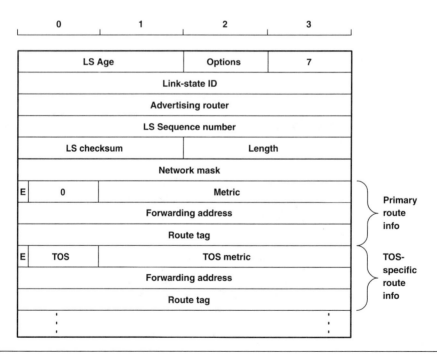

Figure 9-31. *Type 7 LSA format*

1. The NSSA ASBR originates a type 7 LSA with the forwarding address set to a nonzero value and leading to the ASBR itself.

2. The ABRs with the highest Router-ID, connecting the NSSA to the backbone area, performs translation of type 7 LSAs to type 5 LSAs. Every NSSA external route installed in the routing table is considered for translation. If aggregation is not configured, the forwarding address in the type 5 LSA is copied from the corresponding type 7 LSA. If aggregation is configured, the forwarding address in the type 5 LSA is not set.

Note that NSSA ABRs do not change the forwarding address while translating type 7 LSAs to type 5 ones unless aggregation of NSSA external routes is configured. Therefore, routers in the backbone and other areas will calculate optimal routes to the external destination, not necessarily through the translating ABR; see Figure 9-32. If aggregation is configured on the ABRs, suboptimal routing can be seen in the domain because the forwarding address in type 5 LSAs is not set, and all routers outside the NSSA now always calculate their external routes through the translating ABR.

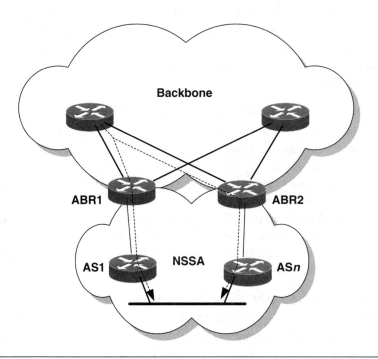

Figure 9-32. *Dual-homed NSSA, optimal routing*

The NSSA technique is described in [RFC 1587]. Also, an IETF draft [NSSA] resolving these and other issues was published. This draft may have become the new NSSA specification by the time you read this book.

Routers internal to the NSSA use type 7 LSAs to calculate NSSA-external routes. Calculation of NSSA-external routes is very similar to calculation of legacy AS-external routes. NSSA ABRs calculate NSSA-external routes after calculation of AS-external routes. If the same destination is described by both a type 5 and a type 7 LSA, the type 5 LSA is always preferred. If the same destination is described by more than one type 7 LSA, an LSA with P bit set and nonzero forwarding address is preferred. In other cases, the LSAs are considered to be equal, and parallel routes are installed.

9.2.5.7 Frequently Asked Questions

Q: **Why does OSPF not propagate external routing information just like internal information, that is, in some sort of summary-LSAs?**

A: That was a protocol design decision. When ABRs announce intra-area routing information in summary-LSAs, the same IP prefix can be announced in more than one LSA, one per ABR. When OSPF was designed, the amount of external routing information was expected to be an order of magnitude higher than the amount of internal routing information, so replication of external routes did not seem to be an attractive solution.

Q: **What is the function of ASBR-summary-LSAs (type 4 LSA)?**

A: When they calculate external routes, OSPF routers consider AS-external-LSAs and need to know the location of the Advertising Router. Routers cannot use their main routing table for this purpose, as LSAs contain the Router-ID of the Advertising Router, so the routing table will contain no information about it. Instead, OSPF routers use an internal router routing table. Routers residing in the same area as the ASBR can install entries in this routing table when doing intra-area SPF. Routers in other areas cannot see the ASBR via intra-area topology, so they use type 4 summary-LSAs to learn ASBR locations and to install inter-area routes in the internal table.

Q: **Can ABRs summarize external routing information?**

A: Only if they are NSSA ABRs that perform type 7–to–type 5 LSA translation. The general rule about route summarization in OSPF is that it can be done only when routing information is put into a newly originated LSA, not when it is flooded throughout the domain.

Q: Why is only one external route put in a type 5 LSA?

A: In theory, many routes could be put into a single LSA. The reason to announce a single route per LSA is to minimize the amount of information that needs to be flooded when a single route flaps. However, this does result in more overhead when the number of injected routes is large and there are few changes in the information.

9.2.6 Summary of Routing Table Calculation and Route Preference Rules

Routing table calculation in OSPF is a multistep process involving various types of algorithms and LSAs. It is interesting that the Dijkstra algorithm per se is performed only when intra-area routes are calculated. Calculation of other route types uses the results of intra-area calculation and simple metric comparison. Following is an outline of the routing table calculation process performed by OSPF routers.

1. Intra-area route calculation is the step caused by a change in the network topology within an area, that is, by a change in a router-LSA or a network-LSA. Route calculation is performed in two steps:

    a. During Dijkstra calculation, the calculating router is building the shortest-path tree over the network topology graph. Only those network prefixes announced in network-LSAs are updated.

    b. During stub link processing, the router walks through all vertices in the SPT and considers stub (type 3) link records in corresponding router-LSAs and updates or installs associated routing table entries.

    When intra-area route calculation is performed, the router updates its internal table containing information about ABRs and ASBRs. The entries in this table are used in the following steps of the algorithm.

2. Inter-area route calculation usually follows intra-area route calculation. The calculating router considers summary-LSAs and ASBR-summary-LSAs of the attached area. (ABRs consider summary-LSAs of the backbone area only; see Section 9.2.3.13 for details.) Summary-LSAs are used to calculate inter-area routes to remote networks, whereas ASBR-summary-LSAs are used to calculate inter-area routes to ASBRs. The route metric is calculated as the sum of the metric announced in the LSA and the cost of the route to the announcing ABR. If more than one LSA describes the same destination, the one providing the lowest route metric is chosen, or parallel routes are installed.

3. AS external route calculation follows inter-area route calculation and relies on the results of the previous two steps saved in the router routing table. All AS-exter-

nal-LSAs are considered in turn. Any LSA may produce either a type 1 or a type 2 external route in the routing table. Metric calculation depends on the route type. For type 1 routes, it is the sum of internal and external costs; for type 2, it is the external cost itself. In the case of multiple LSAs describing the same destination, the tie is broken, using the rules explained later in this section.

4. NSSA external route calculation is similar to that for AS external routes. Any LSA also may produce a type 1 or a type 2 route.

In some situations, the same IP prefix may be described by LSAs of more than one type. In this case, the calculating router has to decide which route type should be preferred. OSPF defines route preference rules as follows.

- Intra-area routes are always most preferred.
- Inter-area routes are preferred over AS or NSSA external routes.
- AS-external routes and NSSA-external routes are of equal preference. Within this set of routes, preferences are defined as follows.
  - Type 1 routes are always preferred over type 2 ones.
  - Within type 1 routes, the route metric is used as the tiebreaker.
  - Within type 2 routes, the route metric and the distance to the originating router are used as the tiebreakers.
  - If the tie is still not resolved, the following priorities are applied.
    - AS-external (type 5) routes are preferred over NSSA external (type 7) ones.
    - Routes derived from type 7 LSAs with a nonzero forwarding address and P bit set are preferred.
- If these rules do not solve the tie, routes are installed in parallel.

Note that the OSPF protocol was designed from the outset to allow equal-cost multipath support. Whereas Cisco IOS has a maximum of six routes per destination, OSPF may provide as many paths as the network topology permits. However, only the first six are used by Cisco routers.

9.2.7 Demand Circuit OSPF Extensions

One of the main OSPF features that allows avoidance of frequent periodic announcements is explicit neighbor relationship maintenance through the Hello subprotocol. This technique, however, prevents OSPF from working optimally over such links as dial-up PSTN or ISDN connections, and X25 or Frame Relay circuits. The problem is that periodic Hello packets keep these connections—usually established on demand for a limited time—active all the time. Another problem with OSPF in this situation is periodic LSA refreshment. If routers' LSDBs contain enough LSAs, periodic LSA updates may also potentially keep a demand circuit from disconnecting.

OSPF extensions to support demand circuit are documented in [RFC1793] and address both problems as follows. First, OSPF routers are allowed to negotiate hello suppression on demand circuit. This means that if both routers agree, as indicated by the DC bit set in the Hello packets, both can stop sending periodic Hello packets. However, OSPF routers still need to be informed about reachability of the neighbor on the other side of the link. This is achieved by using the so-called *presumption-of-reachability* concept. The concept implies that if an OSPF router has successfully established an adjacency with a neighbor and the routers agreed to suppress periodic Hello packets, the neighbor should be considered reachable unless explicit evidence of unreachability is seen. In the case of demand circuit, such explicit evidence is a signal from an underlying layer protocol indicating that, for example, a connection to the neighbor could not be established. In Cisco implementation, five consecutive LSA retransmissions are also considered evidence of unreachability.

The second problem, periodic LSA updates, is solved as follows. A new bit, called *Do-Not-Age*, or DNA, is introduced in the LSA's Age field. When the DNA bit is set in an LSA, the LSA is called a DNA LSA and is not aged in other routers' LSDBs. When it receives a new version of an LSA and needs to flood it over a demand circuit, a router checks whether the contents of the LSA have changed. If the contents are the same, the LSA is not flooded over the demand circuit. If the contents have changed, the LSA is sent over the link, but the DNA bit is set on it first.

The demand circuit extensions also address the problem of backward compatibility. If a router residing in the same area does not support DNA LSAs—indicated by the DC bit's being clear in any LSA originated by such a router—the router that originated the DNA LSAs flushes them from the domain and reoriginates them without the DNA bit. In fact, DNA LSAs can be flushed by the router that first noticed the presence of a DNA-incapable router in the area. Furthermore, ABRs propagate so-called *indication-LSAs* to other areas. These LSAs are essentially type 4 LSAs announcing the ABR itself with the DC bit clear. Because routers in other areas follow the same rule—namely, one LSA with the DC bit clear is enough to consider the area to be DNA incapable—information about the DNA-incapable router is propagated throughout the domain.

> For hello suppression to take effect, both routers on a link must support demand circuit extensions introduced in IOS version 11.2. However, it is enough to configure the **ip ospf demand-circuit** command only on one router. Note also that if at least one router in an area does not support demand circuit extensions, routers have to refresh LSAs periodically.

9.2.8 Details of Cisco OSPF Implementation

This section describes some details of Cisco OSPF implementation that are important for deploying and troubleshooting the OSPF protocol.

9.2.8.1 Packet Pacing

The OSPF packet pacing technique was introduced into Cisco IOS version 11.3A. The idea behind this method is to avoid packet drops at the receiving side, caused by uncontrolled bursts of link-state updates.

When a large number of LSAs need to be flooded to a neighbor, the OSPF router may send it a lot of link-state update packets. The receiving router may not be able to queue and process all the packets, so some updates may be dropped. When packets are dropped, the sending router does not receive the acknowledgment for a subset of LSAs and retransmits them to the neighbor. Retransmission, if not implemented in a sophisticated way, may result in the same problem: dropped packets, leading to more retransmissions.

The packet pacing technique addresses several problems. First, an obligatory interval is introduced between packet transmissions. In the current OSPF implementation, this interval is not configurable and equals 33 milliseconds. If the number of LSAs on a neighbor's retransmission list is nonzero, the router builds a link-state update every 33 milliseconds and sends it to the neighbor. A similar technique is implemented for LSA retransmission: The next group of LSAs is retransmitted after 66 milliseconds, not after the acknowledgments for the first group are received.

The packet pacing technique improves certain characteristics of Cisco OSPF implementation. The technique speeds up protocol convergence and hence decreases the length of the transition period.

9.2.8.2 LSA Group Pacing

In OSPF, every LSA is aged while stored in the database. All LSAs are aged independently of one another. When the age of an LSA reaches LSRefreshTime, the LSA is reoriginated, or refreshed, by the router that created the LSA. When the age of an LSA reaches MaxAge, the router flushes the LSA, which does not have to be a self-originated LSA, from the domain. Also, the checksum of each LSA is verified every 10 minutes.

When a router has a lot of LSAs, maintaining a separate timer for each LSA stored in the database may be very expensive. The LSA group-pacing technique, introduced in IOS version 11.3AA, implies that all LSAs are collected into groups by their ages. The acceptable difference in the age is defined by the group-pacing interval, which is 4 minutes by default, but it can be configured (see Section 9.2.9.12 for more information).

A router maintains timers for LSA groups, not individual LSAs. LSA grouping is used for all LSA-related operations, including LSA aging, LSA refreshing, and LSA checksum verification.

9.2.8.3 SPF Scheduling

Whenever a topology change is detected in an OSPF domain, routers must recalculate their routing tables. Recalculating SPF right after a change in an LSA is observed may put a big load on the CPU if the network experiences some instability and has a considerable number of links and routers.

Cisco OSPF implementation schedules SPF calculation, taking into consideration two configurable timers: the initial SPF schedule delay and the SPF hold interval. The first timer specifies the delay between an SPF request event and an SPF calculation. The second timer specifies the minimum amount of time that must elapse between two consecutive SPF calculations. By default, the initial SPF delay is 5 seconds, and the SPF hold interval is 10 seconds. Both parameters are configurable.

> Decreasing the value of SPF timers may increase the CPU load caused by OSPF route calculation if the network experiences a high level of instability. Increasing the values, on the other hand, may result in slower protocol convergence.

9.2.8.4 Partial SPF Calculation

As discussed earlier, routing table calculation is a complex process, consisting of several steps. When the number of routers and links in the network is large enough, rerunning a complete set of SPF steps may be very expensive. In some situations, only part of a routing table needs to be recalculated. For example, when a new summary-LSA is received and installed in the LSDB, intra-area or external routing information does not need to be recalculated. Instead, it is enough to calculate the metric for the corresponding inter-area route, look up a route to the same destination in the routing table, and decide whether the new inter-area route should be installed or ignored. This is called partial SPF calculation. Cisco implementation of OSPF permits avoiding complete SPF calculation and instead using partial calculation if a summary-LSA, ASBR-summary-LSA, AS-external-LSA, or NSSA-external-LSA has been added to or deleted from the LSDB.

9.2.9 OSPF Configuration

Now that OSPF protocol details have been discussed, let's consider how OSPF is configured in Cisco routers.

9.2.9.1 Basic OSPF Configuration

As with any other IP routing protocol in Cisco IOS, OSPF is started with a **router ospf** *process-ID* command. Interface selection is performed by using the **network** command; in OSPF, however, this command has a special syntax:

network address *wildcard-mask* **area** *area-id*

The address/wildcard mask pair allows the administrator to enable OSPF on specific interfaces or a set of specific interfaces. Unlike in RIP or IGRP, the address part of the network command is not classful but rather can be a subnet or a supernet, depending on the value of the wildcard mask. If the wildcard mask is all zeros, the address portion must refer to a specific interface address.

The area parameter in the command is necessary because in OSPF, every interface is assigned to a specific area. All interfaces covered by a single network command are associated with the area specified in this command. Note that when more than one network command covers the same interface, the most specific one is used. Also note that the more specific network command must be configured before the less specific one.

9.2.9.2 General OSPF Parameters

A number of parameters generic to the overall OSPF process can be configured by using the commands described in this section. Note that in most cases, these commands need not be configured.

router-id *ip-address*

Before this command was introduced in IOS version 12.1, the Router-ID for an OSPF process was selected only automatically, using the following algorithm.

- If the router is configured with loopback interfaces, the highest IP address among those assigned to loopback interfaces is taken.
- If this is not possible—no loopback interfaces are configured or all loopback interface addresses are already allocated by other processes—the highest IP address from the physical interfaces is used.

The administrator can influence the process of Router-ID selection by creating a loopback interface. When the loopback interface that was used to select the Router-ID is removed by a **no interface loopback** *number* command, the router has to reselect the Router-ID and to reoriginate all its LSAs.

The **router-id** command allows the administrator to explicitly specify the value that the process should use as its OSPF Router-ID. Because it does not correlate with any real IP address, this value can be arbitrarily assigned by the administrator, except for 0.0.0.0.

auto-cost reference-bandwidth *reference-bw-value*

By default, OSPF automatically assigns output costs to interfaces on the basis of the value of the bandwidth parameter as 100 megabits per second divided by the value of the bandwidth parameter of the interface.

If automatic cost calculation is disabled with a **no auto-cost** command, the interfaces are assigned default cost values, depending on the interface type. For example, an Ethernet interface is assigned cost 10, a serial interface is assigned cost 1,562, and an FDDI or ATM interface is assigned cost 1. Note that when automatic cost calculation is disabled, the router does not take the configured value into consideration but instead just assigns a value, depending on the interface type.

When a network is built using interfaces with bandwidth more than 100Mb, the value of the reference bandwidth—100Mb in the formula—must be changed to a higher value to allow OSPF to assign more meaningful interface cost values. This is done by configuring the OSPF process with the autocost reference bandwidth **reference-bw-value** command. Note that the value of the reference bandwidth is configured in megabits per second.

> It is important that all routers in the network use the same reference bandwidth value for interface cost calculation. Otherwise, the network will experience suboptimal routing.

capability opaque

Opaque LSAs—those of types 9, 10, and 11—are used in OSPF to distribute information from other protocols or applications. The major example is traffic engineering information used in *multiprotocol label switching* (MPLS) networks. In essence, OSPF is used as a transport mechanism in this case.

Support of opaque-LSAs was introduced into Cisco OSPF version 12.0. Although it is enabled by default, opaque capability may be disabled, if necessary, by the **no capability opaque** command.

default-information originate [**always**] [**metric** *metric-value*] [**metric-type** *type-value*]
        [**route-map** *map-name*]

OSPF routers announce the default route without any configuration only when they perform the role of ABRs connecting a stub area or an NSSA with no summaries to the backbone. In this case, the default route is announced as an inter-area one, using a summary-LSA, and is propagated throughout one area only.

It is often necessary to instruct an OSPF router to originate the default route and to propagate it throughout the OSPF domain. This may be the case when, for example, such a router is the boundary router connecting the network to the Internet or to another upper-level network.

A router configured with the **default-information originate** command announces a type 5 default LSA, provided that it has a default route in its own routing table and that this default route was not installed by the originating process itself. If the **always** keyword is added to the command, the router unconditionally originates the default route but never installs a default route from any other router in the same OSPF domain, to avoid routing loops. The keywords **metric** and **metric-type** can be used to set the value of the metric announced in the AS-external-LSA, as well as the type (type 1 or type 2) used for default route announcement.

The **default-information originate** command may also be augmented with a route map. In this case, the router generates the default route only when the routing table contains a route that is permitted by a **match** clause in the route map. Such *conditional default announcement* can be used when an OSPF domain has more than one exit point; the exit preference should depend on the routing information in the routing table of border routers.

distance {*distance-value* | [**intra-area** *distance1*] [**inter-area** *distance2*] [**external** *distance3*]}

The default value of the administrative distance for the routes installed by OSPF is 110. This command allows the administrator to change the AD value for each specific OSPF route type. Note that this command is optional and is not necessary in the majority of network scenarios.

> The **distance** command does not change the route preference rules within OSPF itself. Regardless of configured administrative distance values, an inter-area route is never preferred over an intra-area one. Changing AD values is justified only when it is necessary to control the preference level of routes coming from different routing processes and covering the same IP prefix.

distribute-list

Basic description of the **distribute-list** command is given in Chapter 7. It is, however, necessary to note that in the case of OSPF, distribute lists do not filter incoming or outgoing link-state updates. Instead, an inbound distribute list configured with a **distribute-list** *acl* **in** command controls installation of the routes calculated by OSPF when it attempts to submit them to the routing table. An outbound access list configured with a **distribute-list** *acl* **out** command controls which routes are redistributed by the OSPF process if it is configured to do so. Route redistribution configuration commands are considered in more detail in Chapter 7 and Section 9.2.10.4.

ignore lsa mospf

Cisco routers do not support Multicast OSPF (MOSPF), for a number of reasons. However, it is quite possible that MOSPF-capable routers from other vendors are installed in the same network with Cisco routers. MOSPF uses type 6 LSAs to propagate IP multicast group membership information. When Cisco routers receive LSAs of this type, an error message is logged. To disable logging of error messages when the router receives a lot of type 6 LSAs, configure the OSPF process with an **ignore lsa mospf** command.

log-adjacency-changes

The **log-adjacency-changes** OSPF router configuration command instructs the router to log a message whenever there is a state change in a neighbor's FSM. Note that the default behavior—no adjacency state change logging—is appropriate in most situations. In very stable networks, however, a state change of an adjacency may signal the administrator that routers are having trouble maintaining their relationship.

maximum-paths

As with all other IP routing protocols, OSPF can install only four parallel routes to the same destination, by default. Similarly, this limit may be changed by using the **maximum-paths** router configuration command. It must be noted that whatever the limit is, OSPF computes all available routes to the same destination internally. If not all of them make it into the routing table, they are installed when some of the installed routes are removed.

traffic-share min [across-interfaces]

This command controls the behavior of the router when multiple routes to the same destination need to be installed. The form **traffic-share min** is the default for OSPF and specifies that only routes with the minimal, or best, metric are installed in the routing table. This is obvious, as OSPF always installs only best routes. (See Chapter 7 for an illustration of how EIGRP installs unequal-cost paths.) The idea behind the **across-interfaces** argument is to try to use as many interfaces are possible. For example, if more than one path linked to a prefix refers to the same interface and a new path—parallel route—referring to a new interface needs to be installed although the maximum number of paths has already been installed, the router will remove a path referring to an already used interface in favor of the new one.

passive-interface {*interface-name* | **default**}

The behavior of the **passive-interface** command in the case of OSPF matches the description given in Chapter 7. Unlike distance-vector routing protocols, which allow reception of routing updates on passive interfaces, OSPF completely disables packet processing on them. As a result, no adjacencies are established on passive OSPF interfaces, and hence no routes are installed over them.

timers {**lsa-group-pacing** *pacing-interval* | **spf** *spf-delay spf-hold*}

OSPF timers tuning is considered in detail in Section 9.2.9.12. In general, this command allows the administrator to control the behavior of the LSA group-pacing algorithm and SPF scheduling.

9.2.9.3 Interface-Specific Parameters

The commands described in this section allow the administrator to configure the parameters that are part of the OSPF interface data structure.

ip ospf cost *cost-value*

Although OSPF calculates interface costs automatically, the administrator can use this command to set this parameter to a specific value. This command is useful when a Cisco router is connected to a router from another vendor. OSPF routers do not need to agree on the interface cost to form an adjacency, but the interface cost may need to be changed to avoid asymmetric routing in the OSPF domain. Another reason to change an interface output cost is to influence the result of the SPF calculation and thus perform traffic engineering in the domain. The OSPF standard does not specify how the interface costs should be calculated, so other router vendors may use a different calculation algorithm. For more information on interface cost calculation, see Section 9.2.9.2.

ip ospf hello-interval *interval-value*

The OSPF Hello interval defines how often the router should send a Hello packet on a specific interface. Neighboring routers need to agree on this parameter to form an adjacency. However, the OSPF standard does not regulate the exact values that should be used for the Hello process, so routers from different vendors may have different values for the parameter, and this may prevent the routers from establishing the adjacency. By default, Cisco routers set the Hello interval to 10 seconds for LAN interfaces and 30 seconds for NBMA interfaces. The command can be used to set the Hello interval for a particular interface to a specific value.

ip ospf dead-interval *interval-value*

The OSPF Dead, or Inactivity, interval specifies the amount of time a neighbor is considered to be operational without receiving a Hello packet. This parameter must be the same for neighboring routers to establish the adjacency. By default, Cisco routers set the Inactivity interval to a value four times higher than the Hello interval. The **ip ospf dead-interval** command allows the administrator to configure a specific OSPF interface with an arbitrary value.

ip ospf priority *priority-value*

The interface priority value influences the probability of an OSPF router's becoming the DR or the BDR on a specific LAN or NBMA segment. Note that the DR election algorithm in OSPF is nonpreemptive, so the priority value is taken into consideration only when the current DR or BDR on a segment goes down or when there is no DR or BDR yet. See Section 9.2.3.7 for details on the DR election algorithm in OSPF. The **ip ospf priority** interface configuration command allows the administrator to set the priority of an interface to a specific value. Note that a priority value of 0 implies that the router is not eligible to become the DR or the BDR on the segment. The default value of the interface priority is 1.

ip ospf retransmit-interval *interval-value*

When an OSPF router floods LSAs to its neighbors, it puts these LSAs on the retransmission list of the corresponding neighbor data structures. When a link-state acknowledgment packet is received from the neighbor, the LSA is removed from the list. If an acknowledgment is not received, the LSA is retransmitted every retransmit-interval number of seconds. The **ip ospf retransmit-interval** interface command sets the retransmit interval to a specific value. The default value of the retransmit interval is 5 seconds.

ip ospf transmit-delay *delay-value*

The interface-transmit delay value is used by the LSA flooding algorithm to avoid endless flooding loops. When sent over an interface, an LSA's age is incremented by adding the value of the transmit delay of the output interface. This behavior ensures that if an OSPF domain experiences a flooding loop, the LSA is finally removed from the domain when its age reaches MaxAge value. The default value for this parameter is 1.

ip ospf network { **broadcast** |
             point-to-point |
             point-to-multipoint [**broadcast** | **non-broadcast**] |
             non-broadcast }

By default, the OSPF process assigns a network type on the basis of the encapsulation type. However, all non-point-to-point WAN interfaces (Frame Relay or X.25) are automatically assigned the non-broadcast network type. It may be necessary to change the network type to point-to-multipoint or broadcast for the sake of more optimal protocol operation or simpler configuration. The **ip ospf network** command allows an interface to be configured with a specific interface type. See Section 9.2.9.4 for more information on NBMA interface configuration.

Note that loopback interfaces may be configured with an **ip ospf network point-to-point** command. In this case, instead of announcing a host route to the IP address of the loopback interface, the router announces the whole prefix associated with it.

ip ospf demand-circuit

[RFC1793] describes demand circuit extensions that allow OSPF routers to suppress Hello processing and to optimize LSA origination and flooding operation over interfaces with dynamically established connections (ISDN, Frame Relay, X.25, and so on). This command configures a point-to-point interface—an internal limitation in the Cisco IOS—as a demand circuit (see Section 9.2.7 for more information).

ip ospf database-filter all out

The **ip ospf database-filter** command allows the administrator to control the process of LSA distribution throughout the domain. Note that the command completely prevents any LSA from being flooded over the interface. This may result in severe routing problems if the LSA is not delivered to the router on the other end of the link through alternative paths. This command is intended to be used to decrease the overhead of the flooding algorithm in topologies with a very high level of connectivity, usually seen when the IP layer of the network is implemented on top of an ATM or a Frame Relay cloud.

ip ospf authentication [**message-digest** | **null**]

The **ip ospf authentication** interface configuration command permits per interface authentication configuration. The area authentication command discussed earlier configures a specific authentication type for all interfaces within an area, whereas the **ip ospf authentication** command provides the possibility of having different authentication types on different interfaces within a single area.

ip ospf authentication-key *keyword*

This command sets the key value that is used on the interface to generate or to verify authentication data for OSPF packets.

9.2.9.4 Configuring OSPF on NBMA Media

Cisco routers may be configured to treat NBMA interfaces, using the following techniques:

- *Nonbroadcast.* The OSPF process is aware that multicast packets cannot be sent over the interface and sends OSPF packets directly to neighbors, using unicast IP addresses. Neighbors must be configured manually by the administrator. The DR and the BDR are still elected among the neighbors. The DR represents the NBMA cloud as a transit network, using a network-LSA.
- *Broadcast.* The OSPF process treats the interface as a broadcast segment and hence uses IP multicasts to send OSPF packets. The data link layer protocol must be configured so that multicast packets are properly replicated and sent through all VCs to all neighbors, using the map table. The map table entries can either be configured manually, with a **broadcast** keyword, or installed dynamically, using such protocols as LMI (Link Management Interface) (see Chapter 5 for details). OSPF elects the DR and the BDR for such segments, just as for LAN media. The topology is also abstracted as in the case of a LAN segment.
- *Point-to-multipoint.* OSPF treats the interface as the placeholder for a set of point-to-point adjacencies. Adjacencies are established as in the case of the point-to-point interfaces; that is, no DR or BDR is elected. Topology abstraction is very much like that for point-to-point interfaces—type 1 links are included in router-LSAs—but every router announces a host route to its own IP address by adding a stub link in the router-LSA.
- *Subinterfaces.* The administrator assigns VCs going through the physical interface to a number of point-to-point and point-to-multipoint subinterfaces. This

way, the underlying topology of virtual circuits can be represented to OSPF as a set of point-to-point interfaces. OSPF establishes point-to-point adjacencies over point-to-point subinterfaces and treats point-to-multipoint subinterfaces as NBMA media.

If the NBMA or the broadcast method is used for a WAN interface, the routers connected to the cloud must be fully meshed. Otherwise, routers may not be able to reach destinations behind some neighbors.

This restriction results from the assumption OSPF makes about connectivity on broadcast and NBMA networks: If routers A and B have adjacencies with router C, they are able to reach each other directly. This assumption is always true for broadcast segments, as all hosts on the segment can see the frames sent on the segment. For NBMA networks, especially when VCs are not established dynamically, connectivity between routers A and C and between B and C does not imply connectivity between A and B, because these two routers may have no VC established between them. However, because the routing table calculation algorithm is generic, router A installs routes to networks behind B directly, using B's address as the next hop, not via C, even if C is the DR on the network. B will also use A's address. This will lead to a situation in which packets going from A to networks announced by B are dropped by the data link layer at A because router A has no map entry for B's address.

Because of the described limitations, the broadcast and nonbroadcast approaches for NBMA networks are suitable only when full mesh of VCs connecting the attached routers is available at the data link layer. Also, even if full mesh of VCs is available when the network is in operational condition, the network may experience problems when a subset of VCs becomes unavailable and data link layer technology does not provide proper VC restoration and rerouting.

The point-to-multipoint approach does not suffer from such problems, because attached routers do not rely on network-LSAs to describe network topology; they include all adjacency and routing information in their router-LSAs. There is a drawback, however. If the number of routers attached to the NBMA cloud is large enough, the amount of information announced by the routers using the point-to-multipoint methodology will be much greater than the amount of information announced in the broadcast or nonbroadcast approach.

Note that the main difference between the broadcast and nonbroadcast approaches in the case of the NBMA cloud is in the way routers discover their neighbors. In the broadcast case, the routers send broadcast packets, and the data link layer software is responsible for replicating them. In the nonbroadcast case, the list of the neighbors must be configured manually. When the nonbroadcast approach is used, the behavior of the Hello subprotocol is also slightly changed, as described in Section 9.2.3.5.

To manually configure an OSPF neighbor, the following OSPF router configuration command should be used:

neighbor ip-address [**priority** *priority-value*] [**poll-interval** *interval-value*]
        [**cost** *cost-value*] [**database-filter** [**all**]]

It is necessary to configure the IP address of the neighbor. All other parameters are optional and can be used to specify the priority associated with the neighbor, the frequency of Hello packet submissions used to poll the neighbor until the first Hello packet is received from it, the link cost that should be used when announcing an adjacency with the neighbor, and whether the router should perform filtering when flooding LSAs to the neighbor or synchronizing the LSDB with it. By default, the priority associated with the neighbor is 0, the poll interval is 2 minutes, the cost equals the cost associated with the interface through which the neighbor is reachable, and no LSA filtering is performed.

9.2.9.5 Basic OSPF ABR Configuration

Basic configuration of OSPF ABRs is as simple as configuring more than one area on a single router. As soon as it finds itself attached to more than one area, the router considers itself to be ABR, sets the B bit in its router-LSAs—one per attached area—and starts performing ABR duties: originating type 3 and type 4 LSAs. Following is a very simple sample configuration of an OSPF ABR:

```
interface ethernet 0
 description Backbone connection 1
 ip address 10.1.1.1 255.255.255.0
!
interface ethernet 1
description Backbone connection 2
ip address 10.1.2.1 255.255.255.0
!
interface ethernet 2
 description Connection to area 1
 ip address 20.1.1.1 255.255.255.0
!
interface ethernet 3
description Connection to area 2
ip address 20.1.2.1 255.255.255.0
!
interface ethernet 4
description Connection to area 3
ip address 20.1.3.1 255.255.255.0
!
router ospf 1
 network 10.0.0.0 0.255.255.255 area 0
```

```
network 20.1.1.0 0.0.0.255 area 1
network 20.1.2.0 0.0.0.255 area 2
network 20.1.3.0 0.0.0.255 area 3
!
```

9.2.9.6 Configuring Route Aggregation

Configuring multiple areas in an OSPF domain is not very effective unless ABRs are instructed to aggregate routing information. If routing information is aggregated, changes in specific routes do not lead to changes in announced summary-LSAs unless the metric announced in the summary-LSA must be changed. (The metric in the LSA announcing an aggregate equals the worst metric seen in the specific routes.)

Following is the command to configure route aggregation on the ABRs:

area *area-id* **range** *address mask* [**not-advertise**]

As you can see, ranges are associated with specific areas. When it announces intra-area routes from area A to all other areas, an ABR looks for area ranges associated with area A; if covered by a range, an intra-area route is not announced in a separate LSA. Instead, the ABR announces a summary-LSA for the whole range. If the **not-advertise** keyword is specified, neither specific nor aggregate routes are announced to other areas. This method can be used to filter inter-area routing information.

9.2.9.7 Configuring Virtual Links

Virtual links were described in Section 9.2.4.5. To establish a virtual link between a couple of ABRs in area A, the administrator must configure both ABRs with the following command:

area *area-id* **virtual-link** *router-id*

Note that even though the Router-ID parameter of the command is configured in the form of an IP address, it is not an IP address of the remote ABR but rather its Router-ID. OSPF does not use the interface IP address for virtual link configuration, because it would introduce dependency on the state of a single interface, whereas the remote router itself can be reached by using other network connections.

When a virtual link is configured, the area ID of the transit area must be specified. This is necessary because two ABRs may be attached to more than one nonbackbone area. Note that virtual links may never cross the backbone area and areas configured as stub or NSSA. The area virtual-link command can be given other parameters that specify the values of the Hello or retransmit interval for the virtual link.

Cisco routers treat virtual links as demand circuit as specified in [RFC1793]. This implies that the Hello exchange is suppressed on virtual links and that the DNA bit is set for all LSAs flooded over the virtual links.

9.2.9.8 Basic OSPF ASBR Configuration (Route Redistribution)

To instruct a router to be an ASBR, the administrator must configure it to redistribute at least one route, that is, to originate at least one AS-external-LSA. The following command instructs the router to originate AS-external-LSAs, based on routing information installed by other route sources:

redistribute route-source-name [*process-id*] [**subnets**] [**route-map** *map-name*] [**metric** *metric-value*] [**metric-type {type-1 | type-2}**]

This syntax shows the parameters that can be given to the **redistribute** command for an OSPF process. The very important keyword is **subnets**, without which the OSPF process does not originate AS-external-LSAs for subnets. Only major networks and supernets are redistributed. In most cases, the **subnets** keyword should be specified.

If the router configured with a **redistribute** command is attached only to stub areas, the command has no effect. The router does not announce itself as ASBR and does not originate type 5 LSAs. If the router is connected to normal and not-so-stubby areas—in essence, an NSSA ABR—it originates both type 5 and type 7 LSAs. The NSSA may, however, be configured with a no-redistribution parameter to prevent origination of type 7 LSAs into that area.

9.2.9.9 Aggregation of Redistributed Routes

By default, the OSPF ASBR creates a separate AS-external-LSA for every redistributed route. This may introduce some problems if the number of redistributed routes is considerable. A large number of AS-external-LSAs may lead to considerable flooding overhead, as well as high CPU load in the calculating routers.

To minimize the number of AS-external-LSAs, ASBRs may be configured to aggregate redistributed routing information, using the following command:

summary-address **address mask** [**tag** *value*] [**metric** *value*] [**not-advertise**] ...

This command works similarly to the **area range** command: If a route to be redistributed is covered by a configured summary address, the ASBR does not announce it in a separate AS-external-LSA but instead creates a single LSA for the whole range. The additional parameters in this command allow the administrator to configure metric and tag values announced in AS-external-LSAs.

9.2.9.10 Configuring Stub Areas

Stub areas are considered in detail in Section 9.2.5.5. For an OSPF to become stub, all routers attached to the area must be configured with the following router configuration command:

area *area-id* **stub**

This command forces the router to clear the E bit in its Hello packets and to exclude type 4 and type 5 LSAs from the initial LSDB synchronization process and asynchronous flooding. Stub area ABRs will also inject a default summary-LSA into the area.

   To make an area totally stub, all ABRs attached to that area must also be configured with the following command:

area *area-id* **stub no-summary**

This command prevents ABRs from originating into the stub area any summary-LSAs except for the default summary-LSA.

9.2.9.11 Configuring NSSA

Not-so-stubby areas were described in Section 9.2.5.6. As in the case of stub areas, all routers should be configured with the following command for an area to become NSSA:

area *area-id* **nssa**

NSSA ABRs may also be configured not to inject inter-area routes into the NSSA, using the following command:

area *area-id* **nssa no-summary**

The effect of this command is essentially the same as that of the **area stub no-summary** command.

9.2.9.12 Tuning OSPF Timers

OSPF uses several timers that control LSA origination and scheduling of SPF calculation. The default values for these timers work perfectly in most cases. However, it may sometimes be necessary to achieve very fast convergence characteristics even at the price of high CPU load and control traffic overhead. To avoid these drawbacks, it may be necessary to make some timers more aggressive.

Changing the default value of the following parameters is not recommended.

By default, the next version of the same LSA must not be originated sooner than 5 seconds after the last origination. If it is necessary to allow the OSPF process to perform LSA origination at a higher rate, the following command may be used:

timers lsa-interval *interval-value*

Because the interval value is given in seconds, the lowest rate of LSA origination may be one per second.

When a new version of an LSA is received, the router does not install it in the LSDB if the LSDB copy was updated less than 1 second ago. Note that the LSA is not acknowledged either, so the neighbor will retransmit the LSA. The following command may be used to increase this interval:

timers lsa-arrival *interval-value*

Setting this parameter to a value higher than the minimum **lsa-interval** value configured in the network may slow down protocol convergence.

The following command may be used to control scheduling of SPF calculation after a change in the topological or routing information.

timers spf *spf-delay spf-hold*

This command controls scheduling of only full SPF, not the partial one.

The **spf-delay** parameter specifies the amount of time that must elapse between a change in the LSDB contents and actual SPF calculation. The **spf-hold** parameter specifies the minimum amount of time that must elapse between two consecutive SPF calculations.

As described in Section 9.2.8.2, Cisco OSPF implementation uses an LSA grouping technique to optimize LSA handling. The LSA group-pacing interval, controlled by the following command, defines the interval used to refresh, age, and verify the checksum of LSA groups:

timers lsa-group-pacing *pacing-interval*

The **pacing-interval** parameter is specified in seconds and can accept values in the range of 10 to 1,800 seconds. The default value is 240 seconds.

9.2.10 Configuration Examples

The configuration examples given here are based on the lab topology shown in Figure 9-33.

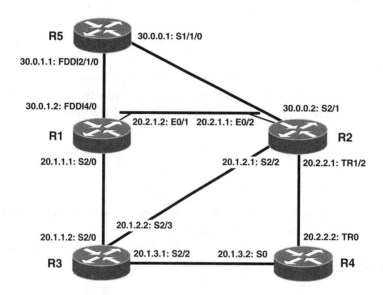

Figure 9-33. *Topology of OSPF lab network*

9.2.10.1 Single-Area OSPF Configuration

The simplest example of an OSPF network is when all routers belong to the same area. This is usually called flat network design. All routers in the network are configured as follows:

```
router ospf 1
router-id N.N.N.N
network 30.0.0.0 0.255.255.255 area 0
```

Note that N in the **router-id** command corresponds to the number of the router: N is 3 for R3 and 4 for R4. Because of the software version running on R1, it was not configured with the **router-id** command, so its Router-ID is the IP address of its loopback interface.

Let's take a closer look at router R5. Listing 9-5 shows the output of the **show ip ospf** command.

```
R5#sho ip ospf
 Routing Process "ospf 1" with ID 5.5.5.5
 Supports only single TOS(TOS0) routes
 SPF schedule delay 5 secs, Hold time between two SPFs 10 secs
 Minimum LSA interval 5 secs. Minimum LSA arrival 1 secs
 Number of external LSA 0. Checksum Sum 0x0
 Number of DCbitless external LSA 0
 Number of DoNotAge external LSA 0
 Number of areas in this router is 1. 1 normal 0 stub 0 nssa
    Area BACKBONE(0)
        Number of interfaces in this area is 2
        Area has no authentication
        SPF algorithm executed 22 times
        Area ranges are
        Number of LSA 11. Checksum Sum 0x371BA
        Number of DCbitless LSA 9
        Number of indication LSA 0
        Number of DoNotAge LSA 0
```

Listing 9-5. *Output of the* **show ip ospf** *command*

The first line of the output shows the OSPF process ID and the Router-ID used by the process. The second line indicates that the router supports only one metric. This is always true for Cisco OSPF implementation and for most OSPF implementations of other vendors, as TOS routing support was removed from OSPF in [RFC2178] because no networks used it. The output also shows configured SPF and LSA timer values, as well as generic LSA counters. The command also shows the area-specific information for each configured area.

Listing 9-6 shows the summary of the LSDB contents.

```
R5#sho ip ospf data

        OSPF Router with ID (5.5.5.5) (Process ID 1)


            Router Link-states (Area 0)

Link ID         ADV Router      Age     Seq#        Checksum Link count
2.2.2.2         2.2.2.2         859     0x80000008 0x39B3    8
3.3.3.3         3.3.3.3         871     0x8000000A 0x2B72    6
4.4.4.4         4.4.4.4         859     0x80000003 0xDAFF    4
5.5.5.5         5.5.5.5         1466    0x80000007 0x2D9     3
30.0.1.2        30.0.1.2        1009    0x8000000F 0x7528    4
203.250.14.3    203.250.14.3    3592    0x80000004 0x6C2     5
                Net Link-states (Area 0)

Link ID         ADV Router      Age     Seq#        Checksum
20.2.1.2        30.0.1.2        1010    0x80000003 0x7381
20.2.2.1        2.2.2.2         859     0x80000001 0x150C
30.0.1.2        30.0.1.2        1010    0x80000005 0x9B43
R5#
```

Listing 9-6. *R5's LSDB*

Note that because we have a flat network, without ABRs or ASBRs, the LSDB contains only type 1 and type 2 LSAs. Also note that the Link-state ID and the Advertising Router ID have the same value in the case of the router-LSA. The Link count field indicates the number of link records inside each router-LSA. If the router-LSA contains zero links, it has no fully adjacent neighbors. The greater the link count value, the more neighbors or internal IP prefixes the router advertises.

The age of the LSA and its sequence number are two parameters that can give the administrator some idea of what's happening in the network. If the sequence number of an LSA is continually increasing and the age is not very high, the LSA is likely being reoriginated often, most probably owing to frequent topology changes.

Listing 9-7 shows the contents of R5's router-LSA.

```
R5#sho ip ospf data router 5.5.5.5

          OSPF Router with ID (5.5.5.5) (Process ID 1)


                Router Link-states (Area 0)

  LS age: 1477
  Options: (No TOS-capability, DC)
  LS Type: Router Links
  Link-state ID: 5.5.5.5
  Advertising Router: 5.5.5.5
  LS Seq Number: 80000007
  Checksum: 0x2D9
  Length: 60
   Number of Links: 3

     Link connected to: another Router (point-to-point)
      (Link ID) Neighboring Router ID: 2.2.2.2
      (Link Data) Router Interface address: 30.0.0.1
       Number of TOS metrics: 0
        TOS 0 Metrics: 66

     Link connected to: a Stub Network
      (Link ID) Network/subnet number: 30.0.0.0
      (Link Data) Network Mask: 255.255.255.0
       Number of TOS metrics: 0
        TOS 0 Metrics: 66

     Link connected to: a Transit Network
      (Link ID) Designated Router address: 30.0.1.2
      (Link Data) Router Interface address: 30.0.1.1
       Number of TOS metrics: 0
        TOS 0 Metrics: 1

R5#
```

Listing 9-7. *Contents of R5's router-LSA*

The router-LSA contains three link records: one IP prefix announcement and two topological elements—a point-to-point adjacency (type 1 link) and an adjacency over a transit segment (type 2 link).

Note that the router-LSA with the Link-state ID 203.250.14.3 is reaching MaxAge. This means that the router that originated the LSA is most probably not available any more or has changed its Router-ID. Listing 9-8 shows the contents of this LSA.

```
R5#sho ip ospf data router 203.250.14.3

        OSPF Router with ID (5.5.5.5) (Process ID 1)


            Router Link-states (Area 0)

  Adv Router is not-reachable
  LS age: MaxAge(3613)
   Options: (No TOS-capability, No DC)
   LS Type: Router Links
   Link-state ID: 203.250.14.3
   Advertising Router: 203.250.14.3
  .LS Seq Number: 80000004
   Checksum: 0x6C2
   Length: 84
    Number of Links: 5
...

R5#
```

Listing 9-8. *Contents of a MaxAge LSA*

When the Age field of the LSA is displayed, the output contains explicit notification that the LSA has already expired and will soon be removed from the LSDB. Also note the Adv Router is not-reachable line at the beginning of the output. This means that when SPF was calculated last time, the router-LSA was not either reached because the age was greater than MaxAge or there was no usable link from other reachable router-LSAs. (Recall that LSAs are not removed from the LSDB right after a router has become unreachable; instead, the LSAs age out if not updated by the originating router.)

OSPF routes calculated by R5 on the basis of the contents of the LSDB are shown in Listing 9-9.

```
R5#sho ip route
...
Gateway of last resort is not set

      2.0.0.0/32 is subnetted, 1 subnets
O        2.2.2.2 [110/12] via 30.0.1.2, 00:17:04, Fddi2/1/0
      4.0.0.0/32 is subnetted, 1 subnets
O        4.4.4.4 [110/18] via 30.0.1.2, 00:17:05, Fddi2/1/0
      20.0.0.0/24 is subnetted, 5 subnets
O        20.2.2.0 [110/17] via 30.0.1.2, 00:17:05, Fddi2/1/0
O        20.1.1.0 [110/65] via 30.0.1.2, 00:17:05, Fddi2/1/0
O        20.1.3.0 [110/81] via 30.0.1.2, 00:17:05, Fddi2/1/0
O        20.1.2.0 [110/75] via 30.0.1.2, 00:17:05, Fddi2/1/0
O        20.2.1.0 [110/11] via 30.0.1.2, 00:17:05, Fddi2/1/0
      30.0.0.0/24 is subnetted, 2 subnets
```

```
C        30.0.0.0 is directly connected, Serial1/1/0
C        30.0.1.0 is directly connected, Fddi2/1/0
R5#
```

Listing 9-9. *OSPF routes in the routing table*

9.2.10.2 Sample Configurations for OSPF over Frame Relay Cloud

In this section, the lab network is configured as shown in Figure 9-34. Router R3 works as a Frame Relay switch. A new router, R6, is added to the network. R3 is configured with a set of fully meshed VCs.

Three types of router configuration are considered in this section. We start with the broadcast method. In this case, routers connected to the cloud (R1, R2, R4, and R6) are not configured with Frame Relay VCs explicitly but know them via the LMI protocol running between them and R3. However, all these routers need to be configured with an **ip ospf network broadcast** command to allow broadcast packets to be used for neighbor discovery. A sample interface configuration follows:

```
interface Serial0
 encapsulation frame-relay
 ip address 10.1.1.4 255.255.255.0
 ip ospf network broadcast
!
```

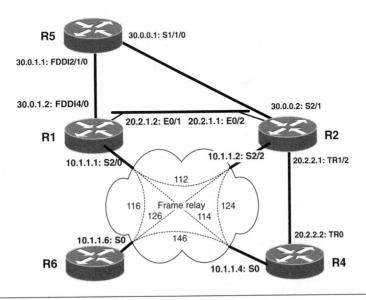

Figure 9-34. *Routers connected via Frame Relay cloud*

As shown in Listing 9-10, OSPF routers elect the DR and the BDR for the NBMA cloud and establish adjacencies as in the case of a LAN segment.

```
R6#sho ip ospf neighbor

Neighbor ID     Pri    State         Dead Time    Address        Interface
4.4.4.4           1    FULL/DROTHER  00:00:35     10.1.1.4       Serial0
2.2.2.2           1    FULL/DROTHER  00:00:29     10.1.1.2       Serial0
30.0.1.2          1    FULL/BDR      00:00:35     10.1.1.1       Serial0
R6#
R6#sho ip ospf int s0
Serial0 is up, line protocol is up
  Internet Address 10.1.1.6/24, Area 0
  Process ID 1, Router ID 6.6.6.6, Network Type BROADCAST, Cost: 64
  Transmit Delay is 1 sec, State DR, Priority 1
  Designated Router (ID) 6.6.6.6, Interface address 10.1.1.6
  Backup Designated router (ID) 30.0.1.2, Interface address 10.1.1.1
  Timer intervals configured, Hello 10, Dead 40, Wait 40, Retransmit 5
    Hello due in 00:00:02
  Neighbor Count is 3, Adjacent neighbor count is 3
    Adjacent with neighbor 4.4.4.4
    Adjacent with neighbor 2.2.2.2
    Adjacent with neighbor 30.0.1.2   (Backup Designated Router)
  Suppress Hello for 0 neighbor(s)
R6#
```

Listing 9-10. *Output of the* **show ip ospf neighbor** *command on R6*

Now the routers are configured to treat the NBMA cloud as a nonbroadcast network—in fact, the default setting. This implies manual configuration of neighbors' IP addresses. Manually specified neighbors are also configured with priorities to ensure that only specific routers are elected as the DR and the BDR. A portion of a sample router configuration follows.

```
interface serial 0
 encapsulation frame-relay
 ip address 10.1.1.4 255.255.255.0
 ip ospf network non-broadcast
 ip ospf priority 0
 !
router ospf 1
 network 0.0.0.0 255.255.255.255 area 0
 neighbor 10.1.1.1
 neighbor 10.1.1.2 priority 0
 neighbor 10.1.1.6
 !
```

After the neighbors are configured, their FSMs go to the Attempt state, as shown in Listing 9-11.

```
R4#sho ip ospf ne

Neighbor ID    Pri   State            Dead Time   Address        Interface
N/A             0    ATTEMPT/DROTHER  00:00:50    10.1.1.6       Serial0
N/A             0    ATTEMPT/DROTHER  00:00:50    10.1.1.2       Serial0
N/A             0    ATTEMPT/DROTHER  00:00:50    10.1.1.1       Serial0
R4#
```

Listing 9-11. *The* **show ip ospf neighbor** *on R4*

When all routers have been configured with similar settings, the neighbor FSMs for the eligible neighbors go to the Full state (see Listing 9-12). Note that ineligible neighbors do not proceed from the Init state if the router is not the DR or the BDR itself, as the adjacencies with these neighbors are not established.

```
R4#sho ip ospf ne
6.6.6.6        1    FULL/BDR        00:01:44    10.1.1.6       Serial0
2.2.2.2        0    INIT/DROTHER    00:01:46    10.1.1.2       Serial0
30.0.1.2       1    FULL/DR         00:01:38    10.1.1.1       Serial0
```

Listing 9-12. *The* **show ip ospf neighbor** *on R4 after a delay*

The routing table calculated by R4 after the protocol has converged is shown in Listing 9-13.

```
R4#sho ip route
...
Gateway of last resort is not set

     2.0.0.0/32 is subnetted, 1 subnets
O       2.2.2.2 [110/65] via 10.1.1.2, 00:00:11, Serial0
     4.0.0.0/32 is subnetted, 1 subnets
C       4.4.4.4 is directly connected, Loopback0
     20.0.0.0/24 is subnetted, 2 subnets
O       20.2.2.0 [110/70] via 10.1.1.2, 00:00:11, Serial0
O       20.2.1.0 [110/74] via 10.1.1.2, 00:00:11, Serial0
                 [110/74] via 10.1.1.1, 00:00:11, Serial0
     6.0.0.0/32 is subnetted, 1 subnets
O       6.6.6.6 [110/65] via 10.1.1.6, 00:00:11, Serial0
O    203.250.14.0/24 [110/65] via 10.1.1.2, 00:00:11, Serial0
     10.0.0.0/24 is subnetted, 1 subnets
```

```
C        10.1.1.0 is directly connected, Serial0
      30.0.0.0/24 is subnetted, 2 subnets
O        30.0.0.0 [110/130] via 10.1.1.2, 00:00:13, Serial0
O        30.0.1.0 [110/65] via 10.1.1.1, 00:00:13, Serial0
R4#
```

Listing 9-13. *R4's routing table*

The final example includes router configuration for the point-to-multipoint case. Note that neighbors need not be configured manually. However, to make the example more interesting, the topology of Frame Relay VCs has been changed to hub and spoke, with R1 being the hub (Figure 9-35).

Following is a typical configuration of a router's interface when the WAN interface is configured as a point-to-multipoint network:

```
interface serial 0
 encapsulation frame-relay
 ip address 10.1.1.4 255.255.255.0
 ip ospf network point-to-multipoint
!
router ospf 1
 network 0.0.0.0 255.255.255.255 area 0
!
```

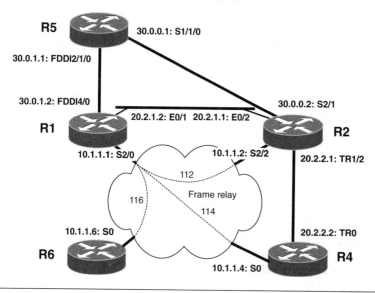

Figure 9-35. *New lab network topology*

After they have been configured with analogous settings, all routers establish point-to-point adjacencies to each other without electing the DR or the BDR. Because the Frame Relay topology is starlike, with R1 inside, it establishes adjacencies with all reachable routers (Listing 9-14), whereas other routers have only a single adjacency to the hub (Listing 9-15).

```
R1#sho ip ospf ne

Neighbor ID     Pri   State          Dead Time   Address     Interface
6.6.6.6           1   FULL/  -       00:01:59    10.1.1.6    Serial2/0
2.2.2.2           1   FULL/  -       00:01:59    10.1.1.2    Serial2/0
4.4.4.4           1   FULL/  -       00:01:59    10.1.1.4    Serial2/0
5.5.5.5           1   FULL/BDR       00:00:39    30.0.1.1    Fddi4/0
```

Listing 9-14. *Neighbor states on R1*

```
R4#sho ip ospf ne

Neighbor ID     Pri   State          Dead Time   Address     Interface
30.0.1.2          1   FULL/  -       00:01:53    10.1.1.1    Serial0
R4#
```

Listing 9-15. *Neighbor states on R4*

9.2.10.3 Configuration of OSPF with Multiple Areas

Now let's consider configuration of multiple areas in an OSPF domain. The area topology is shown in Figure 9-36. Routers R1 and R2 are ABRs. Configuration of router R5 is changed from area 0 to include all interfaces in area 1. Configuration of routers R3 and R4 is not changed. Following is the configuration of R1:

```
hostname R1
!
interface Ethernet0/1
 ip address 20.2.1.2 255.255.255.0
!
interface Serial2/0
 ip address 10.1.1.1 255.255.255.0
 encapsulation frame-relay
 ip ospf network point-to-multipoint
!
```

```
router ospf 1
 network 30.0.0.0 0.255.255.255 area 1
 network 20.0.0.0 0.255.255.255 area 1
 network 10.0.0.0 0.255.255.255 area 0
!
ip classless
end
```

R2 is configured similarly:

```
hostname R2
!
ip subnet-zero
!
interface Loopback100
 ip address 2.2.2.2 255.255.255.255
!
interface Ethernet0/1
 ip address 203.250.15.2 255.255.255.0
 shutdown
!
interface Ethernet0/2
 ip address 20.2.1.1 255.255.255.0
!
interface Serial2/0
 ip address 30.0.0.2 255.255.255.0
!
interface Serial2/2
 ip address 10.1.1.2 255.255.255.0
 encapsulation frame-relay
 ip ospf network point-to-multipoint
 ip ospf priority 0
!
router ospf 1
 network 10.0.0.0 0.255.255.255 area 0
 network 30.0.0.0 0.255.255.255 area 1
!
ip classless
!
end
```

When a router is configured with more than one area, the output of the **show ip ospf** command includes information about all configured areas (see Listing 9-16 for an example).

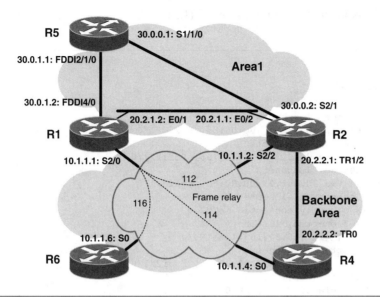

Figure 9-36. *Topology of areas in lab network*

```
R1#sho ip ospf
 Routing Process "ospf 1" with ID 30.0.1.2
 Supports only single TOS(TOS0) routes
 It is an area border router
 Summary Link update interval is 00:30:00 and the update due in 00:28:25
 SPF schedule delay 5 secs, Hold time between two SPFs 10 secs
 Number of areas in this router is 2. 2 normal 0 stub
    Area BACKBONE(0)
        Number of interfaces in this area is 1
        Area has no authentication
        SPF algorithm executed 82 times
        Area ranges are
        Link-state Update Interval is 00:30:00 and due in 00:28:25
        Link-state Age Interval is 00:20:00 and due in 00:12:07
    Area 1
        Number of interfaces in this area is 2
        Area has no authentication
        SPF algorithm executed 7 times
        Area ranges are
        Link-state Update Interval is 00:30:00 and due in 00:28:02
        Link-state Age Interval is 00:20:00 and due in 00:18:02

R1#
```

Listing 9-16. *Output of* **show ip ospf** *from R1 configured as ABR*

Now let's take a look at the routing table of R5 (Listing 9-17).

```
R5#sho ip route
...
Gateway of last resort is not set

     4.0.0.0/32 is subnetted, 1 subnets
O IA    4.4.4.4 [110/66] via 30.0.1.2, 00:00:55, Fddi2/1/0
     20.0.0.0/24 is subnetted, 1 subnets
O        20.2.1.0 [110/11] via 30.0.1.2, 00:00:55, Fddi2/1/0
     6.0.0.0/32 is subnetted, 1 subnets
O IA    6.6.6.6 [110/66] via 30.0.1.2, 00:00:55, Fddi2/1/0
     128.213.0.0/30 is subnetted, 1 subnets
C        128.213.63.0 is directly connected, ATM3/0
     203.250.14.0/32 is subnetted, 1 subnets
S        203.250.14.3 [1/0] via 128.213.63.1, ATM3/0
     10.0.0.0/32 is subnetted, 4 subnets
O IA    10.1.1.2 [110/65] via 30.0.1.2, 00:00:55, Fddi2/1/0
O IA    10.1.1.1 [110/1] via 30.0.1.2, 00:00:56, Fddi2/1/0
O IA    10.1.1.6 [110/65] via 30.0.1.2, 00:00:56, Fddi2/1/0
O IA    10.1.1.4 [110/65] via 30.0.1.2, 00:00:59, Fddi2/1/0
     30.0.0.0/24 is subnetted, 2 subnets
C        30.0.0.0 is directly connected, Serial1/0
C        30.0.1.0 is directly connected, Fddi2/1/0
R5#
```

Listing 9-17. *R5's routing table with inter-area routes*

Note the presence of inter-area routes in the routing table. Also note that inter-area routes have the same prefix length as corresponding subnets in remote areas; that is, ABRs do not summarize routing information.

Now the ABRs are configured to summarize routing information when it is announced to other areas in summary-LSAs.

```
hostname R1
!
router ospf 1
 network 30.0.0.0 0.255.255.255 area 1
 network 20.0.0.0 0.255.255.255 area 1
 network 10.0.0.0 0.255.255.255 area 0
 area 1 range 30.0.0.0 255.0.0.0
 area 0 range 10.0.0.0 255.0.0.0
!

hostname R2
!
router ospf 1
```

```
network 10.0.0.0 0.255.255.255 area 0
network 30.0.0.0 0.255.255.255 area 1
area 0 range 10.0.0.0 255.0.0.0
area 1 range 30.0.0.0 255.0.0.0
!
```

After these configuration changes have been made, the output of the **show ip ospf** command includes information about configured area ranges (Listing 9-18).

```
R1#sho ip ospf
 Routing Process "ospf 1" with ID 30.0.1.2
 Supports only single TOS(TOS0) routes
 It is an area border router
 Summary Link update interval is 00:30:00 and the update due in 00:16:45
 SPF schedule delay 5 secs, Hold time between two SPFs 10 secs
 Number of areas in this router is 2. 2 normal 0 stub
    Area BACKBONE(0)
        Number of interfaces in this area is 1
        Area has no authentication
        SPF algorithm executed 91 times
        Area ranges are
           10.0.0.0/8 Active(0)
        Link-state Update Interval is 00:30:00 and due in 00:16:44
        Link-state Age Interval is 00:20:00 and due in 00:00:27
    Area 1
        Number of interfaces in this area is 2
        Area has no authentication
        SPF algorithm executed 11 times
        Area ranges are
           30.0.0.0/8 Active(1)
        Link-state Update Interval is 00:30:00 and due in 00:16:22
        Link-state Age Interval is 00:20:00 and due in 00:06:22

R1#
```

Listing 9-18. *R1's area ranges*

Both area ranges are active, which means that there is at least one more specific IP prefix that is covered by an area range, causing it to be announced. Note how the routing table of R5 has changed (Listing 9-19). Subnets of the major network 10.0.0.0 are now represented with a single inter-area route to 10.0.0.0/8.

```
R5#sho ip route
...
Gateway of last resort is not set
```

```
         4.0.0.0/32 is subnetted, 1 subnets
O IA    4.4.4.4 [110/66] via 30.0.1.2, 00:03:01, Fddi2/1/0
         20.0.0.0/24 is subnetted, 1 subnets
O        20.2.1.0 [110/11] via 30.0.1.2, 00:03:02, Fddi2/1/0
         6.0.0.0/32 is subnetted, 1 subnets
O IA    6.6.6.6 [110/66] via 30.0.1.2, 00:03:02, Fddi2/1/0
         128.213.0.0/30 is subnetted, 1 subnets
C        128.213.63.0 is directly connected, ATM3/0
         203.250.14.0/32 is subnetted, 1 subnets
S        203.250.14.3 [1/0] via 128.213.63.1, ATM3/0
O IA 10.0.0.0/8 [110/1] via 30.0.1.2, 00:00:15, Fddi2/1/0
         30.0.0.0/24 is subnetted, 2 subnets
C        30.0.0.0 is directly connected, Serial1/1/0
C        30.0.1.0 is directly connected, Fddi2/1/0
R5#
```

Listing 9-19. *R5's routing table with aggregated route*

Let's now consider how virtual links can be used to provide more optimal routing in an OSPF domain. In the topology of the lab network, the Ethernet link between R1 and R2 belongs to area 1. This means that routers in the backbone area cannot see it and do not use it in their Dijkstra calculation. To illustrate this, R1 is configured with a loopback interface that is put in the backbone area (Listing 9-20).

```
R1#conf t
Enter configuration commands, one per line.  End with CNTL/Z.
R1(config)#int lo0
R1(config-if)#ip addr 1.1.1.1 255.255.255.255
R1(config-if)#exit
R1(config)#
R1(config)#router ospf 1
R1(config-router)#network 1.1.1.0 0.0.0.255 are 0
R1(config-router)#^Z
R1#
```

Listing 9-20. *R1 is configured with a loopback interface*

Now take a look at the routing table of R4 (Listing 9-21). Because it cannot see the Ethernet link between R1 and R2, R4 routes to 1.1.1.1 not via a Token Ring link but via the Serial0 interface.

```
R4#sho ip route
...
Gateway of last resort is not set
```

```
        1.0.0.0/32 is subnetted, 1 subnets
O           1.1.1.1 [110/65] via 10.1.1.1, 00:00:05, Serial0
        4.0.0.0/32 is subnetted, 1 subnets
C           4.4.4.4 is directly connected, Loopback0
        20.0.0.0/24 is subnetted, 2 subnets
C           20.2.2.0 is directly connected, TokenRing0
O IA        20.2.1.0 [110/16] via 20.2.2.1, 00:00:05, TokenRing0
        6.0.0.0/32 is subnetted, 1 subnets
O           6.6.6.6 [110/129] via 10.1.1.1, 00:00:05, Serial0
        10.0.0.0/8 is variably subnetted, 4 subnets, 2 masks
O           10.1.1.2/32 [110/6] via 20.2.2.1, 00:00:05, TokenRing0
C           10.1.1.0/24 is directly connected, Serial0
O           10.1.1.1/32 [110/64] via 10.1.1.1, 00:00:06, Serial0
O           10.1.1.6/32 [110/128] via 10.1.1.1, 00:00:06, Serial0
O IA 30.0.0.0/8 [110/17] via 20.2.2.1, 00:00:06, TokenRing0
R4#
```

Listing 9-21. *R4 having a suboptimal path*

To allow backbone routers to consider the Ethernet link between R1 and R2, the ABRs need to be configured with a virtual links, as follows:

```
!
router ospf 1
 network 30.0.0.0 0.255.255.255 area 1
 network 20.0.0.0 0.255.255.255 area 1
 network 10.0.0.0 0.255.255.255 area 0
 area 1 range 30.0.0.0 255.0.0.0
 area 0 range 10.0.0.0 255.0.0.0
 area 1 virtual-link 2.2.2.2
!
hostname R2
!
router ospf 1
 network 10.0.0.0 0.255.255.255 area 0
 network 30.0.0.0 0.255.255.255 area 1
 area 0 range 10.0.0.0 255.0.0.0
 area 1 range 30.0.0.0 255.0.0.0
 area 1 virtual-link 30.0.1.2
!
```

After both routers have been configured, the virtual link's FSM goes to the Full state (Listing 9-22).

```
R1#show ip ospf virtual
Virtual Link to router 2.2.2.2 is up
  Transit area 1, via interface Ethernet0/1, Cost of using 10
  Transmit Delay is 1 sec, State POINT_TO_POINT,
  Timer intervals configured, Hello 10, Dead 40, Wait 40, Retransmit 5
    Hello due in 00:00:02
    Adjacency State FULL
R1#
```

Listing 9-22. *Output of the* **show ip ospf virtual** *command*

Now that the virtual link is up, R4 should be able to use it in its routing table calculation and to install the route to R1's loopback address via the TokenRing interface (see Listing 9-23).

```
R4#sho ip route
...
Gateway of last resort is not set

     1.0.0.0/32 is subnetted, 1 subnets
O       1.1.1.1 [110/17] via 20.2.2.1, 00:00:23, TokenRing0
     4.0.0.0/32 is subnetted, 1 subnets
C       4.4.4.4 is directly connected, Loopback0
     20.0.0.0/24 is subnetted, 2 subnets
C       20.2.2.0 is directly connected, TokenRing0
O IA    20.2.1.0 [110/16] via 20.2.2.1, 00:00:23, TokenRing0
     6.0.0.0/32 is subnetted, 1 subnets
O       6.6.6.6 [110/81] via 20.2.2.1, 00:00:23, TokenRing0
     10.0.0.0/8 is variably subnetted, 4 subnets, 2 masks
O       10.1.1.2/32 [110/6] via 20.2.2.1, 00:00:23, TokenRing0
C       10.1.1.0/24 is directly connected, Serial0
O       10.1.1.1/32 [110/16] via 20.2.2.1, 00:00:24, TokenRing0
O       10.1.1.6/32 [110/80] via 20.2.2.1, 00:00:24, TokenRing0
O IA 30.0.0.0/8 [110/17] via 20.2.2.1, 00:00:24, TokenRing0
R4#
```

Listing 9-23. *R4 taking the virtual link into consideration*

9.2.10.4 Route Redistribution and Stub Areas

To illustrate external routing in the OSPF domain, R4 is configured to perform route redistribution, as shown in Listing 9-24.

```
R4#conf t
Enter configuration commands, one per line.  End with CNTL/Z.
R4(config)#ip route 50.1.1.0 255.255.255.0 Nul0
```

```
R4(config)#ip route 50.1.2.0 255.255.255.0 Null0
R4(config)#ip route 50.1.3.0 255.255.255.0 Null0
R4(config)#ip route 50.1.4.0 255.255.255.0 Null0
R4(config)#ip route 50.1.5.0 255.255.255.0 Null0
R4(config)#router ospf 1
R4(config-router)#redistribute static subnets
R4(config-router)#^Z
R4#
```

Listing 9-24. *R4 configured for route redistribution*

To make sure that R4 originates AS-external LSAs, a **show ip ospf data self** command is used (see Listing 9-25).

```
R4#sho ip ospf data self

        OSPF Router with ID (4.4.4.4) (Process ID 1)


                Router Link-states (Area 0)

Link ID         ADV Router      Age         Seq#         Checksum Link count
4.4.4.4         4.4.4.4         16          0x8000001B 0x44B8    4

                Net Link-states (Area 0)

Link ID         ADV Router      Age         Seq#         Checksum
20.2.2.2        4.4.4.4         687         0x80000003 0xC82D

                Type-5 AS External Link-states

Link ID         ADV Router      Age         Seq#         Checksum Tag
50.1.1.0        4.4.4.4         16          0x80000001 0xCB90    0
50.1.2.0        4.4.4.4         16          0x80000001 0xC09A    0
50.1.3.0        4.4.4.4         16          0x80000001 0xB5A4    0
50.1.4.0        4.4.4.4         16          0x80000001 0xAAAE    0
50.1.5.0        4.4.4.4         16          0x80000001 0x9FB8    0
R4#
```

Listing 9-25. *Output of* **show ip ospf data self** *on R4*

Now let's look at the routing table of R5 (Listing 9-26). The output of the **show ip route** command displays OSPF external routes as expected.

```
R5#sho ip route
...
```

```
Gateway of last resort is not set
...
     50.0.0.0/24 is subnetted, 5 subnets
O E2    50.1.3.0 [110/20] via 30.0.1.2, 00:00:32, Fddi2/1/0
O E2    50.1.2.0 [110/20] via 30.0.1.2, 00:00:32, Fddi2/1/0
O E2    50.1.1.0 [110/20] via 30.0.1.2, 00:00:32, Fddi2/1/0
O E2    50.1.5.0 [110/20] via 30.0.1.2, 00:00:32, Fddi2/1/0
O E2    50.1.4.0 [110/20] via 30.0.1.2, 00:00:32, Fddi2/1/0
...
R5#
```

Listing 9-26. *External routes in R5's routing table*

It is also interesting to use the **show ip ospf border** command to display R5's internal router routing table (Listing 9-27).

```
R5#sho ip ospf bord

OSPF Process 1 internal Routing Table

Codes: i - Intra-area route, I - Inter-area route

I 4.4.4.4 [17] via 30.0.1.2, Fddi2/1/0, ASBR, Area 1, SPF 8
i 2.2.2.2 [11] via 30.0.1.2, Fddi2/1/0, ABR, Area 1, SPF 8
i 30.0.1.2 [1] via 30.0.1.2, Fddi2/1/0, ABR, Area 1, SPF 8
R5#
```

Listing 9-27. *R5's internal routing table*

Note that R5 has an inter-area route to R4, represented by its Router-ID, 4.4.4.4. The reason is that R5 is not in the same area as R4 and R1; as an ABR, R5 announces the location of R4 to area 1 in an ASBR-summary-LSA.

Now let's configure area 1 as stub. Configuration of routers R1, R2, and R5 are changed as shown in Listing 9-28 for R5.

```
R5#conf t
Enter configuration commands, one per line.  End with CNTL/Z.
R5(config)#router ospf 1
R5(config-router)#area 1 stub
R5(config-router)#^Z
R5#
```

Listing 9-28. *Changing R5's config to treat area 1 as stub*

When routers have been configured with area 1 as stub, they withdraw the AS-external-LSAs and ASBR-summary-LSAs. R1 and R2 also announce a summary default route into area 1. Listing 9-29 shows R5's routing table.

```
R5#sho ip route
...
Gateway of last resort is 30.0.1.2 to network 0.0.0.0

     1.0.0.0/32 is subnetted, 1 subnets
O IA    1.1.1.1 [110/2] via 30.0.1.2, 00:00:04, Fddi2/1/0
     4.0.0.0/32 is subnetted, 1 subnets
O IA    4.4.4.4 [110/18] via 30.0.1.2, 00:00:14, Fddi2/1/0
     20.0.0.0/24 is subnetted, 2 subnets
O IA    20.2.2.0 [110/17] via 30.0.1.2, 00:00:14, Fddi2/1/0
O       20.2.1.0 [110/11] via 30.0.1.2, 00:00:14, Fddi2/1/0
     6.0.0.0/32 is subnetted, 1 subnets
O IA    6.6.6.6 [110/66] via 30.0.1.2, 00:00:09, Fddi2/1/0
     128.213.0.0/30 is subnetted, 1 subnets
C       128.213.63.0 is directly connected, ATM3/0
O IA 10.0.0.0/8 [110/1] via 30.0.1.2, 00:00:19, Fddi2/1/0
     30.0.0.0/24 is subnetted, 2 subnets
C       30.0.0.0 is directly connected, Serial1/1/0
C       30.0.1.0 is directly connected, Fddi2/1/0
O*IA 0.0.0.0/0 [110/2] via 30.0.1.2, 00:00:19, Fddi2/1/0
R5#
```

Listing 9-29. *R5's routing table with no external routes and with a summary default route*

Now R1 and R2 are also configured to make area 1 totally stub, as shown in Listing 9-30.

```
R1#conf t
Enter configuration commands, one per line.  End with CNTL/Z.
R1(config)#router ospf 1
R1(config-router)#area 1 stub no-summary
R1(config-router)#^Z
R1#
```

Listing 9-30. *Configuring area 1 as totally stub*

R1 and R2 are supposed to flush the summary-LSAs originated for area 1 and leave only the default summary in that area. R5's routing table changes accordingly (see Listing 9-31).

```
R5#sho ip route
...
Gateway of last resort is 30.0.1.2 to network 0.0.0.0

     20.0.0.0/24 is subnetted, 1 subnet
O        20.2.1.0 [110/11] via 30.0.1.2, 00:00:14, Fddi2/1/0
     128.213.0.0/30 is subnetted, 1 subnets
C        128.213.63.0 is directly connected, ATM3/0
     30.0.0.0/24 is subnetted, 2 subnets
C        30.0.0.0 is directly connected, Serial1/1/0
C        30.0.1.0 is directly connected, Fddi2/1/0
O*IA 0.0.0.0/0 [110/2] via 30.0.1.2, 00:00:19, Fddi2/1/0
R5#
```

Listing 9-31. *R5's routing table when area 1 is totally stub*

9.2.10.5 NSSA

Not-so-stubby areas, described in Section 9.2.5.6, allow an area to inject external routing information into the backbone but to reject it in the other direction. Routers R1, R2, and R5 are configured to treat area 1 in the lab network as NSSA. R5 is also configured to be an NSSA ASBR (Listing 9-32).

```
R5#conf t
Enter configuration commands, one per line.  End with CNTL/Z.
R5(config)#ip route 60.1.1.0 255.255.255.0 Null0
R5(config)#ip route 60.1.2.0 255.255.255.0 Null0
R5(config)#ip route 60.1.3.0 255.255.255.0 Null0
R5(config)#ip route 60.1.4.0 255.255.255.0 Null0
R5(config)#
R5(config)#router ospf 1
R5(config-router)#area 1 nssa
R5(config-router)#redistribute static subnets
R5(config-router)#^Z
R5#
```

Listing 9-32. *R5 configured as an NSSA ASBR*

Take a look at the output of the **show ip ospf** data command (Listing 9-33). It illustrates that R5 originates type 7 LSAs, based on the redistributed routes.

```
R5#sho ip ospf database

        OSPF Router with ID (5.5.5.5) (Process ID 1)
```

```
                    Router Link-states (Area 1)

Link ID             ADV Router         Age        Seq#        Checksum Link count
1.1.1.1             1.1.1.1            6          0x80000023 0x593C    2
2.2.2.2             2.2.2.2            5          0x80000029 0x83C4    2
5.5.5.5             5.5.5.5            4          0x80000001 0x7101    2

                    Net Link-states (Area 1)

Link ID             ADV Router         Age        Seq#        Checksum
20.2.1.1            2.2.2.2            465        0x80000001 0x4DBA
30.0.1.2            1.1.1.1            1          0x80000001 0x9D59

                    Summary Net Link-states (Area 1)

Link ID             ADV Router         Age        Seq#        Checksum
0.0.0.0             1.1.1.1            651        0x80000002 0x1918
0.0.0.0             2.2.2.2            471        0x80000003 0xF833

                    Type-7 AS External Link-states (Area 1)

Link ID             ADV Router         Age        Seq#        Checksum Tag
60.1.1.0            5.5.5.5            4          0x80000001 0xEF35    0
60.1.2.0            5.5.5.5            5          0x80000001 0xE43F    0
60.1.3.0            5.5.5.5            5          0x80000001 0xD949    0
60.1.4.0            5.5.5.5            5          0x80000001 0xCE53    0
R5#
```

Listing 9-33. *Type 7 LSAs originated by R5*

Now let's explore R2's routing information (Listing 9-34).

```
R2#sho ip route
...
Gateway of last resort is not set
...
     50.0.0.0/24 is subnetted, 5 subnets
O E2    50.1.3.0 [110/20] via 20.2.2.2, 00:04:19, TokenRing1/2
O E2    50.1.2.0 [110/20] via 20.2.2.2, 00:04:20, TokenRing1/2
O E2    50.1.1.0 [110/20] via 20.2.2.2, 00:04:20, TokenRing1/2
O E2    50.1.5.0 [110/20] via 20.2.2.2, 00:04:20, TokenRing1/2
O E2    50.1.4.0 [110/20] via 20.2.2.2, 00:04:20, TokenRing1/2
     60.0.0.0/24 is subnetted, 4 subnets
O N2    60.1.4.0 [110/20] via 30.0.0.1, 00:04:20, Serial2/1
O N2    60.1.1.0 [110/20] via 30.0.0.1, 00:04:20, Serial2/1
O N2    60.1.3.0 [110/20] via 30.0.0.1, 00:04:20, Serial2/1
O N2    60.1.2.0 [110/20] via 30.0.0.1, 00:04:20, Serial2/1
...
R2#
```

Listing 9-34. *R2's routing table*

Note that external routes originated by R5 are marked as **O N2** (NSSA, type 2) in R2's routing table.

Listing 9-35 shows R2's link-state database.

```
R2#sho ip ospf data

      OSPF Router with ID (2.2.2.2) (Process ID 1)
...


          Type-7 AS External Link-states (Area 1)

Link ID         ADV Router      Age         Seq#           Checksum Tag
60.1.1.0        5.5.5.5         111         0x80000001 0xEF35    0
60.1.2.0        5.5.5.5         111         0x80000001 0xE43F    0
60.1.3.0        5.5.5.5         111         0x80000001 0xD949    0
60.1.4.0        5.5.5.5         111         0x80000001 0xCE53    0


          Type-5 AS External Link-states

Link ID         ADV Router      Age         Seq#           Checksum Tag
50.1.1.0        4.4.4.4         985         0x80000005 0xC394    0
50.1.2.0        4.4.4.4         985         0x80000005 0xB89E    0
50.1.3.0        4.4.4.4         985         0x80000005 0xADA8    0
50.1.4.0        4.4.4.4         985         0x80000005 0xA2B2    0
50.1.5.0        4.4.4.4         985         0x80000005 0x97BC    0
60.1.1.0        2.2.2.2         91          0x80000001 0xDE5C    0
60.1.2.0        2.2.2.2         91          0x80000001 0xD366    0
60.1.3.0        2.2.2.2         91          0x80000001 0xC870    0
60.1.4.0        2.2.2.2         91          0x80000001 0xBD7A    0
R2#
```

Listing 9-35. *R2's link-state database*

The LSDB contains type 7 LSAs originated by R5, as well as type 5 LSAs originated by R2 as the result of type 7–to–type 5 LSA conversion. Routers in the backbone area install type 5 LSAs originated by R2 and calculate external routes (see Listing 9-36).

```
R4#sho ip route
...
Gateway of last resort is not set
...
     60.0.0.0/24 is subnetted, 4 subnets
O E2    60.1.4.0 [110/20] via 20.2.2.1, 00:08:05, TokenRing0
O E2    60.1.1.0 [110/20] via 20.2.2.1, 00:08:05, TokenRing0
O E2    60.1.3.0 [110/20] via 20.2.2.1, 00:08:05, TokenRing0
```

```
O E2    60.1.2.0 [110/20] via 20.2.2.1, 00:08:05, TokenRing0
O IA 30.0.0.0/8 [110/17] via 20.2.2.1, 00:15:57, TokenRing0
R4#
```

Listing 9-36. *R4's routing table with external routes translated by R2*

Now R1 and R2 are configured to aggregate NSSA routes when they are announced in type 5 LSAs (Listing 9-37).

```
R1#conf t
Enter configuration commands, one per line.  End with CNTL/Z.
R1(config)#router ospf 1
R1(config-router)#summary-address 60.0.0.0 255.0.0.0
R1(config-router)#^Z
R1#
```

Figure 9-37. *R1 configured to aggregate NSSA routes*

External routes in the routing tables of routers in other areas change accordingly (Listing 9-38).

```
R4#sho ip route
...
Gateway of last resort is not set
...
O E2 60.0.0.0/8 [110/20] via 20.2.2.1, 00:00:01, TokenRing0
O IA 30.0.0.0/8 [110/17] via 20.2.2.1, 00:18:54, TokenRing0
R4#
```

Listing 9-38. *R4's routing table containing aggregate originated by R2*

9.2.11 Summary

- OSPF is an open-standard IP routing protocol using the link-state routing algorithm.

- Route calculation in OSPF is based on the SPT built over the topology graph, which in turn is constructed of LSAs.

- To ensure convergence of the network, OSPF performs continual LSDB synchronization by means of initial LSDB exchange and asynchronous LSA flooding.

- OSPF sends updates only when the network topology or routing information changes. In addition, every LSA is refreshed every 30 minutes.

- The route metric in OSPF is represented as a sum of all link costs leading to the corresponding vertex in the topology graph.

- OSPF supports the equal cost multipath technique and may install up to six routes in the routing table.

- OSPF is a hierarchical routing protocol supporting two levels of hierarchy. Routers can be grouped into areas. All areas are connected to a special backbone area.

- OSPF supports external routing information. External routes are explicitly distinguished from internal routes.

- Propagation of external routing information in the domain may be controlled by configuration of stub areas and NSSAs.

9.3 References

[ISO10589] ISO, "Intermediate System to Intermediate System routing information Exchange Protocol for Use in Conjunction with the Protocol for Providing the Connectionless-mode Network Service (ISO 8473)," ISO/IEC 10589, 1992.

[JMOY] J. Moy, OSPF Complete Implementation, Boston, Mass: Addison-Wesley, 2001.

[NSSA] R. Coltun, V. Fuller, and P. Murphy, "The OSPF NSSA Option," work in progress, December 2000, http://www.ietf.org/internet-drafts/draft-ietf-ospf-nssa-update-10.txt.

[RFC1131] J. Moy, "The OSPF Specification," RFC 1131, October 1989, http://www.ieft.org/rfc/rfc1131.ps.

[RFC1142] D. Oran, "OSI IS-IS Intra-domain Routing Protocol," RFC 1142, February 1990, http://www.ieft.org/rfc/rfc1142.txt.

[RFC1195] R. Callon, "Use of OSI IS-IS for Routing in TCP/IP and Dual Environments," RFC 1195, December 1990, http://www.ieft.org/rfc/rfc1195.txt.

[RFC1246] J. Moy, "Experience with the OSPF Protocol," RFC 1246, July 1991, http://www.ietf.org/rfc/rfc1246.txt.

[RFC1247] J. Moy, "OSPF Version 2," RFC 1247, July 1991, http://www.ietf.org/rfc/rfc1247.txt.

[RFC1583] J. Moy, "OSPF Version 2," RFC 1583, March 1994, http://www.ietf.org/rfc/rfc1583.txt.

[RFC1587] R. Coltun and V. Fuller, "The OSPF NSSA Option," RFC 1587, March 1994, http://www.ietf.org/rfc/rfc1587.txt.

[RFC1793] J. Moy, "Extending OSPF to Support Demand Circuits," RFC 1793, April 1995, http://www.ietf.org/rfc/rfc1793.txt.

[RFC1850] F. Baker and R. Coltun, "OSPF Version 2 Management Information Base, RFC 1850, November 1995, http://www.ietf.org/rfc/rfc1850.txt.

[RFC2178] J. Moy, "OSPF Version 2," RFC 2178, July 1997, http://www.ietf.org/rfc/rfc2178.txt.

[RFC2328] J. Moy, "OSPF Version 2," RFC 2328, April 1998, http://www.ietf.org/rfc/rfc1247.txt.

[RFC2370] R. Coltun, "The OSPF Opaque LSA Option," RFC 2370, July 1998, http://www.ietf.org/rfc/rfc2370.txt.

[RFC2740] R. Coltun, D. Ferguson, and J. Moy, "OSPF for Ipv6," RFC 2749, December 1999, http://www.ietf.org/rfc/rfc2740.txt.

[RFC2966] T. Li, T. Przygienda, and H. Smit, "Domain–wide Prefix Distribution with Two-Level IS-IS," RFC 2966, October 2000, http://www.ietf.org/rfc/rfc2966.txt.

Chapter Ten

Enhanced IGRP

This chapter describes principles of operation of another class of routing protocols: hybrids. Hybrid routing technique is based on the distance-vector algorithms but also incorporates some features, such as adjacencies between neighboring routers or guaranteed message delivery, usually found in link-state routing protocols. The sole routing protocol in this group is enhanced IGRP (EIGRP), implemented by Cisco Systems and based on theoretical work done by J. J. Garcia Luna Aceves.

10.1 Basic Description and History

Although the name implies that EIGRP is an enhanced version of IGRP, the only thing these two protocols have in common is the attributes used for route metric calculation: effective path bandwidth, cumulative path delay, and so on. EIGRP is based on the theory of the *diffusing update algorithm* (DUAL), which guarantees loop-free path selection within a network at any time, even while the network is converging. The algorithm is considered in Section 10.2.

As implemented in Cisco IOS, EIGRP provides smooth migration from IGRP. Like classful IGRP, EIGRP performs automatic route summarization by default, although EIGRP itself is a classless routing protocol. Also, if a router has instances of IGRP and EIGRP with the same process ID, IOS will perform automatic route redistribution between the two.

EIGRP supports more than one network-layer protocol. This means that in addition to IP routing, EIGRP can be used as a routing protocol in IPX or AppleTalk networks. EIGRP's general characteristics are listed in Table 10-1.

Table 10-1. *General Characteristics of EIGRP*

Characteristic	EIGRP Implmentation
Algorithm type	Diffused update algorithm (DUAL), a modified version of the distance-vector algorithm
Metric type	Composite, calculated via a weighted function based on a vector of path attributes: bandwidth, delay, reliability, and load
Best path selection	Using DUAL
Multipath support	Equal-cost and unequal-cost multipath routing supported
View of the network	Neighbors' perspective; routers have no full topology information, but EIGRP routers hold more information than those using pure distance-vector algorithms
New neighbor discovery	Explicit, via a Hello subprotocol
Unreachable neighbor discovery	Explicit, via a Hello subprotocol
New route discovery	As in distance-vector protocols
Unreachable route discovery	Via explicit unreachable route announcement
Periodic updates	N/A
Event-driven updates	Triggered updates sent by routers after a network topology change
Transport protocol	Directly over IP, using protocol ID 88, with updates sent using the link-local multicast IP address 224.0.0.10 (AllIGRPRouters)
External routing information	Announced separately from internal routing information
Classful route summarization	A classless routing protocol; but by default performs classful route summarization
CIDR and route aggregation	A classless protocol; supports route aggregation, on a per interface basis, and supernets

10.2 Theoretical Basis

The idea behind the DUAL algorithm can be easily understood if we consider the problems it solves in the traditional distance-vector protocols and the way it does so. First, traditional distance-vector protocols age out individual routing entries and thus need to send a complete set of routes periodically. This consumes too much bandwidth and CPU time. DUAL assumes that routers maintain adjacencies explicitly via a lightweight Hello protocol, so only the changes in routing information need to be exchanged.

Second, RIP and IGRP keep track of only the best routes; when the best path to a given destination becomes unavailable, routers need to wait until the next update to find a path to a network. DUAL saves information on paths through a set of available neighbors and uses it—when it is safe to do so—to immediately calculate the new paths. If stored information cannot be used to find out the new best path—because, for example, it is not obvious that the new path is loop-free—the calculating router sends requests to all its neighbors; that is, it performs active network topology discovery versus the passive discovery usually found in other protocols.

Third, owing to the unreliable nature of message exchange, RIP and IGRP may potentially experience the counting-to-infinity problem, so a number of mechanisms are integrated in these protocols to avoid this problem. Some of these mechanisms, such as holddown timers and route poisoning, cause long convergence times. Because of its nature, DUAL does not need holddown timers. Loop freedom is achieved through fast recalculation of best paths, using stored information and, when a request needs to be sent, locking routing information until the new network topology is discovered.

The main idea behind EIGRP is to improve convergence characteristics of distance-vector routing protocols by solving the preceding problems. Now let's consider how DUAL and its accompanying algorithms do so.

First, several requirements need to be met in order for DUAL to work correctly.

- Routers must maintain adjacencies so new neighbors are discovered and unreachable neighbors are detected within a finite period of time.

- Messages exchanged by routers must be delivered reliably and in the order they were sent.

- All events, such as incoming messages, local link-state changes, and so on, must be processed one at a time, within a finite time, in the order they were experienced.

The requirement for adjacency maintenance is implemented in EIGRP in the form of a Hello subprotocol. In short, routers exchange small Hello packets every 5 seconds or, for lower-bandwidth NBMA interfaces, every 60 seconds. Every Hello packet contains the Hold time. If a neighbor has not been heard from during the Hold time period it announced, the neighbor is declared down.

Reliable delivery of protocol messages is implemented through EIGRP's *reliable transport protocol* (RTP). This protocol provides guaranteed delivery of unicast and multicast packets (see Section 10.3).

When two EIGRP routers establish an adjacency, they exchange routing information in the same way as other distance-vector routing protocols do; that is, the information an EIGRP router advertises to its neighbors is based on the information in the routing table. Note that like any other distance-vector routing protocol, EIGRP uses the split-horizon technique. Also, it is not possible for an EIGRP router to update its other neighbors before it has updated its own routing table.

The route metric in EIGRP is similar to that used in IGRP: A set of route attributes is propagated throughout the network and is used to calculate a scalar metric value. The difference between IGRP and EIGRP is that EIGRP has a wider metric scale and a slightly different formula, considered in Section 10.8.

When an EIGRP router receives an update about a specific network from a given neighbor, this information may be stored internally even though the path through this neighbor is not used for packet forwarding. To understand whether a route through a specific neighbor should be saved for possible later use, EIGRP introduces the concept of *feasible successor*.

Every EIGRP router maintains an *adjacency database* and a *topology database*. The information in the topology database is represented in the form of network prefixes accompanied by a set of paths through directly attached neighbors. Every path has a number of attributes, including the metric as calculated by the neighbor that announced the route—the neighbor's *reported distance* (RD)—and the metric calculated by the router itself. Whenever the set of paths is changed for a given destination in the topology table, the router recalculates the *feasible distance* (FD) for the affected network prefix. Feasible distance is the minimal value of the locally calculated metrics for a given route since the last time the entry entered the Passive state. The topology database contains paths via all neighbors, with paths sorted on the basis of the metric. However, only paths through feasible, or potential, successors are used for actual path calculation and shown in the output of the **show ip eigrp topology** command. (All paths can be shown with the **show ip eigrp topology all-links** command.)

A neighbor is considered a feasible successor for a given destination if the path through it satisfies the feasibility condition (FC).

The feasibility condition requires that for a given network prefix, the metric calculated by the neighbor—the neighbor's reported distance—have a value less than the local FD. If the feasibility condition is met, forwarding traffic destined for that network prefix through such a neighbor is guaranteed to be safe because the neighbor is not using the calculating router as its successor; that is, the neighbor is closer to the destination than the calculating router. Among all feasible neighbors, the one with the lowest distance becomes the *successor*—the next-hop router used for packet forwarding—and the local distance associated with the path through this neighbor becomes the router's RD that is announced in EIGRP updates to the neighbors.

The topology database contains information about paths through all feasible successors. However, not all paths are used to install routes in the routing table. Usually, only paths through the successors are installed, but the value of the variance parameter affects this process, as described in Section 10.8

Let's consider an example. In Figure 10-1, R1 has four neighbors: R2, R3, R4, and R5. We are interested in the information R1 has in its topology table about a destination network, N, directly attached to R7. Before R1 is inserted in the network, R2 routes to N through R5 with distance 8. R3 routes through R6 with distance 3. R4 routes through R7 with distance 4, and R5 routes through R7 with distance 3.

When it starts and receives routing information from R2, R3, R4, and R5, R1 has four paths to N, as follows. The numbers in parentheses indicate the distance calculated by R1 and the distance calculated by the neighbor.

```
N:        R5  (5/3)
          R3  (6/3)
          R4  (7/4)
          R2  (9/8)
```

Now R1 calculates its feasible distance as the minimal locally calculated distance among all available paths. So feasible distance equals 5, and R5 becomes the successor.

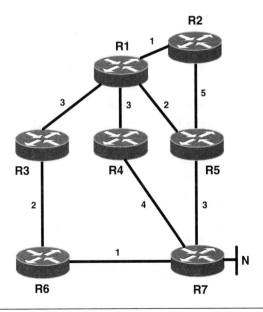

Figure 10-1. *Sample network*

```
N: FD=5      R5 (5/3) Successor
             R3 (6/3)
             R4 (7/4)
             R2 (9/8)
```

Then R1 looks through other paths and identifies feasible successors. In our case, R2 does not satisfy the feasibility condition, because the distance calculated by R2 for N itself is higher than the feasible distance for this network. The paths through R3 and R4, however, do satisfy the feasibility condition, so they become feasible successors.

```
N: FD=5      R5 (5/3) Successor
             R3 (6/3) Feasible Successor
             R4 (7/4) Feasible Successor
             R2 (9/8)
```

After it has finished the computation, R1 installs the route to network N via R5 in the routing table and sends an update to its direct neighbors. Note that this makes R2 select a new successor and route to N via R1. Because of the split-horizon algorithm, R2 needs to suppress R1's route through R2, so the topology table for N looks as follows:

```
N: FD=5      R5 (5/3) Successor
             R3 (6/3) Feasible Successor
             R4 (7/4) Feasible Successor
```

Now imagine that the link between R1 and R5 goes down (Figure 10-2). R1 removes the path through R5 and revisits the list of paths. Because R3 and R4 are feasible successors, R1 can immediately choose the new best path.

```
N: FD=5      R3 (6/3) Successor
             R4 (7/4) Feasible Successor
```

Note that the value of the feasible distance is not changed, because the router still performs local shortest-path computation.

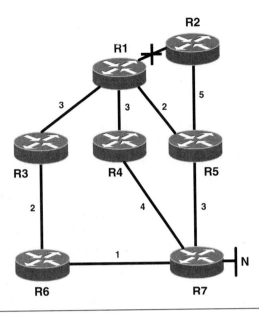

Figure 10-2. *Link going down in the sample network*

After the new successor has been chosen, R1 updates its neighbors with new information. So R2 changes its best-path distance to 7.

Now assume that R1 has lost its connectivity to both R3 and R4. Because R1 does not have any feasible successors, it puts its route to N in the Active state and sends a query to all its neighbors: R2 at this moment. The route remains in the Active state until R1 receives replies from all requested neighbors or a *stuck-in-active* (SIA) timer expires for this route.

```
N: FD=5    (Active) Remaining Replies from: R2
```

The SIA timer expires if the route spends more than 3 minutes, the default value, in the Active state. On expiration of the SIA timer, the neighbors from which the replies have not been received from are reset.

Normally, SIA events should not happen. If SIA events are logged (see Listing 10-1), it means that the EIGRP process is not receiving replies to submitted queries, most probably indicating a problem in the network.

```
DEC 12 10:01:13: %DUAL-3-SIA: Route 10.1.1.0/24 stuck-in-active state in IP-EIGRP 1.
Cleaning up
```

Listing 10-1. *SIA event log message*

When it receives a query from the neighbor it believes is the successor (R1) for network N, R2 removes from the topology table the path to N through R1 and revisits the remaining paths, trying to find the new successor among the feasible successors. Because R5 satisfies the feasibility condition—R5's calculated distance is 3, which is lower than R2's feasible distance, 6—R5 becomes the successor, and R2 sends its reply with new announced distance 8 to R1. R1 installs the new path to N through R2, takes the route out of the Active state, and recalculates its new successor for network N, which is obviously router R2. The network converges on the new topology.

In fact, the DUAL algorithm is a bit more complex than just selecting successors and feasible successors and sending queries and replies. Because a router can experience several events while a route to a particular network is in the Active state and it is important to ensure that a node is waiting to complete the processing of maximum one outstanding query at a time, DUAL introduces a finite state machine for the entries in the topology table. As in previous chapters, the state machine is described in terms of events and states. (The FSM itself is considered after the route states and event are discussed.)

The route FSM state in DUAL is determined by three parameters: route state, Active or Passive; reply status flag, set if the router is waiting for replies to a previously sent query from some neighbors; and the query origin flag, which identifies why the router sent the query and became active for the given route. Table 10-2 lists all possible combinations of these parameters and corresponding route states.

The internal and external events DUAL can experience are

- Change of a link cost
- Change of a link state (topology change)
- Reception of an update
- Reception of a query
- Reception of a reply

From the standpoint of the route FSM, events are subdivided into categories that serve as events to the FSM. Table 10-3 lists DUAL FSM events. The logic of the FSM is illustrated in Figure 10-3. The processing of events causing FSM state transitions is described in more detail in Section 10.5.

Table 10-2. *DUAL Route States*

Active/ Passive	Reply Status	Query Origin	Route State Description
P	0	0	The router is in the Passive state for the network, performing only local calculations and not requesting any information from its neighbors
A	1	0	The router has become Active for the destination without receiving a query from the successor, but after becoming Active has experienced at least one increase in route distance
A	1	1	The router has become Active after processing an event other than a query from the successor; no increase in route distance has been experienced yet; router is the origin of the query
A	1	2	The router has received a query from the successor and it has experienced at least one event that caused an increase in route distance; multiple origins of the query, one of which is the successor.
A	1	3	The router has become Active because a query from the successor has been received, but no increase in route distance has occurred yet; the successor is the origin of the query

Table 10-3. *DUAL Route Events*

Input Event Name	Event Description
IE1	Any input event, after which FC is satisfied or the network is unreachable
IE2	Reception of a query from the successor, after which FC is not satisfied
IE3	Input event other than a query, after which FC is not satisfied
IE4	Input event other than the last reply or a query from the successor
IE5	Input event other than the last reply, a query from the successor, or an increase in route distance
IE6	Input event other than the last reply
IE7	Input event other then the last reply or increase in route distance
IE8	Increase in route distance
IE9	Last reply has been received; FC check not successful
IE10	Query has been received from the successor
IE11	Last reply has been received; FC check successful
IE12	Last reply has been received; FC has been set to infinity

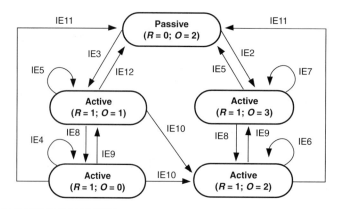

Figure 10-3. *DUAL route FSM*

10.3 Subsystems and Data Structures

EIGRP functionality is divided into several modules. Some of them are generic and work identically for all network-layer protocols; as mentioned earlier, EIGRP can distribute IP, IPX, and AppleTalk routing information, and some modules are protocol-specific:

- *DUAL,* a protocol-independent module implementing the logic of the diffusing update algorithm

- *Hello,* a protocol-independent module that provides new-neighbor discovery and unreachable-neighbor determination functionality

- *Reliable transport protocol* (RTP), a protocol-independent module that provides reliable packet delivery mechanism for EIGRP, working over specific transport protocols, such as IP or IPX, and providing unicast and multicast transmission.

- *Transport module,* a network layer client of EIGRP (IPX-EIGRP or AT-EIGRP, for example) providing transport service that can be used by RTP to send and to receive EIGRP packets.

- *Routing table interface module,* a network layer client providing a routing table management service module to implement the functionality necessary for installing and removing routing information, as well as importing routes from the routing table (route redistribution)

In addition to these software modules, every EIGRP router, as mentioned before, maintains two databases:

- *Adjacency database,* containing information about neighbors. The table is maintained by the Hello module. The DUAL module also uses information from this table.

- *Topology database,* a collection of network prefixes with associated paths through direct neighbors. It is updated by the DUAL module.

Cooperation between EIGRP modules is illustrated in Figure 10-4.

Let's now consider every EIGRP module and database structure in particular. The DUAL module is responsible for maintaining the topology database and performing distributed shortest-path calculation. The module sends and receives queries, updates, and replies through the RTP module; calculates best paths, using information in the topology database; and installs results in the corresponding routing table via the associated routing table interface module.

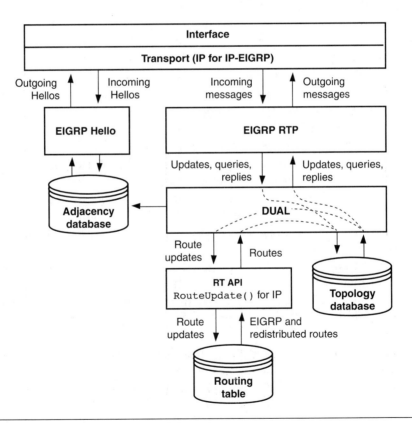

Figure 10-4. *Cooperation between EIGRP modules*

Note that the transport and routing table interface modules are protocol-dependent.

The EIGRP Hello module is in charge of discovering new neighbors and determining unreachable ones. EIGRP routers send Hello packets periodically with a Hello interval of 5 seconds for all links except for low speed (less than T1) NBMA networks. The Hello interval for interfaces attached to low speed NBMA clouds is 60 seconds. (Note that routers use the bandwidth attribute of the interfaces to decide whether an interface is low speed.) A 15 percent jitter is introduced to every Hello period to avoid possible synchronization. Every Hello packet contains the hold time value (see Section 10.4 for the format of EIGRP packets), which tells the neighbor how long it should consider the router alive without receiving any EIGRP packets. The hold time is normally three times the configured Hello interval. Both Hello and Hold timers can be configured on a per interface basis.

The RTP module implements a reliable packet transmission protocol that supports both multicast and unicast submissions. EIGRP's RTP approach, based on a Cisco patent for reliable multicast transmission,[1] allows the protocol to use multicast capabilities more effectively. Initial transmission of data is done by using multicast packets; that is, the data is sent to all neighbors on a segment. Every neighbor is then expected to acknowledge it with a unicast Hello packet that contains the sequence number of the received packet. Until a packet is acknowledged, it is not removed from the neighbor's output queue and is retransmitted to it as unicast. However, EIGRP RTP does not wait until all neighbors acknowledge transmitted packets before it uses the multicast capabilities of the segment again. Instead, when a new multicast packet needs to be sent, the router first sends a special packet that contains the list of neighbors that should not listen to the next multicast packet—essentially, the neighbors that have not acknowledged some packets. The multicast packet itself contains a conditional reception flag that indicates that routers should consult the previously received packet to understand whether the multicast packet should be processed.

The transport module provides basic EIGRP packet encapsulation, transmission, and reception functionality. The IP version of EIGRP, for example, provides encapsulation of EIGRP messages in IP packets, using IP protocol ID 88. EIGRP packets carrying AppleTalk routing information are encapsulated in AppleTalk DDP packets, also using protocol ID 88.

Information in the EIGRP adjacency table is represented in the form of a list of neighbors and associated parameters, as shown in Listing 10-2. (Throughout this chapter, we consider the IP version of EIGRP.) Parameters associated with every neighbor are as follows:

---

[1] Cisco Systems Inc. has a patent on the reliable multicast transmission technique used in EIGRP (US Patent No. 5,519,704, May 21, 1996, Farinacci, et al.).

```
R1#sho ip eigrp neighbors
IP-EIGRP neighbors for process 1
H    Address              Interface    Hold Uptime    SRTT    RTO   Q   Seq Type
                                       (sec)          (ms)          Cnt Num
0    30.0.1.1             Et0/1          13 09:26:15     9    200   0   30
1    20.2.1.1             Se3/1          11 09:36:20    39    570   0   41
3    20.1.2.2             Se3/2          13 10:10:39     5   1140   0   655
2    20.1.1.2             Se3/0          11 10:10:39    14   1140   0   454
R1#
```

Listing 10-2. *EIGRP adjacency table*

- *Address*, the IP address seen in the `source address` field of IP packets received from the neighbor. The same address is used by the local router for unicast packet transmissions to the neighbor.

- *Interface*, the interface through which the neighbor is reachable.

- *Hold time*, the remaining hold time, in seconds. If the router does not receive any EIGRP packets from the neighbor during this time, the neighbor is declared down. When an EIGRP packet is received from the neighbor, the Hold timer for this neighbor is reset.

- *Uptime*, the amount of time the neighbor has been seen operational by the local router.

- *SRTT (smooth round-trip time)*, the number of milliseconds for an EIGRP packet to be sent to the neighbor and for an acknowledgment to be received. This value is used in the flow-control mechanism in the EIGRP RTP module.

- *RTO (retransmit timeout)*, the number of milliseconds defining the retransmit interval for unacknowledged data.

- *Q Cnt*, the depth of the output queue for the neighbor. The output queue is used to store EIGRP packet descriptors corresponding to the packets that have been sent out and are waiting for an acknowledgment. Packet descriptors are removed from the queue only when they are acknowledged by appropriate Hello packets (see Section 10.4 for EIGRP packet format and usage).

- *Seq Num*, the packet sequence number. The reliable nature of the EIGRP RTP requires that all data units transmitted between neighbors be numbered and acknowledged.

Listing 10-3 shows an example of EIGRP topology database. Every element of the table contains the following attributes:

```
R1#sho ip eigrp topo
IP-EIGRP Topology Table for AS(1)/ID(172.16.66.172)

Codes: P - Passive, A - Active, U - Update, Q - Query, R - Reply,
       r - reply Status, s - sia Status

P 20.2.2.0/24, 1 successors, FD is 11023872
        via 20.2.1.1 (11023872/5511936), Serial3/1
        via 20.1.1.2 (21049600/5537536), Serial3/0
        via 20.1.2.2 (21024000/5511936), Serial3/2
...
R1#
```

Listing 10-3. *Sample EIGRP topology table*

- *P* or *A* flag indicating whether the router is in Passive or Active state
- *U* (update) flag indicating that an update has been sent and is waiting to be acknowledged
- *Q* (query) flag indicating that a query has been sent and is waiting for an acknowledgment
- *R* (reply) flag indicating that a reply has been sent and is waiting for an acknowledgment
- Number of successors showing how many neighbors have the best locally calculated metric
- *FD* (feasible distance) showing the value of the FD for a given destination that is calculated as explained in Section 10.8
- Set of paths representing possible packet trails to the destination network

Each path element linked to a topology table entry corresponds to a single neighbor and contains the following information:

- ** flag:* Denotes the paths through successors.
- *via IP-address/Route Source:* Indicates the interface IP address of the remote neighbor if the route was received from a different router. If the route was locally originated, this field indicates the route source. Possible values are:
  - *Connected:* The route is announced because the corresponding interface is covered by a **network** statement in EIGRP configuration.
  - *Rstatic:* The route is static and is installed in the topology table because it was redistributed.
  - *Rconnected:* The route is derived from an interface IP address—it is from the Connected route source—but it is not covered by any **network** statement.

However, the route is installed in the topology database because it was explicitly redistributed.

- *Redistributed:* The route is from a source other than Connected or Static and is installed in the topology table owing to configured route redistribution.

- *Summary:* The route is created by EIGRP itself either as a result of automatic route summarization process or because of a manually configured route summary (see Section 10.13.5 for details).

- *(N/M):* These two numbers correspond to a locally calculated metric through the neighbor and the metric calculated and announced by the neighbor itself.

- *r flag:* This path-specific flag indicates the reply status for a specific neighbor. The flag is set if the neighbor has not replied to the query yet and is cleared when the reply is received. The destination's Q flag is cleared only after r flags are cleared for all neighbors. Other flags described here may also be displayed.

- *Interface-name:* This is the interface through which the corresponding neighbor can be reached.

10.4 Message Format

Even though various network layer versions of EIGRP encapsulate EIGRP packets using different techniques, all EIGRP messages share the same common format, illustrated in Figure 10-5. All EIGRP messages start with a common header, which contains the following fields:

- *Version:* Specifies the EIGRP version that the router that originated the packet is running. Currently version 2 of EIGRP is used.

- *OpCode:* EIGRP shares OpCodes defined in IGRP (see Chapter 8) and adds its own.

  - 1 defines an update packet, as in IGRP.

  - 2 defines a request—not to confuse with query—packet, as in IGRP. This packet type is not used in EIGRP.

  - 3 defines a query packet. EIGRP uses this type of packet to send queries when destinations go Active.

  - 4 defines a reply packet. EIGRP uses this type of packet to send replies to received queries.

  - 5 indicates EIGRP Hellos. EIGRP verifies neighbor reachability by periodically sending these packets.

  - 6 indicates EIGRP IPX SAP (Service Advertisement Protocol). This type of packet is used in the IPX version of EIGRP to send incremental SAP updates.

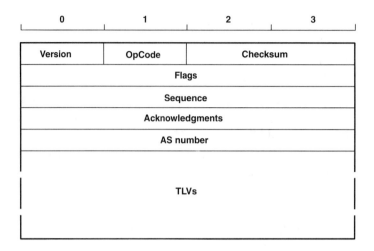

Figure 10-5. *EIGRP message format*

- 7 is a special packet type used for neighbor probing (not discussed in this book).

- 8 defines an acknowledgment packet, a special type of Hello packet used to acknowledge reliably transmitted packets.

- *Checksum:* The IP checksum of the entire EIGRP packet.

- *Flags:* Two bit fields

  - *Init flag* (0x01): Set in the beginning of the EIGRP adjacency establishment process; tells the other side that it needs to download the topology table.

  - *CR (conditionally received) flag* (0x02): Used in the EIGRP RTP mechanism to indicate that the current packet should be received only if the previously received packet contained a special type-length-value (TLV) triplet listing routers that must not receive the packet and the local router was not listed there.

- *Sequence:* The sequence number of the packet. This field is used by the RTP mechanism to ensure that packets are delivered reliably.

- *Acknowledgment:* The sequence number of the last packet received by the originating router. Hello packets with a nonzero value in this field are treated as acknowledgment packets.

- *Autonomous system number:* Identifier of the routing domain the router belongs to. EIGRP is allowed to process only packets from the routers belonging to the same routing domain. This allows several EIGRP processes to work over the same network segments without interfering with one another.

Pseudocode for EIGRP common header is shown in Listing 10-4.

```
/*
 * EIGRP Header
 */

typedef struct EIGRPMessage {
    u_char      Version;
    u_char      OpCode;
    u_int16_t   Checksum;
    u_int32_t   Flags;
    u_int32_t   Sequence;
    u_int32_t   Ack;
    u_int32_t   ASNum;
} TEIGRPMessage;
```

Listing 10-4. *EIGRP message header pseudocode definition*

The body of an EIGRP message is constructed of TLVs. All TLVs start with a common header, as illustrated in Figure 10-6. EIGRP has six standard common TLV types:

- 0x0001 (parameter TLV): Used in EIGRP Hello packets; carries neighbor parameters, such as *K* values used for metric calculation and Hello interval and Hold time values.

- 0x0002 (authentication TLV): Used to perform MD5 authentication of EIGRP packets.

- 0x0003 (sequence TLV): Used in a Hello packet to carry the list of routers that must not receive the next EIGRP packet sent with the CR bit set.

- 0x0004 (SW version TLV): Carries information about the versions of IOS and EIGRP that are running on the originating router.

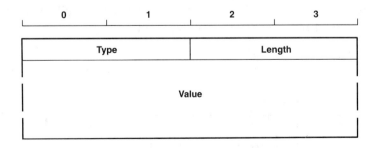

Figure 10-6. *EIGRP TLV format*

- 0x0005 (next multicast sequence TLV): Used to announce the sequence number of the next multicast packet with the CR bit set.
- 0x0006 (peer info TLV): Used to announce router capabilities in EIGRP Hello packets (see Section 10.11 for more information).

EIGRP also has two IP-specific TLVs:

- 0x0102 (IP internal routes TLV): Used by EIGRP to communicate routes internal to the EIGRP domain.
- 0x0103 (IP external routes TLV): Carries routes imported into the EIGRP domain from other sources via route redistribution.

The parameter TLV is illustrated in Figure 10-7. This TLV is included in Hello packets and contains information about the router's K values and the Hold time.

Neighbors must agree on K values for EIGRP adjacency to be established. This is necessary to avoid permanent routing loops in EIGRP domains.

The format of the IP internal routes TLV is shown in Figure 10-8.

Each TLV carries exactly one internal route and contains the following route attributes:

- *Next hop:* This field contains the IP address that must be used by the receiving router as the next-hop address instead of the sending router's interface IP address.
- *Delay:* This 32-bit field contains a cumulative path delay. Note that the EIGRP delay field is longer than the IGRP field (32 bits versus 24). A delay of 0xFFFFFFFF denotes an unreachable network.
- *Bandwidth:* The effective path bandwidth is calculated as 2.56×10^9 divided by the lowest-link bandwidth. Note that this field is also 32 bits, whereas IGRP packets have only 24 bits for the bandwidth parameter.

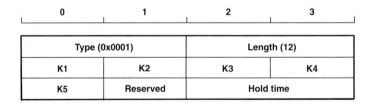

Figure 10-7. *EIGRP parameter TLV*

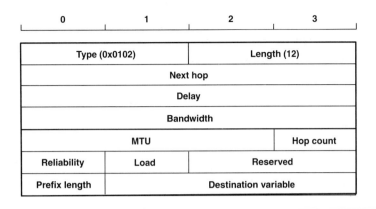

Figure 10-8. *Format of EIGRP IP internal routes TLV*

- *MTU:* This field has the same meaning as in IGRP; that is, it contains the minimal MTU values for the path. Note that as in IGRP, this field is not used in metric computation and is historical.

- *Hop count:* This 8-bit field contains the distance to the destination in hops. The initial value for locally originated routes is 0. Every router increments this value by 1. The default maximum hop count value for EIGRP is the same as for IGRP: 100. But as in IGRP, an EIGRP process may be configured with a different value. Routes with a hop count greater than the maximum allowed value are considered unreachable.

- *Reliability:* This field has the same meaning as in IGRP: the reliability of the least-reliable link in the path, represented as a fraction of 255.

- *Load:* This field has the same meaning as in IGRP: the load of the most-occupied link in the path, represented as a fraction of 255.

- *Prefix length:* This field contains the number of 1 bits in the route mask; that is, it reflects the length of the IP prefix being announced.

- *Destination:* This field contains the IP supernet, network, or subnet address; that is, it contains the value of the announced prefix.

The format of the IP external routes TLV is shown in Figure 10-9. Each TLV carries exactly one external route and contains the following route attributes:

- *Next hop:* This field contains the IP address that must be used by the receiving router as the next-hop address instead of the sending router's interface IP address.

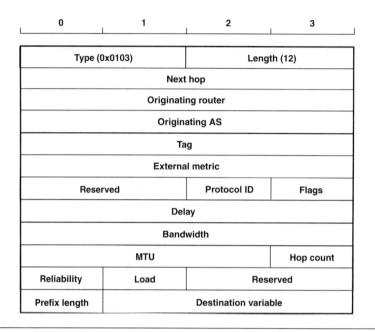

Figure 10-9. *Format of EIGRP IP external routes TLV*

- *Originating router:* This field contains the Router-ID of the router that injected the route into the EIGRP domain.

- *Originating AS:* This field contains the process ID of the routing domain that the redistributed route was taken from.

   The Originating-Router field is checked when an external-route TLV is received (see Section 10.5.2). The Originating AS field is not checked by EIGRP and is present for informational purposes.

- *Tag:* This field contains an arbitrary route tag that may be set by the originating router. This value can then be used for route filtering or other policy mechanisms.

- *External metric:* This field contains the metric of the route being redistributed as it was seen in the routing table by the redistributing router.

- *External protocol ID:* This field contains the ID of the route source the redistributed route was originated by. The following codes are defined.
   1: IGRP
   2: EIGRP

3:   Static

4:   RIP

5:   Hello

6:   OSPF

7:   IS-IS

8:   BGP

9:   IDRP

10:   Connected

- *Flags:* Currently, only one flag, with value 0x02, is used. When set, this flag indicates that the route should be marked as a candidate default on receipt.

The candidate default flag is typically used when default routing information is redistributed into EIGRP from an IGRP domain.

- *Delay, bandwidth, MTU, hop count, reliability, load:* These fields have the same meaning as in the IP internal routes TLV.
- *Prefix length, Destination:* These fields have the same meaning as in the IP internal routes TLV.

10.5   Input Processing

This section describes EIGRP packet-processing rules, including generic packet processing and actions specific to various packet types.

10.5.1   Generic Packet Processing

Before an IP EIGRP packet is passed to the EIGRP processing functions, the IP packet carrying it is received and verified by the IP stack. The IP EIGRP module processes received packets as follows.

1.   Perform a sanity check. As a part of this step, do the following checks.

   a.   Examine the EIGRP version number. If the version in the packet is not correct (2), discard the packet and log a debug message.

   b.   Verify the packet's checksum. If the checksum is not correct, discard the packet and send a debug message.

    c. Verify the AS number. If the number in the packet is not equal to the ID configured for the process, discard the packet and send an error message.

2. Check whether EIGRP is configured to work on the interface the packet was received on. (It is possible to receive packets on an EIGRP-passive interface.) If EIGRP is not enabled on the interface silently discard the packet. This may happen, for example, when EIGRP is disabled on an interface but some EIGRP messages are still in the interface queue.

3. If the interface the packet was received on is configured as passive for this EIGRP process, silently discarded the packet.

4. Verify packet authentication. If the interface is configured with packet authentication, the packet goes through the authentication procedure. If the procedure fails because, for example, the packet is not authenticated or the key is not correct, discard the packet and send a debug message.

5. If the message has gone through all the verification steps, try to the find the adjacency data structure corresponding to the neighbor that sent the message.

6. If the neighbor is found:

    a. Reset the neighbor Hold timer.

Note that this step ensures that any EIGRP packet, not only a Hello, keeps the neighbor up.

    b. The INIT flag is checked in the message. If it is set and the message is not a retransmission of the initial packet, reset the adjacency to the initial state.

    c. If the message is an EIGRP acknowledgment, pass it to the acknowledgment-specific processing routine.

7. If the neighbor is not found:

    a. If the packet has been sent by the router itself, discard it. (On some types of interfaces, self-originated packets sent to a multicast address are received by the sending router.)

    b. If the message is not an EIGRP Hello, drop it. No other packets can be processed, as there is no adjacency yet.

    c. If the IP packet carrying the message was received from a neighbor that does not belong to a primary or secondary subnet assigned to the interface the message was received on, discard the packet.

This check, along with EIGRP authentication, prevents EIGRP packet-spoofing attacks.

   d. The list of statically configured peers is verified. If the packet was sent as IP unicast and there's no manual neighbor configuration for it, ignore the packet.

   e. Create a new peer.

8. Process TLVs inside non-Hello packets further, as follows.

   a. Compute the new route metric, using the parameters in the packet and on the incoming interface.

   b. If the TLV carries an external route and the router is the originator of the announced route, ignore the TLV to avoid redistribution loops.

   c. If the TLV carries an external route and is marked as candidate default, check the default route filter to see whether it allows the route to be received. (See Section 10.12 for more information on how to control default routing information in EIGRP.)

   d. If the route in the TLV is denied by a distribute list, ignore it. (See Chapter 7 for more information on distribute lists.)

   e. Pass the packet to the DUAL algorithm for packet type–specific routines.

10.5.2 Processing EIGRP Updates

EIGRP update packets are processed by the DUAL algorithm as follows.

1. Look up the destination described in the packet in the topology table.

2. If no entry for the destination is in the topology table and the metric of the route in the update is not Infinity, create a new entry.

3. In the topology table entry, look up the path corresponding to the incoming interface and the IP address of the router the update has been received from.

4. If no path has been found and the update being processed is not a poison reverse update, create a new path, and link it to the topology table entry.

5. If the update is a poison reverse update or just refreshes information already in the table, stop processing the packet.

6. Otherwise, if the route is in the Passive state, update the topology table and perform local calculation, trying to find the successor for the affected destination. If a successor is found, leave the route in the Passive state (the FSM experiences event IE1). Otherwise, the route is put in Active mode, with query origin code set to 1, and queries are scheduled to be sent to all its neighbors (the FSM experiences event IE3).

7. If the router is in the Active state and the update came from the successor, check whether the route distance has increased after the update has been processed. If

so, set the route's query origin to 0 if it was equal to 1 and to 2 if it was equal to 3 (the FSM experiences event IE8).

10.5.3 Processing EIGRP Queries

1. If the route is in the Passive state:
    a. If the query metric is unreachable, send a reply immediately.
    b. If the query metric is not unreachable, check the feasibility condition. If it is met, send a reply.
    c. If the FC is not met, put the route in the Active state and send a reply to the neighbor if the neighbor is not the current successor. Also, if the query was received from the successor, change the query origin of the route to 3 (FSM event IE2) or to 1 otherwise (FSM event IE3).
2. If the route is in the Active state and the query was received from the successor, change the route's query origin to 2 (FSM event IE10). If the query was received from a neighbor that is not the current successor, send a reply.

10.5.4 Processing EIGRP Replies

1. Clear the reply flag for the neighbor the reply was received from, and check whether this is the last expected reply.
2. If the reply is the last expected reply, check whether the route can go Passive. If the current value of the query origin of the route is 1 or 3, change the route's state to Passive, set the FD value to infinity, and revisit the list of neighbors to elect the new successor and to calculate the new FD value (FSM event IE12). If the current value of the query origin is 0 or 2, check the FC. If the FC is met, change the route's state to Passive (FSM event IE11). If FC is not met, leave the route in the Active state, restart the diffusing computation process, and set the query origin to 1 if it was 0 and to 3 if it was 2 (FSM event IE9).

10.6 Internal Event Processing

EIGRP processes a number of internal events. These events are generated either because of expiration of an internal EIGRP timer or as a reaction to a signal sent to EIGRP from another process. Descriptions of basic events and corresponding actions follow.

Event: Expiration of the neighbor Inactivity timer

Description: EIGRP maintains a Hold timer for each neighbor. The timer is reset every time an EIGRP packet is received from the neighbor. The value of the timer is determined by the Holdtime field in the parameter TLV received in the last Hello packet. When the Hold timer expires for a particular neighbor, the corresponding element is removed from the neighbor table.

Event: Packet retransmission limit

Description: Another method EIGRP uses to detect malfunctioning neighbors is limitation of the number of attempts a packet can be retransmitted to the neighbor. If a packet has been retransmitted 16 times or more and for longer than the neighbor's hold time, the neighbor is declared inactive and is removed from the neighbor table.

Event: Topology table update

Description: Whenever the router updates its topology table and selects the new set of successors for a given set of routes, the router's main routing table is also updated. Newly reachable destinations and paths are added, and newly unreachable ones are removed.

Event: Installation or removal of a redistributed route

Description: If EIGRP is configured to redistribute routes from some other sources, it receives `callback` function calls whenever a route that needs to be redistributed is installed in or removed from the routing table. EIGRP represents these events as fake updates to the internal DUAL logic.

The preceding event and its processing represent a detail of implementation of EIGRP in Cisco IOS: Redistributed routes are installed in the topology table as if they were received from a neighbor. This is not a feature of the protocol itself, though.

10.7 Sending EIGRP Packets

After the packet has been constructed, it is sent on the interface, encapsulated in an IP packet. If the packet is sent to a particular statically configured neighbor, the destination IP address in the packet is set to the address of that neighbor; otherwise, the packet is sent multicast to IP address AllIGRPRouters (224.0.0.10). When enqueued for transmission on an interface, an EIGRP packet's priority is set according to the packet type. All unicast packets are enqueued with medium priority. Multicast packets and regular Hellos are assigned high priority. EIGRP acknowledgments (sequenced Hellos) are enqueued with medium priority. This priority setting is supposed to ensure that even with a high volume of routing information updates, Hello packets can get through to the neighbors and that adjacencies do not flap. Note, however, that this affects only older versions of

EIGRP, as newer versions reset a neighbor's Hold timer when any packet, not only a Hello, from the neighbor is received.

10.7.1 Sending EIGRP Hellos

EIGRP Hellos are sent periodically as IP multicasts on each EIGRP-enabled interface and as IP unicasts for each manually configured neighbor. By default, Hellos are sent every 5 seconds on all interfaces except for those connected to low speed (less than T1) NBMA clouds, where the Hello interval is 60 seconds. EIGRP Hello packets are built as follows.

1. If EIGRP authentication is enabled on the interface, put the authentication TLV first in the packet.
2. Introduce the parameters TLV containing K values and Hold time into the packet.
3. Add the software version TLV (the version value is always 2 for EIGRP).
4. If the router is configured to be stub, introduce the peer information TLV.

10.7.2 Sending Updates and Queries

EIGRP routers do not send periodic updates. Instead, EIGRP updates are sent only when a network is added to or removed from the topology database, when the successor for a given network changes, or when the locally used metric is updated.

> Note that even though the locally calculated distance may depend on the dynamically changing values of some interface attributes, such as load or reliability, EIGRP will not recalculate the route metric when these parameters change. This property of the protocol ensures stability of the network running EIGRP.

The rules of constructing EIGRP updates and queries are to a large extent the same. An outline of the process follows.

1. In the topology table, go through the routes that need to be announced or requested. Construct the packet by processing each route as follows.
   a. If the route should not be announced on this interface, owing to the split-horizon rule—a successor is reachable through the same interface—skip the route. Under some conditions, such a route may be announced as unreachable.
   b. Look up the corresponding route in the main routing table. If there is no such route, poison the route, advertising it as unreachable.

c. Otherwise, check whether the route is filtered by an outbound filter. If so, the route is suppressed. (If this is an update, the route is excluded from the update. If this is a query, it is announced as unreachable.)

d. If the neighbor is in the receive-only state (see Section 10.11 for more information), do not announce the route.

e. If the neighbor is a stub router, announce the route only if the neighbor has been configured to receive the type of routing information to which the route being processed belongs.

f. If the neighbor is not stub, announce the route only if the route is not suppressed by a summary route announced on the same interface. If the neighbor is stub but configured to accept summary routes, announce the route only if its network prefix is equal to one of the active summaries.

10.7.3 Sending Replies

EIGRP replies are always sent as unicast packets. Each reply contains information about one or more networks whose status has been requested by the neighbor in a query packet. Announcement of any network in the update may be suppressed, owing to configured filters or the split-horizon mechanism. Again, suppression of networks in replies is done through infinite (unreachable) metric announcement.

10.8 Shortest-Path Calculation

Whenever the topology table is updated with new information—a path to a network is added, removed, or changed—EIGRP recalculates the successor and feasible successors for the affected destination as follows.

1. If the destination is not in the Active state, do the following.

    a. If the feasible distance is not set to unreachable or if the feasible distance is set to unreachable but the distance of the new path is not unreachable, calculate the feasibility condition for the route.

    b. Otherwise, ignore the update.

2. If the destination is in the Active state, process the update as indicated in Section 10.5.2.

Calculation of the feasibility condition is performed as follows.

1. Test the feasibility condition. It is considered to be met if the distance of at least one path is lower than the current feasible distance.

2. If the feasibility condition is not met, put the route in the Active state.

3. Otherwise, change the route state as indicated in Section 10.5.2.

The route metric is calculated in EIGRP by using a formula similar to the one used in IGRP (see Chapter 8). The difference between the two is that EIGRP has wider fields for delay and bandwidth route attributes (32 bits versus 24 bits in IGRP), so the value placed in these fields is the value expected in IGRP multiplied by 256. Also, the metric in IGRP is allowed to have value 0, whereas in EIGRP, it is never lower than 1. In both protocols, unreachable networks are assigned metric 0xFFFFFFFF (32 bits set to 1).

By default, EIGRP has the value of the variance parameter set to 1, which means that the routing table maintenance functions install only the routes with the best metric. If this parameter is set to a value greater than 1, routes with the metric value worse than the best are installed in the routing table, provided that the neighbor reporting the route has a better metric than the local router and that the route metric is less than the variance times the best metric for this route.

10.9 Default Route Support

EIGRP supports two modes of announcing default routing information: an IGRP-like mode, whereby some routes can be marked as exterior by using the **ip default-network** command, and EIGRP will then announce them as candidate defaults; and an OSPF-like mode, whereby the default route is represented as a route to pseudonetwork 0.0.0.0/0.

Both modes function equally well in EIGRP. However, for the sake of simplicity in deploying and troubleshooting, the second method is recommended.

In Cisco IOS, the code processing the 0.0.0.0/0 version of the default route provides faster convergence than for IGRP-like defaults.

The simplest method for injecting a default route into an EIGRP domain is to configure a static default route to the Null0 interface on the ASBR and then to redistribute it to EIGRP. All routers in the domain will install this route in their routing tables and will automatically mark them as candidate defaults. Another approach is to redistribute default routing information to EIGRP from another dynamic routing protocol. Both of these methods inject an external default into the EIGRP domain. To inject an internal default, the administrator can configure 0.0.0.0/0 as a summary address on one of the EIGRP-enabled interfaces (see Section 10.13.5 for more information on EIGRP configuration).

10.10 Route Aggregation

Flexible route aggregation capabilities are an attractive feature of EIGRP. As a protocol based on the distance-vector concept, EIGRP allows route aggregation to be configured on a per interface basis (see Section 10.12 for configuration commands).

When a network prefix must be announced on an interface, EIGRP checks whether any summary addresses are configured on this interface. If the network being processed is covered by one of the configured summary addresses, announcement of the network itself is suppressed, EIGRP makes sure that a routing entry corresponding to the summary address is installed in the routing table referencing the Null0 interface, and this summary route, instead of the more specified network prefix, is announced on the interface.

The routing table entries referencing the Null0 interface (discard routes) are necessary to prevent routing loops, as described in Chapter 3. Note that these entries are installed in and removed from the routing table dynamically. That is, the discard route is installed once there's a more specific route that needs to be announced on the interface on which the corresponding summary is configured and is removed after the last specific route is gone.

Note that EIGRP route aggregation commands can be used to summarize both EIGRP routes and routes redistributed into EIGRP.

10.11 EIGRP Stub Router Extension

The basic EIGRP specification does not address the hub-and-spoke and multihoming scenarios, whereby a router is connected to many stub routers that are not supposed to be used for transit routing very well (see Figure 10-10 for a sample network topology). The problem here is that the stub routers receive all routing information from the hubs, although they need only the default routes. Also, when it loses its successors for a given destination and puts the corresponding entry in the topology table to the Active state, a hub router needs to generate and to send queries to all its spoke neighbors, even though they are not supposed to be used for transit routing. This puts an unnecessary load on the hub routers and increases the probability of SIA events (see Section 10.2).

You can resolve most of these problems by using route filtering and summarization, but the EIGRP stub feature, introduced in Cisco IOS version 12.0(6)T, provides a solution that is much cleaner and easier to configure. The idea is to allow the administrator to configure EIGRP routers so that they announce only a limited amount of routing information, specifically, only information about directly connected networks or static routes. Stub routers also announce this status to their neighbors, using a special Peer Info TLV in Hello packets. Neighbors receiving this status announcement will not send any queries to stub routers.

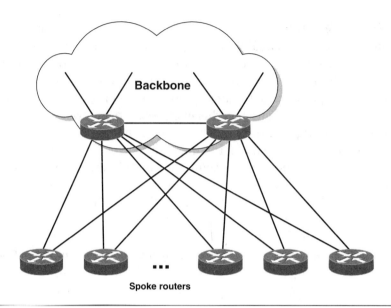

Figure 10-10. *Example of a hub-and-spoke network topology*

For stub routers, modifications to regular EIGRP behavior introduced by the stub router option include the following.

1. For the stub behavior to be enabled, the router needs to be explicitly configured, using the **eigrp stub** command. The router may also be configured with the type of routing information it will announce. In its extreme, a stub router does not announce any routing information; this mode is called receive-only. In this case, a router's neighbors need to have static routes to the networks attached to the stub router. Another option is to permit the stub router to announce redistributed Connected or static routes.

2. When sending Hello packets, a Peer Info TLV is introduced, and the stub router status is announced.

3. When constructing EIGRP messages and checking whether a particular route should be announced, the stub router flag is checked. If set, only allowed routing information is announced. For example, if the router is configured as stub announcing Connected routes and a redistributed static route is being considered for inclusion in the update, that route should be rejected.

4. When a query is received, routes not allowed to be announced by the configuration are responded to with an infinity metric to discourage other routers from using the stub router as transit.

For stub router neighbors, modifications to regular EIGRP behavior introduced by the stub router option include the following.

1. When Hello packets are processed, the neighbor capabilities set is maintained, including whether the router is stub and what type of routing information it announces.

2. No queries are sent to stub routers even for routes stub routers announce. Instead, the hub routers rely on proper announcements from the stub routers.

10.12 EIGRP Configuration

An EIGRP process is started with a **router** command as in other IP routing protocols:

router eigrp *process-id*

However, the process-ID specified as an argument influences EIGRP packet processing; that is, only packets with the same process-ID—also known as AS number in EIGRP documentation—are considered valid by EIGRP process.

The legacy form of the EIGRP **network** command is classful. Starting with IOS version 12.0(3)T, a classless version of this command is available:

network *network* [*wildcard-mask*]

> Note that even though the legacy version of the network command does accept subnet addresses, these addresses are automatically converted to major network values.

The new version of the EIGRP **network** command allows the administrator to enable EIGRP on interfaces with the subnet mask shorter than the default classful mask (supernets) and to enable or disable EIGRP on interfaces in a more (or less) granular fashion.

> The new version also allows the administrator to enable EIGRP on interfaces assigned supernet network prefixes. Also, if 0.0.0.0 0.0.0.0 pair is specified in the **network** command, EIGRP will be enabled on all interfaces.

EIGRP configuration allows the administrator to influence metric calculation by changing the weight values used in the formula. It is very rare when these values need to be changed. Sticking with the default values is strongly recommended. Nevertheless, the following command can be used to change these values:

metric weights *tos k1 k2 k3 k4 k5*

The **tos** parameter was introduced to account for possible future support of TOS-based routing. Cisco IOS currently offers no such support, so the **tos** parameter should always be set to 0. The *K* values should be in the range of 0 to 4,294,967,295. The default values are **k1**, 1; **k2**, 0; **k3**, 1; **k4**, 0; **k5**, 0. For information on how weight parameters are taken into consideration during metric calculation, see Section 10.8.

The **metric** command can also be used to control the maximum hop count considered valid:

metric maximum-hops *hop-count*

The default value for this parameter is 100. EIGRP incorporates mechanisms that prevent route looping, so it is safe to have a relatively high value of this parameter.

If multiple successors and potential paths to a destination are present, the EIGRP successor election algorithm is strict. This means that only paths with the least cost are marked as paths through successors. However, as in IGRP, it is possible to relax this condition, allowing routes with metrics worse than the best one to be installed in the routing table. The variance parameter controls this behavior. The syntax of the **variance** router configuration command for EIGRP is the same as for IGRP:

variance *multiplier*

Whenever an entry in the EIGRP topology table goes to Active state, a timer is started to make sure that the entry does not stay active forever. The default time a route can be in the Active state is 3 minutes. This parameter can be changed by using the following command:

timers active-time [*time-in-minutes* | **disable**]

If the **disable** parameter is specified, the time limitation for the Active state is removed. This command should be used only in networks with very slow links, where 3 minutes is not enough for the diffusing computation to complete.

By default, EIGRP follows the classful route summarization rules; that is, EIGRP performs automatic route summarization at major network boundaries. This makes the transition process from IGRP to EIGRP less painful. However, if EIGRP is used for routing in CIDR environments in which IP address classes do not matter—almost always the case these days—automatic summarization may cause problems, as described in Chapter 3. To solve this problem, autosummarization may be turned off by using the **no** form of the following command:

auto-summary

The **no auto-summary** command is always recommended unless EIGRP is used in a classful environment or during migration from IGRP.

Origination of default information in EIGRP is controlled as in IGRP, using the **default-information** command:

default-information [**allowed**] {**in** | **out**} [*acl-number* | *acl-name*]

The **allowed** keyword is optional and is left for compatibility with old versions of IOS. This keyword is never included in the configuration file generated by the **show running** command. The optional access list number or name allows the administrator to control which routes with the candidate default flag set are announced or installed in the routing table. Without the access list, the command enables or disables announcement and installation of candidate default routes.

The **traffic-share** command controls the way EIGRP installs routes in the routing table and assigns share counters to the path descriptors:

traffic-share { **balanced** | **min** [**across-interfaces**]}

The **balanced** keyword specifies that the traffic share parameters should be assigned to the path descriptors on the basis of the reverse metric ratio of corresponding paths. This is the default behavior for EIGRP. When the **min** keyword is specified, only the path descriptors with the best metric are assigned nonzero traffic share counts. Normally, EIGRP installs the maximum available number of parallel routes to the same destination, controlled by the **maximum-paths** router configuration command (described in Chapter 7). If the topology of the network is such that more paths are available and the number of interfaces used is fewer than the number of paths, the default behavior may not be desirable. Instead, the administrator may prefer to install routes through as many interfaces as possible. The **across-interfaces** option helps here. When this option is specified and the number of installed routes to the same destination reaches the path limit, the router checks, when the next path is being installed, whether multiple routes are referencing a single interface different from the one used in the new path. If there are, one of them is removed, and a new route is installed.

Redistribution in EIGRP is controlled by using the normal **redistribute** command:

redistribute protocol [*protocol-specific-options*] [**metric** *bandwidth delay reliability load MTU*]
        [**route-map** *map-name*]

If the **metric** parameter is specified in the **redistribute** command, a vector of parameters must be specified. These parameters are used when redistributed routes are installed in the topology database of the redistributing router.

> As in RIP and IGRP, it is not necessary to configure metric attributes if routes from the Connected, Static, IGRP, or EIGRP route sources are redistributed. For Connected and Static routes, metric information is taken from the associated interfaces. For IGRP, metrics are automatically converted. For EIGRP, metrics are taken directly from the redistributed routes. Redistribution from all other sources—dynamic routing protocols—require configuration of seed metric parameters.

Instead of specifying the metric parameters in the **redistribute** commands, the administrator has a choice of configuring a single command for the whole EIGRP process to provide default metric parameters used for route redistribution:

default-metric *bandwidth delay reliability load MTU*

The EIGRP stub router feature is configured on the stub routers. Hub routers do not need any configuration:

eigrp stub [**connected** | **receive-only** | **static** | **summary**]

The parameters in the command specify the information announced by the stub router, not the information in which the stub router is interested.

Several interface configuration commands can be used to change EIGRP interface-specific parameters. The **ip bandwidth-percent** command affects EIGRP packet-pacing parameters:

ip bandwidth-percent eigrp *process-id percentage*

By default, EIGRP packets are paced so that they do not use more than 50 percent of the interface bandwidth, configured with the **bandwidth** command. If it is necessary to pace EIGRP packets to a lower rate—if the amount of EIGRP traffic is much lower than 50 percent and it is desirable to avoid packet bursts—or to a higher rate—if the number of neighbors on the interface and the amount of EIGRP traffic is high and it is necessary to avoid packet delays—the **ip bandwidth-percent eigrp** command can be used to change the percentage of interface available for EIGRP.

The following command allows the administrator to change the rate at which EIGRP sends its Hello packets.

ip hello-interval eigrp *process-id seconds*

By default, EIGRP sends Hello packets every 5 seconds on broadcast and point-to-point interfaces. On NBMA interfaces, EIGRP sends packets every 60 seconds. The Hold time used for a particular neighbor is determined by the value announced by the neighbor in its last Hello packet. The Announced Hold time is three times the Hello interval but may be set to a specific value, using the following interface configuration command.

ip hold-time eigrp *process-id seconds*

EIGRP provides an MD5 authentication mechanism to ensure authenticity of exchanged routing information. Before configuring network interfaces with EIGRP authentication, it is necessary to have configured key chains. A key chain is a sequence of keys. Each key has an associated key string—the key sequence—and send and accept time intervals. Following is the sequence of configuration commands used to configure key chains:

key chain *chain-name*
 key *key-id*
 key-string *key-string*
 accept-lifetime *start-time* [**duration** *duration* | *stop-time* | **infinite**]
 send-lifetime *start-time* [**duration** *duration* | *stop-time* | **infinite**]

Key chains allow overlapping time frames for different keys for easier key swapping. Time in this command is specified in the "hh:mm:ss DAY MONTH YEAR" format. After a key chain has been configured, it may be used in EIGRP authentication configuration commands.

The following interface configuration commands are used to enable EIGRP MD5 authentication on an interface and to specify the key chain to be used:

```
ip authentication mode eigrp process-id md5
ip authentication key-chain eigrp process-id chain-name
```

Manual route aggregation in EIGRP is configured by using the following command:

```
ip summary-address eigrp process-id aggregate-value aggregate-mask distance
```

Because multiple EIGRP processes can run on a single interface, the same interface may be configured with multiple **ip summary-address** commands, one for each EIGRP process. The ability to specify the value of AD—the distance parameter in the command—that is used to install the aggregate discard route in the routing table was introduced in IOS version 12.0(4)T.

10.13 Configuration Examples

The sample EIGRP configurations discussed in the rest of this chapter are based on the topology shown in Figure 10-11. First, an example of a basic EIGRP configuration is con-

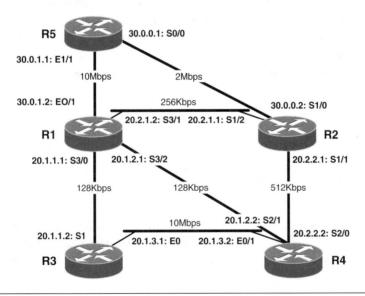

Figure 10-11. *EIGRP lab network*

sidered, and EIGRP topology tables and routing tables are shown. Then EIGRP automatic summarization is turned off to show how EIGRP works in a CIDR environment. Also, distributed EIGRP path calculation is investigated. The examples show how the variance parameter affects installation of EIGRP routes in the routing table, how the default route can be injected into an EIGRP domain, how manual route summarization is configured, and how to configure route redistribution, route filtering, and tagging, using route maps.

10.13.1 Basic EIGRP Configuration

All routers in the lab network are configured with basic EIGRP commands enabling EIGRP on all participating interfaces in the default mode. Listing 10-5 shows an example of such configuration for R1. Other routers have similar configurations.

```
R1#conf t
Enter configuration commands, one per line.  End with CNTL/Z.
R1(config)#router eigrp 1
R1(config-router)#network 20.0.0.0
R1(config-router)#network 30.0.0.0
R1(config-router)#^Z
R1#
```

Listing 10-5. *Initial EIGRP configuration*

The **show ip protocol** command shows the parameters of the corresponding EIGRP process, as shown in Listing 10-6 for R1. Note that the output contains a section showing all networks for which EIGRP has been enabled. Listing 10-7 shows R1's routing table as an illustration of the results of initial EIGRP configuration.

```
R1#sho ip proto
Routing Protocol is "eigrp 1"
  Outgoing update filter list for all interfaces is not set
  Incoming update filter list for all interfaces is not set
  Default networks flagged in outgoing updates
  Default networks accepted from incoming updates
  EIGRP metric weight K1=1, K2=0, K3=1, K4=0, K5=0
  EIGRP maximum hopcount 100
  EIGRP maximum metric variance 1
  Redistributing: eigrp 1
  Automatic network summarization is in effect
  Automatic address summarization:
    30.0.0.0/8 for Serial3/0, Serial3/1, Serial3/2
      Summarizing with metric 281600
    20.0.0.0/8 for Ethernet0/1
      Summarizing with metric 10511872
```

```
 Routing for Networks:
    20.0.0.0
    30.0.0.0
 Routing Information Sources:
    Gateway          Distance      Last Update
    (this router)           5      00:02:48
    20.1.2.2               90      00:01:50
    20.1.1.2               90      00:01:50
    20.2.1.1               90      00:01:50
    30.0.1.1               90      00:01:48
 Distance: internal 90 external 170

R1#
```

Listing 10-6. *Output of* **show ip protocol** *command for an EIGRP process*

```
R1#sho ip route
...
Gateway of last resort is not set

     20.0.0.0/8 is variably subnetted, 6 subnets, 2 masks
D       20.2.2.0/24 [90/11023872] via 20.2.1.1, 00:00:19, Serial3/1
D       20.0.0.0/8 is a summary, 00:01:35, Null0
C       20.1.1.0/24 is directly connected, Serial3/0
D       20.1.3.0/24 [90/11049472] via 20.2.1.1, 00:00:19, Serial3/1
C       20.1.2.0/24 is directly connected, Serial3/2
C       20.2.1.0/24 is directly connected, Serial3/1
     30.0.0.0/8 is variably subnetted, 3 subnets, 2 masks
D       30.0.0.0/24 [90/40537600] via 30.0.1.1, 00:00:05, Ethernet0/1
D       30.0.0.0/8 is a summary, 00:01:06, Null0
C       30.0.1.0/24 is directly connected, Ethernet0/1
R1#
```

Listing 10-7. *EIGRP routes in R1's routing table*

Listing 10-8 shows the contents of R1's topology databases. Also look at R5's database, shown in Listing 10-9.

```
R1#sho ip eigr topo
IP-EIGRP Topology Table for process 1

Codes: P - Passive, A - Active, U - Update, Q - Query, R - Reply,
       r - Reply status

P 20.2.2.0/24, 1 successors, FD is 11023872
         via 20.2.1.1 (11023872/5511936), Serial3/1
         via 20.1.2.2 (21024000/5511936), Serial3/2
         via 20.1.1.2 (21049600/5537536), Serial3/0
```

```
P 20.0.0.0/8, 1 successors, FD is 10511872
        via Summary (10511872/0), Null0
P 20.1.1.0/24, 1 successors, FD is 20512000
        via Connected, Serial3/0
P 20.1.3.0/24, 1 successors, FD is 11049472
        via 20.2.1.1 (11049472/5537536), Serial3/1
        via 20.1.2.2 (20537600/281600), Serial3/2
        via 20.1.1.2 (20537600/281600), Serial3/0
P 20.1.2.0/24, 1 successors, FD is 20512000
        via Connected, Serial3/2
P 20.2.1.0/24, 1 successors, FD is 10511872
        via Connected, Serial3/1
P 30.0.0.0/24, 1 successors, FD is 40537600
        via 30.0.1.1 (40537600/40512000), Ethernet0/1
P 30.0.0.0/8, 1 successors, FD is 281600
        via Summary (281600/0), Null0
P 30.0.1.0/24, 1 successors, FD is 281600
        via Connected, Ethernet0/1
R1#
```

Listing 10-8. *R1's EIGRP topology table*

```
R5#sho ip eigrp topo
IP-EIGRP Topology Table for process 1

Codes: P - Passive, A - Active, U - Update, Q - Query, R - Reply,
       r - Reply status

P 20.0.0.0/8, 1 successors, FD is 10537472
        via 30.0.1.2 (10537472/10511872), Ethernet1/1
        via 30.0.0.2 (41024000/5511936), Serial0/0
P 30.0.0.0/24, 1 successors, FD is 40512000
        via Connected, Serial0/0
P 30.0.1.0/24, 1 successors, FD is 281600
        via Connected, Ethernet1/1
R5#
```

Listing 10-9. *R5's EIGRP topology table*

Note that R5 has no entries for subnets of major network 20.0.0.0/8 in its routing and topology tables. Instead, R5 has two topological entries for the summary route to the whole major network announced by R1 and R2, because of the automatic classful route summarization EIGRP does by default. This mode is indicated in the output of the **show ip protocol** command, highlighted in Listing 10-10.

```
R1#sho ip proto
Routing Protocol is "eigrp 1"
...
```

```
Automatic network summarization is in effect
Automatic address summarization:
   30.0.0.0/8 for Serial3/0, Serial3/1, Serial3/2
     Summarizing with metric 281600
   20.0.0.0/8 for Ethernet0/1
     Summarizing with metric 10511872
...

R1#
```

Listing 10-10. *Output of the* **show ip protocol** *command for an EIGRP process*

The summary route entries created by R1 can also be seen in its routing and topology tables, highlighted in Listings 10-6 and 10-7. Note that these entries are installed with the reference to the Null0 interface, for reasons explained in Chapter 3.

Now all routers in the network are configured to disable automatic classful summarization, as shown in Listing 10-11 for R1.

```
R1#conf t
Enter configuration commands, one per line.  End with CNTL/Z.
R1(config)#router eigrp 1
R1(config-router)#no auto-summary
R1(config-router)#^Z
R1#
```

Listing 10-11. *Disabling classful summarization on R1*

The output of the **show ip protocol** command changes accordingly (Listing 10-12).

```
R1#sho ip proto
Routing Protocol is "eigrp 1"
  Outgoing update filter list for all interfaces is not set
...
  Redistributing: eigrp 1
  Automatic network summarization is not in effect
  Routing for Networks:
     20.0.0.0
     30.0.0.0
...
R1#
```

Listing 10-12. *Output of* **show ip protocol** *command with disabled classful route summarization*

Because it does not perform route summarization, R1 does not install summary entries in its topological and routing tables (see Listings 10-13 and 10-14).

```
R1#sho ip route
...
Gateway of last resort is not set

     20.0.0.0/24 is subnetted, 5 subnets
D       20.2.2.0 [90/11023872] via 20.2.1.1, 00:00:07, Serial3/1
C       20.1.1.0 is directly connected, Serial3/0
D       20.1.3.0 [90/11049472] via 20.2.1.1, 00:00:08, Serial3/1
C       20.1.2.0 is directly connected, Serial3/2
C       20.2.1.0 is directly connected, Serial3/1
     30.0.0.0/24 is subnetted, 2 subnets
D       30.0.0.0 [90/40537600] via 30.0.1.1, 00:00:08, Ethernet0/1
C       30.0.1.0 is directly connected, Ethernet0/1
R1#
```

Listing 10-13. *R1's routing table with disabled classful route summarization*

```
R1#sho ip eigrp topo
IP-EIGRP Topology Table for process 1

Codes: P - Passive, A - Active, U - Update, Q - Query, R - Reply,
       r - Reply status

P 20.1.1.0/24, 1 successors, FD is 20512000
        via Connected, Serial3/0
P 20.2.2.0/24, 1 successors, FD is 11023872
        via 20.2.1.1 (11023872/5511936), Serial3/1
        via 20.1.2.2 (21024000/5511936), Serial3/2
        via 20.1.1.2 (21049600/5537536), Serial3/0
P 20.1.3.0/24, 1 successors, FD is 11049472
        via 20.2.1.1 (11049472/5537536), Serial3/1
        via 20.1.2.2 (20537600/281600), Serial3/2
        via 20.1.1.2 (20537600/281600), Serial3/0
P 20.1.2.0/24, 1 successors, FD is 20512000
        via Connected, Serial3/2
P 20.2.1.0/24, 1 successors, FD is 10511872
        via Connected, Serial3/1
P 30.0.0.0/24, 1 successors, FD is 40537600
        via 30.0.1.1 (40537600/40512000), Ethernet0/1
        via 20.2.1.1 (41024000/40512000), Serial3/1
P 30.0.1.0/24, 1 successors, FD is 281600
        via Connected, Ethernet0/1
R1#
```

Listing 10-14. *R1's topology table with disabled classful route summarization*

Routing tables for R3 and R5 are shown in Listings 10-15 and 10-16.

```
R3#sho ip route
...
Gateway of last resort is not set

     20.0.0.0/24 is subnetted, 5 subnets
C       20.1.1.0 is directly connected, Serial1
D       20.2.2.0 [90/5537536] via 20.1.3.2, 02:05:51, Ethernet0
C       20.1.3.0 is directly connected, Ethernet0
D       20.1.2.0 [90/20537600] via 20.1.3.2, 02:05:54, Ethernet0
D       20.2.1.0 [90/11049472] via 20.1.3.2, 02:05:54, Ethernet0
     30.0.0.0/24 is subnetted, 2 subnets
D       30.0.0.0 [90/41049600] via 20.1.3.2, 02:05:54, Ethernet0
                 [90/41049600] via 20.1.1.1, 02:05:54, Serial1
D       30.0.1.0 [90/11075072] via 20.1.3.2, 02:05:48, Ethernet0
R3#
```

Listing 10-15. *R3's routing table with disabled classful route summarization*

```
R5#sho ip route
...
Gateway of last resort is not set

     20.0.0.0/24 is subnetted, 5 subnets
D       20.1.1.0 [90/20537600] via 30.0.1.2, 02:09:41, Ethernet1/1
D       20.2.2.0 [90/11049472] via 30.0.1.2, 02:09:44, Ethernet1/1
D       20.1.3.0 [90/11075072] via 30.0.1.2, 02:09:44, Ethernet1/1
D       20.1.2.0 [90/20537600] via 30.0.1.2, 02:09:42, Ethernet1/1
D       20.2.1.0 [90/10537472] via 30.0.1.2, 02:09:49, Ethernet1/1
     30.0.0.0/24 is subnetted, 2 subnets
C       30.0.0.0 is directly connected, Serial0/0
C       30.0.1.0 is directly connected, Ethernet1/1
R5#
```

Listing 10-16. *R5's routing table with disabled classful route summarization*

Note that now, R3 and R5 have information about all subnets in the network. This is an example showing that EIGRP works well in CIDR environments.

10.13.2 Local and Distributed Route Calculation

Let's take a closer look at the topology table entries of R1 for subnet 20.2.2.0/24 (Listing 10-17).

```
R1#sho ip eigrp topo
...
P 20.2.2.0/24, 1 successors, FD is 11023872
        via 20.2.1.1 (11023872/5511936), Serial3/1
        via 20.1.2.2 (21024000/5511936), Serial3/2
        via 20.1.1.2 (21049600/5537536), Serial3/0
...
R1#
```

Listing 10-17. *R1's topology table entry for 20.2.2.0/24*

Note that the entry contains three path descriptors through serial interfaces, but there's no path descriptor for R5 reachable through interface Ethernet 0/1. The reason is that according to the value of the FD calculated by R1 for the subnet, R5 is not a feasible successor for this route; indeed, R5 itself routes to this subnet via R1. From the information in the topology table, one could say that as soon as at least one path is left through the feasible successors, R1 should perform all calculations locally, without sending queries to its neighbors, and the entry should stay Passive. Let's verify whether this logic is correct, using the **debug eigrp fsm** command, which shows information about DUAL route FSM state transitions.

First, interface Serial 3/1 is taken down to remove one path to 20.2.2.0/24 from the topology table. The results are shown in Listing 10-18.

```
R1#conf t
Enter configuration commands, one per line.   End with CNTL/Z.
R1(config)#int ser 3/1
R1(config-if)#shut
R1(config-if)#^Z
R1#
...
*Mar  4 09:33:57.422 PST: DUAL: linkdown(): start - 20.2.1.1 via Serial3/1
*Mar  4 09:33:57.422 PST: DUAL: Destination 20.1.1.0/24
*Mar  4 09:33:57.422 PST: DUAL: Destination 20.2.2.0/24
*Mar  4 09:33:57.422 PST: DUAL: Find FS for dest 20.2.2.0/24. FD is 11023872, RD is
11023872
*Mar  4 09:33:57.422 PST: DUAL:          20.2.1.1 metric 4294967295/4294967295
*Mar  4 09:33:57.426 PST: DUAL:          20.1.2.2 metric 21024000/5511936
*Mar  4 09:33:57.426 PST: DUAL:          20.1.1.2 metric 21049600/5537536 found Dmin
is 21024000
*Mar  4 09:33:57.426 PST: DUAL: Removing dest 20.2.2.0/24, nexthop 20.2.1.1
*Mar  4 09:33:57.426 PST: DUAL: RT installed 20.2.2.0/24 via 20.1.2.2
*Mar  4 09:33:57.426 PST: DUAL: Send update about 20.2.2.0/24.  Reason: metric chg
*Mar  4 09:33:57.426 PST: DUAL: Send update about 20.2.2.0/24.  Reason: new if
...
*Mar  4 09:33:57.430 PST: DUAL: linkdown(): finish
...
```

```
*Mar  4 09:33:58.326 PST: %LINEPROTO-5-UPDOWN: Line protocol on Interface Serial3/1,
changed state to down
*Mar  4 09:33:59.418 PST: %LINK-5-CHANGED: Interface Serial3/1, changed state to
administratively down
...
R1#
```

Listing 10-18. *Debug output when a path to 20.2.2.0/24 is removed from EIGRP*
topology table on R1

Note that there was no indication that the route went Passive. The state of the topology
table after this event is shown in Listing 10-19.

```
R1#sho ip eigrp topo
...
P 20.2.2.0/24, 1 successors, FD is 11023872
        via 20.1.2.2 (21024000/5511936), Serial3/2
        via 20.1.1.2 (21049600/5537536), Serial3/0
...
R1#
```

Listing 10-19. *Modified topology entry for 20.2.2.0/24 on R1*

Because the entry did not go Active, the value of the FD remained the same. Taking down
interface Serial 3/2 gives similar results (Listing 10-20).

```
R1#sho ip eigrp topo
...
P 20.2.2.0/24, 1 successors, FD is 11023872
        via 20.1.1.2 (21049600/5537536), Serial3/0
...
R1#
```

Listing 10-20. *Topology entry for 20.2.2.0/24 on R1 after Serial3/2 is taken down*

Now let's see what happens if we remove the path through the last feasible successor
for this subnet. Listing 10-21 shows the debug output.

```
R1#
...
*Mar  4 09:39:08.170 PST: DUAL: linkdown(): start - 20.1.1.2 via Serial3/0
...
*Mar  4 09:39:08.170 PST: DUAL: Destination 20.2.2.0/24
```

```
*Mar  4 09:39:08.170 PST: DUAL: Find FS for dest 20.2.2.0/24. FD is 11023872, RD is
21049600
*Mar  4 09:39:08.170 PST: DUAL:       20.1.1.2 metric 4294967295/4294967295not
found Dmin is 4294967295
*Mar  4 09:39:08.170 PST: DUAL: Dest 20.2.2.0/24 entering active state.
*Mar  4 09:39:08.170 PST: DUAL: Set reply-status table. Count is 1.
*Mar  4 09:39:08.170 PST: DUAL: Not doing split horizon
...
*Mar  4 09:39:08.174 PST: DUAL: linkdown(): finish
*Mar  4 09:39:08.222 PST: %SYS-5-CONFIG_I: Configured from console by console
*Mar  4 09:39:08.386 PST: %LINEPROTO-5-UPDOWN: Line protocol on Interface Serial3/0,
changed state to down
*Mar  4 09:39:08.402 PST: DUAL: dest(20.2.2.0/24) active
*Mar  4 09:39:08.406 PST: DUAL: dual_rcvreply(): 20.2.2.0/24 via 30.0.1.1 metric
41049600/41024000
*Mar  4 09:39:08.406 PST: DUAL: Count is 1
*Mar  4 09:39:08.406 PST: DUAL: Clearing handle 0, count is now 0
*Mar  4 09:39:08.406 PST: DUAL: Freeing reply status table
*Mar  4 09:39:08.406 PST: DUAL: Find FS for dest 20.2.2.0/24. FD is 4294967295, RD is
4294967295 found
*Mar  4 09:39:08.406 PST: DUAL: Removing dest 20.2.2.0/24, nexthop 20.1.1.2
*Mar  4 09:39:08.406 PST: DUAL: RT installed 20.2.2.0/24 via 30.0.1.1
*Mar  4 09:39:08.406 PST: DUAL: Send update about 20.2.2.0/24.  Reason: metric chg
*Mar  4 09:39:08.406 PST: DUAL: Send update about 20.2.2.0/24.  Reason: new if
...
*Mar  4 09:39:10.166 PST: %LINK-5-CHANGED: Interface Serial3/0, changed state to
administratively down
...
R1#
```

Listing 10-21. *Debug output for the distributed path computation for 20.2.2.0/24*

When the path through the last feasible successor is removed from the topology table, the entry for subnet 20.2.2.0/24 transitions to the Active state, and R1 sends requests to all neighbors: only R5 in this particular case, as we took all interfaces except Ethernet 0/1 down. The entry stays in the Active state until R1 receives replies to all its queries for this entry. In our situation, R1 was waiting for a reply only from R5. When the reply is received—the line starting with DUAL: dual_rcvreply(): in the debug output—the entry goes back to the Passive state, the FD value is recalculated—it will be used until the next time the route goes to the Active state—and the new route through R5 is installed in the routing table. Resulting topology and routing tables are shown in Listings 10-22 and 10-23.

```
R1#sho ip eigrp topo
IP-EIGRP Topology Table for process 1

Codes: P - Passive, A - Active, U - Update, Q - Query, R - Reply,
       r - Reply status
```

```
P 20.2.2.0/24, 1 successors, FD is 41049600
          via 30.0.1.1 (41049600/41024000), Ethernet0/1
P 20.1.3.0/24, 1 successors, FD is 41075200
          via 30.0.1.1 (41075200/41049600), Ethernet0/1
P 30.0.0.0/24, 1 successors, FD is 40537600
          via 30.0.1.1 (40537600/40512000), Ethernet0/1
P 30.0.1.0/24, 1 successors, FD is 281600
          via Connected, Ethernet0/1
R1#
```

Listing 10-22. *R1's topology table after distributed computation is complete*

```
R1#sho ip route
...
Gateway of last resort is not set

     20.0.0.0/24 is subnetted, 2 subnets
D       20.2.2.0 [90/41049600] via 30.0.1.1, 00:01:59, Ethernet0/1
D       20.1.3.0 [90/41075200] via 30.0.1.1, 00:02:00, Ethernet0/1
     30.0.0.0/24 is subnetted, 2 subnets
D       30.0.0.0 [90/40537600] via 30.0.1.1, 00:15:57, Ethernet0/1
C       30.0.1.0 is directly connected, Ethernet0/1
R1#
```

Listing 10-23. *R1's routing table containing new route to 20.2.2.0/24*

10.13.3 Configuring Variance Parameter

Now we take R1's interfaces back up and configure a higher value for the variance parameter (Listing 10-24). (For a discussion of the variance parameter, see Section 10.8.)

```
R1#conf t
Enter configuration commands, one per line.  End with CNTL/Z.
R1(config)#router eigrp 1
R1(config-router)#variance 2
R1(config-router)#^Z
R1#
```

Listing 10-24. *Configuring higher variance value in EIGRP*

The value of the variance parameter does not affect the feasibility condition, so the entries in R1's topology table will still have one successor. However, when a **clear ip route** command is issued for one of the subnets to make the EIGRP process recalculate its routes to the destination, multiple routes with unequal metrics are installed (Listing 10-25).

```
R1#clear ip route 20.2.2.0 255.255.255.0
R1#
*Mar  4 09:47:01.601 PST: RT: del 20.2.2.0/24 via 20.2.1.1, eigrp metric
[90/11023872]
*Mar  4 09:47:01.601 PST: RT: delete subnet route to 20.2.2.0/24
*Mar  4 09:47:01.601 PST: DUAL: Find FS for dest 20.2.2.0/24. FD is 11023872, RD is
11023872
*Mar  4 09:47:01.601 PST: DUAL:          20.2.1.1 metric 11023872/5511936
*Mar  4 09:47:01.601 PST: DUAL:          20.1.2.2 metric 21024000/5511936
*Mar  4 09:47:01.601 PST: DUAL:          20.1.1.2 metric 21049600/5537536 found Dmin is
11023872
*Mar  4 09:47:01.601 PST: RT: add 20.2.2.0/24 via 20.2.1.1, eigrp metric [90/11023872]
*Mar  4 09:47:01.601 PST: DUAL: RT installed 20.2.2.0/24 via 20.2.1.1
*Mar  4 09:47:01.601 PST: RT: add 20.2.2.0/24 via 20.1.2.2, eigrp metric [90/21024000]
*Mar  4 09:47:01.605 PST: RT: add 20.2.2.0/24 via 20.1.1.2, eigrp metric [90/21049600]
R1#
```

Listing 10-25. *EIGRP FSM debug output when the variance value is greater than 1*

The resulting routing table is shown in Listing 10-26.

```
R1#sho ip route
...
Gateway of last resort is not set

     20.0.0.0/24 is subnetted, 5 subnets
D       20.2.2.0 [90/11023872] via 20.2.1.1, 00:00:52, Serial3/1
                 [90/21024000] via 20.1.2.2, 00:00:53, Serial3/2
                 [90/21049600] via 20.1.1.2, 00:00:53, Serial3/0
C       20.1.1.0 is directly connected, Serial3/0
D       20.1.3.0 [90/11049472] via 20.2.1.1, 00:04:25, Serial3/1
C       20.1.2.0 is directly connected, Serial3/2
C       20.2.1.0 is directly connected, Serial3/1
     30.0.0.0/24 is subnetted, 2 subnets
D       30.0.0.0 [90/40537600] via 30.0.1.1, 00:04:25, Ethernet0/1
C       30.0.1.0 is directly connected, Ethernet0/1
R1#
```

Listing 10-26. *Multiple path descriptors to 20.2.2.0/24 with unequal costs*

10.13.4 Injecting the Default Route

As discussed in Section 10.9, EIGRP supports both methods for default route injection: an IGRP-like method through configuration of an **ip default-network** command and an OSPF-like method through redistribution of a route to pseudonetwork 0.0.0.0/0. This section provides examples of EIGRP configurations for both methods.

Listing 10-27 shows how R5 is configured with a static default route to network 50.0.0.0 through interface Null0. In reality, R5 would have received this route from one of its neighbors through a dynamic routing protocol and the route would reference a real interface with a real next-hop address. R5 is also configured with an **ip default-network** command, which tells the router to mark the route to network 50.0.0.0 as exterior.

```
R5#conf t
Enter configuration commands, one per line.  End with CNTL/Z.
R5(config)#ip route 50.0.0.0 255.0.0.0 Null0
R5(config)#ip default-network 50.0.0.0
R5(config)#^Z
R5#sho ip route
...
Gateway of last resort is not set

S*    50.0.0.0/8 is directly connected, Null0
      20.0.0.0/24 is subnetted, 5 subnets
D        20.1.1.0 [90/20537600] via 30.0.1.2, 00:13:31, Ethernet1/1
D        20.2.2.0 [90/11049472] via 30.0.1.2, 00:13:28, Ethernet1/1
D        20.1.3.0 [90/11075072] via 30.0.1.2, 00:13:28, Ethernet1/1
D        20.1.2.0 [90/20537600] via 30.0.1.2, 00:13:31, Ethernet1/1
D        20.2.1.0 [90/10537472] via 30.0.1.2, 00:13:34, Ethernet1/1
      30.0.0.0/24 is subnetted, 2 subnets
C        30.0.0.0 is directly connected, Serial0/0
C        30.0.1.0 is directly connected, Ethernet1/1
R5#
```

Listing 10-27. *Route to network 50.0.0.0 marked as exterior*

The EIGRP process on R5 is also configured with a network statement covering network 50.0.0.0, making it automatically announce this route in its updates. Because the route is marked as exterior in the routing table, EIGRP announces it as a candidate default (Listing 10-28).

```
R5#conf t
Enter configuration commands, one per line.  End with CNTL/Z.
R5(config)#router eigrp 1
R5(config-router)#network 50.0.0.0
R5(config-router)#^Z
R5#sho ip route 50.0.0.0
Routing entry for 50.0.0.0/8
  Known via "static", distance 1, metric 0 (connected), candidate default path
  Redistributing via eigrp 1
  Advertised by eigrp 1
  Routing Descriptor Blocks:
```

```
 * directly connected, via Null0
     Route metric is 0, traffic share count is 1
```

R5#

Listing 10-28. *Output of the* **show ip route** *for network 50.0.0.0 announced as candidate default*

Such an announcement makes other EIGRP routers automatically consider this route a candidate default. Listing 10-29 shows the output of the **debug eigrp fsm** command on R1 when it receives the exterior routes to 50.0.0.0 originated by R5.

```
R1#
*Mar  4 09:57:41.221 PST: DUAL: dest(50.0.0.0/8) not active
*Mar  4 09:57:41.221 PST: DUAL: dual_rcvupdate(): 50.0.0.0/8 via 30.0.1.1 metric
281600/256
*Mar  4 09:57:41.221 PST: DUAL: Find FS for dest 50.0.0.0/8. FD is 4294967295, RD is
4294967295 found
*Mar  4 09:57:41.221 PST: RT: add 50.0.0.0/8 via 30.0.1.1, eigrp metric [90/281600]
*Mar  4 09:57:41.221 PST: DUAL: RT installed 50.0.0.0/8 via 30.0.1.1
*Mar  4 09:57:41.225 PST: DUAL: Send update about 50.0.0.0/8.  Reason: metric chg
*Mar  4 09:57:41.225 PST: DUAL: Send update about 50.0.0.0/8.  Reason: new if
*Mar  4 09:57:41.257 PST: DUAL: dest(50.0.0.0/8) not active
*Mar  4 09:57:41.257 PST: DUAL: dual_rcvupdate(): 50.0.0.0/8 via 20.2.1.1 metric
41024000/40512000
*Mar  4 09:57:41.257 PST: DUAL: Find FS for dest 50.0.0.0/8. FD is 281600, RD is
281600
*Mar  4 09:57:41.257 PST: DUAL:          30.0.1.1 metric 281600/256
*Mar  4 09:57:41.261 PST: DUAL:          20.2.1.1 metric 41024000/40512000 found Dmin
is 281600
*Mar  4 09:57:41.261 PST: DUAL: RT installed 50.0.0.0/8 via 30.0.1.1
*Mar  4 09:57:41.281 PST: DUAL: dual_rcvupdate(): 50.0.0.0/8 via 20.2.1.1 metric
4294967295/4294967295
*Mar  4 09:57:41.281 PST: DUAL: Find FS for dest 50.0.0.0/8. FD is 281600, RD is
281600
*Mar  4 09:57:41.281 PST: DUAL:          30.0.1.1 metric 281600/256
*Mar  4 09:57:41.281 PST: DUAL:          20.2.1.1 metric 4294967295/4294967295 found
Dmin is 281600
*Mar  4 09:57:41.281 PST: DUAL: Removing dest 50.0.0.0/8, nexthop 20.2.1.1
*Mar  4 09:57:41.281 PST: DUAL: RT installed 50.0.0.0/8 via 30.0.1.1
*Mar  4 09:57:41.301 PST: DUAL: dest(50.0.0.0/8) not active
*Mar  4 09:57:41.301 PST: DUAL: dual_rcvupdate(): 50.0.0.0/8 via 20.1.2.2 metric
21561600/11049472
*Mar  4 09:57:41.301 PST: DUAL: Find FS for dest 50.0.0.0/8. FD is 281600, RD is
281600
*Mar  4 09:57:41.301 PST: DUAL:          30.0.1.1 metric 281600/256
*Mar  4 09:57:41.301 PST: DUAL:          20.1.2.2 metric 21561600/11049472 found Dmin
is 281600
```

```
*Mar  4 09:57:41.301 PST: DUAL: RT installed 50.0.0.0/8 via 30.0.1.1
*Mar  4 09:57:41.325 PST: DUAL: dest(50.0.0.0/8) not active
*Mar  4 09:57:41.325 PST: DUAL: dual_rcvupdate(): 50.0.0.0/8 via 20.1.1.2 metric
21587200/11075072
*Mar  4 09:57:41.325 PST: DUAL: Find FS for dest 50.0.0.0/8. FD is 281600, RD is
281600
*Mar  4 09:57:41.325 PST: DUAL:        30.0.1.1 metric 281600/256
*Mar  4 09:57:41.325 PST: DUAL:        20.1.1.2 metric 21587200/11075072
*Mar  4 09:57:41.325 PST: DUAL:        20.1.2.2 metric 21561600/11049472 found Dmin
is 281600
*Mar  4 09:57:41.325 PST: DUAL: RT installed 50.0.0.0/8 via 30.0.1.1
*Mar  4 09:57:46.221 PST: RT: default path is now 50.0.0.0 via 30.0.1.1
*Mar  4 09:57:46.221 PST: RT: new default network 50.0.0.0
R1#
```

Listing 10-29. *EIGRP debug output from R1 receiving exterior routes*

The state of the topology table entry that R1 has after receiving this route is shown in Listing 10-30.

```
R1#sho ip eigrp topo 50.0.0.0
IP-EIGRP topology entry for 50.0.0.0/8
  State is Passive, Query origin flag is 1, 1 Successor(s), FD is 281600
  Routing Descriptor Blocks:
  30.0.1.1 (Ethernet0/1), from 30.0.1.1, Send flag is 0x0
      Composite metric is (281600/256), Route is Internal
      Vector metric:
        Minimum bandwidth is 10000 Kbit
        Total delay is 1000 microseconds
        Reliability is 0/255
        Load is 1/255
        Minimum MTU is 1500
        Hop count is 1
        Exterior flag is set
  20.1.1.2 (Serial3/0), from 20.1.1.2, Send flag is 0x0
      Composite metric is (21587200/11075072), Route is Internal
      Vector metric:
        Minimum bandwidth is 128 Kbit
        Total delay is 62000 microseconds
        Reliability is 0/255
        Load is 1/255
        Minimum MTU is 1500
        Hop count is 5
        Exterior flag is set
  20.1.2.2 (Serial3/2), from 20.1.2.2, Send flag is 0x0
      Composite metric is (21561600/11049472), Route is Internal
      Vector metric:
        Minimum bandwidth is 128 Kbit
        Total delay is 61000 microseconds
        Reliability is 0/255
```

```
          Load is 1/255
          Minimum MTU is 1500
          Hop count is 4
       Exterior flag is set
R1#
```

Listing 10-30. *R1's topology table entry for candidate default route*

Listing 10-31 shows R1's routing table after processing R5's candidate default.

```
R1#sho ip route
...
Gateway of last resort is 30.0.1.1 to network 50.0.0.0

     20.0.0.0/24 is subnetted, 5 subnets
D       20.2.2.0 [90/11023872] via 20.2.1.1, 00:11:11, Serial3/1
                 [90/21024000] via 20.1.2.2, 00:11:11, Serial3/2
                 [90/21049600] via 20.1.1.2, 00:11:11, Serial3/0
C       20.1.1.0 is directly connected, Serial3/0
D       20.1.3.0 [90/11049472] via 20.2.1.1, 00:14:43, Serial3/1
C       20.1.2.0 is directly connected, Serial3/2
C       20.2.1.0 is directly connected, Serial3/1
     30.0.0.0/24 is subnetted, 2 subnets
D       30.0.0.0 [90/40537600] via 30.0.1.1, 00:14:43, Ethernet0/1
C       30.0.1.0 is directly connected, Ethernet0/1
D*   50.0.0.0/8 [90/281600] via 30.0.1.1, 00:00:32, Ethernet0/1
R1#
```

Listing 10-31. *R1's routing table with candidate default originated by R5*

Before we proceed to the second method of injecting default routing information in EIGRP, let's remove the **ip default-network** command from R5 and see how the network reacts. Listing 10-32 illustrates how the route to network 50.0.0.0 stops being marked as candidate default in the originating router's (R5's) routing table.

```
R5#conf t
Enter configuration commands, one per line.   End with CNTL/Z.
R5(config)#no ip default-network 50.0.0.0
R5(config)#^Z
23:19:57: %SYS-5-CONFIG_I: Configured from console by console
R5#sho ip route
...
Gateway of last resort is not set

S    50.0.0.0/8 is directly connected, Null0
     20.0.0.0/24 is subnetted, 5 subnets
D       20.1.1.0 [90/20537600] via 30.0.1.2, 00:18:33, Ethernet1/1
```

```
D        20.2.2.0 [90/11049472] via 30.0.1.2, 00:18:31, Ethernet1/1
D        20.1.3.0 [90/11075072] via 30.0.1.2, 00:18:31, Ethernet1/1
D        20.1.2.0 [90/20537600] via 30.0.1.2, 00:18:33, Ethernet1/1
D        20.2.1.0 [90/10537472] via 30.0.1.2, 00:18:36, Ethernet1/1
      30.0.0.0/24 is subnetted, 2 subnets
C        30.0.0.0 is directly connected, Serial0/0
C        30.0.1.0 is directly connected, Ethernet1/1
R5#
```

Listing 10-32. *R5's routing table after removing the* **ip default-network** *command*

Output of the **debug eigrp fsm** and **debug ip routing** commands (Listing 10-33) shows how R1 stops considering the route as candidate default.

```
R1#
*Mar  4 10:01:53.761 PST: DUAL: dual_rcvupdate(): 50.0.0.0/8 via 30.0.1.1 metric
281600/256
*Mar  4 10:01:53.761 PST: DUAL: Find FS for dest 50.0.0.0/8. FD is 281600, RD is
281600
*Mar  4 10:01:53.761 PST: DUAL:        30.0.1.1 metric 281600/256
*Mar  4 10:01:53.761 PST: DUAL:        20.1.1.2 metric 21587200/11075072
*Mar  4 10:01:53.761 PST: DUAL:        20.1.2.2 metric 21561600/11049472 found Dmin
is 281600
*Mar  4 10:01:53.761 PST: RT: 50.0.0.0 is now interior
*Mar  4 10:01:53.761 PST: DUAL: RT installed 50.0.0.0/8 via 30.0.1.1
*Mar  4 10:01:53.761 PST: DUAL: Send update about 50.0.0.0/8.  Reason: rt now int2
*Mar  4 10:01:53.833 PST: DUAL: dual_rcvupdate(): 50.0.0.0/8 via 20.1.2.2 metric
21561600/11049472
*Mar  4 10:01:53.833 PST: DUAL: Find FS for dest 50.0.0.0/8. FD is 281600, RD is
281600
*Mar  4 10:01:53.833 PST: DUAL:        30.0.1.1 metric 281600/256
*Mar  4 10:01:53.833 PST: DUAL:        20.1.1.2 metric 21587200/11075072
*Mar  4 10:01:53.833 PST: DUAL:        20.1.2.2 metric 21561600/11049472 found Dmin
is 281600
*Mar  4 10:01:53.833 PST: DUAL: RT installed 50.0.0.0/8 via 30.0.1.1
*Mar  4 10:01:53.853 PST: DUAL: dual_rcvupdate(): 50.0.0.0/8 via 20.1.1.2 metric
21587200/11075072
*Mar  4 10:01:53.853 PST: DUAL: Find FS for dest 50.0.0.0/8. FD is 281600, RD is
281600
*Mar  4 10:01:53.853 PST: DUAL:        30.0.1.1 metric 281600/256
*Mar  4 10:01:53.853 PST: DUAL:        20.1.1.2 metric 21587200/11075072
*Mar  4 10:01:53.853 PST: DUAL:        20.1.2.2 metric 21561600/11049472 found Dmin
is 281600
*Mar  4 10:01:53.853 PST: DUAL: RT installed 50.0.0.0/8 via 30.0.1.1
R1#
```

Listing 10-33. *Debug output from R1*

Now R5 is configured with an OSPF or RIP-style static default route: a route to pseudonetwork 0.0.0.0/0 (Listing 10-34). R5 is also configured to redistribute static routes with a distribute list, allowing only the default route to be sent; see Section 10.12 for information on how to configure EIGRP redistribution.

```
R5#conf t
Enter configuration commands, one per line.  End with CNTL/Z.
R5(config)#ip route 0.0.0.0 0.0.0.0 Null0
R5(config)#access-list 10 permit host 0.0.0.0
R5(config)#
R5(config)#router eigrp 1
R5(config-router)#distribute-list 10 out static
R5(config-router)#redistribute static
R5(config-router)#^Z
R5#
```

Listing 10-34. *R5 configured to redistribute static default route into EIGRP*

The routing table entry created based on the **ip route** command is shown in Listing 10-35. Note the candidate default and the advertised by fields.

```
R5#sho ip route 0.0.0.0
Routing entry for 0.0.0.0/0, supernet
  Known via "static", distance 1, metric 0 (connected), candidate default path
  Redistributing via eigrp 1
  Advertised by eigrp 1
  Routing Descriptor Blocks:
  * directly connected, via Null0
      Route metric is 0, traffic share count is 1

R5#
```

Listing 10-35. *Routing table entry for the static default route*

The log of events happening on R1 when it receives the default route from R5 is given in Listing 10-36.

```
R1#
*Mar  4 10:04:05.331 PST: DUAL: dest(0.0.0.0/0) not active
*Mar  4 10:04:05.331 PST: DUAL: dual_rcvupdate(): 0.0.0.0/0 via 30.0.1.1 metric
25628160/25602560
*Mar  4 10:04:05.331 PST: DUAL: Find FS for dest 0.0.0.0/0. FD is 4294967295, RD is
4294967295 found
```

```
*Mar  4 10:04:05.331 PST: RT: add 0.0.0.0/0 via 30.0.1.1, eigrp metric [170/25628160]
*Mar  4 10:04:05.331 PST: RT: default path is now 0.0.0.0 via 30.0.1.1
*Mar  4 10:04:05.331 PST: RT: new default network 0.0.0.0
*Mar  4 10:04:05.331 PST: DUAL: RT installed 0.0.0.0/0 via 30.0.1.1
*Mar  4 10:04:05.331 PST: DUAL: Send update about 0.0.0.0/0.  Reason: metric chg
*Mar  4 10:04:05.331 PST: DUAL: Send update about 0.0.0.0/0.  Reason: new if
*Mar  4 10:04:05.371 PST: DUAL: dest(0.0.0.0/0) not active
*Mar  4 10:04:05.371 PST: DUAL: dual_rcvupdate(): 0.0.0.0/0 via 20.2.1.1 metric
41026560/40514560
*Mar  4 10:04:05.371 PST: DUAL: Find FS for dest 0.0.0.0/0. FD is 25628160, RD is
25628160
*Mar  4 10:04:05.371 PST: DUAL:        30.0.1.1 metric 25628160/25602560
*Mar  4 10:04:05.371 PST: DUAL:        20.2.1.1 metric 41026560/40514560 found Dmin
is 25628160
*Mar  4 10:04:05.371 PST: DUAL: RT installed 0.0.0.0/0 via 30.0.1.1
*Mar  4 10:04:05.395 PST: DUAL: dual_rcvupdate(): 0.0.0.0/0 via 20.2.1.1 metric
4294967295/4294967295
*Mar  4 10:04:05.395 PST: DUAL: Find FS for dest 0.0.0.0/0. FD is 25628160, RD is
25628160
*Mar  4 10:04:05.395 PST: DUAL:        30.0.1.1 metric 25628160/25602560
*Mar  4 10:04:05.395 PST: DUAL:        20.2.1.1 metric 4294967295/4294967295 found
Dmin is 25628160
*Mar  4 10:04:05.395 PST: DUAL: Removing dest 0.0.0.0/0, nexthop 20.2.1.1
*Mar  4 10:04:05.395 PST: DUAL: RT installed 0.0.0.0/0 via 30.0.1.1
```

Listing 10-36. *Debug output from R1 receiving the default route from R5*

The routing table entry installed by the EIGRP process is shown in Listing 10-37.

```
R1#sho ip route
...
Gateway of last resort is 30.0.1.1 to network 0.0.0.0

     20.0.0.0/24 is subnetted, 5 subnets
D       20.2.2.0 [90/11023872] via 20.2.1.1, 00:18:39, Serial3/1
                 [90/21024000] via 20.1.2.2, 00:18:39, Serial3/2
                 [90/21049600] via 20.1.1.2, 00:18:39, Serial3/0
C       20.1.1.0 is directly connected, Serial3/0
D       20.1.3.0 [90/11049472] via 20.2.1.1, 00:22:11, Serial3/1
C       20.1.2.0 is directly connected, Serial3/2
C       20.2.1.0 is directly connected, Serial3/1
     30.0.0.0/24 is subnetted, 2 subnets
D       30.0.0.0 [90/41024000] via 20.2.1.1, 00:02:00, Serial3/1
                 [90/40537600] via 30.0.1.1, 00:02:01, Ethernet0/1
C       30.0.1.0 is directly connected, Ethernet0/1
D    50.0.0.0/8 [90/281600] via 30.0.1.1, 00:02:01, Ethernet0/1
D*EX 0.0.0.0/0 [170/25628160] via 30.0.1.1, 00:01:35, Ethernet0/1
R1#
```

Listing 10-37. *Default route installed by EIGRP*

10.13.5 Manual Route Summarization

One of the big advantages of EIGRP is its flexible route aggregation capabilities. As a distance-vector protocol, EIGRP supports route aggregation on a per interface basis. In combination with per interface route filtering available in distance-vector protocols, the same EIGRP router may announce completely different sets of routes on each of its interfaces.

As an example, R1 and R2 are configured to summarize subnets in the network 20.0.0.0 to two less specific prefixes—20.1.0.0/16 and 20.2.0.0/16—when announcing routes to R5 (Listings 10-38 and 10-39).

```
R1#conf t
Enter configuration commands, one per line.  End with CNTL/Z.
R1(config)#int e0/1
R1(config-if)#ip summary-address eigrp 1 20.1.0.0 255.255.0.0
R1(config-if)#ip summary-address eigrp 1 20.2.0.0 255.255.0.0
R1(config-if)#^Z
```

Listing 10-38. *Configuring R1 for arbitrary route summarization*

```
R2#conf t
Enter configuration commands, one per line.  End with CNTL/Z.
R2(config)#int s1/0
R2(config-if)#ip summary-address eigrp 1 20.1.0.0 255.255.0.0
R2(config-if)#ip summary-address eigrp 1 20.2.0.0 255.255.0.0
R2(config-if)#^Z
R2#
```

Listing 10-39. *Configuring R2 for arbitrary route summarization*

Pay attention to the summary routing table entries automatically created by the router (Listing 10-40).

```
R1#sho ip route
...
Gateway of last resort is 30.0.1.1 to network 0.0.0.0

     20.0.0.0/8 is variably subnetted, 7 subnets, 2 masks
D       20.2.2.0/24 [90/11023872] via 20.2.1.1, 00:00:08, Serial3/1
                    [90/21024000] via 20.1.2.2, 00:00:08, Serial3/2
                    [90/21049600] via 20.1.1.2, 00:00:08, Serial3/0
C       20.1.1.0/24 is directly connected, Serial3/0
D       20.1.0.0/16 is a summary, 00:00:12, Null0
D       20.2.0.0/16 is a summary, 00:00:12, Null0
D       20.1.3.0/24 [90/11049472] via 20.2.1.1, 00:00:08, Serial3/1
```

```
                       [90/20537600] via 20.1.2.2, 00:00:08, Serial3/2
                       [90/20537600] via 20.1.1.2, 00:00:09, Serial3/0
C          20.1.2.0/24 is directly connected, Serial3/2
C          20.2.1.0/24 is directly connected, Serial3/1
        30.0.0.0/24 is subnetted, 2 subnets
D          30.0.0.0 [90/41024000] via 20.2.1.1, 00:00:34, Serial3/1
                    [90/40537600] via 30.0.1.1, 00:00:34, Ethernet0/1
C          30.0.1.0 is directly connected, Ethernet0/1
D       50.0.0.0/8 [90/281600] via 30.0.1.1, 00:00:34, Ethernet0/1
D*EX 0.0.0.0/0 [170/25628160] via 30.0.1.1, 00:00:34, Ethernet0/1
R1#
```

Listing 10-40. *Automatic EIGRP summary entries in the routing table*

Similar entries are installed in the topology table as well (Listing 10-41).

```
R1#sho ip eigrp topo
IP-EIGRP Topology Table for process 1

Codes: P - Passive, A - Active, U - Update, Q - Query, R - Reply,
       r - Reply status

P 0.0.0.0/0, 1 successors, FD is 25628160
        via 30.0.1.1 (25628160/25602560), Ethernet0/1
P 20.1.1.0/24, 1 successors, FD is 20512000
        via Connected, Serial3/0
P 20.2.2.0/24, 1 successors, FD is 11023872
        via 20.2.1.1 (11023872/5511936), Serial3/1
        via 20.1.2.2 (21024000/5511936), Serial3/2
        via 20.1.1.2 (21049600/5537536), Serial3/0
P 20.1.0.0/16, 1 successors, FD is 11049472
        via Summary (11049472/0), Null0
P 20.2.0.0/16, 1 successors, FD is 10511872
        via Summary (10511872/0), Null0
P 20.1.3.0/24, 1 successors, FD is 11049472
        via 20.2.1.1 (11049472/5537536), Serial3/1
        via 20.1.2.2 (20537600/281600), Serial3/2
        via 20.1.1.2 (20537600/281600), Serial3/0
P 20.1.2.0/24, 1 successors, FD is 20512000
        via Connected, Serial3/2
P 20.2.1.0/24, 1 successors, FD is 10511872
        via Connected, Serial3/1
P 30.0.0.0/24, 1 successors, FD is 40537600
        via 30.0.1.1 (40537600/40512000), Ethernet0/1
        via 20.2.1.1 (41024000/40512000), Serial3/1
P 30.0.1.0/24, 1 successors, FD is 281600
        via Connected, Ethernet0/1
```

```
P 50.0.0.0/8, 1 successors, FD is 281600
        via 30.0.1.1 (281600/256), Ethernet0/1
R1#
```

Listing 10-41. *Automatic summary entries in EIGRP topology table*

As a result, R5 has two routes in its routing table (Listing 10-42).

```
R5#sho ip route
...
Gateway of last resort is 0.0.0.0 to network 0.0.0.0

S    50.0.0.0/8 is directly connected, Null0
     20.0.0.0/16 is subnetted, 2 subnets
D       20.1.0.0 [90/11075072] via 30.0.1.2, 00:00:45, Ethernet1/1
D       20.2.0.0 [90/10537472] via 30.0.1.2, 00:00:45, Ethernet1/1
     30.0.0.0/24 is subnetted, 2 subnets
C       30.0.0.0 is directly connected, Serial0/0
C       30.0.1.0 is directly connected, Ethernet1/1
S*  0.0.0.0/0 is directly connected, Null0
R5#
```

Listing 10-42. *R5's routing table with summary routes*

10.13.6 Route Redistribution, Filtering, and Route Maps

To demonstrate how route redistribution works in EIGRP, R5 is configured with a set of static routes, as shown in Listing 10-43.

```
R5#conf t
Enter configuration commands, one per line.  End with CNTL/Z.
R5(config)#ip route 50.0.0.0 255.0.0.0 Null0
R5(config)#ip route 60.1.0.0 255.255.0.0 Null0
R5(config)#ip route 60.2.0.0 255.255.0.0 Null0
R5(config)#ip route 60.3.0.0 255.255.0.0 Null0
R5(config)#ip route 60.4.0.0 255.255.0.0 Null0
R5(config)#ip route 60.5.0.0 255.255.0.0 Null0
R5(config)#ip route 70.0.0.0 255.255.0.0 Null0
R5(config)#ip route 70.1.0.0 255.255.0.0 Null0
R5(config)#ip route 70.2.0.0 255.255.0.0 Null0
R5(config)#ip route 70.3.0.0 255.255.0.0 Null0
R5(config)#
```

Listing 10-43. *Configuring static routes on R5*

R5's routing table contains corresponding routing entries, as shown in Listing 10-44.

```
R5#sho ip route
...
Gateway of last resort is not set

S       50.0.0.0/8 is directly connected, Null0
        70.0.0.0/16 is subnetted, 4 subnets
S          70.2.0.0 is directly connected, Null0
S          70.3.0.0 is directly connected, Null0
S          70.0.0.0 is directly connected, Null0
S          70.1.0.0 is directly connected, Null0
        20.0.0.0/16 is subnetted, 2 subnets
D          20.1.0.0 [90/11075072] via 30.0.1.2, 00:07:04, Ethernet1/1
D          20.2.0.0 [90/10537472] via 30.0.1.2, 00:07:04, Ethernet1/1
        60.0.0.0/16 is subnetted, 5 subnets
S          60.4.0.0 is directly connected, Null0
S          60.5.0.0 is directly connected, Null0
S          60.1.0.0 is directly connected, Null0
S          60.2.0.0 is directly connected, Null0
S          60.3.0.0 is directly connected, Null0
        30.0.0.0/24 is subnetted, 2 subnets
C          30.0.0.0 is directly connected, Serial0/0
C          30.0.1.0 is directly connected, Ethernet1/1
R5#
```

Listing 10-44. *Static routes in R5's routing table*

R5 is also configured with access list 10, used as a distribute list controlling which static routes are announced to the EIGRP domain via redistribution (Listing 10-45). The route map **static2eigrp** is used to set the tag for route 60.1.0.0/16 to value 500. This value can later be used on other routers, for example, to perform conditional redistribution to other protocols or EIGRP domains. Note that statement **route-map static2eigrp permit 20** is necessary to allow routes not permitted by the match clause in the previous route map structure to be announced. The **default-metric** statement defines the value of parameters used by EIGRP to announce redistributed routes. These values can be defined either in a **default-metric** command or in the **redistribute** command itself. Even though default metric parameters are required only for distribution of dynamic routes, we specify them in the example for consistency.

```
R5(config)#access-list 10 permit 0.0.0.0
R5(config)#access-list 10 permit 60.0.0.0 0.255.0.0
R5(config)#
R5(config)#access-list 15 permit 60.1.0.0
R5(config)#
R5(config)#route-map static2eigrp permit 10
```

```
R5(config-route-map)#match ip address 15
R5(config-route-map)#set tag 500
R5(config-route-map)#ex
R5(config)#route-map static2eigrp permit 20
R5(config-route-map)#
R5(config)#router eigrp 1
R5(config-router)#default-metric 100 10 255 1 1500
R5(config-router)#distribute-list 10 out static
R5(config-router)#redistribute static route-map static2eigrp
R5(config-router)#^Z
R5#
```

Listing 10-45. *R5 configured to redistribute static routes with route filtering and route map*

When the **redistribute** command takes place, the redistributing subprocess in EIGRP sends pseudoupdates to DUAL for the redistributed routes appropriately applying configured filters. As a result, new entries are created in the EIGRP topology table, as shown in Listing 10-46. These entries make sure that EIGRP announces redistributed routes in its updates. Also, if another source sends the same route to the redistributing router, the topology table will contain multiple path descriptors for the same destination. The path descriptor with the `via Redistributed` legend always wins any path descriptor constructed from a received update.

```
R5#sho ip eigrp topo
IP-EIGRP Topology Table for process 1

Codes: P - Passive, A - Active, U - Update, Q - Query, R - Reply,
       r - Reply status

P 20.1.0.0/16, 1 successors, FD is 11075072
        via 30.0.1.2 (11075072/11049472), Ethernet1/1
        via 30.0.0.2 (41049600/5537536), Serial0/0
P 20.2.0.0/16, 1 successors, FD is 10537472
        via 30.0.1.2 (10537472/10511872), Ethernet1/1
        via 30.0.0.2 (41024000/5511936), Serial0/0
P 30.0.0.0/24, 1 successors, FD is 40512000
        via Connected, Serial0/0
P 30.0.1.0/24, 1 successors, FD is 281600
        via Connected, Ethernet1/1
P 60.4.0.0/16, 1 successors, FD is 25602560
        via Redistributed (25602560/0)
P 60.5.0.0/16, 1 successors, FD is 25602560
        via Redistributed (25602560/0)
P 60.1.0.0/16, 1 successors, FD is 25602560, tag is 500
        via Redistributed (25602560/0)
P 60.2.0.0/16, 1 successors, FD is 25602560
        via Redistributed (25602560/0)
```

```
P 60.3.0.0/16, 1 successors, FD is 25602560
        via Redistributed (25602560/0)
R5#
```

Listing 10-46. *R5's topology table containing redistributed routes*

The **show ip eigrp topology** command, when used with a specific prefix as an argument, displays more detailed information about the topology entry (see Listing 10-47, for example). One can see that route attributes of the entries created for redistributed routes are created by using information specified in the **default-metric** command. Note also how the value of the administrative tag has been changed by the route map.

```
R5#sho ip eigrp topo 60.1.0.0 255.255.0.0
IP-EIGRP topology entry for 60.1.0.0/16
  State is Passive, Query origin flag is 1, 1 Successor(s), FD is 25602560
  Routing Descriptor Blocks:
  0.0.0.0, from Redistributed, Send flag is 0x0
      Composite metric is (25602560/0), Route is External
      Vector metric:
        Minimum bandwidth is 100 Kbit
        Total delay is 100 microseconds
        Reliability is 255/255
        Load is 1/255
        Minimum MTU is 1500
        Hop count is 0
      External data:
        Originating router is 172.16.66.194 (this system)
        AS number of route is 0
        External protocol is Static, external metric is 0
        Administrator tag is 500 (0x000001F4)
R5#
```

Listing 10-47. *Detailed information about redistributed route*

Other routers install routes redistributed by R5 in their routing tables explicitly marking them as external. See Listing 10-48 for a sample routing table from R1.

```
R1#sho ip route
...
Gateway of last resort is 172.16.66.161 to network 0.0.0.0

     20.0.0.0/8 is variably subnetted, 7 subnets, 2 masks
D       20.2.2.0/24 [90/21024000] via 20.1.2.2, 00:22:55, Serial3/2
                    [90/11023872] via 20.2.1.1, 00:22:55, Serial3/1
```

```
                      [90/21049600] via 20.1.1.2, 00:22:55, Serial3/0
C        20.1.1.0/24 is directly connected, Serial3/0
D        20.1.0.0/16 is a summary, 00:13:26, Null0
D        20.2.0.0/16 is a summary, 00:13:26, Null0
D        20.1.3.0/24 [90/20537600] via 20.1.1.2, 00:22:52, Serial3/0
                      [90/20537600] via 20.1.2.2, 00:22:54, Serial3/2
                      [90/11049472] via 20.2.1.1, 00:22:54, Serial3/1
C        20.2.1.0/24 is directly connected, Serial3/1
C        20.1.2.0/24 is directly connected, Serial3/2
         172.16.0.0/27 is subnetted, 1 subnets
C           172.16.66.160 is directly connected, Ethernet0/0
         60.0.0.0/16 is subnetted, 5 subnets
D EX        60.4.0.0 [170/25628160] via 30.0.1.1, 00:13:29, Ethernet0/1
D EX        60.5.0.0 [170/25628160] via 30.0.1.1, 00:13:29, Ethernet0/1
D EX        60.1.0.0 [170/25628160] via 30.0.1.1, 00:13:29, Ethernet0/1
D EX        60.2.0.0 [170/25628160] via 30.0.1.1, 00:13:29, Ethernet0/1
D EX        60.3.0.0 [170/25628160] via 30.0.1.1, 00:13:29, Ethernet0/1
         30.0.0.0/24 is subnetted, 2 subnets
D           30.0.0.0 [90/41024000] via 20.2.1.1, 00:13:29, Serial3/1
                      [90/40537600] via 30.0.1.1, 00:13:29, Ethernet0/1
C           30.0.1.0 is directly connected, Ethernet0/1
S*       0.0.0.0/0 [1/0] via 172.16.66.161
R1#
```

Listing 10-48. *R1's routing table containing external routes from R5*

To show all parameters of the received external route, the administrator can specify the route's network parameters in the **show ip route** command. The example in Listing 10-49 shows the parameters R1 received for the route processed by the route map on R5. Note the value of the route tag. Also take a look at the information in the topology table shown in Listing 10-50.

```
R1#sho ip route 60.1.0.0
Routing entry for 60.1.0.0/16
  Known via "eigrp 1", distance 170, metric 25628160
  Tag 500, type external
  Redistributing via eigrp 1
  Last update from 30.0.1.1 on Ethernet0/1, 00:14:13 ago
  Routing Descriptor Blocks:
  * 30.0.1.1, from 30.0.1.1, 00:14:13 ago, via Ethernet0/1
      Route metric is 25628160, traffic share count is 1
      Total delay is 1100 microseconds, minimum bandwidth is 100 Kbit
      Reliability 255/255, minimum MTU 1500 bytes
      Loading 1/255, Hops 1

R1#
```

Listing 10-49. *External route received by R1 from R5*

```
R1#sho ip eigrp topo
IP-EIGRP Topology Table for AS(1)/ID(172.16.66.172)

Codes: P - Passive, A - Active, U - Update, Q - Query, R - Reply,
       r - reply Status, s - sia Status

P 20.2.2.0/24, 1 successors, FD is 11023872
        via 20.2.1.1 (11023872/5511936), Serial3/1
        via 20.1.1.2 (21049600/5537536), Serial3/0
        via 20.1.2.2 (21024000/5511936), Serial3/2
P 20.1.1.0/24, 1 successors, FD is 20512000
        via Connected, Serial3/0
P 20.1.0.0/16, 1 successors, FD is 11049472
        via Summary (11049472/0), Null0
P 20.2.0.0/16, 1 successors, FD is 10511872
        via Summary (10511872/0), Null0
P 20.1.3.0/24, 1 successors, FD is 11049472
        via 20.2.1.1 (11049472/5537536), Serial3/1
        via 20.1.1.2 (20537600/281600), Serial3/0
        via 20.1.2.2 (20537600/281600), Serial3/2
P 20.2.1.0/24, 1 successors, FD is 10511872
        via Connected, Serial3/1
P 20.1.2.0/24, 1 successors, FD is 20512000
        via Connected, Serial3/2
P 30.0.0.0/24, 1 successors, FD is 40537600
        via 30.0.1.1 (40537600/40512000), Ethernet0/1
        via 20.2.1.1 (41024000/40512000), Serial3/1
P 30.0.1.0/24, 1 successors, FD is 281600
        via Connected, Ethernet0/1
P 60.4.0.0/16, 1 successors, FD is 25628160
        via 30.0.1.1 (25628160/25602560), Ethernet0/1
P 60.5.0.0/16, 1 successors, FD is 25628160
        via 30.0.1.1 (25628160/25602560), Ethernet0/1
P 60.1.0.0/16, 1 successors, FD is 25628160, tag is 500
        via 30.0.1.1 (25628160/25602560), Ethernet0/1
P 60.2.0.0/16, 1 successors, FD is 25628160
        via 30.0.1.1 (25628160/25602560), Ethernet0/1
P 60.3.0.0/16, 1 successors, FD is 25628160
        via 30.0.1.1 (25628160/25602560), Ethernet0/1
R1#
```

Listing 10-50. *Information about received external route in R1's topology table*

10.4 Frequently Asked Questions

Q: **Is there any EIGRP protocol specification like the RFC for OSPF?**

A: EIGRP is a proprietary Cisco protocol, so all protocol specifications are internal to Cisco and are not publicly available.

Q: **EIGRP supports distribution of routing information from multiple network-layer protocols. If EIGRP is configured to distribute, say, IPX routing information, will EIGRP packets still be encapsulated in IP?**

A: No. They will be encapsulated in IPX packets. EIGRP has protocol-independent and protocol-dependent modules. The transport module used to send and to receive packets is protocol dependent.

Q: **EIGRP has a topology table. Does this make EIGRP a link-state routing protocol?**

A: No. Even though each EIGRP process maintains a topology table, the information in it is not represented in the form of PDUs describing the complete network topology. Instead, the table contains information about the paths through the router's neighbors. Also, EIGRP does not perform shortest-path calculation by calculating the shortest-path tree but instead uses the DUAL algorithm.

Q: **EIGRP maintains adjacencies with neighboring routers. Is any state associated with an adjacency and an FSM describing the algorithm of adjacency operation?**

A: EIGRP does not have a formal FSM, but each neighbor goes through the Init state. In this state, neighbors download the topology information from each other.

Q: **Why are routes said to be in the Active state when it is not possible to recalculate paths locally and the router needs to send queries? It would be more logical to call a route active when everything is fine with it.**

A: In fact, the best way to describe this process is to say that the router goes to the Active state—from the distributed computation point of view—for a particular set of routes.

Q: **I have changed the variance parameter to a value higher than 1, so I have multiple routes to the same destination with unequal costs in my routing table. But I see that traffic still goes through a single interface. What could cause the problem?**

A: Because you can see multiple unequal-cost routes in the routing table, EIGRP did its part of work. Now you need to make sure that the switching method the router is using does in fact distribute the load appropriately among multiple routes. See Chapter 5.

Bibliography

All IETF *Request For Comment* (RFC) documents are freely available at the IETF web site <http://www.ietf.org>. For example, to get the text of RFC 791 use URL <http://www.ietf.org/rfc/rfc791.txt>. IETF works in progress are available at <http://www.ietf.org/internet-drafts/>.

Albrightson, B., J.J. Garcia-Luna-Aceves, J. Boyle. "EIGRP—A Fast Routing Protocol Based on Distance Vectors," Proceedings of Networld/Interop 94. Las Vegas, Nevada, May 1994. <http://www.cse.ucsc.edu/research/ccrg/publications/interop94.pdf>.

Baker, F. *Requirements for IP Version 4 Routers.* RFC 1812, June 1995.

Baker, F., R. Coltun. *OSPF Version 2 Management Information Base.* RFC 1850, November 1995.

Bellman, R. "On a routing problem." *Quarterly of Applied Mathematics,* 16(1):87–90, 1958.

Bradley, T., C. Brown, and A. Malis. *Multiprotocol Interconnect over Frame Relay.* RFC 1490, July 1993.

Callon, R. Use of OSI IS-IS for Routing in TCP/IP and Dual Environments. RFC 1195, December 1990.

Chappell, Laura (Editor). *Introduction to Cisco Router Configuration.* Cisco Systems.

Cisco System. *Configuring Fast Switching.* <http://www.cisco.com/univercd/cc/td/doc/product/software/ios122/122cgcr/fswtch_c/swprt1/xcfipsp.htm>.

Cisco Systems. "Congestion Management." *Cisco IOS Quality of Service Solutions Configuration Guide, Release 12.2.* <http://www.cisco.com/univercd/cc/td/doc/product/software/ios122/122cgcr/fqos_c/fqcprt2/index.htm>.

Cisco Systems. "Interior Gateway Routing Protocol," <http://www.cisco.com/univercd/cc/td/doc/cisintwk/ito_doc/igrp.htm>.

Cisco Systems. "Routing Information Protocol (RIP)," `<http://www.cisco.com/univercd/cc/td/doc/cisintwk/ito_doc/rip.htm>`.

Cisco Systems. *An Introduction to IGRP*. `<http://www.cisco.com/warp/public/103/5.html>`.

Cisco Systems. *Cisco Express Forwarding Overview*. `<http://www.cisco.com/univercd/cc/td/doc/product/software/ios122/122cgcr/fswtch_c/swprt1/xcfcef.htm>`.

Cisco Systems. *Cisco IOS Configuration Fundamentals*. `<http://www.cisco.com/univercd/cc/td/doc/product/software/ios122/122cgcr/ffun_c/index.htm>`

Cisco Systems. *Cisco IOS Interface Configuration Guide, Release 12.2*. `<http://www.cisco.com/univercd/cc/td/doc/product/software/ios122/122cgcr/finter_c/index.htm>`.

Cisco Systems. *Cisco IOS Security Configuration*. `<http://www.cisco.com/univercd/cc/td/doc/product/software/ios113ed/dsqcg/qcsecur.htm>`.

Cisco Systems. *Cisco IOS Switching Paths Overview*. `<http://www.cisco.com/univercd/cc/td/doc/product/software/ios122/122cgcr/fswtch_c/swprt1/xcfovips.htm>`.

Cisco Systems. *Configuring Cisco Express Forwarding*. `<http://www.cisco.com/univercd/cc/td/doc/product/software/ios122/122cgcr/fswtch_c/swprt1/xcfcefc.htm>`.

Cisco Systems. Configuring Enhanced IGRP. `<http://www.cisco.com/univercd/cc/td/doc/product/software/ios122/122cgcr/fipr_c/ipcprt2/1cfeigrp.htm>`.

Cisco Systems. *Configuring IGRP*. `<http://www.cisco.com/univercd/cc/td/doc/product/software/ios122/122cgcr/fipr_c/ipcprt2/1cfigrp.htm>`.

Cisco Systems. *Configuring IP addressing*. `<http://www.cisco.com/univercd/cc/td/doc/product/software/ios122/122cgcr/fipr_c/ipcprt1/1cfipadr.htm>`

Cisco Systems. *Configuring IP Routing Protocol-independent features*. `<http://www.cisco.com/univercd/cc/td/doc/product/software/ios122/122cgcr/fipr_c/ipcprt2/1cfindep.htm>`.

Cisco Systems. *Configuring IP Services*. `<http://www.cisco.com/univercd/cc/td/doc/product/software/ios122/122cgcr/fipr_c/ipcprt1/1cfip.htm>`.

Cisco Systems. *Configuring Multiprotocol Label Switching*. `<http://www.cisco.com/univercd/cc/td/doc/product/software/ios122/122cgcr/fswtch_c/swprt3/xcftagc.htm>`.

Cisco Systems. *Configuring OSPF*. `<http://www.cisco.com/univercd/cc/td/doc/product/software/ios122/122cgcr/fipr_c/ipcprt2/1cfospf.htm>`.

Cisco Systems. *Configuring Routing Information Protocol.* <http://www.cisco.com/univercd/cc/td/doc/product/software/ios122/122cgcr/fipr_c/ipcprt2/1cfrip.htm>.

Cisco Systems. *Configuring Snapshot Routing.* <http://www.cisco.com/univercd/cc/td/doc/product/software/ios121/121cgcr/dialns_c/dnsprt2/dcdnsnap.htm>.

Cisco Systems. *Dial-on-Demand Routing Configuration.* <http://www.cisco.com/univercd/cc/td/doc/product/software/ios122/122cgcr/fdial_c/fnsprt5/index.htm>.

Cisco Systems. *Enhanced Interior Gateway Routing Protocol.* <http://www.cisco.com/warp/public/103/eigrp-toc.html>.

Cisco Systems. *IGRP Metric Calculation.* <http://www.cisco.com/warp/public/103/3.html>.

Cisco Systems. *Interior Gateway Routing Protocol (IGRP).* Cisco TAC Technology pages. <http://www.cisco.com/pcgi-bin/Support/PSP/psp_view.pl?p=Internetworking:IGRP>.

Cisco Systems. *Introduction to Enhanced IGRP.* <http://www.cisco.com/univercd/cc/td/doc/cisintwk/ito_doc/en_igrp.htm>.

Cisco Systems. *IP Routing Protocol-Independent Commands.* <http://www.cisco.com/univercd/cc/td/doc/product/software/ios122/122cgcr/fiprrp_r/ind_r/1rfindp1.htm> and <http://www.cisco.com/univercd/cc/td/doc/product/software/ios122/122cgcr/fiprrp_r/ind_r/1rfindp2.htm>.

Cisco Systems. *Multiprotocol Label Switching.* <http://www.cisco.com/univercd/cc/td/doc/product/software/ios122/122cgcr/fswtch_c/swprt3/xcftagov.htm>.

Cisco Systems. *Open Shortest Path First (OSPF).* <http://www.cisco.com/univercd/cc/td/doc/cisintwk/ito_doc/ospf.htm>.

Cisco Systems. *Open Shortest Path First (OSPF).* Cisco TAC Technology pages. <http://www.cisco.com/pcgi-bin/Support/PSP/psp_view.pl?p=Internetworking:OSPF>.

Cisco Systems. *Routing Information Protocol.* Cisco TAC Technology pages. <http://www.cisco.com/pcgi-bin/Support/PSP/psp_view.pl? p=Internetworking:RIP>.

Cisco Systems. *Triggered Extensions to RIP.* <http://www.cisco.com/univercd/cc/td/doc/product/software/ios120/120newft/120t/120t1/trigrip.htm>.

Coltun, R. *The OSPF Opaque LSA Option.* RFC 2370, July 1998.

Coltun, R., D. Ferguson, J. Moy. *OSPF for IPv6.* RFC 2749, December 1999.

Coltun, R., V. Fuller, P. Murphy. *The OSPF NSSA Option.* Work in progress, December 2000. <http://www.ietf.org/internet-drafts/draft-ietf-ospf-nssa-update-10.txt>.

Coltun, R., V. Fuller. *The OSPF NSSA Option.* RFC 1587, March 1994.

Doyle, J. *Routing TCP/IP Volume I (CCIE Professional Development).* Chapter 8. Cisco Press, October 1998.

Floyd, S., V.Jacobson. *The Synchronization of Periodic Routing Messages*. SIGCOMM, 1993.

Ford, L. R. Jr. *Network flow theory*. Technical Report P-923, The Rand Corporation, Santa Monica, CA, August 1956.

Fuller, V., T. Li, J. Yu, K. Varadhan, *Classless Inter-Domain Routing (CIDR): an Address Assignment and Aggregation Strategy*. RFC 1519, September 1993.

Garcia-Luna-Aceves, J.J. "Loop-Free Routing Using Diffusing Computations," *IEEE/ACM Transactions on Networking, Vol. 1, No. 1*. February 1993. <http://www.cse.ucsc.edu/research/ccrg/publications/jj.dual.ton93.pdf>.

Halabi, S., D. McPherson. *Internet Routing Architectures, Second Edition*. Cisco Press, August 2000, ISBN: 157870233X.

Hedrick, C. *Routing Information Protocol*. RFC 1058, June 1988.

Hopps, C. *Analysis of an Equal-Cost Multi-Path Algorithm*. RFC 2992, November 2000.

Huitema, C. *Routing in the Internet*. Prentice Hall, 1997.

International Organization for Standardization. *Intermediate System to Intermediate System Intra-Domain Routeing Exchange Protocol for use in Conjunction with the Protocol for Providing the Connectionless-mode Network Service (ISO 8473)*. ISO DP 10589, February 1990.

Li, T., T. Przygienda, H. Smit. *Domain-wide Prefix Distribution with Two-Level IS-IS*. RFC 2966, October 2000.

Malkin, G. *RIP Version 2. Carrying Additional Information*. RFC 1723, November 1994.

Malkin, G., R. Minnear. *RIPng for IPv6*. RFC 2080, January 1997.

McGregor, Mark. *Cisco IOS Configuration Fundamentals*. Cisco Press. ISBN: 1578700442

Meyer, G. *Extensions to RIP to Support Demand Circuits*. RFC 1582, February 1994.

Meyer, G., S. Sherry, *Triggered Extensions to RIP to Support Demand Circuits*. RFC 2091, January 1997.

Mogul J., *Broadcasting Internet Datagrams In The Presence Of Subnets*. RFC 922. October 1984.

Mogul, J., J. Postel. *Internet Standard Subnetting Procedure*. RFC 950, August 1985.

Moy, J. *Experience with the OSPF protocol*. RFC 1246, July 1991.

Moy, J. *Extending OSPF to Support Demand Circuits*. RFC 1793, April 1995.

Moy, J. *OSPF Version 2*. RFC 1247, July 1991.

Moy, J. *OSPF Version 2*. RFC 1583, March 1994.

Moy, J. *OSPF Version 2*. RFC 2178, July 1997.

Moy, J. *OSPF Version 2*. RFC 2328, April 1998.

Moy, J. *OSPF. Complete Implementation*. Addison-Wesley, October 2000.

Moy, J. *The OSPF Specification*. RFC 1131, October 1989. <http://www.ietf.org/rfc/rfc1131.ps>.

Oran, D. *OSI IS-IS Intra-domain Routing Protocol*. RFC 1142, February 1990.

Perlman, R. *Interconnections, Second Edition : Bridges, Routers, Switches, and Internetworking Protocols (Addison-Wesley Professional Computing Series)*. Addison-Wesley, October 1999.

Plummer, D. *An Ethernet Address Resolution Protocol*. RFC 826, November 1982.

Postel, J. *Internet Control Message Protocol*. RFC 792. September 1981.

Postel, J. *Internet Protocol*. RFC 791, September 1981.

Postel, J. *Transmission Control Protocol*. RFC 793, September 1981.

Pummill, T., B. Manning. *VLSM—Variable Length Subnet Table For IPv4*. RFC 1878, December 1995.

Rekhter Y., T. Li. *A Border Gateway Protocol 4 (BGP-4)*. RFC 1771. March 1995.

Rekhter Y., T. Li. *A Border Gateway Protocol 4 (BGP-4)*. Work in progress. 2001. <http://www.ietf.org/internet-drafts/draft-ietf-idr-bgp4-12.txt>.

Rekhter, Y., et al. *Address Allocation for Private Internets*. RFC 1918, February 1996.

Retana, A., R. White, V. Fuller, D. McPherson, *Using 31-Bit Prefixes on IPv4 Point-to-Point Links*. RFC 3021, December 2000.

Reynolds, J., and J. Postel. *Assigned Numbers*. RFC 1700. October 1994. *See also*: <http://www.iana.org/numbers.html>

Rosen, E., A. Viswanathan, R. Callon. *Multiprotocol Label Switching Architecture*. RFC 3031, January 2001.

Rosen, E., et al. *MPLS Label Stack Encoding*. RFC 3032, January 2001.

Senie, D. *Changing the Default for Directed Broadcasts in Routers*. RFC 2644, August 1999.

Simpson, W. *The Point-to-Point Protocol (PPP)*. RFC 1661, July 1994.

Stevens, W.R. *TCP/IP Illustrated, Volume 1: The Protocols (Addison-Wesley Professional Computing Series)*. Addison-Wesley, January 1994.

Thaler, D., C. Hopps. *Multipath Issues in Unicast and Multicast Next-Hop Selection*. RFC 2991, November 2000.

Varadhan, K., BGP OSPF Interaction. RFC 1403, January 1993.

Index

ABRs *see* OSPF/routing domain structure

Access control list (ACL), 168–169

Adjacencies
 table, 223
 two-way connectivity check, 481
 types, 224
 see also OSPF

Administrative distance (AD), 100, 110,
  275–276, 291, 374
 as additional level of route selection,
   101–103, 102f
 comparison, 103–104
   see also CompareRoutes() function
 defaults, 100, 100t
 static route examples, 106–109, 159
 see also Proto_ADForRoute function

Administrator
 configuration of tunnel interfaces,
   202–203
 implicit control, 3
 interface with routers *see* Command line
   interface
 ip subnet-zero command, 28, 291
 manual routing table clearance,
   144–147
 map table configuration, 194–196,
   286–289

policy routing, 177–182
route cache control, 212–214
routing table initialization, 110–111
setting router configuration, 6–11
 dynamic changes, 6, 61, 78
shutdown interface, 28
and static routing, 41, 44, 241
 adding/deleting static route, 126–127

AFI (address family identifier), 317

AppleTalk (network-layer protocol), 1, 166

ARP (Address Resolution Protocol), 35,
  189–190
 ARPLookUp() function, 190
 inverse, 193
 mechanism, 190l–191l, 191–192

ATM, using static routes, 247

Autonomous system (AS), 44, 45f
 vs. routing domain, 45

AUX (auxiliary asynchronous serial port), 2
 line interface with router, 3–4, 3f, 4f

Bellman-Ford algorithm, 295, 307–310

BGP (routing protocol), 1
 routes, 80

Broadcast types and addressing
 conventions, 182, 439–440
 all subnets, 21

directed, 20–21
frame transmission, 182f
ip broadcast-address, 29, 291–301
ip directed-broadcast command, 30
local, 20
and packet delivery, 188–192

CIDR (classless interdomain routing), 22
and route aggregation, 60, 61f, 61t, 62, 62f
Cisco router
architecture, 1
central processor, 2
console port (CON), 2
I/O devices, 2
memory types, 2
operating system, 3
configuration, 5
file and change commands, 111
host vs. network configuration file, 8
sample configuration file, 6l
see also Administrator
interface with, 3–5
monitoring/troubleshooting tools, 11–14, 131
see also debug commands; ping command; show commands; Traceroute tool
unicast Reverse-Path Forwarding (RPF) check, 35
see also IP addressing details (Cisco routers); Routing table structure (Cisco)
Classful environment
classful addressing, 22, 53
and hierarchical routing table structure, 81
and default route treatment, 56–58, 57f, 62
potential problems, 59
route types, 53–54, 54f, 58
router operation summary, 58–59, 353

routing table lookup algorithm, 54–55, 139, 142–143
example, 55–56, 140–142
and supernet routes, 58, 62, 63t
Classless environment
and automatic route summarization, 59
classless addressing, 22
see also VLSM
and default routes, 62–63
example, 63–64, 64f
routing table lookup algorithm, 64, 237–238
clear ip route command, 144–147
Command line interface (CLI), 1
EXEC process, 3–4, 3f, 4f, 4l
parser, 6
CompareRoutes() function, 103–104l, 104
CON (console port), 2
line interface with router, 3–4, 3f, 4f
configure command, 6, 6l–7l
configure network command, 7, 8l
configure overwrite-network command, 8
configure terminal command, 7, 110
Connected field flags, 85
Connected routes see Directly attached networks
copy command, 8, 8l–9l
copy running-config startup-config command, 9
copy running tftp command, 9
misconceptions, 10–11
Counting, and routing loop, 302

Data link layer protocols, 1
debug commands, 11
debug eigrp fsm, 593, 593l–594l
debug ip commands, 12, 131, 89l, 145l
debug ip rip command, 366l–367l
Default routes
candidate, 147–148
in classful environment, 56–58, 57f, 62
in classless environment, 62–64, 64f

configuration using static routes, 248–250

dynamic propagation, 151

selection algorithm, 151–152

    examples, 152–155

types of addresses

    major network, 149–150

    subnet, 148–149

DelSubnet() function, 99

Demand circuits *see* OSPF; Routing Information Protocol

dialer in-band interface command, 196

DialerProcess() function, 196–198, 197l–198l

    interesting flag, 198–199

    queue checking, 199–200

Dijkstra algorithm, 408, 410–411, 411l–413l

    intra-area route calculation (OSPF), 479–480

    topological information input, 466

    underlying concept, 409–410

Directly attached networks, 66

    and interface routes, 67, 67l–68l, 68, 79

        Ethernet segment connection example, 69, 69f, 70l

        example of IOS route install, 68l–69l

Directly connected routes, 65

Distance-vector routing protocols

    Bellman-Ford algorithm, 295, 307–310

    counting to infinity problem, 301–302, 301f

        solutions, 302–303, 307

    DV_Holddown() function, 330–331

    holddown timers, 305–306

    neighbor and network discovery, 270

    path characteristics augmentation, 298

    principles, 295

    route-refresh requirements, 350

    routing algorithm, 299–301

    snapshot routing, 402

    split-horizon technique, 303–305, 304f

topology discovery

    full-mesh, 296, 296f, 297l

    partial mesh, 297, 297f, 298f

triggered updates, 306–307

see also IGRP

Distribute lists, 274–275

Distributed Services method *see* 7500-series router/(VIPs)

Dotted-decimal notation, 16

DUAL (diffusing update algorithm), 551, 552–553, 558

DV_Holddown() function, 330–331

Dynamic routes

    common functionality, 269–271

    cooperation with static routes, 143–144

    dynamic routing protocol, 41–42, 44–46, 44f, 45f, 78

        configuration commands, 76–78

        and metrics, 85

        no packet forwarding, 66

    events processed, 290–291

    processing, 124–126

EGPs (exterior gateway protocols), 45

    BGP; and inter-domain routing, 45

    EGP, 45

EIGRP (enhanced IGRP), 45, 151, 612

    adjacency database, 554, 561, 562, 563l

        fields, 563

    classful route summarization, 582

    configuration, 581–586

    configuration examples

        basic commands, 587–592

        in CIDR environment, 592–596

        manual route summarization, 605–607

        route redistribution/filtering/and route maps, 607–611, 612l

        topology, 586–587, 586f

        variance parameters, 596–597

    default route support, 578

        examples, 597–604

DUAL algorithm/module, 551, 552–553
  events, 558, 559t
  route states, 559t
  and update processing, 573–574
feasible successor concept, 554
FSM (finite state machine), 558, 560f
  parameters/combinations, 558, 559t
general characteristics, 552t
Hello protocol-independent module,
  560, 585
and IGRP, 402, 551
input processing; generic packet
  processing, 571–573
internal event processing, 574–575
loop-free routing techniques, 271
message format, 566f, 567l
  body *see* TLVs
  header fields, 565–566
multiple routes/metrics, 85, 292, 554
  and administrative control, 581
  example, 555–558
and neighbors, 572, 613
and network command, 77
packet-spoofing attack prevention, 572
path attributes
  FD (feasible distance), 554
  RD (reported distance), 554
protocol-specific modules, 560
  cooperation, 561f
queries/replies, 574
route aggregation, 579, 605–607
routing table interface module/route
  redistribution, 560, 562, 584
RTP (reliable transport protocol), 553,
  560, 562
sending packets, 575–576
  Hellos, 576
  replies, 577
  updates/queries, 576–577
shortest-path calculation, 577–578
stub router extension, 579, 580f

modifications to regular EIGRP
  behavior, 580–581
timers, 582
  SIA (stuck-in-active), 557, 558l, 579
topology database, 554, 561, 564l, 613
  fields/information, 564–565, 589l
transport module, 560, 562
enable command, 6, 6l
EvXXX (Routing Information Protocol/state
  machine events), 333–335
EXEC process *see* Command line interface

Flash memory, 2
Flooding algorithm, 270–271, 481
  assumptions, 414
  goals, 414
  and LSDB maintenance procedures, 473
    link-state update package and
      processing steps, 473–476, 474f
    LSA distribution, 477–478
    LSA installation and SPF scheduling,
      476–477
    new information sources, 473
    special cases, 478–479
  requirements, 415
FlowCollector, 228
Forwarding, 33, 155, 157
  engine algorithm, 170l–171l, 172–173
  packet forwarding actions, 161, 237
    and router components, 162f
  virtual routing and (VRF), 238
  see also Switching technologies
Forwarding algorithm (basic), 47
  data structures (interface)
    address mask, 49, 157
    IP address, 49
    IP status, 49
    IP unnumbered flag, 49
    state, 48
    type, 48
  data structures (packet), 48
  data structures (routing table entries)

default candidate, 49
network prefix, 49
paths (intermediate address), 49
paths (outbound interface), 49
initiation of packet-delivery procedure,
    50
    see also Packet-delivery process
outline of router function, 49–50
Frame check sequence (FCS), 2, 165–166
Frame Relay
    and Data Link Connection Identifier
        (DLCI), 35, 185
    data link protocol, 1
    frame-relay map commands;
        configuration example, 273–274
    and packet-delivery process, 51–52
    as point-to-multipoint, 183
        cloud, 183
    static routes, 247–248
        error, 242–243

Garcia Luna Aceves, J., 271, 551
GetNextHop() function, 176, 176l, 177
Gigabit Switch Router (GSR), 2
    and CEF, 224

HDLC (data link protocol), 1, 70
    on serial interface, 158
Hedrick, Charles, and RIP, 310
Hello
    protocol-independent module (EIGRP),
        560, 562, 576
    subprotocol, 270, 420, 437
        and dynamic neighbor discovery, 449
        incoming (processing), 451–452
        packet formats, 448–449, 448f
        rules per media, 450–451
        tasks, 447
hostname global configuration command, 8
Hub-and-spoke topology, 42, 43f

ICMP (Internet Control Message Protocol),
    addressing, 20
IDB *see* IOS/interface descriptor block
IGPs (interior gateway protocols)
    and explicit neighbor configuration,
        272–273
    hybrids, 551
    interface dependency, 79
    intra-domain routing functions, 45
    see also EIGRP; IGRP; Link-state
        routing protocols; Routing
        Information
        Protocol (RIP)
IGRP (interior gateway routing protocol),
    45, 374, 401
    adjacencies maintenance, 271
    boundary routers, 380, 381f
    characteristics, 375
    configuration, 158, 388–389
    configuration examples
        basic configuration, 389l–390l
        basic configuration/route details, 392l
        basic configuration/routing tables,
            391l
        default routing, 395, 396l–397l
        redistribution, 397l–398l
        selecting routes with more available
            bandwidth, 392l–393l
        subnet mask change, 399l–401l
        unequal cost load-sharing, 393–395
    considerations, 402–403
    and default routing information, 380,
        382
    development of/requirements, 375–376,
        402
    and EIGRP, 402
    and external routes, 383
    input processing, 386–388
    message format
        header, 383–385, 383l, 384f
        source and destination address
            setting, 383

message types
   request, 384–385
   update, 385
  multiple routes/metrics, 85, 379, 380,
   382
  neighbor and network discovery, 270
  and network command, 77
  protocol parameters, 380–383
  route attributes alteration, 386–387,
   387f
  route poisoning, 376, 387–388
  routing information entries format, 385,
   385l, 386f
  special timers, 125, 305–306, 376, 381
  and subnet routes, 83
  see also Path calculations
Inter-domain routing, and BGP, 45
Interface data structures, 279
  see also TRPInterfaceInfo
interface loopback 0 command, 28,
  86l–87l
Interface routes *see* Directly attached
  networks
interface tunnel command, 202–203
Internet
  as example of dynamic routing, 44
  impact on router development, 220
IOS (Internetwork Operating System), 1, 3
  interface descriptor block (IDB), 81
  old vs. new command versions, 9, 10t
  unnumbered point-to-point interfaces,
   27
   alternatives, 31
  see also Command line interface; Load
   sharing
IP addressing details (Cisco routers), 25
  assigning IP address to an interface,
   25l–26l
  assigning secondary IP address, 27l
  and OSPF, 481–482
  root masks and routes provided, 52–53
IP commands

ip address, 25, 26
ip broadcast-address, 29, 291–30l
ip classless, 25, 174, 175, 253
ip default-network, 150–151, 249,
  249l–250l, 597, 598l, 601, 601l–602l
ip directed-broadcast, 30
ip route cache, 209–212
ip route-cache flow, 227
ip subnet-zero, 28, 29l, 31
ip unnumbered, 27–28, 28l, 70l–71l
ip verify unicast reverse-path interface,
  169–170
IP (Internet Protocol)
  datagram, 15
  header, 15–16, 16f
   address class/ranges, 17–18, 17f, 18t
   address mask, 16–17, 17l
   addressing conventions, 20–21
   destination address, 15, 48
   source address, 15
   TOS byte, 225
   see also Classful addressing;
    Classless addressing
  logical addressing, 15
  network layer of OSI reference model, 1,
   15
  packet vs. datagram, 41
  packet fragmentation, 40, 52
  subnetting procedure, 18–19, 19l, 19t
   address ranges, 19–20, 20t–21t
   see also VLSM
IP networks, as datagram networks, 39
IpForward() function, 170l–171l
  goal, 172–173
  process, 172
  see also Policy routing; Process
   switching; Route/lookup
IpInput() function, 167–168
IPinterfaceDown() function, 119–120,
  120l–121l, 128
IPinterfaceUp() function, 118–119, 119l
IpOutput() function, 187, 187l–188l, 188

for point-to-multipoint interfaces,
    193–194
for point-to-point interfaces, 192
IpPolicyRoute() function, 181
IPRIP functions
    IPRIPAddMsgEntry(), 346–347, 346l
    IPRIPAnnounceDefault(), 344l–345l
        conditions for default-route
            announcement, 345
    IPRIPComposeRoute(), 325–326, 325l
    IPRIPGetMask(), 324l–325l, 325
    IPRIPIfDown(), 337, 337l
    IPRIPIfUp(), 336l–338l
    IPRIPIntEventHandler(), 335l
    IPRIPReceive(), 318l–319l
    IPRIPSanityEntry(), 323l–324l, 324
    IPRIPShouldAnnounce(), 343l, 344
    IPRIPUpdate(), 329, 338, 338l–340l
        ForIf/interface message creation
            steps, 341, 342l–343l
IPRoute functions
    IPRouteGarbageTimer(), 332–333
    IPRouteHolddownTimer(), 332
    IPRouteInvalidTimer(), 330
IpRTLookup(), 173, 173l–174l, 176
    and ip classless flag, 174
    NextHop argument, 174
IPX (network-layer protocol), 1, 166
    alternative to secondary addresses, 157
    and MAC address of next-hop router,
        188–189
IS-IS, 45
    Hello subprotocol, 270
ISDN (integrated services digital network)
    interfaces and dialer, 196
    using static routes, 247

Lab see Test lab
LAN interfaces, 182
LastUpdated field, 85
LAT (local-area transport) services,
    interface with router, 3–5, 3f, 4f

Link-state routing protocols, 419
    data unit (LSPDU), 413
        age-check algorithm, 416–417
        asynchronous distribution, 415
        see also Flooding algorithm
    Dijkstra algorithm, 408–413
    and LSDB synchronization, 417–418, 473
        steps, 463
    request packet format, 466f
    routing information calculation,
        418–419
    theoretical basis, 405–408, 406f, 407f
    topology broadcasting, 406–407, 407f
        leaf entries, 408, 408f
        shortest-path tree (SPT), 407–408
    see also IS-IS; LSAs; OSPF
Load sharing, 229
    for CEF, 234–237
    for dynamic routes, 230
    for legacy process switching, 230–232
    per destination (fast switching code),
        232–233
    per packet, 232
    for static route configuration, 229, 229l,
        231l, 268
    techniques in Cisco IOS, 229t
    unequal cost, 379–380, 393–395
LookUp() function, 175
LSAs, 466
    Age field, 528
    and external routing information
        (AS-external-LSAs), 493–495
        formats, 495–496, 496f, 502f
        rules, 496–497
    group pacing, 508–509
    network-LSA, 470, 471f
    origination, 472–473
    origination of summary-LSAs, 487–488
    router-LSA, 468–469, 469f
        and link records, 469–470
        link records, 470–471
        router steps, 471–472

standard header fields, 466–468, 468f
types, 480, 485, 486f, 504
see also Flooding algorithm

MAC (Media Access Control) address, 35
Major network, vs. subnet, 19
Malkin, Gary, 311
Mask
  address, 49, 157
  route, 157
  subnet, 157
maximum-paths router configuration
  command, 80
Metric field, 85
Minnear, Robert, 311
MOSPF (Multicast OSPF), 513

neighbor router configuration command,
  273
Network Address Translation (NAT), 35
network command, 77, 271, 291
  address specifications, 292
Network interface controllers (NICs), 2
Network interface types, 182
  dialer, 184
    lists, 198
    packet delivery, 196–201
    sample configuration, 200
  loopback, 184
    packet delivery, 203–204
  multilink, 184
  null, 184
    packet delivery, 204–205
  subinterface, 184–185, 185l, 186f
  tunnel, 184
    configuration, 202–203
    packet delivery, 201–202
  virtual-access, 184
  see also Broadcast; OSPF;
    Point-to-multipoint; Point-to-point
Network layer
  load sharing in Cisco IOS, 229

protocols, 1, 166
Next field, 86
NHRP (Next-Hop Resolution Protocol),
  201
NMBA (non-broadcast multi-access)
  and static routes, 247–248
  see also ATM; Frame Relay; X.25
no peer neighbor-route interface
  configuration command, 70
NVRAM (nonvolatile random-access)
  memory, 2
  saving active configuration, 8, 81–91
  and show configuration command, 9

offset-list configuration command, 389
Open Systems Interconnection (OSI)
  reference model, 1, 15
Originator field, 85
OSPF (Open Shortest Path First) routing
  protocol, 1, 45, 419–420, 547–548
  adjacencies, 458, 460
  comparison with IS-IS, 421t–422t
  convergence characteristics, 426–428
  DBD packet, 461, 463–465, 464f
  demand circuit extensions, 506–507
  designated router election algorithm,
    454, 456
    procedures, 456–458
  external routing information areas,
    493–495, 504
    normal, 423
    not-so-stubby (NSSA), 424, 500, 501f,
      502–504, 503f
    stub, 423, 499–500
  fragmentation issues, 445
  global data structure, 428
    area data structure, 429–430
    information block, 428–429
  implementation details, 508
    LSA group pacing, 508–509
    packet pacing, 508
  interface data structure, 431–433

interface states, 452–453
  events, 453–454, 455t, 456f
intra-area functionality, 436–437
  subprocesses, 437, 438f
  see also LSAs
loopback states, 443
Multicast, 513
NBMA mode, 440–441, 517–519
  alternatives, 441
  and Hello subprotocol, 449
neighbor data structures, 433
  fields, 434–435
neighbor FSM, 461, 462t–463t, 465,
  467f
neighbor states, 458–459
  events, 460–461
network types, 439
Options field, 446–447, 447f
packet processing, 445–446
periodic updates, 480–481
point-to multipoint networks, 441–442,
  442f
redistribute RIP route (query), 293
route aggregation techniques, 425–426
route calculation, 505–506
  distance-vector approach, 492
  external, 498–499
  inter-area, 486–487
  preference rules, 506
  via network topology, 46, 427–428,
    470–480
route calculation/partial calculation, 509
route types, 425
  external, 425
  inter-area, 425, 427, 536l
  intra-area, 425, 436
Router-ID, 482
router types (internal/backbone),
  424–425, 538–540
routing domain structure, 424f, 483
  area border routers (ABRs), 423,
    490–493, 492f, 504, 536l–537l

autonomous system boundary routers
  (ASBRs), 423, 495, 497–498
  flow of information, 483–485, 484f
session stages, 461
subprotocols, 420
  adjacency establishment, 420
  LSA flooding and LSDB maintenance,
    423, 437–438
  LSA origination and flushing, 420
  routing table calculation, 423
  see also Hello subprotocol
transport protocol and packet formats,
  443
  header fields, 443–444, 443f
virtual links, 442, 485, 488–490, 490f,
  491f, 493
OSPF (Open Shortest Path First) routing
  protocol configuration, 509
  basic, 510
  basic ABR configuration, 519, 519l–520l
  examples
    hub and spoke, 532–533
    multiple areas, 533–538
    NSSA, 544–547
    over Frame Relay Cloud, 529f,
      530–531
    route redistribution and stub areas,
      540–544
    single-area configuration, 525–528
    virtual links/backbone interface,
      538–540
  general parameters, 510–514
  interface-specific parameters, 514–517
  and NBMA interface techniques,
    517–519
  NSSA, 522–523
  route aggregation, 520
  route redistribution (ASBR), 521–522
  stub areas, 522
  timers, 523–524
  virtual links, 520–521

Packet-delivery process
  on broadcast interfaces, 188–192
  decapsulation, 165
  encapsulation, 155f, 165–166, 201f
  general functionality, 187–188
  initiation by forwarding algorithm, 50
  packet flows in Cisco routers, 162, 163f
  packet input, 165–170
  on point-to-point interfaces, 192–193
  steps, 51
  see also Forwarding; IpOutput()
    function; Network interface types
passive-interface router configuration
  command, 271–272, 272l, 292–293
Path calculations (IGRP), 376, 378
  considerations, 403
  effective bandwidth, 376–377
  path delay, 376, 378
  path load, 376, 377–378
  path reliability, 376, 378
Path descriptor
  level in routing table hierarchy, 80, 81
  Metric field, 85
  and parallel routes, 89l–90l
  structured type definition, 84l–85l
  view via show ip route, 90–91, 90l
PathValid() function, 116–117, 116l, 160
Ping, 13–14, 13l
  connectivity test in static route, 74l
Point-to-multipoint interfaces, 182, 186f
  and OSPF, 441–442, 442f
  and packet-delivery process, 193–196
Point-to-point interfaces, 182, 186f, 439,
  440f
  and IP address (OSPF), 481–482
  and packet-delivery process, 51–52,
    192–193
  unnumbered, 27
Policy routing, 173–178, 178l
  and route maps, 178–179
    examples, 179–181
  see also IpPolicyRoute() function

PPP (data link protocol), 1, 70
  example of reconfiguration, 71, 71l–72l
  on serial interface, 158
Prefix descriptor *see* Routing table
  structure
Proto_ADForRoute function, 280–281, 325
Protocol descriptor, 100, 100l, 291
  fields, 277–278
PSTN environment, using static routes,
  247–248

QOS (quality-of-service) techniques, 482

Radix tree, and IP route cache, 209
RAM (random-access memory), 2
redistribute command, 609, 609l–610l
Reverse Path Forwarding (RPF)
  verification, 170
RIP (routing protocol), 1, 45, 292
  and dynamic routing protocol, 78
  hops for metric calculations, 46
  and network command, 77
  special timers, 125
RISC (reduced instruction set computer),
  2
ROM (read-only memory), 2
Route
  0.0.0.0/0, 158, 176, 578
  aggregation, 60, 61f, 61t, 62, 62f,
    425–426, 579
  cache entries *see* Switching technologies
  expiration technique, 270
  filtering, 274–275
  lookup, 173–174
  manipulation, 99, 110
    see also Administrative distance;
      Route source selection
  parallel, 89l–90l, 159
  poisoning, 376
  redistribution, 281, 282, 292
    algorithm, 285
    case example, 281–282

paths for directly connected routes,
285–286
redistribute router configuration
command, 282, 282l–283l, 283
see also Route maps
resolvability, 115–118
types (Cisco), 65
Route maps, 286, 286l–287l
match clauses; 287; parameters,
287–288
redistribution examples, 289
set clauses, 288
see also Policy routing
Route source selection, 110, 291
assigned AD values, 100, 101t
see also IGPs; Route/redistribution
RouteDelete() function, 114–115
RouteInstall() function, 91, 91l–92l
AddSubnet() field, 93
AddToChain() field, 93
algorithm, 93
CheckPath() field, 93, 94–95, 94l
CreateNetwork() field, 93
FindInChain() field, 92
FindRoute() field, 92
FreeRoute() field, 92
GetEntryType() field, 92
Major() field, 92
operation/management examples, 95–97
UnlinkFromChain () field, 93
RouteMetricUnreachable() function,
330–331
router command, 76, 271, 291
router id, 511
router igrp, 381, 388
Router operation, 162f
complex routed network example,
37–39, 38f
in datagram networks, 39
datagram networks rules of thumb,
39–40
default gateway, 35–36, 36f

dropped packets, 40, 164
maximum transmission unit (MTU), 40,
52
metrics calculation, 46, 85
output queuing, 165
route example, 36–37, 37f
see also Forwarding algorithm (basic)
RouteRemove() function, 97–98, 97l–98l
see also DelSubnet() function;
RouteDelete() function
RouteUpdate() function, 104, 104l–105l,
105, 105l–106l, 114–115, 326l–327l
Routing, 33
decision (forwarding decision), 34
default, 46–47, 47f
dynamic propagation, 46, 48f
domain, 45
snapshot, 402
summary, 47, 53
tables, 34
sources, 38f, 41–42, 65
see also Routing table structure
(Cisco routers)
updates, 45
virtual and forwarding (VRF), 238
Routing Information Protocol (RIP),
310–311, 371–372
configuration examples
basic configuration, 357l–358l
basic configuration/routing table
entries, 358, 358l–360l, 360
route redistribution from dynamic
routing protocols, 367, 367f,
368l–371l
static routing connection, 365l–366l
test lab, 356–357, 356f
uniform offset list for every serial
interface/all routers, 362,
362l–365l
version 2 routing tables, 360l–362l
configuration parameters, 311–315, 352
information database, 315

interface information block
  parameters, 311–312
route redistribution, 355–356
setting split-horizon flag, 312, 312l,
  353
timers, 315, 354–355
version, 353
database, 352
default-route announcement conditions,
  345, 354
demand circuit extensions, 350
  alternative routes, 351–352
  presumption of reachability, 351
event processing (external), 335
  interface state change (up/down),
    336–337
  IPRIPIntEventHandler(), 335l–336l
  redistributed route, 337–338
event processing (internal)
  garbage collection route timer
    expiration, 332–333
  holddown route timer expiration,
    331–332
  invalid route timer expiration, 330
  IPRIPUpdate() function, 329, 338,
    338l–340l
  logic, 336t
  periodic/triggered update or general
    request response, 329, 335
general characteristics, 313t
hops for metric calculations/controls,
  46, 312, 314, 372–373
input processing
  algorithm function, 318–319
  reply processing routine, 320, 321l
  request processing routine, 319–320
  sanity check, 319
message format, 315, 315l–316l
  address family identifier (AFI), 317
  general vs. specific request, 317–318
  header, 317
  v1, 316f

message processing, 322–323, 373f
  adding an entry, 346–347
  IPRIPComposeRoute() function,
    325–326, 325l
  IPRIPGetMask() function, 324l–325l,
    325
  IPRIPSanityEntry() function,
    323l–324l, 324
  timers, 328–329
  update steps, 327–328
message types, 317
  for demand circuits, 351
neighbor and network discovery, 270,
  374
offset lists, 362
port 520, 315, 322
sending updates
  logic, 340–341
  using IPRIPUpdate() function, 338,
    338l–340l
state machine, 333, 334f
  events, 333–335
v1/v2, 45, 310
v2, 347–348
  authentication subheader, 349f
  input processing changes, 348–349
  message entry format, 348f
  message sending changes, 349–350
Routing protocols, 1, 45–46
  and classful vs. classless addressing, 25
  configuration, 271–276
  data structures, 276, 276l–277l
    usage, 279
    see also Interface data structures;
      Protocol descriptors
  events processed, 290–291
  and forwarding engine, 66
  link-state protocols, 270
  and route filtering, 274–275
  see also Distance-vector routing
    protocols; EGPs; IGPs; Static routes

Routing table structure (Cisco routers), 65, 87
  composition process example, 89, 89l
  configuration file commands/changes to routing table, 111
  hierarchical database, 81, 82f, 158
    interface descriptor level, 81
    prefix descriptors level, 80, 81, 83l–84l
    subnet descriptor level, 81
    see also path descriptor/level
  linkages example, 87, 88f, 89
  location of route in table, 96
  and routing source and forwarding engine, 66, 67f
  RT (maintenance) process, 85, 113–114, 156t
    algorithm, 113
    deletion consequences, 113
    interface going up/down, 111, 118–121, 119l, 120l, 121l
    IP processing enabled/disabled on an interface, 112, 121–122
    Route installation/deletion requested, 112, 124, 124l–125l
    Route marked as default candidate/deleted, 112–113
    route selection, 101–103, 102f
    Secondary IP address added/deleted to an interface, 112, 123–124
  sample, 65l–66l
  size constraints, 158
  sources supported, 78–79, 79l
  see also Dynamic routes; HDLC; PPP; Route/redistribution; RouteInstall() function; RouteRemove() function; Static routes
RTP (reliable transport protocol/EIGRP), 553

service timestamps command, 12, 12l
7000-series router, switching methods, 214–215, 215f

7500-series router, 2, 162
  architecture, 216f
  distributed switching, 217, 218f
    flow, 218–219
  Route Switch Processors (RSPs), 216, 219
  Versatile Interface Processors (VIPs), 217
  Distributed Services method, 219
ShareCount field, 85
show commands, 11
  show adjacency, 223, 223l–224l
  show configuration, 9
  show interface, 81, 164, 164l
  show interface serial, 0, 26
  show ip cache flow, 227, 227l–228l
  show ip cef, 222l–223l, 234l–235l
  show ip eigrp topology, 554
  show ip ospf, 430l–431l, 525l, 535l
  show ip ospf interface, 433, 433l
  show ip ospf neighbor, 435l–436l, 530l–531l
  show ip protocol, 587, 588l, 589, 590l
  show ip route set of commands, 11, 11l–12l, 65, 65l–70l
    and contents of TNetworkInfo record, 86l
    EIGRP route examples, 588l, 599l–600l, 611l
    and path descriptors, 90–91, 90l
    and routing table hierarchy, 82, 83f, 84l
  show running, 26, 27l
  show running-config, 9, 9l
Split-horizon technique, 303–305, 304f
SPT (shortest-path tree) *see* Link-state routing protocols
SSH (secure shell), interface with router, 3–5, 3f, 4f
Static routes
  address ranges, 133–135, 134f, 134l–135l

backup, 244–247, 245f, 266–267
  dial, 267–268
configuration parameters, 72–73, 73l,
    243, 268
  usage illustrations, 73l–74l
cooperation with dynamic routes,
    143–144
and discard routes, 253–255, 253f
host routes, 266
implementation scenarios, 255
  central and branch offices (partial
      mesh), 259–265, 260f
  ISP and one customer, 255–259, 256f
loops, 246, 250, 251f, 252–253
in NBMA and dial-up environments,
    247–248, 248f
over remote networks, 75, 75l, 76l, 266
processing, 126
  adding/deleting, 126–127
  delete unresolvable routes, 128,
      128l–129l
  deletion examples, 132–133
  installation examples, 130–132
  objectives, 133
  of pending static routes, 129–130
  scheduling, 128
resolution of intermediate network
    address, 79–80
  and classful routing table lookup,
    139–143
routing protocol, 41, 42–44, 43f
sanity check, 135–139
types, 241
  both interfaces and next-hop
      addresses, 242
  interfaces only reference, 242
  intermediate network addresses only,
      243–244, 244f
Subnetting
  automatic route summarization, 53
  and discontiguous networks, 54
  mask, 82, 86l–87l

procedure, 18–20
Supernet routes, 58, 62
Switching tables, 34
Switching technologies (Cisco), 207t
  Autonomous and SSE switching, 206,
      214–215
  Cisco Express Forwarding (CEF), 206
    adjacency table, 223–224
    characteristics, 220–221
    configuration, 225
    cooperation with switching-methods
        code, 221–222, 221f
    enabling, 239
    FIB (Forwarding Information Base),
        220, 222–223
    load sharing, 234–237
  Fast switching, 205, 208–209, 208f, 214
    administrative display, 212–214
    dynamic cache, 211–212
    half-fast switched features, 211
    invalidation timers, 212
    per destination load sharing, 232–233
    and route cache entries, 209–211
  NetFlow switching, 206
    configuration, 227
    and data export, 228
    display, 227l–228l
    flow cache entries, 226–227
    objectives, 225
    and packet processing, 226
  Optimum switching, 206, 215–216
  packet-switched
    datagram networks, 33, 34–35
    IP networks, 39
    virtual-circuits (VC), 33–34
  process switching, 205, 208f
    and load sharing, 230–232
    performance considerations, 206–208
  Tag switching, 206

TADInfo data structure, 280
TELNET, interface with router, 3–5, 3f, 4f, 4l

terminal monitor command, 5, 5l
  and debug output, 11
Test lab, 14
  EIGRP configuration examples,
    586–587, 586f
  OSPF configuration examples, 524, 524f
    and Frame Relay Cloud, 529, 529f
    hub and spoke, 532
    multiple areas, 535f
  RIP configuration examples, 356–357,
    356f
  topology, 14f
TFTP server, and copy of router's active
  configuration, 9
Time-to-Live (TTL) field, 40, 48
TLVs, 567, 567f
  authentication, 567
  IP external routes, 568, 570f
  IP internal routes, 568, 569f
  next multicast sequence, 568
  parameter, 567, 568f
  peer info, 568
  route attributes, 568–569
    external route, 569–571
  sequence, 567
  SW version, 567
TNetworkInfo type, 84, 86l
Topology broadcast *see* Link-state routing
  protocols
TPathDescr, 84l–85l
TPrefixDescr type, 84
  pseudocode example of routing entry,
    83l–84l
Traceroute tool, 13
Traffic flow, 225–226
Triggered updates, 306–307, 335
TRoute types, 84
TRPInterfaceInfo, 278, 278l–279l
  see also Interface data structures
TTY (terminal teletype) lines, interface
  with routers, 3–4, 4f
2500-series routers, 2, 162

ValidateRT() function, 117–118, 117l–118l,
  128
VLSM (variable-length subnet masks), 22, 59
  decision issues, 30
  and forwarding engine, 159
VTY (virtual teletype) lines, interface with
  routers, 3–4, 4f

WAN interfaces, 183

X.25 PAD (packet assembler/disassembler)
  interface with router, 3–5, 3f, 4f
    static routes, 247–248
  and packet-delivery process, 51–52
  point-to-multipoint, 183

DATE DUE
